An Introduction to
Databases with
Web Applications

An Introduction to
Databases with
Web Applications

Martyn Prigmore

PEARSON
Prentice
Hall

Harlow, England • London • New York • Boston • San Francisco • Toronto
Sydney • Tokyo • Singapore • Hong Kong • Seoul • Taipei • New Delhi
Cape Town • Madrid • Mexico City • Amsterdam • Munich • Paris • Milan

Pearson Education Limited

Edinburgh Gate
Harlow
Essex CM20 2JE
England

and Associated Companies throughout the world

Visit us on the World Wide Web at:
www.pearsoned.co.uk

First published 2008

© Pearson Education Limited 2008

ISBN: 978-0-321-26359-9

British Library Cataloguing-in-Publication Data
A catalogue record for this book is available from the British Library.

10 9 8 7 6 5 4 3 2 1
11 10 09 08 07

Typeset in 10/12.5 pt Stone Serif by 73.
Printed by Ashford Colour Press Ltd., Gosport.

The publisher's policy is to use paper manufactured from sustainable forests.

For Andrew

Brief contents

Contents

6   More features of the SQL data language   228

7   Further issues in web database implementation   276

8   Conceptual database design   346

9 Logical database design

10 Physical database design

Preface

Databases form the heart of most contemporary information systems, providing timely access to accurate data for people in a range of organizations. They allow many people to share the same data at the same time and mine that data for useful information. Understanding databases and their associated technologies is essential for students on courses in business computing and information systems. Students on general computing and business courses benefit from studying them, too, as both will encounter databases in their professional lives.

Traditional database applications were often limited to users in one organization and usually to those at a single physical location. Only large organizations could afford the proprietary networking technologies needed to allow databases in one town to be accessed by staff in another. The development of the Internet and, subsequently, of the World Wide Web, changed that. The Internet, and particularly the World Wide Web, promote information sharing without boundaries. Anyone, anywhere can access information at a time that suits them. To share its data, an organization simply needs to hook up its network to the Internet and put a web front-end on its existing database. More and more organizations are seeking to do this, so it has become increasingly important for business computing and information systems graduates to understand the technical challenges this seemingly simple requirement poses.

Another recent development is the appearance of XML as an alternative to relational databases. Compared to relational database technologies, XML-based technologies are immature. It is still not clear whether XML databases will emerge as a fully fledged parallel database technology or be subsumed into the existing relational database technologies. Graduates need to understand the strengths and weaknesses of XML as a format for organizing data and the limitations of current XML database technologies.

Aims of the book

Traditional database textbooks tend to focus closely on database topics. Database design and SQL form the core of the book, followed by coverage of more advanced database topics, such as query optimization and data mining. Web development textbooks – even those focusing on web database applications – tend to cover database design and SQL in a single chapter. They focus closely on coding techniques for server-side scripts and the details of particular scripting languages.

This book takes a different approach. It takes the key concepts and technologies from both areas and presents them in a single, introductory textbook. The first three chapters cover the underlying concepts of both database and web technologies, providing a sound theoretical basis for students to build on.

Chapter 1 gives a general introduction to the key ideas. Chapter 2 introduces the network, database and web technologies that underpin every web database application. Chapter 3 discusses the theory of data models in detail, covering both relational and semistructured data models.

Chapters 4–7 cover scripting, for both web and database servers. They introduce web development with server-side scripting languages, using the data language SQL and the server-side scripting language PHP.

Chapter 4 starts from the problem of how use a web page to deliver data drawn from a database and uses this to introduce the basics of HTML and PHP (with a tiny bit of SQL).

Chapters 5 and 6 cover the SQL data language in detail. They use the ISO SQL:2003 standard, but explain many DBMS-specific features.

Chapter 7 discusses standard techniques of web database development, including how to deliver the results of database queries over multiple pages, how to maintain application state and how to secure your application. Again, the examples use PHP but the focus is on the techniques, not the scripting language.

Chapters 8–11 discuss database design. The traditional topics of ER diagrams and normalization are covered in Chapters 8 and 9.

Chapter 10 explores issues that arise during physical database design. This chapter includes discussion of controlled redundancy, surrogate keys, data storage structures and how to estimate a database application's likely performance.

Chapter 11 extends the traditional discussion of database design to include recent work on designing web database applications.

Chapter 12 concludes the book with an exploration of XML and its related technologies, focusing on its use for data organization. The chapter covers XML schema languages, for describing the structure of XML documents, and approaches to locating data within an XML document. It also explains how to use an ER diagram to design the XML schema.

How to use this book

Although the book sets databases in the context of the Web, it covers the traditional core of an introductory database module. To use it in this way, simply omit Chapters 4, 7 and 11 and the web technology section of Chapter 2.

The book covers scripting languages before it covers design. This is because it is useful to understand how an application will be implemented before trying to design it. However, it's possible to read most of the design chapters before covering implementation. Only Chapter 10 and the final section of Chapter 11, on physical design, require an understanding of SQL.

This leads to two suggested 'routes' through the chapters. To use the book as written, start from Chapter 1 and read the chapters in order. To cover design *before* implementation, read the chapters in this order: 1, 2, 3, 8, 9, 11, but not Section 11.3, then 4, 5, 6, 7, 10, Section 11.3 and 12.

Thanks

Thanks to Andrew Hawkett for his support and encouragement while I wrote this book and for criticizing the early drafts. To my parents, Brian and Jean Prigmore, and my sister, Alison Prigmore, for tea and sympathy. To Kate Brewin, Owen Knight and Simon Plumtree, all at various times editors of the book, for their help and advice. Thanks also to the anonymous reviewers whose critical comments on the first draft were very useful.

Acknowledgements

Adobe and Acrobat Reader are either registered trademarks or trademarks of Adobe Systems Incorporated in the United States and/or other countries.

IBM and DB2 are trademarks of International Business Machines Corporation in the United States, other countries or both.

Macromedia and ColdFusion are trademarks or registered trademarks of Macromedia, Inc. in the United States and/or other countries.

Microsoft, Access and Windows are either registered trademarks or trademarks of the Microsoft Corporation in the United States and/or other countries.

MySQL is a registered trademark of MySQL AB in the United States, the European Union and other countries.

Oracle is a registered trademark of Oracle Corporation and/or its affiliates.

W3C® is a registered trademark of the Massachusetts Institute of Technology, European Research Consortium for Informatics and Mathematics or Keio University on behalf of the World Wide Web Consortium.

1 The web database environment

Chapter objectives

→ To review the information systems lifecycle and the place of application development within that lifecycle.

→ To discuss business rules and their importance for application development.

→ To introduce key themes in the study of web database applications and associated technologies.

→ To introduce the case studies.

Chapter outline

Databases are at the heart of many modern information systems. They store **data**, basic facts, that are processed to provide **information**, some useful combination of facts. The Web offers one way to deliver information to users of the database. This chapter gives an overview of information systems, databases and the Web, examines some benefits of using these technologies and mentions some of the difficulties. Much of the material serves as a gentle introduction to the more detailed discussion of subsequent chapters.

Examples help in any textbook and in this one they come from the fictional Pennine University. Like most universities, the Pennine University uses a number of information systems, including a staff directory. The staff directory is a particularly simple information system that, nevertheless, has some interesting features. It forms a running example through the book, with other university applications providing examples of more complex situations.

■ Section 1.1 introduces the notion of an information system and the software technologies that support computerized information systems. The information systems lifecycle is introduced as a way to approach the complex task of developing computerized information systems.

- Section 1.2 introduces the main case studies, using **use cases**, and explains how to read a use case diagram.

- Section 1.3 discusses the important topic of business rules. It explores the different kinds of business rules there are and discusses how they can be enforced.

- Section 1.4 introduces the notion of a database and discusses database technology. It also introduces the relational data model as an example of one approach to organizing data.

- The World Wide Web and its associated technologies are discussed in Section 1.5 and web database applications in Section 1.6. In particular, Section 1.6 discusses the classic problems that beset applications *not* using a database.

Section 1.7 ends the chapter with a quick run through of the different sorts of people who are involved in developing web database applications.

1.1 Developing information systems

The UK Academy of Information Systems (UKAIS) provides a concise definition of an **information system**.

Information systems are the means by which people and organizations, utilizing technologies, gather, process, store, use and disseminate information. (UKAIS, 1999, p. 1)

So, information systems provide individuals, businesses, governments and other organizations with timely access to accurate information. They support people as they work through the procedures that their organization follows, making their work easier and more efficient. Most contemporary information systems use computer technologies to achieve this. For example, a university may ask students to submit their assignments electronically via a website and check the document for plagiarism using computer technology. The actual marking is done by a person, but then the marks are recorded and collated using a computerized information system.

The technologies that support the computerized parts of an information system include both hardware and the software that runs on it. There are two broad categories of software:

- **system software**
- **application software**

System software – for example, operating systems and printer drivers – runs the computer and its peripheral hardware. It forms the basic software infrastructure on which to develop application software, such as word processors and e-mail clients. It is the application software that people interact with most of the time. The focus of this book is on developing application software using web and database technologies. Such applications software is usually called a **web database application**.

Developing application software is only one part, though an important part, of developing an information system. It is useful to set application software development in the broader lifecycle of an information system. A model of the **information systems lifecycle** describes a phased approach to planning, developing and maintaining an information system. Each phase focuses on specific activities and produces a range of outputs that feed into the subsequent phases. The collection of phases describe the full lifecycle of an information system – from the initial idea, through development and into its day-to-day use.

There are a number of different information systems lifecycle models, though two linked ideas are common to contemporary descriptions. First, software development is an *incremental process*. That is, it moves forward in small steps, with each step building on what has already been achieved. Second, it is an *iterative process*. This means that the information system is a work in progress, with different parts revisited and polished throughout the lifecycle. Figure 1.1 presents one view of the information systems

Figure 1.1 The information systems development lifecycle.

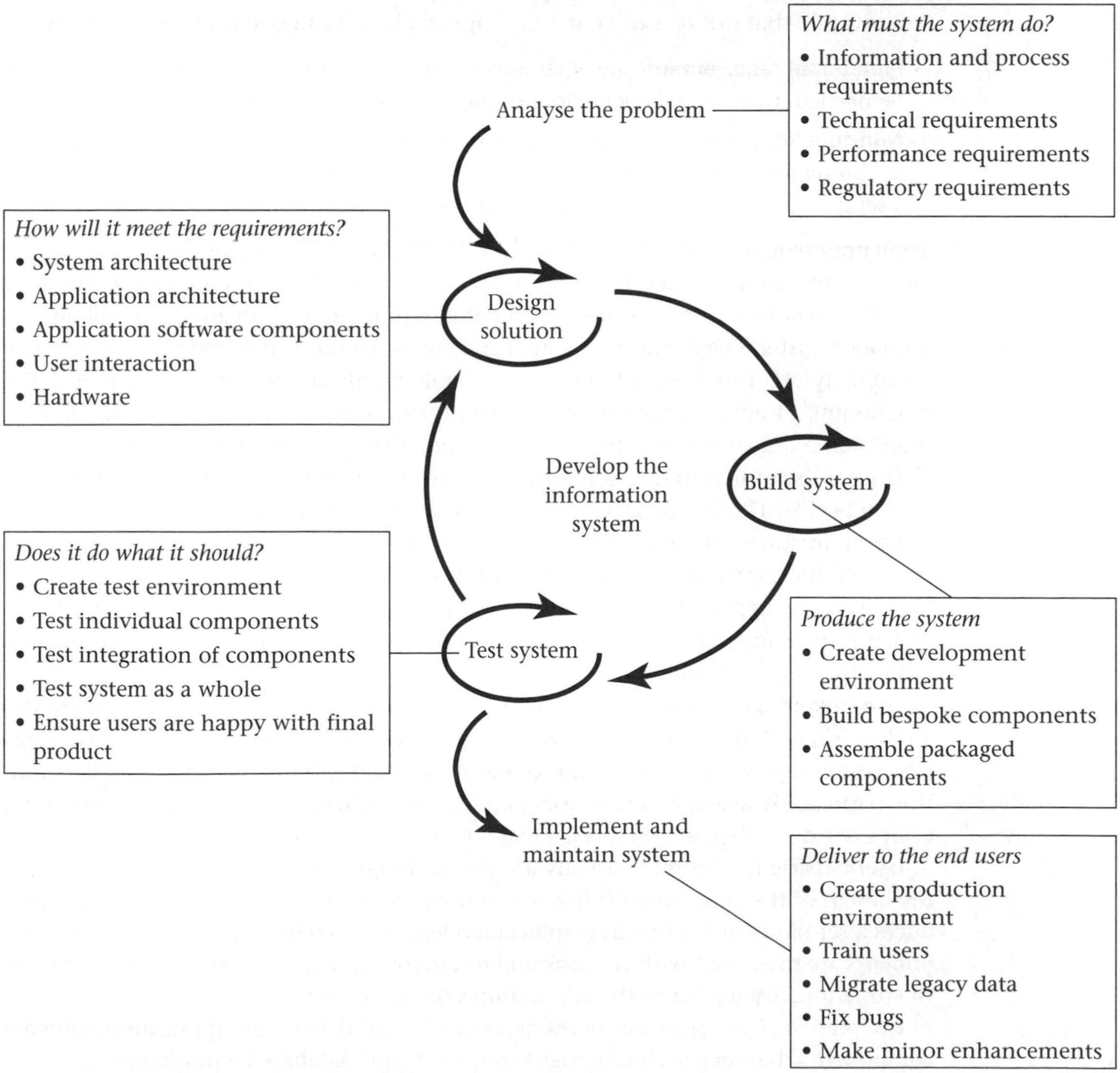

What must the system do?
- Information and process requirements
- Technical requirements
- Performance requirements
- Regulatory requirements

Analyse the problem

How will it meet the requirements?
- System architecture
- Application architecture
- Application software components
- User interaction
- Hardware

Design solution

Develop the information system

Build system

Does it do what it should?
- Create test environment
- Test individual components
- Test integration of components
- Test system as a whole
- Ensure users are happy with final product

Test system

Produce the system
- Create development environment
- Build bespoke components
- Assemble packaged components

Implement and maintain system

Deliver to the end users
- Create production environment
- Train users
- Migrate legacy data
- Fix bugs
- Make minor enhancements

lifecycle. Beginning with the analysis of the problem, it moves into the development phase, with its design–build–test cycle familiar to application software developers, then into the final phase of implementation and maintenance. The circling arrows indicate that the development phase is iterative and incremental. This means that a design is realized by building software, the software is tested and flaws found, which means rethinking the design. Other cycles occur, but each turn around a cycle leads to a better design or better software, so takes the developers closer to a working information system.

The notes in Figure 1.1 indicate some of the activities that are carried out in each phase. Only the development phase is discussed in detail in this book and then only selected activities. The focus is on the development of *bespoke* (written from scratch) web database applications and the key activities in these development projects.

Looking at the information systems lifecycle in more detail, the problem analysis phase usually generates a list of **requirements**, which state *what* the information system must do, but not *how* to do it. There are two broad categories of requirements.

- **Functional requirements** are what information is to be held and what processes will be needed, the data and behaviour of the information system.

- **Non-functional requirements** are any other requirements of the information system – a requirement to uses a particular operating system, respond to users' requests within a set time or comply with certain regulations, for example.

Regulatory requirements are becoming more important than they used to be. For example, any organization that gathers information about people within the EU must comply with EU data protection laws. Recognizing this requirement in advance and building information systems that automate compliance can save users time and effort when they are in daily use. However, data protection requirements are not always essential to the functioning of an information system. An organization could choose to handle data protection requirements by other means, so simplifying the problem analysis.

Once a list of requirements has been agreed, the development of the information system begins. Three subphases of development are highlighted. The first, designing a solution, includes understanding what system software is required and choosing how the application software will utilize this infrastructure, which is discussed in Chapter 2. Designing the application software components is the main focus of Chapters 8–11, which discuss approaches to both database and web application design and include some discussion of hardware.

User experience design deals with presentation, describing the look and feel of the application and the navigation paths through it. Good user experience design ensures a consistent approach to visual effects and navigation through the whole application. It is particularly associated with web applications, where creating visually appealing, even exciting, web pages has been a major concern.

User experience design is usually a separate design activity, undertaken parallel to the design of the application software components themselves. The design phase produces a set of designs, often as graphical models, ready to be built. The software components are then built with the look and feel set out in the user experience design and the functionality set out in the application software design.

Chapters 4–7 develop the necessary skills to build bespoke application software components that realize these designs using web and database technologies.

Testing tends to be done both during and after the build stage. While building the solution, individual developers will test their own components. Once all the components have been built, the system is tested as a whole to ensure that the various parts fit together correctly and work effectively.

The final stage of the lifecycle – implementation and maintenance – sees the information system being used on a day-to-day basis. Notice that this phase includes the activity 'Make minor enhancements'. What counts as 'minor' varies depending on the organization. The key point is that *major* enhancements mean starting a new run through the lifecycle, with the existing information system as one of the inputs for the analysis phase. Major enhancements could include upgrading the system software, moving to new hardware or making significant changes to the behaviour of the application software. In such cases, it is important to analyse the problem before developing and implementing a suitable solution.

Examples of information systems are easy to find. Automatic teller machines (ATM), parking meters and the dashboard of a car are all information systems. On the Web, online retailers use web pages to deliver information about their stock and gather payment information from customers.

E-commerce retail information systems have provided the main examples of web database applications in the past, but, increasingly, there are more sophisticated ones. The Associated Board of the Royal Schools of Music (ABRSM) now offer Music Medals, which are music examinations aimed at school children that 'make maximum use of online technologies' (ABRSM, no date). Registering for the exam, delivery of the exam materials and notification of results is all done over the Web. Another interesting web database application is Wikipedia – 'a Web-based, multi-language, free-content encyclopedia written collaboratively by volunteers' (Wikipedia, 2005). These 'volunteers' add new articles or edit existing ones.

Developing sophisticated web database applications such as these requires considerable skill and experience. To learn the skills, and gain the experience, it is best to start small, so the next section introduces the Staff Directory case study – a nice, small information system.

1.2 Case studies of information systems

The requirements for an information system can be documented as **use cases**. A use case is simply a description of one way in which an information system is used. In particular, it describes how the information system behaves in response to a user request. Often the information system is used by people, but it may be used by other application software. For example, a mail-merge document may get its data from a spreadsheet, so, here, the word processor is a user of the spreadsheet application.

The term **actor** is used to describe a role that a user of the information system, human or otherwise, might take. Actors are not themselves part of the information system.

The terms use case and actor are part of the **Unified Modeling Language (UML)** – 'a visual language for specifying, constructing and documenting the artifacts of systems' (OMG, 2003, p. 20). The official UML definitions of use case and actor are as follows.

> **Use case** The specification of a sequence of actions, including variants, that a system (or other entity) can perform, interacting with actors of the system. (OMG, 2003, p. 19)
>
> **Actor** A construct that is employed in use cases that define a role that a user or any other system plays when interacting with the system under consideration. (OMG, 2003, p. 4)

UML is primarily intended as a way to model object-orientated systems, which is not the subject of this book, but two facts strongly suggest that UML notation should be used where possible. First, application software developers are likely to be presented with use case diagrams as part of the requirements specification, so ought to be able to read them. For this reason, the case studies in this book are presented as use cases. It isn't necessary to understand how these were created, only to be able to read them. Second, the main diagramming tool for database design – entity-relationship diagrams – can be written quite effectively using UML notation. Chapter 8 describes in detail how this is done.

1.2.1 The Staff Directory case study

The Pennine University Staff Directory is a simple web database application, though not as simple as most staff directories. In addition to the usual requirement to deliver staff contact details via a web browser, it must also provide details of support sessions offered to students by academics. These are unbooked 'drop-in' sessions, open to any student who wishes to discuss their studies. A user of the Staff Directory will ask for the contact details first, then may ask to see support sessions, too. As the times of support sessions can change each term, to fit into the academics' new timetables, it was felt that academics themselves should maintain this data.

These requirements are summarized in the **use case diagram** for the Staff Directory (Figure 1.2). It provides an overview of who uses the system, and how they expect to use it.

The actors are shown as stick people. There are three actors: Academic, University member (that is, students and staff, including academic staff) and Visitor (such as prospective students, business people).

The box around the use cases represents the **system boundary**. Everything inside the system boundary will become part of the finished Staff Directory web database application. Everything outside it will be a *user* of the Staff Directory.

The ellipses represent the use cases. The use case Get contact details captures the main behaviour of the Staff Directory information system – finding the contact details of members of staff. It is used by the actors University member and Visitor, indicated by the lines, called **associations**, joining the actors to the use case.

Another behaviour of the Staff Directory is to provide information about support sessions. Rather than bundle this additional behaviour in with the standard behaviour of Get contact details, it makes sense to capture it in a separate use case called Get support sessions. To indicate that the two use cases are connected, an **extend relationship** is drawn from Get support sessions to Get contact details. Extend relationships are

Figure 1.2 Use case diagram for the Staff Directory application.

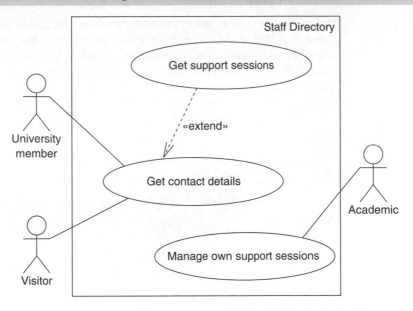

drawn as a *dashed* line with the keyword «extend» written next to it and an open arrowhead pointing at the *extended* use case – that is the one the behaviour of which is being extended. Any user of Get contact details (the extended use case) has the option to use Get support sessions (the extending use case), so there is no need to associate University member and Visitor with Get support sessions. In other words, an association between the actors and Get support sessions is implied by the extend relationship.

The actor Academic is only associated with the use case Manage own support sessions, which allows the days and times of support sessions to be changed. This seems odd as academics may also want to get contact details for their colleagues, so might be expected to be associated with Get contact details. This illustrates the difference between an actor (Academic) and a user (who happens to be an academic). Consider Paul Smith, who lectures in the School of Computing. Taking the role of Academic, he may change his support session details. He could also use the Staff Directory like any other member of staff, to find contact details for a colleague. When he does so, he is acting in the role of University member. One person is acting in two different roles that allow him to use the information system in two different ways.

Each use case has a written description, or **use case specification**, that describes the expected behaviour associated with it. Together, the use case specifications form the formal definition of the users' requirements.

There is a range of styles for writing use case specifications. The style adopted for the case studies in this book is informal and the closest to a traditional textbook case study. The use case for Get staff contact details shown below is typical. Notice that use cases provide considerably more detail about behaviour than the summary given in the first paragraph of this section. Appendix A includes a fuller account of how these use case specifications were derived. However, to use this book, you only need to know how to *read* a use case diagram and the use case specifications, not how to *write* them.

Get staff contact details

This allows any user to get the contact details (name, phone and e-mail) for a named member of staff at the university. The user provides the staff member's surname and first initial and requests his or her contact details. A list showing the name and phone number of each member of staff matching the search criteria is delivered, together with a count of the number of matches from the Staff Directory. The user can see the full contact details for any entry in the list, along with a photo of the member of staff if one is available, by selecting that entry. If there are no matches, a message stating this is displayed.

The full contact details for an academic provide access to a list of support sessions offered by him or her.

There is also an option to view a 'help' page, giving instructions on how to use the search facility.

1.3 Business rules

Every organization will have guidelines on what information should be collected as part of its daily work and what restrictions are placed on how this information is used. These are the organization's **business rules**.

It is important to understand the business rules that apply to a particular information system because, as far as possible, the application software should enforce compliance with them.

Business rule A statement that describes the information used by an organization or restrictions on how that information is used.

Business rules are usually identified during the analysis phase and can be documented in the use cases. Here are some examples of business rules at Pennine University.

1 Each member of staff has a unique staff number.

2 Some staff members do not have telephone numbers.

3 Support sessions offered by academic staff must not start before 9 am nor finish after 6 pm.

4 Every member of staff has an e-mail account with a unique e-mail address. This must be created prior to them taking up their posts.

5 Each assessment is moderated before being issued to students. The rules governing this process are:

(a) the status of an assessment must be draft, moderated or issued

(b) the status of an assessment may change from draft to moderated or from moderated to issued. No other changes are permitted.

Business rules 1, 2 and 3 are examples of **state constraints**. A state constraint is a statement about the information held by the information system that must always be true. Business rule 1 says that the information stored about a member of staff must *always* include his or her staff number. Furthermore, this staff number is unique to that person; no other member of staff will have the same staff number. Of course, it isn't always necessary to show the staff number to the users, but the information system must always know it. In contrast, business rule 2 says that *some* members of staff do not have a phone number. Rules stating that a particular piece of information is, or is not, required are very common and can always be enforced by the application software.

Business rule 4 is more complex. First, it specifies a uniqueness constraint on the e-mail address and says that all members of staff will have one. These are state constraints and the application software can enforce them. It then says that the e-mail account is created *before* the member of staff starts work. Again, this is a state constraint, but in this case the application software cannot easily enforce it. It would need to know the start dates of prospective members of staff and have permission to create e-mail accounts for them. Neither of these is very likely. Typically, the software application would *remind* the e-mail administrator to do this task, but not enforce the business rule.

In contrast to a state constraint, a **transition constraint** restricts the ways in which information can be changed. Consider business rule 5. This describes the restrictions that apply to the process of 'moderating' – that is, checking the suitability of an assessment. The first part of the rule, 5 (a), is a state constraint, as it constrains the value of the assessment's status. The second part of the rule, 5 (b), is a transition constraint, as it restricts how the status of an assessment may change. For example, an assessment the status of which is currently 'draft' can have its status changed to 'moderated', but cannot have its status changed to 'issued'. Transition constraints like this should also be enforced by the application software.

Business rules tell us something about how an organization works and help to define the requirements for an information system. Contemporary information systems use computer technology – hardware, system software and application software – to meet these requirements. This book is concerned with two particular kinds of computer technology: database technology and web technology. The next two sections introduce databases and the Web and pave the way for a detailed discussion of their associated technologies in the following chapter.

1.4   Databases and database technology

A **database** is a collection of **data**, though not just any collection counts as a database. Usually the data are related in some way. The database for the Staff Directory holds data about staff; it does not hold data about students. The data in a database is *persistent*, meaning that, once stored, it is available until it is deleted. This means that the data is usually stored on a hard disk, rather than in a computer's memory.

A database is *structured* to make it easy to use the data. Data about staff are gathered into a single data structure, which clearly distinguishes the different data items. Thus, first and last names are held separately and phone numbers are kept distinct from e-mail addresses.

A description of each data structure is also held in the database – what data it holds and whether or not the business rules place constraints on the data. This sort of data is called **meta-data**. This is because it is data about the Staff Directory database, not data about the staff. Here's a succinct definition of a database.

> **Database** A persistent, self-describing, structured collection of related items of data.

The description of the database structure is usually called the **database schema**. The actual data in the database at any particular time is called the **database instance**. Typically, the database schema does not change very often, while the database instance changes frequently.

A database is designed to meet the need of an organization for timely access to accurate information. It does this by acting as a central repository for data about the things of interest to that organization. These data can be combined to provide the required information.

The Staff Directory database holds data about two sorts of thing: staff contact details and support sessions. The data held relating to staff contact details includes the name, staff number, phone number, e-mail address and a photograph of the member of staff. For support sessions, the day, start and end times are held on the database. The database also provides information about a relationship between these two sorts of thing – that a particular support session is offered by a particular member of staff.

Different approaches to organizing the data in the database will capture this information in different ways. Some approaches have one structure to capture information *about* a thing, and a different structure to capture a relationship *between* things. Others use a single data structure to capture both kinds of information. These different general approaches to organizing the data in a database are called **data models**.

A data model has three aims, which are to:

1 describe how to organize data using meaningful structures

2 provide a language for manipulating the data and the data structures

3 define constraints that ensure the data is consistent and complies with the business rules.

The first aim of a data model is to ensure a consistent approach to data organization: the same basic structures are used to organize data about all those things that the information system holds data about. The data model does not describe how the data is physically arranged on disk. It is concerned with *organization* structures rather then *storage* structures.

The second aim is to ensure that database users can interact with the database, manipulating both data and data structures.

The third aim seeks to ensure that the data in the database is consistent so that it does not give different answers to the same question. Also, constraints can be used to implement the business rules. When a database constraint enforces a business rule, it ensures that the database accurately reflects the business.

The relational data model is a popular data model used to organize many databases. It has a simple solution to organizing data, which is that all data are gathered into tables with rows and columns.

In the Staff Directory database, a `Staff` table holds contact details for members of staff. Each row of the `Staff` table holds the contact details for one member of staff. Every row has exactly the same structure – the six columns `staffNo`, `fname`, `lName`, `phone`, `email` and `photo`. On a given row, the columns hold items of data about a particular member of staff. A typical instance of this table is shown in Figure 1.3.

Notice that there is no data in the phone column for the fourth row of the table, which holds contact details for Paul Smith. This is because he does not have a phone number. Even so, this row still has a phone column – it simply has nothing in it. In the relational data model, a column that has nothing in it on a particular row is said to be **null** for that row. Another important feature is that the values in the `staffNo` column are different for every row of the `Staff` table. This is because that column holds the staff number, which is a unique identifier for each member of staff.

The relationships between members of staff and their support sessions are captured by including the staff number on the appropriate rows of both tables. For example, the first and third rows of the support session table hold data about support sessions offered by Selma Hutchins. So, these rows have the same value in the `staffNo` column as the ninth row of the `Staff` table, as shown by the arrows in Figure 1.3. It is important to realize that there are no special data structures linking a row of the `Staff` table to the associated rows of the `SupportSession` table. Rather, it is the matching of values in the corresponding `staffNo` columns that captures this relationship. Chapter 3 discusses the relational data model in detail.

Whether a database is organized according to the relational data model or not, creating and maintaining it is a complex task. The database schema must be organized according to the underlying data model, business rules must be enforced and multiple users must have access to the database at the same time. The main software technology that supports this is the **database management system (DBMS)**. Examples of DBMS that use the relational data model to organize their databases include the MySQL® DBMS, the Oracle® database (which is actually a DBMS, despite the name), the Microsoft® SQL Server DBMS and the IBM® DB2® DBMS.

A DBMS manages all interactions with the database, whether they involve manipulating the database schema or the database instance. The users never directly access the files where the database is stored. Instead, they ask the DBMS to manipulate these files on their behalf. In fact, as DBMS are complex and often difficult to use, database applications usually add another software application between the user and the DBMS. This is illustrated in Figure 1.4, where the database user uses application software – the **database client** – developed specifically for this database. The database client application software interacts with the DBMS, which in turn manages the database. For example, in the Staff Directory web database application, the database client application software consists of a collection of web pages, the DBMS is a MySQL DBMS and the database consists of the two tables shown in Figure 1.3.

Figure 1.3 The `Staff` and `SupportSession` tables, with one null column value and one set of matching rows indicated.

Null

Staff

staffNo	fName	lName	phone	email	photo
10780	John	Smith		j.b.smith@pennine.ac.uk	[BLOB]
25447	John	Smith	5104	j.smith@pennine.ac.uk	[BLOB]
25448	Judith Anne	Smith	7709	j.a.smith@pennine.ac.uk	[BLOB]
31210	Paul	Smith		p.smith@pennine.ac.uk	[BLOB]
77712	Frank	Rose	8871	f.rose@pennine.ac.uk	[BLOB]
14443	Helen	Abbot	8032	h.abbot@pennine.ac.uk	[BLOB]
23257	Freya	Stark	8660	f.stark@pennine.ac.uk	[BLOB]
33935	Padma	Brar	6641	p.brar@pennine.ac.uk	[BLOB]
35054	Selma	Hutchins	8706	s.hutchins@pennine.ac.uk	[BLOB]
45965	Mikhail	Sudbin	5553	m.sudbin@pennine.ac.uk	[BLOB]
35155	Helene	Chirac		h.chirac@pennine.ac.uk	[BLOB]
55776	Gurpreet	Choudhury	5454	g.choudhury@pennine.ac.uk	[BLOB]
56893	Ruth	Bapetsi	8022	r.bapetsi@pennine.ac.uk	[BLOB]
56673	Joshua	Bittaye	7782	j.bittaye@pennine.ac.uk	[BLOB]
89987	Dan	Lin	8514	d.lin@pennine.co.uk	[BLOB]
78893	Jo Karen	O'Connor	8871	j.k.oconnor@pennine.ac.uk	[BLOB]
33509	Helen	Timms	8661	h.timms@pennine.ac.uk	[BLOB]

Matching rows

SupportSession

staffNo	dayOfWeek	startTime	endTime
35054	Monday	09:00:00	10:00:00
31210	Wednesday	11:00:00	13:00:00
35054	Monday	15:00:00	16:00:00
45965	Monday	11:00:00	12:00:00
45965	Wednesday	11:00:00	12:00:00
23257	Monday	15:00:00	16:00:00
55776	Monday	14:00:00	16:00:00
56893	Tuesday	14:00:00	15:00:00
56893	Thursday	09:00:00	10:00:00
56673	Thursday	15:30:00	16:30:00
56673	Friday	10:00:00	11:00:00

Figure 1.4 How a user accesses a database.

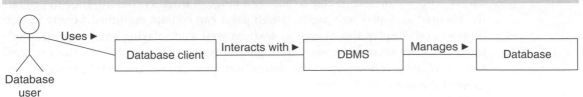

In traditional database applications, there is a persistent connection between the database client application software and the DBMS. Once the database client application software has opened a connection, the DBMS expects to receive a series of requests. The connection can be open for anything from a few seconds to several hours, so the DBMS delegates a portion of its resources to the task of listening out for these requests. Eventually, users request that the connection is closed – in other words, they log off. This is rather like the way in which a good restaurant treats its diners. After arriving at the restaurant, the diners are shown to their table – the connection is opened. The restaurant then delegates a waiter the task of ensuring that their order is taken promptly. The waiter keeps an eye on the diners and responds promptly to any subsequent requests (for a glass of water, a clean fork, another chocolate pudding and so on). Eventually, the diners pay the bill and leave – the connection is closed.

The restaurant doesn't need a waiter for every table. While the diners are happily tucking in to their main course or chatting over coffee, their waiter can deal with other tables. Similarly, a DBMS can have many users connected to it simultaneously without any of them feeling neglected.

The functions of a DBMS and the architecture of traditional database applications are discussed in detail in Chapter 2.

1.5 ▶ The Web and web technology

The World Wide Web (or more simply just **the Web**) is one of several applications based on Internet technology that have become important in recent years. Other important Internet applications include e-mail, file transfer and newsgroups.

For information systems developers, however, the Web has proved to be even more useful. The Web allows information, in the form of documents, to be shared easily on a global scale, using cheap (often free) computer software. This has led to increasing numbers of businesses using websites to market themselves and buy and sell goods and services (National Statistics, 2004). The Web is now seen as an important platform for information systems and, as such, is increasingly used to deliver documents that contain information derived from databases. This is particularly useful for documents the contents of which are changed frequently.

Web documents are usually referred to as **web pages**. They are **multimedia documents**, so can contain different media types, such as text, images, sound and video. The order in which someone views the content of a web page is not fixed. **Hyperlinks** allow users to view document content in an order that suits them, by linking one part of a web page to another or one web page to another.

The basic technologies that support web applications are the **web browser** and **web server**. The web browser is able to display a range of Internet content, though primarily it is used to display web pages. As web pages can contain multimedia content, web browsers can display this as well as text. As well as displaying web pages, the web browser allows users to 'browse' through any web pages available via the Internet. Users can either follow hyperlinks within web pages or tell the web browser the address of the web page they want.

There are a number of web browsers available. Popular graphical web browsers include Mozilla Firefox, Microsoft® Internet Explorer, Netscape® Navigator, as well as Opera from Opera Software ASA.

The role of the web server is similar to that of the DBMS as it manages interaction with a collection of web pages. The Apache web server (an open source project of the Apache Software Foundation) and Microsoft® Internet Information Services (IIS) are the two most common web servers.

The web server listens for requests from web browsers for documents in its collection and responds to those requests by sending a copy of the document to the web browser. A web server does not maintain a persistent connection with the web browsers that display its web pages. Instead, the connection between web browser and web server is closed as soon as the web browser receives the web page. Therefore, subsequent requests from the web browser to the same web server must establish a connection from scratch. This contrasts with the DBMS, which *does* maintain a persistent connection with the application software that uses its databases, allowing the DBMS to track multiple requests. To extend the restaurant analogy, a web server is more like a self-service café. Staff in the café respond to direct requests from customers, but don't keep an eye on them. If customers want a glass of water or another chocolate pudding, then they must return to the counter and attract the attention of a member of staff.

Web pages can be shared because they all have the same **document model**. A document model defines a general approach to structuring documents. For example, the chapters in this book all contain a title, objectives, outline, one or more sections, summary, glossary, further reading and exercises – *in that order*. Each of these document structures can be specified in more detail. For example, a section contains a title, which is followed by a mix of paragraphs, lists, figures and tables.

Specifying a document model for a book ensures consistency between chapters, as an editor can check that each chapter follows the correct structure. It is particularly useful for books with several authors, who might otherwise produce chapters that looked very different from each other. The document model defines what structures can be used to organize a document, while the document itself defines the content of each part.

Staying with the example of this textbook, the actual chapter title is 'The web database environment', there is an actual list of objectives, the actual text for the outline and so on. Once the structure has been specified and the content created, a **stylesheet** can define how the chapter should be presented. For example, chapter titles in 14 point Helvetica bold, objectives in 10 point Garamond, with diamond bullet points, 6 points after each line and with a pale blue background; standard text in 10 point Garamond and so on.

This approach is what gives the Web its global scope. Content producers – people who write web pages – can produce documents to a common document model, though each document can have different content.

Software developers can produce software applications that can read any of these documents easily as their basic structure is known. The presentation of the content in the different document structures, however, can be adapted as required. For example, we could change the objectives from a bulleted to a numbered list, have no background colour and enclose it in a box.

The document model for web pages is defined by the specification of the **Hypertext Mark-up Language (HTML)**. The HTML mark-up describes the content of the web page and the web browser interprets this description and displays the content appropriately. For example, the sixth line in Figure 1.5 (a) – `<title>Welcome to Pennine University</title>` – tells the web browser to display the text 'Welcome to Pennine University' as part of the title bar of the browser window. Figure 1.5 (b) shows how the Firefox web browser interprets this instruction.

The HTML document model is written using the **Standard Generalized Mark-up Language (SGML)**. SGML is used to define different document models for different purposes – HTML for writing web pages, DocBook for writing technical documents such as software manuals. An SGML document model is often called an **SGML application** as it applies SGML to solve a particular problem – namely, how to structure the content of a particular kind of document.

Figure 1.5 The Pennine University home page.

```
view-source:

File  Edit  View  Help

<!DOCTYPE html PUBLIC "-//W3C//DTD XHTML 1.1//EN"
   "http://www.w3.org/TR/xhtml11/DTD/xhtml11.dtd">
<html>
<head>
  <meta http-equiv="Content-Type" content="text/html; charset=ISO-8859-1" />
  <title>Welcome to Pennine University</title>
</head>
<body>
<h1>Pennine University</h1>
<!-- Skeleton home page -->
<p>
Pennine University is a centre for teaching, learning and research based in the
Pennine towns of Yorkshire.
</p>
<p>
Offering a range of courses from Art and Design to Software Engineering, there
is bound to be a course that suits you.  Browse through our <a
href="http://www.pennine.ac.uk/Prospectus.php">prospectus</a> or come to one of
our <a href="http://www.pennine.ac.uk/OpenDays.php">open days</a>.
</p>

<hr />
<p>Author: <cite>Martyn Prigmore</cite>
<br />&copy;2004 and beyond
</p>

</body>
</html>
```

(a) Code listing for an HTML document.

Figure 1.5 (*Continued*)

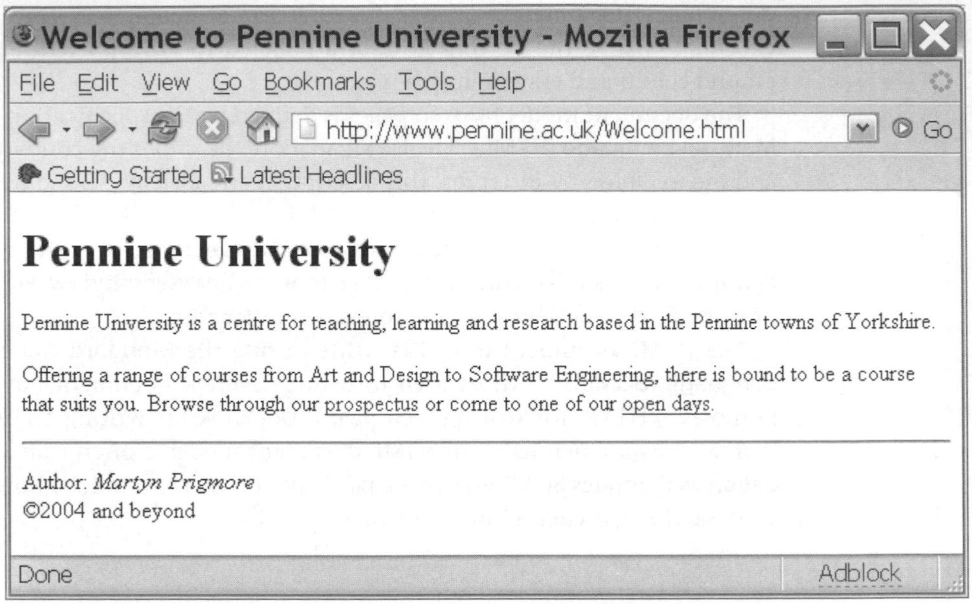

(b) The HTML document displayed in the Firefox web browser.

SGML document models do not define how the content is presented. There is no restriction on the font, indentation or spacing between paragraphs, nor on how lists are presented. The document model even allows presentation using more than one media, so document content may be presented as written text or spoken words. This separation of structure, content and presentation is an important feature of modern document models. Thus, the document model describes the general structure of a document, the document captures the content and a stylesheet describes how to present that content.

The claim that SGML document models and, hence, HTML do not define presentation is not quite correct. They *should not* define presentation. HTML has physical style elements specifically to alter the presentation of text, such as the <b> element for bold type. These make it difficult to control the presentation of document content as the style is then 'hard-coded'. It is better to use HTML simply to define the document structure. For example, use the <em> or <strong> element instead to indicate text that should be emphasized. A stylesheet can instruct the web browser to italicize text within an <em> element and make any text within a <strong> element bold. If it's decided that isn't quite enough, the stylesheet can change the colour, font, font size and so on. It can also indicate increased volume for emphasized content when a web page is presented using a page reader (technology that literally reads out the contents of a web page).

HTML and SGML are important technologies, but both have their weaknesses. SGML is a very powerful language, enabling the definition of document models for all kinds of purposes. This power is achieved as a result of complexity, so SGML can be difficult to use. This would not be a drawback except that it is also difficult to write software tools that allow users to easily create SGML document models and documents based on those document models. Consequently, these tools are expensive. In particular, it would be extremely difficult to write a web browser that could understand documents with any SGML document model. That is why HTML was created.

As all HTML documents have the same document model, it is much easier for content producers to produce HTML documents and for application developers to write a web browser that can understand them. The downside of having just one document model is that it is very restrictive. For example, it is not that easy to create a 'chapter, section, subsection' structure in an HTML document. The HTML physical style elements are another problem, as they mean the mark-up to define content and the mark-up to define presentation are mixed together.

These problems led to the development of a new language for defining document models, called the **Extensible Mark-up Language (XML)**. XML was developed by the World Wide Web Consortium (W3C) and work continues on defining the XML standard and a set of related technologies that support the use of XML for sharing documents across the Internet.

There has been a lot of excitement over XML in recent years, some of which is justified. Like SGML, XML is a language for defining document models, but it is much simpler than SGML. Because it is simpler, it is easier for content producers to *extend* (hence the 'Extensible' in its name) an existing document model to meet their needs or to create their own from scratch. It is also possible for application developers to create web browsers that can understand documents with different document models expressed in XML, not just HTML.

The HTML document model itself has been rewritten using XML instead of SGML and renamed XHTML (most XML-related technologies have names beginning with 'X'). A web page written to the XHTML standard is an **XML document** (as well as an XHTML document). XHTML itself is an **XML application**. There are quite a lot of XML applications.

The Extensible Style Language XSL is another XML application. An XSL document is a kind of stylesheet (there are other stylesheet languages). It instructs a web browser to present an XHTML document exactly as you want (at least, it will when web browsers can understand XSL). So an XSL document tells a web browser how to present the content of a document structured using the XHTML document model.

This illustrates how a lot of the XML-related technologies work. One XML document, written using one XML document model, is used to tell an application what to do with some other XML document, written using a different XML document model. In fact, XSL can instruct *any* application how to present *any* kind of XML document, as long as the application understands XSL.

This is an important point. XML does not actually *do* anything. XML document models are *descriptions* of how to structure certain kinds of document. XML documents are *descriptions* of their content. If something needs to be done with an XML document, then someone has to write a software application that reads the document, understands the description and carries out appropriate actions. In the XHTML and XSL example, someone must write a web browser that understands both document models and can use the XSL document content as instructions on how to format the XHTML document content.

The phrase **XML document** is used to refer to a document written using a particular XML document model, such as a web page written using XHTML. Keep in mind that XML is actually a language for defining *document models*, not writing documents. Behind every XML document is a document model defined with XML.

Although XML was created with documents in mind, it wasn't long before people realized that XML documents could also be used to store data. The definition of a database in Section 1.4 says that a database is a persistent, self-describing, structured collection of related items of data. An XML document is all these things. It is usually a file, so it is persistent. It is self-describing, as the different elements clearly indicate what kind of content they hold. It is structured according to its document model and the data in it are obviously related – why else would they be in the same document? This illustrates the problem of defining concepts in computing. Few database practitioners would regard a single XML document as being a database. Instead, they'd say that it is a data file. A collection of XML documents might seem more like a database. One problem with using XML documents like a database is that there is no single data model for XML. Chapter 3 discusses one data model for XML. Chapter 12 covers database design for XML and discusses XML applications and related technologies that are particularly important from the database perspective.

1.6 Web database applications

The content of printed documents is always static. The content of this chapter will not change, unless a new edition of the book is printed. Web pages may have both **static content** (also called **boiler-plate text**) and **dynamic content**.

Static content is the same every time a copy of the web page is delivered to a web browser. Dynamic content, however, is added to a web page's static content by the web server before sending out a copy of the web page. Thus, different users may receive different versions of the same web page, depending on what dynamic content was added.

For example, the Staff Directory needs a web page to display the contact details for each member of staff. All these web pages have the same structure. The one for Selma Hutchins' contact details is shown in Figure 1.6 (a). It would be very time-consuming to create, and maintain, a different web page for each member of staff. Instead, it makes sense to have a single, skeleton web page to hold the static content and pull the dynamic contact details for a particular member of staff from the database. Figure 1.6 (b) shows the static content of the Staff Contact Details web page. Each time a user asks to see Selma Hutchins' details, they are retrieved from a database and merged with this static content to create the web page.

Notice that in the actual web page shown in Figure 1.6 (a), there is an image and a link to the member of staff's support sessions, but these are not shown in the skeleton page in Figure 1.6 (b). The image is derived from the database, so, like the name, phone number and e-mail address, is dynamic content. This behaviour will be particularly useful when Selma Hutchins' photo is taken as the image file will automatically

Figure 1.6 Static and dynamic content on a web page.

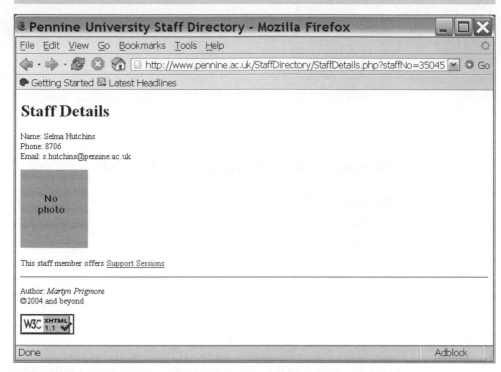

(a) The staff contact details for Selma Hutchins.

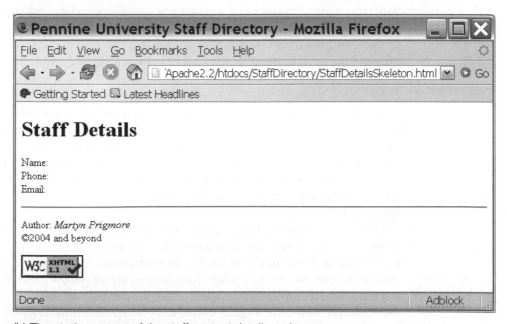

(b) The static content of the staff contact details web page.

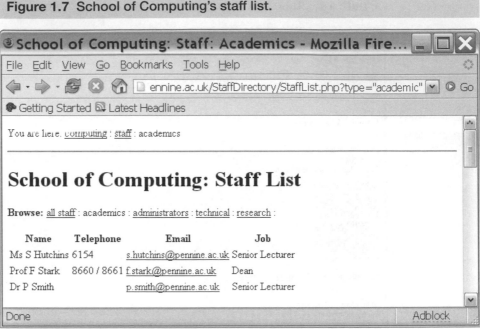

Figure 1.7 School of Computing's staff list.

be added to the static content, replacing the default 'No photo' image. The link to support sessions should *only* appear for academic staff, so this link, and its associated text, count as dynamic content.

There are several well-known problems with managing dynamic content. A bit of the history of web applications at the Pennine University will illustrate these problems. Like most universities, it was an early adopter of web technologies, so some departments already had applications similar to the Staff Directory. Figure 1.7 shows the School of Computing's staff list for academic staff. This application allows users to browse a list of staff members who work in the School of Computing. Users can view all members of staff or just those with a particular job type – namely, academics, administrators, technical staff and researchers. Allowing users to browse the staff list would not be an option for the whole university as the lists would be far too long, even if they were split up by job type. Hence, the Staff Directory application did not follow this approach. Comparing Figure 1.7 with Figure 1.6 (a), it is also apparent that the School of Computing's staff list provides slightly different information from that in the Staff Directory. The staff name includes their title ('Dr', 'Prof', and so on), but only gives the first initial, not the full forename. Also, their job title is included, but there is no photo.

Like the web page in Figure 1.6 (a), the web page in Figure 1.7 includes dynamic content, but the data is stored in a text file, not on a database. A sample of data from the text file is shown in Figure 1.8. It is an example of a 'comma separated values' file. Each line holds the contact details for one member of staff, with commas separating the individual data values from one another. Notice that, in the second line, there are two commas with only a space character between them immediately after the staff name. This is to indicate that Dr P Smith does not have a telephone number.

Figure 1.8 A sample of data from the Staff List data file.

```
35054, Ms S Hutchins, 6154, s.hutchins@pennine.ac.uk, Senior Lecturer, Academic
31210, Dr P Smith, , p.smith@pennine.ac.uk, Senior Lecturer, Academic
23257, Prof F Stark, 8660/8661, f.stark@pennine.ac.uk, Dean, Academic
14443, Miss H Abbot, 8032, h.abbot@pennine.ac.uk, Secretary, Administration
77712, Mr F Rose, 8871, f.rose@pennine.ac.uk, Technician, Technical
```

To create the web page shown in Figure 1.7 from the text file shown in Figure 1.8, the Computing Staff List web application performs the following actions:

1 opens the data file

2 reads a line of text and stores the name, phone number, e-mail, job title and job type

3 if the job type is 'Academic', adds these details to the staff list

4 if there are more lines in the file, goes back to Step 2

5 if there are no more lines, closes the text file.

This seems fairly simple, but there are problems with file-based web applications. The following subsections discuss these problems and explain how the database approach solves them.

1.6.1 Data duplication

Selma Hutchins' details are now stored in a text file on the School of Computing web server and in the Staff Directory database. At best, such data duplication is wasteful. Why keep two copies when one will do? Worse, the two versions can be inconsistent.

Look carefully at Figures 1.6 (a) and 1.7. What is Selma Hutchins' phone number? Figure 1.6 (a) has 8706, but Figure 1.7 has 6154. There is no way of knowing which is correct, other than by phoning both numbers and seeing who answers. If both applications shared a common database, this problem would be solved. That said, many organizations have successfully undermined this advantage of the database approach by developing two or more *different* databases that also have duplicate data.

1.6.2 Program–data dependence

The Computing Staff List application software is closely tied to the structure of the text file it uses. It expects to use a text file and expects that each line in the text file will contain the staff number, name, phone number, e-mail, job title and job type of one member of staff. To use the Staff table from the Staff Directory database, the Computing Staff List application software would need to be completely rewritten. This is called program–data dependence – the structure of the data cannot change without also changing the programs that use it.

In contrast, the structure of the Staff table can be altered without having to rewrite the Staff Directory application. Adding columns to hold the staff members' title, job

Figure 1.9 A revised Staff table with four additional columns.

Staff										
staffNo	fName	lName	phone	email	photo	department	title	jobType	jobTitle
10780	John	Smith	NULL	j.b.smith@pennine.ac.uk	[BLOB]	Catering	Mr	Support	Chef
25447	John	Smith	5104	j.smith@pennine.ac.uk	[BLOB]	Music	Mr	Administration	Secretary
25448	Judith Anne	Smith	7709	j.a.smith@pennine.ac.uk	[BLOB]	Estates	Mrs	Support	Estates Manager
31210	Paul	Smith	NULL	p.smith@pennine.ac.uk	[BLOB]	Computing	Dr	Academic	Senior Lecturer
77712	Frank	Rose	8871	f.rose@pennine.ac.uk	[BLOB]	Computing	Mr	Technical	Technician
14443	Holon	Abbot	8032	h.abbot@pennine.ac.uk	[BLOB]	Computing	Mrs	Administration	Secretary
23257	Freya	Stark	8660	f.stark@pennine.ac.uk	[BLOB]	Computing	Prof	Academic	Dean
33935	Padma	Brar	6641	p.brar@pennine.ac.uk	[BLOB]	Health	Ms	Administration	Administrator
35054	Selma	Hutchins	8706	s.hutchins@pennine.ac.uk	[BLOB]	Computing	Ms	Academic	Senior Lecturer
45965	Mikhail	Sudbin	5553	m.sudbin@pennine.ac.uk	[BLOB]	Music	Mr	Academic	Lecturer
35155	Helene	Chirac	NULL	h.chirac@pennine.ac.uk	[BLOB]	Health	Miss	Technical	Technician
55776	Gurpreet	Choudhury	5454	g.choudhury@pennine.ac.uk	[BLOB]	Music	Dr	Academic	Senior Lecturer
56893	Ruth	Bapetsi	8022	r.bapetsi@pennine.ac.uk	[BLOB]	Health	Mrs	Academic	Senior Lecturer
56673	Joshua	Bittaye	7782	j.bittaye@pennine.ac.uk	[BLOB]	Computing	Mr	Academic	Lecturer
89987	Dan	Lin	8514	d.lin@pennine.co.uk	[BLOB]	Health	Dr	Administration	Senior Administrator
78893	Jo Karen	O'Connor	8871	j.k.oconnor@pennine.ac.uk	[BLOB]	Health	Miss	Administration	Administrator
33509	Helen	Timms	8661	h.timms@pennine.ac.uk	[BLOB]	Music	Mrs	Technical	Technician

type and job title, as well as the school or department they work for, as in Figure 1.9, would allow both the Computing Staff List and the Staff Directory to use this table. However, this change will not affect the Staff Directory as it will use only the original columns. It simply does not see the new columns, so does not see any change at all. This ability to make some changes to a database's structure without affecting the applications that use it is called program–data independence. It is a key advantage of the database approach.

> Note that in Figure 1.9, any columns that are null have the word 'NULL' in them, rather than being left blank as in Figure 1.3. It is common practice to indicates nulls in this way, but be aware that the actual database *does not* have the word NULL in these columns. The column doesn't have any value at all; that is what null means. A similar comment applies to the photo column. Every row has the word '[BLOB]' in it, meaning binary large object, rather than the actual picture of the staff member.

1.6.3 Fixed queries

File-based web applications use the data from their data files to answer specific queries. The Computing Staff List produces a web page showing staff in the School of Computing, filtered by job type. It is difficult to use the same data to answer a different query. For example, to show staff alphabetically, the software application would have to be rewritten. That is the problem with fixed queries.

A web database application does not suffer from this problem quite as badly as does a file-based application. The DBMS handles all the data processing, including filtering the available data. If the web page needs different dynamic content, then the application software simply asks the DBMS to provide it.

1.6.4 Data integrity

The data used by the Computing Staff List web application must be kept up to date. A simple solution is to allow members of staff to amend the text file using a text editor (Notepad or Emacs, for example). Unfortunately, people can make mistakes. Figure 1.10 (a) shows a data file in which someone has hit the ENTER key by mistake immediately after Selma Hutchins' name. This results in the web page shown in Figure 1.10 (b). Notice that Ms S Hutchins has no contact details next to her name as the second line

Figure 1.10 The effect of corrupt data on a file-based application.

```
25447, Mr John Smith, 5104, j.smith@pennine.ac.uk, Secretary, Administration
35054, Ms S Hutchins,
6154, s.hutchins@pennine.ac.uk, Senior Lecturer, Academic
31210, Dr P Smith, , p.smith@pennine.ac.uk, Senior Lecturer, Academic
23257, Prof F Stark, 8660/8661, f.stark@pennine.ac.uk, Dean, Academic
14443, Miss H Abbot, 8032, h.abbot@pennine.ac.uk, Secretary, Administration
77712, Mr F Rose, 8871, f.rose@pennine.ac.uk, Technician, Technical
```

A stray line break after 'Hutchins' means the data file is corrupt

(a) A corrupt data file.

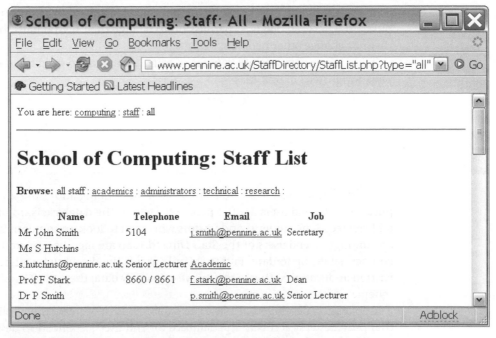

(b) The School of Computing Staff List showing effect of corrupt data.

23

Table 1.1 Benefits of the database approach over the file-based approach.

Benefits of using a database	Explanation
Data sharing	Users share the same data
Concurrent access	Users' actions do not interfere with each other
Data integrity	The DBMS keeps data consistent and accurate
Program–data independence	Data structures can change without affecting applications
Flexible querying	The DBMS can easily deal with new queries

of the data file only has her staff number and name. It is the third line where the real problems occur. The file-based application interprets the first data value, '6154', as a staff number, 's.hutchins @ pennine.ac.uk' as her name, 'Senior Lecturer' as her phone number and 'Academic' as her e-mail address.

Maintaining data integrity is, thus, problematic. How do you ensure that the data accurately reflects the real world? In a database application, the DBMS manages all changes to the data and can prevent accidental corruption.

1.6.5 Concurrent access

It is also possible that two people will try to edit the text file at the same time. Suppose Paul Smith and Selma Hutchins both open a copy of the text file in Notepad. Selma changes her phone number to 8706 and saves the file. Paul's copy still has Selma's old phone number, 6154. When he finishes his changes and saves his file, he overwrites Selma's new phone number with her old one. A database is less prone to this sort of problem. Users can be given permission to change their own details, but not to delete them or change other people's.

Table 1.1 summarizes the benefits of using a database to hold the data for a web application instead of text files.

1.7 Roles

This last section considers who is involved in developing and using a web database application. The end users are the people for whom the database is originally conceived and created. Staff, students and visitors who need to look up someone's phone number are among the end users of the Staff Directory. So are members of staff who keep their contact details up to date. End users only access the database instance using specially written application software to retrieve or modify data; they don't modify the database schema.

Application developers also use the database, as they create the application software that provides easy access to the database for end users. Application developers need to use the database instance and understand the structure of the database schema. They may also need to request changes to the database schema in order to support the needs of the application software they write. In web database applications, the application developer will also need to understand web technologies and how to connect web pages to the database.

The design of the database – its data structures and constraints – is the task of the database designer. There are several stages in database design and a particular database designer may be involved in every stage. They talk to end users to ensure that there are appropriate data structures, and design database constraints to enforce business rules. Database designers also design the storage structures, which are the DBMS internal view of the database. The efficiency of the database will depend on there being an effective design of the storage structures. Different DBMS offer different data storage structures, so the database designer must be familiar with the DBMS being used.

Once a design is available, the database – its data structures and constraints – must be created. This is one of the tasks of the database administrator (DBA). The DBA is an expert user of the DBMS. This often means that the DBA may also be involved in designing the storage structures. The main goal of the DBA is to use the DBMS as effectively and efficiently as possible, to realize the aims of the database designer and meet the needs of the end users and application developers. They also manage user access and database security, as well as day-to-day maintenance (such as taking a back-up of the database) and performance tuning (improving the speed of response to queries, for example).

The web administrator has a parallel role to that of the DBA, being an expert in the particular web server used and associated Internet and web technologies. The web administrator's main goals are to use the web server as effectively and efficiently as possible, realize the aims of the website designer and meet the needs of the end users and application developers. Again, security, maintenance and performance tuning form important parts of their role.

As organizations have gathered more and more data, it has become increasingly important to their success. Organizations have recognized that the technical expertise of the DBA needs to be supplemented by someone with a good understanding of how the data is used. This is the role of the data administrator (DA).

Unlike the DBA, the DA does not need to be an expert in a particular DBMS. Instead, he or she is an expert on the organization and uses this expertise to ensure that the organization's data resources are used efficiently and effectively.

The DA works with the DBA and database designer, planning the database implementation, and is responsible for setting standards (such as naming conventions). They also ensure compliance with any laws or regulations affecting the organization's use of data. For example, the Pennine University must comply with the UK's Data Protection Act 1998. This gives individuals a right to know what data about them is held by the University. The Pennine University also has its own rules on who can use data. Academics cannot access data about a student's fee payments, and finance staff cannot access a student's results. Such internal policies are written by the DA after consulting with management.

Table 1.2 summarizes the tasks taken on by each role. In reality, one person may take on several roles. For example, the DA at the Pennine University uses the Staff Directory, so is also an end user.

Table 1.2 Roles and responsibilities – who does what.

	Data entry	Application development	Database design	Creating data structures	User access and security	Maintenance and performance	Database planning	Setting standards	Policies and procedures
End user	x								
Application developer		x							
Database designer			x				x		
Database administrator (DBA)			x	x	x	x	x		
Data administrator (DA)							x	x	x

Chapter summary

■ This chapter has discussed the importance of information systems and outlined some of the challenges that face those developing them. It has discussed the need for web application developers to understand users' requirements and business rules and introduced use cases as a way of documenting these.

■ The core of the chapter was a discussion of databases and the Web and their enabling technologies – data models, database management systems, document models, web browsers and web servers.

■ The chapter finished with a discussion of web database applications, the advantages they have over file-based approaches, and the people involved in developing them.

■ While the discussion has been reasonably rigorous, it has not gone into details. These details follow in subsequent chapters.

Further reading

This chapter has provided a brief introduction to a number of features of information systems that you may already have met. If not, you may wish to do a little background reading.

Avison and Fitzgerald (2003) provides a good introduction to information systems development, discussing a variety of approaches and describing a range of tools and techniques.

Skidmore and Eva (2004) focus on tools and techniques rather than general approaches, but cover similar material.

Holt (2001) includes a nice introduction to systems and systems engineering in general before moving on to discuss the UML.

Bennett et al. (2005) provide a good introduction to UML, with lots of examples. Note, though, that there is no real need to delve deeply into UML at this stage.

Ideas about business rules and the problems with the file-based approach to database applications are covered in most database textbooks.

Hoffer et al. (2004) have a particularly clear discussion of business rules.

The discussion of the concepts that support database and web technologies and the technologies themselves, continues in the next two chapters.

Review questions

1.1 Explain what differentiates information from data.

1.2 Explain, using examples, the difference between:
(a) system software and application software
(b) functional requirements and non-functional requirements.

1.3 What is a business rule? Describe the two main kinds of business rule.

1.4 Define the terms:
(a) database
(b) database schema
(c) database instance
(d) meta-data.

1.5 Explain what distinguishes a database from a simple collection of data files.

1.6 What is a data model? What are the three aims of a data model?

1.7 What is a document model? What are the aims of a document model?

1.8 Explain the purpose of the following technologies:
(a) web browser
(b) web server
(c) database management system
(d) database client.

1.9 Explain what is meant by saying that the Web is a distributed collection of hypermedia documents.

1.10 Explain the difference between static and dynamic web content.

Exercises

1.11 What problems of file-based applications does the database approach overcome?

1.12 Explain why the database instance will change more frequently than the database schema.

1.13 Using an example, describe the general approach to structuring data used in the relational data model. Briefly explain how the relational data model deals with missing information and a relationship between two organization structures.

1.14 Explain what is meant by the phrase 'separation of content from presentation' in the context of the Web. Why is it a good idea?

1.15 Use a diagram to explain, in general terms, how static and dynamic content are merged to produce the final web page in a web database application.

1.16 Summarize the different roles played by users of a database, then consider an organization you know well and identify which of these roles are played by people in that organization. If no one plays a particular role, explain how the tasks associated with that role are achieved.

Investigations

1.17 Contemporary models of the information systems lifecycle tend to be iterative and incremental. What approach did earlier models take and why did information systems developers move away from these models? (Avison and Fitzgerald (2003) is a good initial source.)

1.18 The use of nulls to indicate missing data in relational databases is controversial. Summarize the arguments for and against nulls. Why do you think that they continue to be used? (Date (2004) is a good initial source.)

1.19 The relational data model is only one of the data models in use today (though it is the one most widely used). Investigate what other data models are in use, describing how each meets the three aims of a data model identified in Section 1.4. (Elmasri and Navathe (2000a, 2000b, 2007) are good initial sources).

1.20 Elizabeth Castro notes that, 'Lately (mid 2006), there has been a crescendo of rising voices complaining about the W3C's slow pace, overemphasis of [sic] the abstract and lack of concrete results.' (Castro, 2007, p. 17). Investigate these criticisms. How do you think these problems affect web database developers? (Castro indicates the following sources: http://microformats.org/; http://www.zeldman.com/2006/07/17/an-angry-fix/; http://joshuaink.com/blog/753/no-i-am-not-bloody-sorry. Warning, free speech zone! These websites may contain language that some of you may find offensive.)

2 Network, database and web technology

Chapter objectives

→ To introduce the notion of client-server computing and examine typical application architectures.

→ To discuss the network technologies that facilitate client-server computing.

→ To discuss database technologies and the ANSI/SPARC database systems architecture.

→ To discuss web technologies and approaches to web programming.

Chapter outline

Web database applications rely on three kinds of technology to deliver information to the end user.

1. Database technologies allow data to be stored and managed effectively and efficiently.

2. Web technologies deliver data to the end user without the need to install specialized software on their computer – any web browser will do.

3. Network technologies are responsible for transporting the information between database and end user.

It is useful for a web database developer to understand these three distinct technologies before they begin to develop web database applications.

Web database applications are examples of client-server computing. One computer, the client, requests services of another the server. Client-server computing is asymmetrical: the client makes requests and the server decides whether or not to grant them. Not all computer software uses the client-server approach. The software used to allow communication over the Internet uses the peer-to-peer approach, which means that each participant has equal status in the interaction and chooses how to respond to requests from its peers. However, for now, the client-server approach remains the dominant approach for web database applications. The web database application developer needs to understand this approach in order to use it effectively.

- Section 2.1 introduces client-server computing. It discusses the standard two- and three-tier architectures for such applications, and explains the importance of assigning the functionality to the appropriate tier.

- Section 2.2 discusses networks, with an emphasis on how information, in the form of network messages, is transported across the network. It examines the problems that arise when distinct networks are interconnected to allow information sharing between networks and how the TCP/IP suite of protocols overcome these problems.

- Section 2.3 looks at database technologies. It focuses first on the server-side technologies, in particular the **database management system (DBMS)**, and introduces the ANSI/SPARC database systems architecture. The section concludes by discussing the client-side database technologies, focusing on how the client communicates its requests to the server.

- Section 2.4 examines the server-side and client-side technologies that support web applications. It includes a discussion of the core web technologies – the HTTP application protocol and HTML – and the need to augment these to allow web applications to interact with a database.

- Section 2.5 concludes the chapter by returning to the discussion of client-server computing and how web database applications utilize the 3-tier architecture.

2.1   Client-server computing

Client-server computing is a common approach to developing computerized information systems. The idea is to split the application software into two or more tiers, with each tier taking responsibility for different aspects of the information system. This division of responsibilities between the different tiers is known as **application partitioning**.

The simplest client-server architecture has two tiers – a single client tier that uses services offered by a single server tier (Figure 2.1 (a)). Generally, the client takes responsibility for the presentation functions – presenting the user interface, accepting user input and displaying data to the user. The server's responsibility is to offer services to the client and these vary depending on the nature of the application. In a database application, the server offers data management services, which are concerned solely with creating and modifying data and data structures or retrieving data. In a web application, it provides web pages. Both the client and server tiers may take on other responsibilities. In particular, the business rules can be enforced by either the client or the server or be shared between the two. Deciding how to partition the responsibilities between the different tiers is an important part of the design phase of the information systems lifecycle. Note that the particular facilities offered by the system software underlying the client and server application software will restrict the choices available.

Figure 2.1 The two-tier client-server architecture.

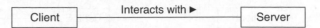

(a) Conceptual view of the two-tier client-server architecture.

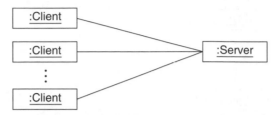

(b) A typical implementation of a two-tier client-server architecture – one server, many clients.

The notion of a 'tier' is usually extended to include the hardware and system software. Typically, the client and server tiers of an application with a two-tier architecture are implemented on two different computers and communicate via a network. For example, the Pennine University's website can be regarded as a two-tier client-server application. The server tier's application software is the collection of web pages and the web server software; its hardware the computer they are installed on and its network connection; and its system software is that computer's operating system and the networking software. The client tier's application software is a web browser; its hardware the computer it is installed on; and its system software that computer's operating system and networking software. Clearly, any personal computer with Internet access could be a client of the Pennine University's web server. This highlights an important benefit of a client-server architecture: the ability of one server to interact with many clients. This situation is shown in Figure 2.1 (b). The notation ':Client' inside a box indicates that this represents a particular instance of the client, rather than the general concept of a 'Client' shown in Figure 2.1 (a).

Occasionally, it is useful to set up a client-server application with both client and server software running on the same machine. Application developers sometimes do this to avoid the expense and complexity of setting up a network environment. For example, it is cheaper and easier to install a web server on a standalone computer and develop and test web pages on the one machine than it is to set up separate client and server machines connected by a network. However, a client-server application developed in this way should also be installed and tested on a network before being put into daily use.

In the early days of client-server computing, two-tier architectures were commonplace. However, more complex applications were developed with three or more tiers. Figure 2.2 (a) shows the three-tier client-server architecture. The first tier of a three-tier architecture is still called the Client. It only interacts with the server of the second tier, named 'Tier 2 Server' in Figure 2.2 (a). The added complication is that the Tier 2 Server can itself act as a client to the Tier 3 Server. This allows greater scope for application partitioning. One typical use of a three-tier architecture is to enforce a stricter partition of responsibilities, so that the Client deals only with presentation, the Tier 2 Server enforces the business rules and the Tier 3 Server manages the data.

Figure 2.2 The three-tier client-server architecture.

(a) Conceptual view of the three-tier client-server architecture.

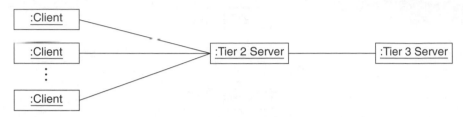

(b) A typical implementation of a three-tier client-server architecture – many clients in the first tier, but only one server in the second and third tiers.

A three-tier architecture is the natural architecture for web database applications. The database server occupies the third tier. It includes the actual database and the DBMS, which manages all interaction with the database. The web server occupies the middle tier, dealing with requests for web pages and integrating dynamic and static web page content. The web browser occupies the position of the client, handling presentation and accepting the user's instructions. Connecting the three tiers are a range of networking technologies.

The remainder of this chapter discusses the web, database and networking technologies that support web database applications and application partitioning.

2.2 Networks, interconnected networks and the Internet

A **computer network**, or simply a 'network', links together a number of individual computers and peripherals (such as printers, faxes, scanners and so on). These computing devices may be linked by wiring them together or using wireless technologies (such as satellite, radio, microwave and other means). To create these links requires further devices – a network interface card in each device, connectors and cabling and devices to manage network traffic and improve performance. Finally, all this hardware is controlled and integrated by network system software. The main goal of this technology is to allow users to share resources.

To develop effective client-server applications, an application developer needs a general overview of how networks function, and some basic knowledge of their supporting technologies. This section provides a basic grounding in network technologies.

Figure 2.3 presents an overview of a fairly simple network. Notice that the network is shown as something separate from the devices it links together. This view is useful for illustrating the range of computing devices a network can connect, but they can also be viewed as part of the network as a network itself, with no computing devices

Figure 2.3 A conceptual image of a computer network.

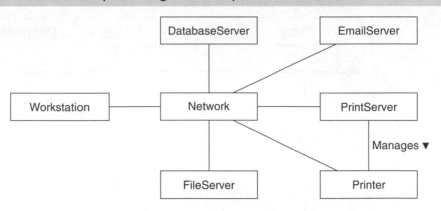

linked to it would not be much use. The network in Figure 2.3 supports the most common networked client-server applications, which are shared file storage, shared printers, e-mail and a database.

The 'Workstation' represents end users' computers connected to the 'Network'. A workstation would typically be a PC or a UNIX workstation with a cable connecting it to the network, but might be a mobile computing device with a wireless connection. It will have the client application software for a number of client-server applications installed on it. For example, the workstation will have a client application to present information about the files stored on the file server – their names, sizes, locations and so on. Windows Explorer does this under the Windows operating system, allowing users to share documents, spreadsheets, images and so on simply by storing them on the file server.

The workstation also has a client application to communicate with the 'PrintServer', which manages at least one 'Printer' (the arrowhead next to the word 'Manages' indicates that the print server manages the printer, not the other way round!). Notice that a printer is a separate computing device from the print server, with its own connection to the network. This allows multiple users to print documents on the same printer. Managing these printing jobs is done by the print server. Each workstation will have a client application allowing users to request that the print server pause or cancel print jobs. In this respect, the print server plays a role similar to the file server, though the print server manages access to shared hardware, rather than shared information.

The computing devices connected to the network communicate by sending messages to each other. As a network is a multi-user system, there will be lots of messages traversing the network, with different destinations. To identify the different destinations, each device has a unique **network address**.

Consider a user who wishes to retrieve some data from a database. He or she will use the database client application on a workstation to create a message requesting the data. The message holds three key pieces of information – the network address of the workstation, the actual request and the network address of the database server. That message is then broadcast to the entire network. The database server hears the broadcast, sees it is addressed to itself and so reads the message. Other devices also hear the broadcast, but, seeing that the message is not for them, ignore it. With the message

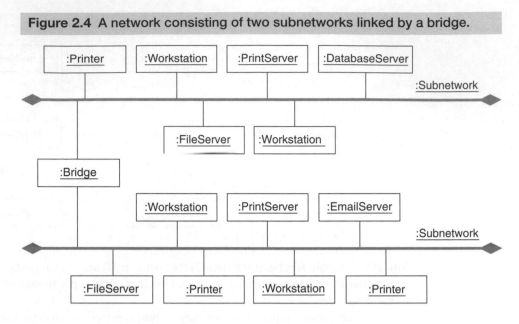

Figure 2.4 A network consisting of two subnetworks linked by a bridge.

delivered to the database server, it retrieves the requested data and bundles it up into a response message. The database server uses the address of the workstation as the destination address and broadcasts the response message back across the network.

Broadcasting messages works reasonably well for a **local area network (LAN)**. LANs use networking technology that limits their size to around 1 kilometre from end to end. They are typically used by a single organization (often within one building) for file and resource sharing, so have a limited number of computing devices attached. Even so, many LANs are split into smaller subnetworks to make them easier to manage. Figure 2.4 shows a LAN that consists of two subnetworks linked by a **bridge**. Each device broadcasts messages only to the subnetwork that it is attached to. The bridge is attached to both subnetworks so sees all the messages and knows which network addresses are on which subnetwork.

Suppose that a workstation on the top subnetwork of Figure 2.4 broadcasts a message for the e-mail server. The bridge knows that the e-mail server is on the other subnetwork, so it rebroadcasts the message to the other subnetwork. However, if a workstation on the lower subnetwork broadcasts a message for the e-mail server, then the bridge will not rebroadcast that message to the top subnetwork. There is no need, because the e-mail server has already heard it.

This simple scheme can cut the number of messages each network device has to check. Although there are a number of different technologies for building networks, the subnetworks of a LAN all use the same networking technology. This means that all the messages use the same language, and bridges only need to rebroadcast the original message; no translation is required.

LANs bring benefits to individual organizations in the form of information and resource sharing. There are further benefits to be gained by interconnecting many organizational networks to create a network of networks. Such an interconnected network is called an **internet** (note the common noun). The most famous internet is *the* **Internet** (note the proper noun). The Internet is the global, publicly accessible internet used by organizations and individuals throughout the world to, for example, send e-mails, browse web pages and download files. E-mail, the Web and file downloading are **Internet applications**. Each is a client-server application using Internet technologies to allow Internet users to share information and collaborate regardless of the physical distance separating them. The Wikipedia is a good example of both information sharing – it is an encyclopaedia – and of a collaborative effort by Internet users, as anyone can contribute an article (Wikipedia, 2005). The huge impact of the Internet meant that the term 'internet' was often confused with 'Internet', so the word **intranet** was coined to mean a private internet, typically used within a single organization. A private internet used by an organization and its partners is sometimes called an **extranet**.

There are some obvious problems with the idea of interconnected networks sharing information and resources around the globe. No one wants their confidential files or data to be accessible to everyone in the whole world. Similarly, there are few benefits to a person living in the UK being able to print a document on a printer attached to a network in some unknown location. Consequently, networks only expose a portion of themselves to the Internet and often even restrict access to this.

Figure 2.5 (a) shows the devices that are typically exposed to the Internet by a network. Notice that a database server is not usually exposed to the Internet. Instead, a three-tier web database application is developed and a web server mediates all requests for information from the database. Clients connecting via the Internet cannot actually see the database server and may not be aware that they are interacting with a database, even though it is on the same network as the web server.

A larger problem that arises from interconnecting networks is how to design an efficient connection architecture.

Each network connected to the Internet does so using a **router** (Figure 2.5 (b)). Each router has connections to several other routers and, through them, their networks. (In fact, the object labelled 'Internet' in Figure 2.5 (b) is really just this network of connections between routers.) When a network message has a destination address that is not for a device on the network, it is handled by the router. The router reads the

Figure 2.5 Interconnecting networks

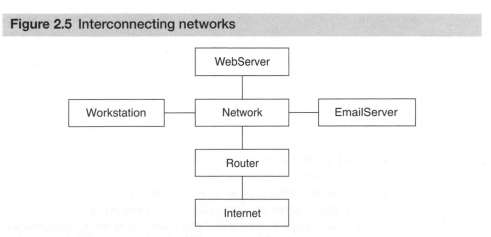

(a) Typical devices exposed by a network to the Internet.

35

Figure 2.5 (*Continued*)

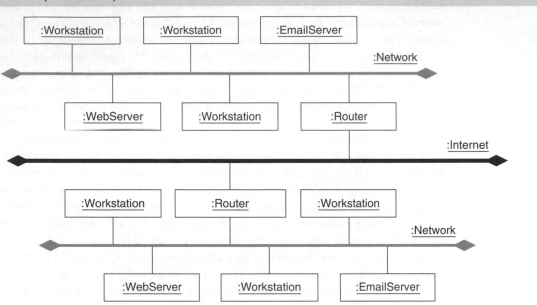

(b) Two networks connected to the Internet via their routers.

Figure 2.6 A small intranet, showing connections between routers.

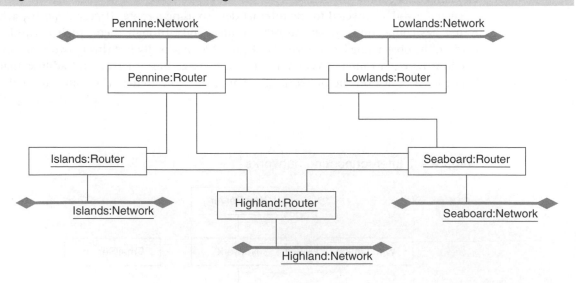

destination address and decides which of the other routers it is connected to is closest to the destination. It then sends the message to that router and *only* that router. Routers do not broadcast messages. To see why, consider Figure 2.6, which shows a small intranet of five imaginary university networks and the connections between their routers.

Suppose that a user on the Highland network sends a message to a user on the Islands network. If the Highland router broadcasts this message, then both the Islands and

Seaboard routers receive the broadcast. The Islands router knows that the message is for its network, so does not rebroadcast. The Seaboard router knows that the message is *not* for its network, so it rebroadcasts the message, sending it to Lowlands and Pennine (assuming that the routers are smart enough not to send a message back to the originator). Both Lowlands and Pennine also rebroadcast, even though Islands already has the message! This is known as flooding, because unnecessary copies of the original message flood the intranet.

Figure 2.6 illustrates another important point about internets, which is that there can be more than one route between two networks. Suppose a computer on the Lowlands network sends a message to a computer on the Islands network. The message goes to the Lowlands router, which can send it to the Pennine or Seaboard routers. The best choice is the Pennine router as it has a direct connection to the Islands router and Seaboard does not. In general, routers will use the destination address to identify the best route for a particular message. The details of how routers identify a 'best route' for a message to take are beyond the scope of this book.

There is a third problem with interconnected networks. The devices in a network communicate by sending messages, so must be able to understand those messages. This is achieved by **protocols**, which define a common language that is sufficient to achieve a specific task. The protocols used to facilitate client-server computing over an interconnected network have a layered structure (Figure 2.7), with each protocol relying on services provided by the layer below it. At the highest level, the application layer includes protocols that allow a client and server to understand one another. At the lowest level, the network layer has protocols specific to each particular network technology, allowing messages to be broadcast to a network. Often the client and server are in different networks, built with different network technologies, which are likely to use different protocols. The protocols of the internetwork layer allow messages to pass between these two networks. The layered structure means that the intricacies of dealing with the physical network infrastructure can be hidden from the application developer, who focuses on the application protocols relevant for his or her specific applications.

Note that the system software implementing the various internetwork and network protocols is installed on each network device. So, when a client application wishes to communicate with its server, it uses a local copy of the networking system software to create a network message. When this network message arrives at the network device

Figure 2.7 Layered protocols supporting Internet applications.

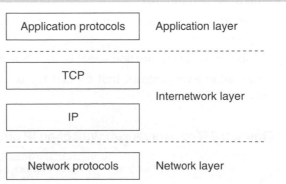

that hosts the application server, the local copy of the networking system software passes the message to the correct server application. It is useful to have a clear understanding of how the protocols of the internetwork layer achieve message delivery between client and server.

The Internet and its applications use a standard suite of protocols in the internetwork layer, but the most important of these are the **Transmission Control Protocol (TCP)** and the **Internet Protocol (IP)**. These are so important that the whole suite of protocols is called TCP/IP, even though it includes others.

> Strictly speaking, neither TCP nor IP uses the client-server architecture. They are both peer-to-peer protocols as the source and destination of a message are treated equally. However, client-server applications can use TCP/IP to send messages between the client and server. The application protocol will encapsulate the different roles of client and server.

As indicated in Figure 2.7, TCP and IP work at different levels. IP interconnects the networks on the Internet by providing a common addressing scheme and mechanisms to identify a route across the Internet from the source to the destination address. Each IP address of a network device has two parts (Figure 2.8). The **network number** identifies which network the device is connected to. The **host number** identifies a particular device in that network. Note that routers, and other devices that are connected to two or more networks, have a different IP address for each network they are connected to. The IP address is a 32-bit binary number, usually written as four integers, separated by dots, so 192.168.7.94 is a valid IP address. Note that the length of the network and host numbers vary (Rodriguez et al. (2001) give a more detailed description of IP addresses).

In general, network devices must have a unique IP address. However, two unconnected intranets may use the same IP addresses for their network devices as devices on one intranet will *never* interact with devices on the other. Thus, the standards governing the IP protocol reserve a set of IP addresses for use on intranets (192.168.7.94 is an IP address for an intranet device, rather than an Internet one).

IP sends messages as IP **datagrams**. Each IP datagram includes the actual data being sent and a header. The header holds important information, including:

- the IP version number
- IP address of the source – that is, the network device that generated the original message
- IP address of the destination – that is, the network device the message is intended for
- the higher-level protocol that created the datagram (often TCP, though there are others)

Figure 2.8 The general structure of an IP address.

$$\textit{IP address} \equiv \boxed{\textit{Network number}} \; \boxed{\textit{Host number}}$$

- the actual data being sent, which is passed to the higher-level protocol once at its destination
- time to live.

The last of these needs further explanation, and the explanation is tied up with IP routing – how IP datagrams are routed from their source to their destination.

Suppose an IP datagram is sent from a device in the Pennine network in Figure 2.6. If the destination is also in the Pennine network, the best route is directly across the local network, so IP sends the datagram that way. If the destination is not in the Pennine network, the IP datagram is sent to the Pennine router. The IP system software on the router checks whether or not the network number is one that it recognizes. This may be a network with a router directly connected to the Pennine router (the Lowlands, Seaboard or Islands routers we saw in Figure 2.6) or one connected via a chain of two or more routers (the Highland via Seaboard router in Figure 2.6). If so, the message is sent directly to the first router in the chain. Otherwise, it is sent to a default router.

In this sense, IP is a best effort protocol as the IP system software on each router does its best to find the destination, but, if it fails, hands the problem on to another router. Note that a routers list of known networks is updated regularly, so the 'best' route may change.

IP is also a connectionless protocol – there is no attempt to notify the destination address that a datagram is on the way. Indeed, the first router may not know if the destination address even exists. This is where the 'time to live' comes in. This is the number of routers the datagram can pass through before IP assumes that the destination address is wrong and throws the datagram away.

> Time to live is supposed to be the number of seconds the IP datagram is allowed to travel before being discarded. However, in practice, each router simply subtracts 1 from the time to live and sends the IP datagram on its way. When the time to live reaches 0, it is discarded.

As IP datagrams can be thrown away, IP is classed as an unreliable protocol. This is a problem for Internet applications. IP datagrams have a maximum size, so a large message generated by applications will be split up into several IP datagrams. These IP datagrams may travel by different routes and so may arrive in a different order from that in which they were sent. It is possible for some of them to not arrive at all if, for example, they are sent by a particularly circuitous route as they may be thrown away before reaching their destination. IP has no mechanism to allow the network device at the destination address to inform the sending device of any such problems. This is where TCP comes into the picture.

TCP adds a layer of processing above IP, allowing reliable communication for client-server applications. Consider what happens when a networked workstation is running several applications, such as an e-mail client, a web browser and an FTP client. The IP address simply identifies the workstation itself, so IP does not know that a particular message is for a particular application. TCP assigns each application running on a workstation, or a server, a unique local identifier called a **port number**. The combination of IP address and port number is called a **socket** and allows TCP to route messages directly between a client and server (or, more generally, between any two computer programs that need to communicate).

Internet application servers tend to use **well-known port numbers** between 1 and 1023 and each will always have this port number. For example, most web servers are always given TCP port 80 (see IANA (2005) for a full list). Clients tend to use an **ephemeral port number** (1024 or greater), which is not fixed for each one. This is because most TCP connections are initiated by the client requesting a service from the server. The client needs to know the IP address and port number of its server, but can tell the server its own IP address and port number in its initial message.

The combination of the source and destination sockets forms the **TCP connection** (Figure 2.9). TCP establishes a connection between the source of a message and the intended destination, which, typically, are the client and server of a client-server application. The TCP system software running on the source computer sends a message to the destination. Once it has been acknowledged by the TCP system software on the destination computer, the connection is established. If the destination IP address or the destination port number are not recognized, TCP reports an error.

TCP uses the connection to provide reliable delivery of IP datagrams. The TCP system software on the destination computer acknowledges receipt of each IP datagram. If the TCP system software on the source computer does not receive acknowledgement within a set time, it will resend the lost IP datagram.

TCP also deals with the problem of large messages by splitting them into segments and sending each segment in its own IP datagram. The TCP system software on the destination computer collects all the segments, sets them into the correct order and reassembles the original message. This is known as stream data transfer as, to the application using TCP, its data appears to have been transmitted in a continuous stream. This is often essential. For example, when a database client sends a sequence of instructions to the DBMS, they must be carried out in the correct order.

TCP provides three other, slightly more technical, features. First, it is a full duplex protocol – that is, the source and destination can be sending messages simultaneously. This is a little like two people talking over one another, but still being able to understand everything that is said.

Second, as each application using TCP gets its own port number, TCP can manage communications for multiple applications, concurrently – this is called multiplexing.

Finally, the TCP system software on the destination computer can let the TCP system software on the source computer know how busy it is. This allows TCP to slow

Figure 2.9 TCP connection.

TCP Connection ≡	Source IP address	Source port	Destination IP address	Destination port

down the rate at which it sends data through the connection, to ease the load at the other end. This is called flow control.

Numeric IP addresses are not easy for people to remember. They are all right for workstations, which hold only client software, but users need to remember the location of application servers (especially web servers). A **domain name** is an easily remembered alternative to an IP address. Domain names have a hierarchical structure and should be read from right to left. Consider the domain name www.pennine.ac.uk. The '.uk' is the top-level domain – in this case, indicating that the server is managed by an organization in the United Kingdom. There is a top-level domain for each country in the world and they are called country code top-level domains (ccTLD). There are also several generic top-level domains (gTLD), such as .com and .org, which are not associated with any particular country.

> Originally there were only gTLD. Only when the Internet spread out from its origins in the USA were ccTLD added. Most organizations in the USA have domain names with a gTLD. The USA's ccTLD is '.us', but it is not widely used.

Each top-level domain has a number of subdomains. Thus, 'www.pennine.ac.uk' is in the '.ac.uk' subdomain, which is reserved for educational establishments in the United Kingdom (the 'ac' stands for 'academic'). Other domains below '.uk' include '.co.uk' for companies, '.gov.uk' for government sites and so on. Below the '.ac.uk' domain, each educational establishment has its own domain, so the Pennine University manages the '.pennine.ac.uk' domain. Finally, the 'www' is used by the Pennine University to indicate that this domain name gets the user to the university's website. As the Pennine University manages all the domain names under the '.pennine.ac.uk' domain, it *could* use the domain name 'OurPublicwebsite.pennine.ac.uk'. By convention, 'www' is shorthand for just that.

> The **domain name system (DNS)** is currently overseen by the Internet Corporation for Assigned Names and Numbers (ICANN). It decides on what top-level domains should be available. Further information on domain names and the DNS is available from its website at www.icann.org

Note that, although all the examples so far have had four parts to their domain names, this is not a requirement. For example, 'www.wikipedia.org' has only three, and 'fr.comp.pennine.ac.uk' has five (it happens to be the French language version of the School of Computing's website). There is *no* direct connection between the four numbers in the IP address and the different parts of a domain name.

The domain name system (DNS) allows an Internet application to translate a domain name, which is used by the application users, into the corresponding IP address, which is used by the router. The idea is that each top-level domain has a **name server** that maintains a database of domain names and their corresponding IP addresses. So, for example, there will be a name server dealing with domain names ending '.uk'. As this would be a very large database, the '.uk' domain (and every other top-level domain) is divided up into zones. For example, there might be a '.ac.uk' zone and a '.co.uk' zone, each with its own name server. Zones are defined in such a way that the associated name server is not overloaded with requests for IP addresses. Thus, when a user gives a domain name to an Internet application, the application looks at the top-level domain and asks the name server for this domain to supply the IP address. The top-level domain name server may refer the request to the name server of one of its zones, but eventually the request is fulfilled. Note that this is done via the Internet; there is no need for a physical connection to the name servers.

IP addresses, domain names and ports are all concepts that allow the networking technology to route messages between a client and server. The **uniform resource locator (URL)** allows the client to specify exactly which resource it wants from a particular server. For example, a web browser uses a URL to tell the web server which web page (resource) it wants.

URLs are used by a number of different Internet applications, called **schemes**, but have a standard format. Figure 2.10 (a) shows the general structure for a URL. The name of the scheme (typically the application protocol name) is first, followed by a colon – ':' – then some scheme-specific information. The structure of the scheme-specific information varies from scheme to scheme, but Figure 2.10 (b) shows the structure commonly used by application protocols that are based on IP. First come two forward slashes – '//'. Immediately following these comes the login information – the username and password, separated by a colon and terminated by an '@' symbol. Login information is optional and usually it is *not* included as including usernames and passwords in a URL is now recognized as being very insecure. The first compulsory part is the 'host', which is the IP address, or domain name, of the application server. Following this is the optional TCP port information, preceded by a colon. As most Internet applications have a default port, this is usually omitted, too. Next comes a single forward slash – '/' – followed by the optional URL path. The URL path indicates how to access the resource and may include data that the client is sending to the server, so is specific to the scheme.

Consider the URL 'http://www.pennine.ac.uk:80/index.html'. The scheme is HTTP, which indicates a web application. The host is 'www.pennine.ac.uk', the Pennine University's web server. This host is attached to the TCP port 80, the standard port number for web servers. Finally, the URL path is 'index.html'. For web URLs, this indicates a

Figure 2.10 The structure of a URL.

$$URL \equiv \boxed{Scheme} \; : \; \boxed{\textit{Scheme-specific information}}$$

(a) The URL.

$$URL \; for \; scheme\text{-}specific \; information \equiv \boxed{//} \boxed{User \; name} : \boxed{Password} @ \boxed{Host} : \boxed{Port} / \boxed{URL \; path}$$

(b) The scheme-specific part of a URL for IP-based application protocols.

Figure 2.11 Structure of the URL path for the HTTP scheme.

HTTP scheme URL path ≡ | *Path* | ? | *Query* | # | *Fragment identifier* |

particular file managed by the web server. Note that login information (user and password) is not allowed in a URL with the HTTP scheme (Berners-Lee, 1994).

> A URL is one form of the uniform resource identifier (URI). The URL identifies the network address of a resource, so, if a resource moves, its URL changes.
>
> The other form of URI is the uniform resource name (URN). A URN defines a unique name for the *resource,* rather than its network *location.* The idea is to translate a URN into a URL, rather like a domain name is translated to an IP address. This allows the URN to stay the same even when the resource is moved, so provides a constant way to locate the resource – no more broken links on a website. Unfortunately, the technology to support URN has not been widely implemented, so, for now, the URL is the main way to locate a resource.

The URL path for the HTTP scheme can be more complex than a simple file name. For web database applications, the important components of the URL path are shown in Figure 2.11. The path component indicates where the requested resource is stored in the web server's file system. The query (or query string) component is used to pass information to the DBMS. For example, the URL 'http://www.pennine.ac.uk/StaffDirectory/StaffDetail.php?staffNo=31210' has a path component 'StaffDirectory/StaffDetail.php', which indicates a PHP script file held in the StaffDirectory folder. The query component – 'staffNo=31210' – passes a staff number to the PHP script, which it uses to query the database.

Strictly speaking, the fragment identifier (shown in Figure 2.11) is not actually part of the URL. Its purpose is to identify a particular section within the resource. For HTML documents, the fragment identifier tells the web browser which part of a long web page to display in the browser window. Users can simply scroll up or down to see the rest.

2.3 Database technology

Database applications apply database and networking technologies to solve a real-world problem – building an information system to help people use their data effectively. Most database applications have a client-server architecture, with the two-tier architecture shown in Figure 2.1 being the basic approach. There may be many instances of the client (identical copies of the client software) installed on different computers. However, there is only one database server, so this architecture supports data sharing. It also supports there being multiple users of the database, as the database server can communicate with many different clients at the same time.

This section examines the server and client technologies used to develop database applications.

Figure 2.12 The database server.

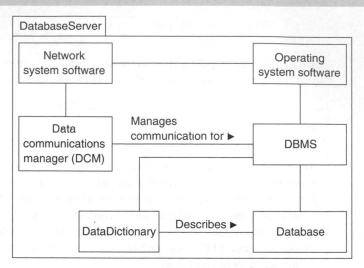

Figure 2.12 highlights the major software and data components of the server tier. The database server includes the operating system (OS) software, which manipulates the physical files and computer's memory according to instructions from the DBMS. The role of the network system software has already been discussed. The interface between the DBMS and the network system software is quite complex, so is usually treated as a separate component – the data communications manager (DCM) in Figure 2.12.

The main application software is the database management system (DBMS). This manages the actual database and its data dictionary by means of a range of functions.

The server's software is not usually written by database application developers. Instead, they use an existing DBMS (with its associated DCM) to create a database (with its associated data dictionary) that meets the end user's requirements. The DBMS has a range of functions that allow application developers to do this.

> The DBMS is classed as application software as its functions allow end users to carry out tasks that benefit them directly. However, it is now rarely used directly by end users. Instead, they interact with increasingly sophisticated database client applications and these interact with the DBMS. It could be argued that, as the DBMS sinks into the background, it becomes more like system software.

A database is a self-describing collection of data. One function of the DBMS is to maintain a description of the database schema (its data structures and constraints) and provide users with access to this meta-data. It keeps the meta-data in the **data dictionary** (sometimes called a **system catalogue**). As users modify the data structures and constraints, the DBMS updates the data dictionary so that it always presents an accurate description of the database schema. The data definition functions allow the user to create and modify data structures and constraints and are at the heart of the DBMS. The underlying data model describes what data structures and constraints are available for a particular database. Most DBMS can manage databases based on the relational data model and some support other data models.

> Data definition functions are used to define the *data structures* and *constraints*, not the actual data.

Once the data structures have been created, users will want to fill them with data. After all, an empty database is not of much use. The DBMS provides data manipulation functions to manage the actual data that forms the database instance. Users can add data and modify or remove existing data. They can also ask to view data from the database. A request to view selected data held in the database is called a **database query**. The DBMS also provides data integrity functions that monitor users' requests to modify the data and ensure that these changes do not violate the database's constraints. This means that the database instance is always consistent.

A database is a *shared* collection of data, so the DBMS must be able to deal with many users making different requests at the same time. It provides concurrency functions to keep users' interactions separate.

A DBMS also provides a number of security functions related to users. When a user asks to use the database, the DBMS must check that he or she is allowed access to it. Identification and authentication functions achieve this. The usual approach is to identify users by a username, which is authenticated by a password. If a user fails to identify him or herself correctly (wrong username) or fails to authenticate his or her identity (wrong password), the DBMS denies access to the database.

Once users have gained access, they request that the DBMS carry out actions on their behalf. Authorization functions check that the user is authorized to make each request. For example, in the University Staff Directory database, Paul Smith is *not* authorized to change Freya Stark's staff details, though he *is* authorized to view them. The DBMS must store all this security information – usernames, passwords and authorization details. Although the exact data will vary from DBMS to DBMS, most store it in the data dictionary. Thus, the data dictionary is a central repository of the data and meta-data that the DBMS needs to carry out its functions.

The database is not usually located on the user's own machine, so a DBMS must have a set of communication functions allowing it to send and receive messages. This may or may not involve sending messages over a network. For example, some database clients are installed on the same computer as the database server.

In addition, database technology was widely adopted before the rise of internetworking technology and the TCP/IP protocol suite, so most DBMS have their own approaches to client-server communication over a network. Strictly speaking, it is not the DBMS that handles this, but the **data communications manager (DCM)**. This software works alongside the DBMS to integrate it with local clients or the network system software. However, for most purposes, it is reasonable to treat the DCM as being part of the DBMS.

The concurrency, security and communications functions allow the DBMS to manage its users. Together with the data definition functions, which manage the database schema, and data manipulation and integrity functions, which manage the database instance, they form the core functionality of the DBMS, summarized in Table 2.1.

Table 2.1 Core DBMS functionality.

DBMS functions	Purpose
Data definition	To allow users to define and modify the database schema and provide access to, and maintain, the data dictionary
Data manipulation	To allow users to manipulate the database instance
Integrity	To ensure changes to the database instance satisfy all database constraints
Concurrency	To allow multi-user access to the database
Security	To provide identification and authentication of users and authorization of their actions
Communication	To allow client and server to communicate

Most DBMS also provide some utility functions, making the DBMS itself more useful. A DBMS will usually provide backup functions. These create a copy of the database, both the data and the meta-data. The database backup can be stored safely in case the actual database is lost if, for example, the disk crashes or a virus damages the database. If the database is lost or damaged, the DBMS recovery functions can recreate the database from the backup copy. This is the simplest form of recovery. Many commercial DBMS have more sophisticated recovery functions. For example, a power failure will stop the DBMS working immediately. If it was part way through writing data to the disk, then it's possible that one or more integrity constraints would be violated so the database instance would be inconsistent. When the power returns, some DBMS can automatically return the database instance to a consistent state.

A database may replace an existing information system. It is unlikely that the users will want to retype all the existing data, so a DBMS is usually able to import this data directly into the new data structures. Similarly, it can export data ready to import into a different database. These import/export functions allow data exchange between databases that use different data models.

All the above functions must be performed efficiently, so a DBMS usually has a set of performance and optimization functions. These allow users to monitor performance and identify suitable optimizations. Different DBMS may offer more or fewer utility functions. The particular needs of the database application will determine which functions are used and which are not.

Chapter 1 discussed the problem of program–data dependence and noted that an important advantage of database applications is that they do not suffer from this problem. A database system architecture gives a high-level description of how to achieve program–data independence and other benefits.

The best-known of these is the ANSI/SPARC database system architecture (Figure 2.13). It identifies three views of the data structures and data that comprise a particular database–external, logical and internal. Each is a view of the *same* database, so it is possible to move between them. The idea is that each view provides an image of the database appropriate to a different group of database users. At the highest level are the views seen by the end users. Few end users need to see the whole database, so it is sensible to hide any irrelevant parts from them. Thus, each external view provides a tailored view

Figure 2.13 The ANSI/SPARC architecture for database systems.

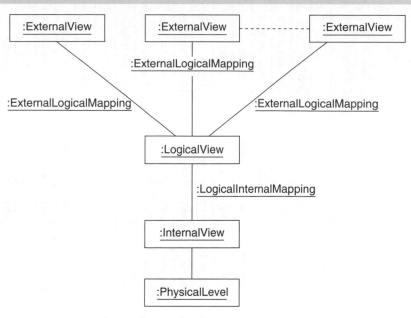

of the data structures and data for a group of end users with similar information needs. Often, a different external view will be defined for each client application, as Figure 2.13 indicates by showing three external views.

Below the external views is the logical view. It provides a complete description of the data structures and data in the database, so there is a single logical view for each database. The logical view is often called the community view as it serves the whole community of database users. Application developers and database administrators use the logical view to understand what data is available and how it can be used to meet the information needs of end users.

For each external view, they develop an external-logical mapping. In Figure 2.13, these are shown as the lines joining the external views to the logical view. Each external-logical mapping describes how the data structures in a particular external view are derived from the data structures of the logical view.

Both the logical and external views provide descriptions of the database in terms of the underlying data model. This is a useful, human-friendly way of thinking about the data structures and data in the database. However, the focus is on organizing the data into meaningful structures. Data models usually ignore data storage issues – what space is available for data storage, how the data is stored and what techniques are used to ensure data can be accessed efficiently.

There are various data storage structures available to deal with these issues. The internal view of the ANSI/SPARC database systems architecture describes which of these data storage structures are used and how. Each data structure from the logical view is linked to data storage structures of the internal view. The logical-internal mapping shown in Figure 2.13 describes these links.

An example of a particular data storage structure is clustered data. Figure 2.14 shows an instance of the `Staff` table, with data clustered by `jobType` – all members of staff

Figure 2.14 Data from the `Staff` table clustered by job type.

Staff

staffNo	fName	lName	phone	email	photo	department	title	jobType	jobTitle
35054	Selma	Hutchins	8706	s.hutchins@pennine.ac.uk	[BLOB]	Computing	Ms	Academic	Senior Lecturer
55776	Gurpreet	Choudhury	5454	g.choudhury@pennine.ac.uk	[BLOB]	Music	Dr	Academic	Senior Lecturer
56673	Joshua	Bittaye	7782	j.bittaye@pennine.ac.uk	[BLOB]	Computing	Mr	Academic	Lecturer
45965	Mikhail	Sudbin	5553	m.sudbin@pennine.ac.uk	[BLOB]	Music	Mr	Academic	Lecturer
23257	Freya	Stark	8660	f.stark@pennine.ac.uk	[BLOB]	Computing	Prof	Academic	Dean
56893	Ruth	Bapetsi	8022	r.bapetsi@pennine.ac.uk	[BLOB]	Health	Mrs	Academic	Senior Lecturer
31210	Paul	Smith	NULL	p.smith@pennine.ac.uk	[BLOB]	Computing	Dr	Academic	Senior Lecturer
89987	Dan	Lin	8514	d.lin@pennine.co.uk	[BLOB]	Health	Dr	Administration	Senior Administrator
78893	Jo Karen	O'Connor	8871	j.k.oconnor@pennine.ac.uk	[BLOB]	Health	Miss	Administration	Administrator
25447	John	Smith	5104	j.smith@pennine.ac.uk	[BLOB]	Music	Mr	Administration	Secretary
14443	Helen	Abbot	8032	h.abbot@pennine.ac.uk	[BLOB]	Computing	Mrs	Administration	Secretary
33935	Padma	Brar	6641	p.brar@pennine.ac.uk	[BLOB]	Health	Ms	Administration	Administrator
25448	Judith Anne	Smith	7709	j.a.smith@pennine.ac.uk	[BLOB]	Estates	Mrs	Support	Estates Manager
10780	John	Smith	NULL	j.b.smith@pennine.ac.uk	[BLOB]	Catering	Mr	Support	Chef
33509	Helen	Timms	8661	h.timms@pennine.ac.uk	[BLOB]	Music	Mrs	Technical	Technician
77712	Frank	Rose	8871	f.rose@pennine.ac.uk	[BLOB]	Computing	Mr	Technical	Technician
35155	Helene	Chirac	NULL	h.chirac@pennine.ac.uk	[BLOB]	Health	Miss	Technical	Technician

with the same type of job being stored in a continuous chunk. This makes it easy to retrieve a list of academics, for example. You just read through the academics, noting their details, and, when you reach the first administrator, you stop. In contrast, to find *all* staff in the School of Health, you must read through all the data or you'd miss Helene Chirac, the department's technician, as she's neither an academic nor an administrator.

It's important to understand that clustering data is about more than simply ordering the rows. For example, the DBMS keeps track of the starting point for each cluster, so can skip through the stored data directly to the first row with jobType 'Administration'. Data storage structures are discussed in more detail in Chapter 10.

Figure 2.15 presents an image of the data and data structures in the Staff Directory database at the three different levels of the ANSI/SPARC database systems architecture. It shows the external views for two applications – the Staff Directory itself (labelled StaffDirectory : ExternalView) and the School of Computing's Staff List (labelled ComputingStaffList : ExternalView). Both these applications use the same Staff Directory database, but have different views of the data. For example, in the external view for the Staff Directory, the Staff table does not hold the titles of members of staff, nor any details about their jobs. Similarly, the external view for the School of Computing's Staff List has no details of support sessions.

All the data in these two external views is derived from the data held in the logical view (labelled StaffData : LogicalView), although the derivation is not always a straight copy. For example, in the external view for the School of Computing's Staff List the name column of the StaffList table is a combination of data from three columns of the logical view (see Figure 2.16).

In the internal view, the data for the StaffList and SupportSession tables is stored in an appropriate format. The data storage structures shown in StaffData : InternalView in Figure 2.15 are explained in Chapter 10 (note that not all data is shown for the internal view).

It is worth analysing more closely the mapping between the two external views and the logical view. The external view for the Staff Directory includes the SupportSession table unaltered – all rows and columns present in the logical view are visible in the external view. The Staff table in the external view does not have the final four columns of that in the logical view, but includes all the rows. Figure 2.15 shows these differences.

The mapping between the external view for the School of Computing's Staff List and the logical view is more complex. First, there is no data from the logical view's SupportSession table in this external view. The data in the StaffList table in the external view is drawn solely from the logical view's Staff table. However, the StaffList table does not include data from every row of the logical view's Staff table, only from those rows in which the department column has the value 'Computing' (check the staffNo column values shown in Figures 2.15 or 2.16 to verify this). This makes sense from the application's perspective as it is only supposed to show staff from the School of Computing.

Note that the StaffList table does not include all the columns of the logical view's Staff table either. The photo, department, title, fName and lName are all absent.

Finally, the data value in the name column of the StaffList table in the external view is a combination of data from the title, fName and lName columns in the

Figure 2.15 Staff and support session data at the different levels of the ANSI/SPARC architecture.

StaffDirectory : ExternalView

Staff

staffNo	fName	lName	phone	email	photo
10780	John	Smith	NULL	j.b.smith@pennine.ac.uk	[BLOB]
25447	John	Smith	5104	j.smith@pennine.ac.uk	[BLOB]
25448	Judith Anne	Smith	7709	j.a.smith@pennine.ac.uk	[BLOB]
31210	Paul	Smith	NULL	p.smith@pennine.ac.uk	[BLOB]
77712	Frank	Rose	8871	f.rose@pennine.ac.uk	[BLOB]
14443	Helen	Abbot	8032	h.abbot@pennine.ac.uk	[BLOB]
23257	Freya	Stark	8660	f.stark@pennine.ac.uk	[BLOB]
33935	Padma	Brar	6641	p.brar@pennine.ac.uk	[BLOB]
35054	Selma	Hutchins	8706	s.hutchins@pennine.ac.uk	[BLOB]
45965	Mikhail	Sudbin	5553	m.sudbin@pennine.ac.uk	[BLOB]
35155	Helene	Chirac	NULL	h.chirac@pennine.ac.uk	[BLOB]
55776	Gurpreet	Choudhury	5454	g.choudhury@pennine.ac.uk	[BLOB]
56893	Ruth	Bapetsi	8022	r.bapetsi@pennine.ac.uk	[BLOB]
56673	Joshua	Bittaye	7782	j.bittaye@pennine.ac.uk	[BLOB]
89987	Dan	Lin	8514	d.lin@pennine.co.uk	[BLOB]
78893	Jo Karen	O'Connor	8871	j.k.oconnor@pennine.ac.uk	[BLOB]
33509	Helen	Timms	8661	h.timms@pennine.ac.uk	[BLOB]

SupportSession

staffNo	dayOfWeek	startTime	endTime
35054	Monday	09:00:00	10:00:00
31210	Wednesday	11:00:00	13:00:00
35054	Monday	15:00:00	16:00:00
45965	Monday	11:00:00	12:00:00
23257	Wednesday	11:00:00	12:00:00
55776	Monday	15:00:00	16:00:00
56893	Monday	14:00:00	16:00:00
56893	Tuesday	14:00:00	15:00:00
56893	Thursday	09:00:00	10:00:00
56673	Thursday	15:30:00	16:30:00
56673	Friday	10:00:00	11:00:00

ComputingStaffList : ExternalView

StaffList

staffNo	name	phone	email	jobTitle	jobType
31210	Dr P Smith	NULL	p.smith@pennine.ac.uk	Senior Lecturer	Academic
77712	Mr F Rose	8871	f.rose@pennine.ac.uk	Technician	Technical
14443	Mrs H Abbot	8032	h.abbot@pennine.ac.uk	Secretary	Administration
23257	Prof F Stark	8660	f.stark@pennine.ac.uk	Dean	Academic
35054	Ms S Hutchins	8706	s.hutchins@pennine.ac.uk	Senior Lecturer	Academic
56673	Mr J Bittaye	7782	j.bittaye@pennine.ac.uk	Lecturer	Academic

StaffData : LogicalView

Staff

staffNo	fName	lName	phone	email	photo	department	title	jobTitle	jobType
10780	John	Smith	NULL	j.b.smith@pennine.ac.uk	[BLOB]	Catering	Mr	Chef	Support
25447	John	Smith	5104	j.smith@pennine.ac.uk	[BLOB]	Music	Mr	Administration	Administration
25448	Judith Anne	Smith	7709	j.a.smith@pennine.ac.uk	[BLOB]	Estates	Mrs	Estates Manager	Support
31210	Paul	Smith	NULL	p.smith@pennine.ac.uk	[BLOB]	Computing	Dr	Senior Lecturer	Academic
77712	Frank	Rose	8871	f.rose@pennine.ac.uk	[BLOB]	Computing	Mr	Technician	Technical
14443	Helen	Abbot	8032	h.abbot@pennine.ac.uk	[BLOB]	Computing	Mrs	Secretary	Administration
23257	Freya	Stark	8660	f.stark@pennine.ac.uk	[BLOB]	Computing	Prof	Dean	Academic
33935	Padma	Brar	6641	p.brar@pennine.ac.uk	[BLOB]	Health	Ms	Administrator	Administration
35054	Selma	Hutchins	8706	s.hutchins@pennine.ac.uk	[BLOB]	Computing	Ms	Senior Lecturer	Academic
45965	Mikhail	Sudbin	5553	m.sudbin@pennine.ac.uk	[BLOB]	Music	Mr	Lecturer	Academic
35155	Helene	Chirac	NULL	h.chirac@pennine.ac.uk	[BLOB]	Health	Miss	Technician	Technical
55776	Gurpreet	Choudhury	5454	g.choudhury@pennine.ac.uk	[BLOB]	Music	Dr	Senior Lecturer	Academic
56893	Ruth	Bapetsi	8022	r.bapetsi@pennine.ac.uk	[BLOB]	Health	Mrs	Senior Lecturer	Academic
56673	Joshua	Bittaye	7782	j.bittaye@pennine.ac.uk	[BLOB]	Computing	Mr	Lecturer	Academic
89987	Dan	Lin	8514	d.lin@pennine.co.uk	[BLOB]	Health	Dr	Senior Administrator	Administration
78893	Jo Karen	O'Connor	8871	j.k.oconnor@pennine.ac.uk	[BLOB]	Health	Miss	Administrator	Administration
33509	Helen	Timms	8661	h.timms@pennine.ac.uk	[BLOB]	Music	Mrs	Technician	Technical

SupportSession

staffNo	dayOfWeek	startTime	endTime
35054	Monday	09:00:00	10:00:00
31210	Wednesday	11:00:00	13:00:00
35054	Monday	15:00:00	16:00:00
45965	Monday	11:00:00	12:00:00
23257	Monday	15:00:00	16:00:00
55776	Monday	14:00:00	16:00:00
56893	Tuesday	14:00:00	15:00:00
56893	Thursday	09:00:00	10:00:00
56673	Thursday	15:30:00	16:30:00
56673	Friday	10:00:00	11:00:00

StaffData : InternalView

```
Index file header
No of blocks: 1
Block 1: <pointer to block 1>

Block 1
10780, <pointer to data file block 1>
25447, <pointer to data file block 1>
25448, <pointer to data file block 1>
31210, <pointer to data file block 1>
77712, <pointer to data file block 1>
14443, <pointer to data file block 2>
23257, <pointer to data file block 2>
33257, <pointer to data file block 2>
33935, <pointer to data file block 2>
35054, <pointer to data file block 2>
```

```
Data file header
No of blocks: 2
Block 1: <pointer to block 1>
Block 2: <pointer to block 2>

Block 1
10780, John , Smith , NULL , j.b.smith@pennine.ac.uk
25447, John, Smith, 5104, j.smith@pennine.ac.uk
25448, Judith Anne, Smith, 7709, j.a.smith@pennine.ac.uk
31210, Paul, Smith, NULL, p.smith@pennine.ac.uk
77712, Wednesday, 11:00:00, 13:00:00,
77712, Frank, Rose, 8871, f.rose@pennine.ac.uk

Block 2
14443, Helen, Abbot, 8032, h.abbot@pennine.ac.uk
23257, Freya, Stark, 8660, f.stark@pennine.ac.uk
23257, Monday, 15:00:00, 16:00:00,
33935, Padma, Brar, 6641, p.brar@pennine.ac.uk
35054, Selma, Hutchins, 8706, s.hutchins@pennine.ac.uk
35054, Monday, 09:00:00, 10:00:00,
```

Figure 2.16 The external-logical mapping: a column value in the external view is derived from three of the column values in the logical view.

ComputingStaffList : ExternalView

StaffList

staffNo	name	phone	email	jobTitle	jobType
31210	Dr P Smith	NULL	p.smith@pennine.ac.uk	Senior Lecturer	Academic
77712	Mr F Rose	8871	f.rose@pennine.ac.uk	Technician	Technical
14443	Mrs H Abbot	8032	h.abbot@pennine.ac.uk	Secretary	Administration
23257	Prof F Stark	8660	f.stark@pennine.ac.uk	Dean	Academic
35054	Ms S Hutchins	8706	s.hutchins@pennine.ac.uk	Senior Lecturer	Academic
56673	Mr J Bittaye	7782	j.bittaye@pennine.ac.uk	Lecturer	Academic

StaffData : LogicalView

Staff

staffNo	fName	lName	phone	email	photo	department	title	jobType	jobTitle
10780	John	Smith	NULL	j.b.smith@pennine.ac.uk	[BLOB]	Catering	Mr	Support	Chef
25447	John	Smith	5104	j.smith@pennine.ac.uk	[BLOB]	Music	Mr	Administration	Secretary
25448	Judith Anne	Smith	7709	j.a.smith@pennine.ac.uk	[BLOB]	Estates	Mrs	Support	Estates Manager
31210	Paul	Smith	NULL	p.smith@pennine.ac.uk	[BLOB]	Computing	Dr	Academic	Senior Lecturer
77712	Frank	Rose	8871	f.rose@pennine.ac.uk	[BLOB]	Computing	Mr	Technical	Technician
14443	Helen	Abbot	8032	h.abbot@pennine.ac.uk	[BLOB]	Computing	Mrs	Administration	Secretary
23257	Freya	Stark	8660	f.stark@pennine.ac.uk	[BLOB]	Computing	Prof	Academic	Dean
33935	Padma	Brar	6641	p.brar@pennine.ac.uk	[BLOB]	Health	Ms	Administration	Administrator
35054	Selma	Hutchins	8706	s.hutchins@pennine.ac.uk	[BLOB]	Computing	Ms	Academic	Senior Lecturer
45965	Mikhail	Sudbin	5553	m.sudbin@pennine.ac.uk	[BLOB]	Music	Mr	Academic	Lecturer
35155	Helene	Chirac	NULL	h.chirac@pennine.ac.uk	[BLOB]	Health	Miss	Technical	Technician
55776	Gurpreet	Choudhury	5454	g.choudhury@pennine.ac.uk	[BLOB]	Music	Dr	Academic	Senior Lecturer
56893	Ruth	Bapetsi	8022	r.bapetsi@pennine.ac.uk	[BLOB]	Health	Mrs	Academic	Senior Lecturer
56673	Joshua	Bittaye	7782	j.bittaye@pennine.ac.uk	[BLOB]	Computing	Mr	Academic	Lecturer
89987	Dan	Lin	8514	d.lin@pennine.co.uk	[BLOB]	Health	Dr	Administration	Senior Administrator
78893	Jo Karen	O'Connor	8871	j.k.oconnor@pennine.ac.uk	[BLOB]	Health	Miss	Administration	Administrator
33509	Helen	Timms	8661	h.timms@pennine.ac.uk	[BLOB]	Music	Mrs	Technical	Technician

SupportSession

staffNo	dayOfWeek	startTime	endTime
35054	Monday	09:00:00	10:00:00
31210	Wednesday	11:00:00	13:00:00
35054	Monday	15:00:00	16:00:00
45965	Monday	11:00:00	12:00:00
45965	Wednesday	11:00:00	12:00:00
23257	Monday	15:00:00	16:00:00
55776	Monday	14:00:00	16:00:00
56893	Tuesday	14:00:00	15:00:00
56893	Thursday	09:00:00	10:00:00
56673	Thursday	15:30:00	16:30:00
56673	Friday	10:00:00	11:00:00

logical view's `Staff` table. Figure 2.16 shows how this data value has been derived. To support this mapping, the DBMS must be able to strip off the first letter of `fName` and combine it with `title` and `lName` into a single data value.

The main goal of all this is data independence – a key feature of the database approach. Separating the external and logical views achieves **logical data independence** – that is, data structures in the logical view can change without necessarily affecting the external views. Some changes to the logical view *will* affect the external views, but such changes can be kept to a minimum. Separating the logical and internal levels achieves **physical data independence** – that is, the data storage structures of the internal view can change without necessarily affecting the logical view.

> **Logical data independence** This insulates the external view from changes to the logical view.
>
> **Physical data independence** This insulates the logical view from changes to the internal view.

The ANSI/SPARC database systems architecture is concerned with managing the database. It is not concerned with how the data is used, nor with how it is presented. Its main achievement is to provide an architecture for database systems with data independence as a built-in feature.

The internal view is the lowest level of the ANSI/SPARC database systems architecture. Beneath it (in Figure 2.13) is the physical level – the actual physical files that implement the data storage structures on disk. In most cases, the computer's operating system (such as Windows or UNIX) is used to read from and write to these physical files. The physical level is not really part of the ANSI/SPARC database systems architecture, though it is usually shown for completeness.

Like the database server, the database client includes both system software and application software (as shown in Figure 2.17). In contrast to the server software, the application developer does create the database client application software and this forms the focus of much of the rest of the book.

Figure 2.17 The database client.

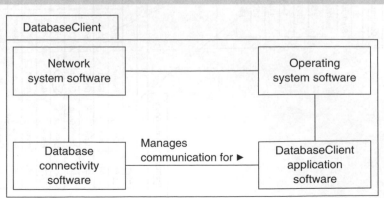

Some DBMS manufacturers also offer client development solutions to complement their DBMS software. Oracle Forms are only ever used to develop database client applications that connect with an Oracle database, and Microsoft Access bundles an integrated development environment and a simple DBMS into a single package. However, in most cases, the tools used to develop the database client application software are not tied to any one DBMS. That is why Figure 2.17 includes a separate component, labelled database connectivity software. This is the part of the database client that handles communication with whatever DBMS sits on the database server. It allows the database client application software to establish a connection with the DBMS, pass instructions to it (to create a table or retrieve some data from the database, for example) and correctly interpret the results sent back by the DBMS. It is worth emphasizing that the communication protocols used may not be TCP/IP as database technology predates the wide adoption of TCP/IP by a couple of decades.

There is a range of possible approaches to creating the database connectivity software. Each DBMS includes one or more **application programming interfaces (API)**. An API is a little like a protocol, but is focused on allowing the client direct access to certain server-side functions, rather than simply passing messages between client and server. A DBMS API exposes a set of DBMS functions that can be called directly from the program code of the database client application software. A DBMS may provide different API for different programming languages. For example, the MySQL DBMS has an API for the programming languages C, C++, Perl, PHP, Python and Tcl. In later sections, the PHP API is used to connect a database client to the MySQL DBMS.

An alternative to using an API tailored to a particular programming language is to use the general API offered by the open database connectivity (ODBC) standard. Most DBMS vendors offer ODBC client software – called an ODBC driver – that allows database client application software to connect to their DBMS. The ODBC driver interfaces with the call-level interface (CLI) API of the DBMS, so it simply adds a standard layer of function calls between the database client and DBMS. This means that it is, in theory, possible to change the DBMS and the ODBC driver, but not have to change any of the code in the database client application software.

The main value of ODBC is to those using a programming language that does not have an API defined for their chosen DBMS. For example, there is no Visual Basic API defined for the MySQL DBMS, so any database client application software written in Visual Basic would need to use ODBC. Figure 2.18 illustrates the difference between

Figure 2.18 Two approaches to client-side database connectivity.

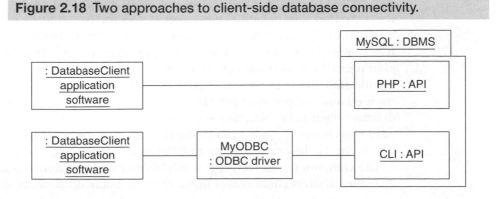

Figure 2.19 Establishing a connection between a database client and database server.

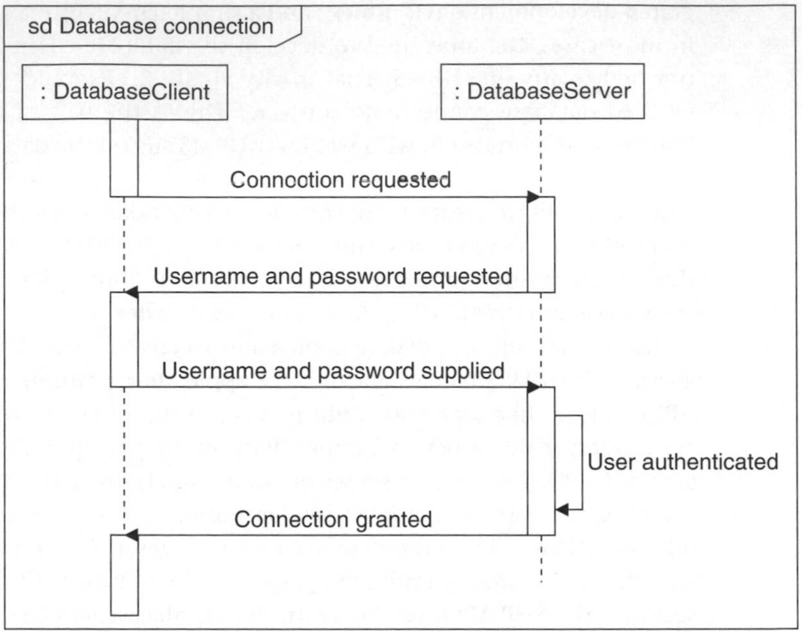

connecting database client application software to the MySQL DBMS PHP API directly and using ODBC to achieve the connection.

To round off this section, it is worth noting that, for applications written using the Java programming language, there is JDBC. This provides similar functionality to that of ODBC, but only for the Java language.

The client and database server communicate by sending messages. To begin communication, the client must connect to the database server. This can be a complex process, so Figure 2.19 presents a much simplified view, highlighting the main messages sent between a database client and database server. The diagram (a UML sequence diagram, indicated by the 'sd' in the top left corner) shows a particular database client and its database server. The dashed lines below them are timelines, indicating the passage of time. The rectangles overlaying the timelines indicate whether the client or the server currently has the initiative. Initially, the database client has the initiative, as it is the client that must request a connection. It does this by sending a message, indicated by the arrow labelled 'Connection requested'. Now the database server has the initiative. It may choose to grant a connection immediately, request user authentication or even reject the request outright. In the diagram, the database server requests user authentication and so the initiative passes back to the database client, which must get the username and password from the end user. The third message sends these from the database client to the database server, which will check them against a list of authorized users before it sends a fourth message granting (or denying) the user a connection to the database server. In this case the request is granted.

The computing time devoted to establishing a connection is significant, so the communication channel is kept open, allowing many different messages to be sent.

Recall the restaurant analogy used to explain this in Chapter 1 – the DBMS keeps listening for further requests from each of its clients. Eventually, either the client requests that the connection is closed (the user logs out, for example) or the server closes the connection, perhaps because no messages have been sent for a long time.

An open connection allows the database server to keep track of all requests sent by a particular client. When an application maintains a record of the current and past state of its communications, it is called **stateful**. One useful feature of stateful applications is the ability to **rollback** any changes, rather like the 'undo' facility of a word processor. The client can request a series of modifications to the database instance, but only **commit** ('save') them once all have been completed successfully. Note that the rollback facility of database applications only usually applies to the database instance. Any change to the database schema is generally made permanent immediately.

A series of modifications to the database instance that can only be committed if all of them succeed (they must be rolled back otherwise) is called a **transaction**. For example, if Paul Smith leaves the university, his staff contact details and associated support sessions should be removed from the Staff Directory database. Consider what happens if the DBMS successfully removes his staff contact details (shown greyed out in Figure 2.20), but cannot remove the data about his support sessions. The database will be inconsistent, as shown, with a row in the `SupportSession` table where the value for the `staffNo` column does not match the value in any (undeleted) row in the `Staff` table. In this situation, the row deleted from the `Staff` table should be reinstated, using a rollback.

The messages sent between database client and server can be quite complex. If the request is a database query, the client must specify exactly what data is required, and the server's response must include a copy of the requested data. The broad range of functions offered by a DBMS discussed above must all be accessible to the client. This means that an application protocol focused on a specific task is insufficient to support communication between database client and server. Instead, the database client and server use a **data language** to communicate.

A data language is a computer language designed to allow the manipulation of the data and data structures in a database. It allows database users to tell the DBMS *what* they want it to do without necessarily having to explain *how* to do it.

These languages are initially defined as part of the data model, though typically this only includes statements to manipulate the data and data structures. When a data language is implemented as the language used by a DBMS, it usually includes statements for manipulating data storage structures, creating usernames and passwords for database users, starting and stopping the DBMS software itself and so on. Most relational DBMS, and many others, implement the SQL data language, examined in Chapters 5 and 6.

Data languages need not be full programming languages. Instead, application developers use data language statements within a program written in a full programming language, such as Java, Visual Basic or PHP. Hence, they are sometimes called data sublanguages. Figure 2.21 shows an SQL statement used within a fragment of PHP code. The SQL statement is:

```
SELECT fName, lName, phone, email FROM Staff
```

and is one of the parameters of the PHP function 'mysql_query'. This is the approach introduced in Chapter 4 and used through much of the rest of the book.

Figure 2.20 Deleted row in Staff table leaving unmatched row in SupportSession table.

Staff

staffNo	fName	lName	phone	email	photo
10780	John	Smith	NULL	j.b.smith@pennine.ac.uk	[BLOB]
25447	John	Smith	5104	j.smith@pennine.ac.uk	[BLOB]
25448	Judith Anne	Smith	7709	j.a.smith@pennine.ac.uk	[BLOB]
31210	Paul	Smith	NULL	p.smith@pennine.ac.uk	[BLOB]
77712	Frank	Rose	8871	f.rose@pennine.ac.uk	[BLOB]
14443	Helen	Abbot	8032	h.abbot@pennine.ac.uk	[BLOB]
23257	Freya	Stark	8660	f.stark@pennine.ac.uk	[BLOB]
33935	Padma	Brar	6641	p.brar@pennine.ac.uk	[BLOB]
35054	Selma	Hutchins	8706	s.hutchins@pennine.ac.uk	[BLOB]
45965	Mikhail	Sudbin	5553	m.sudbin@pennine.ac.uk	[BLOB]
35155	Helene	Chirac	NULL	h.chirac@pennine.ac.uk	[BLOB]
55776	Gurpreet	Choudhury	5454	g.choudhury@pennine.ac.uk	[BLOB]
56893	Ruth	Bapetsi	8022	r.bapetsi@pennine.ac.uk	[BLOB]
56673	Joshua	Bittaye	7782	j.bittaye@pennine.ac.uk	[BLOB]
89987	Dan	Lin	8514	d.lin@pennine.co.uk	[BLOB]
78893	Jo Karen	O'Connor	8871	j.k.oconnor@pennine.ac.uk	[BLOB]
33509	Helen	Timms	8661	h.timms@pennine.ac.uk	[BLOB]

SupportSession

staffNo	dayOfWeek	startTime	endTime
35054	Monday	09:00:00	10:00:00
31210	Wednesday	11:00:00	13:00:00
35054	Monday	15:00:00	16:00:00
45965	Monday	11:00:00	12:00:00
45965	Wednesday	11:00:00	12:00:00
23257	Monday	15:00:00	16:00:00
55776	Monday	14:00:00	16:00:00
56893	Tuesday	14:00:00	15:00:00
56893	Thursday	09:00:00	10:00:00
56673	Thursday	15:30:00	16:30:00
56673	Friday	10:00:00	11:00:00

Unmatched row

Deleted row

Figure 2.21 An SQL statement embedded in PHP code.

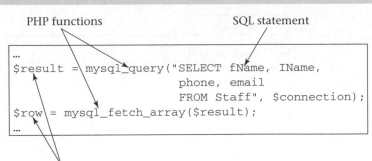

Embedding data language statements in procedural application code can be less efficient than running procedural code directly on the DBMS. Recognizing this, many DBMS support stored procedures by extending the data sublanguage to include the usual programming language constructs, such as if statements, for loops and so on. SQL is an example of a data language that has grown into a full programming language in this way (see Chapters 10 and 11 for a discussion of these SQL features).

Within a data language, the statements used to manipulate the database instance form the **data manipulation language (DML)**. These statements allow users to instruct the DBMS to retrieve, add, modify and remove data. Clearly, the DML lets users tell the DBMS what they want it to do with the data. With a procedural DML, users must also tell the DBMS *how* to retrieve, or manipulate, the data. A non-procedural DML lets the DBMS work this out for itself, so is simpler to learn. It's rather like the difference between the schoolteacher who tells students exactly what to do and the university lecturer who makes vague statements about learning outcomes and suggests that you read a few books.

The **data definition language (DDL)** is the set of statements for creating and modifying the database schema. These statements allow users to create data structures and constraints and usually include statements for dealing with data storage structures, too. Most DBMS will include further management statements in the DDL, such as statements to create usernames and passwords for database users, start and stop the DBMS itself or set default character sets.

2.4 Web technology

Web applications apply web and networking technologies to solve a real-world problem – that of building an information system to help people share their documents. All web applications have a client-server architecture and, as with database applications, the two-tier architecture shown in Figure 2.1 is the basic approach. Again, multiple clients may communicate with a single server, allowing many users to access the same documents. To communicate, the web browser and web server use the **hypertext transfer protocol (HTTP)** as the main aim is to transfer hypertext documents.

Figure 2.22 A web server.

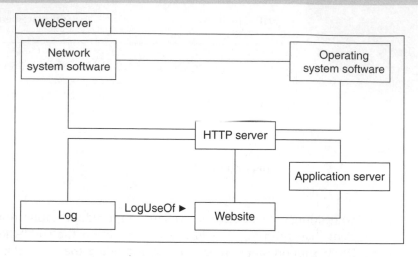

These documents, called web pages, are written using the **hypertext mark-up language (HTML)**, discussed briefly in Chapter 1.

At its simplest, a web server manages access to a set of web pages. In this respect, it is similar to a file server, in this case allowing users access to a structured collection of files called a **website**. Figure 2.22 shows the major software and document components of a web server. The **HTTP server** is the web server application software and is what most people call 'the web server'. However, 'web server' is also used to mean a particular computer with the appropriate software installed on it. Where the difference is important, the term 'HTTP server' is used instead.

The HTTP server is the main application software that manages access to the web pages. It does not usually provide services that allow web pages to be modified or to modify the structure of the document collection (what folders there are). In this sense, it has less functionality than a DBMS, which manages all aspects of its databases.

As with the DBMS, few application developers write their own HTTP server. Instead, they use an existing HTTP server to manage access to a custom-built website. The HTTP server also keeps a log of all requests to access documents on the website and its responses to those requests (such as denying access).

The final software component shown in Figure 2.22 is the application server. Most websites include dynamic web pages and these may need to be processed by a specialized application server on behalf of the HTTP server before the HTTP server can pass the resource to the web client.

Most DBMS keep log files, too, but this is seen as a minor part of their functionality. HTTP servers offer much less functionality than a DBMS and, consequently, the logging function has greater prominence.

HTTP servers provide a range of functions. The most basic are the connection functions, allowing the client and server to communicate. The HTTP server listens for requests from web clients to establish a TCP connection (see Figure 2.9). Usually an HTTP server is assigned TCP port 80, so only hears TCP/IP messages with destination port 80. Note that it is the TCP system software that actually establishes the connection, but only if the HTTP server accepts the connection request. The HTTP server may choose to reject a connection request, in which case no TCP connection is established. For example, some HTTP servers only accept requests from authorized clients, rejecting any connection requests from unrecognized IP addresses. (Remember, the IP address of the client is part of the information sent in the IP datagram, so is known to the TCP system software and, hence, also to the HTTP server.) The HTTP server then keeps track of all open connections.

The HTTP server's request-handling functions determine what the client is requesting and identify the resources required to fulfil that request. For example, a client may request a copy of a resource from the website or to add a resource to the website or remove a resource from the website or it may request information about a resource or about the web server itself.

Requests involving website resources entail locating the resource before preparing a response. The simplest approach stores all the website's resources in a single folder called the **document root (docroot)**. The combination of docroot and URL path gives a pathname for the associated file (see Figure 2.23). For example, the docroot of the Pennine University's website is '/usr/local/httpd/files'. Consider a resource with URL 'http://www.pennine.ac.uk/StaffDirectory/search.html'. The URL path is 'StaffDirectory/search.html', so the actual file is located at '/usr/local/httpd/files/StaffDirectory/search.html'. A single HTTP server can manage more than one website by allocating each website its own docroot.

The HTTP server's response-handling functions allow it to perform the requested action. It ensures that any processing is carried out, builds the response message and sends it. Once the response has been sent, the HTTP server closes the TCP/IP connection. This is an important point. A standard TCP/IP connection is closed as soon as the response has been sent. Once closed, any information associated with that connection is lost, including the application state. This means that the communication between web client and web server is **stateless**.

The HTTP server usually also has logging functions, used to maintain a log of client requests and its responses, and security functions to allow for user authentication and authorization.

These last complete the list of an HTTP server's core functionality (summarized in Table 2.2), although, as with DBMS, the more powerful HTTP servers offer additional utility functions. These may include functions to help the web administrator manage the site or the web server cope with surges in demand from clients.

Figure 2.23 Comparing the web URL and the pathname of a web resource.

Web URL ≡	http	:	//	Host	: Port	/	URL path

Pathname ≡	Docroot	/	URL path

Table 2.2 Core HTTP-server functionality.

HTTP server functions	Purpose
Connection	To allow client and server to establish a TCP/IP connection to use to communicate.
Request handling	Determine what action is being requested and what resources are required to service the request.
Response handling	Build a response and send to the client.
Logging	Record transactions.
Security	To provide identification and authentication of users, and authorization of their actions.

Websites may include a range of resources. Requests for different kinds of resource need to be processed in different ways. The HTTP server must know how to process requests for each type of resource it manages. The processing can be quite simple. For example, processing the request to view a static web page or image file merely involves taking a copy of the requested file. However, some web pages include dynamic content. It is important to understand that dynamic content does not mean animated content. A video clip includes moving pictures, but that is *not* dynamic content. All the data needed by a media player to play the video clip is included in the video clip file – it, in fact, has only static content. However, a web page that draws some of its content from a database has dynamic content as the actual file stored on the website does not include all the data needed to display the web page.

There are two kinds of dynamic content that can be included on a web page:

- server-side dynamic content, which is handled by the web server
- client-side dynamic content, which is handled by the web browser.

Client-side dynamic content (browser script) is discussed below.

Server-side dynamic content is merged into the static content *before* the resource is sent to the web client, so the web client never sees the server-side dynamic content. Although HTTP servers were originally designed to deal only with static resources, it is possible to extend their functionality to process server-side dynamic content. One version of this approach is server-side includes (SSI). This allows simple instructions to be included on a web page, which the HTTP server can interpret and carry out before it sends the web page to the web client. For example, an SSI instruction can write the current date at the end of the page or include (copy and paste) text from some other file into the requested web page.

This is still quite limited, so another option is to augment the web server rather than the HTTP server by including one or more application servers to process server-side dynamic content. Figure 2.22 shows a web server that includes an application server and Figure 2.24 (b) shows how an application server interacts with the HTTP server.

The HTTP server recognizes web pages with server-side dynamic content and passes them to the appropriate application server for processing. The application server interprets any processing instructions to generate dynamic content (such as to include data drawn from a database) and carries them out, merging the dynamic content with the

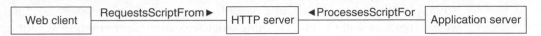

Figure 2.24 Relationships between the web client, HTTP server and application server.

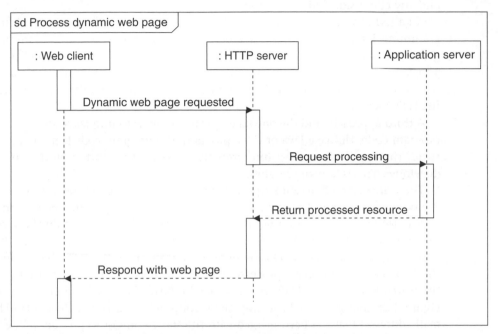

(a) Three-tier web application architecture.

(b) HTTP and application servers dealing with a request for a dynamic web page.

surrounding static content. The resulting HTML file is sent back to the HTTP server, which delivers it to the web client.

Thus, when an application server is involved in generating web pages, the web application already uses a three-tier architecture (Figure 2.24 (a)). Interestingly, in this three-tier architecture there will be one HTTP server in the second tier, but there may be *many* application servers in the third tier.

The HTTP server needs some mechanism to recognize which web pages need processing by which application server. The simplest approach is to have a separate folder under the docroot associated with each available application server. The HTTP server knows to pass resources from these folders to the associated application server. Alternatively, the file extension can identify files that require special processing.

Augmenting the web server with one or more application servers is the more powerful and flexible solution to the problem of server-side dynamic content. It is more powerful because application servers can be built to offer as much, or as little, additional functionality as is required. They offer flexibility as the website developer can bolt on additional application servers with the required processing capabilities without necessarily having to rewrite existing web pages.

Two issues must be addressed in order to implement this approach effectively. The first is to decide how to define the server-side dynamic content of a web page. HTML is not a programming language, so cannot be used for this purpose. One approach is to use a standard programming language, such as Java or C++, to write a program that actually writes out the HTML to a new file, line by line. This program becomes the website resource and the programming language's runtime environment is the application server. Because a program can easily generate dynamic content, this approach is very powerful. Unfortunately the program must also generate all the static content and any client-side dynamic content.

An alternative is to extend the HTML language, adding tags that turn it into a programming language. These non-standard tags allow for standard programming language capabilities – assigning variables, writing 'if' statements and loops and so on. The Macromedia® Coldfusion® web development environment takes this approach, with the ColdFusion application server dealing with non-standard tags on behalf of the HTTP server.

A third approach, and the one taken in this book, is to interleave static HTML with program code. Unlike a Java or C++ program, the program code is not compiled. Instead, the application server interprets the code as it is written by the application developer. This is known as scripting.

There are several different scripting languages, but all work in the same way. Look at the two files shown in Figure 2.25. On the left is a PHP script. The first section is pure HTML, followed by a section of PHP (and some SQL!) enclosed within the special tag '<?php...?>'. In the next section, some lines include both HTML and PHP. The final section is pure HTML. On the right is an example of the HTML generated when the PHP application server processes this script. It is this HTML file that is sent to the web client, not the PHP script. Notice how the final PHP statement (circled in Figure 2.25) has generated some dynamic content – in this case, Selma Hutchins' e-mail address – that has been merged with the static content to produce a line of pure HTML. Chapter 4 introduces PHP scripting and it's used in subsequent chapters to solve a number of problems that arise when developing web database applications.

The second, more technical, issue is how to define the communication interface between the HTTP server and the application servers. As one HTTP server may need to communicate with many different application servers, the obvious solution is to develop a suitable application programming interface (API) for the HTTP server. Then, each application server can be written to use this API.

Probably the most widely used HTTP server API is the **common gateway interface (CGI)**. The CGI API defines how an HTTP server passes web resources to the application server. In particular, it provides a mechanism for passing the value of any variables (such as data entered by the end user in an HTML form) from the HTTP server to the application server.

One weakness of the CGI API is that the HTTP server and application server must be installed on the same machine, which may not be suitable for some web applications. Also, the CGI API is mainly used by those writing their own application servers, using a standard programming language (the first approach discussed above). It has the benefit of portability as, once an application developer is skilled in using the CGI API, he or she can work with most HTTP servers. The downside, however, is that you need to learn the API.

In contrast, scripting languages come with ready-made application servers, which are often closely integrated with a range of HTTP servers by means of a server-specific

Figure 2.25 A PHP script file and its HTML output.

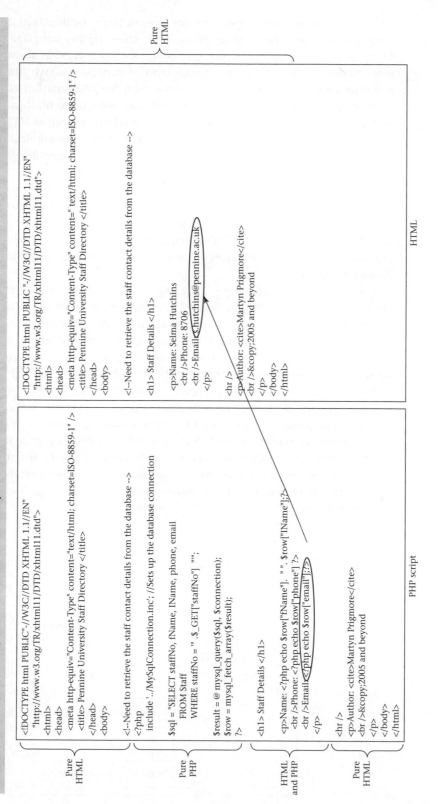

API. The application developer does not need to learn the details of the API, but uses a range of functions and facilities provided by the scripting language to get data from and pass it back to the HTTP server. In effect, someone else has already done the hard work of developing a nice, easy-to-use layer of functions above the API. This makes scripting languages easier to learn and use than the combination of CGI and a standard programming language and they certainly offer more built-in functionality. In particular, they usually support database connectivity, as well as HTTP server connectivity. So, learning just one scripting language allows the application developer to build web database applications. These benefits make scripting languages a good choice for first-time web database application developers.

The role of the web server is to store the web resources, and the role of the web client is to use them. Figure 2.26 shows a typical web client. The main application software on the web client is the web browser. It uses the network system software to establish a connection to the HTTP server, request web resources and display them to the end user. Most of these resources are web pages and images, which the web browser is able to display itself.

Some resources need plug-ins. Examples of plug-ins include the Macromedia® Flash® Player software and the Adobe® Acrobat® Reader® software. These play a similar role to application servers on the web server, providing additional functionality to that offered by the web browser itself. While some web database applications make use of resources that require plug-ins, they are not essential, so won't be considered further. Be aware that they form a part of the web client architecture, though.

Plug-ins are not the same as browser script. Browser script is like the server-side scripting discussed above. Program code is interleaved with static HTML, only, in this case, the program code is sent to the web browser along with the static HTML. The web browser recognizes and interprets the browser script code itself – there is no need for separate application servers on the web client to interpret the browser script. Browser script can't connect to databases, so is not directly relevant to the topic of this book. For simplicity and clarity, browser script isn't used in the examples or exercises.

Figure 2.26 A typical web client.

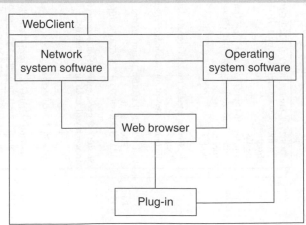

One last point about Figure 2.26. There are web clients that do not include web browsers. For example, spiders explore websites automatically and can build an index of keywords. Search engines use spiders to keep their indices up to date. There is a range of such automated web clients, but the focus here is on the web browser and how it can provide end users with access to a database.

The main function of a web browser is to display web pages. The language used to define the structure and content of a web page is the hypertext mark-up language (HTML), as already mentioned. The structure is defined using **elements**. Each element contains a particular kind of content and is delimited by a start and an end **tag**. For example, the title element contains the document's title. Its start and end tags are '`<title>...</title>`' (in the document head of Figure 2.27). The start and end tags for all elements follow this same format – the element name enclosed in angle brackets, with a forward slash distinguishing the end tag from the start tag. So, for example, the body element will have start and end tags '`<body> ... </body>`'.

Every valid HTML document has the same basic outline as that highlighted in Figure 2.27. First, a **document type declaration** indicates which version of HTML is being used (in Figure 2.27, it is XHTML 1.1).

The actual HTML document follows the document type declaration, enclosed in the 'html' element, and split into a **document head** and a **document body**.

The document head contains information about the document and is enclosed in the head element. Every document head must include a title element. Most web browsers display the title in the browser window's title bar.

Figure 2.27 The structure of an HTML document.

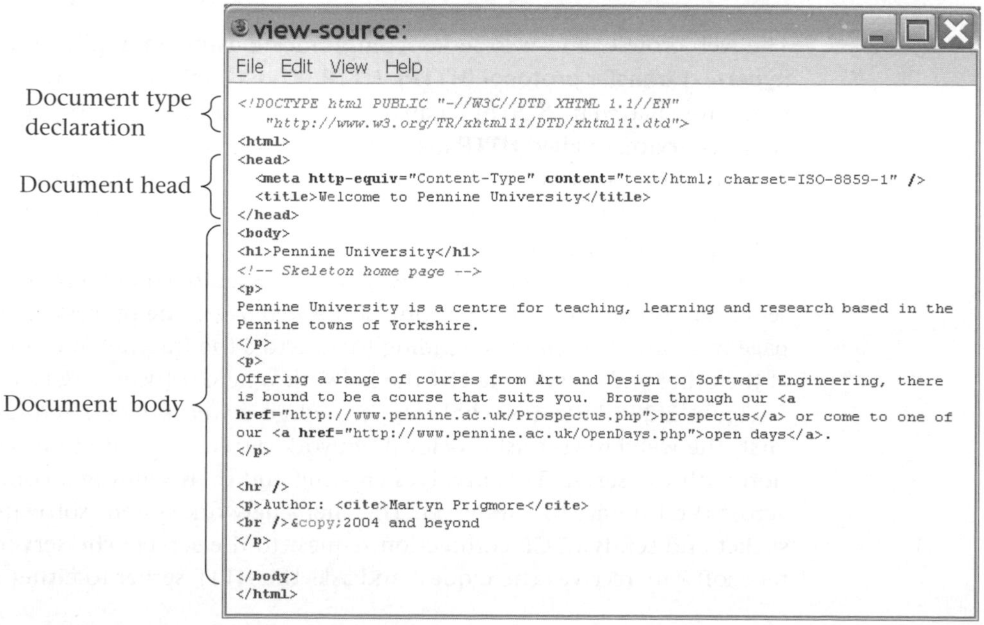

```
view-source:
File  Edit  View  Help

<!DOCTYPE html PUBLIC "-//W3C//DTD XHTML 1.1//EN"
    "http://www.w3.org/TR/xhtml11/DTD/xhtml11.dtd">
<html>
<head>
   <meta http-equiv="Content-Type" content="text/html; charset=ISO-8859-1" />
   <title>Welcome to Pennine University</title>
</head>
<body>
<h1>Pennine University</h1>
<!-- Skeleton home page -->
<p>
Pennine University is a centre for teaching, learning and research based in the
Pennine towns of Yorkshire.
</p>
<p>
Offering a range of courses from Art and Design to Software Engineering, there
is bound to be a course that suits you.  Browse through our <a
href="http://www.pennine.ac.uk/Prospectus.php">prospectus</a> or come to one of
our <a href="http://www.pennine.ac.uk/OpenDays.php">open days</a>.
</p>

<hr />
<p>Author: <cite>Martyn Prigmore</cite>
<br />&copy;2004 and beyond
</p>

</body>
</html>
```

Document type declaration

Document head

Document body

65

The body element encloses the document body, which is the actual content of the web page. The document body can include a range of elements to define the sort of content on the web page. For example, in Figure 2.27, the '<p>...</p>' tags delimit paragraph elements, the '<h1>...</h1>' tags delimit a level-one heading and the '<a...>...</a>' tags delimit an anchor (that is, a hyperlink). The start tag for the anchor element includes an 'href' **attribute**. Attributes are name-value pairs that provide additional information about the element – in this case, the URL of the document that the hyperlink links to.

Some elements, like the html, head and body elements, can only contain other elements. They define the document's high-level structure. The title, paragraph, heading and anchor elements can all contain text (as well as certain other elements). This text forms the document content. The web browser will present the text in a different format for different elements. For example, text in a level-one heading element is usually black text, displayed bold and in a large font size, while text in an anchor element is underlined and in a different colour (often blue). Users can instruct their web browser to present each element's content in a particular way, so the same document can look quite different to two different users.

Cascading stylesheets (CSS) control presentation and, together with HTML provide web browsers with all the information they need to handle web pages.

> There is only room for this brief sketch of HTML here. Readers not familiar with HTML should consult one of the sources in the Further reading section below for more information. The examples used in this book use plain HTML and the web browser's default presentation, rather than user-defined style sheets, so there is no need to understand CSS in this book.

The web browser and web server communicate using an application protocol – the **hypertext transfer protocol (HTTP)**. HTTP plays a similar role in web communication to the role played by SQL in database communications. It allows the client to request specific services – called **HTTP methods** – from the server. For example, the HTTP GET method allows a client to get a copy of a particular resource from the server. HTTP was designed to utilize the TCP/IP suite of internetworking protocols. It sits in the top layer of the protocol stack shown in Figure 2.7.

The main function of HTTP allows a web browser to request a web page and the web server to respond by sending a copy of the web page. The process of splitting the web page into bite-sized chunks, sending these across the Internet and reassembling them at the other end is performed by the network system software (TCP/IP).

Figure 2.28 illustrates what happens when a web browser requests a web page. First, the web browser asks its local network system software to establish a connection with the server. This involves creating and then sending a connection request across the Internet to the server. The client network system software creates a TCP socket and sends a TCP connection request to the server. The server's network system software receives the request and asks the HTTP server to either accept or reject

Figure 2.28 Sending an HTTP request.

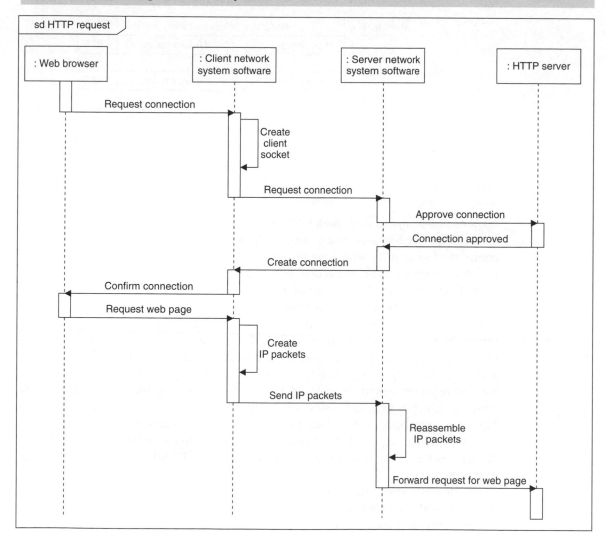

it. In Figure 2.28, the request is accepted and this message makes its way back across the Internet to the web browser. At this point, the web browser sends the request for the actual web page. Again, this goes via the local network system software. The request is broken up into IP packets, ready to be sent across the Internet (note that the connection request and response messages are also sent as one or more IP packets, which is not shown on the diagram). The IP packets are reassembled into the original request message by the server's network system software and the message forwarded to the HTTP server. All this occurs before the HTTP server even begins to process the request.

There are just two kinds of message in HTTP. An HTTP **request message** is created by a web client and sent to a web server. The web server then creates an HTTP

Figure 2.29 The structure of an HTTP message.

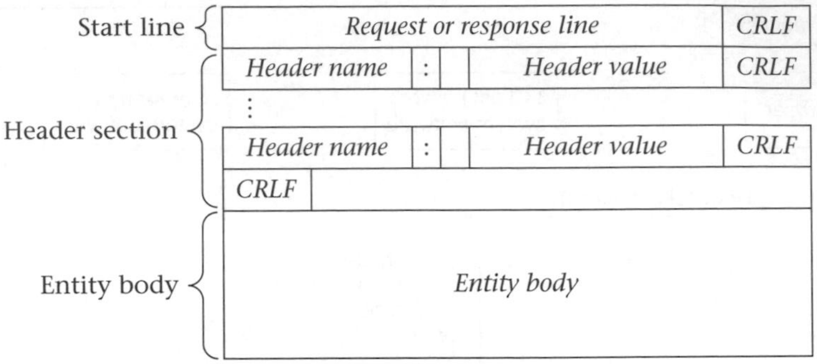

response message to send back to the web client. As indicated in Figure 2.28, HTTP messages are actually sent as a number of IP packets, each of which includes the TCP connection to identify which application generated the message and which application it is targeted at. The interactions between the client and server network system software shown in Figure 2.28 are invisible to the web browser and HTTP server, which simply see the HTTP messages themselves.

Both kinds of HTTP message have the same structure (see Figure 2.29). The first line is the start line, which always ends with the carriage return and linefeed (CRLF) characters. Following the start line is the header section, with one or more headers, each terminated by a CRLF. The header section always ends with a blank line, even if there were no headers in the message. Finally, the entity body includes the actual data being sent in this message. The entity body is optional and many request messages have no entity body. This is because many request messages are simple requests to view a static web page, so there is no need to pass data to the HTTP server. In contrast, most response messages *do* include an entity body – the HTML source of the requested web page.

The header section may contain zero or more headers. Each header takes the form of a name-value pair separated by a colon – ':' – as indicated in Figure 2.29. General headers provide information about the message itself. For example, the date header gives the date and time that the message was created. Entity headers describe the entity body or, when the entity body is missing, the requested resource. For example, the allow header lets a server tell the client what methods are allowed to be used on this resource, while the content-length header gives the size of the entity body. General and entity headers may be used in both request and response messages.

Request headers are used only with request messages. They give the server information about the client and its capabilities or about the request message itself. For example, the accept header lets the server know what media types the client can accept and the host header holds the domain name and port of the website the request message is targeted at – useful if the HTTP server manages more than one website.

Response messages also have their own headers – the response headers. These can give information about the response message itself or the HTTP server sending the message. For example, the server header includes the name and version of the HTTP

Figure 2.30 HTTP message start lines.

Request line ≡ | HTTP method | Request URL | HTTP version |

(a) The structure of an HTTP request line.

Response line ≡ | HTTP version | Status | Reason phrase |

(b) The structure of an HTTP response line.

server application software and the title header is used when the requested resource is a web page, and includes the content of the HTML title element.

The start line for a request message has the structure shown in Figure 2.30 (a). First comes the name of the HTTP method, followed by a single space and then the URL of the requested resource to apply the method to. Another space is followed by the HTTP version, indicating which version of HTTP the client has used to build the request message.

A response line (Figure 2.30 (b)) begins by stating which version of HTTP was used to build the response. Typically, both client and server would use HTTP 1.1. The response line continues with a single space, then the status code, which indicates what happened when the requested action was performed. The reason phrase is a description of the status. The start line of a typical request message might be:

```
GET www.pennine.ac.uk/StaffDirectory/Serch.html HTTP/1.1
```

This start line tells the HTTP server to use the GET method on the resource with URL 'www.pennine.ac.uk/StaffDirectory/serch.html' and that this message is written using HTTP 1.1. Note that the request URL is actually just the scheme-specific part of the URL. As this is an HTTP message, there is no need to specify the HTTP scheme in the URL.

The response message sent by the server might have the start line:

```
HTTP/1.1 404 Not found
```

Again, this message is written using HTTP 1.1. The status code indicates that there is no resource with the URL path '/StaffDirectory/Serch.html' on the 'www.pennine.ac.uk' server, perhaps because the user seems to have mistyped the URL – 'Serch.html' should be 'Search.html'.

The two methods most commonly used by HTTP request messages are GET and POST. GET is a so-called **safe method** as it should not result in any changes on the web server (other than the HTTP server logging the request). Note, though, that safe methods can lead to changes on the web server if they are misused.

The GET method asks the server for a copy of the resource specified by the request URL. Request messages using the GET method have no entity body, as all the information needed to service the request is contained in the start line and header section.

Request messages using the POST method *do* have an entity body. The entity body includes data that the web server should process. Most HTML forms submit their data in the entity body of a request message that uses the POST method. The POST method is not considered a safe method. It usually passes data to an application server (see Figure 2.22), which may initiate changes on the web server other than simply logging the request. For example, it may modify a database.

A third method that can be useful to web application developers is the HEAD method. This is very similar to GET, but only the start line and headers are included in the response message. The entity body is omitted. This allows the client to check whether it really wants to request this resource or not. For example, the resource might be in a media type that the web client cannot process, or the resource may be too big. The HEAD method is considered safe.

Table 2.3 summarizes the safety and purpose of these three methods.

There are 41 status codes defined in the HTTP/1.1 specification. Table 2.4 lists some of the common ones. Some status codes have headers associated with them. For example, a response message with the status code '301 Redirection' informs the client that the requested resource has moved from the location specified by the request URL. The response message should include a location header, which gives the URL at which the requested resource can now be found. Typically, the web client will send a second request message using this new URL.

Table 2.3 Common HTTP methods.

Method	Safe?	Purpose
GET	Yes	Asks the server to send a copy of the resource specified by the request URL in its response message.
POST	No	Passes data to a specified resource held on the web server for processing.
HEAD	Yes	Similar to the GET method, but asks the server to send the start line and header section only in its response message.

Table 2.4 Some common HTTP status codes.

Code	Category	Reason phrase	Meaning
101	Informational	Switching protocols	The server is switching to a different version of HTTP.
200	Successful	OK	The request was carried out.
301	Redirection	Moved permanently	The resource at the requested URL has moved.
401	Client error	Unauthorized	The client must authenticate itself (login) to access the resource with the requested URL.
404	Client error	Not found	The server could not find a resource with the requested URL.
503	Server error	Service unavailable	The server is temporarily unable to service the request.

2.5 Web database applications

Although both database applications and web applications can be developed with a two-tier client-server architecture, web database applications require a three-tier architecture (see Figure 2.2). Figure 2.31 shows the three-tier architecture for web database applications. The major components of the web server and database server, discussed above, are included in the model. Notice that the 'RequestData' association in Figure 2.31 has the name 'DatabaseClient' at one end. This is simply a means of indicating that the application server is playing the role of a database client when it interacts with the DBMS. For example, it may ask the DBMS to retrieve data from the database, then integrate that data into a skeleton web page before the final web page is passed to the HTTP server, ready to be sent to the web client.

Figure 2.31 highlights two problems for web database applications. First, the DBMS only communicates directly with the web server, not with the web client, which represents the real end users. If the DBMS is to distinguish between its many different end users, then the web server must maintain a separate connection to the DBMS for each web client. Notice that any database application with a three-tier architecture suffers from this problem.

One solution is to include in the middle tier some software known as a transaction processing monitor. The transaction processing monitor keeps track of individual users, rather than the DBMS doing so. It maintains a separate connection with each client and a pool of connections to the DBMS. This allows it to keep track of requests from different clients and ensure that responses from the database server are routed to the correct client. Transaction processing monitors can handle many hundreds of concurrent users. However, there may be hundreds of thousands of web clients accessing a web server at the same time. Consequently, in the Web environment, transaction processing monitors are not yet a viable general solution to this problem.

The second problem concerns communication protocols. The channel of communication between the web client and the HTTP server is stateless. Once the HTTP server has responded to the web client's request, the connection is closed. However, a DBMS expects to maintain an open connection with its end users. Even if it maintains an open connection with the web server, it cannot maintain an open connection with

Figure 2.31 The three-tier web database application architecture.

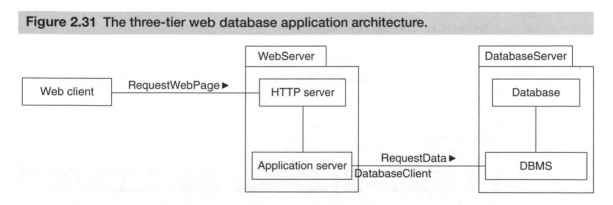

the *real* end users, represented by the web clients. (This is another reason for transaction processing monitors not being easy to use in web database applications.)

The design and development of web database applications must take account of both these problems. Techniques for handling them effectively are discussed in the following chapters.

Most web database applications are designed to allow an end user to access a database via a web browser. It is worth tracing what happens to the data as it passes from user to database server and back again. Consider the HTML form in Figure 2.32. This form allows an end user to type the surname and first initial of a member of staff and search the database for their contact details. The form element's action attribute is the URL 'http://www.pennine.ac.uk/StaffDirectory/SearchName.php'. When the user clicks on the 'Submit Query' button, the web browser's first task is to extract the domain name and translate it into an IP address. Each web browser keeps a local cache of such translations, for URLs that have been accessed regularly by the end users. If the IP address for 'www.pennine.ac.uk' is not in the local cache, the web browser will use the domain name system to look it up. As discussed above, this involves sending a message to the '.uk' name server. Once the domain name has been resolved into an IP address, the web browser opens a TCP connection to the HTTP server. At this point, the actual HTTP request message can be sent.

HTML forms can use either the GET or POST methods to send data to the HTTP server. The form in Figure 2.32 uses GET, so the web browser creates the HTTP request:

```
GET
www.pennine.ac.uk/StaffDirectory
/SearchName.php?surname=Smith&initial=J HTTP/1.1
```

(Note that the HTTP request line will be a single line. Here, it has been split over two lines to fit it on the page.)

Figure 2.32 The Staff Directory search form.

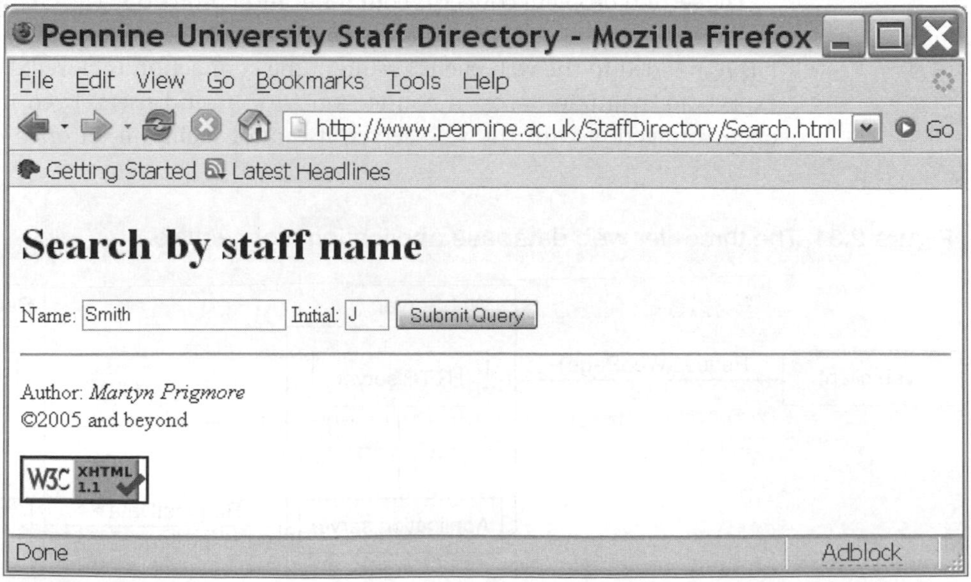

The form data has been copied into name-value pairs in the query string of the URL. There are no headers and no entity body. The HTTP request message is sent, using TCP/IP, to the HTTP server.

When the HTTP server receives this message, it recognizes that the requested resource is a PHP script, not a plain HTML file. The HTTP server delegates the task of running the PHP script to an application server. It tells the application server the script file's location in the local file system – in our example, the file is called `SearchName.php` and it is located in the `StaffDirectory` folder under the docroot. The HTTP server also passes the name-value pairs from the URL of the HTTP request message. The application server now runs the PHP script, using the name-value pairs as input parameters.

The `SearchName.php` script opens a connection to the DBMS on the database server (see Figure 2.19) and uses an SQL query to ask the DBMS which staff have the surname 'Smith' and first initial 'J'. The DBMS searches the database and finds three matching rows in the `Staff` table (see Figure 2.14). It passes these three rows to the application server, which uses the data to create a web page listing these members of staff. The application server passes the web page to the HTTP server, which sends it as the entity body of an HTTP response message to the web browser. Finally, the HTTP server closes the TCP connection. This process happens each time data is submitted to an HTTP server and used to query or modify a database.

Chapter summary

- The aim of this chapter has been to describe the concepts and technologies that underlie web database applications. As web database applications are always client-server applications, the first section discussed the client-server architecture in general and the final section showed how this concept applies to web database applications. Just as the client-server architecture forms a conceptual basis for web database applications, networks and network technologies form the technical basis. Without networks, there would be no World Wide Web (though there could still be databases). It is hard to discuss networks without getting a little technical, but understanding how networks work is well worth the effort.

- The rest of the chapter introduced the two technologies that are explored in the rest of the book – namely, database and web technology.

Further reading

Most books on application development discuss the client-server architecture. Ince (2002) goes into more depth, discussing both networks and client-server application development, though using Java technologies.

The section on networking and internetworking is based largely on Rodriguez et al. (2001), though it is a detailed, technical book. Williams (2001) has three nice chapters on networking.

All the above discuss the OSI seven-layer reference model for layered network architectures. If this is not familiar to you, don't worry, as, while important, it is not essential knowledge for database specialists.

Berners-Lee (1994) is the original Internet 'request for comments' (RFC), detailing the URL syntax, with Fielding (1995) describing the authoritative URL syntax for relative URLs.

The classic reference for databases is Date (2004), with a critical discussion of standard approaches and technologies. Elmasri and Navathe (2007) and Connolly and Begg (2004) are good alternative texts. Much of the material covered in this book is also covered in these books, although web topics tend to be dealt with in isolation from the main text.

Though now quite old, Wilde (1999) provides a good general introduction to Web and Internet technologies. Gourley and Totty (2002) is a good reference for HTTP and the web architecture, while Ince (2002) covers Java technologies and web robots.

Review questions

2.1   What is client-server computing?

2.2   What is a network? Why would you use a network?

2.3   Define the terms internet, Internet, intranet and extranet, highlighting the similarities and differences between them.

2.4   What is a protocol? Explain the purpose of each of the following protocols:
(a) IP
(b) TCP
(c) HTTP.

2.5   Explain the following terms:
(a) IP address
(b) port number
(c) socket
(d) TCP connection.

2.6   Explain the purpose of each of the following:
(a) the DBMS
(b) the DCM
(c) a data manipulation language
(d) a data definition language.

2.7   In the ANSI/SPARC architecture for database systems, what is meant by:
(a) logical data independence
(b) physical data independence?

2.8 On a web server, what is the purpose of each of the following:
(a) HTTP server
(b) application server.

2.9 Explain what a mark-up language is, clearly distinguishing between the terms 'attribute', 'element' and 'tag'.

2.10 Explain why each of the four numbers in an IP address lies between 0 and 255.

Exercises

2.11 Describe the purpose of application partitioning and the different responsibilities involved. Explain, using a diagram, how application partitioning in a two-tier database application would differ from that in a three-tier database application.

2.12 Briefly describe the function of a bridge in a local area network. A router performs a similar role in an internet, but functions differently. Describe this difference.

2.13 Explain the addressing mechanism used on the Internet. You should include an explanation of the domain name system and uniform resource locator.

2.14 Describe the functions of a DBMS. Why does a DBMS vendor include utility functions in its product?

2.15 Describe, with the aid of a diagram, the ANSI/SPARC database systems architecture. You should explain the purpose of each of the various views, and the mappings between them. What is the main purpose of this architecture?

2.16 Suggest changes to the logical view in Figure 2.15 that:
(a) do not affect either external view
(b) affect the `StaffDirectory` external view, but do not affect the `ComputingStaffList` external view
(c) affect the `ComputingStaffList` external view, but do not affect the `StaffDirectory` external view.

In each case, explain your example.

Investigations

2.17 The database approach to storing data has a number of advantages over the file-based approach (discussed in Chapter 1). Investigate how the functions of the DBMS ensure that these advantages are realized in practice.

2.18 Database communications are designed to be stateful, whereas web communications are designed to be stateless. Investigate how this difference affects the design of web database applications compared to rich client (that is, traditional GUI) database applications. One approach to this question is to consider what happens at the application protocol level when a user submits data that is used to modify a database instance, for both web and rich client database applications.

2.19 Using a diagram, explain the three-tier architecture for web database applications. You should explain the purpose of each of the three tiers and the separation of application functionality across the tiers. How useful is this approach in practice?

2.20 Most contemporary approaches to web development make use of the model–view–controller design pattern. Investigate this approach to application development, its relationship to the three-tier architecture and its use by PHP web application developers.

3 Data models

Chapter objectives

→ To discuss the role of data models in organizing data.

→ To explain the differences between values, literals and variables.

→ To discuss data types as a simple approach to organizing data.

→ To discuss the relational and semistructured data models.

Chapter outline

A **data model** is a general approach to organizing data in a database. It defines:

1 a set of structures that are used to organize data about things that the end user is interested in and which can capture relationships between data held in different structures

2 a language that the end user can use to manipulate structures and the data they contain

3 a collection of integrity constraints that limit what data can be held or how that data can be changed.

The structures a data model provides to organize data and describe relationships should be sufficiently flexible to represent any information a database user might wish to keep. They should be sufficiently simple, too, so that software engineers can create a DBMS capable of managing these structures efficiently. This need for a balance between flexibility and simplicity means that there is only a small number of widely used data models. The most widely used of these is the relational data model and the one currently generating most interest is the semi-structured data model of **XML.** Both these data models are covered in detail in this chapter.

Each data model has at least one data language defined for it. Some have more than one. The relational data model, for example, has two formal languages, the relational algebra and relational calculus, and many languages implemented by particular DBMS. The two most widely implemented languages used by relational DBMS (RDBMS) are SQL and QBE. QBE, an acronym for Query By Example, is a visual language, probably best known as the query language for Microsoft Access. It is not much use to application developers, though, as it can't be used from within program code, so isn't covered in this book. SQL can, so its use from within program code is covered in detail in Chapters 4 to 7.

The integrity constraints perform two important tasks. First, they help to ensure that the database instance is consistent. For example, an integrity constraint can ensure that, for each support session recorded on the database, there exists a corresponding member of staff. Integrity constraints can also enforce some business rules, though, as we saw in Chapter 1, not all.

In a sense, a data model represents the combined wisdom of those involved in creating and managing databases. All databases seek to capture information about things of interest to a business or other organization and a data model describes an effective and efficient way of doing this.

The simplest kind of information is an individual **data item**. This represents a particular fact about something – a staff number, a name, an e-mail address. On their own, data items are of little use – whose staff number, whose e-mail address? By gathering related data items into a single structure, however, a database can present all information about a particular thing of interest to the database users in a coherent package.

In the Staff Directory, the things of interest are members of staff and the support sessions that they offer to students, but *not* the students. A data model describes the 'shape' of these larger structures. For example, the relational data model organizes data items into tables. In the Staff Directory, one table represents the members of staff and a second table represents support sessions. For the database to be useful, it must also capture information on which particular member of staff offers which particular support session.

This seems to suggest that a data model needs two structures – namely, one to represent the things of interest, by organizing data items into meaningful structures, and a second to represent relationships between these structures. The network and hierarchical data models take this approach (see, for example, Connolly and Begg (2004) p. 46 or Elmasri and Navathe (2000a, 2000b)). The relational model does not. It uses a single data structure – the table – to represent both the things of interest and the relationships between them. XML is different again, with a single approach to structuring data, but two approaches to representing relationships between these structures. Which data model is best for a particular database will depend on what information the database will hold.

The term 'data model' is often used to mean a description, or model, of the data requirements of a particular organization. This is not the same as a general approach to organizing data. Such a description is certainly a model of data, but it is specific to a given organization and often to a particular database used by that organization. To avoid confusion, in this book such a description is called a **database design**. Chapters 8–11 discuss the process of database design.

■ Here, Section 3.1 discusses data items and how they are represented on a computer. The discussion centres on database applications, but applies more generally to all computer software. It also discusses data types and their operators – the first steps towards a data model and its data language respectively.

■ Section 3.2 discusses the relational data model. It describes the table – the structure used to organize data – in some detail. The consequences of allowing columns to be null are explored. Detailed discussion of the data language is postponed to Chapters 5 and 6, but the main relational integrity constraints are explained and some consequences of enforcing them explored.

■ Section 3.3 discusses XML, which can be viewed as a semistructured data model.

3.1 Representing data items

Data items represent some fact about a thing of interest to an organization. For example, in our case study, they can represent the phone number of a member of staff or the day and start time of a support session. In a database, data items are stored on a computer as **values**. Each value represents some fact about a particular thing. The facts 'Paul Smith is the name of a member of staff' and 'p.smith@pennine.ac.uk is Paul Smith's e-mail address' are represented by storing appropriate values in the appropriate data structure.

When a human being enters data into a database, he or she passes the value as a **literal**. A literal is a human-readable representation of a particular value. The literals '21 January 2005', '21-JAN-2005' and '2005-01-21' all represent the same value: the twenty-first of January in the year 2005 of the common era. Even this simple example shows that there can be many literals representing the same value. The same is true of numbers. Thus, 1.5 is the same as 1 ½ which is the same as 3/2. In each case, the actual value stored on the database would be the same, though the data model does not specify the details of these internal storage formats.

Most DBMS have a preferred format for literals. Numeric literals are usually decimal numbers, not fractions. Literals for character strings are natural language text. Typically, character string literals are enclosed in single or double quotes to distinguish them from any surrounding text. For example, 'abc xyz' is a character string literal with seven characters – six letters and a single space character. This raises the interesting problem of how to store the name Rosalind O'Neil without the apostrophe being mistaken for the 'end of string' single quote. The SQL language solves this problem by the convention that two single quote marks represent an apostrophe, so the literal 'Rosalind O''Neil' will be stored as the data value Rosalind O'Neil.

The preferred format for date literals varies. The Oracle DBMS prefers '21-JAN-2005', while the MySQL DBMS prefers '2005-01-21'. This is because there is no internationally agreed format for date literals. For example, in the USA, '3/4/2005' is March the fourth 2005, while in Europe it is the third of April 2005. The DBMS data language will provide ways to convert date literals from one format to another. The application programmer can use these to ensure that dates entered by the end user are correctly interpreted by the DBMS. Again, date literals are enclosed in single quotes.

A **variable** is a named container for data values. At any one time, a variable holds a single value, but the value can be changed. Consider the following database query put to the Staff Directory database:

Which staff have surname `staffSurname`

Here, `staffSurname` is a variable that can take the value of any surname. The Staff Directory Search Page (Figure 3.1) asks this question. The value of `staffSurname` is set to the literal entered in the text box labelled 'Name'. This means that a single database query can be used to search for the contact details of any member of staff.

Dates, character strings and numbers are different kinds of values for data items and are used in different ways. Numbers can be added, multiplied, averaged or even have their cube root taken. Dates can be compared, but not multiplied. It makes sense to ask whether 21 January 2005 is earlier or later than 3 August 2004, but not to multiply the dates together. Strings can be sorted into alphabetical order or concatenated (added together). Concatenating the string 'This is part' with the string 'of a sentence', gives the string 'This is partof a sentence.' Notice that, because there was no space character after the last character of 'This is part' or before the first character of 'of a sentence', the concatenated string is not correct English – 'partof' should be 'part of'. This is a common error made by programmers when assembling sentences from string data held on a database.

A reasonable first step in organizing data is to identify the different kinds of data values. A **data type** does this by giving a name to a set of values that share some common characteristics.

Data type Named set of data values.

Figure 3.1 The staff search form.

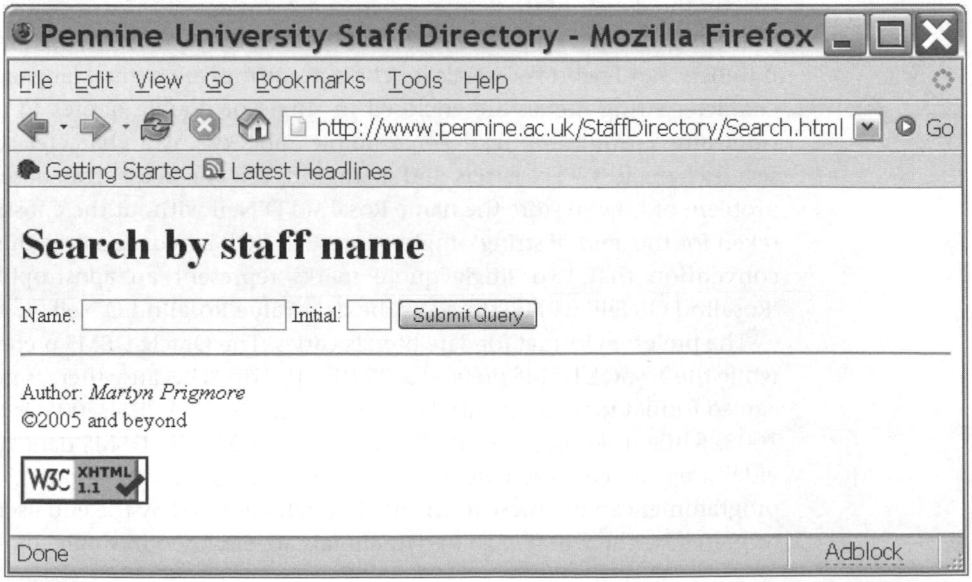

Pennine University Staff Directory - Mozilla Firefox

File   Edit   View   Go   Bookmarks   Tools   Help

http://www.pennine.ac.uk/StaffDirectory/Search.html   Go

Getting Started   Latest Headlines

Search by staff name

Name: [   ]   Initial: [   ]   Submit Query

Author: *Martyn Prigmore*
©2005 and beyond

W3C XHTML 1.1

Done   Adblock

Table 3.1 Common system-defined data types.

Data type	Description of values
Numeric	An ordinal or cardinal number.
Character string	Any string of characters.
Boolean	Either of the two values: true and false.
Date	Any valid date.
Time	Any valid time of day.
Interval	An interval of time, such as 'two years and four months' or 'four days seven hours eighteen minutes and five seconds'.
Binary large object (BLOB)	A 'catch-all' for more complex data, such as images, sound, video and so on.

For example, emailAddress would make a sensible data type. Every e-mail address identifies an electronic mailbox, so they are clearly the same sort of data. However, emailAddress is not usually one of the data types defined by a data model. It is too specific as not all database applications need to store data about e-mail addresses. Instead, a data model usually allows **user-defined data types**. The database designer can define data types such as emailAddress if they are needed. Some data types are so common that data models almost always include them. The commonest **system-defined data types** are listed in Table 3.1, together with a brief description of their values.

The numeric data type includes the sorts of numbers used in basic mathematics. If values of a particular data item can sensibly be added together or sorted into numerical order, then its data type is numeric. Clearly, phone numbers are *not* numeric. Staff numbers at the Pennine University *might* be numeric. Although it doesn't make sense to add them together, it might make sense to sort them into numerical order. Before deciding the data type for staff numbers, the database designer should check if this is the case.

A data item that is numeric can be given a **precision** (the number of digits used) and a **scale** (the number of digits after the decimal point). Salaries at the Pennine University range up to £135,000.00, which means a precision of 8 and a scale of 2.

If it does not make sense to sort staff numbers into numerical order, then their data type will be character string. Character strings are simply strings of characters. The data model may allow the database designer to specify which character sets are supported – Western European, Cyrillic or Arabic, for example. Character strings can be of varying length or fixed length. Telephone numbers are varying length character strings. For example, '+44 (0) 1484 042526' and '01484 042526' are both the same phone number, with the first written out for international dialling. A staff number is always five characters long, so is of fixed length. The abbreviation **Varchar** is used to indicate a varying length character string, and **Char** a fixed-length character string.

The Boolean, date and time data types are straightforward. Like dates, the Boolean data type has a variety of literals. Depending on the DBMS, the value for true may be represented by the literals TRUE, 1 or 0. Like character strings, the literals for dates and times are usually enclosed in single quotes.

The interval data type has values that measure an interval of time. There are two different sorts of interval or, rather, there are two different interval data types. One measures intervals of time in years and months, the other in days, hours, minutes and seconds. The two cannot be mixed as months do not all have the same number of days. If you buy a monthly bus pass, adding an extra 28 days on 1 February gets you a whole month extra, while on 1 August, it gets you three days short of a month. The irregular structure of the calendar was a real problem for early application developers. Fortunately, the developers who wrote today's DBMS have dealt with these problems. If a database application needs to manipulate dates, then the easiest approach is to use the DBMS date manipulation functions.

The data types in Table 3.1 are known as **scalar data types** (sometimes called atomic or primitive data types). To the end user, each value of a scalar data type is complete in itself – it has no subparts that are directly accessible to the end user. The numeric value 57 is complete in itself. Fifty seven is always, and only ever, fifty seven. It is less obvious that the date value '21 January 2005' is complete in itself. Obviously it is always the same date, but it seems to have user-accessible subparts – the year, month and day. In fact, this is simply one way of representing the underlying date value. Another possible representation would be to show a date as the number of seconds elapsed since some fixed point in the past (the UNIX operating system uses this form of representation). So, although the date *literal* '21 January 2005' has subparts, the date *value* it represents does not.

In contrast, **non-scalar data types** do have user-accessible subparts. Table 3.2 lists some system-defined non-scalar data types. They are non-scalar because they allow the end user to store a collection of data values as a *single* value, but retain access to the values of the members of the collection. The non-scalar data types in Table 3.2 are particularly simple, as the members must be of the same type. For example, if staff at the Pennine University can have more than one phone number, each of which is a character string, then it makes sense to represent them as a set of character strings. The end user can see the value of some, or all, of the members of this set. A set is the simplest kind of non-scalar data type, with no implied ordering of members and no repeated member values. This is because there is no point having two members representing the same phone number, for example.

A multiset (sometimes called a bag, but multiset is the SQL terminology) is also an unordered collection, but it allows repeated members. The list of books a lecturer has could be represented as a multiset because he or she might have two copies of the same textbook (one for the office, one for home, say).

An array is an ordered collection of members and, like a multiset, may include repeated member values. Although arrays are the most complex of the three non-scalar

Table 3.2 System-defined non-scalar data types.

Data type	Description of values
Array	An ordered collection of members – that is, an ordered list.
Multiset	An unordered collection of members, which may contain duplicate values.
Set	An unordered collection of members, with no duplicates.

data types considered here, they are actually the simplest to implement on a computer. Accordingly, most programming languages include arrays, but many do not include the set or multiset data types. The array data type was added to the SQL data language in SQL:1999, but it was only in SQL:2003 that multiset was added. There is still no set data type in SQL.

Each data type has a set of **operators** associated with it. An operator takes one or more values, manipulates them in some way and outputs a single value. The output value is not necessarily the same data type as the inputs. Operators actually combine literals and variables as they are the representations of data values used by database users. A valid combination of literals, variables and operators is called an **expression**. Thus, '2 + 3', '$x - 7$' and '$(3 \times z) - 2$' are all valid numeric expressions (assuming x and z are numeric variables). An expression is said to *evaluate to* its output value, so '2 + 3' evaluates to 5 and '15 < 12' evaluates to false. An expression that evaluates to a numeric value is called a numeric expression, one that evaluates to a Boolean value is a Boolean expression and so on.

Boolean expressions are extremely important in SQL and other data languages. They allow the end user to place conditions on the actions of the DBMS: 'only do this action if this Boolean expression evaluates to true'. Most Boolean expressions involve **comparison operators**. These compare two values of a given data type, but always return a Boolean value.

Comparisons are often used when an application needs to make choices. For example, comparisons are used when an end user wants the DBMS to retrieve rows from a database table, but only those rows where the data values satisfy certain conditions. Suppose a user of the Staff Directory database wants to know which support sessions start before 10.00 am. The DBMS must look at each row of the `SupportSession` table and, if that support session starts before 10.00 am, show the data to the end user. The Boolean expression `startTime<'10:00'` evaluates to true if the support session starts before 10 am and to false otherwise. The DBMS can evaluate this Boolean expression, so the user can pose a query in the form:

'Show me the data from those rows of the `SupportSession` table where the Boolean expression `startTime<'10:00'` evaluates to True'

One of the difficulties many ordinary database users have is framing their question in this form. Database application developers create client applications that make it easier for end users to state what data they want, then translate these data requirements into a form that the DBMS can understand.

The 'less than' operator – '<' – is a good example of a comparison operator. It compares the relative positions of two values in the usual ordering for their data type. For numeric values, 2 < 3, evaluates to true, while 7 < 5 evaluates to false. For character strings, 'apple' < 'banana' is true, because 'apple' comes before 'banana' in a standard English dictionary.

Table 3.3 lists the other common comparison operators, their usual symbols and the symbols used in SQL and most other computer languages. Computer languages use different symbols because of the limitations inherent in computer keyboards. The table also shows which data types the comparison operator can be used with. For

Table 3.3 Common comparison operators.

Comparison operator	SQL symbol	Familiar symbol	Used with data types
Equal to	=	=	All data types.
Not equal to	<>, or !=	≠	All data types.
Less than	<	<	Numeric, character string, date, time, interval.
More than	>	>	Numeric, character string, date, time, interval.
Less than or equal to	<=	≤	Numeric, character string, date, time, interval.
More than or equal to	>=	≥	Numeric, character string, date, time, interval.

example, it doesn't make sense to ask whether true is less than false, so this operator doesn't work with the Boolean data type.

In most languages, it is not permitted to compare values of different data types. For example, 5 < 'one' is not a valid Boolean expression as 5 is a numeric literal, but 'one' is a character string literal. A language that insists comparison operators only compare values of the same type is said to be **strongly typed**. Not all languages are strongly typed. For example, SQL is, but PHP is not. The advantage of strong typing is that it can prevent misleading results. For example, in SQL the Boolean expression 5 < 'one' is simply not allowed. A DBMS encountering this expression would tell the user that there was an error in the SQL statement. In contrast, PHP is not strongly typed, so it evaluates the Boolean expression 5 < 'one' and announces that it is false. What does this mean? The two literals can only meaningfully be compared if both have the same data type. PHP converts the character string literal 'one' to the numeric literal 0 and evaluates the Boolean expression 5 < 0, which is clearly false. Unfortunately, PHP evaluates 5<'seven' as false, too as 'seven' is also converted to 0! This can be very misleading, but there is a reason for PHP not being strongly typed.

Consider what happens when SQL is confronted with the Boolean expression '5' < '17'. As both literals are character strings, SQL evaluates this expression as false. In a dictionary ordering, all character strings beginning with '1' come *before* those beginning with '5', so this is correct, but it is misleading. PHP automatically converts both character string literals to numeric values and evaluates the Boolean expression 5 < 17, getting the expected value true. The reason it does this is that, when data is passed from an HTML form to PHP, any values entered in a text box are passed as character strings, even if they are actually numbers. Because PHP can automatically convert character string literals such as '5' and '17' to numeric values, it is easier to deal with data from an HTML form. Even so, it is better to be sure of the data type of any variables to avoid misleading results.

In contrast to comparison operators, the basic arithmetic operators take numeric values as inputs and output another numeric value, so the numeric expression 2 + 3

Table 3.4 Single data type operators for common system-defined types.

Data type	Operator symbol	Familiar symbols
Numeric	+, −, *, /	+, −, ×, ÷
Character string	‖	
Boolean	NOT, AND, OR	¬, ∧, ∨
Array	‖	
Multiset	UNION, INTERSECT, −	∪, ∩, −
Set	UNION, INTERSECT, −	∪, ∩, −
BLOB	‖	

evaluates to five. The ' − ' operator can either combine two numeric values or modify a single value, so 7 − 4 evaluates to three, while −17 evaluates to minus seventeen.

An operator that takes two input values, like '+', is called a **binary operator**. Operators with only one input value are **unary operators**. The symbol ' − ' can represent either a unary operator or a binary operator – the context making it clear which is intended. Table 3.4 lists the most common non-comparison operators usually provided for each data type listed in Tables 3.1 and 3.2, together with their more familiar symbols, where these exist. All these operators take values of the given data type as inputs, and output a value of the same data type. The operators for dates, times and intervals behave differently, so are dealt with below.

The concatenation operator – ‖ (two vertical bar characters) – acts on character strings (or arrays or BLOBs). It pastes the second character string (or array or BLOB) on to the end of the first, so 'the quick' ‖ 'brown fox' evaluates to 'the quickbrown fox'. Notice how there is no space between the words 'quick' and 'brown'. This is correct as neither of the input character string literals included a space at this position. Application developers must be careful when concatenating character string data to ensure that any necessary spaces are present or to add them themselves.

> ‖ is not always used to denote concatenation. The MySQL DBMS uses ‖ to denote the Boolean OR operator. It provides the CONCAT() function to perform string concatenation. Check the DBMS manual to find the correct symbols to use for operators.

The Boolean data type has the usual logical operators. Truth tables for these are shown in Figure 3.2. To use these, note that the Boolean variables p and q can be any Boolean expression. The second line of the truth table for AND tells us that, whenever p is true and q is false, then p AND q is also false and so on.

The operators for multiset and set are UNION, INTERSECT and DIFFERENCE. Note that the union of two set values is also a set, so duplicate values are removed: For example:

{2, 7, 15} UNION {7, 15, 22} = {2, 7, 15, 22}

Figure 3.2 Truth tables for Boolean operators.

p	NOT p
TRUE	FALSE
FALSE	TRUE

p	q	p AND q
TRUE	TRUE	TRUE
TRUE	FALSE	FALSE
FALSE	TRUE	FALSE
FALSE	FALSE	FALSE

p	q	p OR q
TRUE	TRUE	TRUE
TRUE	FALSE	TRUE
FALSE	TRUE	TRUE
FALSE	FALSE	FALSE

As multisets allow duplicate values, the union operator for multisets does *not* eliminate duplicates. In SQL, the union of two multisets looks like this:

[2, 7, 15] UNION [7, 7, 15, 22] = [2, 7, 7, 7, 15, 15, 22]

The intersection operator for sets (and multisets) identifies common members. This includes common repeated members for multisets. For example:

{2, 7, 15} INTERSECT {7, 15, 22} = {7, 15}.

[2, 7, 7, 15] INTERSECT [7, 7, 7, 15, 15, 22] = [7, 7, 15]

Finally, the DIFFERENCE operator identifies members in the first set (or multiset) that are not in the second:

{2, 7, 15} DIFFERENCE {7, 15, 22} = {2}.

[2, 7, 7, 15] DIFFERENCE [7, 15, 15, 22] = [2, 7]

In mathematics, adding together all the repeated members from both multisets, as the SQL UNION operator does, is called fusion. Multiset union takes the *maximum* number of members in the two multisets:

[2, 7, 15, 15] ∪ [7, 7, 15, 22] = [2, 7, 7, 15, 15, 22].

This difference is only a concern to those used to the mathematical definition.

The date and time data types have only one operator – '–'. The '–' operator is a little unusual, because it takes two dates (or two times), but returns an interval. All the non-comparison operators for date, time and interval data types involve a mix of these three data types. For example, '17 January 2007' – '21 January 2007' evaluates to the interval '4 days'. The Pennine University's Web Timetable database can use this to calculate the duration of a teaching session (which is clearly an interval) from its start and end times. An alternative approach would be to store the start time (a time) and the duration (an interval) and calculate the end time by adding them together. Adding, or subtracting, a year–month interval from or to a date will give another date. Adding or subtracting a day–hour–minute–second interval to a time will give another time. These two operators are usually supported whenever the interval data type is. A summary of the different mixed data type operators involving the date, time and interval data types is given in Table 3.5.

Table 3.5 Mixed data type operators for date, time and interval types.

Expression	Output data type
Date – date	Interval
Time – time	Interval
Date + year–month interval	Date
Date – year–month interval	Date
Time + day–second interval	Time
Time – day–second interval	Time

Organizing data values into data types is an obvious first step towards a data model and defining the operators a first step towards defining a data language. Most data models include one or more data types and allow the DBMS application developers to define additional data types as they see fit. These additional data types will be part of a data language for the data model. The data types discussed above are the most common ones used in business information systems. Geographical information systems (GIS), which hold data about maps, have more complex data types – points, lines and paths, for example (Elmasri and Navathe (2007) include a brief introduction to GIS).

3.2 The relational data model

The relational data model was developed by E.F. Codd in the late 1960s in response to the difficulties existing data models had when dealing with large, shared databases. The relational data model is quite simple, and remains one of the easiest data models to understand. It is also very flexible as *any* data at all can be represented by a relational database. Not surprisingly, most commercial DBMS are based on the relational data model; these are called **RDBMS.** Earlier data models (such as the hierarchic and network data models) have largely faded away, though some important legacy applications still use databases based on these data models. Later data models (such as object-orientated and semistructured) are important in niche markets and their use is growing. For now, though, it is the relational data model that every database professional must understand.

Although motivated by practical problems, Codd gave the relational data model a firm mathematical foundation using set theory and predicate logic. In fact, the name 'relational data model' refers to the fact that all data is organized into **relations**, which are the mathematical equivalent of **tables**. So, a relation is a table and 'relational' means 'table-based'. It is worth emphasizing this, because 'relation' is often mistaken as meaning 'relationship'. It does not: *'relation' is just another name for 'table'*. To avoid confusion, this book uses the word table throughout.

The relational data model requires only a single data type: Boolean. An RDBMS is free to include other data types in its implementation of the relational data language. The data types discussed above are supported by many RDBMS. The relational data model can also accommodate any **integrity constraint** that can be written as a Boolean expression. Traditionally two sorts of integrity constraint have been important – **candidate key constraints** and **foreign key constraints**. More general **enterprise constraints** are often supported by commercial RDBMS. For example, the SQL standard includes **check constraints** and **assertions** (see Chapters 5 and 6).

3.2.1 Organizing data in the relational data model

The relational data model organizes all data in the database into tables. Each table holds data about some particular kind of thing that database users are interested in. In the Staff Directory database, the users are interested in staff contact details, which are held in the `Staff` table. Similarly, users are interested in support sessions offered by academic staff, which are held in the `SupportSession` table.

The data in a table is organized into rows. Each row represents a particular instance of the sort of thing that the table holds data about. A row in the `Staff` table represents the contact details for a particular member of staff. A row in the `SupportSession` table represents a particular support session, offered by a member of academic staff. The set of all rows is called the **table instance**.

Within each row, data is organized into columns. In each row of a table, there is a single value for each column. Each column has a name and a data type and the column value must have the same data type as the column.

The table name together with the set of these **column descriptions** is called the **table heading**. The number of columns in the table heading is called the table's **degree** and the number of rows in the table instance is its **cardinality**.

> **Table heading and table instance** A table consists of a *table heading* and a *table instance*. The table heading includes the table name and the column descriptions. The table instance is the set of rows held in the table at a given time.

The relational data model also includes integrity constraints, to limit what data can be held in a table instance. The description of the table, its columns and constraints is called the **table schema**. The collection of all table schema for a particular database is the **database schema**. Figure 3.3 gives a picture of the `SupportSession` table with the various features labelled. Note that each column description shows the column name and data type. The column values all have the appropriate data type, which are varying length character strings for the `Varchar` columns and times for the `Time` columns. The table name is shown as part of the table heading, but the relational data model includes both named and unnamed tables. For example, the RDBMS responds to a database query by creating an unnamed table and passing this table to the database client. This means that tables really are the *only* data structure in the relational data model.

There are four properties that the table instance must satisfy:

1 for each row of the table instance, there is exactly one value for each column and that value has the same data type as the column

2 there are no duplicate rows in the table instance

3 the order of the rows in the table instance is not significant

4 the order of the columns for a particular row is not significant.

Figure 3.3 The parts of a table.

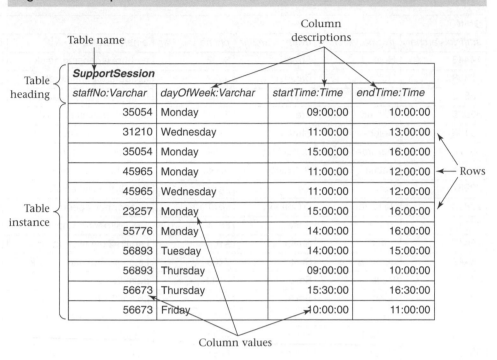

Properties 3 and 4 mean that, for example, the two instances of the Staff table in Figures 3.4 (a) and (b) are identical. The fact that the columns and rows are in different orders is irrelevant. Both table instances hold *exactly* the same data about members of staff.

Property 2 means that the table instance shown in Figure 3.5 is illegal, because the third and last rows are identical. It is worth noting that most RDBMS do not enforce this rule, nor does the ISO standard for SQL. Even so, it is good practice to use integrity constraints to prevent duplicate rows in a table instance, unless there is a very good reason for allowing them. Tables that hold audit information – who did what, when – or that log errors are good examples of tables that might need to hold duplicate rows.

Interpreted strictly, property 1 means that the Staff table instances shown in Figures 3.4 (a) is also illegal. On the fifth row, the row of data about Helene Chirac, the phone column is null (indicated explicitly by writing the keyword NULL in that column, rather than by leaving the column empty). Null is not a value, but an indication that there is no value for this column, on the current row. Nulls are the mechanism most RDBMS use to deal with missing data (though this approach has its critics – see, for example, Date (2004)). Since null is not a value, an amended version of property 1 is needed:

1 (amended version) For each row of the table instance, each column either has exactly one value or is null. When there is a value, it has the same data type as the column.

Notice that null, as it is not a value, does not have a data type. Although null is widely used to represent missing information, it does complicate things. Consider what happens when a user asks of the Staff Directory whether any members of staff have the

89

Figure 3.4 Two identical instances of the `Staff` table.

Staff

staffNo:Varchar	fName:Varchar	lName:Varchar	phone:Varchar	email:Varchar	photo:BLOB
14443	Helen	Abbot	8032	h.abbot@pennine.ac.uk	[BLOB]
56893	Ruth	Bapetsi	8022	r.bapetsi@pennine.ac.uk	[BLOB]
56673	Joshua	Bittaye	7782	j.bittaye@pennine.ac.uk	[BLOB]
33935	Padma	Brar	6641	p.brar@pennine.ac.uk	[BLOB]
35155	Helene	Chirac	NULL	h.chirac@pennine.ac.uk	[BLOB]
55776	Gurpreet	Choudhury	5454	g.choudhury@pennine.ac.uk	[BLOB]
35054	Selma	Hutchins	8706	s.hutchins@pennine.ac.uk	[BLOB]
89987	Dan	Lin	8514	d.lin@pennine.co.uk	[BLOB]
78893	Jo Karen	O'Connor	8871	j.k.oconnor@pennine.ac.uk	[BLOB]
77712	Frank	Rose	8871	f.rose@pennine.ac.uk	[BLOB]
25447	John	Smith	5104	j.smith@pennine.ac.uk	[BLOB]
25448	Judith Anne	Smith	7709	j.a.smith@pennine.ac.uk	[BLOB]
31210	Paul	Smith	NULL	p.smith@pennine.ac.uk	[BLOB]
10780	John	Smith	NULL	j.b.smith@pennine.ac.uk	[BLOB]
23257	Freya	Stark	8660	f.stark@pennine.ac.uk	[BLOB]
45965	Mikhail	Sudbin	5553	m.sudbin@pennine.ac.uk	[BLOB]
33509	Helen	Timms	8661	h.timms@pennine.ac.uk	[BLOB]

(a) An instance of the `Staff` table.

Staff

staffNo:Varchar	email:Varchar	fName:Varchar	lName:Varchar	phone:Varchar	photo:BLOB
10780	j.b.smith@pennine.ac.uk	John	Smith	NULL	[BLOB]
14443	h.abbot@pennine.ac.uk	Helen	Abbot	8032	[BLOB]
23257	f.stark@pennine.ac.uk	Freya	Stark	8660	[BLOB]
25447	j.smith@pennine.ac.uk	John	Smith	5104	[BLOB]
25448	j.a.smith@pennine.ac.uk	Judith Anne	Smith	7709	[BLOB]
31210	p.smith@pennine.ac.uk	Paul	Smith	NULL	[BLOB]
33509	h.timms@pennine.ac.uk	Helen	Timms	8661	[BLOB]
33935	p.brar@pennine.ac.uk	Padma	Brar	6641	[BLOB]
35054	s.hutchins@pennine.ac.uk	Selma	Hutchins	8706	[BLOB]
35155	h.chirac@pennine.ac.uk	Helene	Chirac	NULL	[BLOB]
45965	m.sudbin@pennine.ac.uk	Mikhail	Sudbin	5553	[BLOB]
55776	g.choudhury@pennine.ac.uk	Gurpreet	Choudhury	5454	[BLOB]
56673	j.bittaye@pennine.ac.uk	Joshua	Bittaye	7782	[BLOB]
56893	r.bapetsi@pennine.ac.uk	Ruth	Bapetsi	8022	[BLOB]
77712	f.rose@pennine.ac.uk	Frank	Rose	8871	[BLOB]
78893	j.k.oconnor@pennine.ac.uk	Jo Karen	O'Connor	8871	[BLOB]
89987	d.lin@pennine.co.uk	Dan	Lin	8514	[BLOB]

(b) The same table instance with columns and rows in a different order.

same phone number as Helen Abbot. Given the `Staff` table instance in Figure 3.4 (a), the obvious answer is 'No'. Obvious, but wrong! The null in the phone column of the rows representing Paul Smith, Helene Chirac and John Smith means their phone number is not known. Any one of them might share a phone number with Helen Abbot, but, then again, they might not. The RDBMS should recognize this uncertainty and answer 'Unknown'. Formally, introducing null to represent missing information alters the interpretation of Boolean expressions. There are now *three* Boolean values: TRUE, FALSE and UNKNOWN. Thus, the truth tables shown in Figure 3.2 need to be amended. Figure 3.6 shows the truth tables for this three-valued logic.

Consider the truth table for NOT. Whenever the Boolean expression *p* evaluates to TRUE, it follows that the Boolean expression NOT *p* must evaluate to FALSE and vice versa. To say that a Boolean expression *p* evaluates to UNKNOWN means that it cannot be decided whether it is true or false. Consequently, NOT *p* must also evaluate to UNKNOWN because, if, for example, NOT *p* was TRUE, then *p* would have to be FALSE.

Figure 3.5 An illegal table instance (though allowed by most RDBMS).

Staff					
staffNo:Varchar	*fName:Varchar*	*lName:Varchar*	*phone:Varchar*	*email:Varchar*	*photo:BLOB*
14443	Helen	Abbot	8032	h.abbot@pennine.ac.uk	[BLOB]
56893	Ruth	Bapetsi	8022	r.bapetsi@pennine.ac.uk	[BLOB]
55776	Gurpreet	Choudhury	5454	g.choudhury@pennine.ac.uk	[BLOB]
56673	Joshua	Bittaye	7782	j.bittaye@pennine.ac.uk	[BLOB]
33935	Padma	Brar	6641	p.brar@pennine.ac.uk	[BLOB]
35155	Helene	Chirac	NULL	h.chirac@pennine.ac.uk	[BLOB]
55776	Gurpreet	Choudhury	5454	g.choudhury@pennine.ac.uk	[BLOB]

Duplicate row

Figure 3.6 Truth table for the Boolean operators using three-valued logic.

p	NOT p	p	q	p AND q	p	q	p OR q
TRUE	FALSE	TRUE	TRUE	TRUE	TRUE	TRUE	TRUE
FALSE	TRUE	TRUE	FALSE	FALSE	TRUE	FALSE	TRUE
UNKNOWN	UNKNOWN	TRUE	UNKNOWN	UNKNOWN	TRUE	UNKNOWN	TRUE
		FALSE	TRUE	FALSE	FALSE	TRUE	TRUE
		FALSE	FALSE	FALSE	FALSE	FALSE	FALSE
		FALSE	UNKNOWN	FALSE	FALSE	UNKNOWN	UNKNOWN
		UNKNOWN	TRUE	UNKNOWN	UNKNOWN	TRUE	TRUE
		UNKNOWN	FALSE	FALSE	UNKNOWN	FALSE	UNKNOWN
		UNKNOWN	UNKNOWN	UNKNOWN	UNKNOWN	UNKNOWN	UNKNOWN

Figure 3.7 The `Staff` table redefined so that the phone column has data type 'set of character strings'.

Staff					
staffNo:Varchar	fName:Varchar	lName:Varchar	phone:Varchar Set	email:Varchar	photo:BLOB
14443	Helen	Abbot	{'8032'}	h.abbot@pennine.ac.uk	[BLOB]
56893	Ruth	Bapetsi	{'8022'}	r.bapetsi@pennine.ac.uk	[BLOB]
56673	Joshua	Bittaye	{'7782'}	j.bittaye@pennine.ac.uk	[BLOB]
33935	Padma	Brar	{'6641'}	p.brar@pennine.ac.uk	[BLOB]
35155	Helene	Chirac	NULL	h.chirac@pennine.ac.uk	[BLOB]
55776	Gurpreet	Choudhury	{'5454', '5771'}	g.choudhury@pennine.ac.uk	[BLOB]
35054	Selma	Hutchins	{'8706'}	s.hutchins@pennine.ac.uk	[BLOB]
89987	Dan	Lin	{'8514'}	d.lin@pennine.co.uk	[BLOB]
78893	Jo Karen	O'Connor	{'8871'}	j.k.oconnor@pennine.ac.uk	[BLOB]
77712	Frank	Rose	{'8871'}	f.rose@pennine.ac.uk	[BLOB]
25447	John	Smith	{'5104'}	j.smith@pennine.ac.uk	[BLOB]
25448	Judith Anne	Smith	{'7709'}	j.a.smith@pennine.ac.uk	[BLOB]
31210	Paul	Smith	NULL	p.smith@pennine.ac.uk	[BLOB]
10780	John	Smith	{}	j.b.smith@pennine.ac.uk	[BLOB]
23257	Freya	Stark	{'8660', '8661'}	f.stark@pennine.ac.uk	[BLOB]
45965	Mikhail	Sudbin	{'5553'}	m.sudbin@pennine.ac.uk	[BLOB]
33509	Helen	Timms	{'8661'}	h.timms@pennine.ac.uk	[BLOB]

For Boolean expressions involving AND, the truth table offers the obvious interpretation: the Boolean expression p AND q evaluates to TRUE precisely when both p and q are TRUE. When either one of the input values is FALSE, p AND q evaluates to FALSE. In all other circumstances, one of the input values must be UNKNOWN and p AND q evaluates to UNKNOWN. A similar case-by-case description can be given for the Boolean operator OR.

Both versions of property 1 state that, on any row, each column has a *single* value. This has led many textbooks to insist that a column must have a scalar data type. The argument is that non-scalar data types are designed to hold more than one value. For example, suppose that the `Staff` table is defined so that the data type of the phone column is 'set of character strings' rather than 'character string'. A possible instance of this version of the `Staff` table is shown in Figure 3.7. The value in the phone column in the row for Freya Stark is a set with two members, the two character strings '8660' and '8661'. However, the column's data type is not `Varchar`, it is `Varchar Set`. So, the column value is the whole set {'8660', '8661'} and this is a *single* set value. Thus, the table instance in Figure 3.7 does still satisfy property 1.

The table also illustrates an important distinction between null and 'no value'. The fifth row from the top holds data for Helene Chirac and the entry in the phone column for this row is null. This indicates that her phone number is not yet known. In contrast, the fourth row from the bottom, which holds data about one of the two John Smiths employed at the Pennine University, has the value {} in the phone column, which indicates the empty set. This is a valid set value – specifically, it is the set with no members. It tells us that John Smith is *known to not have a phone number*. This is *not* the same as null, which indicates that it is unknown whether or not the person has a phone number.

Allowing columns to have a non-scalar data type opens up an interesting possibility. A table heading can be thought of as declaring a user-defined data type. Consequently, a column's data type can be a table. A named table is simply a variable with this data type and its table instance a particular value of the data type. Not all RDBMS support table data types. Even when they do, it is a feature that should be used sparingly. Unnecessary complexity is best avoided.

3.2.2 Integrity constraints in the relational data model

The **integrity constraint** is the mechanism that ensures the database instance is consistent and it enforces business rules. Different data models provide different integrity constraints, but all work in the same way. They place a restriction on the database instance so that some *logically possible* database instances are disallowed. There is no logical reason for a member of staff not offering a support session starting at 7 pm, but doing so is not allowed at the Pennine University. The Staff Directory database will use an integrity constraint to enforce this business rule.

An integrity constraint is declarative rather than procedural. It declares restrictions on what data values can be stored in the database. There is no need to state how to enforce the restriction as the DBMS will handle that.

> **Integrity constraint** A statement about the database instance that must always be true. It is usually written as a Boolean expression.

The relational data model has two main integrity constraints, both based on the notion of a relational key. A relational key is simply a set of columns that serve a particular role within the database schema. A **candidate key** is a set of columns the values of which are unique to a particular row of the table. The candidate key acts as a unique identifier for a row as, given the values for the columns of the candidate key, there can be only one matching row in the table instance. A **candidate key constraint** is a Boolean expression that tells the DBMS to ensure that the value of a candidate key is unique within the table instance. A table may have several candidate keys. One of these is chosen to be the main identifier for the table and is called the **primary key**.

The uniqueness condition is not quite enough to properly define a candidate key. Consider the Staff table (shown in Figure 3.4 (a)). It has six columns, staffNo, fName, lName, phone, email and photo. Clearly the set of all these columns satisfies the uniqueness property as every row in a table is unique. However, it is not much help as an identifier, as you must know all the data values in a row before you can identify that row. A candidate key should be a minimal set, in the sense that if you removed any one of the columns, then the resulting set would not be unique. This leads to the following definition.

Candidate key A candidate key for a table is a set of columns that has two properties:

1 uniqueness – the combination of values for these columns is different for each row of the table instance

2 irreducibility – no subset of the columns has the uniqueness property.

Candidate key constraint States that the *candidate key* (the combination of values of the candidate key columns) is unique within the table instance.

Sets of columns that have uniqueness, but not irreducibility are sometimes called *super keys* – meaning that they contain a candidate key as a subset.

The value of `staffNo` will be different for each row as, after all, the purpose of a staff number is to uniquely identify a member of staff. Any set of columns with just one column in it is obviously irreducible, so {`staffNo`} is a candidate key. Similarly, {`email`} is a candidate key, because the Pennine University has a business rule that each member of staff has exactly one e-mail address. E-mail addresses are usually unique to an individual, but not always. Within an organization, individuals will typically have their own e-mail address, though there may be shared e-mail addresses, too. At the Pennine University, for example the members of the Admissions team each have their own e-mail address, but share responsibility for checking the 'admission@pennine.ac.uk' e-mail address, used by applicants to request brochures, make enquiries and so on. Similarly, some families share an e-mail address because their Internet service provider only provides one e-mail address per connection. Using a shared e-mail address to identify customers in a billing system is not a good idea. Who settles the bill if the couple split up?

Notice that {`fName`}, {`lName`} and {`fName, lName`} are not candidate keys (check the table instance shown in Figure 3.4 (a)). Names almost never work as candidate keys, because different people often share the same name. Actors' stage names are unique, so can be used as candidate keys, but that is the only obvious example and is pretty limited in application.

The phone column presents an interesting situation. Suppose that the Pennine University has the following business rule:

● no two members of staff share a phone number.

This suggests that phone has the uniqueness property. However, it does not. To see why, suppose the user adds a new row to the database, with the column values:

```
staffNo = '56890'
fName = 'Anna'
lName = 'Jones'
phone = '1229'
email = 'a.jones@pennine.ac.uk'
```

(The `photo` column will be null for this new row of the table instance.) The RDBMS must check whether or not the value of the phone column for this new row will be unique. It does this by looking at each of the existing rows and asking the question:

'Is the value of the phone column on this row equal to '1229'?'

This is equivalent to evaluating the Boolean expression `phone = '1229'` for each row in the table. With the data shown in Figure 3.4 (a), this Boolean expression evaluates to `FALSE` for the first four rows. For the fifth row it evaluates to `UNKNOWN`, because the phone column is null for the fifth row. This means that it cannot be said with certainty that the new phone number is unique, so it cannot be a candidate key. In general, no column of a candidate key can be null.

SQL includes a constraint called `UNIQUE`. This *does* allow columns to be null, but enforces uniqueness across rows where there are no null columns. This added flexibility in defining integrity constraints can be useful.

A candidate key with a single column is called a **simple candidate key**, while ones with two or more columns are **composite candidate keys**. The `SupportSession` table shown in Figure 3.3 is an example of a table with no simple candidate keys. The set of columns {`staff`, `dayOfWeek`, `startTime`} is a composite candidate key. It is unique, as a member of staff can only offer one support session at any one time. Notice that the uniqueness condition refers to the combination of values in all three columns. The first and third rows of the table instance in Figure 3.3 have the same values in `staff` and `dayOfWeek`, but differ in the `startTime` column, while the fourth and fifth have the same values in `startTime` and `staff`, but differ in the `dayOfWeek` column. Analysing all possible subsets of the candidate key shows that {`staff`, `dayOfWeek`, `startTime`} is irreducible. {`staff`, `dayOfWeek`} cannot be guaranteed to be unique as one member of staff may offer two support sessions on the same day. Similarly, {`staff`, `startTime`} may not be unique as staff may offer support sessions at the same time on different days. {`dayOfWeek`, `startTime`} is not unique as two different members of staff may offer support sessions on the same day and at the same time. Thus, none of the two-member subsets satisfies the requirement of uniqueness. This is sufficient to establish irreducibility as, if any one-member subset had the uniqueness property, so would the two-member subsets containing this member.

The `SupportSession` table has another candidate key: {`staff`, `dayOfWeek`, `endTime`}. For both the `Staff` and `SupportSession` tables, one of the candidate keys must be chosen as the primary key – the main identifier for the table. The other candidate keys are sometimes referred to as **alternate keys**. There are no fixed rules as to which candidate key to choose as the primary key. One useful guide is to pick the candidate key:

1 that makes the most sense to the business

2 where the data values rarely change

3 with the fewest columns

4 with the shortest length, for typical data values.

For the `Staff` table, `staffNo` probably makes more business sense than `email`. Note that neither will change and both have only a single column, but that each value of `staffNo` is shorter in length than a value of `email` (5 characters compared to more than 14).

Of the two candidate keys for the `SupportSession` table, {`staff`, `dayOfWeek`, `startTime`} makes more business sense as a primary key as it is more useful to know when a support session starts than when it ends. Note that both the candidate keys for the `SupportSession` table change rarely, have the same number of columns and the same length for their data values. If both made equal business sense as primary keys, then it wouldn't matter which was chosen.

The candidate key allows an RDBMS to uniquely identify a row from a fragment of the data held on that row. Candidate key constraints help the RDBMS to ensure that there are no duplicate rows in a table instance. The second kind of key is not concerned with individual tables, but with the relationships between them. Figure 3.8 shows how this works for the `Staff` and `SupportSession` tables. Each of these tables has a column called `staffNo`. For the `Staff` table, {`staffNo`} is a candidate key (in fact, the primary key), so a particular value for `staffNo` identifies a single row of the `Staff` table. For the `SupportSession` table, the `staffNo` column is not a candidate key, so many rows can have the same value in the `staffNo` column. For example, the two rows with the value '45965' are indicated in Figure 3.8, along with the matching candidate key value in the `Staff` table. This matching of data values tells us that the two support sessions are offered by Mikhail Sudbin. This mechanism for capturing a relationship is simple and elegant. No special data structures are needed. Everything is dealt with through the relational data model's only data structure, the table.

There is quite a bit of terminology associated with the scenario in Figure 3.8. The set of columns {`staffNo`} from the `SupportSession` table is called a **foreign key**. Notice that a foreign key, like a candidate key, is a *set of columns* (although in the example there is only one member in the set). In any row, the values of the foreign key columns act as a key to related data from another (a foreign) table. The `Staff` table's candidate key {`staffNo`} is called the **matching candidate key** because it is the column values of that candidate key, rather than any other, which will match those of the foreign key. The table with the foreign key is called the **referencing table** and the table with the matching candidate key the **referenced table**. That is because, for example, rows of `SupportSession` *refer back to* rows of `Staff`.

> The referencing table is sometimes called the *child table* and the referenced table the *parent table*. The idea is that the rows of the child table 'belong to' the matching row of the parent table.

The **foreign key constraint** (also called the **referential integrity constraint**) is a Boolean expression that tells the RDBMS to ensure that the values entered for the foreign key columns of the referencing table can be found as the column values of the matching candidate key on *some* row in the referenced table. In the example above, the foreign key constraint insists that, for each row of `SupportSession`, there is a row in `Staff` such that the values in the `staffNo` columns of the two tables are the same.

Figure 3.8 Implementing relationships between tables with foreign keys.

Matching candidate key   Referenced table

Staff

staffNo:Varchar	fName:Varchar	lName:Varchar	phone:Varchar	email:Varchar	photo:BLOB
14443	Helen	Abbot	8032	h.abbot@pennine.ac.uk	[BLOB]
56893	Ruth	Bapetsi	8022	r.bapetsi@pennine.ac.uk	[BLOB]
56673	Joshua	Bittaye	7782	j.bittaye@pennine.ac.uk	[BLOB]
33935	Padma	Brar	6641	p.brar@pennine.ac.uk	[BLOB]
35155	Helene	Chirac	NULL	h.chirac@pennine.ac.uk	[BLOB]
55776	Gurpreet	Choudhury	5454	g.choudhury@pennine.ac.uk	[BLOB]
35054	Selma	Hutchins	8706	s.hutchins@pennine.ac.uk	[BLOB]
89987	Dan	Lin	8514	d.lin@pennine.co.uk	[BLOB]
78893	Jo Karen	O'Connor	8871	j.k.oconnor@pennine.ac.uk	[BLOB]
77712	Frank	Rose	8871	f.rose@pennine.ac.uk	[BLOB]
25447	John	Smith	5104	j.smith@pennine.ac.uk	[BLOB]
25448	Judith Anne	Smith	7709	j.a.smith@pennine.ac.uk	[BLOB]
31210	Paul	Smith	NULL	p.smith@pennine.ac.uk	[BLOB]
10780	John	Smith	NULL	j.b.smith@pennine.ac.uk	[BLOB]
23257	Freya	Stark	8660	f.stark@pennine.ac.uk	[BLOB]
45965	Mikhail	Sudbin	5553	m.sudbin@pennine.ac.uk	[BLOB]
33509	Helen	Timms	8661	h.timms@pennine.ac.uk	[BLOB]

Foreign key   Matching
                     rows

SupportSession

staffNo:Varchar	dayOfWeek:Varchar	startTime:Time	endTime:Time
35054	Monday	09:00:00	10:00:00
31210	Wednesday	11:00:00	13:00:00
35054	Monday	15:00:00	16:00:00
45965	Monday	11:00:00	12:00:00
45965	Wednesday	11:00:00	12:00:00
23257	Monday	15:00:00	16:00:00
55776	Monday	14:00:00	16:00:00
56893	Tuesday	14:00:00	15:00:00
56893	Thursday	09:00:00	10:00:00
56673	Thursday	15:30:00	16:30:00
56673	Friday	10:00:00	11:00:00

Referencing
table

An RDBMS that ensures foreign key constraints are always satisfied is said to maintain referential integrity.

> **Foreign key** A Set of columns in the referencing table, the values of which refer to those of the matching candidate key columns in some row of the referenced table.
>
> **Foreign key constraint** States that, for each row in the referencing table, there must be a row in the referenced table such that the value in the foreign key columns is the same as the value of the matching candidate key columns.

As the values of the foreign key columns are identical to values from the matching candidate key columns, they must have the same data type. When the two keys are composite, the declaration of the foreign key constraint must specify which columns of the foreign key match which of the candidate key. This is not always obvious as there is no rule that insists on the column names being the same, only their data types. Figure 3.9 shows the foreign key relationship between the `Equipment` and `Room` tables. These tables are part of the Web Timetable database at the Pennine University. The values in the `Equipment` table's `portable` column indicate whether the equipment is fixed in a particular room or can be moved from room to room. For fixed equipment, such as ceiling-mounted projectors, the database captures the link between the equipment and the room it is fixed in by enforcing a foreign key constraint. The foreign key for the `Equipment` table is {`building`, `room`}, the matching candidate key for the `Room` table is {`building`, `roomNo`}. These have different column names, so the foreign key constraint must make it clear that the match is between data in the two `building` columns and in the `room` and `roomNo` columns. This issue is addressed in the data language (see Chapter 5).

> This may seem a minor point, but it is important. Remember, a DBMS is computer software and computer software cannot make an educated guess. While to a person it seems obvious to match `room` and `roomNo`, computer software has no knowledge base of common sense from which to make such an inference.

Unlike a candidate key, the columns of a foreign key may be null. Figure 3.9 also shows this situation. For example, the entries in the second row for both the foreign key columns are null. This does not violate the foreign key constraint, even though there can never be a row in the `Room` table for which the entries in the `building` and `roomNo` columns are null. The reason for this is tied up with the interpretation of null and three-valued Boolean logic. When a row is added to the `Equipment` table, the DBMS checks that the foreign key constraint is satisfied by answering the following question:

Is there is a row in the `Room` table for which the entries in the `building` and `roomNo` columns have the same values as those supplied for the `building` and `room` columns respectively of this new row in the `Equipment` table?

Figure 3.9 A composite foreign key, with different column names and nulls.

Equipment

assetNo:varchar	assetType:varchar	description:varchar	building:varchar	room:varchar	portable:boolean
1570131	Data projector	HP vp6100	Wilson	205	FALSE
1799131	Data projector	HP vp6100	NULL	NULL	TRUE
4560293	OHP	3M OHP 1608	Locke	24	FALSE
4503993	PC	Dell OptiPlex™ GX280	Wilson	205	FALSE
5010009	OHP	3M OHP 2000	NULL	NULL	TRUE
2992220	Data Projector	ToshibaTDP-SW20	Priestley	G12	FALSE
2892112	Laptop	SONY X505	NULL	NULL	TRUE

Primary key

Foreign key

Room

building:varchar	roomNo:varchar	capacity:numeric
Wilson	205	25
Wilson	113	25
Wilson	205	100
Priestley	G12	150
Priestley	113A	20
Locke	24	30
Locke	27	25
Locke	14	30

Matching rows

The constraint is only violated if this statement evaluates to FALSE, in which case the DBMS would not add the row to the table instance. When a null has been supplied for one of the foreign key columns in the Equipment table, the statement evaluates to UNKNOWN. The constraint has *not* been violated as UNKNOWN is not FALSE and so the row is added to the table instance. A similar process of checking occurs when a row of the Equipment table is modified.

It is possible to design any database so that foreign key columns do not allow null and, indeed, many database practitioners prefer this approach (in particular, those who never liked nulls in the first place). Figure 3.10 shows how the Equipment table could be split into two separate tables – PortableEquipment and FixedEquipment. There is now a foreign key linking FixedEquipment and Room that does not allow nulls in the foreign key columns. There is no foreign key for PortableEquipment. In addition, there is no longer a need for the portable column in either of the two equipment tables.

The main use of foreign key constraints is to ensure that new rows in the referencing table have valid values in the foreign key columns. A second use is to check that

Figure 3.10 Redesigning the `Equipment` table to avoid nulls in the foreign key columns.

Foreign key

FixedEquipment				
assetNo:varchar	*assetType:varchar*	*description:varchar*	*building:varchar*	*room:varchar*
1570131	Data projector	HP vp6100	Wilson	205
4560293	OHP	3M OHP 1608	Locke	24
4503993	PC	Dell OptiPlex™ GX280	Wilson	205
2992220	Data projector	Toshiba TDP-SW20	Priestley	G12

PortableEquipment		
assetNo:varchar	*assetType:varchar*	*description:varchar*
5010009	OHP	3M OHP 2000
1799131	Data projector	HP vp6100
2892112	Laptop	SONY X505

No foreign key

changes to the column values of the matching candidate key do not violate referential integrity. For example, suppose that the Wilson building at the Pennine University is renamed the Heath building. The RDBMS must amend the data in the first three rows of the `Room` table (see Figure 3.9) to reflect that change. In doing so, it would leave the first and fourth rows of the `Equipment` table without a matching candidate key, so, to maintain the foreign key constraint, the RDBMS must reject the requested change. This is a little inconvenient, as, to make the change, three distinct steps are needed.

1 For each row in the `Room` table where the `building` column has the value 'Wilson', add a new row, identical to it except that the `building` column has the value 'Heath'.

2 For each row in the `Equipment` table where the `building` column has the value 'Wilson', change this value to 'Heath'.

3 Delete all rows from the `Room` table where the `building` column has the value 'Wilson'.

To avoid this rigmarole, there is a **referential action** associated with every foreign key constraint. The referential action tells the RDBMS how to maintain referential integrity when a user requests changes to matching candidate key values that would violate the foreign key constraint. The default referential action is NO ACTION. This means that there is no special action defined for the foreign key constraint. If a request to change the referenced table instance would violate the foreign key constraint, then the change will be rejected.

The CASCADE referential action says that changes to the referenced table instance are cascaded down to the referencing table instance. In our example, this would mean that changing the value in the `building` column from 'Wilson' to 'Heath' in the

Room table would automatically lead to a similar change being made in the Equipment table.

Two further referential actions are widely supported. SET NULL says that when a row of the referenced table is modified or removed, the foreign key columns of any matching rows in the referencing table are set to null. SET DEFAULT has a similar effect, except that the foreign key column values are set to their default value.

Referential actions are a good solution to the problem of maintaining referential integrity, while still allowing the user to make reasonable changes to the database instance. They are applied automatically by the DBMS, with no need for the application developer to code an exception-handling procedure. However, they only deal with the situation where the user changes the value in the matching candidate key of a foreign key constraint. A more general approach is to define a **transaction**. A transaction is a series of database modifications that are treated as a single unit of work. During the transaction, some integrity constraints may be temporarily violated – there may be unmatched foreign keys or duplicate rows, for example. However, at the end of the transaction, these violations have been resolved and all integrity constraints are satisfied.

Up to this point, table schema have all been given by showing a picture of the table (table heading and table instance). Database designers use a standard format for written table schemas (usually called a relation schema). Figure 3.11 shows the general format for a written table schema. First comes the table name, followed by the list of column descriptions in parentheses. In many cases, this is all that is given (sometimes, even the column data types are omitted), but it is handy to include a description of the main constraints. For the primary key constraint, the primary key column(s) can simply be listed, but, for the foreign key constraint, both the foreign key column(s) *and* the matching candidate key column(s) need to be given. The written table schemas for the Staff and SupportSession tables are shown below.

```
Staff (staffNo:Varchar, fName:Varchar, lName:Varchar,
phone:Varchar, email:Varchar, photo:BLOB)
Primary Key: (staffNo)

SupportSession (staffNo:Varchar, dayOfWeek:Varchar,
startTime:Time, endTime:Time)

Primary Key: (staffNo, dayOfWeek, startTime)
Foreign Key: (staffNo) references Staff(staffNo)
Candidate Key: (staffNo, dayOfWeek, endTime)
```

Figure 3.11 A written table schema.

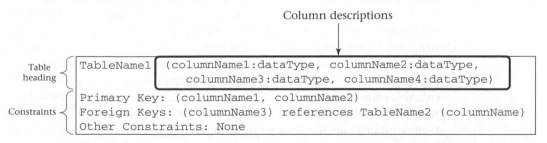

An alternative way to show primary keys is to underline the primary key columns. This works well enough, but the practice of showing foreign keys by placing an asterisk – '*' – next to foreign key columns is less effective. Which table does the foreign key refer to and, if there is more than one foreign key, how do you indicate this? In this book, the fuller notation shown above is used instead.

Although the primary and foreign key constraints are the main ones in the relational data model, most RDBMS include at least two other integrity constraints. The **not-null constraint** states that a particular column must never be null; every row must have a valid data value for this column. The **unique constraint** acts a little like the primary key constraint. It applies to a set of columns and ensures that, in every row of the table, the combination of column values is unique. The significant difference is that any of the columns may be null, in which case the unique constraint is ignored. Candidate keys can be enforced by placing a unique constraint on the candidate key and not null constraints on each of the candidate key columns.

3.2.3 Relational data languages

Although the relational data model uses only one structure to organize data, it has a number of data languages. Each relational data language provides a way for users to create tables, manipulate the table instance and query the database instance. The relational algebra provides a formal declarative language for manipulating relational databases, with the relational calculus offering a formal procedural alternative. These languages are important for advanced topics such as query processing and optimization. Application developers can benefit from studying the relational algebra, but SQL remains the most important relational language for developers, designers and users. The focus of this book is firmly on developing web database applications, and so on SQL, which is covered in detail in Chapters 5 and 6.

SQL provides relational DBMS (and some non-relational products) with a standard, widely implemented language for interacting with their users. When a user wishes the DBMS to carry out some action against the database, he or she writes an **SQL statement**. There are several different SQL statements, such as to create a new table, add a row to an existing table, retrieve data from the database instance and so on. As SQL is an international standard, an SQL statement should work regardless of the DBMS being used. This is not quite the case, so database developers must always keep a copy of the SQL manual for their DBMS to hand. The version of SQL discussed in this chapter is the international standard ISO SQL:2003, unless otherwise stated.

SQL assumes that each user has a unique **authorization identifier**. The SQL standard does not include a way to create authorization identifiers for individual users, leaving this to individual DBMS. Most DBMS do this by including the SQL statement CREATE USER in their version of SQL, but this statement is not part of the ISO SQL standard.

Different users will have different **privileges**. A user privilege is the ability to instruct the DBMS to carry out some particular action. For example, some users will be able to instruct the DBMS to create a new database or modify a particular database schema or retrieve data from a particular database instance. SQL also includes the concept of a **role**, which is when a group of users share the same privileges. One user can play many different roles and a role may be played by many different users. SQL includes statements to manage roles and privileges.

Figure 3.12 Tables, columns and constraints.

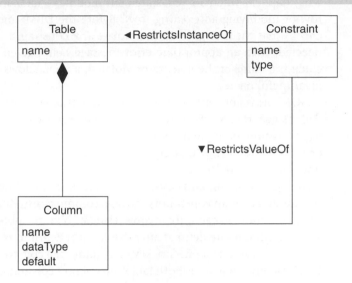

Each user must have his or her own **connection** to the DBMS and each connection has an associated **session**. Any SQL statements sent over the user's connection are executed within the associated session. The user can modify the properties of that session – for instance, specifying a default database from the many managed by the DBMS. Most DBMS provide their own way to associate a particular database with a session. For example, the MySQL DBMS has the 'USE' statement. The main function of a connection and its associated session is to support the communication and concurrency functions of the DBMS.

SQL is a database language for the relational model, so its main data structure is the table, made up of one or more columns. A table may also have constraints. Figure 3.12 shows the associations between a table, its columns and constraints using a simple UML class diagram. You will notice that there is a little more notation in this diagram than in those seen in earlier chapters. For a start, each box has two compartments. The upper compartment tells us what the thing is and the lower compartment tells us what information is known about that thing. So, the only information known about a Table is its name, while, for a Column, its name, dataType and default are known. For a constraint, the name and type are known. The black diamond symbol on the association line between Table and Column means 'is composed of', so this association is read 'a table is composed of columns'.

Primary key and foreign key constraints can be defined in ISO SQL. The standard also includes the not-null constraint, which states that a particular column cannot be null in any row of the table; the unique constraint, which is used to enforce candidate key constraints; and the check constraint, which places a more complex restriction on the value of a particular column. Many state constraints can be implemented using the SQL check constraint, but transition constraints must be implemented using SQL triggers (see Chapter 10) or handled in the application code. These SQL constraints are all discussed in Chapters 5 and 6.

Every SQL constraint restricts what rows can exist in a table instance. Consider what happens when an SQL statement modifies a table instance (either adding a new row or modifying an existing row). Before the DBMS modifies the table instance, it checks that the changes will not violate any constraint. If they will, the statement is rejected, with an appropriate error message being given. Warning messages will include the name of the constraint violated, as SQL allows the DBA to give constraints meaningful names.

SQL constraints only restrict an individual table's instance. The SQL standard also defines **assertions**, which restrict what data can exist in a database instance. This is a useful feature for implementing more complex enterprise constraints that involve two or more tables. Unfortunately, it is not supported by many commercial DBMS, so is not covered in this book.

The ISO SQL standard distinguishes between two kinds of constraints – table constraints and column constraints. An SQL column constraint is defined as part of the column definition, so can only involve a single column – not-null is the obvious example. Table constraints are defined after the column definitions and may involve more than one column, such as a primary key constraint for a composite primary key. This distinction is purely syntactic as both table and column constraints restrict what *rows* can exist in a table instance. In fact, a column constraint is just shorthand for a table constraint. The specific syntax for defining constraints is discussed in Chapters 5 and 6.

Data is added to tables as rows. The collection of rows held in a table at a particular time is the table instance. SQL provides facilities to manipulate the table instance, supporting the data manipulation function of the DBMS. One important feature of an SQL table instance is that, if there is no primary key constraint on the table, it can include two rows that are identical. This means that, in SQL, a table instance is a *multiset* of rows. In the relational data model, tables cannot have repeated rows – they are *sets*. (It is important to remember this difference when reading books on the theory of relational databases.) In most cases, a table includes a primary key constraint, so there are *no* repeated rows. However, sometimes repeated rows are necessary. The module evaluation questionnaire used by the Pennine University includes a free text section for 'any other comments'. This sort of data gives useful feedback, but cannot be analysed easily, so is kept in a separate table. The table does not have, and does not need, a primary key. An instance of the table is shown in Figure 3.13. Notice that comments in the first and fourth rows are identical. Those in the second and fifth have the same meaning, but are not identical.

Figure 3.13 A table with no primary key

ModuleEvaluation	
moduleCode:char	studentComment: varchar
17335	Too little lab time
17335	Great tutor
17335	Well-structured assessment, but need more feedback
17335	Too little lab time
17335	Brilliant tutor

Figure 3.14 The different sorts of table in SQL.

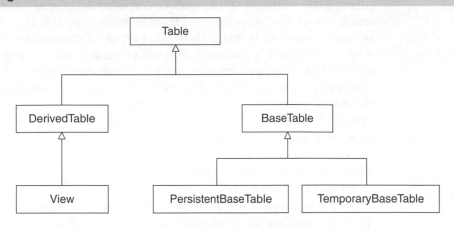

There are two different sorts of table in SQL – **base tables** and **derived tables**. Both have further specializations, as shown in Figure 3.14. This is another UML class diagram and introduces another important piece of notation. It is the small triangle, which indicates a **generalization relationship**. Often, things have general and more specialized forms – cars can be hatchbacks, saloons and estates; people can be male or female; animals can be reptiles, mammals, fish, birds and insects, for example. In such cases, a particular instance of the more specialized form is also an instance of the general form. So, a Skoda Fabia is a hatchback, but is also a car; Angela Merkel is a woman, but is also a person; my pet cat Suki is a mammal, but is also an animal. Similarly, an instance of a View is also a DerivedTable, which is also a Table.

Base tables have their table instance stored on disk. A persistent base table also has its table definition stored in the data dictionary. Its table instance is shared by all database users, so changes by one user are seen by other users. A temporary base table may or may not have its table definition stored in the data dictionary. However, each session (each user) gets its own instance of the table. Data is *copied* into the temporary base table instance, then used exclusively by one session. Temporary base tables are often used to assemble data for reports or export.

The other sort of table is the derived table. The data in a derived table is only ever stored in memory; it is never written to permanent storage in the database. This means that a derived table is not part of the database instance, even though its data is derived from the database instance. When a database query is executed in SQL, the result is always a derived table. A **view** is a special sort of derived table, the definition of which is stored in the data dictionary. The view instance is derived from one or more base tables and assembled on demand. A view's instance is shared, so may change if another user changes the data in the underlying base tables. SQL's facilities to manipulate table and view structures support the data definition function of the DBMS.

The ANSI/SPARC database system architecture is based on three different views of the database. The data storage structures of the internal view are discussed in Chapter 10. The external and logical views are concerned with organizing the data and both are based on the underlying data model. In a relational DBMS that uses SQL, base tables are the organization structures of the logical view. The organization structures of the external views can be both base tables and derived tables, in particular relational views (the two uses of the word 'view' can be confusing, so, in this section, 'relational view' and 'external view' are used). The idea of an external view in the ANSI/SPARC database system architecture is that it delivers an image of the database instance tailored to meet the needs of a particular group of end users. The obvious mechanism is the derived table, both as a database query and a relational view. A DBMS responds to a database query by creating an unnamed derived table and passing this derived table to the database client. So, a query is clearly a tailored view of the database instance. However, each time a database query is run, the DBMS must interpret the instructions it contains before carrying them out. A relational view is defined by a database query, but the definition is named and stored in the data dictionary. This storing process allows the DBMS to interpret the query once, then carry out its instructions many different times, improving performance.

For the end user, a relational view can be used much like a base table. A user can query the database via a relational view. The RDBMS assembles the relational view from the underlying base tables and then answers the query based on the data in the relational view. Thus, the user is actually seeing the base tables *through the relational view* rather than looking at them directly. To the end user, the relational view looks just like a base table. Relational views are often used to present data in different formats for different users or hide some data from certain users. They can also be used to present a simplified version of the base tables when the logical view of the database is particularly complex.

A familiar example of the view mechanism is the Microsoft Access select query. An Access select query is defined using the relational data language Query By Example (QBE) rather than SQL. The QBE definition of the view (that is, the MS Access select query) named StaffSupport is shown in Figure 3.15. The StaffSupport view

Figure 3.15 A view definition in QBE.

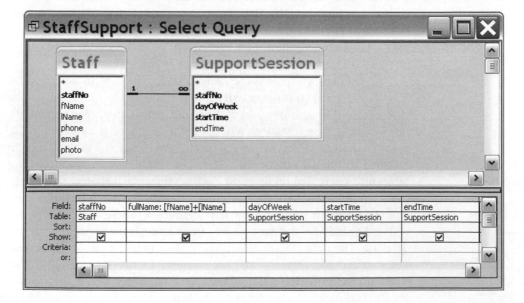

combines data from the two base tables `Staff` and `SupportSession`. Instances of the view and the base tables it is derived from are shown in Figure 3.16. The `StaffSupport` view includes some, but not all, of the columns from each base table. The data in the `fullName` column of the `StaffSupport` view is derived by concatenating the data in the `fName` and `lName` columns in the `Staff` table. Note that if the data in the underlying base tables changes, then so will the data in the view.

Clearly, the relational view is one way to implement the external views of the ANSI/SPARC database system architecture and, hence, achieve logical data independence. An external view will consist of one or more relational views. Typically, users will also have direct access to some of the persistent tables. While this violates logical-data independence, it is necessary because of the problem of modifying the database instance through a relational view. Consider what would happen if Selma Hutchins got married and changed her surname to 'Hutchins Davis'. If the users could only see the `StaffSupport` relational view, they might try to change the `fullName` from 'Selma Hutchins' to 'Selma Hutchins Davis'. The RDBMS would then have a problem. Should the value of the `lName` column be 'Davis' or 'Hutchins Davis'? Clearly, this modification cannot be done through the `StaffSupport` relational view.

Under certain circumstances, it is possible to modify the underlying base table instance through a relational view, either by adding a new row or modifying an existing one. Such a relational view is called an updateable view. The rules for updateable views are quite complex. In fact, the ISO SQL:2003 specification distinguishes at least four different kinds of updateable view. As a general rule, a relational view is updateable provided the following three conditions hold:

1 each column of the underlying base table appears at most once in the select list of the database query defining the relational view

2 each row in the relational view instance can be traced back to a unique row in the underlying base table – the underlying row

3 in each row of the relational view instance, the value of each column is taken directly from a single column in the underlying row, with no operators or functions used.

One problem that all computer systems must address is the shortage of meaningful names. The Staff Directory and Web Timetable databases at the Pennine University both include a table named 'Staff', but these tables have different structures and hold different data. Unless the DBMS can distinguish between two different tables with the same name, creating databases will involve a constant search for synonyms – in this case, calling one table 'Staff' and the other 'Employee'. However, SQL provides a way to organize tables that allows one DBMS to manage multiple databases without there being conflicts over names. Each database corresponds to an **SQL schema**. Within a particular SQL schema, each table must have a unique name, but tables in different SQL schema can have the same name.

An **SQL catalog** is a container for SQL schema. The SQL standard does not define a statement to create an SQL catalog. Each DBMS implements the catalog concept in its own way. Inside every SQL catalog is a system-defined SQL schema called `INFORMATION_SCHEMA`. This holds the meta-data for all other SQL schema in the SQL catalog. In effect, the `INFORMATION_SCHEMA` form the DBMS data dictionary.

Figure 3.16 The StaffSupport view compared with the underlying base tables.

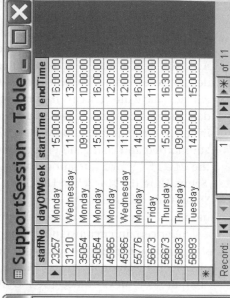

StaffSupport : Select Query

staffNo	fullName	dayOfWeek	startTime	endTime
23257	Freya Stark	Monday	15:00:00	16:00:00
31210	Paul Smith	Wednesday	11:00:00	13:00:00
35054	Selma Hutchins	Monday	09:00:00	10:00:00
35054	Selma Hutchins	Monday	15:00:00	16:00:00
45965	Mikhail Sudbin	Monday	11:00:00	12:00:00
45965	Mikhail Sudbin	Wednesday	11:00:00	12:00:00
55776	Gurpreet Choudhury	Monday	14:00:00	16:00:00
56673	Joshua Bittaye	Thursday	15:30:00	16:30:00
56673	Joshua Bittaye	Friday	10:00:00	11:00:00
56893	Ruth Bapetsi	Tuesday	14:00:00	15:00:00
56893	Ruth Bapetsi	Thursday	09:00:00	10:00:00

Record: 1 of 11

SupportSession : Table

staffNo	dayOfWeek	startTime	endTime
23257	Monday	15:00:00	16:00:00
31210	Wednesday	11:00:00	13:00:00
35054	Monday	09:00:00	10:00:00
35054	Monday	15:00:00	16:00:00
45965	Monday	11:00:00	12:00:00
45965	Wednesday	11:00:00	12:00:00
55776	Monday	14:00:00	16:00:00
56673	Friday	10:00:00	11:00:00
56673	Thursday	15:30:00	16:30:00
56893	Thursday	09:00:00	10:00:00
56893	Tuesday	14:00:00	15:00:00

Record: 1 of 11

Staff : Table

staffNo	fName	lName	phone	email	photo
10780	John	Smith	NULL	j.b.smith@pennine.ac.uk	
14443	Helen	Abbot	8032	h.abbot@pennine.ac.uk	
23257	Freya	Stark	8660	f.stark@pennine.ac.uk	
25447	John	Smith	5104	j.smith@pennine.ac.uk	
25448	Judith Anne	Smith	7709	j.a.smith@pennine.ac.uk	
31210	Paul	Smith	NULL	p.smith@pennine.ac.uk	
33509	Helen	Timms	8861	h.timms@pennine.ac.uk	
33935	Padma	Brar	6641	p.brar@pennine.ac.uk	
35054	Selma	Hutchins	8706	s.hutchins@pennine.ac.uk	
35155	Helene	Chirac	NULL	h.chirac@pennine.ac.uk	
45965	Mikhail	Sudbin	5553	m.sudbin@pennine.ac.uk	
55776	Gurpreet	Choudhury	5454	g.choudhury@pennine.ac.uk	
56673	Joshua	Bittaye	7782	j.bittaye@pennine.ac.uk	
56893	Ruth	Bapetsi	8022	r.bapetsi@pennine.ac.uk	
77712	Frank	Rose	8871	f.rose@pennine.ac.uk	
78893	Jo Karen	O'Connor	8871	j.k.oconnor@pennine.ac.uk	
89987	Dan	Lin	8514	d.lin@pennine.co.uk	

Record: 1 of 17

Figure 3.17 Containers in ISO SQL.

The DBMS must ensure that users can only see the meta-data in INFORMATION_SCHEMA for the SQL schema (databases) they use. Figure 3.17 shows the associations between SQL catalogs, SQL schemas and tables. Just as a table is composed of columns, an SQL schema is composed of tables and an SQL catalog is composed of SQL schema. However, a table must have at least one column, whereas an SQL schema can be empty.

All these database objects will have a name. An SQL **identifier** is a valid name for a database object. It must begin with a letter but can include letters, digits and the underscore character, '_'. SQL **regular identifiers** are not case-sensitive, so SupportSession, supportsession and SUPPORTSESSION are all the same to SQL, which can make names difficult to read. To avoid this, some developers use the underscore character to separate the words, like this support_session.

The ISO SQL standard also provides the **delimited identifier** to allow for case-sensitive identifiers. To define a delimited identifier, simply enclose it in double quotes. Thus, the identifier "SupportSession" is *not* the same identifier as "SUPPORTSESSION". Some database applications may need to use delimited identifiers, but this book does not. All SQL identifiers in this book are regular identifiers, written in mixed case, to improve legibility.

Whether regular identifiers are actually case-insensitive or not depends on the DBMS. For example, in the MySQL DBMS, the underlying operating system determines the case sensitivity of regular identifiers. So, on UNIX they are case-sensitive, but on Windows they are not.

One last point is that SQL supports Unicode character sets, so identifiers (and data) can be written using any Unicode character set. For example, a database designed for use in China will have identifiers and data written using Chinese ideographs. These internationalization aspects of SQL are beyond the scope of an introductory textbook like this one, but one little quirk arising from character set support needs to be highlighted. When an SQL statement is written in a text editor, the text editor saves the statement using its default character set. Under Windows, this is usually the ISO-8859-1 character set (also called Latin-1). When a DBMS reads a file, it assumes that the file is written in its default character set and, for a DBMS used as part of a web database application, this may well be UTF-8. Although these two character sets are the same for the most common characters, so the SQL keywords use the same character codes, special characters, such as 'TM' have different character codes. Thus, the DBMS may not automatically recognize the 'TM' character when written as part of a string literal. Those DBMS that support multiple character sets can translate literals written using one character set – say, ISO-8859-1 – into their default character set, but need to be told to do so. The DBMS manual provides advice on how to request such character set translations.

109

3.3   Semistructured data models and XML

The relational data model is capable of representing the information required for any application by organizing data into tables. Tables have a fixed structure – every row in the table instance has the same columns. This can seem a little restrictive, especially when there is lots of missing data. Using nulls to represent missing data works, but why not simply omit the column for that row?

Semistructured data models take this alternative approach. The organization structures have a basic shape, but there is the flexibility to omit parts of the structure in particular instances. This seems a cleaner solution to the problem of missing data than the relational data model, especially as nulls lead to a rather complicated three-valued logic.

Semistructured data models also deal quite naturally with repetition. If a member of staff has two phone numbers, for example, then both can be included within the organization structure for that member of staff. This is rather like allowing one or two `phoneNo` columns on some rows of the `Staff` table and none on others.

This flexibility in the actual shape of the organization structures means that semistructured data models can easily represent quite complex data. Not being able to do this was a particular weakness of early implementations of the relational data model, which were limited to columns with an atomic data type and tables. Contemporary relational DBMS do implement a more sophisticated version of the relational data model that is able to represent complex data quite easily, using non-scalar data types, but, even so, semistructured data models seem more flexible than the relational data model. This has led some to suggest that they provide a superior alternative to the problem of database organization.

Another argument sometimes put against the relational data model is that its data language, SQL, is not really a programming language. Many application developers found SQL too different from the procedural programming languages they were familiar with. They wanted to open the files and manipulate the data directly, not rely on a DBMS to do this for them. This objection has also lost some of its force as the ISO SQL:2003 standard defines a complete programming languages not just a data language. Furthermore, the experience of web application developers with early, file-based web applications has served to remind everyone of the significant advantages offered by the database approach (see Chapter 1).

Perhaps the best argument in favour of an alternative to the relational data model is the fact that, while it is a good fit for business data, the data for some specialist applications do not fit naturally into tables. Chemical formulae, musical scores and engineering data are all areas where the relational data model is an awkward fit for the information that must be held on the database. These niche applications often have specialist database software using alternative data models to meet their particular needs. However, for a long time, the relational data model remained the main approach to organizing data in databases. The release in 1998 of the XML specification led to renewed interest in the possibility of a general-purpose semistructured data model that could replace the relational data model. Before discussing the XML semistructured data model, it is worth reviewing its origins.

XML was not designed as a data model. As mentioned in Chapter 1, it is a language for defining document models, in the form of mark-up languages, either from scratch or by extending existing document models. Nor was there a formal, mathematical basis for the XML language itself. XML was seen as a natural development of the pre-existing SGML technology for describing documents. (This contrasts with the relational data model, which was a radical departure from existing database technologies and came with a clear mathematical basis.)

The W3C's aims for XML were to develop a way of describing the structure and content of web documents that would not be restricted to a predefined set of elements – a major weakness of HTML. The language had to be easy to use, by both document authors and those writing software to process these documents, as complexity was the major argument against using SGML.

This focus on *documents* is important. XML was never envisaged as a database technology, let alone as a replacement for existing database technologies. Its main aim was to provide a much clearer separation between the descriptions of the structure, content and presentation of a web document.

Each XML mark-up language represents a document model for a specific kind of document content. In other words, there is an intended interpretation of documents written in each mark-up language, so XHTML documents are intended to be interpreted as descriptions of web documents; Scalable Vector Graphics (SVG) documents are intended to be interpreted as descriptions of graphical images (that is, basic geometrical shapes rather than bitmap images); and MathML documents are intended to be interpreted as mathematical formulae.

XML also allows different XML mark-up languages to be mixed together in the same document. This is what makes XML a major advance on HTML as the underlying technology for describing web documents. A single XML document on the Web may include general text content that is described by XHTML mark-up, a line drawing described by SVG mark-up and a mathematical formula described by MathML mark-up. Provided the web browser knows how to interpret all three mark-up languages, the web author can deliver complex and sophisticated web documents, without resorting to embedding GIF images for the line drawings and formulae.

There is some standard terminology used within the XML community. An **XML document** is a plain text file of Unicode characters, containing **well-formed XML**. The rules on what constitutes 'well-formed XML' cover both logical and physical features and are described below.

An **XML application** is a particular XML document model. Although called an 'application', it is *not* a software application as XML documents do not actually *do* anything – they merely describe their content.

An **XML processor** is application software that can read and correctly interpret an XML document. The XML processor uses the appropriate XML document models to interpret an XML document and carry out actions that, eventually, yield something of use to the end user. For example, a web browser is an XML application that interprets XHTML documents and displays the content to the user. Drawing an analogy with databases, the XML documents form the database and data dictionary, while the XML processors constitute the DBMS.

An important example of an XML processor is an **XML parser**. An XML parser will check whether or not a particular document satisfies the well-formedness constraints in the XML specification – that is, the document really is an XML document. A **validating XML parser** will also check that the XML document satisfies the constraints specified in the appropriate document model – that is, it is a valid instance of the appropriate XML application. A validating XML parser needs a description of document structures allowed by a particular document model, which is provided by a **schema document** (just as a table schema describes the structure of a table in the relational data model).

An XML document written using a particular document model is called an **instance document** for that document model, and is said to be **schema-valid** – that is, meets all the structural requirements set out in the document model's schema. There will be many different instance documents that conform to a given schema (just are there are many instances of a table, all with the same general structure but holding different data).

The original XML specification did not include a formal data model, though, within a year, the Document Object Model (DOM) had been extended to cover XML documents. DOM is an object-orientated data model originally developed to allow ECMAScript (browser-side scripting languages such as JavaScript and VBScript) programs to refer to the different parts of HTML documents. DOM is focused on manipulating physical documents, not organizing data, so wasn't considered a suitable basis for a proper XML data model.

As new XML technologies were developed, it became clear that different groups, even within the W3C, were interpreting the XML specification in subtly different ways. This could have made different XML applications incompatible. To remedy this, XML acquired a formal data model in 2001 with the adoption of the XML Information Set (W3C, 2004b) as a W3C recommendation. This provided a formal description of XML, ensuring a consistent interpretation across different XML initiatives. However, its support for data types was poor and it still dealt with the physical organization of XML documents. Thus, when the W3C began work on developing XML database technologies, another XML data model was developed. This data model, known as the XPath 2.0 and XQuery 1.0 Data Model (XDM for short), is the one described here as it is probably the most appropriate one for XML database applications. The description focuses on those aspects of XML that can be regarded as relevant to the logical view of the ANSI/SPARC architecture. In particular, the following important simplifications have been made.

- An XML document can be split into two or more physical files. This is not something a data model needs to cover as the data model is concerned with the logical structure of an XML document.

- XML documents can include processing instructions and comments. Again, these are physical issues and are largely excluded from the discussion.

- The W3C's XML namespaces recommendation allows one XML document to use structures defined in two or more different document models without there being any name conflicts. For example, a web page could include SVG and HTML content. To simplify the discussion, it is assumed that each XML document has a single document model and so uses a single namespace. (Chapter 12 discusses namespaces).

These simplifications make it easier to describe XML as a data model by highlighting the logical aspects and avoiding some of the features that are concerned with physical implementation issues.

3.3.1 Organizing data in XML

XML uses three structures to organize data – **document**, **element** and **attribute**. The general idea is that the document holds some data (either narrative text, as in a web page, or data items, as in a database). This data is enclosed in elements, which describe the structure of the data (this is the same mechanism that is used in HTML). Each element has a name and can contain other elements and text (the actual data). In database applications, elements tend to contain *either* other elements *or* text, but not both. Document applications allow elements to contain **mixed content** – a mix of elements and text. An element may also have attributes, which capture information about the element and its content – meta-data rather than data. Each attribute has a name and a value. Attribute values and the text content of an element are stored as character data – in fact, as Unicode characters. Character data is the only data type required by the XDM for attribute values and element content, though the data model does allow any of the 49 data types defined in the W3C's XML schema specification to be used, too.

It is important to realize that there is no direct correlation between the organization structures of XML and those of the relational data model. Thus, a document is not the same thing as a database, an element is not the same thing as a table and an attribute is not the same thing as a column. It is possible to transform a schema for an XML document into a schema for a relational database, but the transformation depends on the intended meaning of the various document structures. Some elements may become tables, while others become columns. Some attributes may become columns, while others become part of an SQL user-defined data type.

The natural mathematical description of this way of organizing data is the **tree**. A tree consists of **nodes**, representing the different organization structures and the data, and **edges**, representing a parent–child relationship between nodes.

Figure 3.18 shows part of an XML document for holding staff contact details represented as a tree. Each node is drawn as a rectangle, some split into two compartments. Each node has been labelled with its node type in the upper compartment, and the main properties of the node included as name-value pairs in the lower compartment. The upper compartment also includes a unique identifier for each node, which is the number preceding the node type. The **root** of the tree is the document node (trees are traditionally drawn 'upside down') so has its type labelled as 'Document'. It is the first node in the tree, so has also been labelled with the number '1' as its unique identifier. Node 1 has a single **child**, the element node with the identifier '2'. The **parent** of node 2 is node 1. This parent–child relationship is indicated by the line drawn between the two nodes.

The root node of a well-formed XML document will always have a single child node of the type element, which is often referred to as the **root element** or **document element**. This is a bit confusing because the root/document element is *not* the root node of the tree, nor is it the document node! It is, however, the first element node in the document. The document node may also have other children, which must be comment nodes or processing instruction nodes.

The XDM also allows the document node to have text nodes among its children and to have more than one element node. In such cases, the tree represents an **XML document fragment** – it is part of a well-formed XML document rather than the whole thing. The XDM needs to allow XML document fragments because they will often

Figure 3.18 Part of the XML tree for an XML document. The attributes and children of the element nodes labelled 11 and 17 are not shown.

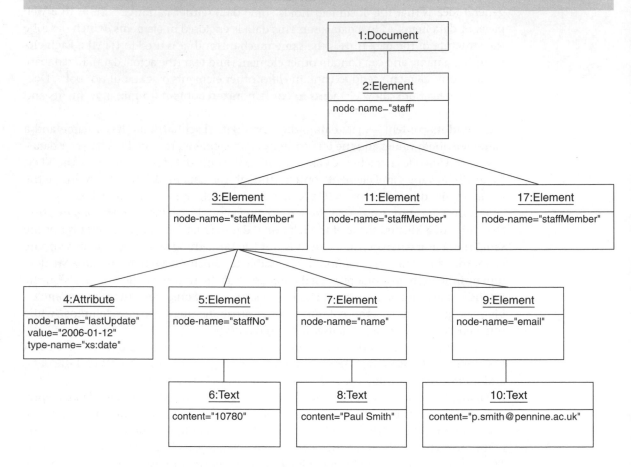

appear as the result of queries on an XML document. For example, the result of the query 'List all the `staffMember` elements' on the XML document in Figure 3.18 produces an XML document fragment, the document node of which has three element nodes as its children (the nodes labelled 3, 11 and 17). Contrast this with the relational data model, where the result of a query is always a complete table, not a fragment of a table.

Each element node has a **node-name**, usually called the **element name**. The element name indicates what kind of element the node represents. It is an **XML name** so cannot contain spaces, nor can it begin with a colon – ':' – dash – '–' – or digit. Names in XML serve the same purpose as SQL identifiers. Node 2 is an element node with the node-name `staff`, indicated by the name-value pair in the lower compartment. Hence, this node is a `staff` element. Other element nodes have different node names. The node name needn't be unique as there may be many elements of the same kind. Nodes 3, 11 and 17 all have the same element name, `staffMember`, so are `staffMember` elements.

Element nodes also have a **type-name**. The type-name identifies the data type of the element's content. This may be a complex type, consisting of a sequence of element and text nodes, each with its own data type. (A sequence is simply an ordered set.)

It is important to distinguish between the element's node name, which indicates what kind of element this is, and the elements type-name, which indicates what sort of data the element contains. Two different kinds of element can have the same data type. For example the `staffNo` and `name` elements both contain character string data. They are different kinds of element, but the same data type.

> An XML name is the simplest kind of identifier in XML. There are quite a few others, mostly connected with the XML namespaces recommendation. These are discussed in Chapter 12.

An element node may have other element nodes and text nodes among its children. As mentioned above, when XML documents are used to hold data, they usually have either element nodes *or* text nodes as children, not both. In Figure 3.18, node 3, a `staffMember` element, has three element nodes as children – nodes 5, 7 and 9. Each of these has a text node as their only child.

Rather annoyingly, an element's attributes are *not* children of the element node. Even so, the element node *is* considered to be the parent node for its attributes. Node 4 in Figure 3.18 is an attribute node and its parent is node 3, though node 4 is *not* among the children of node 3. Attributes have a node-name and a value and that value has a data type. Node 4 in Figure 3.18 has a node-name of `lastUpdate` and a value of `"2006-01-12"`, which has a data type of `xs:date` (one of the data types defined in the W3C's XML schema recommendation). An attribute node cannot have any children of its own.

> Strictly speaking, every attribute has two values – a typed value and a string value. The *typed value* is the actual data value and the *string value* is a literal representing this data value. The physical XML document can only contain Unicode characters, so it is always the string value that is stored in the physical XML document. It is the responsibility of an XML parser to convert the literal to the appropriate value before manipulating it. This contrasts with a relational database, where the data value can be stored using the representation the DBMS thinks is most efficient. The DBMS then converts the data value to a suitable literal before showing it to the end user.

Text nodes represent the text content of elements. In a well-formed XML document, the parent of a text node is always an element node, but in an XML document fragment its parent may be the document node. Where an element has two text nodes, they *must* have an element node (or a comment or processing instruction node) between them, but such mixed content is rare in XML databases. The fact that element nodes can appear 'between' text nodes indicates an important feature of the XDM. Unlike the relational data model, where the order of columns is not significant, the order of nodes *is*. In fact, the numbers of the nodes in Figure 3.18 indicate the document order for this XML document. Again, there is a nasty quirk with regard to attribute nodes. The attribute nodes come after their parent element node and before this element node's children, but there is no particular order for the set of attribute nodes. Different XML processors may place the attribute nodes of a given element node in different orders.

Document order only really makes sense when considering a physical XML document, but, before discussing that, there is a little more tree terminology to cover. This terminology is used to describe how to navigate the tree to retrieve data from the document, so is important for the data language. So far, the terms root, child and parent have been explained. The **siblings** of a node are the other children of its parent – that is, all the nodes at the same level in the tree. In Figure 3.18, node 11 has two siblings – node 3 and node 17. The **descendants** of a node are all its children, their children and so on. The descendants of node 3 are nodes 5, 6, 7, 8, 9 and 10. Node 4 is *not* a descendant of node 3 because attribute nodes are not children of their parent element. The **ancestors** of a node are its parent, its parent's parent and so on. The ancestors of node 4 are nodes 3, 2 and 1 (note that an element *is* an ancestor of its attributes). A **leaf** node is a node that has no children. Attribute and text nodes are always leaf nodes.

Consider the physical XML document shown in Figure 3.19. This is a textual representation of the same XML document that is represented by the tree diagram shown in Figure 3.18 (so, Figures 3.18 and 3.19 are two different representations of the same XML document). However, in Figure 3.18, there wasn't room to show all the nodes, so the parts of the document tree below nodes 11 and 17 were omitted (that is why nodes

Figure 3.19 A typical XML document for holding data.

```
1   <?xml version="1.0"encoding="utf-8"?>
2   <staff>
3     <staffMember lastUpdate="2006-01-12">
4         <staffNo>10780</staffNo>
5         <name>Paul Smith</name>
6         <email>p.smith@pennine.ac.uk</email>
7     </staffMember>
8     <staffMember lastUpdate="2005-03-07">
9         <staffNo>35054</staffNo>
10        <name>Selma Hutchins</name>
11        <phone>8706</phone>
12        <email>s.hutchins@pennine.ac.uk</email>
13    </staffMember>
14    <staffMember lastUpdate="2005-03-07">
15        <staffNo>23257</staffNo>
16        <name>Freya Stark</name>
17        <phone>8660</phone>
18        <phone>8661</phone>
19        <email>f.stark@pennine.ac.uk</email>
20    </staffMember>
21  </staff>
```

12 to 16 are missing from that diagram). Each physical XML document is a file containing Unicode characters and nothing else. These characters represent two different sorts of text:

- **mark-up** is the term used to describe the structure and meta-data of the document, such as elements and attributes, and appears between angle brackets
- **character data** is the actual content of the document – text nodes.

It is common practice to indent elements, as shown in Figure 3.19, though not strictly necessary. In fact, the entire XML document could be written on a single line, with no line breaks or indenting. However, as XML documents are supposed to be readable, it makes sense to use white space, such as line breaks and spaces, to make it easier for us to make out the document structure. White space is *not* significant and an XML parser will 'normalize' it in text nodes. Every sequence of white space characters (spaces, tabs, carriage returns and linefeeds) is replaced by a single space character and any leading or trailing spaces are trimmed.

The first line of the physical XML document is the **XML declaration**. As it appears between angle brackets, it must be mark-up. An XML declaration is not strictly necessary and not actually part of the logical structure of the XML document. However, it is worth including in all XML documents as, without it, it is not clear whether the document is intended to be XML, SGML or some proprietary mark-up language that happens to look a bit like XML. In a database, where the end user never looks at the actual data files, such a statement is unnecessary as the DBMS knows the data model used for its data and that is all that matters. However XML documents *are* intended to be read by humans, so a clear statement that the file *is* an XML document is necessary. When included, the XML declaration must be the very first thing in the XML document.

Another good reason for including the XML declaration is that XML parsers use the first five characters in the file to try to identify the Unicode character set being used. This information is actually included in the encoding attribute. In Figure 3.19 the encoding attribute tells the XML parser that the file was written using the utf-8 character set. However, the encoding attribute's name and value are themselves written using utf-8 characters, so the XML parser must know that the document is written in utf-8 *before* it can read the encoding attribute and find out that the document is written using utf-8. It's a little like including the statement 'This document is written in English' at the start of a document and expecting non-English speakers to understand what this means.

The second line in Figure 3.19 is also mark-up. It is the start tag for the `staff` element. In a physical XML document, every element is indicated by start and end tags. The start tag begins with a left angle bracket followed immediately (no spaces allowed) by the element name and ends with the right angle bracket (spaces are allowed between the element name and the right angle bracket).

The end tag also begins with a left angle bracket, but it is followed immediately by a forward slash and the element name (again, no spaces) and ends with the right angle bracket – so `'</staff>'` in the last line shown in Figure 3.19 is the end tag for the `staff` element.

117

A document may have several instances of the same element. In Figure 3.19, there are three instances of the `staffMember` element. Everything between the start and end tags is the **element content**.

Because elements can contain other elements, they provide a natural way to represent complex data. The `staff` and `staffMember` elements only contain other elements and such elements are sometimes called **complex elements**. The `staffNo`, `name`, `phone` and `email` elements only contain character data and these are called **simple elements**.

In a well-formed XML document, every start tag has a matching end tag. Moreover, if one element's start tag appears as the content of another, then so must its end tag. Put simply, one element can contain another, but they cannot overlap. So, for example, this is not well-formed XML, because the `staffNo` and `name` elements overlap.

```
<staffMember lastUpdate="2006-01-12">
  <staffNo>31210<name></staffNo>Paul Smith</name>
  <email>p.smith@pennine.ac.uk</email>
</staffMember>
```

An element's attributes are listed as name-value pairs inside its start tag (the attribute's data type is not included in the XML instance documents). The attribute name comes first, followed by an equals sign and the attribute value. If there are two or more attributes, then they are separated by spaces. In a well-formed XML document, attribute values will be character data enclosed in quotation marks. Also, the attribute name must be unique within the element (though different elements can have attributes with the same name).

Attributes were originally intended to hold meta-data, though there is some debate as to what counts as meta-data. The `staffMember` elements in Figure 3.19 all have a single attribute holding the date when the element content was last changed. This is classic meta-data as it tells us nothing about the member of staff the element refers to, only something about the element itself.

Many word processors include a custom, or smart, quotes feature. This replaces straight quote marks – "like these" – with fancy, curly quote marks – "like these". The same holds for single quotes – 'straight quotes' are turned into 'custom quotes'. Although the two sorts of quote marks are equivalent in normal use, they are different characters. The custom quote marks are not part of the standard ASCII character set so only straight quotes can be used to delimit attribute values. So, if you write an XML document in a word processor program, make sure you turn off the custom quotes feature!

Character data within an element becomes a text node in the tree representation. The first `staffNo` element contains the character data '10780', which becomes the content of the text node labelled 6 in Figure 3.18. In a well-formed XML document the characters '<' and '&' cannot appear in character data. Use their character entity alternatives, '<' and '&' instead.

Returning to the subject of the document order, this is most easily understood by describing how to take a textual representation of an XML document and turn it into a tree representation. This involves reading through the document, top to bottom, left to right, and creating the appropriate nodes, just as an XML parser does. During this process each node is given a number and these numbers are the document ordering. Here is a general description of how to turn a textual representation of a well-formed XML document into an equivalent tree representation. As usual, namespaces, comments and processing instructions are omitted, to simplify the discussion.

1 Create the document node and make it the current node.

2 Ignore the XML declaration.

3 Apply the following rules repeatedly:

   (a) on encountering the start tag of an element, create an element node with the current node as its parent, then make this new element node the current node

   (b) on encountering a name-value pair inside a start tag, create an attribute node with the current node as its parent (the parent remains the current node)

   (c) on encountering a block of text, create a text node with the current node as its parent (the parent remains the current node)

   (d) on encountering the end tag of an element, make this element's parent the current node.

Following this process, the parent of a text node is the element containing the text – the element represented by the enclosing start and end tags. An attribute node's parent is the element the start tag for which the attribute appears in. An element node's parent is either the document node or the element node the start and end tags of which contain the whole of the element. So, for example, in Figure 3.18, the `staff` element's parent is the document node, and the parent of all three `staffMember` elements is the `staff` element. The document order is simply the order in which the nodes were created. Notice that only the document node and element nodes can become the 'current node'. Attribute and text nodes never become the current node because they cannot have child nodes.

The document order is called the preorder in the mathematical theory of trees.

In this version, the document order for attribute nodes is simply the order in which the attributes appear within each element start tag. As the XML specifications do not prescribe an order for attribute elements, this seems a reasonable choice. A more sophisticated approach is to order them alphabetically by their names, but this process is harder to describe.

This process is the reason why start and end tags for two different elements cannot overlap. If they did, it might not be possible to determine the parent for a particular node. For example, which node does the text 'Who is my parent?' in the following example belong to?

```
<staffMember lastUpdate="2006-01-12">
   <staffNo>31210<name>Who is my parent?</staffNo>Paul
Smith</name>
   <email>p.smith@pennine.ac.uk</email>
</staffMember>
```

It could belong to the `staffNo` element as it lies between that element's start and end tags. However, it also lies between the `name` element's start and end tags, so could have this element as parent. In the textual representation of an XML document, elements must nest properly or else it is not possible to convert it into a tree.

As an example of the process, apply it to the textual representation of the well-formed XML document shown in Figure 3.19.

Rule 1 says to create the document node and make it the current node. As this is the first node created, it is node 1.

Now begin reading the document. The first thing in the document is the XML declaration, but rule 2 says to ignore this.

The next thing in the document is the start tag of a `staff` element. Rule 3(a) says to create an element node with the current node, node 1, as its parent. This is the second node created, so is node 2. Make node 2 the current node.

Continuing to read the document, the next thing encountered is the start tag for a `staffMember` element. Rule 3(a) applies again, so create a new element node with the current node, node 2, as its parent. This is the third node created, so is node 3. Make node 3 the current node.

Reading on, there is a name-value pair – `lastUpdate="2006-01-12"` – defined in the start tag of the `staffMember` element. Rule 3(b) says to create an attribute node with the current node, node 3, as parent. This is the fourth node created, so it is node 4. The current node is still node 3, though.

Next comes a start tag for a `staffNo` element. Apply rule 3(a) and create an element node with the current node, node 3, as its parent. This is the fifth node created, so is node 5. Make node 5 the current node.

The next thing encountered is some text, `10780`. Rule 3(c) says to create a text node with the current node, node 5, as its parent. This is the sixth node created, so is node 6. Node 5 remains the current node.

Next comes an end tag for the `staffNo` element, so rule 3(d) applies. The current node is node 5. The parent of node 5 is node 3, so node 3 becomes the current node.

Continue to read through the document, applying the appropriate rule to each tag, name-value pair and block of text. The result is the tree representation, part of which, as we have seen, is shown in Figure 3.18, where each node has a number. This numbering is the document order.

The document order is important because it is used to define a third way of representing an XML document – as a sequence of nodes. The sequence of nodes that appear in the tree representation of an XML document provides a complete description of that document, and one that it is easier for computers to manipulate than text. Furthermore, a sequence of nodes can also represent a document fragment. As the result of a query on an XML document may be a document fragment, sequences provide the XDM and its query languages with a consistent representation of the data. Just as everything in the relational model is a table, everything in the XDM is a sequence of nodes.

So far, the discussion has focused on organizing data about things that the end user is interested in. XML documents can also capture relationships between two such things quite naturally, by representing both things as elements and including one element in the content of the other. At the Pennine University, as we have seen, members of staff offer support sessions. Data about support sessions can be captured using elements. The `supportSessions` element includes one or more `session` elements, each of which has exactly one `dayOfWeek`, `startTime` and `endTime` element. An XML instance document is shown in Figure 3.20. It is immediately clear that Paul Smith offers just the one support session, whereas Selma Hutchins offers three.

Capturing relationships between things by including one element in the content of another is seen by some as more natural than the foreign keys of the relational data model. However, element inclusion is not always an effective approach to representing relationships. For example, the relationships between staff and the modules they teach is hard to represent using element inclusion. If `staff` elements are included in `module`

Figure 3.20 Support session data contained within `staff` elements.

```
<?xml version="1.0" encoding="utf-8"?>
<staff>
  <staffMember lastUpdate="2006-01-12">
    <staffNo>31210</staffNo>
    <name>Paul Smith</name>
    <email>p.smith@pennine.ac.uk</email>
    <supportSessions>
      <session>
        <dayOfWeek>Wednesday</dayOfWeek>
        <startTime>11:00</startTime>
        <endTime>13:00</endTime>
      </session>
    </supportSessions>
  </staffMember>
  <staffMember lastUpdate="2005-03-07">
    <staffNo>35054</staffNo>
    <name>Selma Hutchins</name>
    <phone>8706</phone>
    <email>s.hutchins@pennine.ac.uk</email>
    <supportSessions>
      <session>
        <dayOfWeek>Monday</dayOfWeek>
        <startTime>09:00</startTime>
        <endTime>10:00</endTime>
      </session>
      <session>
        <dayOfWeek>Monday</dayOfWeek>
        <startTime>15:00</startTime>
        <endTime>16:00</endTime>
      </session>
      <session>
        <dayOfWeek>Tuesday</dayOfWeek>
        <startTime>11:00</startTime>
        <endTime>12:00</endTime>
      </session>
    </supportSessions>
  </staffMember>
</staff>
```

A `staffMember` element that contains support session data

A `supportSessions` element containing several different `session` elements

121

elements, then there will be data duplication – some staff teach many modules, for example. The same holds if the `module` elements are included in the `staff` element – some modules are taught by many staff.

Another problem is that including one element inside another makes it hard to extract data about the included element. The query 'Are there any support sessions offered on a Friday afternoon?' doesn't need any information about staff, but the staff data must be parsed to get at the support session data. To alleviate some of these problems the XDM includes a foreign key mechanism as an alternative way to represent relationships.

It's clear that the XML data model is much more complicated than the relational data model. This is odd as the organization structures of document, element and attribute should be pretty easy to assemble into an elegant, tree-structured data model. The various XML recommendations make a poor job of this task because they must incorporate a lot of information about the physical representation of XML documents. There was also a desire to ensure backwards compatibility with SGML, both of which are reasonable goals. That said, there are one or two points at which the choices made about terminology lead to an unnecessarily complex description, such as the fact that an attribute is not a child of its parent element. However, the underlying idea is clean, simple and elegant. A document is structured into elements, which may contain other elements or text. Elements can also have attributes, which capture meta-data. An XML document provides a very flexible way to hold the data and meta-data needed for any database application.

3.3.2 Integrity constraints in XML

The database schema provides the basic description of the organization structures used in a particular database. In XML, the schema describes what elements there are, how they nest and what their attributes are. Each XML instance document must conform to the schema. An integrity constraint places an *additional* restriction on the instance documents, so that some *logically possible* instance documents are disallowed. This subsection reviews some of the possible integrity constraints, while the next discusses XML languages for defining both schema and integrity constraints.

An XML document can represent missing information simply by omitting an element or attribute. Occurrence constraints determine whether or not a particular element or attribute can be omitted. They also determine whether or not a particular element can occur more than once in a particular context. (Attributes cannot occur more than once in a given element, though their value may be a list of space-separated literals.) For example, the `session` element may occur zero or many times inside a `supportSessions` element (Figure 3.20).

Co-occurrence constraints are a more general kind of integrity constraint, where the occurrence of elements is made conditional on the surrounding structures. For example, in the Staff Directory database, we can add a `jobType` attribute to the `staff` element to distinguish between academics and other members of staff. Now, it becomes possible to define an integrity constraint to enforce the conditional statement:

> If the `staff` element's `jobType` attribute has the value 'Academic', then the `staff` element must contain a `supportSessions` element containing at least one `session` element. Otherwise, the `staff` element should not contain a `supportSessions` element.

This sort of integrity constraint is obviously very powerful and there is nothing similar to it in relational databases.

XML also allows the content of an element to be restricted to particular strings of characters. For example an e-mail address must be a sequence of characters with an '@' symbol somewhere in the middle. Regular expressions (see, for example, http://www.regular-expressions.info) offer one way to define such integrity constraints. SQL:2003 also supports regular expressions by means of its `SIMILAR` comparison operator.

As an XML document can be represented as a tree, there is also scope to place constraints on the permitted tree structures. Such constraints can be based on the notion of a **path**. A path is simply a particular route through the tree – starting at a given node, follow the parent–child links to some other node. There is no back-tracking allowed: a path always moves down the tree (assuming the root is drawn at the top of the diagram). It is possible to define structural constraints that require a particular path to exist or forbid a particular path or require certain structures to appear at the end of a particular path. Finally, it should also be possible to enforce more general business rules, possibly using combinations of the mechanisms described above.

As mentioned above, XML also includes analogues of the relational data model's primary and foreign key constraints. These allow one element to refer to another and are an alternative to the inclusion mechanism for defining relationships between elements. The analogue of the foreign key is actually more flexible as it can include more than one value. This allows the referencing element to refer to several different referenced elements. Using this mechanism, it would be possible to model the relationship between staff and the modules they teach.

The breadth and generality of these integrity constraints should indicate that there is currently no single, agreed set of integrity constraints for XML documents. Work is under way at ISO (the body that has standardized the SQL language) to develop an international standard for Document Schema Definition Languages (DSDL) for defining both the underlying structure and the integrity constraints. Schema languages form part of the suite of data languages for XML and this is the topic of the next subsection.

3.3.3 Data languages for XML

There is no single data language for XML. Instead, some of the various roles of the relational data language SQL are taken on by one or more alternative languages and technologies. When considering relational languages, it was possible to focus closely on SQL and describe its structure in some detail because SQL is basically the only relational data language a database developer needs to know. The range of alternative languages for XML means it is impossible to cover them in such detail. Instead, this subsection presents an overview of the most important languages from the application developer's perspective.

The first point to make is that there is no specific language for creating XML documents, at least not in the way SQL provides facilities to create tables and other database objects. An XML instance document is created by the user typing out the mark-up and content (structure *and* data) using a simple text editor. This raises a problem: what if the end user types it incorrectly? There must be some way of checking that a particular XML instance document really is a valid instance of the relevant document model.

123

The solution to this problem is to use a validating XML parser to check the XML instance document against a description of the document model. Any incorrect XML instance documents can be rejected, usually with error messages stating what is wrong with the XML instance document.

This way of working is quite different from relational databases. In a relational database the DBMS controls all interactions with the database instance. One SQL statement instructs the DBMS to create a table according to a relational table schema and further SQL statements instruct the DBMS to add data to this table. There is no way that the end user can add even a single row that does not conform to the table schema. There are DBMS that use XML as their underlying data model, and they work in the same way, but these technologies are not yet mature and there is no single approach to 'creating' a document.

It is worth taking a closer look at the split between the XML schema, which describes a document model, and the XML instance document, which realizes it. Consider the XML instance document in Figure 3.19. This is just one possible instance document for the Pennine University's Staff Directory. As new staff join and old staff leave, the data will change, but its basic structure will not. This basic structure is easy enough to describe in English. There will always be a single `Staff` element, with one or more `staffMember` elements. Each `staffMember` element will have a single attribute, `lastUpdate`, and some elements in its content – exactly one `staffNo`, `name` and `email` elements and zero or more `phone` elements. The `staffNo`, `name`, `email` and `phone` elements will all have text content.

XML needs some way in which to express such descriptions so that a computer can understand them. In the relational data model, this role is played by a single SQL statement. Unfortunately, the added complexity of XML means that a single data language statement simply isn't expressive enough to describe any possible XML document. Instead, an entire language is required. A schema language for XML is a computer language capable of describing the document model for a class of XML instance documents. An **XML schema** is written in a particular schema language for XML and describes the document structures allowed by a particular document model.

There are three general approaches to defining an XML schema, exemplified by three different schema languages. The W3C's XML Schema language (W3C 2004d and 2004e) (note the capital 'S' of 'XML Schema language', to distinguish this schema *language* from a particular XML schema *document*) is based on describing the allowed content. Each element and attribute allowed by the document model is described in detail. For example, an English language description of the `session` element in Figure 3.20 would be: 'The session element contains: a `dayOfWeek` element, which contains text; a `startTime` element, which contains a time value; and an `endTime` element, which contains a time value'. These descriptions are written in a special language developed to allow schema writers to describe all the usual situations – parent–child relationships, occurrence constraints and so on. The situations covered are those that schema writers have, over the years, recognized as being important for XML (and SGML) documents.

The clever thing about the W3C XML Schema is that the language is itself an XML application and the schemas written in it are XML documents. This is a classic example of XML's flexibility: one XML document, the schema document, describes the allowed content of a second XML document, the instance document. A validating XML parser can use both documents to check that the instance document conforms to the description set out in the schema document. Once this is done, a second XML processor can read the XML instance document, which describes its own content, and deliver that content in an appropriate form to the end users.

There is a further advantage of using XML to develop a schema language. A schema language for XML is intended as a way of describing document models for XML applications. As the W3C XML Schema language is itself an XML application, it can describe its own document model. The W3C has published an XML schema, written in the W3C XML Schema language, which describes the document model for the W3C XML Schema language. This is a little like publishing, in English, a book on English grammar. As long as you can read English, you can check whether or not you are writing it properly.

This is quite a complex idea and it is fair to ask why anyone would do this. The reason is that someone has to write each XML schema and it is pretty likely that mistakes will be made. Because each schema document written using the W3C XML Schema language is itself an instance document, a validating parser can check it for errors. All the parser needs is a schema document that describes the document model for the W3C XML Schema language. As long as the W3C get this 'master' XML schema right, everyone else who writes an XML schema can check that theirs is a valid instance of the W3C XML Schema language. Thus, there should never be any syntax errors in XML schema.

Unfortunately, the W3C XML Schema language is not actually up to the job of describing itself. Another problem with it is that it is fiendishly complex. It was developed as a replacement for the Document Type Definition (DTD) schema language of SGML, so focused closely on replicating the facilities of that language. This led to a complex and cumbersome syntax.

> The DTD schema language itself is not really up to defining the structure of XML documents designed to hold data, so it will not be covered here or in subsequent chapters. From the XML perspective, it may seem a little odd to ignore the DTD schema language as it is very good for defining the structure of a narrative document and remains the most widely used schema language. However, it simply does not make sense to use it for XML documents designed to hold data when there are schema languages such as W3C XML Schema and RELAX NG available. DTD has limited support for data types and, then, only for attribute values. Worse, it does not really support namespaces. Both W3C XML Schema and RELAX NG have a wide range of data types, which can be applied to both attribute values and the content of simple elements, and they support namespaces. They also deal more easily with unordered element content, which is more common in databases than it is in documents.

Dissatisfaction with W3C XML Schema led to alternative proposals. Some of these crystallized into RELAX NG (OASIS, 2001) an alternative schema language with a much simpler syntax. It also has a solid basis in mathematics (something that the W3C XML Schema language lacks). Like W3C XML Schema, RELAX NG schema documents are XML documents. However, rather than providing descriptions of elements and attributes, RELAX NG schema describe patterns. Each instance document is checked to ensure that its structure matches the patterns defined in the RELAX NG schema.

One significant advantage of using patterns rather than descriptions is that complex patterns can be built from simpler patterns, following the underlying mathematical rules for combining patterns. Although the W3C XML Schema language does provide facilities for combining descriptions, they add further complexity to an already complex schema language.

The elegance of RELAX NG owes a lot to its grounding in a mathematical understanding of the structure of XML documents. As with the the W3C XML Schema language, there is a RELAX NG schema describing the document model of RELAX NG. Again, however, this XML schema cannot describe the entire language.

The third approach to creating an XML schema is to provide a set of rules that the instance document must comply with. Schematron (ISO/IEC JTC 1, 2004) takes this approach. Both RELAX NG and Schematron form part of the ISO/IEC proposed international standard for schema definition languages. Rules in Schematron consist of two parts:

● a path to locate those nodes the rule applies to

● a way to determine whether or not these nodes satisfy certain criteria.

In Schematron, both parts of the rule (location and criteria) are defined using the W3C XPath language (see below). This language is not itself an XML application, so neither is Schematron.

Another schema language for XML that takes the rule-based approach is the Document Structure Description language, DSD2 (Møller, 2002). This rule-based schema language *is* an XML application. Moreover, it is the only schema language for XML that can fully describe its own syntax (at least, the only one the author has encountered).

Just as there is no single schema definition language, there is no single query language for extracting data from an XML document. The W3C XML Path language, XPath (W3C, 2005d) provides a way to extract data from an XML document by specifying a path through the tree structure of the document to the required data. An XPath expression may actually match more than one path through the document. At the end of each matching path is a node and the result of an XPath expression is this sequence of nodes, listed in document order. As the basic data structure of the XDM is a sequence of nodes, this means that XPath expressions always return values that the data model can represent. For example, an XPath expression capturing the statement 'move to the `phone` element of the last `staffMember` element' would result in a sequence of two nodes, which would be the two `phone` element nodes in the instance document shown in Figure 3.19 that represent Freya Stark's phone numbers.

Although XPath can search through an XML document and generate a sequence of nodes, it is more limited than the SQL select statement. For example, it can only extract data from one XML document at a time. Recognizing its limitations, the W3C has also developed XQuery (W3C, 2005e), a query language for XML documents. (At the time of writing XQuery was a W3C *candidate* recommendation rather than a formal W3C recommendation, so is subject to changes. It seems likely to become a formal W3C recommendation by the end of 2006 (Eisenberg and Melton, 2005).) XQuery is a functional language that builds on XPath and provides the user with the ability to extract information from one or more XML documents. It is possible that XQuery will become an important query language for databases that use XML as their underlying data model, but it is not yet clear to what extent it will be adopted by DBMS vendors.

A third approach to querying XML documents that has already been implemented by relational DBMS vendors is SQL/XML. SQL/XML forms part of the ISO SQL:2003 international standard for the SQL data language. SQL/XML provides a way to move between representations of data as relational database tables and XML documents. First, it adds a new XML data type to the relational data model. A column with this data type can hold all, or part, of an XML document or even a collection of XML documents. Additional operators for this data type allow queries such as 'return all rows where the value of a specific column is a valid XML document'. It is also possible to embed XQuery expressions in the SQL statement, allowing *parts* of the XML data held in a column to be extracted and used in the SQL query. In effect, these SQL facilities take XML documents and present them as relational data (remember, the result of every SQL query is a table, even when some *column values* are XML documents). SQL/XML also includes functions that take relational data and turn it into XML, reversing the process just discussed. Using these functions, it is possible to generate all or part of an XML document from data held in 'ordinary' columns.

The W3C Extensible Style Language Transformations (XSLT) (W3C, 2005i) provides a view mechanism for XML databases. XSLT is a powerful stylesheet language that can take an XML document written to one document model and transform it into an XML document written to another document model. A typical use of XSLT is to take an XML document written using a proprietary document model, such as the Staff Directory shown in Figure 3.19, and transform it into an XHTML document. This sort of transformation allows any XML document to be delivered using a web browser.

One problem with this approach to implementing a view mechanism is that it actually creates a new, physical XML document. There are two problems with this. First, if the original document is modified while the transformed document is being viewed, there is no mechanism for automatically updating the transformed document. Second, if the transformed document is saved to disk, there will be data duplication. Relational views can avoid both problems because they assume a stateful connection between the end user and the DBMS.

All the data languages discussed focus on querying an XML document or creating new XML documents from existing ones. At the moment, the main way to update an XML document is to open it in a text editor and type out the changes by hand. This weakness should be addressed in the near future, as the W3C has published a working draft of the XQuery Update Facility (W3C, 2006b). The lack of an update function does at least mean that using XPath and XSLT as a view mechanism for an XML database is currently reasonably safe as the original document can't easily be changed. Other features of SQL that are missing from the equivalent XML technologies are the ability to manage users and their privileges and the ability to handle concurrent access. Both issues will need to be addressed by XML DBMS once the XQuery Update Facility has been approved.

3.3.4 Some comments on XML as a data model

This section began by mentioning some criticisms of the relational data model that helped explain why some people wanted to use XML as a database technology. There are some good reasons for doing so. The tree structure of XML documents is a natural fit for semistructured data. There are lots of pre-existing XML technologies, originally developed to process documents, that can be adapted to process data. There is also the fact that XML is a web technology, making it a good choice for putting databases on the Web. These arguments are persuasive, but not conclusive as there are some serious problems with using XML as a database technology.

One problem is that XML does not follow the ANSI/SPARC architecture for database systems. There is a clear separation of the description of an XML document's content from the description of how to present that content – mark-up describes structure, while stylesheets deal with presentation. This corresponds to the separation between the external and logical views in the ANSI/SPARC architecture. However, the logical and internal views both use the same structure – the XML document. Even worse, from the database perspective, XML documents are specifically designed to mix logical organization structures and the physical storage structures that lie beneath the three levels of the ANSI/SPARC architecture. XML documents must contain only Unicode characters and may include references to physical file locations, both file system issues rather than database issues. The decision to mix logical and physical structures makes sense in terms of the original motivation for XML, which was to produce a format for web pages that both humans and machines could easily use. It remains a problem, though, for those keen to use XML as a native format for databases as it can make processing an XML document inefficient. In particular, the fact that all the data is stored as strings, regardless of its actual data type, makes it harder for XML processors to manipulate the data. For example, a database using the XDM as its data model will store all data items as strings of characters. This means that the database stores *literals* not values. When the end user requests data from the database, the DBMS must first convert the literals to values of the correct type before it can manipulate them.

There is also the problem of updating an XML document. In a true database, end users never get their hands on the physical data files, so cannot break the logical structure. Allowing end users to type mark-up directly into an XML document means that it would be prone to structural errors. Validating XML parsers can find such errors, but why allow users to put them there in the first place?

Perhaps the biggest problem for XML is that relational database technologies are stable, efficient and widely used. Native XML DBMS are a new technology and still developing. They lack concurrency, security and optimization technologies that could match those of the commercial RDBMS. With the development of SQL/XML, they risk being beaten on their own territory. Now that relational databases can deal with XML data, there may be no need for a DBMS that uses the XDM as its underlying data model.

Chapter summary

- This chapter has explored approaches to organizing data. The chapter began by examining data items – the individual facts from which useful information is created. It emphasized the difference between values and literals, and introduced the notion of a variable as a named container for data values. The first step taken towards organizing data items into meaningful structures was to develop a range of data types – sets of data values that share some common characteristic. The most common scalar and non-scalar data types were introduced, along with operators for manipulating data values of specific data types. The section on data items also introduced the important notion of a Boolean expression.

- The discussion then moved on to the relational data model. This remains the most commonly used data model today. The section began with a careful discussion of the single data structure, the table. The consequences of allowing a column to be null were explored, including the horrors of three-valued logic. Nulls also cropped up in the section on relational integrity constraints, particularly in the discussion of referential integrity. This section concluded by looking at the SQL data language and the view mechanism for the relational data model.

- The final section discussed XML as an emerging database technology. The problems of separating the physical and logical features of XML documents were discussed, along with the tree-structured data model provided by the XDM. The immaturity of many of the data-focused aspects of XML technology meant that the discussion of integrity constraints and data languages could not be as detailed as it was for the relational data model. The section concluded with a brief discussion of the pros and cons of using XML documents as the native organization structures of a database.

Further reading

The classic reference for the relational data model is Date (2004). Discussed, at some length, are the many advantages of the relational approach and the several weaknesses of the data language SQL and commercial RDBMS. The discussion of data types extends to complex data types not covered here – user-defined types, table types and so on.

Hoffer et al. (2004) offer a more practical approach to the subject, focusing on business applications.

Otherwise, any database textbook aimed at university students will cover the relational model in reasonable detail. Database books aimed at practitioners tend to take a programmer's view of databases and generally cover the relational model very briefly, if at all.

Discussions of XML tend to be from the practitioners' perspective. Probably the best introductory book on XML and related technologies is Møller and Schwartzbach (2006).

Harold and Means (2004) is well thought of, though it is not really an introductory text.

The actual XML recommendation (W3C, 2004f) is also worth a look.

Bourret (2003) provides a nice, gentle introduction to the relevance of XML for database practitioners, while the first chapter of Steegmans et al. (2004) provides a fuller account of these issues.

Review questions

3.1 Define the terms:
(a) data item
(b) value
(c) literal
(d) variable
(e) operator
(f) comparison operator
(g) expression.

3.2 What is a data type? What distinguishes user-defined data types from system-defined data types?

3.3 Describe how data is organized in the relational data model.

3.4 Explain the following terms used in the relational data model:
(a) candidate key
(b) candidate key constraint
(c) primary key
(d) simple key
(e) composite key.

3.5 Explain the following terms used in describing foreign keys:
(a) referencing table
(b) referenced table
(c) foreign key
(d) matching candidate key
(e) foreign key constraint.

3.6 What is the purpose of nulls? In what ways do the introduction of nulls complicate the relational data model?

3.7 Explain the difference between base tables and derived tables. How does a view differ from an ordinary derived table?

3.8 Describe the rules for SQL identifiers (that is, the names for database objects). Explain the differences between SQL regular and delimited identifiers.

3.9 Define the following terms:
(a) XML document
(b) XML application
(c) XML processor
(d) XML parser
(e) XML schema.

3.10 Explain the following terms, each of which applies to nodes in an XML document (you may need to draw a suitable diagram):

(a) root

(b) child

(c) parent

(d) sibling

(e) descendant

(f) ancestor

(g) leaf.

Exercises

3.11 Explain the difference between scalar and non-scalar data types. Give an example of each kind of data type to illustrate your explanation.

3.12 Explain the connections between business rules, integrity constraints and Boolean expressions.

3.13 Using a suitable example, explain how a relational DBMS would enforce a foreign key constraint under the following circumstances:

(a) adding a new row to the referencing table

(b) removing an existing row from the referenced table

(c) changing the value of a matching candidate key.

Use the terminology introduced in this chapter and include a discussion of referential actions in your answer.

3.14 Explain the purpose of views in the relational data model. Discuss how effectively they implement the external views of the ANSI/SPARC database systems architecture.

3.15 Describe how data is organized in the XPath 2.0 and XQuery 1.0 data model (XDM). How does it deal with missing information?

3.16 Use the textual representation of the XML document shown in Figure 3.20 to produce a tree-structured representation of this same document, so that it is in the same style as that shown in Figure 3.18.

Investigations

3.17 Research the ways in which SQL deviates from the relational data model. Critically evaluate both the reasons for and the effects of these deviations. (Date (2004) is a good initial source for this.)

3.18 Investigate the different approaches an RDBMS can take to implementing relational views. What approaches do the major commercial RDBMS take?

3.19 Use a range of sources to compare and contrast the relational data model and the semistructured XML data models, such as the XDM. Critically evaluate the various arguments put forward in favour of each data model. Which side of the debate do you find most convincing? Why?

3.20 Investigate one of the many data models *not* discussed in this chapter, critically evaluating its potential for use in web database applications. Possible data models for investigation include the associative data model (see www.lazysoft.com/index. html), object-orientated and object-relational data models (Date (2004) or Elmasri & Navathe (2007) are good starting points.)

4

Web database implementation

Chapter objectives

→ Discuss how the PHP application server and HTTP server work together to generate an HTTP response message.

→ Review the use of HTML forms to gather user input.

→ Introduce the main features of the PHP scripting language – variables and statements.

→ Discuss how to handle user input – validation and data cleansing.

→ Discuss approaches to code reuse – functions and include files.

→ Introduce the PHP functions for communicating with the MySQL DBMS.

Chapter outline

Any web database application needs user input. The users must tell the application what they want it to do and provide any data values the application needs to complete this task. Searching for data in a database is by far the commonest use of web database applications. This chapter uses a simple database search to illustrate how data passes from the web browser to the web server and on to the DBMS. The DBMS retrieves the requested data from the database and passes it back to the web server, which uses this data to generate a web page that is sent to the web browser.

For simple web database applications, the application developer can assume that the networking and operating system technologies will work efficiently. More complex applications may need to be written to make the most of the specific technologies that support the application – in particular the TCP/IP suite of protocols.

Chapter 2 outlined the different approaches to handling server-side dynamic content. This chapter focuses on extending the capabilities of the web server with the PHP application server.

The PHP application server – called the Zend Engine – is an open source development, now managed by Zend Technologies Inc. (www.zend.com). It supports the PHP language, a server-side scripting language designed to make it easy to embed code within HTML mark-up and so speed up web application development. The PHP code, embedded in the HTML mark-up, can generate additional HTML elements or content for those elements. Once the PHP application server has processed the script, the HTTP server sends the generated web page to the web browser. One important advantage of server-side scripting is that the end user never sees the actual code used to generate a web page, they only see the generated HTML.

Each PHP script is, in essence, a set of instructions for generating an HTTP response message. When a web browser requests a PHP script, the HTTP server and the PHP application server work together to produce this HTTP response message. The PHP code is interpreted and any output it generates is merged into the HTML. The resulting HTML is sent as the entity body of the HTTP response. The application developer can even instruct the PHP application server to generate HTTP headers, though many PHP scripts only generate the HTML of the entity body.

The power of server-side scripting is that a single PHP script can produce many different versions of a web page. PHP scripts are mostly used to generate web pages that include content drawn from a database. As the database instance changes, so does the web page generated by the PHP script. The PHP application server can also use data gathered from the user, typically using an HTML form, as parameters to the PHP script. A different web page is generated in response to different user data.

The PHP application server does not actually interpret the raw PHP code written by the developer. This code is parsed, to ensure that it is correct PHP, then the instructions are compiled into an intermediate format. It is this intermediate format that is executed by the PHP application server. The complied PHP code is faster to execute than raw, human-readable PHP. However, the description above captures the essence of how PHP works.

- Section 4.1 reviews the ways in which HTML forms gather data from the user and pass this data to the web server. The example also serves to review the basics of the HTML mark-up language, although readers not familiar with HTML should do some background reading before tackling this chapter. See the Further reading section at the end of this chapter for recommended sources of information on HTML.

- Section 4.2 introduces the PHP server-side scripting language. It explains how to embed PHP code within an HTML document using the special PHP tag `<?php ...  ?>`; include comments within PHP code to explain its function; generate HTML or content for the web page using the PHP `echo` statement; use PHP variables to store and manipulate data values; access parameter values passed to the PHP script from an HTML form using the PHP superglobal variables; and how to use string literals.

- Section 4.3 looks at how to handle data values passed to the PHP script from an HTML form. It discusses the important topics of data validation and data cleansing, clearly distinguishing between them. This section discusses the PHP if ... `else` ... statement and PHP functions and so completes the introduction to the basic PHP syntax.

■ Section 4.4 introduces the PHP functions that allow a web developer to instruct the PHP application server to communicate with a MySQL DBMS. It describes a six-step process for this, introducing the PHP loop constructs `while`, `foreach` and `for`. The section ends by discussing how to deal with errors that occur when communicating with the MySQL DBMS.

4.1 Gathering user input with HTML forms

HTML forms are the obvious way to gather data from the end user and pass it to the web server for processing. An HTML form can have a number of controls. Figure 4.1 (a) shows a very simple HTML form, displayed in the Firefox web browser. It has two controls: a text box and a submit button. Text boxes allow the user to type character string, date and numeric literals, so can be used to gather these types of data. In Figure 4.1 (a), the form gathers a single character string literal from the user via the text box labelled 'Surname' and here the literal that has been entered is 'Smith'. Once the user has typed in the literal he or she clicks on the submit button (the Firefox web browser gives submit buttons the caption 'Submit Query' unless another value is specified in the HTML) and the browser sends the value to the web server. Obviously, the intention is to search the Staff Directory database for staff whose surname is the same as the value entered by the user. Data about all matching members of staff will be sent back to the user as a web page.

To begin with, a simple 'stub program' is often written to allow the HTML form to be tested without the need to connect to the DBMS. This stub program accepts the data from the HTML form, then simply generates an appropriate message. Figure 4.1 (b) shows a typical stub program response. Note that this stub program is a PHP script called 'SurnameStub.php' (see the URL in Figure 4.1 (b) to confirm this). All the dynamic web pages in this chapter are generated by such PHP scripts.

An HTML form can use either of the HTTP methods GET and POST to pass data to the web server. The POST method sends the data as part of the entity body of the HTTP request. The GET method sends the form data in the query component of the URL. This query component consists of a name-value pair for each control on the HTML form. The web browser's address line in Figure 4.1 (b) shows part of this URL. The full URL is:

http://www.pennine.ac.uk/StaffDirectory/SurnameStub.php?surname=Smith

The query component is the part following the '?' character. Here there is a single name-value pair, with name 'surname', which is the name of the text box, and 'Smith' value.

This is one weakness of the GET method – if there are lots of controls, the query component can be very long. For simple forms that gather data sent across the Internet as plain text (the data is neither confidential nor business critical), use the GET method. For forms with several controls or that gather confidential data, use the POST method.

Figure 4.1 Illustrating the use of HTML forms and the HTTP GET method.

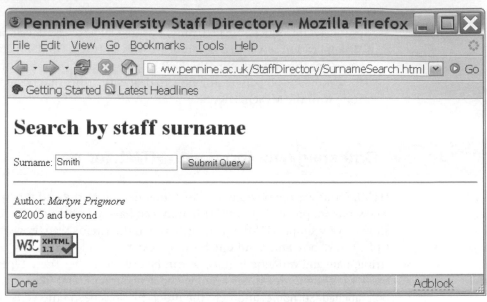

(a) A simple HTML form to gather data and submit it for processing.

(b) The response from the web server when the 'Submit Query' button is clicked on.

The actual HTML for the surname search web page is stored in the file 'SurnameSearch.html', shown in Figure 4.2. The line numbers down the left-hand side of the image are *not* part of the HTML, but have been included to make it easier to discuss the content of the file.

Figure 4.2 The SurnameSearch.html file.

```
1  <!DOCTYPE html PUBLIC "-//W3C//DTD XHTML 1.1//EN"
2      "http://www.w3.org/TR/xhtml11/DTD/xhtml11.dtd">
3  <html>
4  <head>
5    <meta http-equiv="Content-Type" content="text/html; charset=utf-8" />
6    <title> Pennine University Staff Directory </title>
7  </head>
8  <body>
9  <h1> Search by staff surname </h1>
10
11 <form method="get" action="SurnameStub.php">
12 <p> Surname: <input type="text" name="surname" size="25" maxlength="20"  />
13     <input type="submit" />
14 </p>
15 </form>
16
17 <hr />
18 <p>Author: <cite>Martyn Prigmore</cite>
19 <br />&copy;2005 and beyond
20 </p>
21 <p>
22   <a href="http://validator.w3.org/check?uri=referer">
23       <img src="http://www.w3.org/Icons/valid-xhtml11"
24           alt="Valid XHTML 1.1" height="31" width="88" />
25   </a>
26 </p>
27 </body>
28 </html>
```

The very first thing in the file is the document type declaration in lines 1 and 2. This declares that the file contains HTML mark-up written to the XHTML1.1 standard, rather than to any other version of the HTML language. The <html> start tag in line 3 is the start tag for the html element. The html element ends with the </html> end tag in line 28.

In XHTML1.1, all tags must be written with lower-case letters, so using the tags <HTML> ... </HTML> to delimit (that is, mark the start and end of) the html element is not valid XHTML1.1.

Every html element contains two other elements. The head element starts in line 4 with the <head> start tag and ends in line 7 with the </head> end tag. The body element starts in line 8 with the <body> start tag and ends in line 27 with the </body> end tag.

These three elements – html, head and body – define the basic structure of any HTML document.

In XHTML1.1, the head element must include a title element, as shown in line 6 of Figure 4.2. Failing to include a title element generates a validation error. Typically, the content of the title element is displayed in the title bar of the web browser's window, often followed by the name of the web browser software. This is how the Firefox web browser behaves, as shown in Figure 4.1 (a).

The meta element is used to provide additional information about the document. The meta element in line 5 tells the web browser that this document contains text, structured using html, and that the character set used is utf-8. (The utf-8 character set is a Unicode character set recommended by the W3C as the one to use for web pages.) Usually this information is included automatically by the HTTP server as HTTP response message headers. The meta element overrides the HTTP server's default settings, so should be used with care. If in doubt, omit it.

> Different languages use different sets of characters. For example, English uses an alphabet of 26, letters, while Greek uses a different alphabet of 24 letters, α, β, γ and so on. Some character sets (such as ASCII) cannot represent the Greek letters, while others can (utf-8, for example). So, a page written in Greek might use a different character set from one written in English. Korpela (2001) and W3C (2005a) are good introductory tutorials on character sets. (The official website for the Unicode Consortium is www.unicode.org)
>
> Note that it is not enough to just state that a web document uses a particular character set, but must actually be stored using that character set. Many web development tools allow the user to choose which character set to use when saving a file, but some do not. The Unicode Consortium maintains a list of Unicode enabled products (Unicode Consortium, 2005).

The meta element is interesting as it cannot contain any content. In older versions of HTML, such **empty elements** did not have an end tag. In XHTML *all* elements *must* have an end tag. Strictly speaking, the correct form for the meta tag in line 5 is:

```
<meta http-equiv="Content-Type"
content="text/html; charset=utf-8"> </meta>
```

However, requiring web authors to type end tags for empty elements goes against human nature, so the W3C included the shortened form in the XHTML specification:

```
<meta http-equiv="Content-Type"
content="text/html; charset=utf-8" />
```

Notice that there is a space character before the /> combination that closes this tag. This is necessary to avoid confusing older browsers, which might not understand this shortened form for empty elements. Other examples of empty elements, written using the short form, include the horizontal rule element – <hr/> in line 17 – and the break element –
 in line 19. The horizontal rule element instructs the browser to draw a line across the web page, while the break element instructs it to start a new line.

The body element can be empty, though there is little point in a web page with no content in its body.

The body of the SurnameSearch.html file includes several elements. In line 9, the heading1 element includes the main heading for this page. Notice that in the HTML mark-up there is a leading space character in the element content – the space before the word 'Search'. The web browser ignores leading, and trailing, spaces in most element content. It also ignores multiple spaces and new lines (that is why HTML includes the break element, to force a new line in the web browser). The content of the heading1 element is presented in a large, bold, serif font in the web browser. This default presentation is not particularly good, from a visual design perspective, so some web developers would use the heading3 (<h3> ... </h3>) element instead, as this usually looks better. However, 'Search by staff surname' is the top-level heading on this web page, so the heading1 element correctly identifies it as such. A tool to generate a 'table of contents' for a web page could easily be confused if the wrong heading element was used here. To alter the way the web browser presents the element content, use a stylesheet. Don't use the wrong element just because the default presentation of that element looks better.

Line 11 is the start tag for the form element. The form element has two required attributes and they provide additional information about the element. An element's attributes are listed as name-value pairs inside the element's start tag. The method attribute tells the web browser whether to send the form's data using the HTTP GET or POST method. The form in Figure 4.2 uses the GET method. The action attribute tells the web browser where to send the form data, so its value should be a valid URL. In line 11, the action attribute has the value 'SurnameStub.php'. This is just the file name of the PHP script that processes the form data, not a full URL. The web browser assumes that the file SurnameStub.php is located in the same directory as the current web page. As the current page has the URL:

```
http://www.pennine.ac.uk/StaffDirectory/SurnameSearch.html
```

the action attribute shown in line 11 is simply an abbreviation for:

```
action="http://www.pennine.ac.uk/StaffDirectory/SurnameStub.
php"
```

The ability of a web browser to correctly interpret a **relative URL** makes maintaining a website simpler. If all the Staff Directory files are moved to a new directory on the web server, the form element's action attribute will still point at the right PHP script as its value is defined relative to the location of the SurnameSearch.html file.

Within the form element is a paragraph element (the start tag is in line 12 and the end tag is in line 14). This acts as a container for the form's controls and any text used to label those controls. In line 12, the text 'Surname:' acts as a label for the text box, indicating to the user what sort of text is being gathered. Immediately after this text comes an input element. The input element is an empty element that must be enclosed within a form element. Each input element includes a type attribute. In line 12, the type attribute has the value 'text', indicating that the web browser should display a text box. In line 13, the type is 'submit', so the web browser will display a submit button. Notice that, in Figure 4.1 (a), both input elements appear on the same line. A web browser always ignores line breaks. To make the submit button appear below the text box, use a break element (<br/>).

When the user clicks on the submit button, the value of the text box is sent to the file identified by the form's action attribute. Submit buttons don't need any other attribute values, but text boxes must include a name. This is used to create the name-value pair sent to the server (see the address line of the web browser in Figure 4.1 (b)). In line 12, two optional attributes are used to control the behaviour of the text box. The size attribute sets the width of the text box to 25 characters and the maxlength attribute means that, in this case, a maximum of 20 characters can be typed into the text box by the user. The maxlength attribute is useful for limiting data values gathered from the user to the maximum length of the corresponding data in the database (such as a column of a table).

The remainder of the HTML document – lines 17 to 28 – is a general page footer, which will appear on every page on the website. The footer includes an anchor element (<a> ... </a>), the href attribute of which gives the URL for the W3C HTML validation service (W3C, 2005a). Anchors are used to create hyperlinks. This anchor element's content is an image element (<img ... />), so the link will display as an icon rather than text. The image element's src attribute is the URL for this icon. The icon indicates that the HTML for this web page is valid XHTML 1.1. If the icon is not available, then the value of the alt attribute provides the text to display as the alternative form of the hyperlink.

When the web browser receives the SurnameSearch.html from the Pennine University's web server (host name www.pennine.ac.uk), it reads through the HTML and finds the image element in lines 23 and 24. The image file is not delivered with the HTML file, so the web browser creates a new HTTP request to retrieve this image. Note that this second request is sent to a *different* web server, the W3C's web server with host name www.w3.org

---

XHTML 1.1 is the latest stable version of the HTML language and will form the basis for future development (W3C, 2001). It is important to ensure that any web pages intended for public viewing are written in valid HTML as invalid HTML may be displayed incorrectly in some web browsers. A more detailed justification for validating HTML pages is given in W3C (2004a).

Web pages with dynamic content are harder to validate than static web pages. With a static web page, the structure and content of the document are fixed. With a dynamic web page, both the structure (the HTML elements) and the content may change from one request to the next. This is because a PHP script can output a range of HTML documents, depending on the precise processing involved. To ensure that a PHP script generates valid HTML for each valid input, it must be tested. As with any computer program, a range of typical values for the inputs are tested as it is not possible to test all possible inputs. For example, the HTML form in Figure 4.1 (a) accepts a string of 20 characters. There are around 100 different characters (letters, numerals, punctuation marks and so on) that the user can type, so over 100^{20} different inputs to the SearchStub.php script. Validating the HTML output by SearchStub.php for all these possible inputs is simply not feasible. Instead, a representative sample of test cases is used. If the HTML generated for the input value of each test case is valid, then it is reasonable to assume that the PHP script will always generate valid HTML.

4.2 Introduction to PHP

The data entered into the HTML form in Figure 4.2 is passed to the web server using the HTTP GET method. There, it becomes a parameter to the PHP script SurnameStub.php, which uses it to generate a message. This message simply tells the user what he or she typed into the form. Figure 4.1 (a) shows the HTML form with the data 'Smith' entered into the text box and Figure 4.1 (b) the response generated from the PHP script by the PHP application server when this data is submitted. The actual

Figure 4.3 First draft of a PHP script to accept data from the SurnameSearch.html form.

```
1  <?php
2  /*-- Begin script file header
3  -- ********************************************************************
4  -- Title   Staff search
5  -- Comment Accepts search criteria from users, and delivers a list
6  --         of staff whose details match the search criteria.
7  --
8  -- Version Date        Author          Comment
9  -- 0.1     2005-11-05  M. Prigmore     STUB PROGRAM
10 --                                     accepts user data and generates
11 --                                     an appropriate message
12 -- Parameters:
13 -- Script expects the following GET and POST parameters:
14 --
15 -- ParameterName   Method  Description
16 -- surname         GET     A character string; the surname to search for
17 -- ********************************************************************
18 -- End script file header */
19 ?>
20 <!DOCTYPE html PUBLIC "-//W3C//DTD XHTML 1.1//EN"
21    "http://www.w3.org/TR/xhtml11/DTD/xhtml11.dtd">
22 <html>
23 <head>
24   <meta http-equiv="Content-Type" content="text/html; charset=utf-8" />
25   <title>Surname search stub program</title>
26 </head>
27 <body>
28 <h1>Data passed to stub program</h1>
29 <?php
30   echo "\n<p>";
31   $surname = $_GET["surname"];
32   echo "\nYou entered the surname \"$surname\".";
33   echo "\n</p>";
34 ?>
35
36 <hr />
37 <p>Author: <cite>Martyn Prigmore</cite>
38 <br />&copy;2005 and beyond
39 </p>
40 </body>
41 </html>
```

PHP script SurnameStub.php is shown in Figure 4.3. The line numbers are not part of PHP, but are used here to refer to specific lines in the script.

It's clear that HTML mark-up and PHP code are interleaved in this script. The PHP code is easily identified, as it must be enclosed in the special PHP tag <?php ... ?>. Although this PHP script is very simple, it illustrates many of the features of the PHP language, so a line-by-line discussion of the script is worthwhile.

The script begins with a section of PHP code, between the <?php in line 1 and the ?> in line 19. This long section does not actually do anything; it is just a comment. The comment begins in line 2 with the PHP start-of-comment symbol /* and ends in line 18 with the end-of-comment symbol */. Everything between these two symbols is ignored by the PHP application server. It reads through this whole section without generating anything. Even so, this section provides useful information for the application developer. It gives a title for this script file and a brief comment explaining its purpose. Next comes some version control information – this file is version 0.1, created on 5 November 2005 by M. Prigmore. Later versions would include comments stating what has been changed. Finally, there is a list of parameters that the script expects to receive. In this case, there is just one – a parameter named 'surname', which is passed using the HTTP

GET method. It is not necessary to include a script header like this, but many application developers find them useful. Trying to figure out what a script (or any program) does simply by looking at the code can be tricky, so good comments, including script headers, help to make maintaining scripts much easier than is the case when they are missing.

The characters `//` also begin a PHP comment, but this sort of comment ends at the end of the current line. Use the `/* ... */` form for all multiline comments.

Lines 20 to 28 are not PHP at all – they are plain HTML. When the PHP application server comes across a line in the script file that is not enclosed within a PHP tag, it writes this line as HTML directly into the entity body of the HTTP response message it is generating from the script. Thus, the very first thing in the entity body is a doctype declaration (line 20). This is just what is needed – every HTML document should begin with a doctype declaration. The remaining lines, up to line 28, are also written directly into the entity body.

This raises the question, what about the HTTP headers? In Chapter 2 it was made clear that the HTTP headers must precede the entity body in any HTTP message. Although the script has not instructed the PHP application server to generate any HTTP headers, there will be some. The HTTP response message will include any default headers generated by the HTTP server itself. Once the PHP application server starts to generate the entity body, it cannot generate any further HTTP headers. Even if there is a single blank line before the first PHP tag, attempting to generate an HTTP header in the PHP that follows will cause an error. This can be a problem in advanced PHP scripts, but, for now, the scripts are simple enough that there's no need to worry about the HTTP headers.

In line 29, the script slips back into PHP code and line 30 is a PHP echo statement. Notice that the statement is terminated with a semicolon – ';'. Every PHP statement must end with a semicolon, otherwise the PHP application server cannot properly interpret the script.

The echo statement instructs the PHP application server to write the string `'<p>'` directly into the entity body of the HTTP response. In other words, it generates the start tag for an HTML paragraph element. The `\n` represents the new line character and means that the `<p>` tag will be written in a new line of the entity body. Using new line characters makes the HTML generated from the PHP script easier to read. Without them, all the generated content would appear in one long line, rather than in successive lines. Character combinations such as `'\n'` are called **escape sequences** (see the PHP manual at www.php.net for a list of PHP escape sequences).

Missing out a semicolon is a common cause of errors in PHP scripts. If your script does not produce anything at all, then check for missing semicolons. The PHP application server will write an error message to the PHP error log when it encounters a missing semicolon. The PHP error log is very useful for debugging PHP scripts. For example, when the semicolon is missed off the end of line 30, the message is:

```
[17-Nov-2005 14:11:18] PHP Parse error: syntax error,
unexpected T_VARIABLE, expecting ',' or ';' in
SurnameStub.php on line 31
```

All error messages follow this format. First comes the date and time the error occurred, followed by the type of error. A 'PHP Parse error' means that the code written by the application developer is simply wrong. The PHP application server then gives an explanation of the error. In this case, it came across a variable (the $surname that starts line 31) when it was expecting either a comma or a semicolon. As there are two possibilities, the PHP application server does not know what to do, so stops compiling the script. Notice that the line number is 31, which is the line *after* the one with the missing semicolon. This is because it is only when the PHP application server encounters the $ character of $surname in line 31 that it realizes something has gone wrong. Chapter 7 covers PHP error reporting in more detail.

> The error log is often just a text file. The PHP application server may create this text file in the same directory as the script that generated the error, though this depends on how PHP was installed. The PHP administrator will know the default error logging behaviour of your PHP application server.

The `<p>` and `</p>` tags, generated in lines 30 and 33 respectively, delimit an HTML paragraph element that encloses the content generated by the echo statement in line 32; Figure 4.4 shows this paragraph element enclosing the generated content 'You entered the surname "Smith"'. It is important that any content generated by PHP is enclosed in an appropriate HTML element, otherwise the generated HTML will not be valid.

Figure 4.4 The HTML file generated from the SurnameSearch.php script, with input parameter surname=Smith.

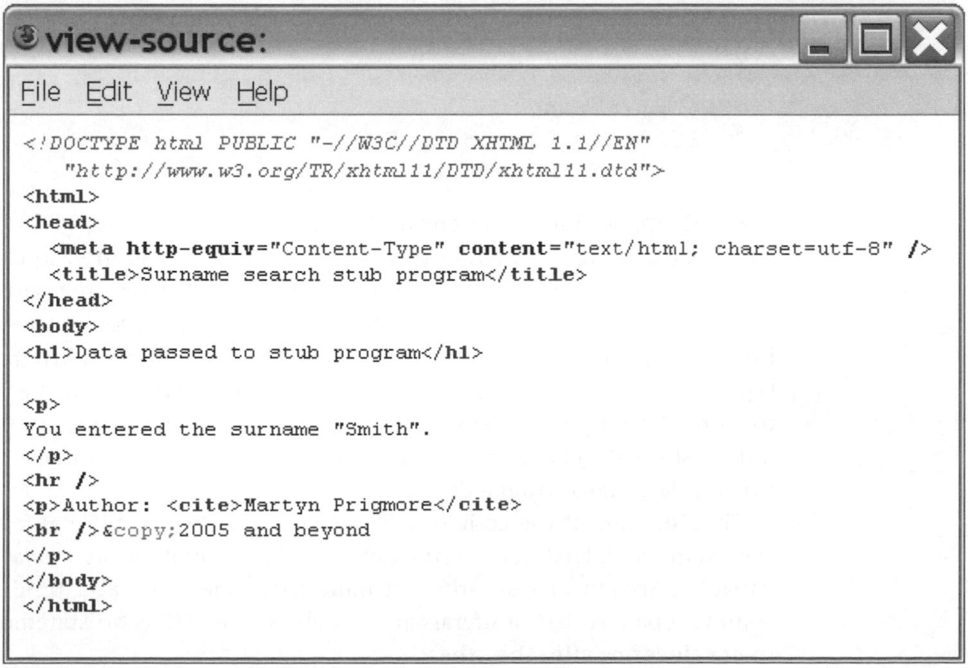

```
view-source:

File  Edit  View  Help

<!DOCTYPE html PUBLIC "-//W3C//DTD XHTML 1.1//EN"
    "http://www.w3.org/TR/xhtml11/DTD/xhtml11.dtd">
<html>
<head>
  <meta http-equiv="Content-Type" content="text/html; charset=utf-8" />
  <title>Surname search stub program</title>
</head>
<body>
<h1>Data passed to stub program</h1>

<p>
You entered the surname "Smith".
</p>
<hr />
<p>Author: <cite>Martyn Prigmore</cite>
<br />&copy;2005 and beyond
</p>
</body>
</html>
```

Line 31 in Figure 4.3 is a PHP assignment statement. It declares a new variable, called $surname and assigns it a value. All PHP variable names begin with the dollar character $ and, unlike most programming languages, don't need to be declared before they are used. The PHP application server recognizes that a new variable has been assigned a value and works out what the data type should be by looking at that value. So, the assignment statement:

```
$myString = "This should be a string.";
```

will declare a new variable called $myString with the data type character string and assign it the value 'This should be a string.' This is a nice feature, but also a bit dangerous. The following code will not show any error, but will not work as expected:

```
$myString = "This should be a string.";
echo $mySrting;
```

The PHP application server interprets the first line as an instruction to declare the variable $myString, as before. On the next line, the variable name has been mistyped: $mySrting should be $myString. The PHP application server recognizes that this variable has not been declared (as it has never been assigned a value) so ignores it. Nothing is generated by this echo statement.

If your PHP script runs, but is blank where you expected text, check that you have spelt variable names correctly. PHP actually generates a 'Notice' in the error log when it encounters an undeclared variable. Using PHP's error log to debug scripts is discussed in Chapter 7.

The data type of a PHP variable is not fixed. The following code is valid PHP:

```
$myString = "This should be a string.";
echo $myString;
$myString = 5.26 * 0.01;
echo "\nBut now it's a number: ", $myString;
```

The PHP application server creates the variable $myString, gives it the value 'This should be a string.' and writes this value to the HTTP response. In the third line, PHP gives $myString the value 0.0526 and changes the data type to floating point number.

In PHP, the data type of a variable is simply the data type of the value it currently holds. If the value changes, so can the data type. This ability of PHP to change the data type of a variable partway through a script was intended to make it easier for beginners to write PHP scripts. However, it does mean that sometimes the application developer must test the data type of a variable before manipulating its value. This is particularly true for data drawn from a database.

The final line of the code snippet above shows two additional features of the PHP echo statement. First, it can write out the value of numeric, as well as character string, variables. Second, it can write out more than one value at a time. Supplied with a comma-separated list of literals and variables, the PHP echo statement will write out their values one after the other.

PHP is *not* Unicode enabled and only recognizes the 256 characters that can be defined using a single byte. The underlying operating system will determine the specific character encoding, though it is probably safe to assume ASCII. This means that the meta element in line 24 of Figure 4.3 is not entirely honest. The output of this PHP script will probably be in the ASCII character set, not utf-8. Fortunately, ASCII is a subset of the utf-8 character set, so any character generated by PHP should be correctly interpreted by the web browser.

In line 31 of Figure 4.3, the variable $surname is assigned the value $_GET ["surname"]. $_GET is one of PHP's **superglobal variables**. The value of a superglobal variable can be accessed from anywhere in the PHP script – they automatically have global **scope**. In contrast, the scope of other variables may be restricted to just a small portion of the script. This is the case for variables declared within a function (discussed below). The PHP application server stores the name-value pairs sent using the HTTP GET method in the $_GET superglobal variable. $_GET is an associative array, meaning that each element in the array has an index (its position in the array), a key (it's unique identifier) and a value. Each name-value pair is turned into an element of $_GET and the name becomes the element key and the value becomes the element value. For example, in Figure 4.1, the HTML form uses the HTTP GET method to send a single name-value pair 'surname=Smith' to the PHP script SurnameStub.php. The $_GET superglobal for SurnameStub.php will be:

$_GET =

Index	0
Key	surname
Value	Smith

Thus, in this instance, the value referred to by the array expression $_GET ["surname"] is 'Smith', so that is the value assigned to $surname in line 31. If the HTML form used the HTTP POST method, its name-value pairs would become the elements of the $_POST superglobal. There are other superglobals, but $_GET and $_POST are the two that contain data gathered from the user via an HTML form.

Always use the element key to refer to an element of a superglobal. There is no guarantee that all the name-value pairs you are expecting have actually been supplied and so there is no way to be sure what index is given to a particular name-value pair.

Line 32 of Figure 4.3 is a further example of the echo statement and PHP character string literals. PHP allows character string literals to be enclosed either in single or double quotes. Character string literals enclosed in double quotes can include single quotes. Similarly, a character string literal enclosed in single quotes can include double quotes. For example, the following echo statements work fine:

```
echo "This string's enclosed in 'plain' double quotes";
echo 'This in "plain" single ones';
```

This is a nice feature as names such as O'Connor and sentences that include apostrophes, can be represented using a double-quoted string literal without the need to worry about how PHP will interpret the apostrophe.

> Many word processors include a custom, or smart, quotes feature. This replaces straight quote marks, "like these", with fancy quote marks, "like these". The same holds for single quotes, so 'straight quotes' are turned into 'custom quotes'. Although the two sorts of quote marks are equivalent in normal use, they are different characters and the custom quote marks are not part of the standard ASCII character set. This means that PHP cannot recognize custom quotes. Only straight quotes can be used to delimit string literals. So, if you must write PHP code using a word processor, make sure that you turn off the custom quotes feature!

String literals enclosed in single quotes are treated as simple strings of characters. Most escape sequences are *not* recognized. For example, the new line character \n is not treated as a new line character, but as a backslash followed by the letter 'n'. The PHP statements:

```
echo 'This is the first line.';
echo '\nAnd this is the second line';
```

will generate the text 'This is the first line.\nAnd this is the second line', which is not what was intended. To include new line characters in a string literal, therefore, always use double quotes.

To include an apostrophe character (a single quote) inside a single-quoted string literal, 'escape' the special meaning of the single quote by preceding it with a backslash. So, the escape sequence \' will be output as a single apostrophe. For example, the PHP code:

```
echo 'It\'s easy enough to include an apostrophe in this
      string literal';
```

will output the string 'It's easy enough to include an apostrophe in this string literal', which is what was required.

> SQL only allows single-quoted string literals and does not use the same escape sequences as PHP. See Chapter 5 for details.

When PHP encounters a double-quoted string literal, it recognizes all the escape sequences, including \n for a new line and \" for a double quote mark. Both these occur in the string literal in line 32 of Figure 4.3.

PHP also recognizes variable names within a double-quoted string literal and replaces the variable name with its current value. Given that $surname has the value 'Smith', line 32 is equivalent to:

```
echo "\nYou entered the surname \"Smith\".";
```

Again, this is a nice feature, making it much easier to work with strings in PHP than in some other languages. PHP can even replace a reference to an array element inside a double-quoted string with that element's value, but the array reference must be enclosed in curly brackets. For example, lines 31 and 32:

```
$surname = $_GET["surname"];
echo "\nYou entered the surname \"$surname\".";
```

are equivalent to the single line:

```
echo "\nYou entered the surname \"{$_GET["surname"]}\"."
```

This latter code is shorter, but not quite as easy to understand. Which to use is a matter of personal style and may depend on exactly how the array is being used.

4.3 Handling user input in PHP

When a PHP script accepts data from an HTML form, there is no guarantee that the data entered is the sort of data the PHP script expects. For example, if the user clicks on the submit button on the SurnameSearch.html form *before* entering a surname, they see the web page shown in Figure 4.5 (a). In this case, the result gives a poor impression to the user rather than causing a problem in the script. Similar sorts of problem occur when the user enters '30/02/2005' for a date or '£3.50p' for a price when the PHP script expects a plain number. In these cases, the problem may cause the script to generate the wrong result.

All these are examples of everyday mistakes that an end user might innocently make. A PHP script can cope with such problems by performing basic **data validation** on all user input. The goal of data validation is to correctly interpret the data entered by the user and generate an appropriate response. This may mean asking the user to try again.

A more serious problem occurs when the user deliberately sets out to hack a web application. Figure 4.5 (b) shows what happens when the user enters the text:

```
<script>alert("Ha!");</script>
```

into the surname text box, then clicks on the submit button. While this particular example is fairly harmless, the same isn't true when the text box gathers data that is stored in a database and used in future to generate further web pages. In that situation, users other than the original user will see the message box and if the message is insulting or offensive, it could prove very serious for an e-commerce business. Potential customers would be put off using a website that was clearly insecure.

To avoid these problems, the PHP script should also perform **data cleansing**, to remove any potentially malicious data before it is processed by the script. Data cleansing is distinct from data validation. Data cleansing is about stripping away potentially malicious data, while data validation is about generating an appropriate response to invalid, confusing or unexpected data.

147

Figure 4.5 Two unfortunate web pages generated by SearchStub.php

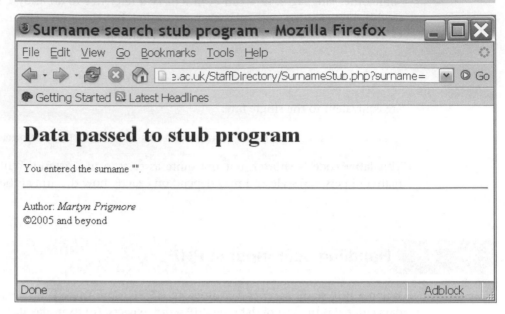

(a) The web page generated when the user leaves the surname box blank.

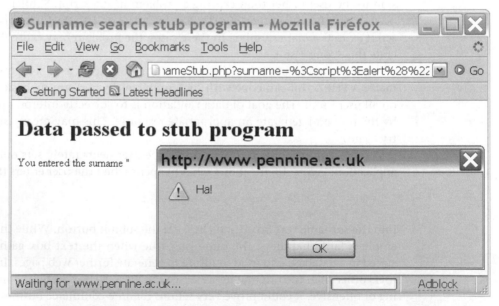

(b) The result of malicious data entered into an HTML form.

Actually, the version of SurnameSearch.html shown in Figure 4.2 can't be hacked in this way. The surname text box will only accept up to 20 characters and `<script> alert("Ha!");</script>` has 30 characters. However, a knowledgeable user could simply type the URL into the web browser as `SurnameSearch.html?surname="<script>alert("Ha!");</script>"`. This gets round the limit placed on the text box, so data cleansing is still necessary.

Two technical points arise from Figure 4.5 (b). First, the data passed from the SurnameSearch.html form has been encoded by the web browser: '<' is represented by '%3C' and '>' by '%3E'. This is shown in the address bar. Second, the ECMAScript for the alert box appears part-way through the HTML, just after the first double quote mark (see Figure 4.3). When the browser reaches the HTML script element, it stops rendering the page until the alert has been responded to by the user. This is why the second double quote mark, the horizontal rule, and the page footer are all missing from the page in Figure 4.5 (b).

The simplest form of data validation is to check whether or not the user has entered any data at all. The second version of the SurnameStub.php script (Figure 4.6) adds this simple form of data validation. If the user does not enter a surname, then the script generates a message to indicate this. Otherwise, it generates the same message as before.

Version 0.2 of the SearchStub.php script introduces three concepts not met in version 0.1 – the 'if' statement, code blocks and PHP built-in functions.

The `if ... else ...` statement is simply a way of instructing the PHP application server to carry out one of two actions, based on some condition. The basic structure is shown in Figure 4.7. This is the same basic structure as is used in most programming languages. The statement begins with the keyword `if`, immediately followed by the test condition. The test condition is a Boolean expression, so is either true or false. In PHP, the test condition must be enclosed in parentheses, like so `(...)`. Next – typically this part is written on the following line of the script file – comes a **code block**. A code block is simply a sequence of one or more PHP statements. Any PHP statement can occur in such a code block. If there is more than one statement, the code block must be enclosed in braces – `{...}` – but, if there is only one statement, the braces can be omitted. The first code block in Figure 4.7 is enclosed in braces and is the code executed when the condition evaluates to `TRUE`.

For some `if ... else ...` statements, there is nothing to do when the condition is false. In this case, the `else` part is simply omitted. For example, the `if ... else ...` statement:

```
if ($count = 0)
   echo "Nothing to count.";
```

will generate the message 'Nothing to count' if the variable `$count` is zero. If `$count` is not zero, then the code block is skipped.

More generally, the keyword `else` indicates that there is a code block to execute when the condition is false, as well as when it is true. In Figure 4.7, the second code block has a single PHP statement, so the braces are omitted. Notice that the statements in both

Figure 4.6 Stub program with basic data validation.

```php
1  <?php
2  /*-- Begin script file header
3   -- ***********************************************************************
4   -- Title    Staff search
5   -- Comment  Accepts search criteria from users, and delivers a list
6   --          of staff whose details match the search criteria.
7   --
8   -- Version Date         Author          Comment
9   -- 0.1     2005-11-05   M. Prigmore     STUB PROGRAM
10  --                                      accepts user data and generates
11  --                                      an appropriate message
12  -- 0.2     2005-11-05   M. Prigmore     Adds basic data validation
13  --
14  -- Parameters:
15  -- Script expects the following GET and POST parameters:
16  --
17  -- ParameterName    Method  Description
18  -- surname          GET     A character string; the surname to search for
19  -- ***********************************************************************
20  -- End script file header */
21  ?>
22  <!DOCTYPE html PUBLIC "-//W3C//DTD XHTML 1.1//EN"
23     "http://www.w3.org/TR/xhtml11/DTD/xhtml11.dtd">
24  <html>
25  <head>
26    <meta http-equiv="Content-Type" content="text/html; charset=utf-8" />
27    <title>Surname search stub program</title>
28  </head>
29  <body>
30  <h1>Data passed to stub program</h1>
31  <?php
32    echo "\n<p>";
33    if (empty($_GET["surname"]))
34      echo "\nYou did not enter a surname.";
35    else
36    {
37      $surname = $_GET["surname"];
38      echo "\nYou entered the surname \"$surname\".";
39    }
40    echo "\n</p>";
41  ?>
42
43  <hr />
44  <p>Author: <cite>Martyn Prigmore</cite>
45  <br />&copy;2005 and beyond
46  </p>
47  </body>
48  </html>
```

Figure 4.7 The PHP if statement.

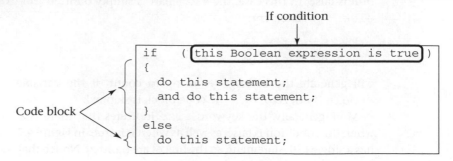

150

code blocks are indented slightly (by two spaces). Like comments, the PHP application server ignores indentation, but it does make the code easier to read, especially when a second if ... else ... statement occurs inside one of the code blocks.

> The statement shown in Figure 4.7 is intended to highlight the *structure* of the PHP if ... else ... statement. Neither the condition, nor the statements in the two code blocks are valid PHP. It isn't possible just to write English sentences as the PHP application server will not understand them.

Lines 33–39 in Figure 4.6 illustrate how to use an if ... else ... statement for real. Notice that there is no semicolon at the end of the line 33. That is because the if ... else ... statement doesn't end until the end of the final code block in line 39. Also, there is no semicolon after the } in line 39 as the closing brace itself indicates the end of the code block and, hence, the end of the if ... else ... statement.

The condition in line 33 tests whether or not $_GET["surname"] has a value. Even a single space character will do. If the user *did* type something, then the condition would be FALSE so the PHP application server would skip past the first code block to the else keyword and execute the second code block. The second code block is simply the same code as in version 0.1 of the script (Figure 4.3). If there is no value for $_GET["surname"], the user must have failed to type anything, so the message 'You did not enter a surname.' would be generated. No braces are needed to delimit this code block as it has only the one statement. Note that in this case, the PHP application server will now skip past the else keyword and its code block to line 40. Only *one* of the if ... else ... statements' two code blocks can be executed on any run through the script.

Line 33 includes a call to one of PHP's built-in functions – the empty() function. A function accepts a list of parameters and returns a single value. Functions can be used much like variables as they represent a value, but the value can change depending on the values of the parameters. In general, a parameter can be a literal, variable, function or any other kind of expression (though not always – see below). The PHP user manual (PHP Documentation Group, 2005) describes all functions in the same way (Figure 4.8). First comes the data type of the value returned by the function, then the function's name. The parameters are presented as a comma-separated list enclosed in parentheses.

Figure 4.8 PHP function description.

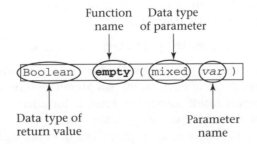

In empty($_GET["surname"]) the parameter is an array variable, referring to the surname element of the associative array $_GET. The return value is a Boolean value – that is, TRUE if the parameter is empty, FALSE otherwise. The empty() function accepts a single parameter of any data type (the word mixed in Figure 4.8 indicates this) and returns a Boolean value. This means that the condition of the if ... else ... statement in line 33 asks 'Is $_GET["surname"] empty?' Using the PHP Boolean operator '!' ('not'), the condition can ask 'Is $_GET["surname"] non-empty?' This turns the if ... else ... statement around and means that the code block likely to be used in most cases appears first. Compare the statement in lines 33 to 39 with the following, equivalent, statement:

```
if (!empty($_GET["surname"]))
{
  $surname = $_GET["surname"];
  echo "\nYou entered the surname \"$surname\".";
}
else
  echo "\nYou did not enter a surname.";
```

Whether you ask 'Is this empty?' or 'Is this non-empty?' is, once again, a matter of personal coding style (it used to affect performance, but this is less of an issue with modern programming languages). Testing for the most likely situation seems sensible, but often means coding with the 'not' operator ('!').

It is very easy to type $_GET("surname") instead of $_GET["surname"]. This really confuses the PHP application server as it thinks $_GET("surname") is a *function* not an array variable. If you get the error message 'PHP Fatal error: Can't use function return value in write context', then check if you've used parentheses when you should have used square brackets.

The code in Figure 4.6 deals with the situation where users submit the data without entering anything, but not where they type a string of spaces. The data validation should deal with this in the same way as an empty submission.

PHP includes the trim() function to strip away any leading or trailing spaces from a string (it also strips away leading tab characters, new lines and other white space). Leading spaces are spaces that appear before any other characters, trailing spaces ones that appear after them. The trim() function's return value is a copy of the original string, but with leading and trailing spaces stripped away. The description of this function in the PHP manual is:

```
string trim ( string str [, string charlist] )
```

There are two parameters. The first, *str*, is the string that needs to be stripped and the other, *charlist* is an *optional* parameter (PHP function descriptions list optional parameters inside square brackets). If included, it is a string listing which characters should be stripped away. Using *charlist* overrides the basic behaviour of the trim() function, so, if *charlist* does not include the space character, leading and trailing spaces are not stripped. Some examples should clarify how the basic `trim()` function works.

```
echo trim(" a b c");
//Generates "a b c"; leading space stripped away
echo trim("a b c ");
//Generates "a b c"; trailing space stripped away
echo trim(" a b c ");
//Generates "a b c"; leading and trailing spaces stripped
away
```

If the user types a string of spaces into the surname text box, then using the `trim()` function will remove all those spaces and leave an empty string. This suggests the following test:

```
if (empty($_GET["surname"]) or
empty(trim($_GET["surname"])))
  echo "\nYou did not enter a surname.";
```

The condition first tests whether or not `$_GET["surname"]` is empty, then whether or not `trim($_GET["surname"])` is empty. If either the first *or* the second test returns TRUE, then the whole condition is TRUE. Unfortunately, *this won't work*. While most functions can accept any valid expression as a parameter, `empty()` is intended to ascertain whether a *variable* has a value or not, so it only works if the parameter is a variable name. In the function call `empty(trim($_GET["surname"]))` the parameter is a function return value. Calling the `empty()` function with any expression other than a variable will mean that the PHP application cannot run the script. Instead, it writes a 'PHP fatal error' message to the error log. Always check the PHP user manual (PHP Documentation Group, 2005) for the full description of a particular built-in function and any restrictions on how it can be used.

It's easy to get round this restriction on `empty()`. The following code *does* work:

```
$surname = trim($_GET["surname"]);
if (empty($_GET["surname"]) or empty($surname))
  echo "\nYou did not enter a surname.";
else
  echo "\nYou entered the surname \"$surname\".";
```

> PHP includes two Boolean OR operators – `or` and `||`. They behave alike, except in terms of operator precedence. See PHP Documentation Group (2005) for details.

There is a problem with the above code, though. When the user does not enter anything into the surname text box, the PHP application server recognizes that the array key `surname` does not exist for the superglobal `$_GET`. It then writes the error message:

```
'PHP Notice: Undefined index: surname in SurnameStub.php
on line 33'
```

to the error log. While such notices don't cause the application to fail, some PHP programmers like to eliminate them, as well as more serious errors. One way to do this is always to use `empty()` to check that the user entered a value *before* using `$_GET` to access that value. This means coding a nested `if ... else ...` statement:

```php
if (empty($_GET["surname"]))
  echo "\nYou did not enter a surname.";
else
{
  $surname = trim($_GET["surname"]);
  if (empty($surname))
    ccho "\nYou did not cnter a surname.";
  else
    echo "\nYou entered the surname \"$surname\".";
}
```

The first `if ... else ...` statement tests whether `$_GET["surname"]` is empty. If it is, it generates the usual message. If not, it then strips out leading and trailing spaces and tests whether *that* string is empty.

Even this code is not ideal. There are two different points at which it has been ascertained that the user entered a blank surname, so the same message is generated in two different places. Some PHP developers would prefer to ignore PHP notices, and use the simpler code above. It is possible to instruct the PHP application server to do just this, so no notices are written to the error log, only more serious errors. See PHP Documentation Group (2005) for details.

The PHP application server does not write an error message to the log when it encounters the code `empty($_GET["surname"])`. As the purpose of the `empty()` function is to test whether a variable has a value or not, it is unnecessary to generate an error message for those variables that don't. The function will tell the application developer this directly, by returning the value `FALSE`.

Testing whether a string is or is not empty is very common. Another common test is whether or not the user entered numeric data into a text box. For example, at the Pennine University, staff use a web database application to record the marks awarded to students for assignments. Figure 4.9 shows the HTML form that gathers marks for an individual student. Notice that each assignment has a maximum mark. In the example shown, the assignment is marked out of 80 rather than 100. This means that the PHP script should convert the mark into a percentage before saving it in the database.

All data sent from an HTML form, whether it is sent using the HTTP GET or POST method, arrives as a string. Thus, the mark awarded to Emma Kirkby arrives as the string value `"62"`, not as a numeric value `62`. As it is a string that represents a numeric literal, PHP can recognize it and change the type of the variable when it's used in a calculation. Assume that the text box is named 'mark' and form data is passed using the GET method. Also assume that the PHP script has a local variable `$maxMark` that stores the maximum mark for this assignment. The following code calculates the percentage mark awarded for the assignment:

```php
$mark = ($_GET["mark"]/$maxMark)*100;
```

Figure 4.9 The HTML form used to enter a student's mark into the assessment system.

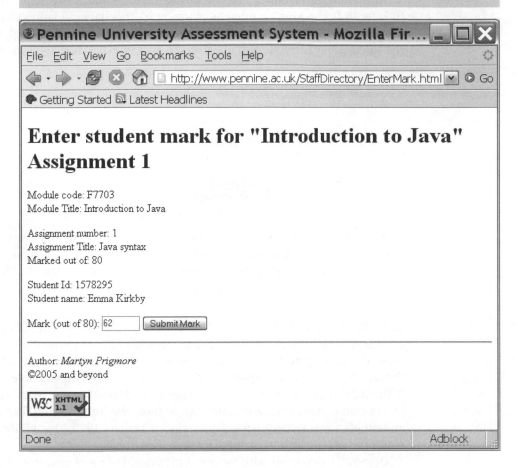

When the PHP application server encounters this code, it automatically converts the string value of $_GET["mark"] to a numeric data type and calculates the correct percentage.

Rather than rely on PHP's automatic type conversion, the following code explicitly changes the type of the string value of $_GET["mark"] to a floating point number (to allow for marks such as 43.5) before doing the calculation:

```
$mark = (float)$_GET["mark"];
$mark = ($mark/$maxMark)*100;
```

The second assignment statement illustrates a common feature of computer languages – a variable can appear on both sides of an assignment. This line says 'Make the new value of $mark equal to the old value of $mark divided by the value of $maxMark then multiplied by 100'. The (float) syntax in the first statement instructs the PHP application server to change the data type of the variable to floating point number. Changing the type of a variable is known as **type casting** and may be familiar from other programming languages. The PHP application server can correctly interpret most numeric string literals, but if it does not recognize a string as representing a number, then it casts it to the numeric value 0 (zero).

As there is no guarantee that the user won't enter the string 'Hello' in the text box in Figure 4.9, checking for numeric strings is another data validation issue. The following code checks that a non-empty numeric value has been entered before performing the calculation. The code also illustrates the use of PHP's and Boolean operator:

```php
if ((!empty($_GET["test"])) and
(is_numeric($_GET["test"])))
{
  $mark = (float)$_GET["test"];
  $mark = ($mark/$maxMark)*100;
}
else
  echo "\nYou did not enter a number.";
```

> PHP includes two Boolean AND operators – and and &&. They behave alike, except in terms of operator precedence. See PHP Documentation Group (2005) for details.

Date literals entered by the user should also be validated before being used. Unlike most data languages, programming languages like PHP don't usually include a date or time data type. Instead, PHP stores combined datetime values as an integer – that is, the number of seconds elapsed since 1 January 1970. So, for example, '16 November 2005, 2:24:57 pm' is stored as the integer 1132151097 because at this date and time one billion one hundred and thirty two million one hundred and fifty one thousand and ninety seven seconds have elapsed since 1 January 1970. Thankfully, PHP provides a number of functions to manipulate such date literals.

Data validation deals with innocent mistakes. Data gathered from the user is validated to see whether or not it is the sort of data expected and, if it is not, a suitable message is generated. Data cleansing deals with potential attempts to hack the application. All data gathered from users are stripped of any potentially harmful text. Only when potentially harmful text has been removed is the data validated and any further processing carried out.

As shown in Figure 4.5 (b), HTML tags in data gathered from users can cause problems for web database applications. PHP includes the strip_tags() function to remove HTML tags from a string:

```php
string strip_tags (string str [, string allowable_tags])
```

The basic strip_tags() function accepts a single string parameter and returns a copy of that string, but with any HTML or PHP tags removed. For example:

```php
echo strip_tags("<strong>bold</strong>");
//Generates the text "bold"
echo strip_tags("<?php echo 'Ha'; ?>");
//Generates an empty string
```

Occasionally, an application needs to allow users to enter a limited set of HTML tags. The optional second parameter is a string listing those start tags that are allowed (the corresponding end tag is obviously allowed whenever the start tag is). Again, an example will help:

```
echo strip_tags("<strong><em>bold</em></strong>",
"<strong>");
//Generates the text "<strong>bold</strong>"
echo strip_tags("<?php echo '<strong>Ha</strong>'; ?>",
"<strong>");
//Generates an empty string
```

In the first statement, only the HTML <strong> tags are allowed, so the <em> tags are removed. In the second statement, the <strong> tag is removed because it appears inside a <?php ... ?> tag, which is not allowed. When a tag is removed, everything between the < and >, which delimit the start and end of the tag, is removed. For a special PHP tag, that means everything is removed.

A related problem occurs with characters that have a special meaning in HTML or cannot easily be typed using a standard keyboard. The HTML mark-up language includes **HTML character entities** to represent such characters within an HTML document.

One hard-to-type character is the copyright symbol – © – which has the HTML character entity ©. This is used in the page footer of the HTML and PHP scripts in this chapter (see, for example, Figure 4.2, line 19).

Special characters include the < character. A web browser will interpret the < character as the start of an HTML tag. If the < character needs to be used on a web page – for example, to show a mathematical expression – it must be written as the HTML character entity <.

Table 4.1 lists the four commonest HTML character entities. When data gathered from users are written into a new HTML document – as the surname is – then any special characters in the users' data should be replaced by the corresponding HTML character entity.

The PHP function htmlspecialchars() replaces any occurrence of these four characters in the parameter str with its equivalent HTML character entity:

```
string htmlspecialchars (string str [, int quote_style
[, string charset]])
```

See the PHP manual (PHP Documentation Group, 2005) for details of the optional parameters.

Table 4.1 Common HTML character entities

Character	HTML character entity
<	&lt;
>	&gt;
&	&amp;
"	&quot;

An HTML character entity is nothing to do with an HTTP entity body, which is the part of an HTTP message that carries data between the client and server. The word 'entity' is used to represent two quite different concepts.

Figure 4.10 shows the first half of SurnameStub.php Version 0.3, which adds data cleansing functionality to the script. The script declares a **user-defined function** cleanse_data(). A user-defined function works in just the same way as a PHP function – it accepts a list of parameters and returns a single value. The user-defined function cleanse_data() expects a single string parameter and returns a copy of that string with special characters replaced by their HTML character entities and all HTML and PHP tags removed. Using the same style as the PHP manual, the description of cleanse_data() is:

string **cleanse_data**(string *value*)

Line 23 in Figure 4.10 shows how to declare a user-defined function in PHP. The keyword 'function' is followed by the name of the function and a list of parameters in

Figure 4.10 Data cleansing with a PHP user-defined function.

```php
1  <?php
2  /*-- Begin script file header
3   -- ***********************************************************************
4   -- Title    Staff search
5   -- Comment  Accepts search criteria from users, and delivers a list
6   --          of staff whose details match the search criteria.
7   --
8   -- Version Date       Author          Comment
9   -- 0.1     2005-11-05 M. Prigmore      STUB PROGRAM
10  --                                     accepts user data and generates
11  --                                     an appropriate message
12  -- 0.2     2005-11-05 M. Prigmore      Adds basic data validation
13  -- 0.3     2005-11-05 M. Prigmore      Adds data cleansing
14  --
15  -- Parameters:
16  -- Script expects the following GET and POST parameters:
17  --
18  -- ParameterName    Method  Description
19  -- surname          GET     A character string; the surname to search for
20  -- ***********************************************************************
21  -- End script file header */
22
23  function cleanse_data($value)
24  {
25   /*-- Begin function header
26    -- ***********************************************************************
27    -- Comment Removes HTML tags from the string $value, and replaces special HTML
28    --         characters with their equivalent HTML entity; e.g. "<" becomes "&lt;"
29    -- Version Date       Author          Comment
30    -- 0.1     2005-11-05 M. Prigmore      First draft
31    -- ***********************************************************************
32    -- End function header */
33   if (empty($value))
34     return "";
35   else
36     return htmlspecialchars(strip_tags($value));
37  }
38
39  ?>
```

parentheses – '(...).' Each parameter is represented by a PHP variable. As PHP variables can take any data type, there is no way to specify which data type the function should expect. The function description above does include a data type for the parameters, but this is purely for information and not part of the syntax for declaring a function in PHP. The same goes for the data type of the function's return value – this is included in a function description, but is not part of the syntax for declaring a function in PHP.

The body of the function begins with the { in line 24 and ends with the matching } in line 37. The first thing in the function body is a comment. Like the script file header, the function header is there to help the application developer understand what the function does. The PHP application server ignores it.

The first thing the function does is use an if ... else ... statement to check if there is anything to do (line 33). If the parameter value is empty, then there cannot be any HTML tags or special characters. In this case, the return statement in line 34 sets the function's return value to the empty string and terminates the function. If $value is not empty, the return statement in line 36 is executed. This also sets the function's return value and exits the function. The return value it sets is a little more complex, as it involves two PHP functions:

```
return htmlspecialchars(strip_tags($value));
```

This statement says 'Pass the value of the variable $value to the PHP function strip_tags(). Pass the value returned by strip_tags() to the PHP function htmlspecialchars(). Finally, set the return value of cleanse_data() to the value returned by htmlspecialchars()' This single line is equivalent to the three PHP statements:

```
$strip = strip_tags($value);
$replaceEntities = htmlspecialchars($strip);
return $replaceEntities;
```

Note that a 'return' statement terminates the function. No code after a 'return' statement will ever be executed.

Line 55 of Figure 4.11 shows how to use the user-defined function cleanse_data() in the main body of the PHP script. Notice that the value passed to cleanse_data() has already been tested to see if it is empty. This seems to make the test in line 33 of Figure 4.10 redundant. However, a function can be used many times in a single script so there is no guarantee that every value passed to it will have been tested in this way. The function should be written to cope with anything (well, almost anything).

The cleanse_data() function will be needed in every script that handles data gathered from users. As it stands, it is only available in the script SearchStub.php. This is because user-defined functions have local scope (they can only be used in the script where they are declared). One solution is to declare the function separately at the start of every script, but that is not very sensible. If the function must change – and most functions are modified at some point – then every copy of the function, in every script, must be changed individually.

A better solution is to use an **include file**. Include files are simply PHP scripts that store useful code and can be included automatically in other scripts. Often they are used to store utility functions. These are useful, general-purpose functions that will be

Figure 4.11 Using the `cleanse_data()` function.

```
40 <!DOCTYPE html PUBLIC "-//W3C//DTD XHTML 1.1//EN"
41    "http://www.w3.org/TR/xhtml11/DTD/xhtml11.dtd">
42 <html>
43 <head>
44   <meta http-equiv="Content-Type" content="text/html; charset=utf-8" />
45   <title>Surname search stub program</title>
46 </head>
47 <body>
48 <h1>Data passed to stub program</h1>
49 <?php
50   echo "\n<p>";
51   if (empty($_GET["surname"]))
52     echo "\nYou did not enter a surname.";
53   else
54   {
55     $surname = cleanse_data($_GET["surname"]);
56     echo "\nYou entered the surname \"$surname\".";
57   }
58   echo "\n</p>";
59 ?>
60
61 <hr />
62 <p>Author: <cite>Martyn Prigmore</cite>
63 <br />&copy;2005 and beyond
64 </p>
65 </body>
66 </html>
```

Figure 4.12 A PHP include file.

```
1 <?php
2 /*-- Begin script file header
3  -- ********************************************************************
4  -- Title    Include file - Data cleansing utilities
5  -- Comment Functions to cleanse user data before processing
6  --
7  -- Version Date        Author         Comment
8  -- 0.1     2005-11-16  M. Prigmore    First draft.
9  --
10  -- ********************************************************************
11  -- End script file header */
12
13 function cleanse_data($value)
14 {
15   /*-- Begin function header
16    -- ******************************************************************
17    -- Comment Removes HTML tags from the string $value, and replaces special HTML
18    --          characters with their equivalent HTML entity; e.g. "<" becomes "&lt;"
19    -- Version Date        Author         Comment
20    -- 0.1     2005-11-05  M. Prigmore    First draft
21    -- ******************************************************************
22    -- End function header */
23   if (empty($value))
24     return "";
25   else
26     return htmlspecialchars(strip_tags($value));
27 }
28 ?>
```

used in lots of different scripts. If a function will only ever be used in one script, then it should be declared as a local function in that script. Include files are also used to store web page header and footer sections as these, too, may need to change and it is simpler if they are stored in a single file.

Figure 4.12 shows the PHP include file DataCleansing.inc. The '.inc' file name extension is usually used to indicate an include file. Notice that all the content of the file is enclosed in a single PHP tag. This is because the PHP application server assumes that the include file contains HTML. Without the PHP tag, it would simply write the contents of the include file directly to the HTTP response. With the PHP tag, it knows that they should be processed as PHP. An include file can have HTML mark-up, just like an ordinary PHP script, though an include file that stores utility functions tends not to. The actual function declaration is exactly the same as in Figure 4.10.

Line 24 of Figure 4.13 shows how to include the content of DataCleansing.inc in the script file SurnameStub.php. You should always enclose the file name in quotes. The `include` statement works by copying the included file, DataCleansing.inc, into the script SurnameStub.php at line 24. It is important, when using include files, to avoid declaring a function twice. In PHP5, doing so will cause a fatal error.

Figure 4.13 Using PHP include files.

```php
1  <?php
2  /*-- Begin script file header
3  -- *******************************************************************
4  -- Title   Staff search
5  -- Comment Accepts search criteria from users, and delivers a list
6  --         of staff whose details match the search criteria.
7  --
8  -- Version Date         Author         Comment
9  -- 0.1     2005-11-05   M. Prigmore    STUB PROGRAM
10 --                                     accepts user data and generates
11 --                                     an appropriate message
12 -- 0.2     2005-11-05   M. Prigmore    Adds basic data validation
13 -- 0.3     2005-11-05   M. Prigmore    Adds data cleansing
14 -- 0.4     2005-11-16   M. Prigmore    Put data cleansing function into an include file
15 --
16 -- Parameters:
17 -- Script expects the following GET and POST parameters:
18 --
19 -- ParameterName   Method  Description
20 -- surname         GET     A character string; the surname to search for
21 -- *******************************************************************
22 -- End script file header */
23
24 include 'DataCleansing.inc'; //Functions to cleanse user data before processing
25
26 ?>
27 <!DOCTYPE html PUBLIC "-//W3C//DTD XHTML 1.1//EN"
28    "http://www.w3.org/TR/xhtml11/DTD/xhtml11.dtd">
29 <html>
30 <head>
31   <meta http-equiv="Content-Type" content="text/html; charset=utf-8" />
32   <title>Surname search stub program</title>
33 </head>
34 <body>
35 <h1>Data passed to stub program</h1>
36 <?php
37   echo "\n<p>";
38   if (empty($_GET["surname"]))
39     echo "\nYou did not enter a surname.";
40   else
41   {
42     $surname = cleanse_data($_GET["surname"]);
43     echo "\nYou entered the surname \"$surname\".";
44   }
45   echo "\n</p>";
46 ?>
47
48 <hr />
49 <p>Author: <cite>Martyn Prigmore</cite>
50 <br />&copy;2005 and beyond
51 </p>
52 </body>
53 </html>
```

4.4   PHP and the MySQL DBMS

PHP provides a range of facilities to allow web database developers to retrieve data from a database and merge this dynamic content with static content on a web page. Figure 4.14 shows the architecture of a typical web database application. There are three tiers. The first tier is the web client, typically a web browser. The middle tier is the web server, which receives HTTP requests for web resources from the web client and generates an HTTP response. The third tier is the database server, which receives requests for data from the web server and provides that data. It includes the actual database (where the data are stored) and the DBMS, which manages all access to the database. The web server manages these two channels of communication with different components. The HTTP server manages communication with the web client using HTTP. The application server manages communication with the database server via the DBMS API (see Chapter 2). These two components of the web server work together to create the HTTP response.

4.4.1   Querying the database instance

Version 0.4 of the SurnameStub.php script (Figure 4.13) forms a basis for a PHP script that actually queries the Staff Directory database and displays a list of those staff whose surnames match the text gathered from the user.

The only significant change that needs to be made is at line 43. Rather than echo back the text gathered from the user, it should be used to query the database. Figure 4.15 shows version 1.0 of the SurnameSearch.php script – the first attempt at implementing the database search. Note the cosmetic changes to the `title` and `h1` elements in the static HTML when compared to version 0.4 of SurnameStub.php in Figure 4.13. Otherwise, the only change is to the code block following the else statement, which now runs from line 41 to 57.

> The data validation in this version of the PHP script deals with the situation where – users submit the data without entering anything, but not where they type a string of spaces.

Figure 4.14 A three-tier web database application.

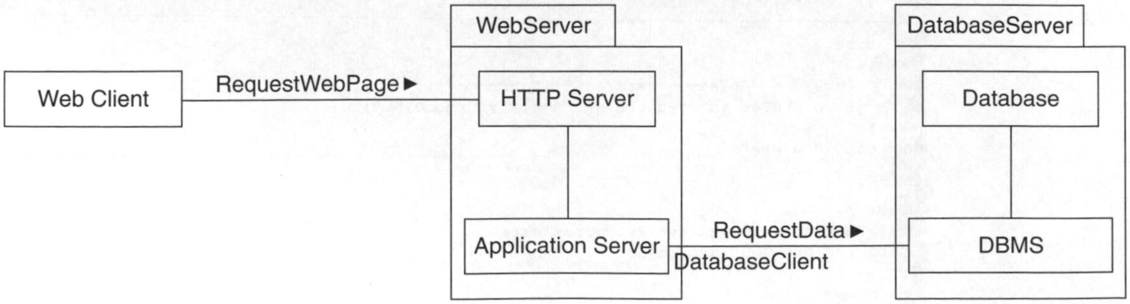

Figure 4.15 Version 1.0 of SurnameSearch.php: querying a database and displaying the result.

```
23    -- End script file header */
24
25  include 'DataCleansing.inc';  //Functions to cleanse user data before processing
26
27  ?>
28  <!DOCTYPE html PUBLIC "-//W3C//DTD XHTML 1.1//EN"
29      "http://www.w3.org/TR/xhtml11/DTD/xhtml11.dtd">
30  <html>
31  <head>
32    <meta http-equiv="Content-Type" content="text/html; charset=utf-8" />
33    <title>Surname search</title>
34  </head>
35  <body>
36  <h1>Search results</h1>
37  <?php
38    echo "\n<p>";
39    if (empty($_GET["surname"]))
40      echo "\nYou did not enter a surname.";
41    else
42    {
43      $surname = cleanse_data($_GET["surname"]);
44      //STEP 1 connect to the DBMS
45      $connection = mysql_connect('localhost', 'martyn', 'martynpassword');
46      //STEP 2 specify which database to use
47      mysql_select_db('StaffDirectory', $connection);
48      //STEP 3 Query the database
49      $result = mysql_query("SELECT fName, lName, email FROM Staff WHERE lName = '$surname'", $connection);
50      //STEP 4 Fetch the rows
51      $row = mysql_fetch_array($result, MYSQL_ASSOC);
52      //STEP 5 Display the data from the row
53      foreach($row as $key => $value)
54        echo $key, ": ", $value, ", ";
55      //STEP 6 Close the connection
56      mysql_close($connection);
57    }
58    echo "\n</p>";
59  ?>
60
61  <hr />
62  <p>Author: <cite>Martyn Prigmore</cite>
63  <br />&copy;2005 and beyond
64  </p>
65  </body>
66  </html>
```

There are six steps to querying a database from a PHP script:

1 open a connection to the DBMS

2 specify which database to use

3 pass a database query to the DBMS and capture the result set

4 fetch the rows from the result set for processing

5 for each row, display the data retrieved

6 close the connection to the DBMS.

The code in Figure 4.15 illustrates each of these these six steps.

Line 45 establishes a connection to the MySQL DBMS, using the PHP function `mysql_connect()`. The function description is:

```
resource mysql_connect([string server[, string userName
[, string password]]])
```

The mysql_connect() function accepts three optional parameters. The *server* parameter identifies the network location of the MySQL DBMS. This can be an IP address or domain name. In line 45, the *server* parameter has the value 'localhost', which means that the MySQL server is installed on the same computer as the PHP application server. The *userName* parameter tells the MySQL DBMS which user is requesting a connection, while the *password* parameter authenticates that user. It is possible for a web database application to gather a MySQL user name and password from the end user and use this to connect to the DBMS. It is more common to create a MySQL user specifically for web applications and connect to the MySQL DBMS from PHP scripts using this general user. The 'guest' user is such a user.

The mysql_connect() function returns a connection to the MySQL DBMS. To the PHP application server, a database connection is an externally defined **resource** used by the script, not something PHP itself creates or manages. Whenever the script needs to communicate with the MySQL DBMS it will need to use this external resource. The script stores a reference to this resource in a variable. In line 45, a reference to the connection to the MySQL DBMS is stored in a variable called $connection. Sometimes it's useful to have more than one connection open at a time – to copy data between databases on different servers, for example. In this situation, make sure you give the two variables different names.

> PHP can connect to other DBMS, either directly or using ODBC. See the PHP user manual (PHP Documentation Group, 2005).
>
> It's important to recognize that the $connection variable holds a *reference* to an external resource, rather than the actual resource itself. However, it is often clearer to speak as if $connection holds the actual connection.

One MySQL DBMS can manage several different databases. Each connection can be associated with a particular database so that any queries sent to the MySQL DBMS over that connection will be run against the chosen database. The PHP function mysql_select_db() associates a database with a connection. The description is:

```
bool mysql_select_db (string databaseName
[, resource connection])
```

The first parameter is mandatory and names a MySQL database. If the MySQL DBMS doesn't recognize the name, then the function returns the value FALSE, but otherwise it returns TRUE. The second parameter is the connection to the MySQL DBMS, passed using the variable $connection. If this is omitted, then the PHP application server uses the *most recent* connection made. Line 47 shows this function in use. Notice that there is no attempt to capture or test the return value. Even if the database name is wrong, the script will continue to the next step. This is an obvious weakness and so will be remedied in the next script.

Now that a database is associated with the connection to the DBMS, the script can query this database. A database query is simply an instruction to the DBMS to retrieve certain data from the database. Any such instruction must be made using the DBMS data language. For the MySQL DBMS, this data language is SQL. The PHP function mysql_query() instructs the PHP application server to pass an SQL statement to the

MySQL DBMS. The MySQL DBMS executes the SQL statement and passes the result back to the PHP application server. This result is a derived table called the **result set** – in effect, it is a set of rows. The result set is another external resource. The `mysql_query()` function returns a reference to this resource. The function description is:

```
resource mysql_query (string sqlStatement
[, resource connection])
```

Line 49 shows how to use this function. The first parameter is a string literal, defining the SQL statement to pass to the MySQL DBMS. The second parameter to the function is the connection to the MySQL DBMS established in line 45. The variable `$result` will hold (a reference to) the result set returned by the DBMS.

The actual SQL statement needs to be explained. The first part is the **select list**:

```
SELECT fName, lName, email
```

This tells the DBMS to retrieve the values of the columns `fName`, `lName` and `email`, but not the values of any other columns. The **from clause**:

```
FROM Staff
```

indicates that these columns come from the `Staff` table. The last part is the **where clause**. The where clause specifies a condition on the data retrieval operation. Without a where clause, the DBMS will retrieve the values of the columns in the select list for every row of the `Staff` table. The where clause instructs it to retrieve the values of the columns in the select list, but only for those rows where the condition is `TRUE`. The where clause in line 49 is:

```
WHERE lName = '$surname'
```

This restricts the result to those rows of the `Staff` table where the value of the `lName` column is exactly the same as the string literal `'$surname'`. Of course, the PHP application server will automatically replace the variable name `$surname` with its value before it passes the string literal to the MySQL DBMS. For example, if the value of `$surname` is Smith, then:

```
"SELECT fName, lName, email
FROM Staff
WHERE lName = '$surname'"
```

becomes:

```
"SELECT fName, lName, email
FROM Staff
WHERE lName = 'Smith'"
```

This is the SQL select statement sent to the MySQL DBMS. Notice the use of *single quotes* around the SQL string literal, 'Smith'. SQL does not allow you to use double quotes to delimit a string literal. Chapters 5 and 6 look in detail at the SQL data manipulation language and the SQL `SELECT` statement in particular. Note that column *values* in SQL are case-sensitive, so the two statements:

```
"SELECT fName, lName, email
FROM Staff
WHERE lName = 'Smith'"
```

```
"SELECT fName, lName, email
FROM Staff
WHERE lName = 'SMITH'"
```

will return different result sets.

> Although the ISO SQL:2003 standard states that SQL is case-sensitive, with respect to column values, a DBMS may allow the DBA to alter this behaviour. For some databases SQL may treat 'Smith' and 'SMITH' as identical values.

As the result set returned by the mysql_query() function in line 49 is another external resource it can't be manipulated directly by PHP. To use the data from the result set it must be fetched, one row at a time, into a PHP array. The PHP function mysql_fetch_array() in line 51 does just this. The function description is:

array **mysql_fetch_array** (resource *result*
[, int *result_type*])

Notice that mysql_fetch_array() does not need the connection variable. This is because the result set has already been passed from the DBMS to the PHP application server. It is an external resource, but directly available to the PHP application server. The second, optional, parameter specifies what sort of array to return. In line 51, the PHP constant MYSQL_ASSOC tells the function to return an associative array. This associative array is stored in the variable $row. Notice that, in this case, $row really does hold a PHP array and can be manipulated directly by PHP statements. The keys are the column names from the query's select-list and the values are the column values. This makes it very easy to work with result sets as the column names can often be used as labels for their values.

It's important to realize that mysql_fetch_array() only fetches one row at a time. In line 51, it will fetch the *first* row from the result set. The data in this row needs to be displayed to the end user, so must be written to the HTTP response. This means writing out the key and value of each element of the array $row.

The simplest way to do this is with a PHP foreach statement, as shown on lines 53 and 54. A foreach statement loops through the elements of an array, from start to finish, and executes the code block once for each element. The syntax is explained in Figure 4.16. The keyword foreach begins the statement and is followed by a list of parameters in parentheses. The array to loop through comes first (typically stored in a

Figure 4.16 The PHP foreach statement.

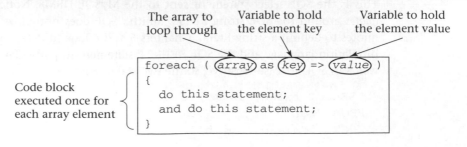

Figure 4.17 The web page generated by Version 1.0 of SurnameSearch.php.

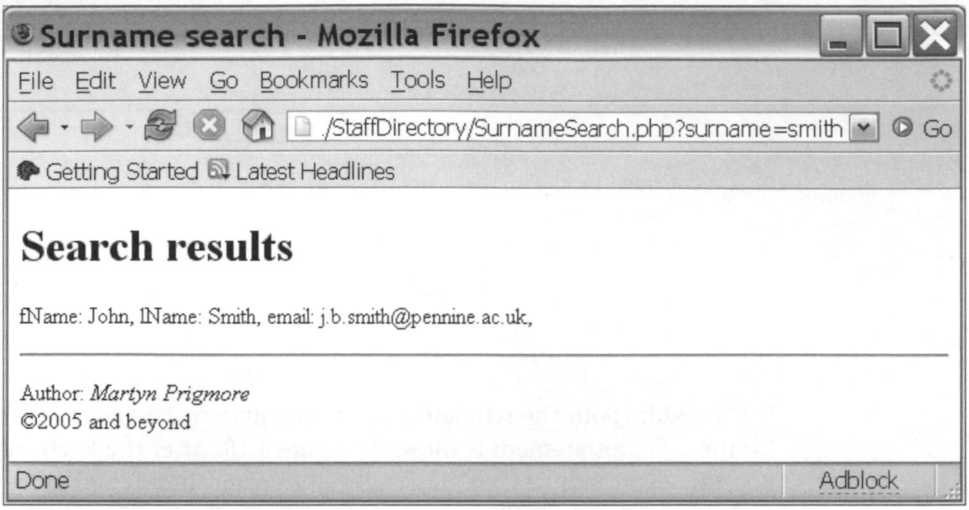

variable, but this could be a function call that returns an array). The keyword `as` comes next, then a variable that will hold the key for the current element. The symbol `=>` comes next and it is followed by a variable that holds the value of the current element. These two variables can be used inside the code block, but nowhere else – their scope is local to the `foreach` statement.

The code block of the `foreach` statement, in line 54, is a single `echo` statement, so does not need to be enclosed in braces. It simply writes the key and value for the current element, separated by a colon and space. The web page generated by this script is shown in Figure 4.17. Only one row of data is displayed because only the first row was fetched from the result set. If there is more than one row, then the script should make further calls to `mysql_fetch_array()`.

The final step in querying a database is to close the connection to the DBMS once all processing has been completed. This is done in line 56, using the PHP function `mysql_close()`. In fact, the connection could have been closed in line 50 as, once the query has been run, there is no further communication with the DBMS. Whether to close a connection as soon as possible or at the end of the script is largely a matter of personal preference. However, if the script is likely to take a long time to run, with no further DBMS communications, then it makes sense to close the connection as this frees resources on the database server.

Version 1.0 of the PHP script SurnameSearch.php illustrates all six steps involved in querying a database from a server-side web script. The main problem with this first attempt is that it only ever displays data from the first row of the result set. This isn't really satisfactory as users will want to see *all* matching rows of data. A fully working script must loop through all the rows of a result set, fetching one row at a time into an array. It can then use the `foreach` statement to loop through the data in this array and display one element at a time.

Figure 4.18 The PHP `while` statement.

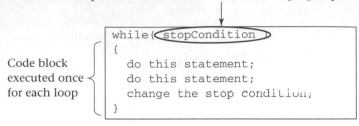

A Boolean expression tested before each loop through the code block.
When the expression evaluates to FALSE, the looping stops.

```
while(stopCondition)
{
    do this statement;
    do this statement;
    change the stop condition;
}
```

Code block
executed once
for each loop

PHP provides both the standard loop statements `while` and `for`. The standard form
for the `while` statement is shown in Figure 4.18. After the keyword `while` comes a
Boolean expression `stopCondition` (in parentheses). Provided this expression
evaluates to `TRUE`, PHP executes the statements in the code block (enclosed in curly
brackets). It then checks the value of `stopCondition` again and, if it is still `TRUE`,
executes the code block for a second time. PHP continues to loop through this process
until `stopCondition` evaluates to `FALSE`. At this point, it skips past the code
block to the next line of code. Because PHP executes a `while` statement over and
over again until the value of the Boolean expression `stopCondition` becomes
false, at least one of the statements in the code block should affect the value of
`stopCondition`. Otherwise, the script will get stuck in an infinite loop. In this
case, the PHP application server eventually decides that the loop has gone on too
long, and terminates the script with a fatal error.

Version 1.1 of SurnameSearch.php (Figure 4.19) demonstrates how to use the PHP
`while` statement to loop through the rows of an SQL result set. In line 53 the first
row is fetched from the result set. The `while` statement starts in line 54 with the
keyword `while` followed by the stop condition `$row <> FALSE`. This expression
uses the not-equal-to comparison operator `<>` and is true when the value of `$row` is
not the Boolean value `FALSE`. This test seems a bit odd as `$row` ought to contain
the first row fetched from the result set (in line 53). However, if there is no row to
fetch, then the PHP function `mysql_fetch_array()` actually returns the
Boolean value `FALSE`. So, if the result set is empty, `$row` equals `FALSE` and the
stop condition evaluates to `FALSE`. This means that the code block of the `while`
statement is never executed. If there *is* a row to fetch from the result set, then, in
line 54, the value of `$row` will be an array. This is definitely *not* equal to the
Boolean value `FALSE`, so the code block of the `while` statement is executed. This
code block displays the data held in the array (lines 57 and 58), then calls the PHP
function `mysql_fetch_array()` again (line 60). This fetches the *second* row
from the result set, changing the value of `$row`. It is this statement that ensures the
`while` statement will eventually terminate as, once all the rows have been fetched
from the result set (and their data displayed), `$row` will be `FALSE`. The `echo` statement in line 59 ensures that, in the generated web page, the data for each row of the
result set appears on a separate line (Figure 4.20).

Figure 4.19 Version 1.1 of SurnameSearch.php: using the PHP `while` statement to loop through an SQL result set.

```
30 <!DOCTYPE html PUBLIC "-//W3C//DTD XHTML 1.1//EN"
31    "http://www.w3.org/TR/xhtml11/DTD/xhtml11.dtd">
32 <html>
33 <head>
34   <meta http-equiv="Content-Type" content="text/html; charset=utf-8" />
35   <title>Surname search</title>
36 </head>
37 <body>
38 <h1>Search results</h1>
39 <?php
40   echo "\n<p>";
41   if (empty($_GET["surname"]))
42     echo "\nYou did not enter a surname.";
43   else
44   {
45     $surname = cleanse_data($_GET["surname"]);
46     //STEP 1 connect to the DBMS
47     $connection = mysql_connect('localhost', 'martyn', 'martynpassword');
48     //STEP 2 specify which database to use
49     mysql_select_db('StaffDirectory', $connection);
50     //STEP 3 Query the database
51     $result = mysql_query("SELECT fName, lName, email FROM Staff WHERE lName = '$surname'", $connection);
52     //STEP 4 Fetch the rows
53     $row = mysql_fetch_array($result, MYSQL_ASSOC);
54     while ($row <> FALSE)
55     {
56     //STEP 5 Display the data from the row
57       foreach($row as $key => $value)
58         echo $key, ": ", $value, ", ";
59       echo "<br />";
60       $row = mysql_fetch_array($result, MYSQL_ASSOC);
61     }
62     //STEP 6 Close the connection
63     mysql_close($connection);
64   }
65   echo "\n</p>";
66 ?>
67
68 <hr />
69 <p>Author: <cite>Martyn Prigmore</cite>
70 <br />&copy;2005 and beyond
71 </p>
72 </body>
73 </html>
```

Using a PHP `while` statement to loop through an SQL result set always follows this pattern:

1 fetch the first row from the result set into a variable
2 while this variable actually holds a row of data:
    (a) display the data
    (b) fetch the next row from the result set.

Fetching the first row *before* beginning the `while` statement ensures that, if there are no rows in the result set, the code block of the `while` statement is never executed.

The `for` statement offers an alternative for those who don't like the `while` statement. A `for` statement is designed to execute a block of code a fixed number of times, then stop. This contrasts with the `while` statement, which can get into an infinite

169

Figure 4.20 The web page generated by Version 1.1 of SurnameSearch.php

Figure 4.21 The PHP `for` statement.

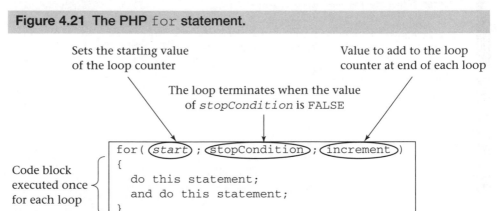

loop. The general format is shown in Figure 4.21. The keyword `for` is followed by three expressions, in parentheses. The first declares a loop counter, which is a variable that indicates the number of times the code block has been executed. The second indicates when to stop – typically, this states that the loop counter must be less than a fixed value. The third indicates how much to increase the loop counter by when the code block has been executed, which usually is 1.

An example of how to use the `for` statement to loop through an SQL result set is shown in Figure 4.22. Using a `for` statement, there is no need to fetch the first row from the result set to check that there are some rows in there. Instead, in line 53, the PHP function `mysql_num_rows()` is used to find out how many rows there are in the result set. The function description is:

```
int mysql_num_rows (resource result)
```

Figure 4.22 Version 1.2 of SurnameSearch.php using the PHP `for` statement to loop through an SQL result set.

```
31 <!DOCTYPE html PUBLIC "-//W3C//DTD XHTML 1.1//EN"
32    "http://www.w3.org/TR/xhtml11/DTD/xhtml11.dtd">
33 <html>
34 <head>
35   <meta http-equiv="Content-Type" content="text/html; charset=utf-8" />
36   <title>Surname search</title>
37 </head>
38 <body>
39 <h1>Search results</h1>
40 <?php
41   echo "\n<p>";
42   if (empty($_GET["surname"]))
43     echo "\nYou did not enter a surname.";
44   else
45   {
46     $surname = cleanse_data($_GET["surname"]);
47     //STEP 1 connect to the DBMS
48     $connection = mysql_connect('localhost', 'martyn', 'martynpassword');
49     //STEP 2 specify which database to use
50     mysql_select_db('StaffDirectory', $connection);
51     //STEP 3 Query the database
52     $result = mysql_query("SELECT fName, lName, email FROM Staff WHERE lName = '$surname'", $connection);
53     $numRows = mysql_num_rows($result);
54     //STEP 4 Fetch the rows
55     for ($i=1; $i<=$numRows; $i=$i+1)
56     {
57       $row = mysql_fetch_array($result, MYSQL_ASSOC);
58       //STEP 5 Display the data from the row
59       foreach($row as $key => $value)
60         echo $key, ": ", $value, ", ";
61       echo "<br />";
62     }
63     //STEP 6 Close the connection
64     mysql_close($connection);
65   }
66   echo "\n</p>";
67 ?>
68
69 <hr />
70 <p>Author: <cite>Martyn Prigmore</cite>
71 <br />&copy;2005 and beyond
72 </p>
73 </body>
74 </html>
```

The number of rows in the result set, stored in the variable $numRows, is used to place a limit on the number of times the `for` statement in line 55 loops through its code block. This statement declares a loop counter – the variable $i – and sets its initial value to 1. Before each execution of the code block, the value of $i is compared with the value of the variable $numRows and the code block is executed, provided $i<=$numRows (<= is the PHP less-than-or-equal-to comparison operator). If there are no rows, then $numRows is 0 and, as 1<=0 is false, the code block is never executed. If there are some rows, then the code block is executed once for each of them. After executing each code block, the final expression $i=$i+1 instructs PHP to add 1 to the loop counter $i. If there are four rows in the result set, then the `for` statement will loop through its code block four times. The code block runs from line 56 to 62. In line 57, the PHP function `mysql_fetch_array()` fetches the next row from the result set. The `foreach` statement in lines 59 and 60 displays the data in this row and the `echo`

Figure 4.23 Basic formatting of search results, showing full staff names, e-mail and a hyperlink to their full details.

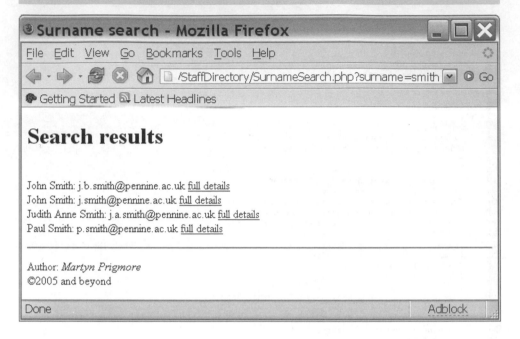

statement in line 61 ensures that the data for different rows appear on separate lines in the generated web page.

There is no noticeable difference in performance between the `while` and `for` statements. Which to use is a matter of personal style. The syntax of the `while` statement is a little simpler, but the first row must be fetched before the loop starts and the stop condition can be difficult to understand. The `for` statement has a more complex syntax and the number of rows in the result set needs to be checked before starting the loop, but it is easy to understand how many times the loop will be executed.

Using a PHP `foreach` statement to display the name and value of each column does not really deliver the data in an effective way. In particular, the point of listing out the names and e-mail addresses is to allow the end user to pick one member of staff and view his or her full contact details. One approach is simply to list the names and e-mail addresses followed by a hyperlink, as shown in Figure 4.23. Compared with the list in Figure 4.20, the latter list is much clearer. Each 'full details' hyperlink points to the URL `StaffDetail.php?staffNo=nnnnn`, where `nnnnn` is the staff number of the member of staff. When the user clicks on a hyperlink, the web browser requests the StaffDetail.php script, passing it the staff number of the member of staff whose details are required. StaffDetail.php can then retrieve that person's full contact details and deliver them as another web page.

The code in SurnameSearch.php can easily be adapted to deliver the data in this more useful format. Figure 4.24 shows the changes to the code for steps 3 and 4. In line 53, the SQL select statement has been altered to retrieve the `staffNo` from the database. In line 60, rather than churn out the column names and values with a

Figure 4.24 Version 1.3 of SurnameSearch.php: using PHP to create a hyperlink.

```
52   //STEP 3 Query the database
53   $result = mysql_query("SELECT staffNo, fName, lName, email FROM Staff WHERE lName = '$surname'", $connection);
54   //STEP 4 Fetch the rows
55   $numRows = mysql_num_rows($result);
56   for ($i=1; $i<=$numRows; $i=$i+1)
57   {
58       $row = mysql_fetch_array($result, MYSQL_ASSOC);
59       //STEP 5 Display the data from the row
60       echo "\n<br />", $row["fName"], " ", $row["lName"], ": ", $row["email"];
61       $url="StaffDetail.php?staffNo=" . rawurlencode($row["staffNo"]);
62       echo " <a href=\"$url\">full details</a>";
63   }
```

foreach loop, the script displays the values of the name and email columns of the current row in a more natural format – full name followed by e-mail address. Line 61 assembles the URL for the 'full details' hyperlink. The URL path is just the name of the PHP script. This is a relative URL, so the web browser will assume that the file StaffDetail.php is located in the same directory as SurnameSearch.php.

The query string is more complex as it needs to include the value of the staffNo column as part of a name-value pair. The value of a name-value pair may include characters that have a special meaning in a URL. For example, the '&' character separates two different name-value pairs in the query string. If the value of a name-value pair includes an '&', then the web browser will get confused. So, for example, the '&' (and the spaces) in the name-value pair:

```
companyName=Shaw & Sons
```

will confuse the web browser. PHP includes the function rawurlencode() to deal with this problem. The function rawurlencode() leaves letters, digits, full stops, hyphens and the underscore character unchanged. It replaces every other character with a percent symbol – % – followed by the hexadecimal number representing the character in the document's character set. Applying rawurlencode() to 'Shaw & Sons' replaces the spaces with the hexadecimal character reference %20 and the ampersand with %26:

```
echo rawurlencode('Shaw & Sons');
// displays Shaw%20%26%20Sons
```

The function rawurlencode() is used in line 61 to encode the value of $row["staffNo"]. Line 62 uses the resulting URL to create an anchor element. Notice that the value of the anchor element's href attribute is enclosed in double quotes as this is required for the HTML to comply with the latest standard. Version 1.3 of SurnameSearch.php generates the web page in Figure 4.23. The HTML source of this web page is shown in Figure 4.25. In this case, the rawurlencode() function has not had any noticeable effect. All the characters in the values of the name-value pairs are digits, so there were no special characters to replace.

> PHP includes two functions to encode parts of a URL that need to be encoded – rawurlencode() and urlencode(). The only difference is that urlencode() replaces each space character with a '+' character instead of its hexadecimal representation.

Figure 4.25 The HTML output by Version 1.3 of SurnameSearch.php, with search criteria 'Smith'.

```
view-source:
File  Edit  View  Help

<!DOCTYPE html PUBLIC "-//W3C//DTD XHTML 1.1//EN"
   "http://www.w3.org/TR/xhtml11/DTD/xhtml11.dtd">
<html>
<head>
  <meta http-equiv="Content-Type" content="text/html; charset=utf-8" />
  <title>Surname search</title>
</head>
<body>
<h1>Search results</h1>

<p>
<br />John Smith: j.b.smith@pennine.ac.uk <a href="StaffDetail.php?staffNo=10780">full details</a>
<br />John Smith: j.smith@pennine.ac.uk <a href="StaffDetail.php?staffNo=25447">full details</a>
<br />Judith Anne Smith: j.a.smith@pennine.ac.uk <a href="StaffDetail.php?staffNo=25448">full
details</a>
<br />Paul Smith: p.smith@pennine.ac.uk <a href="StaffDetail.php?staffNo=31210">full details</a>
</p>
<hr />
<p>Author: <cite>Martyn Prigmore</cite>
<br />&copy;2005 and beyond
</p>
</body>
</html>
```

4.4.2 Handling DBMS communication errors

A significant weakness of all four versions of SurnameSearch.php is that there is no error handling. Whenever a PHP script communicates with a DBMS, there is the potential for errors. These errors are not fatal – the script will continue to run – but no data will be retrieved from the database. When a DBMS communication error occurs, PHP can write a standard error message to a log file or display it to end users. Displaying standard error messages to end users can confuse them as the messages tend to be terse and may be difficult to understand. However, writing standard error messages to a log file may mean that end users are not aware that there was a problem. Neither situation is satisfactory. For this reason, it is worth including some custom error handling whenever a PHP script communicates with a DBMS. Custom error handling simply means writing an `if ... else ...` statement that checks whether or not there was a problem and generates a meaningful error message if there was.

Figure 4.26 shows version 1.4 of the SurnameSearch.php script. This version checks for errors that may have occurred when communicating with the DBMS. If an error has occurred, it generates a custom error message, displayed as part of the web page, and ends execution of the script. If everything went fine, the script generates an HTML comment saying so. The browser won't display HTML comments on the web page, but they are visible when the user views the HTML source for a web page. Generating 'everything is fine' messages isn't strictly necessary and most production systems would not include them, but they are a useful debugging tool.

Figure 4.26 Version 1.4 of SurnameSearch.php – handling DBMS communication errors.

```php
42 <?php
43   echo "\n<p>";
44   if (empty($_GET["surname"]))
45     echo "\nYou did not enter a surname.";
46   else
47   {
48     $surname = cleanse_data($_GET["surname"]);
49     //STEP 1 connect to the DBMS
50     $connection = mysql_connect('localhost', 'martyn', 'martynpassword');
51     //Report any errors that occurred when communicating with the MySQL DBMS
52     if ($connection==FALSE)
53       exit("\nCould not connect to MySQL DBMS. \n<br />MySQL error " . mysql_errno() . " : " . mysql_error());
54     else
55       echo "\n<!-- Notice: Succesfully connected to MySQL DBMS. -->";
56     //STEP 2 specify which database to use
57     $database = mysql_select_db('StaffDirectory', $connection);
58     //Report any errors that occurred when communicating with the MySQL DBMS
59     if ($database == FALSE)
60       exit("Unable to locate the database. \n<br />MySQL error " . mysql_errno() . " : " . mysql_error());
61     else
62       echo "\n<!-- Notice: Using specified database. -->";
63     //STEP 3 Query the database
64     $result = mysql_query("SELECT fName, lName, email FROM Staff WHERE lName = '$surname'", $connection);
65     //Report any errors that occurred when communicating with the MySQL DBMS
66     if ($result == FALSE)
67       exit("SQL statement failed. \n<br />MySQL error " . mysql_errno() . " : " . mysql_error());
68     else
69         echo "\n<!-- Notice: SQL statement worked. -->\n";
70     $numRows = mysql_num_rows($result);
71     //STEP 4 Fetch the rows
72     for ($i=1; $i<=$numRows; $i=$i+1)
73     {
74       $row = mysql_fetch_array($result, MYSQL_ASSOC);
75       //STEP 5 Display the data from the row
76       echo "\n<br />", $row["fName"], " ", $row["lName"], ": ", $row["email"];
77       $url=rawurlencode("StaffDetail.php?staffNo=" . $row["staffNo"]);
78       echo " <a href=\"$url\">full details</a>";
79     }
80     //STEP 6 Close the connection
81     mysql_close($connection);
82   }
83   echo "\n</p>";
84 ?>
```

The first step in communicating with the DBMS is to establish a connection. There are two things that can go wrong when trying to connect to the DBMS. PHP may not be able to find a MySQL DBMS on the given host if either the MySQL DBMS isn't running or the host name is wrong. If the host can be found, then the login details (username or password or both) might be incorrect. In either case, the `mysql_connect()` function in line 50 returns the value FALSE. Line 52 checks if `$connection` is FALSE:

```php
    if ($connection == FALSE)
```

Notice that the equality comparison operator in PHP is two consecutive equals symbols – ==. A single equals symbol is the variable assignment operator. (SQL uses the single equals symbol for *both* these operators, which can be a little confusing.) Using '=' when it should be '==' is another common PHP bug. The assignment operation (`$connection = FALSE`) always evaluates to FALSE, so an if...else... statement using this as its condition will always execute the else code block.

> The equality comparison operator '==' can compare values that have different data types. So, for example, TRUE == 1 is true as PHP regards the numeric value 1 as equivalent to the Boolean value TRUE (in fact, any value other than 0 is equivalent to TRUE; see PHP Documentation Group (2005) for details). PHP includes the special operator '===' to mean 'are equal *and* the same type'. TRUE === 1 is false as the two operands are of different types. This is another situation where PHP's relaxed attitude to data typing means developers must write their code carefully.

When an error occurs, the statement exit() (line 53) ends the script. Although exit() looks like a function, it isn't really; it is part of the core PHP language (like echo, if...else... and so on). It instructs the PHP application server to write a message (the string parameter) to the HTTP response, then end the script gracefully. The PHP application server will not read any more of the script file after executing an exit() statement. The message generated in line 53 begins with the string literal "\nCould not connect to MySQL DBMS. \n
MySQL error". Note that this string literal includes an HTML <br /> element, so the message is formatted nicely on the final web page. Next comes a call to the function mysql_errno(). This function returns the error number associated with the last function to communicate with the MySQL DBMS, which, in this case, is mysql_connect(). This number is concatenated on to the first part of the string. The string literal ': ' is added next, purely to make the final message look better. Finally, the function mysql_error() returns the error message associated with the last error. An example is shown in Figure 4.27. Here, the hostname of the MySQL DBMS is incorrect – 'locahost' instead of 'localhost'. Notice that the page footer is missing from this web page (compare it with Figure 4.20). The HTML for the page footer comes *after* the exit() statement, so, when an error occurs, it is not included in the web page generated by the PHP script. If there were no errors connecting to the MySQL DBMS, then the statement in line 55 would be executed. This simply writes an HTML comment to the generated web page. Strictly speaking, this sort of thing is not necessary, but can be useful during debugging.

Figure 4.27 Reporting an error connecting to the MySQL DBMS.

Surname search - Mozilla Firefox

File Edit View Go Bookmarks Tools Help

http://www.pennine.ac.uk/StaffDirectory/SurnameSearch.php?surname=Smith

Getting Started Latest Headlines

Search results

Could not connect to MySQL DBMS.
MySQL error 2005 : Unknown MySQL server host 'locahost' (11004)

Done   Adblock

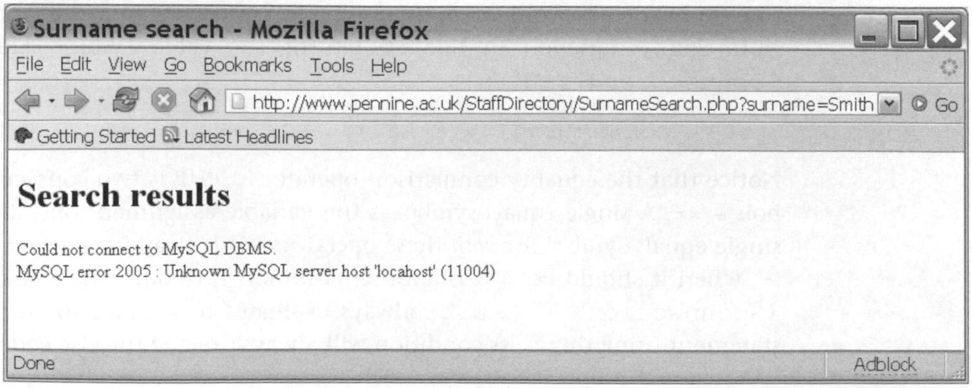

There is always an 'error number' when PHP communicates with the MySQL DBMS. If the communication went smoothly, then the 'error number' would be set to zero (0). Thus, if a call to `mysql_errno()` returns the error number 0, then that means there were no problems communicating with the MySQL DBMS. If your error-handling routines keep reporting an error of 0, then check the `if...else...` condition. You have probably got the logic wrong.

There are three further points where the PHP script in Figure 4.26 communicates with the DBMS. In line 57, the PHP script states which database it wishes to use and, in line 64, it asks the MySQL DBMS to run an SQL select statement for it. At both points, similar error-handling code is included. In line 81, PHP communicates with the MySQL DBMS for the final time as it tells the DBMS that it is closing the connection. There is no error handling at this point. If the connection fails to close, there is nothing the developer can do; the PHP application server will tidy everything up once the script has finished. Even so, it is good practice to close any DBMS connections as soon as they are done with – keeping them open takes up resources and can slow down the database server's response times.

Figure 4.28 shows the HTML generated by a successful execution of the script file shown in Figure 4.26. Notice that the HTML has a line break before each `<br />` tag. This is because there is a `\n` character before the `<br />` in line 76 of Figure 4.26 (the `<br />` only ensures that they are displayed in a separate line on the *web page*). The three HTML comments generated by the debug code are clearly visible. When there is no data, it is clear that the SQL select statement has been executed, but no rows were returned.

Figure 4.28 The HTML generated by a successful call to Version 1.4 of SurnameSearch.php.

```
view-source: -
File  Edit  View  Help

<!DOCTYPE html PUBLIC "-//W3C//DTD XHTML 1.1//EN"
  "http://www.w3.org/TR/xhtml11/DTD/xhtml11.dtd">
<html>
<head>
  <meta http-equiv="Content-Type" content="text/html; charset=utf-8" />
  <title>Surname search</title>
</head>
<body>
<h1>Search results</h1>

<p>
<!-- Notice: Succesfully connected to MySQL DBMS. -->
<!-- Notice: Using specified database. -->
<!-- Notice: SQL statement worked. -->

<br />John Smith: j.b.smith@pennine.ac.uk <a href="StaffDetail.php%3FstaffNo%3D">full details</a>
<br />John Smith: j.smith@pennine.ac.uk <a href="StaffDetail.php%3FstaffNo%3D">full details</a>
<br />Judith Anne Smith: j.a.smith@pennine.ac.uk <a href="StaffDetail.php%3FstaffNo%3D">full details</a>
<br />Paul Smith: p.smith@pennine.ac.uk <a href="StaffDetail.php%3FstaffNo%3D">full details</a>
</p>
<hr />
<p>Author: <cite>Martyn Prigmore</cite>
<br />&copy;2005 and beyond
</p>
</body>
</html>
```

One last point about DBMS communication errors that relates to the `mysql_query()` function. A MySQL DBMS communication error occurs with this function only if the SQL statement is not valid. There are many reasons for an SQL statement not being valid – the keyword SELECT might be spelt wrongly or one of the column names in the select list might not appear on a table in the from clause, for example. Sometimes, the SQL statement is valid, but wrong. For instance, if the variable name `$surname` is spelt wrongly in line 64, the PHP application server will replace it with an empty string rather than the value entered by the user into the search form. The actual SQL statement passed to the MySQL DBMS will be:

```
SELECT fName, lName, email FROM Staff WHERE lName = ''
```

This means that there is no data in the result set. Other similar errors might mean there is more data than expected. To work out what is going on, the developer needs to see the actual SQL statement. In this situation, it is useful to include the actual SQL statement in the debugging message. To do this, replace lines 63–68 with the following:

```
$sqlStatement = "SELECT fName, lName, email
                 FROM Staff
                 WHERE lName = '$surname'"
$result = mysql_query($sqlStatement, $connection);
//Report any errors communicating with the MySQL DBMS
if ($result == FALSE)
  exit("SQL statement failed.
        \n<br />$sqlStatement
        \n<br />MySQL error " . mysql_errno() . " : " .
        mysql_error());
else
  echo "\n<!-- Notice: SQL statement \n$sqlStatement
        \nworked. -->\n";
```

This is much the same, except that it stores the actual SQL select statement in the variable `$sqlStatement`. This is used as a parameter to `mysql_query()` and in the success notice.

4.4.3 Modifying the database instance

Web database applications can modify the database instance, too. The process is similar to that for querying the database, namely, gather data from the end user, typically via an HTML form, and use the `mysql_query()` function to send an SQL insert, update or delete statement to the DBMS. In the simplest scenario, a single HTML form gathers data in order to modify a single table. That is the scenario covered here. Some more complex scenarios are discussed in Chapter 7.

Figures 4.29 (a) and (b) show two web pages involved in adding a new support session to the database. The first page (Figure 4.29 (a)) is a plain HTML form, SupportSessionInsert.html. It gathers the necessary data and submits it for processing to the web script SupportSessionInsert.php. This web script adds a new row to the

Figure 4.29 The Modifying the database instance.

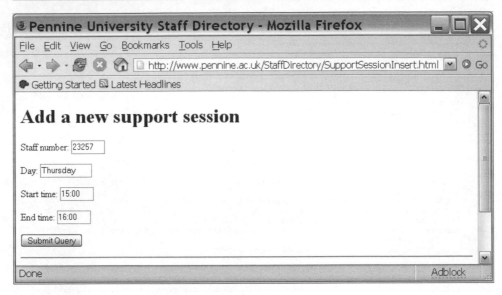

(a) Web page to gather data about a new support.

(b) Web page to display a success message.

`SupportSession` table and, if the modification succeeds, generates the web page shown in Figure 4.29 (b).

The design is a little naïve. For one thing, there is no login procedure, so anyone who knows a valid staff number can add support sessions for that member of staff. This weakness is addressed in Chapter 7, which discusses ways to limit access to web resources by forcing users to log in. Another weakness is the rather clunky visual design, but, as stated earlier, visual design issues aren't addressed in this textbook.

Figure 4.30 Adding a new row to the `SupportSession` table.

```php
35 <?php
36  if (empty($_GET["staffNo"]) or empty($_GET["day"]) or empty($_GET["start"]) or empty($_GET["end"]))
37  {
38    echo "\n<h1>New support session - Error</h1>";
39    echo "\n<p>You did not enter all the required information.
40         Please <a href=\"SupportSessionInsert.html\">try again</a>.</p>";
41  }
42  else
43  {
44    $staffNo = cleanse_data($_GET["staffNo"]);
45    $day = cleanse_data($_GET["day"]);
46    $start = cleanse_data($_GET["start"]);
47    $end = cleanse_data($_GET["end"]);
48    //STEP 1 connect to the DBMS
49    $connection = mysql_connect('localhost', 'martyn', 'martynpassword');
50    //Report any errors that occurred when communicating with the MySQL DBMS
51    if ($connection==FALSE)
52      exit("\nCould not connect to MySQL DBMS. \n<br />MySQL error " . mysql_errno() . " : " . mysql_error());
53    else
54      echo "\n<!-- Notice: Succesfully connected to MySQL DBMS. -->";
55    //STEP 2 specify which database to use
56    $database = mysql_select_db('StaffDirectory', $connection);
57    //Report any errors that occurred when communicating with the MySQL DBMS
58    if ($database == FALSE)
59      exit("Unable to locate the database. \n<br />MySQL error " . mysql_errno() . " : " . mysql_error());
60    else
61      echo "\n<!-- Notice: Using specified database. -->";
62    //STEP 3 Modify the database
63    $sqlStatement = "INSERT INTO SupportSession (staffNo, dayOfWeek, startTime, endTime)
64                 VALUES ('$staffNo', '$day', '$start', '$end')";
65    $result = mysql_query($sqlStatement, $connection);
66    //STEP 4 Confirm successful execution or report any errors that occurred when communicating with the MySQL DBMS
67    if ($result == TRUE)
68    {
69    echo "\n<!-- Notice: SQL statement \n$sqlStatement \nworked. -->\n";
70      echo "\n<h1>New support session added</h1>";
71      echo "\n<p>The following support session data has been successfully added to the database:";
72      echo "\n<br />Staff number: $staffNo";
73      echo "\n<br />Day: $day";
74      echo "\n<br />Start time: $start";
75      echo "\n<br />End time: $end</p>";
76    }
77    else
78      exit("\nSQL statement failed.
79           \n<br />$sqlStatement
80           \n<br />MySQL error " . mysql_errno() . " : " . mysql_error());
81    //STEP 5 Close the connection
82    mysql_close($connection);
83  }
84 ?>
```

Figure 4.30 shows the PHP code from version 0.1 of the SupportSessionInsert.php server-side script. It illustrates the five steps needed to modify the database instance from a PHP script:

1 open a connection to the DBMS

2 specify which database to use

3 pass a database modification statement to the DBMS and capture the result

4 inform the user that the modification succeeded, or display an error message if it failed

5 close the connection to the DBMS.

These are largely the same steps as those used to query the database, though, in this case, there is no need to scroll through the result set. For a data modification statement, the PHP function `mysql_query()` always returns a Boolean value: TRUE if the statement succeeded, and FALSE if it failed.

The structure of SupportSessionInsert.php is similar to that of SurnameSearch.php (Figure 4.26). Line 36 checks that the user has entered some data for each of the text boxes on the form. If any box has not been filled in, then the script displays an error message. Note that the second echo statement is split over two lines (lines 39 and 40). As each PHP statement is terminated by a semicolon, long statements can be split over multiple lines. This can make the code easier to read. Another feature of this echo statement is that it writes an HTML anchor element to the HTTP response:

```
<a href=\"SupportSessionInsert.html\">try again</a>
```

Web applications shouldn't rely on the web browser's back button for navigation, but, rather, include navigation links to allow the end user to complete a particular behaviour successfully. No further data validation is attempted, which is another weakness in the script. It really ought to check that the value of the day column is a day of the week and that the start and end times are valid times. Further data validation is covered in Chapter 7.

Lines 44–82 deal with the situation when the data entered has passed validation. Initially there are no changes from the scripts to query the database. First, the user-defined `cleanse_data()` function deals with any potentially malicious data (lines 44–47), then the script connects to the DBMS and specifies which database to use.

The first significant difference occurs in step 3, in lines 62–65. The SQL statement is not a select statement, but an insert statement, which adds a single row to a table. The insert statement begins with the keywords `INSERT INTO` followed by the name of the table and a list of columns for which data is being supplied. In this case, there is data for *all* the columns of the `SupportSession` table, so all are named. Note that the column names are listed in parentheses. This is a different format from the select statement.

After the list of columns comes the keyword `VALUES` followed by a list of data values (again in parentheses). The DBMS uses the order to determine which data goes in which column – the first data value going in the first named column and so on. As usual, PHP variables hold the actual data values. The variable names in line 64 will be replaced by their values when the script is executed. Notice that within the SQL insert statement all the data values are enclosed in single quotes as the column data type is either `VARCHAR` or `TIME`. If there was some numeric data, then this would not be enclosed in single quotes.

There is another significant change in line 67. Previously, after calling the `mysql_query()` function in SurnameSearch.php (Figure 4.26, line 63), the script used an if statement to check for DBMS communication errors. If there were errors, it exited, but if not, it wrote a debug message as an HTML comment. The script then went on to fetch the data from the result set (step 4, line 70 and so on), but this was not part of the if statement.

SupportSessionInsert.php, also checks for DBMS communication errors. If there are DBMS communication errors, it writes out an error message (the else block), including the actual SQL statement submitted to the DBMS. If there are no DBMS communication errors, the script uses the data to generate a web page confirming the changes that have been made to the database instance (the if block). The difference is subtle, but, in SupportSessionInsert.php, what to do when things go right is included in the if statement after the `mysql_query()` function, along with the error handling. SurnameSearch.php could easily be rewritten with the same structure as SupportSessionInsert.php or vice versa. Line 82 rounds off the PHP code by closing the connection to the DBMS.

The basic structure of SupportSessionInsert.php can be reused to deal with any simple modification to the database instance. The SQL statements required are covered in the next chapter, but the approach is easy to envisage. To modify, for example, an existing row of the `SupportSession` table, simply present the existing data using a form similar to that in Figure 4.29 (a). The end users can then make any changes they want and submit the form data for processing. The only change required to the code in SupportSessionInsert.php is to replace the SQL insert statement (lines 63–64) with an SQL update statement, which changes the values in an existing row. Usually, end users will search for a row to update, by entering a staff number, for example. The application displays a list of matching rows from the `SupportSession` table and users pick one. This is the same process as searching for a member of staff by entering a surname, so, again, there is scope to reuse existing code.

Chapter summary

- This chapter has reviewed the use of HTML forms and discussed how to deal with data sent from an HTML form to a PHP script. While doing this, the basics of the PHP scripting language were introduced and explained. As this is a book about databases, not programming, the code has been kept pretty simple. However, it is robust enough to build many standard web database applications. Later chapters will introduce more sophisticated programming techniques, building on the basics introduced here.

- The main purpose of the chapter has been to explain how a PHP script instructs the PHP application server to communicate with a MySQL DBMS and use the data retrieved to generate an HTTP response message (a web page with dynamic content). It is important to keep the roles of the three players clear:

  1 the PHP script is a set of instructions written by a web application developer

  2 the PHP application server follows these instructions, which may include communicating with a DBMS

  3 the DBMS responds to requests for information from the PHP application server – these requests may ask the DBMS to retrieve data from the database instance or make changes to it.

Further reading

The World Wide Web Consortium (W3C) oversees the HTML standard and related technologies, such as cascading stylesheets (CSS). Its website (www.w3.org) includes the formal standards as well as discussions of current developments and some tutorials. The official PHP website (www.php.net, with a UK mirror at http://uk.php.net) has a searchable online manual, which provides details on all the functions covered in this chapter.

There are many good books on HTML and PHP and plenty of Web resources. The best way to find a book you like is to head to the library, type 'HTML' or 'PHP' into the search part of the catalogue, then browse the relevant shelves. The approach varies from student-focused to practitioner-focused and from a strong emphasis on efficient programming techniques to the lighter, conceptual touch of this chapter.

Some PHP books the author liked are Bulger et al. (2004), Williams and Lane (2004) and Welling and Thompson (2005). A favourite introduction to HTML and CSS is Castro (2007), with Gourley and Totty (2002) as a good reference book.

One good online source is the W3Schools website (www.w3schools.com), which has introductory tutorials on HTML, SQL, PHP and CSS. Vaswani (2004) is a good, on-line introduction to PHP.

Review questions

4.1 What is the main difference between sending HTML form data using the HTTP GET method and the HTTP POST method? How is the data accessed within a PHP script?

4.2 For each of the following PHP code snippets, write down what you'd expect to be displayed on the web page generated by PHP. Give a brief explanation of your answer in each case.

(a) `$name='Fred';`
    `echo 'Hello $name.';`

(b) `$name='Fred';`
    `echo "Hello $name.";`

(c) `$name='Fred';`
    `echo "Hello $nane.";`

(d) `$name='Fred';`
    `echo 'Hello', $name;`

4.3 Explain the difference between data validation and data cleansing. In what ways are they similar?

4.4 In HTML, what is the purpose of character entities? How do HTML character entities differ from the character encoding used for URLs?

4.5 Explain the purpose of the PHP built-in functions `strip_tags()` and `htmlspecialchars()`.

4.6 List the six steps for querying a MySQL database, and the PHP DBMS communication functions associated with each step. If the step does not involve communicating with the DBMS, then state this.

4.7 List the three PHP loop statements discussed in the chapter and explain their purpose.

4.8 List the PHP comparison operators used in the chapter. What others would you expect PHP to include?

4.9 List the PHP Boolean operators used in the chapter. What others would you expect PHP to include?

4.10 Explain the purpose of the PHP exit statement.

Exercises

Before attempting these exercises, you must create the Staff Directory database. Code for this is included in Appendix A.

A number of these exercises introduce PHP functions not covered in the main text of the chapter. Check the PHP online manual at www.php.net (or the UK mirror site at http://uk.php.net) for information on these functions.

4.11 Using a diagram (a UML sequence diagram such Figure 2.28, for example), explain how data from an HTML form is sent to the database. Include the web browser, HTTP server, PHP application server and DBMS in your diagram.

4.12 This exercise introduces some more of the PHP string manipulation functions. Using SurnameSearch.html as a template, write an HTML form to gather a single string of data from end users. Using version 0.1 of the SurnameStub.php script (Figure 4.3) as a template, write a PHP stub program to process the data entered as described below. In each case, display the results to end users.
(a) Use the built-in PHP function `strlen()` to find the length of the string entered.
(b) Use the built-in PHP functions `strtolower()` and `strtoupper()` to change the case of the letters entered by the user.
(c) Use the built-in PHP function `strpos()` to find the position of the first occurrence of the letter 'e' in the string. Then find the position of every letter 'e'. (*Hint:* You can use a loop statement to do this.)
(d) Use the built-in PHP functions `strpos()` and `substr()` to split the string at the first space character and display the two halves on separate lines of the web page.
(e) Suggest why these string manipulation functions can be useful in a web database application.

4.13 This exercise extends the data validation to deal with literals for strings and numbers (date validation is covered in Chapter 7). It provides practice with PHP built-in functions and with `if ... else` statements. Using SurnameSearch.html as a template, write an HTML form with two text boxes labelled 'Character string' and 'Number'. Using version 0.2 of the SurnameStub.php script (Figure 4.6) as a template, write a PHP stub program to process the data entered and echo the values back to the user. The data validation code should meet the following requirements.
(a) Use the built-in PHP function `array_key_exists()` to test that both the array elements are present. What happens if the user submits the form with nothing (not even a space character) in the text boxes? Under what circumstances would the `array_key_exists()` function actually do some good?

(b) Use the built-in PHP functions `trim()` and `empty()` to check that the character string text box has data in it, not just white space characters.

(c) Repeat this validation for the number text box. Then use the built-in PHP function `is_numeric()` to test if the data in the number text box is numeric.

(d) Start a new PHP script. Turn this basic data validation into two functions that you can reuse in other scripts – one to validate string literals and one to validate numeric literals. The functions should return a Boolean value – true if the literal passes validation, false if it fails. (Alternatively, create a single function capable of validating both string *and* numeric literals.)

4.14 This exercise integrates the data validation code from Exercise 4.13 into a database search and tidies up the presentation of the search results. Using version 1.1 of SurnameSearch.php (Figure 4.19) as a basis, write a PHP script to implement the following requirements. To test your script, you will need a copy of Surname Search.html that submits its data to this PHP script.

(a) Use the validation function created in Exercise 4.13 (d) to validate the data entered into the surname text box. For data that passes validation, remember to trim off any leading or trailing spaces and to carry out data cleansing.

(b) Retrieve the `fName`, `lName` and `email` columns from the `Staff` table. At the start of the list, display a count of the number of matching rows found. (*Note:* You will need to pay careful attention to nesting of the HTML paragraph elements in your script.)

(c) Provided that some rows were found, display the rows in an HTML paragraph element. Begin with a header row, displaying the text 'Name, E-mail' in bold. (*Hint:* Use the HTML strong element, `<strong>...</strong>`.) Then, for each row, show the full name and the e-mail address, using a break element to start each row of data on a separate line.

(d) Start a new PHP script. Display the rows in an HTML table element, rather than a paragraph element, so that the names and e-mail addresses of different rows line up nicely. (Alternatively, if you are familiar with CSS, use it to control the layout.)

(e) Try validating the web pages generated by your PHP scripts using the W3C HTML validator, located at http://validator.w3.org. Adjust your PHP script to eliminate any HTML validation errors.

If your web pages are on a public web server, just type the URL of the page you wish to validate into the 'Validate by URL' text box. If not, then view your web page in one browser window, select 'View source' and copy the HTML. Open the HTML validator in another browser window and paste your HTML into the 'Validate by direct input' text area.

4.15 This exercise deals with DBMS communication errors. Using your solution to Exercise 4.14 (or version 1.3 of SurnameSearch.php – the actual code is shown in Figure 4.26) add code to handle DBMS communication errors. Your code should meet the following requirements.

(a) When an error occurs while communicating with the DBMS, the error number and associated message are displayed to the end user.

(b) The script includes a PHP constant DEBUG. If no error occurs and DEBUG is TRUE, then write a suitable notice as an HTML comment. (*Hint:* The PHP statement `define("DEBUG", true);` names a constant called DEBUG and sets its value to `TRUE`. To refer to the constant, simply use its name – for example, the PHP statement `echo DEBUG;` writes the value of the constant `DEBUG` to the HTTP response.)

(c) When querying the database, if `DEBUG` is `TRUE`, then the SQL statement should be written out as an HTML comment whether or not there is a DBMS communication error.

4.16 Use the experience gained in the previous exercises to improve the SupportSessionInsert.php script. In particular:

- ensure that the staff number is a five-digit numeric literal and inform the user of any errors
- check that the day is one of the string literals 'Monday', . . . 'Friday' and inform the user of any errors
- only run the database query if the staff number and day pass validation
- handle any DBMS communication errors as in Exercise 4.15.

Investigations

4.17 String manipulation and data validation with the functions covered in this chapter are rather cumbersome. Regular expressions provide a much more elegant solution. Investigate regular expressions and the associated PHP functions.

4.18 Typing ECMAScript into a text box is only one way in which hackers can try to subvert a PHP script. Investigate other ways hackers seek to subvert web applications. The UK government agency Centre for the Protection of the National Infrastructure (CPNI) has produced a briefing document on securing web applications (NISCC, 2006), available at www.cpni.gov.uk/docs/secureWebApps.pdf and it includes a detailed technical discussion of 'data validation', which this book calls 'data cleansing'.

4.19 The functions used to connect to the MySQL DBMS in this chapter are actually quite old (and, hence, reliable). The PHP language includes the MySQL Improved Extension for connecting to the MySQL DBMS version 4.1 or later. This extension supports both procedural and object-orientated approaches to coding (see http://uk.php.net/manual/en/ref.mysqli.php). The PHP Extension and Application Repository (PEAR) project provides a prebuilt set of database connectivity functions in the MDB2 package (see http://pear.php.net/package/MDB2). Investigate one (or both) of these, comparing them to the older set of functions used here with regard to ease of use, maintainability and robustness.

4.20 PHP is only one of a number of server-side scripting languages. Others include Ruby on Rails, Microsoft ASP.NET, JSP (Java Server Pages) and Macromedia ColdFusion. Investigate one of the others, comparing it to PHP.

5 Introduction to the SQL data language

Chapter objectives

→ To introduce the facilities SQL provides to query the database instance.

→ To introduce the facilities SQL provides to modify the database instance.

→ To introduce the facilities SQL provides to create and modify the database schema.

Chapter outline

SQL is the standard data language for relational DBMS and widely used by non-relational products. It evolved from a language developed by IBM in the mid 1970s and was adopted as an international standard in the late 1980s. The International Organization for Standards (ISO) oversees development of the language and publishes the definitive standard. At the time of writing, the latest version was SQL:2003.

SQL is a large language and, since the mid 1990s, has been computationally complete. The specification includes `if ... else` statements, loops and so on. In 1999, it acquired object-orientated features and, in 2003, facilities to deal with XML. Some of these advanced features are covered in later chapters. However, many DBMS do not implement the full language and most database applications only use the basic data language features.

This chapter focuses on the SQL **data language**, the original core of SQL. The SQL data language has two parts:

1 the SQL **data definition language** for creating and modifying the database schema

2 the SQL **data manipulation language** for querying and modifying the database instance.

The basic features of both are introduced in this chapter and more advanced features are discussed in the following chapter. As all web database developers will need to query the database instance, but some may never create the database schema, SQL DML is covered first.

- Section 5.1 introduces the SQL DML **select statement** for querying the database instance. It explains the basic options for manipulating the result set, which are how to define which columns to include, how to order the rows of the result set and how to remove duplicate rows from a result set. It also discusses how to include expressions, rather than simple column values, in the rows of a result set.

- Section 5.2 discusses the **where clause**. This allows the developer to identify which rows the DBMS should include in the result set.

- Section 5.3 concludes this chapter's look at the SQL DML by discussing how to modify the database instance using the SQL DML **insert**, **update** and **delete statements**.

- Section 5.4 introduces the SQL DDL statements to create, and remove, databases and tables. These are **create schema** and **create table**.

- Section 5.5 discusses the SQL DDL **alter table** statement, used to modify a table definition.

5.1 SQL queries: the basic select statement

The SQL select statement allows users to query the database. The simplest form of the select statement is shown in Figure 5.1. The statement begins with the SQL keyword SELECT, which is followed by a comma-separated list of column names. This is called the **select list**. Immediately after the last column name in the select list comes the **from clause**. The from clause indicates which database table the columns in the select list come from. The result of any SQL select statement is a derived table, called the **result set**. The data in a derived table is stored in memory, not on disk.

The Staff Directory web database application can use a simple SQL select statement to retrieve a list of staff and their e-mail addresses from the database (Code listing 5.1.1, below).

The select list includes three columns – fName, lName, email. When the select statement is executed, the from clause tells the DBMS which table to retrieve data from. The select list tells the DBMS to retrieve the values of the columns fName, lName and email, but not the values of any other columns.

Figure 5.2 (b) shows the result set (that is, the derived table) for the select statement in Code listing 5.1.1. Because the derived table is generated in response to a database

Figure 5.1 The basic SQL select statement.

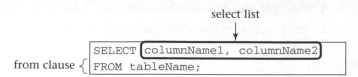

query, it doesn't have a name and there are no data types shown for the columns. The data type of the derived table's columns is determined by the underlying base table.

Figure 5.2 (a) shows the instance of the `Staff` table (the underlying base table) being queried. Notice how every row of the `Staff` table instance is represented in the result set. Simple select statements, with just a select list and a from clause, always include the requested column values for every row of the underlying base table.

Code listing 5.1.1   A simple select statement

```
SELECT fName, lName, email
FROM Staff;
```

> In the SQL statements in this book, SQL keywords are written in upper-case letters and identifiers in mixed case. This is simply to make the code easier to read. ISO SQL is not case-sensitive for keywords or identifiers. Some DBMS, including the MySQL DBMS, can be case-sensitive for identifiers. For example, the identifiers `STAFF` and `Staff` are the same in ISO SQL, but can be different in the version of SQL implemented by the MySQL DBMS. The DBA can decide whether a particular instance of a DBMS is, or is not, case-sensitive for identifiers.

Figure 5.2 Querying the `Staff` table. Examples of a table instance and query result.

Staff					
staffNo:Varchar	fName:Varchar	lName:Varchar	email:Varchar	phone:Varchar	photo:BLOB
10780	John	Smith	j.b.smith@pennine.ac.uk	NULL	[BLOB]
14443	Helen	Abbot	h.abbot@pennine.ac.uk	8032	[BLOB]
23257	Freya	Stark	f.stark@pennine.ac.uk	8660	[BLOB]
25447	John	Smith	j.smith@pennine.ac.uk	5104	[BLOB]
25448	Judith Anne	Smith	j.a.smith@pennine.ac.uk	7709	[BLOB]
31210	Paul	Smith	p.smith@pennine.ac.uk	NULL	[BLOB]
33509	Helen	Timms	h.timms@pennine.ac.uk	8661	[BLOB]
33935	Padma	Brar	p.brar@pennine.ac.uk	6641	[BLOB]
35054	Selma	Hutchins	s.hutchins@pennine.ac.uk	8706	[BLOB]
35155	Helene	Chirac	h.chirac@pennine.ac.uk	NULL	[BLOB]
45965	Mikhail	Sudbin	m.sudbin@pennine.ac.uk	5553	[BLOB]
55776	Gurpreet	Choudhury	g.choudhury@pennine.ac.uk	5454	[BLOB]
56673	Joshua	Bittaye	j.bittaye@pennine.ac.uk	7782	[BLOB]
56893	Ruth	Bapetsi	r.bapetsi@pennine.ac.uk	8022	[BLOB]
77712	Frank	Rose	f.rose@pennine.ac.uk	8871	[BLOB]
78893	Jo Karen	O'Connor	j.k.oconnor@pennine.ac.uk	8871	[BLOB]
89987	Dan	Lin	d.lin@pennine.co.uk	8514	[BLOB]

(a) The `Staff` table instance being queried.

Figure 5.2 (*Continued*)

fName	lName	email
John	Smith	j.b.smith@pennine.ac.uk
Helen	Abbot	h.abbot@pennine.ac.uk
Freya	Stark	f.stark@pennine.ac.uk
John	Smith	j.smith@pennine.ac.uk
Judith Anne	Smith	j.a.smith@pennine.ac.uk
Paul	Smith	p.smith@pennine.ac.uk
Helen	Timms	h.timms@pennine.ac.uk
Padma	Brar	p.brar@pennine.ac.uk
Selma	Hutchins	s.hutchins@pennine.ac.uk
Helene	Chirac	h.chirac@pennine.ac.uk
Mikhail	Sudbin	m.sudbin@pennine.ac.uk
Gurpreet	Choudhury	g.choudhury@pennine.ac.uk
Joshua	Bittaye	j.bittaye@pennine.ac.uk
Ruth	Bapetsi	r.bapetsi@pennine.ac.uk
Frank	Rose	f.rose@pennine.ac.uk
Jo Karen	O'Connor	j.k.oconnor@pennine.ac.uk
Dan	Lin	d.lin@pennine.co.uk

(b) Result set for Code listing 5.1.1.

A user making a database query such as this one probably wants to see the results in alphabetical order. The select statement's order by clause allows the user to specify how to order the rows returned by the select statement. The order by clause comes after the from clause.

Code listing 5.1.2 shows how to use an order by clause. It asks the DBMS to retrieve the values in the fName, lName and email columns of all rows from the Staff table and order the rows in the result set by lName and fName.

Code listing 5.1.2 Ordering the result set

```
SELECT fName, lName, email
FROM Staff
ORDER BY lName, fName;
```

The rows in the result set are ordered first by the value of the lName column. Any rows that have the same value in the lName are ordered by their fName column. The SQL standard doesn't specify what to do with rows that have the same values in both columns. Typically, these appear in the order the rows were stored in in the underlying database storage structure.

Figure 5.3 Result set for Code listing 5.1.2.

fName	lName	email
Helen	Abbot	h.abbot@pennine.ac.uk
Ruth	Bapetsi	r.bapetsi@pennine.ac.uk
Joshua	Bittaye	j.bittaye@pennine.ac.uk
Padma	Brar	p.brar@pennine.ac.uk
Helene	Chirac	h.chirac@pennine.ac.uk
Gurpreet	Choudhury	g.choudhury@pennine.ac.uk
Selma	Hutchins	s.hutchins@pennine.ac.uk
Dan	Lin	d.lin@pennine.co.uk
Jo Karen	O'Connor	j.k.oconnor@pennine.ac.uk
Frank	Rose	f.rose@pennine.ac.uk
John	Smith	j.b.smith@pennine.ac.uk
John	Smith	j.smith@pennine.ac.uk
Judith Anne	Smith	j.a.smith@pennine.ac.uk
Paul	Smith	p.smith@pennine.ac.uk
Freya	Stark	f.stark@pennine.ac.uk
Mikhail	Sudbin	m.sudbin@pennine.ac.uk
Helen	Timms	h.timms@pennine.ac.uk

The result set for the select statement in Code listing 5.1.2 is shown in Figure 5.3. Notice that four staff members whose surname is 'Smith' now appear together, ordered by their first names. The order by clause can include *any* columns from the table mentioned in the from clause, not just those in the select list. So, Code listing 5.1.3 is also a valid SQL statement.

Code listing 5.1.3   Ordering the result set by a column that isn't in the select-list

```
SELECT fName, lName, email
FROM Staff
ORDER BY staffNo;
```

The select list is not limited to column names, but can include expressions. For example, the list of staff and their e-mail addresses shown in Figure 5.3 may look a bit odd as the first and last names are in separate columns. The SQL concatenation operator allows the character string values of these two columns to be added together into a single character string. Code listing 5.1.4 shows a first attempt at this and Figure 5.4 the result set for this select statement. Notice that there are now just two columns in the result set. For each row of the `Staff` table, the values from the `fName` and `lName` columns have been merged to form a single value in the result set's derived table.

Figure 5.4 Result set for Code listing 5.1.4.

fName || lName	email
HelenAbbot	h.abbot@pennine.ac.uk
RuthBapetsi	r.bapetsi@pennine.ac.uk
JoshuaBittaye	j.bittaye@pennine.ac.uk
PadmaBrar	p.brar@pennine.ac.uk
HeleneChirac	h.chirac@pennine.ac.uk
GurpreetChoudhury	g.choudhury@pennine.ac.uk
SelmaHutchins	s.hutchins@pennine.ac.uk
DanLin	d.lin@pennine.co.uk
Jo KarenO'Connor	j.k.oconnor@pennine.ac.uk
FrankRose	f.rose@pennine.ac.uk
JohnSmith	j.b.smith@pennine.ac.uk
JohnSmith	j.smith@pennine.ac.uk
Judith AnneSmith	j.a.smith@pennine.ac.uk
PaulSmith	p.smith@pennine.ac.uk
FreyaStark	f.stark@pennine.ac.uk
MikhailSudbin	m.sudbin@pennine.ac.uk
HelenTimms	h.timms@pennine.ac.uk

Code listing 5.1.4   Using the concatenation operator to add together character string values

```
SELECT fName||lName, email
FROM Staff
ORDER BY lName, fName;
```

There are two problems with the information in the result set shown in Figure 5.4. First, there is no space between the first and last names of members of staff. If a space is required between two column values, then this must be included in the expression in the select list, as shown in Code listing 5.1.5.

Code listing 5.1.5   Including a space between column values

```
SELECT fName||' '||lName, email
FROM Staff
ORDER BY lName, fName;
```

The second problem is with the column names for the result set. The first column has the name fName || lName, which isn't very informative. SQL allows an expression (and a column) in the select list to be given an **alias**. The alias is then used as the column name in the result set. This is particularly useful when passing database queries from a PHP script and using the result set to create a web page. By choosing meaningful

Figure 5.5 Result set for Code listing 5.1.6.

name	email
Helen Abbot	h.abbot@pennine.ac.uk
Ruth Bapetsi	r.bapetsi@pennine.ac.uk
Joshua Bittaye	j.bittaye@pennine.ac.uk
Padma Brar	p.brar@pennine.ac.uk
Helene Chirac	h.chirac@pennine.ac.uk
Gurpreet Choudhury	g.choudhury@pennine.ac.uk
Selma Hutchins	s.hutchins@pennine.ac.uk
Dan Lin	d.lin@pennine.co.uk
Jo Karen O'Connor	j.k.oconnor@pennine.ac.uk
Frank Rose	f.rose@pennine.ac.uk
John Smith	j.b.smith@pennine.ac.uk
John Smith	j.smith@pennine.ac.uk
Judith Anne Smith	j.a.smith@pennine.ac.uk
Paul Smith	p.smith@pennine.ac.uk
Freya Stark	f.stark@pennine.ac.uk
Mikhail Sudbin	m.sudbin@pennine.ac.uk
Helen Timms	h.timms@pennine.ac.uk

aliases, the column names of the result set can be used directly to label column values on the web page. For example, Code listing 5.1.6 gives the alias 'name' to the expression fName ||' '|| lName. A PHP script can use this alias to label the column values. Figure 5.5 shows the result set for Code listing 5.1.6. Note that both the problems identified in Figure 5.4 have been corrected.

Code listing 5.1.6 *Providing a meaningful name for an expression*

```
SELECT fName||' '||lName AS name, email
FROM Staff
ORDER BY lName, fName;
```

The concatenation operator for ISO SQL:2003 is '||'. However, this symbol is the Boolean OR operator in the MySQL DBMS – one of the few cases where the dialect of SQL implemented by the MySQL DBMS conflicts with the ISO standard. The MySQL DBMS uses the CONCAT() function to concatenate string values. For example, the MySQL equivalent of Code listing 5.1.6 is:

```
SELECT concat(fName, ' ', lName) AS name, email
FROM Staff
ORDER BY lName, fName
```

Figure 5.6 Listing the days on which staff offer support sessions.

staffNo	dayOfWeek
23257	Monday
31210	Wednesday
35054	Monday
35054	Monday
45965	Monday
45965	Wednesday
55776	Monday
56673	Friday
56673	Friday
56673	Thursday
56893	Thursday
56893	Tuesday

staffNo	dayOfWeek
23257	Monday
31210	Wednesday
35054	Monday
45965	Monday
45965	Wednesday
55776	Monday
56673	Friday
56673	Thursday
56893	Thursday
56893	Tuesday

(a) Result set for code listing 5.1.7 (note the duplicate rows).

(b) Result set for Code listing 5.1.8 (note that there are no duplicate rows).

Suppose now that the user wants a list showing the days when members of staff offer support sessions. The SupportSession table only includes the staff numbers as the names are given in the Staff table. Section 6.1 investigates how to use SQL to retrieve data simultaneously from two tables, but, for now, let us assume that the staff number is sufficient.

Code listing 5.1.7 is a first attempt at this query. It asks the DBMS to retrieve the values in the staffNo and dayOfWeek columns of all rows in the SupportSession table, ordered by the staffNo. The result set for this query is shown in Figure 5.6 (a).

Code listing 5.1.7 *Listing the days on which members of staff offer support sessions*

```
SELECT staffNo, dayOfWeek
FROM SupportSession
ORDER BY staffNo;
```

The problem here is that there are some duplicate rows in the result set. The staff member with staffNo '35054' offers two support sessions on a Monday and '56673' offers two on a Friday. The list should simply show which days a member of staff offers support sessions, not how many. The duplicate rows need to be removed from the result set.

Placing the SQL keyword DISTINCT before the select list, as in Code listing 5.1.8, instructs the DBMS to do exactly that (see the result set in Figure 5.6 (b)). Using DISTINCT only instructs the DBMS to remove duplicate *rows* from the result set, so there are still two different rows with staffNo '56673' and five rows with dayOfWeek 'Monday', but none of these rows is a duplicate.

Code listing 5.1.8   Using DISTINCT to remove duplicates rows from the result set

```
SELECT DISTINCT staffNo, dayOfWeek
FROM SupportSession
ORDER BY staffNo;
```

5.2   The where clause

Most database queries do not retrieve data from every row of a table. Instead, they instruct the DBMS to retrieve data from only those rows where a given condition is true. This condition is specified as a Boolean expression in the select statement's where clause. A typical condition is that a column value for the row must satisfy some restriction – the value of the lName column must equal 'Smith', for example. When the DBMS executes the select statement, it will check each row of the underlying base table in turn. If the condition is true, then the DBMS retrieves values for the columns (and expressions) in the select list. In this way, the DBMS constructs the result set row by row, scanning through the underlying base table from top to bottom and adding a row to the result set for every row of the underlying base table that satisfies the condition in the where clause.

The select statement is not the only SQL statement to use a where clause, so it is worth covering this clause in detail. The general format for an SQL select statement with a where clause is shown in Figure 5.7. Notice that the various parts of the select statement must be placed in the correct sequence:

- select list
- from clause
- where clause
- order by clause.

The simplest condition is an equality condition – that is, the value in a particular column must equal some given value. Code listing 5.2.1 uses an equality condition to request a list of members of staff who have the surname 'Smith'. The where clause

Figure 5.7 SQL select statement with a where clause and order by clause.

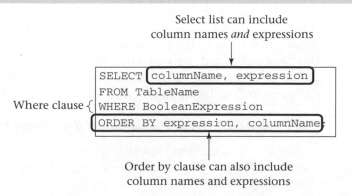

Select list can include column names *and* expressions

```
SELECT columnName, expression
FROM TableName
WHERE BooleanExpression
ORDER BY expression, columnName;
```

Where clause

Order by clause can also include column names and expressions

Figure 5.8 Result set for Code listing 5.2.1.

fName	lName	email
John	Smith	j.b.smith@pennine.ac.uk
Paul	Smith	p.smith@pennine.ac
Judith Anne	Smith	j.a.smith@pennine.ac.uk
John	Smith	j.smith@pennine.ac.uk

begins with the keyword WHERE, which is followed by a Boolean expression lName = 'Smith'. Notice that the string literal is enclosed in single quotes. When the DBMS executes the statement, it looks at each row of the Staff table in turn. If the value in the lName column for the current row of the Staff table is *not* 'Smith', then the DBMS skips that row. If the value in the lName column for the current row *is* 'Smith', then the DBMS retrieves the values of the columns fName, lName and email and adds them as a new row to the result set.

The final result set, for the instance of the Staff table in Figure 5.2 (a), is shown in Figure 5.8.

Code listing 5.2.1 *Listing members of staff with surname 'Smith'*

```
SELECT fName, lName, email
FROM Staff
WHERE lName = 'Smith';
```

One common database query is to look for missing data, such as Which members of staff do not have a phone number? Looking at the table instance shown in Figure 5.2 (a), there are three – John Smith (staffNo 10780), Paul Smith (31210) and Helene Chirac (35155). It is tempting to use an equality condition to list these members of staff, as in Code listing 5.2.2. That doesn't work. The reason is that SQL uses three-valued logic, as discussed in Chapter 3. Suppose that, in some row, the value of the phone column is '8996'. The Boolean expression '8996' = NULL has the truth value UNKNOWN, which is not TRUE, so the DBMS skips that row. This is the behaviour we expect – that is, staff whose phone column is not null do not appear in the result set. Unfortunately the Boolean expression NULL = NULL also has the truth value UNKNOWN. This is because null represents missing information and nothing is known about either value in the comparison expression, so it is impossible to say whether they are equal or not! Consequently, even in those rows of the Staff table where the phone column is null, the DBMS does not add anything to the result set. The select statement in Code listing 5.2.2 *always* returns an empty result set.

Code listing 5.2.2 *A select statement that always returns an empty result set*

```
SELECT fName, lName, email
FROM Staff
WHERE phone = NULL;
```

This is clearly a problem and SQL gets round it by introducing a special operator for comparing values to null – IS NULL. This takes a single expression, of any data type, and outputs TRUE if the expression is null or FALSE if it isn't. The IS NULL operator never outputs the value UNKNOWN. Usually, the expression is just a column name.

Code listing 5.2.3 shows how to use the IS NULL operator to list members of staff for whom the phone number column is null. Nulls and three-valued logic make SQL more complicated. Always think carefully about how a where clause will treat nulls and whether or not this is the behaviour that's required.

Code listing 5.2.3   Testing for null in an SQL where clause

```
SELECT fName, lName, email
FROM Staff
WHERE phone IS NULL;
```

The IS NULL operator is one of four IS operators. The other three test the value of a Boolean column (or Boolean expression). They are:

- expression IS TRUE
- expression IS FALSE
- expression IS UNKNOWN.

These three operators output TRUE if the expression has the truth value stated or FALSE if it doesn't. It is important to use these IS operators in preference to the = comparison operator for Boolean columns. This is because, in ISO SQL:2003, the Boolean value represented by the literal UNKNOWN is the same as null (represented by the SQL keyword NULL). This means that when a Boolean column is assigned the value UNKNOWN, it is actually made null. That is not the most sensible idea. *Any* column, no matter what its data type, can be null. Only a column the data type of which is Boolean can hold the Boolean value UNKNOWN. Even worse, although the comparisons columnName=TRUE and columnName=FALSE work as expected, columnName= UNKNOWN does not! This is because UNKNOWN is the same as null, so columnName= UNKNOWN is the same as columnName=NULL. As noted above, this *always* evaluates to UNKNOWN. There is a good discussion of these issues in Date (2004, pp. 575–63).

Support for the ISO SQL:2003 Boolean data type in commercial DBMS is rather patchy. The Oracle database does not include a Boolean data type and the MySQL DBMS silently converts columns defined as BOOLEAN to TINYINT(1), a single-digit numeric data type. The MySQL DBMS manual (MySQL AB, 2007) states that the numeric value 0 equates to FALSE and all other numeric values equate to TRUE– there is no equivalent of the ISO SQL:2003 Boolean value UNKNOWN. In practice, the MySQL DBMS version 5.0.15 only treats 1 as TRUE; other numeric values are simply not recognized as being either TRUE or FALSE.

Another common kind of database query asks whether the value of a column lies in a particular range – Show support sessions that start between 09.00 and 12.00, for example.

Code listing 5.2.4 shows how to write this query. The result set will include values from every column of the SupportSession table for those rows where the value of the `startTime` column lies between 09.00 and 12.00. Syntax like this is what makes SQL a nice language – it is almost, though not quite, plain English. Understand the structure of the select statement and it is easy to write simple database queries.

Code listing 5.2.4   *A where clause with a range comparison expression*

```
SELECT staffNo, dayOfWeek, startTime, endTime
FROM SupportSession
WHERE startTime BETWEEN '09:00' AND '12:00';
```

In the Boolean expression `startTime BETWEEN '09:00' AND '12:00'`, the keyword `AND` is *not* the Boolean operator of the same name. It is part of the syntax for an SQL range comparison using the `BETWEEN` operator. The SQL range comparison expression takes three parameters as inputs and returns a single Boolean value. The general format is:

```
testExpression BETWEEN lowerValue AND upperValue
```

The intended meaning is that the range comparison expression is true whenever the value of `testExpression` lies between the `lowerValue` and `upperValue` or is equal to either of them.

Both `IS NULL` and `BETWEEN` are called 'predicates' in the ISO SQL standard. A predicate is simply a statement that a particular object (or objects) have a particular property. In other words, it is a Boolean expression. `IS NULL` and `BETWEEN` are really predicate symbols, used to form predicates such as `phone IS NULL` and `start-Time BETWEEN '09:00' AND '12:00'`. The distinction between an 'operator' and a 'predicate symbol' is important in mathematical logic, but not in web database development. In this book, the term 'operator' is used for all these symbols.

When a select statement needs to retrieve data from every column of a table, the select list can be replaced with an asterisk. The select statement:

```
SELECT staffNo, dayOfWeek, startTime, endTime
FROM SupportSession
```

is equivalent to the shorter:

```
SELECT * FROM SupportSession
```

Many database developers use this shorthand, but it can cause problems. If a new column is added to the `SupportSession` table, then the first version only includes values for the four named columns in the rows of the result set. The second version includes values for all five columns. There are three good reasons to use the longer version rather than the shorthand.

- Placing unnecessary column values into a result set can slow things down as more data is being transferred than is needed.
- If a PHP script is set up to expect four columns in a result set and suddenly finds that there are five, this will generate unexpected results and could cause the script to fail.

- Database applications need to be maintained by different people. Listing the columns in the select list makes it clear to new members of the development team exactly what data is being retrieved, without the need to hunt down a description of the table. It is always better to write self-documenting code where possible.

A where clause can include more complex conditions than those seen so far by using the Boolean operators NOT, AND and OR to create longer Boolean expressions. For example, the range comparison expression:

```
startTime BETWEEN '09:00' AND '12:00'
```

in Code listing 5.2.4 is equivalent to the Boolean expression:

```
startTime >= '09:00' AND startTime <= '12:00'
```

In this second Boolean expression, the keyword AND is the Boolean operator, joining together the two simple comparison expressions startTime>='09:00' and startTime<='12:00'. Adding brackets can make clear which two Boolean expression are being joined together by the AND operator:

```
(startTime >= '09:00') AND (startTime <= '12:00')
```

Using AND allows more complex database queries to be performed. For example, Code listing 5.2.5 lists all members of staff who have the surname 'Smith' and their phone number is not known. These are completely unrelated conditions, but both can be included in the same Boolean expression by using the Boolean operator AND.

Code listing 5.2.5   *Using AND to test that two unrelated conditions are both true*

```
SELECT fName, lName, email
FROM Staff
WHERE (phone IS NULL) AND (lName='Smith');
```

The brackets in the where clause of Code listing 5.2.5 are not required, but can make the where clause easier to understand. The DBMS uses the truth tables discussed in Chapter 3 to evaluate the value of the complex Boolean expression by first evaluating the values of the two simpler Boolean expressions phone IS NULL and lName='Smith'. The complex expression is TRUE when phone IS NULL is TRUE and lName='Smith' is also TRUE, FALSE if either of these is FALSE and UNKNOWN if either is UNKNOWN.

The result set is shown in Figure 5.9. Only two rows satisfy both the simpler expressions. Other staff members satisfy one of the conditions, but are excluded from the result set because they don't satisfy the other. For example, Helene Chirac's phone

Figure 5.9 Result set for Code listing 5.2.5.

fName	lName	email
John	Smith	j.b.smith@pennine.ac.uk
Paul	Smith	p.smith@pennine.ac.uk

Figure 5.10 Result set for Code listing 5.2.6.

fName	lName	email
John	Smith	j.b.smith@pennine.ac.uk
John	Smith	j.smith@pennine.ac.uk
Judith Anne	Smith	j.a.smith@pennine.ac.uk
Paul	Smith	p.smith@pennine.ac.uk
Helene	Chirac	h.chirac@pennine.ac.uk

number is null, but her surname is not Smith, so she is excluded from the result set. Judith Anne Smith is also excluded from the result set because her phone number is 7709, which is clearly not null.

The difference between AND and OR is illustrated by Code listing 5.2.6 and Figure 5.10. With OR, rows that satisfy either (or both) of the simpler expressions are included in the result set. Rows for Helene Chirac and Judith Anne Smith are both included in Figure 5.10 because they each satisfy *one* of the two conditions, though both were excluded from Figure 5.9 as neither satisfies *both* conditions.

Code listing 5.2.6 Using OR to test that either one of the distinct conditions is true

```
SELECT fName, lName, email
FROM Staff
WHERE (phone IS NULL) OR (lName='Smith');
```

Some database queries require both the AND and OR Boolean operators to define which rows should be included in the result set. Suppose the user wants to see a list of support sessions that are offered either on a Friday afternoon or Monday morning. The Boolean expression:

```
dayOfWeek='Monday' AND startTime<'12:00'
```

identifies all support sessions offered on a Monday morning. No parentheses are needed in this expression as the DBMS knows to evaluate the two simple comparison expressions dayOfWeek='Monday' and startTime<'12:00' individually, then evaluate the full expression. Support sessions offered on a Friday afternoon can be identified by the expression:

```
dayOfWeek='Friday' AND startTime>='12:00'
```

Note that support sessions starting at 12.00 are counted as afternoon sessions. To generate a list of the Monday morning *and* Friday afternoon support sessions, the DBMS simply needs to check that one or the other of these two Boolean expressions is true, using:

```
  (dayOfWeek='Monday' AND startTime<'12:00')
OR (dayOfWeek='Friday' AND startTime>='12:00')
```

Code listing 5.2.7 shows the full select statement.

Code listing 5.2.7   A complex condition

```
SELECT staffNo, dayOfWeek, startTime, endTime
FROM SupportSession
WHERE (dayOfWeek='Monday' AND startTime<'12:00')
OR (dayOfWeek='Friday' AND startTime>='12:00');
```

The parentheses – (. . .) – in this expression *are* needed to avoid confusion. If the DBMS is shown this statement:

```
dayOfWeek='Monday' AND startTime<'12:00'
OR dayOfWeek='Friday' AND startTime>='12:00'
```

it is not clear what is meant. Apart from the *intended* interpretation, this expression *could* be interpreted to mean:

```
dayOfWeek='Monday'
AND (startTime<'12:00' OR dayOfWeek='Friday')
AND startTime>='12:00'
```

No rows satisfy this expression. The first and final conditions mean that the support session must run on a Monday afternoon, but the second condition means that it must run on either a Friday or in the morning. Clearly, these conditions cannot all be met. Always use parentheses to indicate the correct interpretation of a complex Boolean expression.

The third Boolean operator is NOT. The select statement in Code listing 5.2.8 result in all support sessions apart from those that run on a Monday morning being listed.

Code listing 5.2.8   Using NOT

```
SELECT staffNo, dayOfWeek, startTime, endTime
FROM SupportSession
WHERE NOT (dayOfWeek='Monday' AND startTime<'12:00');
```

Many database queries can be written without using NOT. For example, the Boolean expression:

```
NOT (surname='Smith')
```

is usually written using the not-equal-to operator – <>:

```
surname<>'Smith'
```

Range comparisons can also be negated and SQL allows a fairly natural way to write such expressions. For example:

```
NOT (startTime BETWEEN '09:00' AND '12:00')
```

can also be written:

```
startTime NOT BETWEEN '09:00' AND '12:00'
```

Both expressions are true whenever the value of startTime lies outside of the range specified.

Figure 5.11 Result set for Code listing 5.2.9.

fName	lName	email
John	Smith	j.b.smith@pennine.ac.uk
John	Smith	j.smith@pennine.ac.uk
Judith Anne	Smith	j.a.smith@pennine.ac.uk
Joshua	Bittaye	j.bittaye@pennine.ac.uk
Jo Karen	O'Connor	j.k.oconnor@pennine.ac.uk

There is one more comparison operator provided by SQL that is regularly used in database queries. The LIKE operator performs pattern matching for character strings. It recognizes two wild card characters. The percentage character – % – matches any group of characters. For example, the select statement in Code listing 5.2.9 lists all members of staff whose e-mail addresses begin with the letter 'j'. The result set is shown in Figure 5.11. If the comparison expression is changed to email LIKE 'j.b%', then only the first and fourth rows shown in Figure 5.11 would appear in the result set.

Code listing 5.2.9   Pattern matching with the LIKE string comparison operator

```
SELECT fName, lName, email
FROM Staff
WHERE email LIKE 'j%';
```

As with the range comparison expression, SQL allows a natural way to negate a LIKE comparison. The Boolean expression:

```
NOT (lName LIKE 'j%')
```

is equivalent to the more natural:

```
lName NOT LIKE 'j%'
```

The other wild card character is the underscore – _. This matches any *single* character. For example, in the select statement in Code listing 5.2.10, the single underscore matches a single letter (or other character, though e-mail addresses always begin with a letter). The result set is shown in Figure 5.12. Notice that Judith Anne Smith does not appear in the result set. Her e-mail address is 'j.a.smith@pennine.ac.uk'. This doesn't match the pattern in Code listing 5.2.10 as there are *three* characters before the

Figure 5.12 Result set for Code listing 5.2.10.

fName	lName	email
John	Smith	j.smith@pennine.ac.uk
Paul	Smith	p.smith@pennine.ac.uk

Figure 5.13 An instance of the `Equipment` table from the Web Timetable database.

Equipment							
assetNo:varchar	assetType:varchar	description:varchar	building:varchar	room:varchar	portable:boolean	cost:numeric	acquired:date
1570131	Data projector	HP vp6100	Wilson	205	FALSE	1300.00	2004-07-14
1799131	Data projector	HP vp6100	NULL	NULL	TRUE	1300.00	2005-01-12
4560293	OHP	3M OHP 1608	Locke	24	FALSE	NULL	NULL
4503993	PC	Dell OptiPlex™ GX280	Wilson	205	FALSE	625.00	2004-04-30
5010009	OHP	3M OHP 2000	NULL	NULL	TRUE	185.00	2001-08-20
2992220	Data projector	ToshibaTDP-SW20	Priestley	G12	FALSE	1100.00	2005-01-12
2892112	Laptop	SONY X505	NULL	NULL	TRUE	NULL	NULL

'.smith@pennine.ac.uk' and the underscore only matches *single* characters (for the same reason, John Smith, with the e-mail address 'j.b.smith@pennine.ac.uk', also does not appear in the result set). If the underscore were to be replaced with a '%', then all four Smiths would appear in the result set.

Code listing 5.2.10   Matching a single character

```
SELECT fName, lName, email
FROM Staff
WHERE email LIKE '_.smith@pennine.ac.uk';
```

Most comparison expressions involving character string, Boolean and numeric data types are straightforward. Date comparisons for DBMS that conform to the ISO SQL standard are equally straightforward. However, with some DBMS there can be a problem. Consider the `Equipment` table from the Web Timetable database shown in Figure 5.13. The `acquired` column records the date a particular piece of equipment was bought by the Pennine University. The date appears to be a simple date, showing the year, month and day when the equipment was bought. However, some DBMS (such as the Oracle database) will actually store a date and time value. Even when a column value is actually a date and time, the DBMS may only display the date portion. Thus `'2004-07-14 00:00'`, `'2004-07-14 09:45'` and `'2004-07-14 12:00'` may all be displayed by default as `'2004-07-14'`. With dates, what you see displayed is not necessarily a true representation of the value stored. This can lead to unexpected results. For example, consider the select statement in Code listing 5.2.11.

Code listing 5.2.11   Date comparisons

```
SELECT assetNo, assetType, acquired
FROM Equipment
WHERE acquired <= '2004-07-14'
```

The date literal in the comparison expression does not have a time value, but assume that the column values do. To compare them, the DBMS must make some assumption about the time value for this date literal. Typically, it would interpret `'2004-07-14'` to mean `'2004-07-14 00:00'` (the very first minute of 14 July 2004). Given the table instance in Figure 5.13, the result set for the query should include the first, fourth and fifth rows of the table. However, if the date and time value for the first row of the acquired column is actually `'2004-07-14 09:45'`, then this row will *not* be included in the result set for the query in Code listing 5.2.11. This problem does not occur for DBMS that have separate data types for date and date and time values, as the ISO SQL standard specifies. Section 6.2 looks at some of SQL's built-in value functions, including functions to manipulate date values, which can help deal with this problem.

5.3   Modifying the database instance with SQL DML

The SQL DML includes three statements that modify the database instance (in fact, each modifies the table instance of a particular table):

- the **insert statement** adds a new row to the table instance of a particular table
- the **delete statement** removes one or more rows from the table instance of a particular table
- the **update statement** modifies one or more rows of the table instance of a particular table.

In ISO SQL:2003, the only way to modify the table instances of two different tables is to write two separate SQL statements.

> The dialect of SQL used by the MySQL DBMS (Version 4.0.4 onwards) does allow delete statements and update statements that affect multiple tables. See MySQL AB (2007) for details.

The SQL DML insert statement adds a new row to a table instance. Figure 5.14 shows the basic format of the insert statement. It starts with the keywords `INSERT INTO` followed by the name of the table the new row will be added to. Next comes a comma-separated list of the column names the insert statement is supplying data values for. If no value is supplied for a particular column, it is set to the default value for that column (or to null, if there is no default value specified).

The keyword `VALUES` comes next, followed by a comma-separated list of the values being supplied for the columns in the column list. Obviously, the two lists must be the same length. Code listing 5.3.1 shows how to use the insert statement to add contact

Figure 5.14 The SQL DML insert statement.

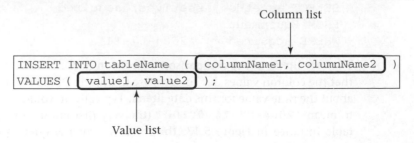

details for a new member of staff to the Staff Directory database's `Staff` table. The first value – `'89988'` – is the value for the `staffNo` column in the new row, the second value, `'Hasif'`, is the value of the `fName` column on the new row, and so on.

Code listing 5.3.1 An insert statement

```
INSERT INTO Staff (staffNo, fName, lName, email)
VALUES ('89988', 'Hasif', 'Choudhury',
       'h.choudhury@pennine.ac.uk');
```

The phone and photo columns don't appear in the column list, so, when the DBMS adds the new row to the `Staff` table, these columns are null. Code listing 5.3.2 shows how to explicitly instruct the DBMS to make the `phone` column null – that is, to do so include the column name in the column list and use the SQL keyword `NULL` in the value list.

Code listing 5.3.2 An equivalent insert statement to that in Code listing 5.3.1

```
INSERT INTO Staff (staffNo, fName, lName, email, phone)
VALUES ('89988', 'Hasif', 'Choudhury',
       'h.choudhury@pennine.ac.uk', NULL);
```

The column list is optional. Code listing 5.3.3 shows an insert statement with no column list. If the column list is omitted, then the value list *must* include a value for every column on the table. The first value is inserted into the first column, the second value into the second column and so on.

Code listing 5.3.3 Another equivalent insert statement to that in Code listing 5.3.1

```
INSERT INTO Staff
VALUES ('89988', 'Hasif', 'Choudhury',
       'h.choudhury@pennine.ac.uk', NULL, NULL);
```

This version of the insert statement can cause problems, though. First, it is possible to add new columns to a table. If a new column is added to the `Staff` table, then both Code listings 5.3.1 and 5.3.2 continue to work – data values will be inserted into the named columns and the defaults (or null) used for any other columns, including the new one. However, the insert statement in Code listing 5.3.3 will fail as the DBMS expects a value for every column, but the value list includes values for only the original six columns, not for the new seventh column.

Another problem is that it is very easy to get the order of the values wrong. Code listing 5.3.4 will work, but it puts the forename in the `staffNo` column, the surname in the `fName` column, the e-mail address in the `lName` column and the staff number in the `email` column. For these reasons, it is always better to include the column list.

Code listing 5.3.4 Adding a new row with all the data values in the wrong columns

```
INSERT INTO Staff
VALUES ('Hasif', 'Choudhury', 'h.choudhury@pennine.ac.uk',
       '89988', NULL, NULL);
```

Figure 5.15 The SQL DML update statement.

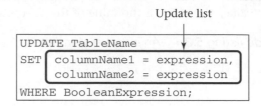

The SQL DML update statement changes column values in selected rows of a table instance. The general form is shown in Figure 5.15. The statement begins with the keyword UPDATE, followed by the name of the table the instance of which is being modified. Next comes the keyword SET, followed by a comma-separated list of assignment statements. Each assignment statement sets the value of *one* of the columns in the table to the value given by the expression. Finally, there is a where clause. Just as a where clause in a select statement tells the DBMS which rows to retrieve, the where clause in an update statement tells the DBMS which rows of the table instance to modify. If there is no where clause, then the update statement will affect every row in the table instance. This is rarely what is required, so most update statements include a where clause.

Suppose that Judith Smith, with staff number 25448, gets married and changes her surname to Smith-Atkins. This also means that her e-mail address changes. The Staff table in the Staff Directory database must be updated to reflect these changes in the real world.

Code listing 5.3.5 shows how the update is effected. The where clause ensures that only one row of the table is affected – the row that holds data about this particular member of staff. The update list mentions just two columns, so the column values for the staffNo, fName, phone and photo columns are unchanged.

Code listing 5.3.5 An update statement

```
UPDATE Staff
SET lName = 'Smith-Atkins',
    email = 'j.a.smith-atkins@pennine.ac.uk'
WHERE staffNo = '25448';
```

The format for setting the new column value is always the same – columnName = expression. This is true even when the column is being set to null. In this case, the expression is simply the SQL keyword NULL.

Code listing 5.3.6 shows how to set Judith Smith-Atkins' phone number to null. The '=' sign represents the assignment operator, not the equality comparison operator, so, in this case, it is correct to write phone = NULL (see the discussion of the IS NULL operator above for why it is not correct to write phone = NULL when using the equality comparison operator).

Code listing 5.3.6 Setting a column to null

```
UPDATE Staff
SET phone = NULL
WHERE staffNo = '25448';
```

Figure 5.16 The SQL DML delete statement.

```
DELETE FROM TableName
WHERE BooleanExpression;
```

The delete statement removes one or more rows from a table instance. The general format is shown in Figure 5.16. Notice that the delete statement only deletes whole rows – you don't 'delete' a single column value from a row. If the value of a column no longer applies (say Judith Smith-Atkins has moved office and no longer has a telephone), set the column to null using an update statement.

The delete statement begins with the SQL keywords DELETE FROM, followed by the name of the table. This can be followed by a where clause, though this is optional. Without a where clause, the delete statement will remove every row from the table.

For example, suppose that Judith Smith-Atkins has resigned. Code listing 5.3.7 shows how to remove the row that holds data about her from the Staff table instance. Notice that, in this case, only one row is removed because the where clause identifies a single row (the staffNo is the primary key for this table). If the where clause identifies more than one row, then all are removed from the table instance.

Code listing 5.3.7   Removing a row from the Staff *table*

```
DELETE FROM Staff
WHERE staffNo = '25448';
```

When there is no where clause, every row is removed from the table instance. The table definition (that is, the structure of the table) remains, but the table instance has no rows. It is sometimes necessary to remove all rows from a table instance, though. For example, at the end of each academic year, all information on staff support sessions is removed from the Staff Directory database. Staff timetables change each year, so the next year staff would be likely to offer support sessions at different times. Leaving the old data in the SupportSession table could cause confusion at the start of term, before staff have got round to entering their new support session times. Code listing 5.3.8 shows how to do this.

Code listing 5.3.8   Removing all rows from the SupportSession *table*

```
DELETE FROM SupportSession;
```

5.4 Creating, and removing, databases and tables with SQL DDL

Databases and tables need to be created before data can be added to them or retrieved from them. A database corresponds to an **SQL schema**. Figure 5.17 shows the basic format of the SQL DDL create schema statement. The SQL keywords CREATE SCHEMA are followed by the name of the new SQL schema. In fact, this is all that is required.

Figure 5.17 The SQL DDL create schema statement.

```
CREATE SCHEMA SchemaName
AUTHORIZATION AuthorizationId;
```

The authorization clause, which indicates which database user owns the new SQL schema, is optional. If included, it begins with the SQL keyword AUTHORIZATION (spelt with a 'z', not an 's'), followed by a valid authorization identifier. If the authorization clause is omitted, then the DBMS assumes that the user executing the statement owns the SQL schema.

Code listing 5.4.1 shows the SQL DDL statement to create an SQL schema called WebTimetable, owned by the user with the authorization identifier Web-TimetableDba. The WebTimetable SQL schema holds all the tables and other database objects needed by the Web Timetable application.

Code listing 5.4.1 Creating an SQL schema with SQL DDL

```
CREATE SCHEMA WebTimetable
AUTHORIZATION WebTimetableDba;
```

When an SQL Schema is first created, it does not have anything in it. In particular, the database tables need to be created, too. SQL DDL has the create table statement to do this.

The basic format for the create table statement is shown in Figure 5.18. The statement begins with the SQL keywords CREATE TABLE, followed by the name of the table being created. After this, and enclosed in parentheses, comes a comma-separated list of column definitions and table constraint definitions. Usually, database developers list the column definitions first, then the constraint definitions. Each column definition defines the characteristics of a single column. For most columns, there are four main characteristics:

1 column name – any valid SQL identifier

2 data type – any valid SQL data type

Figure 5.18 The basic SQL DDL create table statement.

```
CREATE TABLE TableName
(column1 dataType,
 column2 dataType DEFAULT (expression),
 column3 dataType NOT NULL,
 column4 dataType NOT NULL,
 column5 dataType DEFAULT (expression) NOT NULL,
 CONSTRAINT constraintName PRIMARY KEY (column3, column4)
);
```

Column definitions

Constraint definition

3 default clause – the keyword DEFAULT is followed by a default value for this column, enclosed in parentheses, which is usually a literal, but can be a more complex expression

4 column constraint – the keyword NOT NULL places a not-null constraint on the column.

Only the column name and data type are required. In Figure 5.18, column1 has a minimal column definition, while the other four include one or both of the two optional characteristics. The column constraint for column3 is a not-null constraint. There are other valid column constraints, but, as a matter of coding style, only not-null constraints will be defined as column constraints. The column definition for column5 has all four characteristics in the correct order.

> In the dialect of SQL used by the MySQL DBMS, the expression that defines the default value should *not* be enclosed in parentheses. See MySQL AB (2007) for details.

The table constraint definition in Figure 5.18 defines a primary key constraint. It begins with the keyword CONSTRAINT, followed by an SQL identifier that names the constraint. This part (CONSTRAINT constraintName) is optional and, if it is omitted, then the DBMS assigns the constraint a system-defined identifier. It is always best to give a constraint a meaningful name, rather than relying on the DBMS to generate one as it is often easier to remove a constraint later if its name is known.

After the constraint name, the keywords PRIMARY KEY indicate that this is a primary key constraint. The columns that form the primary key are then listed in parentheses. In this book, primary key constraint names consist of the table name prefixed by pri. This is just another coding convention. Naming a constraint priRoom does *not* make it a primary key, the keywords PRIMARY KEY do this.

Any valid SQL table constraint can be included in a create table statement, but, in this book, only primary key constraints are defined in the create table statement. Other constraints are added once the table has been created, using the SQL DDL alter table statement (see below). This is another coding convention and makes it easier to define foreign key constraints.

The Room and Equipment tables from the Web Timetable database use most of the different available data types and include columns with default values and not-null constraints. Sample table instances are shown in Figure 5.19. Note that the Equipment table now includes both the costs of the equipment and the dates when they were purchased. The SQL DDL statement to create the tables is shown in Code listing 5.4.2.

> SQL does not require the column and constraint definitions to appear on separate lines, but it is much easier to read the statement when it is presented with line breaks. Lining up the column names and data types is another good way to make the statement more readable, but is not required.

Figure 5.19 Sample instances of the `Equipment` and `Room` tables from the Web Timetable database.

Equipment

assetNo:varchar	assetType:varchar	description:varchar	building:varchar	room:varchar	portable:boolean	cost:numeric	acquired:date
1570131	Data projector	HP vp6100	Wilson	205	FALSE	1300.00	2004-07-14
1799131	Data projector	HP vp6100	NULL	NULL	TRUE	1300.00	2005-01-12
4560293	OHP	3M OHP 1608	Locke	24	FALSE	NULL	NULL
4503993	PC	Dell OptiPlex™ GX280	Wilson	205	FALSE	625.00	2004-04-30
5010009	OHP	3M OHP 2000	NULL	NULL	TRUE	185.00	2001 08-20
2992220	Data projector	ToshibaTDP-SW20	Priestley	G12	FALSE	1100.00	2005-01-12
2892112	Laptop	SONY X505	NULL	NULL	TRUE	NULL	NULL

Room

building:varchar	roomNo:varchar	capacity:numeric
Wilson	205	25
Wilson	113	25
Wilson	105	100
Priestley	G12	150
Priestley	113A	20
Locke	24	30
Locke	27	25
Locke	14	30

Code listing 5.4.2:   Creating tables with SQL DDL

```
CREATE TABLE Room
(
    building    VARCHAR(15) NOT NULL,
    roomNo      VARCHAR(4) NOT NULL,
    capacity    INTEGER,
    CONSTRAINT priRoom PRIMARY KEY (building, roomNo)
);


CREATE TABLE Equipment
(
    assetNo     VARCHAR(15) NOT NULL,
    assetType   VARCHAR(15) NOT NULL,
    description VARCHAR(50),
    building    VARCHAR(15),
    room        VARCHAR(4),
    portable    BOOLEAN DEFAULT (FALSE) NOT NULL,
    cost        NUMERIC(7,2),
    acquired    DATE,
    CONSTRAINT priEquipment PRIMARY KEY (assetNo)
);
```

The first create table statement in Code listing 5.4.2 creates the Room table. There are three column definitions and a primary key constraint. The first column definition defines a column called building with data type VARCHAR(15), so, in each row of the table, the value of the building column will be a character string of varying length, with a maximum length of 15 characters. The not-null constraint means that, in every row of the Room table, the building column will have a value; it is never null. Similarly, the value of the roomNo column will be a character string of varying length with a maximum of four characters and is never null.

The capacity column will have the data type INTEGER. The values of this numeric data type are integers. There is no precision defined by SQL (no limit on the number of digits in an INTEGER value), though the operating system software will impose a limit on the size of integers. Obviously, there is no scale for an integer – there are *no* digits after the decimal point (see Chapter 3 for a discussion of precision and scale). The capacity column *is* allowed to be null, although, in the table instance shown in Figure 5.19, every row has an integer value in the capacity column.

Finally, the table-constraint definition shows how to define a composite primary key.

The second create table statement in Code listing 5.4.2 creates the Equipment table. Note that the data type and size of the Equipment table's building and room columns must exactly match those of the corresponding building and roomNo columns of the Room table.

The first five column definitions should be familiar. The sixth column definition defines the portable column to have its data type as Boolean. Values in this column, therefore, will be Boolean values, which, in SQL, are TRUE, FALSE or UNKNOWN. The default clause ensures that if a row is added to the Equipment table with no value specified for portable, then the DBMS will use the default value FALSE. A column that does not have a default clause has a default of null, such as the description column of the Equipment table.

The last part of the column definition for portable is a not-null constraint. This means that it can never be null. In ISO SQL:2003, the truth value UNKNOWN is actually represented by null (Date, 2004, p. 592), so the portable column can only be either TRUE or FALSE.

A good rule of thumb is to *always define Boolean columns to be not null*. If a column value needs three different states – for example, an assignment from a particular student can be 'submitted', 'marked' or 'unknown' – then use a character data type and apply a **check constraint** to restrict the column values.

The column definition for cost has the data type NUMERIC(7,2). Here, the precision is 7, meaning that the value in the cost column can have up to seven digits. The scale is 2, so two of these digits *must* come *after* the decimal point. Thus, the cost column can hold values from 0 to 99999.99. (In fact, it can also hold negative values in the same absolute range.)

The last column defined is acquired with the data type DATE. Both cost and acquired can be null, as shown in Figure 5.19.

> The SQL standard insists that no column forming part of a primary key can ever be null. This means that the not-null column constraints on the `building` and `roomNo` columns of the `Room` table, and on the `assetNo` column of the `Equipment` table, are unnecessary. Including them does no harm, however, and makes clear that these columns cannot be null, even to people who don't understand SQL that well. Depending on the DBMS, it may even be necessary, so always include them.

The distinction between SQL column and table constraints is purely syntactic: both restrict what *rows* can exist in a table instance. In fact, a column constraint is just shorthand for a table constraint. Code listing 5.4.3 shows how to define the `Room` table using SQL check constraints on the table, rather than the not-null constraints on the columns.

Code listing 5.4.3   Creating a table without using column constraints

```
CREATE TABLE room
(building  VARCHAR(15),
roomNo     VARCHAR(4),
capacity   INTEGER,
CONSTRAINT priRoom PRIMARY KEY (building, roomNo),
CONSTRAINT chkRoomBuilding CHECK (building IS NOT NULL),
CONSTRAINT chkRoomRoomNo CHECK (roomNo IS NOT NULL)
);
```

While every column constraint is equivalent to some table constraint, the converse is not true. Column constraints can *only* refer to the column being defined. So, the primary key of `Equipment` *could* be defined as a column constraint, as shown in Code listing 5.4.4. However, the primary key of `Room` could *not* as this constraint must refer to two columns. To maintain a consistent feel between statements, it is best to define not-null constraints as unnamed column constraints and all other constraints as named table constraints.

Code listing 5.4.4   Defining a primary key using a column constraint

```
CREATE TABLE Equipment
(
   assetNo     VARCHAR(15) PRIMARY KEY NOT NULL,
   assetType   VARCHAR(15) NOT NULL,
   description VARCHAR(50),
   building    VARCHAR(15),
   room        VARCHAR(4),
   portable    BOOLEAN DEFAULT (FALSE) NOT NULL,
   cost        NUMERIC(7,2),
   acquired    DATE
);
```

One final point about the create table statements discussed above. There is no way to specify which SQL schema the table belongs to. This seems odd as every table *must* belong to some SQL schema. The way it works is that there is an SQL schema associated with each session as, when users log on to the DBMS, they must tell it what SQL schema they will be working on. Any create table statement executed during that session creates a table in the associated SQL schema. Users can change SQL schema during a session – the MySQL DBMS includes the USE statement to do this, for example.

> One more final point about the create table statement. There is a lot more to it than has been discussed here. However, most of the other options are not usually needed and may not be implemented by some commercial DBMS. Furthermore, commercial DBMS usually include additional options in their versions of the SQL create table statement. Every database developer should read the manual for the DBMS being used to become reasonably familiar with all the options of the create table statement that are available. This goes for the other statements, too.

Sometimes, it is necessary to remove a table entirely from a database. Tables are removed using the SQL DDL drop table statement. Removing a table has two effects:

1 all rows in the table instance are removed from the database.
2 all meta-data relating to the table definition are removed from the data dictionary.

Code listing 5.4.5 shows how to remove the Room table. The RESTRICT keyword means that if the Room table is referred to by a foreign key or check constraint on another table, then the DROP statement will fail. The DBMS will instead display an error message. This is the default behaviour, so the RESTRICT keyword is optional.

Code listing 5.4.5   Two equivalent SQL DDL statements to remove a table

(a) Explicitly using the RESTRICT option

```
DROP TABLE Room RESTRICT;
```

(b) Relying on the default behaviour to apply the RESTRICT option

```
DROP TABLE Room;
```

To remove Room and all tables that refer to it, use the statement given in Code listing 5.4.6. It will remove the Room table and all tables with a foreign key or check constraint mentioning Room, then all tables referring to these tables and so on.

The CASCADE option is very powerful. It is often better to use the RESTRICT option, then work out which other tables are affected. If all these tables can go, then repeat the drop table statement with the CASCADE option.

Code listing 5.4.6   Removing a table and all tables that refer to it

```
DROP TABLE Room CASCADE;
```

Sometimes, whole SQL schemas need to be removed. Code listing 5.4.7 shows how to remove an SQL schema with the SQL DDL drop schema statement. As with the drop table statement, the keyword RESTRICT instructs the DBMS to remove the SQL schema only if there are no tables (or other database objects) in it.

Code listing 5.4.7 Removing an empty SQL schema

```
DROP SCHEMA WebTimetable RESTRICT;
```

To remove the `WebTimetable` SQL schema and all its tables (and other database objects) with a single SQL DDL statement, use the `CASCADE` option. Here, too, the `CASCADE` option is very powerful. The statement in Code listing 5.4.8 removes the SQL schema `WebTimetable` and everything within it. Then, it removes or modifies any object in any other SQL schema that refers to an object in `WebTimetable`. These knock-on effects of the `CASCADE` option mean that it should be used with care.

Code listing 5.4.8 Removing an SQL schema and all related database objects

```
DROP SCHEMA WebTimetable CASCADE;
```

5.5 Altering tables with SQL DDL

The SQL create table statements in this book do not include foreign key or enterprise constraints. As discussed in Chapter 3, the columns {building, room} are a foreign key on the `Equipment` table that refers to the `Room` table. To define the associated foreign key constraint when the `Equipment` table is created, the `Room` table must already exist. More generally, to define foreign key constraints as part of the create table statement, the referenced tables must be created before the referencing tables.

With a large database, lots of tables and many foreign keys, working out which tables to create first becomes a chore. It is much better if the initial create table statements only include the not-null and primary key constraints. Other constraints are added using the SQL DDL alter table statement once all the tables have been created. The ISO SQL:2003 standard only allows one modification to a table schema in an alter table statement. Some DBMS allow you to make several modifications in a single alter table statement (the Oracle database and MySQL DBMS both allow this). All the examples in this book stick to the ISO SQL:2003 standard.

The format of the alter table statement changes slightly depending on what modifications are being made to the table. Figure 5.20 shows the format of the alter table statement used to add a foreign key constraint to a table.

The statement begins with the SQL keywords `ALTER TABLE`, followed by the name of the table being modified. The keywords `ADD CONSTRAINT` indicate that a new table constraint is being added. They are followed by the constraint name.

The next two lines in Figure 5.20 form the constraint definition. The keywords `FOREIGN KEY` indicate that a foreign key constraint is being added rather than any other table constraint. Next, comes a list of the foreign key columns. Of course, if there is only a single column in the foreign key, then there will be only a single column in this list.

The keyword `REFERENCES` is followed by the name of the referenced table and a list of the matching candidate key columns. The order of the columns in these lists is significant. The first foreign key column is matched with the first matching candidate

Figure 5.20 Adding a foreign key constraint using the SQL DDL alter table statement.

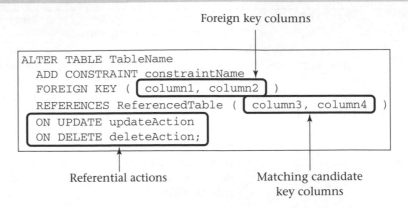

key column and so on. Get the order wrong, and the foreign key constraint will probably not work at all or, certainly, not as expected.

The constraint definition ends by specifying the referential actions. ON UPDATE tells the DBMS what to do with rows in the referencing table when the matching row in the referenced table is modified. Similarly, ON DELETE says what to do when a row of the referenced table is removed. In both cases, the referential action (indicated by updateAction and deleteAction in Figure 5.20), must be one of NO ACTION, CASCADE, SET NULL, SET DEFAULT and RESTRICT.

The first four were discussed in Chapter 3, but RESTRICT is new. RESTRICT is very similar to NO ACTION and the difference is in how the DBMS behaves while it is running an SQL DML statement. Every modification to the database instance – for example, to delete some rows from a table or modify column values on some rows of a table – goes through three stages.

1 The first stage is the set-up stage. During set-up, the DBMS identifies the *target rows* – those that will be modified directly by the SQL statement. Modifying these rows may cause indirect modifications to other rows in the form of referential actions and these *matching rows* are also identified.

2 Next comes the execution stage, during which the DBMS modifies the target rows, but does not change the matching rows.

3 The final stage is clean-up. During clean-up, the matching rows are modified, based on the relevant referential action.

The referential action NO ACTION says that the foreign key constraint should only be checked at the end of the clean-up stage and, if it is violated at that stage, then all the modifications must be undone. However, it is possible for the foreign key constraint to be violated during the execution stage; the constraint is only checked right at the end of the clean-up stage. In contrast, the RESTRICT referential action insists that the foreign key constraint is *never* violated, not even temporarily, during the execution stage. Table 5.1 summarizes the referential actions supported by SQL:2003 and explains their effects when a row in the referenced table is modified or removed.

215

Table 5.1 Referential actions supported by SQL and their effects.

Referential action	Referenced row is modified	Referenced row is removed
CASCADE	Modify value of foreign key columns on referencing rows to match.	Remove all referencing rows.
SET DEFAULT	Set value of the foreign key column on any referencing row to the column's default value.	Set value of the foreign key column on any referencing row to the column's default value.
SET NULL	Set value of the foreign key column on any referencing row to null.	Set value of the foreign key column on any referencing row to null.
RESTRICT	If there are referencing rows, do not allow the referenced row to be modified.	If there are referencing rows, do not allow the referenced row to be removed.
NO ACTION	If there are referencing rows, do not allow the referenced row to be modified.	If there are referencing rows, do not allow the referenced row to be removed.

Code listing 5.5.1 shows how to add the foreign key constraint to the Equipment table. The SQL identifier frnEquipmentRoom names the constraint and the name indicates that the constraint is a foreign key on the Equipment table, which references the Room table. Notice that the building column of the Equipment table is matched with the building column of the Room table, while the room column of the Equipment table is matched with the roomNo column of the Room table. Note that NO ACTION is the default referential action, so the last line in Code listing 5.5.1 could be omitted.

Code listing 5.5.1 Adding a foreign key constraint to a table

```
ALTER TABLE Equipment
ADD CONSTRAINT frnEquipmentRoom
  FOREIGN KEY (building, room)
  REFERENCES Room (building, roomNo)
  ON UPDATE CASCADE
  ON DELETE NO ACTION;
```

Primary key constraints and foreign key constraints are largely concerned with ensuring that the database instance is internally consistent – that there are no duplicate rows in a table, no unmatched foreign keys. In doing this, they can also enforce some business rules – every member of staff has a unique staff number, every support session is offered by some member of staff, for example.

To allow for more business rules to be enforced, SQL includes a third sort of constraint, which is the check constraint. Figure 5.21 shows the general format of the alter table statement that adds a check constraint. Only the format of the constraint definition has changed. This begins with the SQL keyword CHECK, followed, in parentheses, by a Boolean expression. This is the **check condition**. The check condition expresses the business rule in terms that the DBMS can understand. The format of the check

Figure 5.21 Adding a check constraint using the SQL DDL alter table statement.

```
ALTER TABLE TableName
  ADD CONSTRAINT constraintName
  CHECK (booleanExpression);
```

condition is the same as the Boolean expression in the where clause in an SQL DML statement. This allows a wide range of business rules to be enforced, as the following examples indicate. However, SQL does not support transition constraints, so all the examples are of state constraints.

The first example uses a check constraint to enforce the business rule:

the building name must be 'Wilson', 'Priestley' or 'Locke'.

There are two obvious ways to do this, illustrated by the two alter table statements in Code listing 5.5.2. The first alter table statement creates a constraint called chkBuildingName1; – using the prefix chk to begin the names of check constraints is simply a coding convention. The check condition on this alter table statement uses three equality comparisons joined by OR to express the business rule. It is true – and, hence, the constraint is satisfied – if the value of the building column is one of the three string literals about 'Wilson', 'Priestley' and 'Locke'.

The second alter table statement uses the SQL IN operator to form its check condition. The Boolean expression building IN ('Wilson', 'Priestley', 'Locke') asks the question. 'Is it true that the value of building is one of the values in the list ('Wilson', 'Priestley', 'Locke')?'

Clearly, both these constraints enforce the business rule. Which to use is a matter of personal preference, though some DBMS take longer to evaluate the IN operator.

Code listing 5.5.2   Enforcing the business rule 'The building name must be "Wilson", "Priestley" or "Locke"'

```
ALTER TABLE Room
  ADD CONSTRAINT chkBuildingName1
  CHECK (building='Wilson'
  OR building='Priestley'
  OR building='Locke');

ALTER TABLE Room
  ADD CONSTRAINT chkBuildingName2
  CHECK (building IN ('Wilson', 'Priestley', 'Locke'));
```

It's important to note that both these check constraints would allow a row with the building column set to null. When a row is added, or modified, the DBMS determines the truth of the statement 'The value supplied for the building column is equal to one of the allowed values.' The constraint is only violated if this statement is FALSE, in which case the DBMS rejects the change to the table instance. When the column would be null, the truth value of the statement is UNKNOWN as any comparison involving nulls evaluates to UNKNOWN (except those using the special IS NULL

217

operator). Thus, the constraint is *not* violated and the table instance would be changed, except for the fact that there is also a not null constraint on the `building` column. It is *this* constraint that stops the `building` column from being null.

> The MySQL DBMS does not enforce check constraints, although it does recognize the syntax. Instead, it includes an `enum` data type. Like a check constraint, this data type allows nulls, unless there is a not null constraint on the column. See MySQL AB (2007) for details.

Another business rule that applies to the `Room` table is:

the value of the `capacity` column must lie in the range 10 to 250.

As discussed above, range comparisons can be written using the SQL `BETWEEN` operator or the `<=` and `>=` comparison operators. Both versions are shown in Code listing 5.5.3. The check condition (`capacity BETWEEN 10 AND 250`) is self-explanatory. Note that (`capacity BETWEEN 250 AND 10`) is a valid Boolean expression, but never true as it states that the capacity must be greater than 250 and less than 10, which is impossible. Again, both forms of this check constraint allow `capacity` to be null and, as there is no not-null constraint, the capacity of a particular room may not be recorded in the database.

Code listing 5.5.3   Enforcing the business rule 'The value of the `capacity` column must lie in the range 10 to 250.'

```
ALTER TABLE Room
  ADD CONSTRAINT chkRoomCapacity1
  CHECK (capacity BETWEEN 10 AND 250);

ALTER TABLE Room
  ADD CONSTRAINT chkRoomCapacity2
  CHECK (capacity <= 250 AND capacity >= 10);
```

SQL also includes the unique constraint (Figure 5.22). This is used mostly to enforce candidate key constraints other than the primary key constraint. The keyword `UNIQUE` is followed by a list of columns. Like a primary key constraint, it is the combination of column values that must be unique. At the Pennine University, the business rule:

every member of staff has an e-mail account with a unique e-mail address

can be enforced by a unique constraint. Code listing 5.5.4 adds this unique constraint to the `email` column of the `Staff` table.

Figure 5.22 Adding a unique constraint using the SQL DDL alter table statement.

```
ALTER TABLE TableName
  ADD CONSTRAINT constraintName
  UNIQUE (column1, column2, column3);
```

Figure 5.23 Using the SQL DDL alter table statement to remove a constraint.

```
ALTER TABLE TableName
  DROP CONSTRAINT constraintName;
```

Code listing 5.5.4   A unique constraint

```
ALTER TABLE Staff
  ADD CONSTRAINT unqStaffEmail
  UNIQUE (email);
```

The unique constraint, like the check constraint, allows columns to be null. Sometimes, a column value should be unique if it is known, but may be null. This would be true if some of the staff at the Pennine University did not have an e-mail address. For a candidate key, no column can be null, so, as well as the unique constraint on the table, each column of the candidate key should have a not-null constraint.

The alter table statement can also remove a named constraint. The general format is shown in Figure 5.23. Note that the constraint name is required, which is why it is a good idea to give constraints meaningful names. Being able to remove constraints from a table is useful when legacy data is being imported into a new database. Some legacy data may violate the constraints, but it is usually easier to find and modify such data once it is in the database. Dropping the constraint allows the data to be imported into the table and modified. The constraints can then be reinstated. This is also a good way to check that *all* the imported data has been modified as the attempt to reinstate a constraint will fail unless all data in the table satisfies it. Code listing 5.5.5 shows how to remove the unique constraint on the `email` column of the `Staff` table.

Code listing 5.5.5   Removing a constraint from a table

```
ALTER TABLE Staff
DROP CONSTRAINT unqStaffEmail;
```

> Some DBMS allow a constraint to be disabled and then enabled. This is less drastic than removing and recreating it, so is a useful feature if there is lots of legacy data to import.

Unlike removing a table or an SQL schema, removing a constraint never has knock-on effects on other tables. Even removing a foreign key constraint will not affect the referenced table. Even on the referencing table there is no immediate effect on the table instance – the data in the table instance conforms to the constraint, whether it is enforced by the DBMS or not. For this reason, there is no need to include the CASCADE and RESTRICT keywords.

The other use of the alter table statement is to add, modify or remove columns. Adding a new column (Figure 5.24) is much like adding a constraint – the keywords ADD COLUMN are followed by a column definition, in the same format as was the case for a create table statement. Also as in the create table statement, only the column

219

Figure 5.24 Adding a column to a table using the SQL DDL alter table statement.

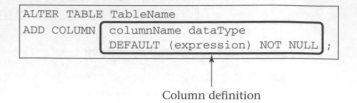

Column definition

name and data type are required. Code Listing 5.5.6 adds a new column to the Room table. Notice that the default value is zero. In this situation, zero indicates that the floorspace is not known, but, usually, null is used for this purpose. Using a valid value to indicate missing information is not usually a good idea as it can lead to ambiguity. However, in some circumstances, such as this one, there is no possibility of confusion – the floorspace in a room is always greater than zero.

Code listing 5.5.6   Adding a column to a table

```
ALTER TABLE Room
ADD COLUMN floorSpace NUMERIC(5,1) DEFAULT (0) NOT NULL;
```

The ISO standard for SQL allows an existing column to be modified in only two ways:

- the default can be set to a different value
- the default can be removed; Figure 5.25 shows the general syntax for both modifications.

Even a column that was originally defined without a default clause can be given one using the SET DEFAULT keywords in the alter table statement. Code listing 5.5.7 shows how to modify, and remove, the default value on the Room table's floorSpace column.

Code listing 5.5.7   Modifying the Room table's floorSpace column

```
ALTER TABLE Room
  ALTER COLUMN floorSpace SET DEFAULT (25);
ALTER TABLE Room
  ALTER COLUMN floorSpace DROP DEFAULT;
```

Figure 5.25 Using the SQL DDL alter table statement to modify a column.

```
ALTER TABLE TableName
 ALTER COLUMN columnName
 SET DEFAULT (expression);
```

```
ALTER TABLE TableName
 ALTER COLUMN columnName
 DROP DEFAULT;
```

Figure 5.26 Removing a column using the SQL DDL alter table statement.

```
ALTER TABLE TableName
 DROP COLUMN columnName RESTRICT;
```

```
ALTER TABLE TableName
 DROP COLUMN columnName CASCADE;
```

The final modification supported by the alter table statement is that of removing an entire column. Removing a column, like removing a table, can have knock-on effects. For example, if the column is part of a primary key, then removing the column means that the primary key constraint must also be removed as the remaining columns cannot form a candidate key for the table (remember: all candidate keys are irreducible). For this reason, the CASCADE and RESTRICT keywords are part of the DROP COLUMN clause, as shown in Figure 5.26. Code Listing 5.5.8 shows how to remove a column. The first statement will fail if there are knock-on effects, as RESTRICT is the default. The second will always succeed, but may have knock-on effects.

Code listing 5.5.8   Removing a column from a table

```
ALTER TABLE Room
  DROP COLUMN floorSpace;

ALTER TABLE room
  DROP COLUMN floorSpace CASCADE;
```

The alter table statement is one area where DBMS manufacturers have added functionality beyond that specified in the SQL standard. Table 5.2 summarizes the different uses of the alter table statement in the ISO SQL:2003 standard and recent versions of selected commercial DBMS.

There are other differences between the ISO SQL standard and the SQL syntax supported by commercial DBMS. It is sensible to consult the manual for a particular DBMS before attempting any major projects. That said, understanding the ISO standard for

Table 5.2 Functionality of the alter table statement.

Functionality	SQL:2003	MySQL	Oracle	MS SQL Server
Add a column	Yes	Yes	Yes	Yes
Set or remove a column default	Yes	Yes	Yes	Yes
Alter column data type or length	No	Yes	Yes	Yes
Remove a column	Yes	Yes	No	Yes
Add a constraint	Yes	Yes	Yes	Yes
Disable and enable a constraint	No	Foreign key constraint only	Yes	Yes
Remove a constraint	Yes	Yes	Yes	Yes

SQL is still the best basis for learning the language as most DBMS support most of the features discussed above.

Chapter summary

- This chapter has covered the basic features of the SQL data language. The SQL DML select, insert, update and delete statements were introduced, with examples. The where clause was discussed separately, including the problems caused by nulls and three-valued logic. The SQL DDL create schema, create table, alter and drop statements were also introduced.

- Although the ISO SQL standard forms a good basis for learning SQL, it's important to always check the manual for a particular DBMS. Few DBMS implement the whole ISO SQL standard, and all include extensions and additional features that may prove useful. In particular, support for the Boolean data type is very patchy. (This is odd as it is the only data type actually required by the relational data model.)

Further reading

There are many books and web resources covering SQL.

Connolly and Begg (2004) is a good source for students.

The main reference work on the ISO SQL standard is Melton and Simon (2002), although this covers the earlier SQL:1999 standard.

The actual ISO SQL standard can be purchased from the ISO website (www.iso.org), though it is unlikely to be much use to beginners.

Date (2004) covers SQL, but is not very enthusiastic about the language.

Websites include the always excellent W3Schools (www.w3schools.com) and the sites of the major DBMS vendors.

A copy of the BNF grammar for the ISO SQL:2003 standard is available online from Savage (2005).

Review questions

5.1 Explain the following terms used in the definition of the SQL data language:
   (a) SQL schema
   (b) catalog
   (c) information schema
   (d) SQL DDL
   (e) SQL DML.

5.2 Name the four main statements of the SQL DML and explain their purpose.

5.3 Which parts of the select statement must always be included? Why?

5.4 Explain the purpose of the order by clause of the select statement.

5.5 In the context of the select list, what is an alias? Why might you use one?

5.6 Name three of the SQL DDL statements discussed in this chapter and explain their purpose.

5.7 List the four main characteristics of a column definition in a create table statement and explain them.

5.8 Explain the purpose of the RESTRICT and CASCADE keywords in the drop statement.

5.9 Explain the purpose of the SQL check constraint and unique constraint.

5.10 Summarize the functionality of the SQL alter table statement discussed in this chapter.

Exercises

These exercises use the Equipment and Room tables to provide practice in writing SQL statements. Sample instances of these are shown in Figure 5.19.

5.11 The following questions provide practice in using the most basic form of the select statement, where data from all the rows in the table are included in the result set. All solutions have the same basic structure – an instruction to the DBMS to 'SELECT the data in these columns FROM this table'. There are no where clauses needed in any of the select statements for this question.

(a) Write an SQL statement to display the data in the assetNo and assetType columns from all rows of the Equipment table. Do not display data from the other columns.

(b) Write an SQL statement to display the data in the assetNo, assetType and description columns from all rows of the Equipment table. Do not display data from the other columns.

(c) Write two different SQL statements to display the data in the building, roomNo and capacity columns from all rows of the Room table. One statement should use column names and one not.

(d) Display the data in the building and room columns from all rows of the Equipment table. Ensure that if two rows have the same data in the building and room columns, then that data is shown only once.

(e) Display the data in the building and roomNo columns from all rows of the Room table. Again, ensure that if two rows have the same data in the building and roomNo columns, then that data is shown only once.

5.12 The following questions provide practice in writing select statements that have a where clause. The where clause specifies which rows of the table should be included in the result set. All solutions will have the same basic structure – an instruction to the DBMS to 'SELECT the data in these columns FROM this table WHERE the data on the row satisfies this Boolean expression'.

(a) Display the data in the `assetNo, assetType` and `description` columns for those rows of the `Equipment` table where the value of the `building` column is Wilson.

(b) Display the data in the `assetNo, assetType` and `description` columns for those rows of the `Equipment` table where the value of the `building` column is Wilson and the value of the `room` column is 205.

(c) Display the data in the `assetNo, assetType` and `description` columns for those rows from the `Equipment` table where the value of the `building` column is Wilson or the value of the `building` column is Locke.

(*Note:* Usually the above instructions would be phrased like this: 'List the asset number, type and description for equipment in the Wilson and Locke buildings.' Note that, although the informal description uses 'and' logically this is an 'or' as one piece of equipment cannot be in both buildings at the same time, so the query requires a list of equipment that is either in the Wilson building or in the Locke building. This is a style of writing database queries that you will need to get used to. Both forms are included for the rest of this question, then only the less formal version.)

(d) List the asset number, type and description for all equipment where the date it was acquired is unknown. Phrasing this more formally, display the data in the `assetNo, assetType` and `description` columns for those rows from the `Equipment` table where the `acquired` column is `NULL`.

(e) List the asset number, description and cost of all equipment costing £500 or more. List the equipment alphabetically by description. Phrasing this more formally, display the data in the `assetNo, description` and `cost` columns for those rows from the `Equipment` table where the `cost` is greater than or equal to £500. Order the results alphabetically by `description`.

(f) List the asset number, description and cost of all equipment costing between £500 and £1500, inclusive. Phrasing this more formally, display the data in the `assetNo, description` and `cost` columns for those rows from the `Equipment` table where the `cost` is greater than or equal to £500 and less than or equal to £1500.

5.13 The following questions provide practice in using expressions and column aliases in the select list and the `LIKE` comparison operator in the where clause.

(a) Display a list of equipment showing the asset number, type, description and location for each piece of equipment. The location is defined as being the combination of the building and room number, such as 'Wilson 205'. Ensure that the columns of the result set have suitable names.

(b) The equipment budget for 2005 was £10,000. Display a list of equipment purchased in 2005 showing the asset number, type, description and the percentage of the budget spent on each item. Ensure that the columns of the result set have suitable names.

(c) List the asset number, type and description for all equipment where the description begins with the string 'HP'. (This should include all equipment manufactured by Hewlett Packard.)

(d) List the asset number, type and description for all equipment where the description includes the string 'HP'.

(e) List the asset number, type and description for all equipment where the asset type ends with the string 'HP'.

(f) List the asset number, type and description for all equipment where the asset type includes the string 'projector' and the description begins with the string 'HP'.

(g) List the asset number, type and description for all equipment where the asset type includes the string 'projector' or the description begins with the string 'HP'.

5.14 This question gives you some practice in modifying the table instance. In each case, write an appropriate SQL DML statement to complete the task.

(a) Add the following row of data to the `Room` table:

`building` = 'Priestley', `roomNo` = '114' and `capacity` = 40.

(b) Add the following row of data to the `Equipment` table:

`assetNo` = '3124657', `assetType` = 'OHP', `description` = '3M OHP 2000', `portable` = FALSE.

Leave the remaining columns null. Why doesn't the foreign key constraint prevent this row, which does not match any row on the `Room` table, being added?

(c) Now set the building and room for the piece of equipment added in part (b) to Priestley 114.

(d) Increase the capacity of every room by 5.

(e) The Priestley building has burnt down, destroying all the equipment stored there. The insurance claim has been paid and a new building is under construction. Remove all data associated with this building from the Web Timetable database.

5.15 This question provides practice in writing SQL create table and alter table statements. For each table schema, write a suitable create table statement to implement the table schema shown below. This statement should implement all the column definitions and the primary key constraint. *Do not* include constraint definitions to implement candidate keys, foreign keys or business rules in the create table statements. Add each of these constraints using an alter table statement.

(*Note:* There is no foreign key linking the `Course` and `Module` tables as each module may be used by many courses and each course delivers many modules. Chapters 8 and 9 explain how to deal with such 'many-to-many' relationships between tables.)

```
Course (code CHAR(4) NOT NULL,
        title VARCHAR(50) NOT NULL,
        leadDepartment VARCHAR(30) NOT NULL,
        minorDepartment VARCHAR(30),
        level VARCHAR(15) NOT NULL,
        qualification VARCHAR(50),
        mode VARCHAR(9)DEFAULT 'Full Time' NOT NULL
        )
PRIMARY KEY (code)
CANDIDATE KEY (title, mode)
BUSINESS RULE mode must be one of {'Full Time', 'Part Time'}
```

```
Module (code CHAR(8) NOT NULL,
        title VARCHAR(50) NOT NULL,
        department VARCHAR(30) NOT NULL,
        level VARCHAR(15) NOT NULL,
        leader VARCHAR(10)
        )
PRIMARY KEY (code)
CANDIDATE KEY (department, title)
FOREIGN KEY leader REFERENCES Staff(staffNo)
            ON UPDATE CASCADE
            ON DELETE SET NULL

Staff (staffNo VARCHAR(10) NOT NULL,
       title VARCHAR(4) NOT NULL,
       fName VARCHAR(50) NOT NULL,
       lName VARCHAR(20) NOT NULL,
       email VARCHAR(50) NOT NULL,
       department VARCHAR(30) NOT NULL,
       lineManager VARCHAR(10) NOT NULL
       )
PRIMARY KEY (staffNo)
CANDIDATE KEY (email)
BUSINESS RULE title must be one of {'Mr', 'Ms', 'Miss', 'Mrs',
'Dr', 'Prof'}
FOREIGN KEY lineManager REFERENCES Staff(staffNo)
            ON UPDATE CASCADE
            ON DELETE NO ACTION
```

5.16 Write alter table statements to achieve the following actions:
   (a) remove the foreign key constraint on the `Staff` table's `lineManager` column
   (b) remove the `Staff` table's `lineManager` column
   (c) reinstate the `Staff` table's `lineManager` column
   (d) remove the default value from the `Course` table's `mode` column
   (e) reinstate the default value for the `Course` table's `mode` column.

Investigations

5.17 Investigate the differences between the ISO SQL standard and the version of the SQL language implemented by the DBMS you use. You may choose to investigate differences in syntax or look at the different conformance packages of the ISO SQL standard itself and the level of conformance your DBMS claims. How do other DBMS compare to yours in terms of compliance with the standard? (Melton and Simon (2002) is a useful source on the ISO SQL standard.)

5.18 What tools exist to help write, and debug, SQL statements? To what extent is the data language query by example (QBE) used as a basis for such tools? You should look into query builders and administration tools. Critically evaluate the usefulness of such tools for a novice web database developer.

5.19 The ISO SQL specification states that every SQL catalog must contain at least one SQL schema – the `INFORMATION_SCHEMA`. This is the data dictionary for *all* the SQL schema in the catalog. Investigate the `INFORMATION_SCHEMA` and the extent to which your DBMS implements the approach to managing meta-data taken in the ISO SQL standard. (Melton and Simon (2002) is a useful source for the ISO SQL standard.)

5.20 SQL is the most widely used data language for the relational data model, but the formal data languages defined for the relational data model are the relational algebra and the relational calculus. Date (2004) has a chapter on each of these. Investigate these languages, comparing them to SQL.

6 More features of the SQL data language

Chapter objectives

→ Describe more advanced use of the SQL DML, such as:
  - joins
  - value functions
  - subqueries
  - grouping and summarizing data.
→ Describe more advanced use of the SQL DDL, such as:
  - advanced enterprise constraints
  - SQL views.

Chapter outline

This chapter continues the discussion of the SQL data language. It introduces some more advanced SQL features for manipulating both the database instance and database schema. Until recently, not all commercial DBMS implemented all the features discussed here. In particular, the MySQL DBMS only implemented subqueries in Version 4.1 and views in Version 5.0. Prior to these releases, web database developers using the MySQL DBMS had to use alternative approaches to achieve the same effect. Often this meant coding a table join instead of a subquery or using procedural code (such as PHP) to manipulate result sets rather than using a view. Now that the MySQL DBMS supports these features it makes sense to use them, but be aware that older code will still use the alternative approaches. It may simply not be feasible to recode all the existing web pages to make use of these recently supported features.

■ Section 6.1 discusses join queries. A join query allows data to be retrieved from two or more tables at once, so join queries are quite common in database applications.

- Section 6.2 discusses some of the built-in SQL value functions. There are useful SQL value functions to manipulate string values and convert string literals to dates and back. It is often better to use these than pull the raw data back to the PHP script and manipulate the values there.

- Section 6.3 looks at the SQL aggregate functions, which allow queries to retrieve summary information from tables.

- Section 6.4 explores subqueries, which are now supported by all the major commercial DBMS. A subquery allows data from one table to be manipulated in ways determined by data values from another. Subqueries can be used in both data manipulation and data definition, and examples of both uses are explained.

- Finally, having introduced a range of more complex queries, Section 6.5 shows how to hide this complexity using SQL views.

6.1   Joining data from two or more tables

Relational databases organize data into tables. Typically, there will be relationships between the tables in a database. For example, the `Staff` and `SupportSession` tables of the Staff Directory database are related as each support session is offered by a particular member of staff (Figure 6.1). This means that the data only really make sense when they are joined together, to show both the data held about the member of staff and the data held about their support sessions. It is very easy to retrieve data from two tables using SQL – simply name both the tables in the from clause. Code listing 6.1.1 shows how. Note that the select list is rather long, so has been split over three lines (SQL allows line breaks in an SQL statement). A select statement that retrieves data from two (or more) tables is called a **join**.

Code listing 6.1.1   Retrieving data from two tables – a cross join

```
SELECT Staff.staffNo, fName, lName, phone,
       email, SupportSession.staffNo,
       dayOfWeek, startTime, endTime
FROM Staff, SupportSession;
```

Code listing 6.1.1 illustrates the SQL **qualified identifier** – any column name can be prefixed with the name of the table that it belongs to. The format is `tableName.columnName`, so, for example, `Staff.staffNo` is the `staffNo` column of the `Staff` table, whereas `SupportSession.staffNo` is the `staffNo` column of the `SupportSession` table. Without the qualified identifier, there would be no way for the DBMS to distinguish between these two different columns in the select list and it would report an error. The qualified identifier syntax can be extended to include the database, too:

```
databaseName.tableName.columnName
```

For example, `StaffDirectory.Staff.staffNo`. This allows SQL queries to gather data from tables in different databases (as long as the two databases are managed by the same DBMS). Notice that the column names in the result set are based solely on the underlying column name, not on the qualified identifier (Figure 6.2).

229

Figure 6.1 Related data in the `Staff` and `SupportSession` tables.

Staff

staffNo:Varchar	fName:Varchar	lName:Varchar	email:Varchar	phone:Varchar	photo:BLOB
10780	John	Smith	j.b.smith@pennine.ac.uk	NULL	[BLOB]
14443	Helen	Abbot	h.abbot@pennine.ac.uk	8032	[BLOB]
23257	Freya	Stark	f.stark@pennine.ac.uk	8660	[BLOB]
25447	John	Smith	j.smith@pennine.ac.uk	5104	[BLOB]
25448	Judith Anne	Smith	j.a.smith@pennine.ac.uk	7709	[BLOB]
31210	Paul	Smith	p.smith@pennine.ac.uk	NULL	[BLOB]
33509	Helen	Timms	h.timms@pennine.ac.uk	8661	[BLOB]
33935	Padma	Brar	p.brar@pennine.ac.uk	6641	[BLOB]
35054	Selma	Hutchins	s.hutchins@pennine.ac.uk	8706	[BLOB]
35155	Helene	Chirac	h.chirac@pennine.ac.uk	NULL	[BLOB]
45965	Mikhail	Sudbin	m.sudbin@pennine.ac.uk	5553	[BLOB]
55776	Gurpreet	Choudhury	g.choudhury@pennine.ac.uk	5454	[BLOB]
56673	Joshua	Bittaye	j.bittaye@pennine.ac.uk	7782	[BLOB]
56893	Ruth	Bapetsi	r.bapetsi@pennine.ac.uk	8022	[BLOB]
77712	Frank	Rose	f.rose@pennine.ac.uk	8871	[BLOB]
78893	Jo Karen	O'Connor	j.k.oconnor@pennine.ac.uk	8871	[BLOB]
89987	Dan	Lin	d.lin@pennine.co.uk	8514	[BLOB]

Matching rows

SupportSession

staffNo:Varchar	dayOfWeek:Varchar	startTime:Time	endTime:Time
56673	Friday	15:30:00	16:30:00
56673	Thursday	15:30:00	16:30:00
35054	Monday	09:00:00	10:00:00
45965	Wednesday	11:00:00	12:00:00
31210	Wednesday	11:00:00	13:00:00
35054	Monday	15:00:00	16:00:00
56893	Thursday	09:00:00	10:00:00
45965	Monday	11:00:00	12:00:00
23257	Monday	15:00:00	16:00:00
55776	Monday	14:00:00	16:00:00
56893	Tuesday	14:00:00	15:00:00
56673	Friday	10:00:00	11:00:00
35054	Tuesday	11:00:00	12:00:00

Figure 6.2 The first few rows of the result set for Code listing 6.1.1.

staffNo	fName	lName	phone	email	staffNo	dayOfWeek	startTime	endTime
10780	John	Smith	NULL	j.b.smith@pennine.ac.uk	35054	Monday	09:00:00	10:00:00
25447	John	Smith	5104	j.smith@pennine.ac.uk	35054	Monday	09:00:00	10:00:00
25448	Judith Anne	Smith	7709	j.a.smith@pennine.ac.uk	35054	Monday	09:00:00	10:00:00
31210	Paul	Smith	NULL	p.smith@pennine.ac.uk	35054	Monday	09:00:00	10:00:00
77712	Frank	Rose	8871	f.rose@pennine.ac.uk	35054	Monday	09:00:00	10:00:00
14443	Helen	Abbot	8032	h.abbot@pennine.ac.uk	35054	Monday	09:00:00	10:00:00
23257	Freya	Stark	8660	f.stark@pennine.ac.uk	35054	Monday	09:00:00	10:00:00
33935	Padma	Brar	6641	p.brar@pennine.ac.uk	35054	Monday	09:00:00	10:00:00
35054	Selma	Hutchins	8706	s.hutchins@pennine.ac.uk	35054	Monday	09:00:00	10:00:00
45965	Mikhail	Sudbin	5553	m.sudbin@pennine.ac.uk	35054	Monday	09:00:00	10:00:00
35155	Helene	Chirac	NULL	h.chirac@pennine.ac.uk	35054	Monday	09:00:00	10:00:00
55776	Gurpreet	Choudhury	5454	g.choudhury@pennine.ac.uk	35054	Monday	09:00:00	10:00:00
56893	Ruth	Bapetsi	8022	r.bapetsi@pennine.ac.uk	35054	Monday	09:00:00	10:00:00
56673	Joshua	Bittaye	7782	j.bittaye@pennine.ac.uk	35054	Monday	09:00:00	10:00:00
89987	Dan	Lin	8514	d.lin@pennine.co.uk	35054	Monday	09:00:00	10:00:00
78893	Jo Karen	O'Connor	8871	j.k.oconnor@pennine.ac.uk	35054	Monday	09:00:00	10:00:00
33509	Helen	Timms	8661	h.timms@pennine.ac.uk	35054	Monday	09:00:00	10:00:00
10780	John	Smith	NULL	j.b.smith@pennine.ac.uk	31210	Wednesday	11:00:00	13:00:00
25447	John	Smith	5104	j.smith@pennine.ac.uk	31210	Wednesday	11:00:00	13:00:00
25448	Judith Anne	Smith	7709	j.a.smith@pennine.ac.uk	31210	Wednesday	11:00:00	13:00:00
31210	Paul	Smith	NULL	p.smith@pennine.ac.uk	31210	Wednesday	11:00:00	13:00:00
77712	Frank	Rose	8871	f.rose@pennine.ac.uk	31210	Wednesday	11:00:00	13:00:00
14443	Helen	Abbot	8032	h.abbot@pennine.ac.uk	31210	Wednesday	11:00:00	13:00:00
23257	Freya	Stark	8660	f.stark@pennine.ac.uk	31210	Wednesday	11:00:00	13:00:00
33935	Padma	Brar	6641	p.brar@pennine.ac.uk	31210	Wednesday	11:00:00	13:00:00
35054	Selma	Hutchins	8706	s.hutchins@pennine.ac.uk	31210	Wednesday	11:00:00	13:00:00
45965	Mikhail	Sudbin	5553	m.sudbin@pennine.ac.uk	31210	Wednesday	11:00:00	13:00:00
35155	Helene	Chirac	NULL	h.chirac@pennine.ac.uk	31210	Wednesday	11:00:00	13:00:00
55776	Gurpreet	Choudhury	5454	g.choudhury@pennine.ac.uk	31210	Wednesday	11:00:00	13:00:00
56893	Ruth	Bapetsi	8022	r.bapetsi@pennine.ac.uk	31210	Wednesday	11:00:00	13:00:00
56673	Joshua	Bittaye	7782	j.bittaye@pennine.ac.uk	31210	Wednesday	11:00:00	13:00:00
89987	Dan	Lin	8514	d.lin@pennine.co.uk	31210	Wednesday	11:00:00	13:00:00
78893	Jo Karen	O'Connor	8871	j.k.oconnor@pennine.ac.uk	31210	Wednesday	11:00:00	13:00:00
33509	Helen	Timms	8661	h.timms@pennine.ac.uk	31210	Wednesday	11:00:00	13:00:00
10780	John	Smith	NULL	j.b.smith@pennine.ac.uk	35054	Monday	15:00:00	16:00:00
25447	John	Smith	5104	j.smith@pennine.ac.uk	35054	Monday	15:00:00	16:00:00
25448	Judith Anne	Smith	7709	j.a.smith@pennine.ac.uk	35054	Monday	15:00:00	16:00:00

The select statement in Code listing 6.1.1 does not do what you might expect. The first few rows of the result set are shown in Figure 6.2. There are actually 204 rows in the result set, which is why the final row in Figure 6.2 is shown cut off.

Look carefully at the first 17 rows in Figure 6.2 and compare them to the 17 rows in the Staff table and the *first* row in the SupportSession table, shown in Figure 6.1. It is clear that the DBMS has taken each row of the Staff table in turn and joined on to this data the data from the *first* row of the SupportSession table. Then, it has taken each row of the Staff table in turn and joined on to this data the data from the *second* row of the SupportSession table. Just to be clear, the select statement in code listing 6.1.1 joins each row of the SupportSession table to *every* row of the Staff table. This is called a **cross join**.

In itself, the cross join is not very useful. In fact, the result set in Figure 6.2 is misleading as it suggests, for example, that every member of staff is available for the support session offered by the staff member with staff number 35054 on a Monday between 9 and 10 o'clock. In fact, the staff member with staff number 35054 is Selma Hutchins and only Selma Hutchins offers this support session. The cross join, is, however, the basis for a more useful approach to joining data from related tables.

The obvious way to produce meaningful information out of the result set in Figure 6.2 is to instruct the DBMS to only include those rows of the cross join where the values in the Staff.staffNo and SupportSession.staffNo columns are the same. Of the first 17 rows, this is only true for the ninth row – the row with Selma Hutchins' data. To see how to do this, it helps to understand how the DBMS processes a select statement. Chapter 5 explained that the order of the different parts of the select statement is fixed:

1 select list
2 from clause
3 where clause
4 order by clause.

However, the DBMS does *not* process the instructions in this order. The very first thing the DBMS does with a select statement is process the from clause. If there is a single table, this simply means that it retrieves all the rows from that table. When there are two (or more) tables, the DBMS creates the cross join. Only after the cross join has been produced does the DBMS look at the where clause. It uses the instructions in the where clause to decide which rows of the cross join will actually go into the final result set. It then uses the select list to decide which columns to include and the order by clause to sort the rows of the result set as required. To sum up, the order of processing is:

1 from clause
2 where clause
3 select list
4 order by clause

This description of how a DBMS processes a select statement is intentionally naïve. It correctly describes the general approach taken, but not the specifics. Most DBMS have a more sophisticated approach, which optimizes the speed with which a result set is retrieved. These query optimization techniques are beyond the scope of this book.

Figure 6.3 The result set for Code listing 6.1.2.

staffNo	fName	lName	phone	email	staffNo	dayOfWeek	startTime	endTime
35054	Selma	Hutchins	8706	s.hutchins@pennine.ac.uk	35054	Monday	09:00:00	10:00:00
31210	Paul	Smith	NULL	p.smith@pennine.ac.uk	31210	Wednesday	11:00:00	13:00:00
35054	Selma	Hutchins	8706	s.hutchins@pennine.ac.uk	35054	Monday	15:00:00	16:00:00
45965	Mikhail	Sudbin	5553	m.sudbin@pennine.ac.uk	45965	Monday	11:00:00	12:00:00
45965	Mikhail	Sudbin	5553	m.sudbin@pennine.ac.uk	45965	Wednesday	11:00:00	12:00:00
23257	Freya	Stark	8660	f.stark@pennine.ac.uk	23257	Monday	15:00:00	16:00:00
55776	Gurpreet	Choudhury	5454	g.choudhury@pennine.ac.uk	55776	Monday	14:00:00	16:00:00
56893	Ruth	Bapetsi	8022	r.bapetsi@pennine.ac.uk	56893	Tuesday	14:00:00	15:00:00
56893	Ruth	Bapetsi	8022	r.bapetsi@pennine.ac.uk	56893	Thursday	09:00:00	10:00:00
56673	Joshua	Bittaye	7782	j.bittaye@pennine.ac.uk	56673	Thursday	15:30:00	16:30:00
56673	Joshua	Bittaye	7782	j.bittaye@pennine.ac.uk	56673	Friday	10:00:00	11:00:00
56673	Joshua	Bittaye	7782	j.bittaye@pennine.ac.uk	56673	Friday	15:30:00	16:30:00

As the DBMS creates the cross join before processing the where clause, the where clause can be used to extract meaningful data from the cross join. Typically, this means matching the foreign key columns of one table with the primary key columns of the other.

Code listing 6.1.2 produces the result set shown in Figure 6.3. This is the correct way to join the `Staff` and `SupportSession` tables as it clearly identifies who offers which support session. Notice that those staff who do not offer any support sessions (Dan Lin and Helene Chirac) do not appear in the result set.

Code listing 6.1.2 *Retrieving data from two tables – an equi-join*

```
SELECT Staff.staffNo, fName, lName, phone,
       email, SupportSession.staffNo,
       dayOfWeek, startTime, endTime
FROM Staff, SupportSession
WHERE Staff.staffNo = SupportSession.staffNo;
```

The select statement in Code listing 6.1.2 is called an **equi-join** as it joins two tables based on an equality condition. It is used mostly where there is a foreign key relationship between the two tables in the from clause. In an equi-join, the where clause always includes a **join condition** of the form:

```
foreign key column = matching primary key column
```

In Chapter 5, Code listing 5.1.8 showed how to use the SQL keyword DISTINCT to produce a list showing the days when members of staff offer support sessions. The code there was inadequate as it could only show the staff number, not the person's name. Using an equi-join, however, both the staff member's name and the days he or she offers support sessions can be retrieved from the database. Code listing 6.1.3 shows the original select statement and the improved version. The second select statement shows that column aliasing, expressions in the select list and the order by clause can all be used with an equi-join select statement.

233

Code listing 6.1.3   Listing the days on which members of staff offer support sessions

```
SELECT DISTINCT staffNo, dayOfWeek
FROM SupportSession
ORDER BY staffNo;

SELECT DISTINCT fName || ' ' || lName AS name, dayOfWeek
FROM Staff, SupportSession
WHERE Staff.staffNo = SupportSession.staffNo
ORDER BY lName, fName;
```

The where clause can also include other conditions, not just the join condition. For example, the select statement in Code listing 6.1.4 lists details of all support sessions that run on a Monday morning and the staff members who offer them.

Code listing 6.1.4   An equi-join with additional conditions in the where clause

```
SELECT Staff.staffNo, fName, lName, phone,
       email, SupportSession.staffNo,
       dayOfWeek, startTime, endTime
FROM Staff, SupportSession
WHERE Staff.staffNo = SupportSession.staffNo
AND    dayOfWeek = 'Monday'
AND    startTime < '12:00';
```

The foreign key on the SupportSession table has only one column, so there is only one join condition needed to identify the correct rows from the cross join of the SupportSession and Room tables. The foreign key on the Equipment table has two columns – {building, room}. These match the primary key columns of the Room table – {building, roomNo} (see Figure 6.4).

Figure 6.4 Related data in the Room and Equipment tables.

Room

building:varchar	roomNo:varchar	capacity:numeric
Wilson	205	25
Wilson	113	25
Wilson	205	100
Priestley	G12	150
Priestley	113A	20
Locke	24	30
Locke	27	25
Locke	14	30

Matching rows

Equipment

assetNo:varchar	assetType:varchar	description:varchar	building:varchar	room:varchar	portable:boolean	cost:numeric	acquired:date
1570131	Data projector	HP vp6100	Wilson	205	FALSE	1300 00	2004-07-14
1799131	Data projector	HP vp6100	NULL	NULL	TRUE	1300.00	2005-01-12
4560293	OHP	3M OHP 1608	Locke	24	FALSE	NULL	NULL
4503993	PC	Dell OptiPlex™ GX280	Wilson	205	FALSE	625.00	2004-04-30
5010009	OHP	3M OHP 2000	NULL	NULL	TRUE	185.00	2001-08-20
2992220	Data projector	ToshibaTDP-SW20	Priestley	G12	FALSE	1100. 00	2005-01-12
2892112	Laptop	SONY X505	NULL	NULL	TRUE	NULL	NULL

To identify the correct rows for the equi-join of the Room and Equipment tables, the values in the two building columns *and* the values in the room and roomNo columns must match. This requires two join conditions. Code listing 6.1.5 shows how to write the equi-join to join these two tables. The same principle applies when a foreign key has three or more columns – the where clause has one join condition for each column in the foreign key. Notice that the room and roomNo columns are not qualified by their table name. This is because there is only one room column and only one roomNo column in the Room and Equipment tables. As there is no possible ambiguity about which column is meant, there is no need to use qualified identifiers.

Code listing 6.1.5   An equi-join for tables with composite foreign and primary keys

```
SELECT Room.building, roomNo, capacity, assetType,
description
FROM Equipment, Room
WHERE Equipment.building = Room.building
AND    room = roomNo;
```

For those who find it a chore to type qualified identifiers in full, SQL offers a short-cut. Any table in the from clause can be given an alias – called a **correlation name** – and that name used in the qualified identifier instead of the full table name. Code listing 6.1.6 illustrates table aliasing using correlation names, with the Equipment table being given the correlation name e, and the Room table the correlation name r. Otherwise, this select statement is the same as to that in Code listing 6.1.5. With a short correlation name for each table, it is feasible to use the qualified identifier for every column in the select list, which makes it absolutely clear which table each column belongs to.

Code listing 6.1.6   Using a table alias to shorten qualified identifiers

```
SELECT r.building, roomNo, capacity, assetType,
description
FROM Equipment e, Room r
WHERE e.building = r.building
AND    room = roomNo;
```

The equi-join, with its join conditions, is not the only notation for joining two related tables. A number of alternative notations are provided in the SQL standard. These are all abbreviations for the equi-join, but some developers prefer to use them than write out the full join condition. In each case, the join condition of the where clause is replaced by some additional notation in the from clause.

To see how these different notations work, suppose the user wants a list of staff and their support sessions. The first select statement in Code listing 6.1.7 is a plain equi-join, which does the job just fine. The second select statement illustrates the natural join syntax. The SQL keyword NATURAL JOIN in the from clause informs the DBMS that the two tables have columns with the same name (in this example, the staffNo columns). The DBMS automatically identifies the columns with matching names and uses them to generate a join condition. The third select statement is a condition join, the syntax of which is actually more complicated that the original equi-join, so condition joins aren't used in this book. The final select statement is called a column name join. The column name join is similar to the natural join, except that the DBMS does not have to identify the columns that have the same name. Instead, it is told which columns appear in both tables as the shared column names are listed (in parentheses) after the keyword `USING`. One useful feature of the column name join is that there is no need to use qualified identifiers for the columns listed after the keyword `USING`.

Code listing 6.1.7   Alternative notations for an equi-join

```
SELECT Staff.staffNo, fName||' '||lName AS name,
dayOfWeek, startTime, endTime
FROM Staff, SupportSession
WHERE Staff.staffNo = SupportSession.staffNo;

SELECT Staff.staffNo, fName||' '||lName AS name,
dayOfWeek, startTime, endTime
FROM Staff NATURAL JOIN SupportSession;

SELECT Staff.staffNo, fName||' '||lName AS name,
dayOfWeek, startTime, endTime
FROM Staff JOIN SupportSession
ON (Staff.staffNo = SupportSession.staffNo);

SELECT staffNo, fName||' '||lName AS name, dayOfWeek,
startTime, endTime
FROM Staff JOIN SupportSession USING (staffNo);
```

All the joins discussed so far are known as **inner joins**. Only data for matched rows appears in the result set. This was noted above, but is worth reiterating. Consider the data in the base tables, shown in Figure 6.1. There are 17 members of staff, but only 7 of them offer support sessions. These seven staff members are the only ones to appear in the list shown in Figure 6.3. Sometimes, this is not what is required. The Web Timetable's `Equipment` and `Room` tables provide a good example of how inner joins can fail to provide the information required by a business query. Consider the business query:

provide a list of all rooms and the equipment stored in those rooms.

The inner join in Code listing 6.1.5 produces the result set shown in Figure 6.5. This only lists those rooms that have equipment in them, but this is *not* what was requested. The business query requests a list of *all* rooms, together with any equipment stored in those rooms. Even if a room has no equipment in it, the room should still appear in the list. This might be needed to decide which rooms need a new digital projector, for example, or to distribute equipment more evenly among teaching rooms.

Figure 6.5 Result set for Code listing 6.1.5.

building	roomNo	capacity	assetType	description
Wilson	205	25	Data projector	HP vp6100
Locke	24	30	OHP	3M OHP 1608
Wilson	205	25	PC	Dell OptiPlex™ GX280
Priestley	G12	1	Data projector	ToshibaTDP-SW20

The solution is to use an **outer join**. An outer join is one in which data for unmatched rows from one, or both, tables is included in the result set. For such rows, the column values from the other table are set to null in the result set. This is exactly what is required – unmatched rows from the Room table *should* be included, but the assetType and description columns for these rows of the result set should be *null* as there is no equipment in those rooms (Figure 6.6).

Code listing 6.1.8 shows the ISO standard SQL syntax for the outer join statement. Consider the first of the two select statements. The from clause includes the new SQL keywords RIGHT OUTER JOIN as well as the two table names, with their correlation name aliases. The keywords OUTER JOIN indicate that unmatched rows from *one or more* of the tables should be included in the result set. The keyword RIGHT indicates that it is the unmatched rows of the table to the right of the OUTER JOIN keywords that need to be included – the Room table in Code listing 6.1.8. Unmatched rows in the table to the left of the OUTER JOIN keywords (the Equipment table) will not be included. The on clause plays the role of the join condition as it indicates how to join rows that *do* match. Outer joins can also include a where clause, but it should not repeat the join condition.

Code listing 6.1.8   Two equivalent outer joins, listing all rooms and any equipment in those rooms

```
SELECT r.building, roomNo, capacity, assetType,
description
FROM Equipment e RIGHT OUTER JOIN Room r
ON (e.building = r.building) AND (room = roomNo)
ORDER BY r.building, roomNo;

SELECT r.building, roomNo, capacity, assetType,
description
FROM Room r LEFT OUTER JOIN Equipment e
ON (e.building = r.building) AND (room = roomNo)
ORDER BY r.building, roomNo;
```

Figure 6.6 Result set for Code listing 6.1.8.

building	roomNo	capacity	assetType	description
Locke	14	30	NULL	NULL
Locke	24	30	OHP	3M OHP 1608
Locke	27	25	NULL	NULL
Priestley	113A	20	NULL	NULL
Priestley	G12	150	Data projector	ToshibaTDP-SW20
Wilson	105	100	NULL	NULL
Wilson	113	25	NULL	NULL
Wilson	205	25	Data projector	HP vp6100
Wilson	205	25	PC	Dell OptiPlex™ GX280

Figure 6.6 shows the result set for this code listing. Notice how rooms that have no equipment in them are still included in the list, with nulls in the `assetType` and `description` columns. Comparing this result set to the data in the base tables (Figure 6.4), it is clear that all rows in the `Room` table have been included, but only those rows in the `Equipment` table that match one of the rows in the `Room` table have been added (that is, none of the portable equipment is shown in Figure 6.6).

The order by clause is optional and has been included here to present the information in a sensible order. The second of the two statements is equivalent to the first because, in this statement, the `Room` table is to the left of the keywords `OUTER JOIN`. The two alternative SQL outer join statements, left and right outer joins, are provided for ease of use, rather than for any difference they would make to their behaviour.

With outer joins, it is important to be careful which of the matching primary and foreign key columns are included in the select list. Consider the outer join in Code listing 6.1.9. This includes the `building` column from the `Equipment` table rather than from the `Room` table. Although this seems a minor change (both columns hold the same data) it changes the result set significantly (Figure 6.7). The problem this causes occurs in those rows of the result set that hold data from unmatched rows in the `Room` table, such as the first row. Data from the `Room` table's `roomNo` and `capacity` columns is included, but these are the only columns from the `Room` table – the `building` column, like the `assetType` and `description` columns, belongs to the `Equipment` table, so is set to null. This leaves the user puzzling over which building room number 14, with a capacity of 30, is in, making the list in Figure 6.7 useless.

Code listing 6.1.9   An outer join that does not retrieve the data required

```
SELECT e.building, roomNo, capacity, assetType, description
FROM Equipment e RIGHT OUTER JOIN Room r
ON (e.building = r.building) AND (room = roomNo)
ORDER BY r.building, roomNo;
```

Figure 6.7 Result set for Code listing 6.1.9 – getting the select list wrong.

building	roomNo	capacity	assetType	description
NULL	14	30	NULL	NULL
Locke	24	30	OHP	3M OHP 1608
NULL	27	25	NULL	NULL
NULL	113A	20	NULL	NULL
Priestley	G12	150	Data projector	ToshibaTDP-SW20
NULL	105	100	NULL	NULL
NULL	113	25	NULL	NULL
Wilson	205	25	Data projector	HP vp6100
Wilson	205	25	PC	Dell OptiPlex™ GX280

It is also possible to write an outer join statement that includes unmatched rows from both tables, which is called a full outer join. A business query that requires a full outer join is:

> provide a list of all equipment, where it is located and which rooms currently have no equipment in them.

Clearly this list needs to join data from the Room and Equipment tables to show which room the fixed equipment is located in. It must also include unmatched rows from both tables because the query specifically requests information on *all* equipment and rooms that have *no* equipment in them.

The full outer join for this query is shown in Code listing 6.1.10 and the result set in Figure 6.8. Notice that the assetNo column of the Equiment table is included in this statement. This makes it possible to distinguish between identical items of equipment (such as the two HP vp6100 data projectors).

Code listing 6.1.10   A full outer join

```
SELECT r.building, roomNo, capacity, assetNo, assetType,
description
FROM Equipment e FULL OUTER JOIN Room r
ON (e.building = r.building) AND (room = roomNo)
ORDER BY r.building, roomNo;
```

This result set clearly includes data for every row of the two tables. The three rows of the Equipment table that hold data on portable equipment are not matched with any rows in the Room table. These are listed first, with the three columns from the Room table set to null. The reason these rows come first is to do with the order by clause. The ISO SQL standard states that, for the purposes of ordering rows, null should be regarded as either 'less than' any data value or 'greater than' any data value. The DBMS manufacturer is free to choose which. In the version of SQL implemented

Figure 6.8 Result set for Code listing 6.1.10.

building	roomNo	capacity	assetNo	assetType	description
NULL	NULL	NULL	2892112	Laptop	SONY X505
NULL	NULL	NULL	1799131	Data projector	HP vp6100
NULL	NULL	NULL	5010009	OHP	3M OHP 2000
Locke	14	30	NULL	NULL	NULL
Locke	24	30	4560293	OHP	3M OHP 1608
Locke	27	25	NULL	NULL	NULL
Priestley	113A	20	NULL	NULL	NULL
Priestley	G12	150	2992220	Data projector	ToshibaTDP-SW20
Wilson	105	100	NULL	NULL	NULL
Wilson	113	25	NULL	NULL	NULL
Wilson	205	25	1570131	Data projector	HP vp6100
Wilson	205	25	4503993	PC	Dell OptiPlex™ GX280

by the MySQL DBMS, the order by clause regards null as 'less than' any data value – hence, the result set shown in Figure 6.8. This behaviour does not affect the treatment of null in a comparison expression as `null < capacity` always evaluates to UN-KNOWN.

Unlike the inner join, an outer join is *not* a subset of the cross join. The cross join matches each row of one table with every row of the other, so there are *no* unmatched rows in a cross join.

Support for the ISO SQL outer join syntax is a little patchy. Several DBMS had implemented outer joins before they were included in the ISO SQL:1992 standard. They all used different, usually incompatible, syntax, so the ISO SQL standard adopted the new syntax described above. Since then, some DBMS have implemented support for the ISO SQL syntax, but some have not. Even those that support the ISO SQL syntax retain their old, non-standard syntax. The MySQL DBMS supports the ISO SQL syntax for left and right outer joins, but not the full outer join.

Occasionally, data in one row of a database table is related to data in another row of the same table by a foreign key relationship. An example occurs in the `Module` table of the Web Timetable database. Each module may (or may not) have a prerequisite – that is, a module at a lower level that must be taken first. For example, before students can study the second year module 'Application development', they must have passed the first year module 'Introduction to programming'.

A sample instance of the `Module` table appears in Figure 6.9, with this foreign key relationship highlighted. Code listing 6.1.11 shows the create and alter table

Figure 6.9 An instance of the module table with a self-referencing foreign key.

Module			
code:varchar	title:varchar	level:char	preReq:varchar
CCFC0108	Introduction to programming	F	NULL
CIFC0084	Information systems	F	NULL
BAFC0178	Introduction to business	F	NULL
BMFC0107	Introduction to management	F	NULL
CIIC0053	Application development	I	CCFC0108
CCIC7009	Computing mathematics	I	NULL
CCHO0418	Formal specification	H	NULL
BAIC3427	Business audit	I	BAFC0178
CCH09668	Advanced programming	H	CCIC7009
CIHO6008	Soft systems	H	NULL

statements for this table. The column `preReq` is the foreign key column – its values match the value of the primary key column `code` in some other row. The referential actions are the obvious ones. These are that, if the module code changes in the referenced row (the prerequisite module), then change the value of the `preReq` column in the referencing row and, if the referenced row is deleted, then set the value of the `preReq` column in the referencing row to null (remove the prerequisite requirement).

Code listing 6.1.11   A table with a foreign key relationship to itself

```
CREATE TABLE Module(
code VARCHAR(8) NOT NULL,
title VARCHAR(100) NOT NULL,
level CHAR(1) NOT NULL,
preReq VARCHAR(8),
CONSTRAINT priModule PRIMARY KEY (code)
);

ALTER TABLE Module
ADD CONSTRAINT frnModuleSelf
  FOREIGN KEY (preReq)
  REFERENCES Module (code)
  ON UPDATE CASCADE
  ON DELETE SET NULL;
```

The obvious business query associated with this situation is:

produce a list of modules and their prerequisites and include the module code, title and level for the module and its prerequisite.

241

Code listing 6.1.12 shows two select statements that answer this query in different ways. The first is an inner join, so only lists modules that have prerequisites, which is one possible interpretation of the business query. The second is an outer join, so lists all modules and the prerequisites for those modules that have them, which provides the fullest possible information in answer to the query.

This illustrates an important point about users' requirements: they aren't always clear. Which query – and, hence, which information – is actually required would need to be clarified with the end users.

Code listing 6.1.12   Two examples of self joins

```
SELECT main.code, main.title, main.level,
  prereq.code AS pCode, prereq.title AS pTitle,
  prereq.level as pLevel
FROM Module main, Module prereq
WHERE main.preReq = prereq.code;

SELECT main.code, main.title, main.level,
  prereq.code AS pCode, prereq.title AS pTitle,
  prereq.level as pLevel
FROM Module main LEFT OUTER JOIN Module prereq
ON main.preReq = prereq.code;
```

Figure 6.10 Result sets for Code listing 6.1.12.

code	title	level	pCode	pTitle	pLevel
CIIC0053	Application development	I	CCFC0108	Introduction to programming	F
BAIC3427	Business audit	I	BAFC0178	Introduction to business	F
CCH09668	Advanced programming	H	CCIC7009	Computing mathematics	I

(a) A self-inner join.

code	title	level	pCode	pTitle	pLevel
CCFC0108	Introduction to programming	F	NULL	NULL	NULL
CIFC0084	Information systems	F	NULL	NULL	NULL
BAFC0178	Introduction to business	F	NULL	NULL	NULL
BMFC0107	Introduction to management	F	NULL	NULL	NULL
CIIC0053	Application development	I	CCFC0108	Introduction to programming	F
CCIC7009	Computing mathematics	I	NULL	NULL	NULL
CCHO0418	Formal specification	H	NULL	NULL	NULL
BAIC3427	Business audit	I	BAFC0178	Introduction to business	F
CCH09668	Advanced programming	H	CCIC7009	Computing mathematics	I
CIHO6008	Soft systems	H	NULL	NULL	NULL

(b) A self-outer join.

Both the select statements are **self joins**, which are select statements that join two copies of the same table. Because the from clause includes the same table name twice, both occurrences must be given a correlation name. The correlation names are used to remove the inevitable ambiguity in the select list.

The copy of `Module` aliased `main` provides data for the main module, while that aliased `prereq` provides data on prerequisites. As the roles played by the two tables are different, it is important to get the join condition right – the foreign key column of `main` should match the primary key column of `prereq`, not the other way round.

Finally, the columns in the select list from `prereq` are also aliased, to indicate that these column hold data on prerequisite modules. The result sets are shown in Figures 6.10 (a) and (b).

6.2 SQL built-in value functions

The select lists of the SQL select statements used so far have included columns and expressions that use operators to combine column values, such as `fName || ' ' || lName`, or `endTime-startTime`. The ISO SQL standard defines a number of **value functions.** Like the built-in functions of PHP, value functions are simply predefined functions that take zero or more values (the parameters, or arguments), each of a given data type, and return a single value. For example, the value function `CHARACTER_LENGTH(myString)` takes a single character string value and returns a numeric value, which is the number of characters in the string. So, `CHARACTER_LENGTH('Jo Karen O''Connor')` returns the value 17 as there are 14 letters, 2 spaces and a *single* apostrophe character. Remember, in SQL, an apostrophe character inside a string literal is represented by *two* single quote marks. The single quote marks that delimit the string literal are *not* part of the literal, so don't count towards its length.

The ISO SQL standard classifies value functions according to the data type of their return value, so value functions that return a numeric value are called numeric value functions, those that return a character string are called string value functions and so on. The following examples look first at a range of numeric and string value functions to manipulate character string data, then value functions that help deal with dates and times. The examples cover the most commonly used value functions.

One common problem when manipulating character string data is the problem of case sensitivity – is 'Smith' the same as 'smith'? In a web database application, there is no guarantee that end users will always use the same case when typing in data values. When the DBMS is case-sensitive, this means that some comparison operations won't work as expected – 'Smith' is *not* equal to 'smith'. To overcome this problem, SQL includes two string value functions to manipulate the case of a character string – namely, `LOWER(myString)` and `UPPER(myString)`. Examples of these two value functions in action are shown in Code listing 6.2.1. Figure 6.11 shows the result set for the first of the select statement (based on the data in Figure 6.1). Note that the first names are no longer capitalized. The second select statement in Code listing 6.2.1 shows how the `UPPER()` function helps to overcome the problem of case sensitivity, by changing both the literal entered by the user and the column value to upper case.

Figure 6.11 Result set for Code listing 6.2.1.

LOWER(fName)	UPPER(lName)
john	SMITH
john	SMITH
judith anne	SMITH
paul	SMITH
frank	ROSE
helen	ABBOT
freya	STARK
padma	BRAR
selma	HUTCHINS
mikhail	SUDBIN
helene	CHIRAC
gurpreet	CHOUDHURY
ruth	BAPETSI
joshua	BITTAYE
dan	LIN
jo karen	O'CONNOR
helen	TIMMS

Code listing 6.2.1   Using the value functions LOWER() *and* UPPER()

```
SELECT LOWER(fName), UPPER(lName)
FROM Staff

SELECT staffNo, fName, lName, phone, email
FROM Staff
WHERE UPPER(lName)=UPPER('Smith')
```

Whether the DBMS is case-sensitive regarding character string data or not depends partly on the underlying operating system and partly on the settings chosen by the DBA when a particular database was created. This means that the database developer may have little choice in the matter.

The MySQL DBMS uses the functions UCASE and LCASE rather than UPPER and LOWER. This mismatch between the ISO standard and the value functions of a particular DBMS is typical. Consult the manual for your particular DBMS for information on the actual value functions available to you and their particular syntax. The developers of the MySQL DBMS are working towards full compliance with the ISO standard, so may eventually support the ISO SQL syntax for value functions.

Some applications need to manipulate character strings in more complex ways. One common requirement is to trim leading and/or trailing spaces from a string literal. Suppose a user entered the string literal ' Smith ' into the surname search web page discussed in Chapter 4. To the DBMS, ' Smith ' and 'Smith' are different character strings – the spaces are significant. The SQL value function `TRIM()` can remove leading and trailing spaces:

- `TRIM(LEADING ' ' FROM ' Smith ')` will return the string `'Smith '`
- `TRIM(TRAILING ' ' FROM ' Smith ')` will return the string `' Smith'`
- `TRIM(BOTH ' ' FROM ' Smith ')` will return the string `'Smith'`.

The `TRIM()` function can actually trim any character, not just spaces, so, for example, `TRIM(LEADING 'x' FROM 'xxSMITHxx')` will return the string `'SMITHxx'`.

The PHP in Code listing 6.2.2 shows one way to deal with unwanted spaces at the start, and end, of a character string passed from an HTML form. Of course, trimming off unwanted spaces can also be done using PHP (by, for example, adapting the `cleanse_data()` user-defined function described in Chapter 4).

Code listing 6.2.2   Using the value function `TRIM()` in an SQL select statement passed from a PHP script

```php
<?php
$surname = $_GET["surname"];
$sql = "SELECT fName, lName, email
        FROM Staff
        WHERE lName = TRIM(BOTH ' ' FROM '$surname')";
$result = mysql_query($sql, $connection);
?>
```

SQL, like most other languages, also includes functions to:

- calculate the length of a character string
- find one string of characters within another
- extract a portion of a string.

The select statements in Code listing 6.2.3 and their result sets in Figure 6.12, illustrate how these three functions work. The first statement uses the `CHARACTER_LENGTH()` value function to find the number of characters in the `lName` column value for each row of the `Staff` table. Notice that the apostrophe in 'O'Connor' counts as one character. `CHARACTER_LENGTH()` always takes a single parameter, which must be a character string.

The second select statement shows how to use the `POSITION()` value function. `POSITION()` takes two parameters:

`POSITION(stringToFind IN stringToSearch)`

and finds the starting position of the string of characters given by the parameter `stringToFind` within the character string value in the `stringToSearch` parameter. In the example, `stringToFind` is the character string literal 'ch' and `stringToSearch` is the value of the `lName` column on each row of the `Staff` table. For most rows, 'ch' does not appear in the lName column value, so POSITION() returns zero (0). For the row where lName has the value 'Chirac', POSITION() returns one (1) as 'ch' starts at the very first character of 'Chirac' (note that this assumes the DBMS is case-insensitive).

The third select statement demonstrates the SUBSTRING() function. This function takes three parameters:

```
SUBSTRING(stringValue FROM start FOR numCharacter)
```

The stringValue parameter is a character string and the other two are integers. The idea is to take the character string value stringValue and 'cut out' numCharacter characters starting from the start. This example 'cuts out' five characters from the value of the fName column, starting from the fourth character. The result set is shown in Figure 6.12.

Code listing 6.2.3 String manipulation in SQL

```
SELECT lName, CHARACTER_LENGTH(lName)
FROM Staff;

SELECT lName, POSITION('ch' IN lName)
FROM Staff;

SELECT fName, SUBSTRING(fName FROM 4 FOR 5)
FROM Staff;
```

Figure 6.12 The result sets for the select statements in Code listing 6.2.3.

lName	CHARACTER_LENGTH(lName)
Smith	5
Smith	5
Smith	5
Smith	5
Rose	4
Abbot	5
Stark	5
Brar	4
Hutchins	8
Sudbin	6
Chirac	6
Choudhury	9
Bapetsi	7
Bittaye	7
Lin	3
O'Connor	8
Timms	5

lName	POSITION('ch' IN lName)
Smith	0
Smith	0
Smith	0
Smith	0
Rose	0
Abbot	0
Stark	0
Brar	0
Hutchins	4
Sudbin	0
Chirac	1
Choudhury	1
Bapetsi	0
Bittaye	0
Lin	0
O'Connor	0
Timms	0

fName	SUBSTRING(fName FROM 4 FOR 5)
John	n
John	n
Judith Anne	ith A
Paul	l
Frank	nk
Helen	en
Freya	ya
Padma	ma
Selma	ma
Mikhail	hail
Helene	ene
Gurpreet	preet
Ruth	h
Joshua	hua
Dan	
Jo Karen	Karen
Helen	en

The examples in Code listing 6.2.3 illustrate the basic operation of these string manipulation functions, but aren't very realistic. For an example of a realistic use of these value functions, consider the business query:

> produce a list showing staff names and their phone numbers – the staff name should be split into the full first name, middle initial (if any) and surname.

The tricky bit is extracting the first name and middle initial from the fName column. First and middle names will be separated by a space character – 'Judith Anne' and 'Jo Karen' and so on. The obvious approach is to find the first space in the fName column value, with everything up to the space being the first name, and the first character after the space being the middle initial. A first attempt at using the substring function to extract the first name might be:

```
SUBSTRING(fName FROM 1 FOR POSITION(' ' IN fName))
```

The POSITION(' ' IN fName) finds the position of the first space character, so the SUBSTRING() function then extracts everything from the first character up to and including the first space. Unfortunately, this only works for those fName column values that actually have a space character in them. For those that don't, POSITION(' ' IN fName) returns zero, so the SUBSTRING() function extracts zero characters.

The way around this problem is to add a space character at the end of every fName value, using the concatenation operator fName||' '. For example, 'John' becomes 'John ' and 'Judith Anne' becomes 'Judith Anne '. In both cases, POSITION(' ' IN fName||' ') will always find the *first* space character at the end of the person's *first* name. The full expression is:

```
SUBSTRING(fName||' ' FROM 1
          FOR POSITION(' ' IN fName||' '))
```

A similar problem occurs when extracting the middle initial. If the value of fName does not have a space character, then:

```
SUBSTRING(fName FROM POSITION(' ' IN fName)+1 FOR 1)
```

returns the first character of the *first* name, rather than the first character of the *middle* name.

The select statement that implements the business query is shown in Code listing 6.2.4 and the result set in Figure 6.13. The values of the lName and phone columns are not manipulated, although lName, like the two expressions, is aliased.

Code listing 6.2.4 *Retrieving the first name, middle initial and surname and combining them into a single value*

```
SELECT SUBSTRING(fName||' ' FROM 1
                 FOR POSITION(' ' IN fName||' ')) AS
                 forename,
       SUBSTRING(fName||' ' FROM
                 POSITION(' ' IN fName||' ')+1 FOR 1) AS
                 middleInitial,
       lName as surname,
       phone
FROM Staff;
```

Figure 6.13 Result set for Code listing 6.2.4.

forename	middleInitial	surname	phone
John		Smith	NULL
John		Smith	5104
Judith	A	Smith	7709
Paul		Smith	NULL
Frank		Rose	8871
Helen		Abbot	8032
Freya		Stark	8660
Padma		Brar	6641
Selma		Hutchins	8706
Mikhail		Sudbin	5553
Helene		Chirac	NULL
Gurpreet		Choudhury	5454
Ruth		Bapetsi	8022
Joshua		Bittaye	7782
Dan		Lin	8514
Jo	K	O'Connor	8871
Helen		Timms	8661

This example shows how tricky it can be to manipulate character string values using SQL. Things are a little easier using PHP as an `if ... else ...` statement can distinguish between different cases. For example 'If there is a space in the string then extract everything up to the space, else use the whole string.' A better solution for applications that need to manipulate middle names separately from the first name is to include them as separate columns in the `Staff` table. This is closer to the ideal of the relational model, which sees each column value as a single value of the given data type, with no subparts. An image of the `Staff` table with separate `fName` and `mName` (middle name) columns is shown in Figure 6.14. Notice that, in this instance, the `mName` column is null in almost all the rows. This isn't ideal, either. The database designer would need to choose which solution best suited the needs of the application.

The ISO SQL standard includes three useful functions for generating date and time values:

- `CURRENT_DATE` returns the current date, such as '2005-01-18'
- `CURRENT_TIME` returns the current time down to the second, such as '12:15:22'
- `CURRENT_TIMESTAMP` returns a time stamp value, giving the current date and time, again down to the second, such as '2005-01-18 12:15:22'.

These three functions are commonly used in `INSERT` and `UPDATE` statements. Code listing 6.2.5 shows how to add a new piece of equipment to the `Equipment` table and give the current date as the value for the `acquired` column. All three functions return

Figure 6.14 The `Staff` table with separate columns for first and middle names.

Staff

staffNo:Varchar	fName:Varchar	mName:Varchar	lName:Varchar	email:Varchar	phone:Varchar	photo:BLOB
10780	John	NULL	Smith	j.b.smith@pennine.ac.uk	NULL	[BLOB]
14443	Helen	NULL	Abbot	h.abbot@pennine.ac.uk	8032	[BLOB]
23257	Freya	NULL	Stark	f.stark@pennine.ac.uk	8660	[BLOB]
25447	John	NULL	Smith	j.smith@pennine.ac.uk	5104	[BLOB]
25448	Judith	Anne	Smith	j.a.smith@pennine.ac.uk	7709	[BLOB]
31210	Paul	NULL	Smith	p.smith@pennine.ac.uk	NULL	[BLOB]
33509	Helen	NULL	Timms	h.timms@pennine.ac.uk	8661	[BLOB]
33935	Padma	NULL	Brar	p.brar@pennine.ac.uk	6641	[BLOB]
35054	Selma	NULL	Hutchins	s.hutchins@pennine.ac.uk	8706	[BLOB]
35155	Helene	NULL	Chirac	h.chirac@pennine.ac.uk	NULL	[BLOB]
45965	Mikhail	NULL	Sudbin	m.sudbin@pennine.ac.uk	5553	[BLOB]
55776	Gurpreet	NULL	Choudhury	g.choudhury@pennine.ac.uk	5454	[BLOB]
56673	Joshua	NULL	Bittaye	j.bittaye@pennine.ac.uk	7782	[BLOB]
56893	Ruth	NULL	Bapetsi	r.bapetsi@pennine.ac.uk	8022	[BLOB]
77712	Frank	NULL	Rose	f.rose@pennine.ac.uk	8871	[BLOB]
78893	Jo	Karen	O'Connor	j.k.oconnor@pennine.ac.uk	8871	[BLOB]
89987	Dan	NULL	Lin	d.lin@pennine.co.uk	8514	[BLOB]

values of the appropriate data type – date, time or time stamp. None of them returns a string literal. Note that the values returned by CURRENT_TIME and CURRENT_TIMESTAMP actually include information on the time zone. This is useful for distributed database applications that are used by many people in different countries, but is beyond the scope of this book.

Code listing 6.2.5 Using the CURRENT_DATE value function

```
INSERT INTO Equipment
(assetNo, assetType, description, cost, acquired)
VALUES ('34569856', 'Laptop', 'DELL laptop', 500,
        CURRENT_DATE);
```

Although date, time and time stamp values can easily be generated by the DBMS, users of a database application often submit such data as literals. The DBMS will be able to correctly interpret some literals, but not all. For example, the first insert statement in Code listing 6.2.6 will work fine with a database managed by the MySQL DBMS, but will not work with an Oracle database. The second works fine on an Oracle database, but not on a MySQL one (where the row may be inserted, but the acquired column is given the value '0000-00-00').

Code listing 6.2.6 Using date literals

```
INSERT INTO Equipment
(assetNo, assetType, description, cost, acquired)
VALUES ('34569856', 'Laptop', 'DELL laptop',
        500, '2006-01-18');

INSERT INTO Equipment
(assetNo, assetType, description, cost, acquired)
VALUES ('34569856', 'Laptop', 'DELL laptop',
        500, '18-JAN-2006');
```

These problems are inevitable. As noted in Chapter 3, there are numerous different, and contradictory, formats for date literals. No DBMS can automatically sort out exactly what date is meant to be represented by a date literal. Unfortunately, every DBMS has implemented its own functions to deal with such matters and the ISO SQL standard has shied away from suggesting any common ones. DBMS tend to provide at least two functions to deal with date literals:

● a function to take a date literal (written as a character string) in a specified format and return a valid date value

● a function to take a valid date value and return a date literal representing that date value in the specified format.

The format of the date literal is specified using special character combinations. For example, the MySQL DBMS includes the STR_TO_DATE(dateLiteral, format) and DATE_FORMAT(dateValue, format) functions to achieve these two tasks. In both cases, the format parameter is a string that defines the date format to use. For example, the format string '%d-%m-%Y' instructs the MySQL DBMS to interpret the

Figure 6.15 Result set for Code listing 6.2.7.

acquired	European	American	WithTime	Elegant
2004-07-14	14-07-2004	07-14-2004	14-07-2004 00:00	July 14th, 2004
2005-01-12	12-01-2005	01-12-2005	12-01-2005 00:00	January 12th, 2005
2004-04-30	30-04-2004	04-30-2004	30-04-2004 00:00	April 30th, 2004
2001-08-20	20-08-2001	08-20-2001	20-08-2001 00:00	August 20th, 2001
2005-01-12	12-01-2005	01-12-2005	12-01-2005 00:00	January 12th, 2005

date in the standard European format of day of the month, then month and, finally, the four-digit year, all separated by dashes.

Code listing 6.2.7 demonstrates the DATE_FORMAT() function in action, and Figure 6.15 shows the results. The first column of the result set is presented in the MySQL DBMS preferred date format. The others are all presented in the format specified. Because acquired is a date, there is no time associated with the column value. Even so, the fourth column includes a time in the literal because the format specifically requested one. The best the DBMS can do in this situation is return the time literal '00:00'.

Code listing 6.2.7   Using the DATE_FORMAT() function on the MySQL DBMS

```
SELECT acquired,
  DATE_FORMAT(acquired, '%d-%m-%Y') AS European,
  DATE_FORMAT(acquired, '%m-%d-%Y') AS American,
  DATE_FORMAT(acquired, '%d-%m-%Y %H:%i') AS WithTime,
  DATE_FORMAT(acquired, '%M %D, %Y') AS Elegant
FROM Equipment
WHERE acquired IS NOT NULL;
```

The DATE_FORMAT() function is usually used when retrieving data from the database to format the date values into a date literal that the end user will recognize. In contrast, STR_TO_DATE() is usually used to take a date literal entered by the end user and ensure that the DBMS can recognize the date value it represents. In most web database applications, users never actually type in date literals – they select valid dates from list boxes or calendar controls. These controls will themselves use a particular date format. The STR_TO_DATE() function can convert this format into a date value for the MySQL DBMS. For example, Code listing 6.2.8 takes a date literal in the format 'January 12th, 2005' and puts the appropriate date value into the acquired column of the Equipment table.

Code listing 6.2.8   Using the STR_TO_DATE() function in the MySQL DBMS

```
UPDATE Equipment
SET acquired = STR_TO_DATE('January 12th, 2005',
                           '%M %D, %Y')
WHERE acquired IS NULL;
```

> The SQL in Code listings 6.2.7 and 6.2.8 are specific to the dialect of SQL implemented by the MySQL DBMS. Other DBMS have their own versions of the `STR_TO_DATE()` and `DATE_FORMAT()` functions. Most DBMS will include a range of other functions for manipulating dates, times and time stamps – check your manual for details.

6.3 Aggregate queries

The queries discussed so far allow rows of data to be retrieved from tables or modified in some way. Sometimes the user wants a summary of the information held on a database. Common business queries that require summary information often ask the following basic questions:

- 'How many . . . ?'
- 'What is the largest . . . ?'
- 'What is the smallest . . . ?'
- 'What is the average . . . ?'
- 'What is the total . . . ?'

The ISO SQL standard includes a number of **aggregate functions** (called **set functions** in the ISO SQL standard) that can formulate such business queries as SQL select statements, called **aggregate queries**. Each aggregate function summarizes the data held in a particular column across a set of rows. Business queries that ask 'How many?' can be answered using the aggregate function `COUNT()`. For example, consider the business query:

'How many members of staff have a phone number?'

The aggregate function `COUNT()` counts how many rows have a valid data value in a particular column. It does not count rows where the column is null.

The select statement in Code listing 6.3.1 uses the aggregate function `COUNT()` to answer the business query asked above. The only new feature is the `COUNT()` aggregate function itself. The DBMS deals with this select statement as follows. First, it evaluates the from clause, retrieving all the rows from the `Staff` table. Next, it identifies which of these rows satisfy the where clause. Here, as there is no where clause, that means all of them. It works through these rows, counting those for which the `phone` column is not null. Finally, it puts this value in the result set and returns it to the user. The result set for Code listing 6.3.1 is very simple – a single row, with a single column, holding the value 14 (the number of staff who have a phone number).

Code listing 6.3.1   Using an aggregate query to count how many staff have a phone number

```
SELECT COUNT(phone)
FROM Staff;
```

Figure 6.16 Result set for Code listing 6.3.2 (note the column names).

COUNT(staffNo)	COUNT(phone)	noPhone
17	14	3

An aggregate query can ask for more than one piece of summary information. Code listing 6.3.2 asks for the number of members of staff, the number of them who have a phone and the number of them who do not have a phone. The result set is shown in Figure 6.16. There are 17 members of staff, 14 of whom have a phone and 3 of whom don't. Notice that the column names for the first two columns of the result set are just the expressions from the select list. The third element of the select list has a column alias and so has a more meaningful name as its column heading in the result set.

Code listing 6.3.2   Using an aggregate query to count how many staff have a phone number

```
SELECT COUNT(staffNo), COUNT(phone),
       COUNT(staffNo) − COUNT(phone) AS noPhone
FROM Staff;
```

Using the COUNT() aggregate function with a column name will return the number of rows for which this column is not null. To count the total number of rows, use COUNT(*) in the select list. For example, code listing 6.3.3 is equivalent to 6.3.2 as COUNT(staffNo) will always return the same number as COUNT(*) because the staffNo column is never null (it is the primary key). COUNT(*) can be useful as it counts *all* the rows, even when the value of a particular column is null.

Code listing 6.3.3   Using COUNT(*)

```
SELECT COUNT(*), COUNT(phone),
       COUNT(staffNo) − COUNT(phone) AS noPhone
FROM Staff;
```

Sometimes it is useful to count how many distinct column values there are in a table. For example, it is possible that members of staff at the Pennine University share phone numbers, so, although 14 of them have a phone, there may be fewer than 14 phone numbers.

The result set for Code listing 6.3.4 tells us that 14 people have a phone, but there are only 13 distinct phone numbers. That is because Frank Rose and Jo Karen O'Connor share a phone number (see Figure 6.1).

Code listing 6.3.4   Using DISTINCT to count distinct column values

```
SELECT COUNT(phone), COUNT(DISTINCT phone)
FROM Staff;
```

Business queries that ask 'What is the largest?' or 'What is the smallest?' are answered using the MAX() and MIN() aggregate functions. MAX(columnName) returns the largest value in the column `columnName`, while `MIN(columnName)` returns the smallest. Both these aggregate functions work with columns of any scalar data type, but are most useful with numeric and date columns and both ignore nulls. So, for example, Code listing 6.3.5 answers the business query:

'What was the cost of the most expensive, and least expensive, items of equipment?'

Code listing 6.3.5   Using MAX and MIN

```
SELECT MAX(cost), MIN(cost)
FROM Equipment;
```

Code listing 6.3.6 answers the business query

'When was our oldest piece of equipment purchased?'

Notice that finding when the *oldest* piece of equipment was purchased means finding the *earliest* purchase date – that is the *minimum* value of the `acquired` column. (See Figure 6.4 for a snapshot of the `Equipment` table instance.) Always think carefully when using the `MAX()` and `MIN()` aggregate functions with date columns.

Code listing 6.3.6   Using MIN to find the earliest date

```
SELECT MIN(acquired)
FROM Equipment;
```

The final two aggregate functions – `AVG()` and `SUM()` – only work with columns of the data types numeric or interval. `AVG()` calculates the average value of the column and `SUM()` adds up all the values. Again, both ignore nulls.

Code listing 6.3.7 answers the business query:

'What is the average cost of a piece of equipment and how much has been spent on equipment in total?'

With the table instance shown in Figure 6.4, the average cost is £902 and the total spent is £4510.

Code listing 6.3.7   Using SUM and AVG

```
SELECT AVG(cost), SUM(cost)
FROM Equipment;
```

The `Equipment` table includes two sorts of equipment – portable and fixed. It seems reasonable to ask:

'What is the average cost of portable equipment and how much has been spent in total on portable equipment?'

Aggregate queries can include a where clause. As noted above, the DBMS applies the where clause *before* looking at the select list, so only rows that satisfy the where clause are used to calculate the aggregate function values.

The select statement in Code listing 6.3.7 forms the basis for an aggregate query that answers this question. All that is needed is to use a where clause to instruct the DBMS to only summarize information for those rows where the `portable` column is

TRUE. The select statement in Code listing 6.3.8 does this. It calculates the average cost of portable equipment to be £742.50 and the total spent to be £1485. Note that both values are lower than the corresponding values for all equipment.

Code listing 6.3.8   An aggregate query with a where-clause

```
SELECT AVG(cost), SUM(cost)
FROM Equipment
WHERE portable=TRUE;
```

The MAX(), MIN(), AVG() and SUM() aggregate functions can all be used with expressions as well as columns. For example, the expression (endTime - startTime) HOUR TO MINUTE calculates the length of time a support session lasts and expresses it as an interval in hours and minutes.

It is interesting to know the length of the longest, and shortest, support sessions and the average length of a support session. It is also interesting to calculate the total amount of time devoted by staff to supporting students. This would be expected to be more than 24 hours in total, so would be a DAY TO MINUTE interval. Code listing 6.3.9 shows the ISO SQL syntax to calculate all of these aggregate values.

Code listing 6.3.9   Using an expression in an aggregate function

```
SELECT MAX((endTime-startTime) HOUR TO MINUTE),
       MIN((endTime-startTime) HOUR TO MINUTE),
       AVG((endTime-startTime) HOUR TO MINUTE),
       SUM((endTime-startTime) DAY TO MINUTE)
FROM SupportSession;
```

Unfortunately, the ISO SQL syntax for dealing with the interval data type is not well supported by commercial DBMS. For example, the MySQL DBMS uses the TIME data type to store intervals of time in the format HHH:MM:SS. This approach means that, in a MySQL database, the TIME literal '48:33:12' stands for '48 hours 33 minutes and 12 seconds'. This is quite different from the approach taken in the ISO SQL standard, where the TIME data type represents a time of day in the 24-hour clock format. In the ISO SQL standard, '48:33:12' is not a valid TIME literal as the maximum value of a time of day is '23:59:59' (actually, to allow for leap-seconds, it is '23:59:61' (see, for example, Wikipedia (2005) for an explanation of leap seconds). This means that it is important to always check the manual for your particular DBMS for information on how it handles the DATE, TIME and INTERVAL data types.

> Another difference between the ISO SQL standard and the commercial implementations is that most DBMS do not allow the + and − operators for dates, times and intervals. Instead, they use special functions to manipulate date and time values. Code listing 6.3.10 shows how to write the select statement in Code listing 6.3.9 using the version of SQL implemented by the MySQL 5.0 DBMS. This DBMS includes the function TIMEDIFF() to calculate the difference between two times. Again, you need to check the manual for your particular DBMS for information on its date and time manipulation functions.

Code listing 6.3.10   A select statement written in the version of SQL implemented by the MySQL DBMS

```
SELECT MAX(TIMEDIFF(endTime, startTime)),
       MIN(TIMEDIFF(endTime, startTime)),
       AVG(TIMEDIFF(endTime, startTime)),
       SUM(TIMEDIFF(endTime, startTime))
FROM SupportSession;
```

One restriction on the aggregate queries seen so far is that it is not possible to include columns in the select list. This should be obvious. The aggregate function returns a single value, regardless of how many rows satisfy the where clause, so there is only ever one row in the result set. A column returns one value for every row that satisfies the where clause, so there may be many rows in the result set. It is impossible for the result set of an aggregate query to include data for all these rows. However, there are business queries that want rows to be grouped together and summary information calculated for each group, rather than the whole table. For example:

list all staff members and the number of support sessions they offer.

To answer a query like this, the following steps need to be taken:

1 group together rows with identical values in the column that needs to be displayed
2 for each group of rows, use an aggregate function to calculate the required summary data.

An SQL select statement uses the **group by clause** to achieve this.

Code listing 6.3.11 shows the SQL statement that lists all staff (identified by their staff number) and the number of support sessions they offer. The select list and from clause are familiar, but the third line is new. The SQL keywords GROUP BY begin the group by clause and are followed by the column name staffNo. The group by clause instructs the DBMS to group together rows that have the same value in their staffNo column. It then counts how many rows there are in each group. As every row in the group has the same value in the staffNo column, the DBMS can display *this* value, together with the value of COUNT(*), for each group. Only columns that appear in the group by clause can be included in the select list.

Code listing 6.3.11   Grouping then summarizing data

```
SELECT staffNo, COUNT(*)
FROM SupportSession
GROUP BY staffNo
```

The result set for code listing 6.3.11 (Figure 6.17) includes one row for each group – that is, one row for every member of staff whose staff number appears in the staffNo column of some row of the SupportSession table. This means every member of staff who offers support sessions.

Figure 6.17 Result set for Code listing 6.3.11.

staffNo	COUNT(*)
23257	1
31210	1
35054	2
45965	2
55776	1
56673	3
56893	2

Some business queries only require data for *some* of the groups. For example:

produce a list showing those staff who offer more than one support session and include a count of the number of support sessions offered.

This list would identify staff who are 'student-friendly', offering a choice of times when they will give individual support to students. There are four such in Figure 6.17. SQL includes the **having clause** to specify which groups of data have their summary information included in the result set. This is a different purpose from that of the where clause. The where clause restricts which rows are grouped together, but the having clause restricts which groups have summary data calculated for them. Note that the having clause, like the where clause, uses a Boolean expression to identify which groups should have their data summarized. This Boolean expression can involve any column that appears in the group by clause or any suitable aggregate function. Usually, restrictions on column values should be made using the where clause. So, if no data is required for a whole group of rows based on a shared column value, then the individual rows can be eliminated in the where clause, using that same shared column value. When possible, use the where clause to cut down the number of rows that need to be grouped. This means that the having clause usually restricts the groups based on an expression involving an aggregate function.

Code listing 6.3.12 shows the select statement to answer the business query above, and Figure 6.18 the result set. Comparing Figure 6.18 with Figure 6.17, it's clear that the having clause has correctly identified which groups to include summary data for.

Code listing 6.3.12   Controlling which groups of data have their summary information included in the result set

```
SELECT staffNo, COUNT(*)
FROM SupportSession
GROUP BY staffNo
HAVING COUNT(*)> 1
```

The having clause is the sixth, and final, part of the select statement. As discussed in the section on table joins, the order in which these different parts appear in the select

Figure 6.18 Result set for Code listing 6.3.12.

staffNo	COUNT(*)
35054	2
45965	2
56673	3
56803	2

statement is fixed. The group by and having clauses come immediately after the where clause, so the order is:

1 select list

2 from clause

3 where clause

4 group by clause

5 having clause

6 order by clause.

The order of processing for the DBMS is different:

1 from clause

2 where clause

3 group by clause

4 having clause

5 select list

6 order by clause.

So, first the DBMS identifies which tables it is dealing with, then which rows of those tables. Once the rows are known, it groups them according to the group by clause and uses the having clause to determine which groups need to be summarized. The DBMS then looks at the select list to see what summary information is needed. It adds *one row* to the result set *for each group of rows that satisfies the having clause*. Finally, it orders the result set according to the instructions in the order by clause.

The whole process can be illustrated by a business query that requires all six parts of the select statement:

produce a list showing those staff who offer more than one support session, excluding support sessions that run on a Friday, and include a count of the number of support sessions offered and order the list, first, by the number of support sessions and then by staff number.

Figure 6.19 shows how the DBMS processes the select statement in Code listing 6.3.13. The from clause mentions only one table, so, in step 1, the DBMS identifies that it's dealing with the current instance of the base table `SupportSession`. If there were more than one table, then, in step 1, the DBMS would create the cross join.

Code listing 6.3.13 A more complex example

```
SELECT staffNo, COUNT(*)
FROM SupportSession
WHERE dayOfWeek <> 'Friday'
GROUP BY staffNo
HAVING COUNT(*)>1
ORDER BY COUNT(*), staffNo
```

In step 2, the DBMS applies the where clause. All except two rows of the `SupportSession` table satisfy the where clause, so the DBMS creates a derived table consisting of these rows.

Step 3 sees the DBMS group together those rows that have the same value in the `staffNo` column. The different groups are indicated by the shading in Figure 6.19. Notice that these groups are not ordered by `staffNo` – *grouping* is different from *ordering*.

Next, the DBMS inspects each group and checks whether or not it satisfies the having clause. Those that do not are discarded, leaving the derived table shown in step 4. This derived table is the basis for creating the result set.

The DBMS next looks at the select list and calculates the summary information required for each group of rows. In this case, for each group of rows, it identifies the common `staffNo` value and counts how many rows are in that group. The result set is shown in step 5.

Finally, in step 6, the DBMS orders the rows of the result set. Notice that the order by clause in Code listing 6.3.13 orders the rows of the result set based on the value of `COUNT(*)`. This is the first time an order by clause has used a value other than a column value to order the result set. In SQL, the order by clause can use any expression that could appear in the select list.

Again, this description of how a DBMS processes a select statement with a group by clause is intentionally naïve. It correctly describes the general approach taken, but not the specifics. Note that some DBMS will not allow aggregate functions in the order by clause, so, again, check the manual.

One problem with the select statement in Code listing 6.3.13 is that it identifies staff by their staff number. A better solution joins the `Staff` and `SupportSession` tables, and summarizes the data in this joined table.

Code listing 6.3.14 shows how to do this. Notice that the where clause includes the usual join condition as well as one that excludes support sessions running on a Friday.

The group by clause includes the three columns `staffNo`, `fName`, and `lName`. As the values of `fName` and `lName` are determined by the value of `staffNo`, it seems odd to include them, but the ISO SQL standard insists that only columns that appear in the group by clause may appear in the select list, so they have to go in, even though they don't affect the actual grouping of rows. (Some DBMS (including the MySQL DBMS) do not enforce this rule.)

Figure 6.19 Processing the select statement in Code listing 6.3.13.

SupportSession

staffNo:Varchar	dayOfWeek:Varchar	startTime:Time	endTime:Time
56673	Friday	15:30:00	16:30:00
56673	Thursday	15:30:00	16:30:00
35054	Monday	09:00:00	10:00:00
45965	Wednesday	11:00:00	12:00:00
31210	Wednesday	11:00:00	13:00:00
35054	Monday	15:00:00	16:00:00
56893	Thursday	09:00:00	10:00:00
45965	Monday	11:00:00	12:00:00
23257	Monday	15:00:00	16:00:00
55776	Monday	14:00:00	16:00:00
56893	Tuesday	14:00:00	15:00:00
56673	Friday	10:00:00	11:00:00
35054	Tuesday	11:00:00	12:00:00

Step 1 The from clause (base table or cross join)

Step 2 The set of rows satisfying the where clause

staffNo	dayOfWeek	startTime	endTime
56673	Thursday	15:30:00	16:30:00
35054	Monday	C9:00:00	10:00:00
45965	Wednesday	11:00:00	12:00:00
31210	Wednesday	11:00:00	13:00:00
35054	Monday	15:00:00	16:00:00
56893	Thursday	09:00:00	10:00:00
45965	Monday	11:00:00	12:00:00
23257	Monday	15:00:00	16:00:00
55776	Monday	14:00:00	16:00:00
56893	Tuesday	14:00:00	15:00:00
35054	Tuesday	11:00:00	12:00:00

Step 3 Grouping the rows – seven groups, identified by the shading

staffNo	dayOfWeek	startTime	endTime
56673	Thursday	15:30:00	16:30:00
31210	Wednesday	11:00:00	13:00:00
56893	Thursday	09:00:00	10:00:00
56893	Tuesday	14:00:00	15:00:00
35054	Monday	09:00:00	10:00:00
35054	Tuesday	11:00:00	12:00:00
35054	Monday	15:00:00	16:00:00
45965	Wednesday	11:00:00	12:00:00
45965	Monday	11:00:00	12:00:00
23257	Monday	15:00:00	16:00:00
55776	Monday	14:00:00	16:00:00

Step 4 The groups that satisfy the having clause

staffNo	dayOfWeek	startTime	endTime
56893	Thursday	09:00:00	10:00:00
56893	Tuesday	14:00:00	15:00:00
35054	Monday	09:00:00	10:00:00
35054	Tuesday	11:00:00	12:00:00
35054	Monday	15:00:00	16:00:00
45965	Wednesday	11:00:00	12:00:00
45965	Monday	11:00:00	12:00:00

Step 5 Summary data – one row for each group

staffNo	COUNT(*)
56893	2
35054	3
45965	2

Step 6 Ordering the result set

staffNo	COUNT(*)
35054	3
45965	2
56893	2

Code listing 6.3.14   An aggregate query involving two tables

```
SELECT Staff.staffNo, fName, lName, COUNT(*)
FROM Staff, SupportSession
WHERE Staff.staffNo = SupportSession.staffNo
AND dayOfWeek <> 'Friday'
GROUP BY staffNo, fName, lName
HAVING COUNT(*)>1
ORDER BY COUNT(*), lName, fName
```

Business queries that request summary information can be difficult to translate directly into an SQL statement. It can help to work through the following process:

1 identify what summary information is required (the select list)

2 specify which rows are involved (the where clause)

3 explain how to group these rows (the group by clause)

4 specify which groups have their summary information included in the result set (the having clause).

6.4 Subqueries

The select statement can appear as part of another SQL statement and such a select statement is called a **subquery.** A variation of the create table statement uses a subquery to specify the table's structure.

Code listing 6.4.1 shows such a create table statement. It begins as usual with the keywords `CREATE TABLE`, followed by the name of the new table. Then, rather than a list of column and constraint definitions, comes the keyword `AS`. This is followed by a subquery. The subquery can be any valid select statement, but cannot include an order by clause. The subquery's result set is a derived table and it is this derived table that forms the basis for creating the new base table. The new base table inherits the column definitions, not-null constraints and table instance of the subquery's result set. However, no other constraints are copied, so there will be no primary or foreign key constraints, nor unique or check constraints.

The create table statement in Code listing 6.4.1 thus creates a new base table called `StaffBackup` in the same database as the `Staff` table. It has identical column definitions and the same table instance – both the basic structure and the data are copied. For any column in the `Staff` table that has a not-null constraint, the corresponding column on the `StaffBackup` table also has a not-null constraint. There are no other constraints on the `StaffBackup` table.

Code listing 6.4.1   A create table statement using a subquery to specify column definitions

```
CREATE TABLE StaffBackup
AS SELECT * FROM Staff
```

Code listing 6.4.2 shows a more complex example. It creates a new base table called `StaffSupport`, which holds details of all support sessions and the staff who offer them. Rather than simply copying the existing data, it reformats it. Thus, the fName and lName columns are concatenated together and the endTime column is replaced with a duration column, showing how long the session lasts.

Code listing 6.4.2   A more complex example of a subquery

```
CREATE TABLE StaffSupport
AS SELECT Staff.staffNo, fName||lName AS name,
       dayOfWeek, startTime, endTime-startTime AS duration
  FROM Staff, SupportSession
  WHERE Staff.staffNo = SupportSession.staffNo
```

Creating copies of tables – or even copying part of one table into a new base table – creates duplicate data in the database. This goes against one of the main motivations of the database approach – reducing data duplication to a minimum. A better approach to presenting information in a different format, therefore, is to use a view (views are discussed further in Section 6.5, below). One valid reason for copying a base table, though, is that some DBMS do not allow a table to be renamed. To rename a table, copy it (using the new name) and then remove the old version. Note that any constraints (other than not-null constraints) will need to be defined on the new table.

The insert statement can use a subquery instead of a list of values. Suppose that some significant changes were requested to the data in the Staff table. For example, all the phone numbers and e-mail addresses were modified in advance of a planned upgrade to the telephone and e-mail systems. In such a situation, it makes sense to create a backup copy of the base table, as in Code listing 6.4.1. Suppose the upgrade to the telephone and e-mail systems is delayed. The old phone and e-mail data can easily be reinstated.

In Code listing 6.4.3, the modified data in the Staff table is removed using a delete statement and data from the StaffBackup table is copied back into the Staff table using an insert statement. This insert statement will add one row to the Staff table for each row in the subquery's result set – that is, each row of the StaffBackup table. Note that the columns in the column list of the insert statement are matched with the columns of the subquery's select list by position, *not* by name. If the order of the fName and lName columns in the subquery's select list is changed, then the data from the StaffBackup table's fName column will be placed in the Staff table's lName column and vice versa.

Code listing 6.4.3   Using a subquery in an insert statement

```
DELETE FROM Staff;

INSERT INTO Staff (staffNo, fName, lName, phone, email,
photo)
SELECT staffNo, fName, lName, phone, email, photo
FROM StaffBackup;
```

Of course this code won't work. The delete statement will fail because the rows of the Staff table are referenced by rows of the SupportSession table. The associated foreign key constraint on the SupportSession table prevents the referenced rows being deleted as there is no CASCADE keyword. However, adding the CASCADE keyword would mean data from the SupportSession table would be deleted, too.

A better solution is to use an update statement to reinstate the old phone numbers and e-mail addresses, without changing any of the other data. Code listing 6.4.4 shows such an update statement. The format is not the same as that discussed in Chapter 5. There, each column was assigned a value individually. Here, the columns being modified are listed in the set list and the values are provided as the result set of a subquery. Again, the columns in the set list are matched with those in the subquery's select list by position, not by name. The subquery must return one value for each column in the select list – that is for each row of the Staff table there must be one row in the subquery's result set.

Code listing 6.4.4   Using a subquery in an update statement

```
UPDATE Staff
SET (phone, email) = (SELECT phone, email
                      FROM StaffBackup
                      WHERE Staff.staffNo =
                              StaffBackup.staffNo);
```

A standard select statement can only refer to columns in the tables named in its own from clause. The subquery in Code listing 6.4.4 is an example of a **correlated subquery** as it refers to a column of a table mentioned in the outer SQL statement – Staff.staffNo. In an update statement, a subquery can refer to columns in the tables in its own from clause or the table being updated. The subquery in code listing 6.4.4 says:

retrieve the values of the phone and email columns from that row of the StaffBackup table for which the staffNo column value matches the value of the staffNo column in the current row of the Staff table.

The DBMS will work down the Staff table, row by row. For each row, it will calculate the result set for the subquery – it finds the matching row of the StaffBackup table and retrieves the phone and email column values. It then updates the current row of the Staff table with those values.

Not all update statements use correlated subqueries. Code listing 6.4.5 is not correlated. The only columns referred to in the subquery come from its own copy of the Equipment table. This update statement sets the values of the cost and acquired columns to be the same as those of the piece of equipment with asset number '1570131', but only in those rows of the Equipment table where the description column has the value 'HP vp6100'.

As the subquery returns the same result set for every row modified by the update statement, the DBMS can calculate the subquery's result set once and use that result set to modify every affected row. This makes non-correlated subqueries much faster than correlated ones. Figure 6.20 highlights the data in the subquery's result set and the rows affected by the update statement. After the update has been completed, all three rows will have the values '1300.00' and '2004-07-14' in their cost and acquired columns.

Figure 6.20 The effect of an update statement with a non-correlated subquery.

Subquery retrieves this data once, and uses it to modify each row affected by the update statement

Equipment

assetNo:varchar	assetType:varchar	description:varchar	building:varchar	room:varchar	portable:boolean	cost:numeric	acquired:date
1570131	Data projector	HP vp6100	Wilson	205	FALSE	1300.00	2004-07-14
1799131	Data projector	HP vp6100	NULL	NULL	TRUE	1300.00	2005-01-12
4560293	OHP	3M OHP 1608	Locke	24	FALSE	NULL	NULL
4503993	PC	Dell OptiPlex™ GX280	Wilson	205	FALSE	625.00	2004-04-30
5010009	OHP	3M OHP 2000	NULL	NULL	TRUE	185.00	2001-08-20
2992220	Data projector	ToshibaTDP-SW20	Priestley	G12	FALSE	1100.00	2005-01-12
2892112	Laptop	SONY X505	NULL	NULL	TRUE	NULL	NULL
3144578	Data projector	HP vp6100	Locke	14	FALSE	NULL	NULL

Update statement modifies these rows

Code listing 6.4.5 An update statement the subquery of which is not correlated with the outer statement.

```
UPDATE Equipment
SET (cost, acquired) = (SELECT cost, acquired
                        FROM Equipment
                        WHERE assetNo = '1570131')
WHERE description = 'HP vp6100';
```

Perhaps the commonest use of a subquery is as part of a where clause. This could be the where clause of a delete statement, update statement or a select statement. The examples covered will illustrate the main uses of a subquery in a where clause. In each case, we can see that the subquery restricts which rows are affected by the outer SQL statement. For example, consider the following business query:

How many support sessions are offered by Mikhail Sudbin, whose e-mail address is m.sudbin@pennine.ac.uk?

To answer this query, the DBMS must count those rows of the SupportSession table that are offered by Mikhail Sudbin. The obvious approach is to use the value of the staffNo column for Mikhail Sudbin, but his staff number isn't known. The value of the candidate key email *is* known, though.

The first select statement in Code listing 6.4.6 uses the value of email to retrieve the value of the staffNo column from the Staff table, which is the done in the subquery. Then, this value of the staffNo column is used to restrict the rows of the outer select statement. The second select statement shows how the same result can be achieved using an inner join. Where either approach will work, it is a matter of personal preference as to which is used.

Code listing 6.4.6   A subquery in the where clause and the equivalent join statement

```
SELECT COUNT(*)
FROM SupportSession
WHERE staffNo = (SELECT staffNo
                 FROM Staff
                 WHERE email = 'm.sudbin@pennine.ac.uk');
SELECT COUNT(*)
FROM SupportSession, Staff
WHERE SupportSession.staffNo = Staff.staffNo
AND email = 'm.sudbin@pennine.ac.uk';
```

Strictly speaking, the where clause in the first select statement of Code listing 6.4.6 should result in a data type error. It asks whether a *column value*, the value of staffNo, is equal to a *derived table*, the result set of the subquery. Obviously it isn't as the derived table has a non-scalar data type (the table type), whereas the staffNo is a scalar (a varchar). The syntax is acceptable, though, because the result set of the subquery will always consist of a single row (email is a candidate key) with a single column. So, because the subquery returns a derived table with one row and one column, the DBMS can treat it as though it were a single data value. That is why the equality comparison works. If the subquery returns more than one column, or more than one row, the select statement cannot use an equality comparison.

Business queries sometimes want to retrieve information based on the value of an aggregate function. For example:

display a list of equipment that is more expensive than the average cost of equipment.

A business query such as this is best answered using a subquery (there are other approaches, but the subquery is by far the simplest).

Code listing 6.4.7 shows the select statement for the above query. First, the subquery calculates the average cost of *all* the equipment, then the outer select statement retrieves those rows of the Equipment table where the value of the cost column is greater than this average cost. This select statement cannot be replaced by a join as it is not possible to use an aggregate function in the where clause.

Code listing 6.4.7   A subquery that cannot be replaced by a join

```
SELECT assetNo, assetType, description, cost, acquired
FROM Equipment
WHERE cost > (SELECT AVG(cost)
              FROM Equipment);
```

Subqueries that return more than one row are sometimes useful. For example, the following business query can be answered using such a subquery:

list all members of staff who offer support sessions on a Monday.

The way to answer this question is to, first, retrieve a list of staff numbers from the SupportSession table for those staff who offer support sessions on a Monday. Based on the instance of the SupportSession table in Figure 6.19, there are four: 35054, 45965, 23257 and 55776. Next, retrieve data from those rows of the Staff table where the value of the staffNo column appears in this list. The SQL comparison operator IN checks whether or not a given value appears in a list of values.

Code listing 6.4.8 shows how to use IN with a subquery. Again, the subquery can only retrieve data from a single column, but there may be more than one row in the result set. The DBMS treats the subquery's result set as a list of single data values rather than a derived table with several rows.

Code listing 6.4.8 A subquery using the IN comparison operator

```
SELECT staffNo, fName, lName
FROM Staff
WHERE staffNo IN (SELECT staffNo
                  FROM SupportSession
                  WHERE dayOfWeek = 'Monday');
```

Suppose that the business query is simply:

list all members of staff who offer support sessions.

Code listing 6.4.9 shows two solutions to this query. The first uses a subquery to compile a list of staff numbers that appear in the SupportSession table. It then uses IN to identify those rows of the Staff table where the staffNo value appears in this list.

The second query uses a correlated subquery, which is evaluated separately for each row of the Staff table. The subquery retrieves all data for those rows of the SupportSession table for which the staffNo value matches that of the current row of the Staff table. The keyword EXISTS means that the current row of the Staff table is included in the result set of the outer select statement whenever there is at least one row in the result set of the subquery – that is, whenever the current member of staff actually offers a support session.

As is usually the case, which form you use is a matter of personal preference. That preference should be informed by the capabilities of the particular DBMS being used. In particular, the speed with which a DBMS executes these two select statements may be different, in which case, the fastest should be used. Decisions like this are part of physical database design and are discussed in Chapter 9.

Code listing 6.4.9 A subquery using EXISTS

```
SELECT staffNo, fName, lName
FROM Staff
WHERE staffNo IN (SELECT staffNo
                  FROM SupportSession);

SELECT staffNo, fName, lName
FROM Staff
WHERE EXISTS (SELECT *
             FROM SupportSession
             WHERE SupportSession.staffno =
                   Staff.staffno);
```

One final use of subqueries is in the check constraint. Suppose that, in the Asset Tracking database (the SQL schema AssetTracking), there is a table:

```
AssetType(type, description)
```

The Asset Tracking database is separate from the Web Timetable database (the SQL schema `WebTimetable`), though both hold data on equipment owned by the university. The university uses the `AssetType` table as the main list of the different sorts of equipment it owns. It must ensure that the values in the `Equipment` table's `assetType` column all exist in the `AssetType` table's `type` column. A foreign key constraint won't work because the tables are in different databases, but a check constraint will.

Code listing 6.4.10 shows how this is achieved. Notice the use of the qualified identifier `"AssetTracking.AssetType"`. Without the name of the SQL schema, the DBMS would look for the `AssetType` table in the current database (the `WebTimetable` SQL schema). As it isn't there, the alter table statement would not work.

Code listing 6.4.10   A subquery in a check constraint

```
ALTER TABLE Equipment
ADD CONSTRAINT chkEquipmentAssetType
  CHECK (assetType IN (SELECT type
                       FROM AssetTracking.AssetType));
```

The check constraint in Code listing 6.4.10 ensures that, when a row is added to the `Equipment` table or an existing row is modified, the value supplied for the `assetType` column is in a list selected from another table using a subquery. For the statement in Code listing 6.4.10 to work, both SQL schema must be in the same SQL catalog. If not, then the SQL schema name must be qualified with the correct SQL catalog name. For example, `Estates.AssetTracking.AssetType` would refer to the `AssetType` table in the `AssetTracking` SQL schema of the SQL catalog named `Estates`.

6.5   Views

In SQL, a **view** is a derived table, the definition of which is stored in the data dictionary (see Chapter 3 for a discussion of the view mechanism). Once defined, a view can be queried much like a base table, although, as discussed in Chapter 3, not all views are updateable. Until the release of Version 5, views had not been available on the MySQL DBMS. As many web database applications used the MySQL DBMS, this meant that web database developers tended not to use views. This should change, however, because views are useful in two ways.

First, they can improve the performance of database queries. Whenever the DBMS is passed a select statement in human-readable SQL, it needs to build an execution plan. Essentially, the DBMS translates the SQL instructions into a series of instructions that can be executed by the system software. This takes time. A view can be thought of as a select statement for which the DBMS has already prepared an execution plan.

A second advantage of views is that they can simplify database queries. Rather than repeatedly coding a join query to retrieve data from two (or more) tables, the web database developer can store the join query as a view and retrieve data through the view. This makes coding SQL select statements simpler, which is particularly useful on projects where some developers aren't familiar with SQL. In fact, for a web database application, it makes sense to build enough views so that a PHP script need only ever query a single base table or view. In this way, there are no join queries in the PHP code at all, making it much simpler to maintain.

Code listing 6.5.1 illustrates how to create a view using SQL. It creates a view based on the `Equipment` table that will show only portable equipment.

Code listing 6.5.1   A view showing portable equipment

```
CREATE VIEW PortableEquipment
AS SELECT assetNo, assetType, description, cost, acquired
   FROM Equipment
   WHERE portable = TRUE;
```

The `CREATE VIEW` keyword is followed by the SQL identifier `PortableEquipment` naming the view.

The `AS` keyword is followed by the **view definition**, an SQL select statement. The select list tells the DBMS which columns of the underlying base table are included in the view. The `portable` column is not included as its value would be `TRUE` in every row of the view instance. The `building` and `room` columns are omitted as they would always be null.

The from clause tells the DBMS what the underlying base table is and the where clause which rows of the underlying base table should appear in the view instance. In this example, these are all the rows of the `Equipment` table for which the value for the `portable` column is `TRUE`.

Querying the view creates a derived table. The column names of this derived table will be the same as those of the underlying base table – in this case, `assetNo, asset-Type, description, cost` and `acquired`. Code listing 6.5.2 shows a database query using this view and the equivalent query on the underlying base table.

Code listing 6.5.2   Querying a view compared to querying its underlying base table

(a) A database query against the view `PortableEquipment`

```
SELECT assetNo, description
FROM PortableEquipment;
```

(b) The equivalent database query against the underlying base table `Equipment`

```
SELECT assetNo, description
FROM Equipment
WHERE portable = TRUE;
```

Sometimes the column names in the view must be different from those in the underlying base table. To specify the view's column names, use the format illustrated in Code listing 6.5.3.

Code listing 6.5.3   A view with column names that are different from those in its underlying base table

```
CREATE VIEW PortEquip (ID, atype, adesc, cost, acq)
AS SELECT assetNo, assetType, description, cost, acquired
   FROM Equipment
   WHERE portable = TRUE;
```

This creates a view with the same basic structure, but its columns are named `ID`, `atype`, `adesc`, `cost` and `acq`. A database query using this view must use these column names, not the column names of the underlying base table. Compare the query in Code listing 6.5.2 (a) with the corresponding query in Code listing 6.5.4

Code listing 6.5.4   Querying a view the columns of which have been renamed

```
SELECT ID, adesc
FROM PortEquip;
```

Views are often used to present data in different formats for different users. In most of the examples used so far, the structure of the `Staff` table has been:

```
Staff (staffNo:Varchar, fName:Varchar, lName:Varchar,
       phone:Varchar, email:Varchar, photo:BLOB)
Primary Key: (staffNo)
```

However, in Chapter 1, an alternative structure was proposed that included four additional columns. The table schema for this expanded version – named `FullStaff` to avoid confusion is:

```
FullStaff (staffNo:Varchar, fName:Varchar, lName:Varchar,
           phone:Varchar, email:Varchar, photo:BLOB,
           department:Varchar, title:Varchar,
           jobType:Varchar, jobTitle:Varchar)
Primary Key: (staffNo)
```

Chapter 2 explained how this approach is supported by the ANSI/SPARC database systems architecture. The additional columns allow both the Staff Directory and the School of Computing's Staff List applications to use the same base table (the `FullStaff` table, which is part of the logical view of the ANSI/SPARC database systems architecture). All that's needed is an *external* view for each application.

The external view for the Staff Directory includes the `SupportSession` table and a relational view showing data from the first six columns of the underlying `FullStaff` table. This can be created using the SQL statement shown in Code listing 6.5.5 (a). However, the School of Computing's Staff List application needs a more complex relational view. It needs a single name made up of title, first initial and surname. This data is available from the `FullStaff` table of the logical view, but not from any single column. The `title`, the first character of `fName` and the `lName` must be concatenated to give the name of each academic in the format required. Also, this relational view uses a where clause in its definition, to ensure that only staff from the School of Computing can be retrieved through the view. Code listing 6.5.5 (b) shows the SQL statement used to create this view.

Code listing 6.5.5   Two relational views based on the same underlying table

(a) A vertical view: some columns, all rows

```
CREATE VIEW Staff
AS SELECT staffNo, fName, lName, phone, email, photo
   FROM FullStaff;
```

269

(b) A more complex view: some columns, some rows

```
CREATE VIEW ComputingStaff (name, email, phone, job,
                            jobType)
AS SELECT title || SUBSTRING(fName FROM 1 FOR 1) || lName,
          email, phone, job, jobType
  FROM FullStaff
  WHERE department = 'Computing';
```

The ISO standard for SQL does not provide a facility for modifying the definition of a view (though some commercial DBMS do). To do this, remove the view from the database, then recreate it with the new definition. As a view is a virtual table, removing it has no effect on the database instance, though it will change the meta-data held in the data dictionary. Code listing 6.5.6 shows how to remove a view.

Code Listing 6.5.6   Removing a view

```
DROP VIEW ComputingStaff;
```

Under certain circumstances, it is possible to modify the underlying base table instance through the view by either adding a new row or modifying an existing one. Updateable views were discussed in Chapter 3. Briefly, a view will be updateable provided:

1 each column of the underlying base table appears at most once in the select list of the database query defining the relational view

2 each row in the relational view instance can be traced back to a unique row in the underlying base table – the underlying row

3 in each row of the relational view instance, the value of each column is taken directly from a single column of the underlying row, with no operators or functions used.

The ComputingStaff relational view of Code listing 6.5.5 satisfies the first condition – no column name appears more than once in the select list. It also satisfies the second as each row in the view is derived from a single row in the Staff table. It does not satisfy the third, however, as the name column is assembled from the values of three different columns of the underlying row. This means that the ComputingStaff relational view is not updateable. The Staff view is updateable as it satisfies all three conditions. However, it is not possible to add a new member of staff through this view. In the underlying base table FullStaff, the department column has a not-null constraint. The Staff view doesn't include this column, so an insert statement using the Staff view can't include data for a mandatory column, and rows cannot be added through the Staff view. Existing rows can have the data in their staffNo, fName, lName, phone, email and photo columns modified, though.

The relational view PortableEquipment, created in Code listing 6.5.1, is also updateable and illustrates another problem when updating the underlying base table through a view. Consider what happens when the SQL INSERT statement shown in Code listing 6.5.7 is executed.

Code listing 6.5.7 *Adding a row into a base table via a view*

```
INSERT INTO PortableEquipment (assetNo, assetType,
description)
VALUES (15733, 'OHP', 'Basic, two-bulb OHP');
```

The relational view `PortableEquipment` only has three columns, so only values for these columns can be supplied with the `INSERT` statement. A new row is added to the underlying base table `Equipment` with `assetNo` set to 15733, `assetType` to 'OHP' and `description` to 'Basic, two-bulb OHP'. The remaining columns of the equipment table are set to their default values – `building` is set to `NULL`, `room` is set to `NULL` and `portable` is set to `FALSE`. (See Code listing 5.4.2 in Chapter 5 for the relevant create table statement.) This creates a problem. The row just added to the `Equipment` table via the view `PortableEquipment` has its `portable` column set to `FALSE`. The definition of `PortableEquipment` view states that such rows cannot be retrieved through the view. To the end user, seeing only those rows that can be retrieved through the `PortableEquipment` view, it will appear as though the `INSERT` statement failed.

Allowing users to add rows via a view that won't appear in the view instance is certain to cause confusion. SQL includes the `WITH CHECK OPTION` to prevent this. When this is included in the view definition (Code listing 6.5.8), only rows that can be retrieved through the view instance can be added to the underlying base table via the view. In the case of the `PortableEquipment` view, this stops users adding any rows to the underlying base table via the view.

Code listing 6.5.8 *An updateable view with the* `WITH CHECK OPTION`

```
CREATE VIEW portable_equipment
AS SELECT asset_no, asset_type, description
   FROM equipment
   WHERE portable = TRUE
WITH CHECK OPTION;
```

Chapter summary

■ This chapter has examined a range of more advanced applications of the data language SQL. Joins, subqueries and aggregate queries were discussed in some depth. These kinds of queries are very common, so a web database developer needs to understand how to implement them. Some examples of SQL's value functions were discussed, with an emphasis on manipulating dates and character strings. The chapter has also looked at more advanced examples of SQL DDL, including using a subquery in a check constraint and creating SQL views.

Further reading

See the suggested further reading at the end of Chapter 5.

Review questions

6.1 Explain the following terms used in relation to the SQL select statement:
(a) qualified identifier
(b) correlation name
(c) join
(d) join condition
(e) equi-join.

6.2 Explain the differences between a cross join, inner join and outer join (assume that the join involves only two tables).

6.3 In SQL, what is a value function? Name three ISO SQL value functions and explain the purpose of each.

6.4 In SQL, what is an aggregate (or set) function? Name three ISO SQL aggregate (or set) functions and explain the purpose of each.

6.5 What is the purpose of the SQL group by clause?

6.6 How does the SQL having clause differ from the SQL where clause?

6.7 Describe the order in which a DBMS processes the various clauses of the select statement.

6.8 What is a subquery? Suggest two situations for which a subquery could be used.

6.9 How does a correlated subquery differ from a non-correlated one?

6.10 What facilities does ISO SQL provide for creating and manipulating views?

Exercises

These exercises use the `Room` and `Equipment` tables from this chapter and the `Course`, `Module` and `Staff` tables created in the exercises for Chapter 5 as practice for writing SQL statements. The table schema are:

```
Room (building VARCHAR(15) NOT NULL,
      roomNo VARCHAR(4) NOT NULL,
      capacity INTEGER
     )
PRIMARY KEY (building, roomNo)

Equipment (assetNo VARCHAR(15) NOT NULL,
           assetType VARCHAR(15) NOT NULL,
```

```
                    description VARCHAR(50),
                    building VARCHAR(15),
                    room VARCHAR(4),
                    portable BOOLEAN DEFAULT (FALSE) NOT NULL,
                    cost NUMERIC(7,2),
                    acquired DATE
                )
        PRIMARY KEY (assetNo)
        FOREIGN KEY (building, room) REFERENCES Room (building, roomNo)

        Course (code CHAR(4) NOT NULL,
                title VARCHAR(50) NOT NULL,
                leadDepartment VARCHAR(30) NOT NULL,
                minorDepartment VARCHAR(30),
                level VARCHAR(15) NOT NULL,
                qualification VARCHAR(50),
                mode VARCHAR(9) DEFAULT 'Full Time' NOT NULL
                )
        PRIMARY KEY (code)
        CANDIDATE KEY (title, mode)
        BUSINESS RULE mode must be one of {'Full Time', 'Part Time'}

        Module (code CHAR(8) NOT NULL,
                title VARCHAR(50) NOT NULL,
                department VARCHAR(30) NOT NULL,
                level VARCHAR(15) NOT NULL,
                leader VARCHAR(10)
                )
        PRIMARY KEY (code)
        CANDIDATE KEY (department, title)
        FOREIGN KEY leader REFERENCES Staff(staffNo)
                ON UPDATE CASCADE
                ON DELETE SET NULL

        Staff (staffNo VARCHAR(10) NOT NULL,
                title VARCHAR(4) NOT NULL,
                fName VARCHAR(50) NOT NULL,
                lName VARCHAR(20) NOT NULL,
                email VARCHAR(50) NOT NULL,
                department VARCHAR(30) NOT NULL,
                lineManager VARCHAR(10) NOT NULL
                )
        PRIMARY KEY (staffNo)
        CANDIDATE KEY (email)
        BUSINESS RULE title must be one of {'Mr', 'Ms', 'Miss', 'Mrs',
        'Dr', 'Prof'}
        FOREIGN KEY lineManager REFERENCES Staff(staffNo)
                ON UPDATE CASCADE
                ON DELETE NO ACTION
```

6.11 The following questions provide practice with inner joins.
   (a) Produce a list of modules and their module leaders. Do not list modules that currently have no module leader.
   (b) Produce a list of modules and their module leaders for all modules in the computing department. Do not list modules that currently have no module leader.
   (c) Produce a list of modules and their module leaders for all modules at Honours level in the computing department. Do not list modules that currently have no module leader.
   (d) Produce a list of modules and their module leaders for all modules in the computing and business departments. Do not list modules that currently have no module leader.

6.12 The following questions provide practice with outer joins.
   (a) Repeat the database queries in Exercises 6.11 (a)–(d), but this time include all modules in the list, even those that currently have no module leader.
   (b) Produce a list of all staff and the modules they lead. Include staff who do not currently lead any modules.
   (c) Produce a list of staff from the computing department, showing the modules they lead. Include staff who do not currently lead any modules.
   (d) Produce a list of staff from the computing and business departments, showing the modules they lead. Include staff who do not currently lead any modules.
   (e) Produce a list showing all staff and all modules, clearly indicating which staff currently lead which modules, those modules that have no leader and those staff who do not currently lead a module.
   (f) Produce a list showing all staff and their line manager. (*Hint:* You will need to use a self join.)

6.13 The following questions provide practice with SQL value functions.
   (a) Display a list of staff showing their title, first initial and surname.
   (b) List all staff whose surname starts with the same character as their first name.
   (c) List all modules with titles longer that 20 characters.
   (d) Managers have decided that course titles should be stored in upper case. Write an update statement to implement this requirement.
   (e) Managers have now decided that having course titles in upper case is too aggressive and want them in sentence case, where only the first letter is upper case. Write an update statement to implement this requirement.
   (f) What problems can making such changes to the stored data produce? (*Hint:* What happens to the course with the title ICT?) How could you meet these requirements without changing the data in the base table?

6.14 The following questions provide practice with SQL aggregate functions and queries. For each, write a suitable SQL statement.
   (a) How many courses have a second (minor) department involved in their delivery?
   (b) Produce a list of departments and the numbers of courses they deliver as lead departments.
   (c) Produce a list of departments and the numbers of courses they deliver as lead departments, excluding courses that lead to an HND qualification.
   (d) Produce a list of departments and the numbers of courses they deliver as lead departments. Only show information for departments with three or fewer courses.

(e) Produce a list showing how many modules each department offers at each level.

(f) Produce a list of staff showing how many modules they lead.

6.15 The following questions provide practice with SQL subqueries. For each, write a suitable SQL statement.

(a) Using a subquery, display the staff details for the module leader of the module with the code CCHO0418.

(b) Write two subqueries to display the staff details for all module leaders. One should be a correlated subquery, the other not.

(c) Using a subquery, display the module details for all modules except those led by staff who work in the computing department.

6.16 Give an example, other than the ones given in this chapter, of a situation for which you would use a self join. Provide a suitable table schema and a rationale for an organization wanting to use the result set of the self join.

Investigations

6.17 Investigate the support your DBMS provides for storing and manipulating dates, times and intervals. Using a suitable example, write SQL queries to demonstrate the date and time manipulation functions.

6.18 Investigate the SQL view mechanism and its implementation in various DBMS. There are two important issues. First, what does the DBMS actually do when a user queries a view? Does the DBMS physically assemble the view as a derived table and then query it or does it use the view definition to translate the query into one that only mentions base tables? The second issue is whether or not the user can update the base tables through the view.

6.19 The ISO SQL:2003 standard's DML includes a number of statements not covered in this textbook. For example UNION, INTERSECT, EXCEPT and MERGE are all widely supported SQL DML statements, though less widely used. Investigate these statements, identifying scenarios for which they could prove useful.

6.20 The ISO SQL standard, and many of the commercial DBMS, include support for multiple character sets. This is particularly important in the context of web databases as the Web is a global medium and databases may need to store information in many different languages. Investigate the extent to which your DBMS supports internationalization. Does it follow the ISO SQL standard? If not, critically assess its deviations from the standard.

Further issues in web database implementation

Chapter objectives

→ To explore PHP's built-in error-reporting facilities.

→ To discuss a range of programming techniques used in web database applications.

→ To explore ways of maintaining state across multiple HTTP requests.

Chapter outline

This chapter looks at some common issues that arise when implementing web database applications. It builds on the material covered in Chapters 4, 5 and 6. The focus is on the issues rather than production-quality solutions. Most of the code developed in this chapter is definitely *not* suitable for deploying as part of a live web database application and it is important to be clear about this. There are plenty of sources of production-quality code to solve particular problems, but, unless application developers understand the issues, they will struggle to use those resources effectively.

Many of the issues discussed involve the problem of maintaining **application state**. Application state is the term used to refer to information about the current and previous state of an application. Typical examples of application state include the identity of the end user, what he or she has done and any data gathered from him or her. Examples of aspects of application behaviour that need to keep track of application state include presenting the results of a database query across multiple web pages, keeping track of decisions made as the user browses a website and implementing a single login process to allow access to many different web resources.

As HTTP is a stateless protocol, application state does not persist between HTTP requests. It is worth looking in a little more detail at how this affects web database applications. Each HTTP request–response cycle has the same general structure (Figure 7.1). First, a web browser sends an HTTP request to the web server. This request can include application data, either in the URL query string or the HTTP request

Figure 7.1 The HTTP request–response cycle for a dynamic resource.

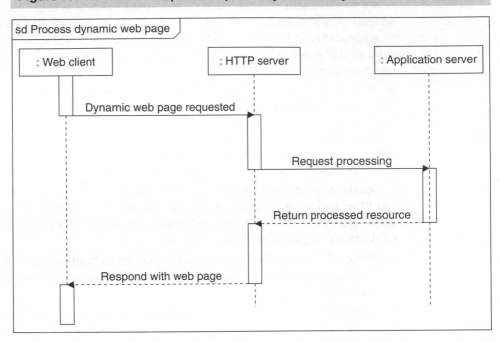

message's entity body (such as data from a form sent using POST). When the request includes application data, then the requested resource is usually a server- side script (or other dynamic resource). On the web server, the HTTP server receives the request and decides how to deal with it. For a PHP script, the HTTP server passes the application data to the PHP application server, which uses it to build an HTTP response message. Once the PHP application server has built the HTTP response message, it passes this to the HTTP server and tidies up. 'Tidying up' involves clearing out any application state stored by the PHP application server for this particular HTTP request. The HTTP server forwards the HTTP response to the web browser, then it also tidies up. The consequence of this is that there is no record of application state on the web server. With simple applications this is not a problem. In the Staff Directory, the web page that gathers the search criteria submits this data to a PHP script for processing. The script uses the data to search the database, then builds an HTTP response (a web page) to deliver the search results. Once the web server sends the HTTP response, the application state – that is, the search criteria – is lost. This is not a problem because everything the end user wanted done has been done.

Now consider what happens if the Pennine University decides to password protect its Staff Directory. Before end users can submit a search they must first login. When users request the search form from the Staff Directory, the application asks them for their username and password. Only when the end users have supplied a valid username and password do they see the search form. They can then enter the search criteria, but must login again before they see the web page with the results. In fact, every time they request a protected resource, they need to login. This is clearly not very user-friendly. End users expect to login once, not every time they want to do anything.

There are three basic solutions to the problem of maintaining application state between two different HTTP requests. The simplest solution is to get the web browser to remember any state information and send it along with every HTTP request. One way to achieve this is to get the web browser to add the state information as name-value pairs to the query string of the URL for the requested resource. This is called **URL rewriting** and is a simple and effective approach if there is only a small amount of application state data. If there is a lot of application state data, then it is possible to place it inside an HTML form as **hidden form controls**. When the user submits the form, the application state data is submitted, too.

The HTTP protocol itself includes a way to maintain login data between requests. HTTP authentication causes the web browser to store login details for a particular web server and send them with each request to that web server.

Sessions generalize this idea. The web server gives each end user a unique session identifier, and the web browser sends this unique session identifier with each request. The web server can associate the application state for that user with the session identifier so that it is always available.

- Section 7.1 begins the chapter by looking at PHP's built-in error-reporting facilities. Understanding these can save a lot of time and frustration when trying to debug a PHP script.

- Section 7.2 uses URL rewriting to implement a script that can deliver the result set of a database query across multiple web pages. This is a common technique, used on most e-commerce retail sites.

- Section 7.3 delves deeper into data validation and shows how to use a single script to both gather and process data entered by end users. Single script solutions are useful as they allow the script to display messages about validation failures next to the relevant HTML form control.

- Section 7.4 looks at the reload problem. This problem affects many of the scripts used so far. The solution uses PHP to write HTTP headers – an important technique that is used in later sections, too.

- Section 7.5 discusses hidden form controls in the context of 'wizards', which guide end users through long or complex processes.

- Section 7.6 discusses sessions – the technique that provides the most robust approach to maintaining application state. Any application that uses URL rewriting or hidden form fields could be rewritten to use sessions.

- Section 7.7 concludes the chapter with a discussion of HTTP authentication.

7.1 Error reporting and debugging

The error reporting discussed in Chapter 4 mainly dealt with errors that arise while the server-side script is communicating with the DBMS. This is a small part of the larger problem of error handling.

There are different kinds of errors that can occur. Some of the hardest to detect are those that arise from incorrect program logic, such as an incorrect condition on an if statement or a misspelt variable name. These don't cause the script to stop, but do mean that it produces unexpected, often incorrect, results.

Another kind of error – called a runtime error – occurs when a valid script encounters a situation that it just cannot deal with. Errors communicating with the DBMS are runtime errors. With these, the script will continue to execute, but won't work properly. Chapter 4 showed how to check for such errors and deal with them. Trying to use an unknown function, perhaps because the function name is misspelt, will also cause a runtime error. This one *will* stop the script executing, though.

In the early stages of developing a PHP script, incorrect syntax is a common source of errors. Some syntax errors can prevent the script from executing – a missing semicolon, for example. Others may allow it to execute, but could stop it working properly. For example, failing to enclose the key of an associative array in quotes can cause problems. It's common to see $\_GET[staffNo]$ instead of $\_GET["staffNo"]$. PHP will first interpret $\_GET[staffNo]$ as referring to the element of $\_GET$, the key of this being the value of the staffNo *constant*. Only if there is no such constant does it interpret it as the element the key of which is the string literal "staffNo".

PHP, like most programming languages, provides facilities to automatically detect and report as many errors as practicable. This section examines PHP's built-in error-reporting facilities and how to use them to debug a PHP script. PHP classifies errors into several different levels, according to when they occur and how serious they are. As mentioned in Chapter 4, the instructions in the human-readable PHP code have to be transformed into a format that the PHP application server can understand. The first step in this processes is parsing, which means checking that the code in the PHP script is grammatically correct PHP. If the code is *not* grammatically correct, then the PHP parser will report an error. The fragment of PHP code in Figure 7.2 (a) has an example of an error that the parser will pick up. There should be a semicolon at the end of line 27. The PHP parser generates the error message shown in Figure 7.2 (b).

Figure 7.2 PHP code with a parse error.

```
24 <?php
25 // Example of an un-terminated statement
26 echo "This line has a semi colon ";
27 echo "but this line does not ..."
28 echo " which will cause problems";
29 ?>
```

(a) The PHP code.

Date and time the
error occurred   The kind of error

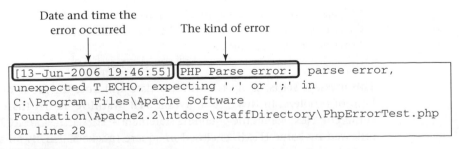

```
[13-Jun-2006 19:46:55] PHP Parse error: parse error,
unexpected T_ECHO, expecting ',' or ';' in
C:\Program Files\Apache Software
Foundation\Apache2.2\htdocs\StaffDirectory\PhpErrorTest.php
on line 28
```

(b) The PHP error message.

The format of PHP error messages follows this standard pattern. First comes the date and time the error occurred (this is only included in log file error messages, not display messages – see below), then a brief description of the kind of error. As this error was identified by the PHP parser, it is called a `PHP Parse error`. The error message itself begins with a description of the problem:

```
parse error, unexpected T_ECHO, expecting ',' or ';'
```

This message indicates that the parser came across a `T_ECHO` when it was expecting to find either a comma or a semicolon. `'T_ECHO'` is the parser's name for an echo statement (see Appendix Q of PHP Documentation Group (2005) for a full list of these parser tokens). Next comes the full pathname of the PHP script in which the error occurred:

```
in C:\Program Files\Apache Software Foundation\
Apache2.2\htdocs\StaffDirectory\
PhpErrorTest.php
```

The final piece of information is the number of the line where the parser first realized that something was wrong. In the example, it is line 28. Notice that this is the line *after* the one with the missing semicolon. This is because a PHP statement can run over several lines. Only at the start of line 28, when the parser reads the keyword `echo`, does it realize that something is wrong. The echo statement that began in line 27 could have a comma-separated list of strings running over on to the next line, but there must be a semicolon *before* the second `echo` keyword. The PHP parser does not care whether this semicolon appears at the end of line 27 or the start of line 28, but it must be there.

The PHP parser only checks the *syntax* of a PHP script. It ensures that the instructions are written in grammatically correct PHP, but does not check that the instructions can actually be carried out. This means that, when the script is run, there could still be errors. When PHP encounters a problem while running a script, it can issue a warning or an error. Warnings are issued when PHP encounters something that *might* be a problem, but then again might not. It is possible that the script will run correctly despite the warning. Missing include files fall into this category. Provided the PHP in the missing include file is not actually needed, the script may still run. PHP continues to run the script, but issues a warning:

```
[15-Jun-2006 10:26:54] PHP Warning:
include(DataCleansing.inc)
[<a href='function.include'>function.include</a>]: failed
to open stream: No such file or directory in
C:\Program Files\Apache Software
Foundation\Apache2.2\
htdocs\phpTestScripts\PhpErrorTest.php on line 34
```

This message starts, as always, with the date and time the problem occurred, then the kind of problem. In this case it gives a 'PHP warning' rather than a 'PHP Parse error' comment. Next comes the offending statement – `include(DataCleansing.inc)` – followed by some HTML enclosed in square brackets. This is an attempt to provide more friendly messages by giving a link to the relevant PHP manual page, though it only works if the HTML version of the PHP manual is installed with the PHP software. The warning message itself is `failed to open stream: No such file or directory ...`, which indicates that the file called `DataCleansing.inc` could not be found. The warning message ends, as usual, with the script's pathname and the line number where the problem was first recognized.

One common use of include files is to share functions between different scripts. Indeed, this is the purpose of the include file DataCleansing.inc. If the include file cannot be found, then any subsequent attempts to use its functions will cause a fatal error. In this case, PHP immediately stops running the script and issues an error message like this:

```
[15-Jun-2006 10:26:54] PHP Fatal error: Call to undefined
function cleanse_data() in C:\Program Files\Apache
Software Foundation\Apache2.2\htdocs\phpTestScripts\
PhpErrorTest.php on line 44
```

Note that the error is now a 'PHP Fatal error'. PHP will not execute any statement after the line where the error occurred, so lines from 45 onwards are ignored.

PHP also issues notices. Notices indicate when the script uses an old-fashioned coding approach, a deprecated function (one that might not be supported in future releases) or some other less serious problem. When a variable is used before it is given a value, PHP issues a notice like this:

```
[15-Jun-2006 11:14:28] PHP Notice: Undefined variable:
myVariable in C:\Program Files\Apache Software
Foundation\Apache2.2\htdocs\phpTestScripts\PhpErrorTest.php
on line 48
```

Note that the error is now a 'PHP Notice'. Provided the programmer actually wants to use a variable before assigning it a value, then the notice can be ignored. It is difficult to think of a good reason to do this, though.

Other common notices concern arrays. PHP issues a notice when the code refers to an array element that does not exist. This might happen because the code uses the wrong key name or the wrong index number. The code in Figure 7.3 defines an array with two elements. The key for the first element is `firstKey` and, for the second element, `secondKey`. Line 54 refers to the array element with key `thirdKey` and there is no such element, so PHP issues the notice:

```
[15-Jun-2006 11:28:39] PHP Notice: Undefined index:
thirdKey in C:\Program Files\Apache Software
Foundation\Apache2.2\htdocs\phpTestScripts\PhpErrorTest.php
on line 54
```

Figure 7.3 Errors with arrays are often reported as notices.

```
52 //Using the wrong key, and index, for an array element
53 $myArray=array('firstKey'=>23, 'secondKey'=>'This is the second element');
54 echo "Wrong array element key: ", $myArray['thirdKey'];
55 echo "Wrong array element : ", $myArray[2];
```

Line 55 refers to an array element by its index number – in this case, $myArray[2]. Unfortunately, PHP numbers element index numbers from zero, so the only valid index values are $myArray[0] and $myArray[1]. Thus, when it reaches line 55, PHP issues the notice:

```
[15-Jun-2006 11:28:39] PHP Notice: Undefined offset: 2 in
C:\Program Files\Apache Software
Foundation\Apache2.2\htdocs\phpTestScripts\PhpErrorTest.php
on line 55
```

In both cases, the script will continue to run, but may not behave as expected.

Errors, warnings and notices (generally referred to as error messages) are all very useful when debugging a PHP script, so it makes sense to ensure that PHP reports them. The PHP initialization file determines how PHP initially reports error messages and there are functions to change this behaviour from within a PHP script.

One option is to display error messages in the HTTP response generated when the script is run. This means that the errors are visible in the web browser, so this should only be done during development. Once the application has gone into the production environment and is being used by the end users, it should not display raw PHP error messages on the generated web pages.

Instead, production applications should write error messages to a log file. It's useful to do this during development, too. One problem with using a log file is that the web server must have write privileges on the file. With a shared, development web server this is not always possible, especially if the web server is used by many different developers working on different projects (as it is in a university, for example). See the PHP manual (PHP Documentation Group, 2005) for details of how to use error log files.

Along with a choice of how to report errors, PHP allows the application developer to specify which errors to report. The range of error levels is shown in Table 7.1. The levels E_ERROR, E_WARNING, E_PARSE and E_NOTICE represent the four levels of error discussed above and are by far the most common. The level E_ALL is an abbreviation for 'report all errors' and E_STRICT for 'include coding hints', which will issue a notice about deprecated functions or how to improve your PHP code.

One common problem for PHP application developers is how to manage these error-reporting facilities. Some application developers want to see all messages displayed on the web page, while others don't want to see any. This causes a problem for the web server administrator, who can only define *one* default policy in the PHP initialization file. A sensible compromise is to instruct PHP to display errors in the HTTP response, but then to set the error reporting level to E_PARSE. This means that parse errors are reported on the web page by default, but other errors are not reported. Each application developer can then control error reporting in their own scripts. The PHP function error_reporting() changes the error-reporting level. It is defined as:

```
int error_reporting ( [int level] )
```

where the value of the parameter *level* is one of the constants from Table 7.1. In fact, these constants can be combined to give a mixture of different levels. For example:

```
error_reporting(E_ALL | E_STRICT);
```

Table 7.1 Errors in PHP.

Constant	Description
E_ERROR	Fatal runtime errors. These indicate errors that cannot be recovered from, such as a memory allocation problem. Execution of the script is halted.
E_WARNING	Runtime warnings (non-fatal errors). Execution of the script is not halted.
E_PARSE	Compile time parse errors. Parse errors should only be generated by the parser.
E_NOTICE	Runtime notices. Indicate that the script encountered something that could indicate an error, but could also happen in the normal course of running a script.
E_CORE_ERROR	Fatal errors that occur during PHP's initial startup. This is like an E_ERROR, except that it is generated by the core of PHP.
E_CORE_WARNING	Warnings (non-fatal errors) that occur during PHP's initial startup. This is like an E_WARNING, except that it is generated by the core of PHP.
E_COMPILE_ERROR	Fatal compile time errors. This is like an E_ERROR, except that it is generated by the Zend Scripting Engine.
E_COMPILE_WARNING	Compile time warnings (non-fatal errors). This is like an E_WARNING, except that it is generated by the Zend Scripting Engine.
E_USER_ERROR	User-generated error message. This is like an E_ERROR, except that it is generated in PHP code by using the PHP function trigger_error().
E_USER_WARNING	User-generated warning message. This is like an E_WARNING, except that it is generated in PHP code by using the PHP function trigger_error().
E_USER_NOTICE	User-generated notice message. This is like an E_NOTICE, except that it is generated in PHP code by using the PHP function trigger_error().
E_ALL	All errors and warnings, as supported, except level E_STRICT.
E_STRICT	Runtime notices. Enable you to have PHP suggest changes to your code that will ensure the best interoperability and forward compatibility of the code.

Source PHP Documentation Group (2005).

instructs PHP to report all errors and all coding hints. Application developers who don't want coding hints or notices can use:

```
error_reporting(E_ALL & ~E_NOTICE);
```

This will ensure that only warnings and error messages are displayed. Calls to the error_reporting() function should come before any other PHP code, for obvious reasons.

> The symbols ' | ', '&' and '~' are the PHP bitwise operators. There are explanations of these in the PHP manual (PHP Documentation Group, 2005).

Sorting out which errors PHP reports and how it reports them is only the first step in error handling. PHP allows application developers to write their own error-handling functions. These could automatically distinguish between development and production environments and issue different styles of error message. They can even be set up to e-mail errors to the application support team. Since PHP version 5, object-orientated programming has been incorporated into PHP, so it now supports Java-style exception handling with 'try' and 'catch' blocks. Good sources to consult on these more advanced issues are mentioned in the Further reading section at the end of this chapter.

7.2 Managing large result sets

A common feature of web database applications is the search results page. The Staff Directory search page is typical of this feature. Data is drawn from the database and delivered to the end user as a list of results, with hyperlinks to further details. Where the number of results is likely to be small, delivering them all on a single web page is an acceptable solution. Where the number of results is large, however, they need to be delivered across multiple pages, with each page delivering a fixed-sized chunk of the result set. So, for example, the Staff Directory search could deliver four results per page. If a particular search returned ten results, then the first four would be delivered on page one, the next four on page two and the final two on page three. This presents a problem for web database applications. HTTP is a stateless protocol, so the web server does not remember which page the user was looking at and so cannot automatically deliver the correct chunk of the result set.

Two mechanisms are required to deliver a result set across multiple pages. The first must allow the application to retrieve a particular chunk of the result set – the first 5 rows only, then rows 6–10 and, finally, rows 11–12, for example. Second, the application needs to implement a mechanism for navigating from page to page that maintains the application state between HTTP requests. The application state keeps track of which chunk of the result set to retrieve for the next page.

The SQL standard does not provide a mechanism to allow the application to specify which chunk of the result set it wants. Instead, the application would need to retrieve the whole result set and navigate through to the chunk it required. This is not difficult, but can involve the web server doing a lot of work as it trawls through a large result set. However, the MySQL DBMS has an extension to the ISO SQL standard that does allow the application to tell the DBMS which chunk of the result set is required. This is a very handy feature for web database applications, shifting the work of navigating through the result set to the required chunk from the *web* server to the *database* server.

Figure 7.4 shows the general form of the limit clause of a MySQL DBMS select statement. It comes after the order by clause and begins with the keyword LIMIT. This is followed by two values. The value offset is the number of the row to start from – rows

Figure 7.4 The format of the MySQL DBMS limit clause of the select statement.

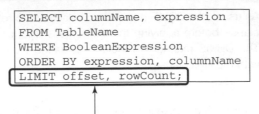

```
SELECT columnName, expression
FROM TableName
WHERE BooleanExpression
ORDER BY expression, columnName
LIMIT offset, rowCount;
```

The MySQL limit clause instructs the DBMS to return only the specified chunk of the result set

are numbered from zero, like PHP arrays. The other value, `rowCount`, is the number of rows to retrieve. So, for example, the limit clause `LIMIT 8,4` tells the DBMS to start from the ninth row of the result set and return four rows in total.

Code listing 7.2.1 shows three equivalent MySQL DBMS select statements to retrieve the first four rows of the result set. Code listing 7.2.1 (a) shows the standard format. Code listing 7.2.1 (b) illustrates that when only one number is supplied for the limit clause, it is the `rowCount` rather than the `offset`. Finally, code listing 7.2.1 (c) shows a longer form of the limit clause, which uses the keyword `OFFSET` to indicate the offset. It is important to understand that the DBMS will retrieve all rows that satisfy the where clause and put them in order *before* it uses the limit clause to decide which rows to deliver to the end user.

Code listing 7.2.1 Three equivalent statements using the MySQL DBMS limit clause

(a) Specifying the offset

```
SELECT fName, lName, email FROM Staff
WHERE lName LIKE '%sm%'
ORDER BY lName, fName
LIMIT 0, 4;
```

(b) Using the default offset of zero

```
SELECT fName, lName, email FROM Staff
WHERE lName LIKE '%sm%'
ORDER BY lName, fName
LIMIT 4;
```

(c) Using the longer style

```
SELECT fName, lName, email FROM Staff
WHERE lName LIKE '%sm%'
ORDER BY lName, fName
LIMIT 4 OFFSET 0;
```

> The PostgreSQL DBMS provides a similar extension to ISO SQL. It uses the format shown in Code listing 7.2.1 (c). See www.postgresql.org for details.
>
> As usual, the DBMS may not actually have to retrieve all rows that satisfy the where clause before applying the limit clause, though conceptually that is how it works. The DBMS manual will include guidance on any optimization features associated with the limit clause.

The limit clause provides the mechanism for delivering a chunk of the result set that greatly simplifies the process of delivering result sets over multiple pages. All the database client (the web server) need do is keep track of where in the result set it is. To request the next page of data, it simply reruns the original database query, but with a different offset. The database query should include an order by clause to ensure that each time it is run the rows of the result set appear in the same order. This helps to ensure that, as the end user navigates back and forth through the set of web pages, the same rows are displayed each time a page is viewed. Although an order by clause helps keep things consistent, it can't be guaranteed that the data won't change. Another user could modify the database instance while the first page is being viewed. This may alter which rows appear on the second page. In the worst case, some rows may end up being missed out.

The mechanism for page navigation is typically implemented using a 'previous page' and 'next page' metaphor. The different web pages are generated by the *same* PHP script. Each HTTP request for this PHP script supplies the appropriate offset, and the script delivers the required chunk of data. The offset is often coded as a name-value pair into the URL of the 'previous page' and 'next page' hyperlinks. Using the URL to keep track of application state is called **URL rewriting**. It is one of a range of techniques for overcoming the stateless nature of HTTP.

Figure 7.5 shows the first page generated by Version 1.5 of the SurnameSearch.php script. This version differs from Version 1.4 in two significant ways.

First, it allows the end user to enter any string and returns all members of staff whose surnames include this string. The URL in the address box at the top of the browser window has a single name-value pair in the query string, indicating that the end user entered the character 's' as the surname to search for. The script uses the SQL LIKE comparison operator to retrieve all staff members whose surnames include this character.

The second difference is the 'Next' hyperlink at the bottom of the web page. When the screenshot was taken, the mouse was hovering over this hyperlink, so its URL appears in the status bar at the foot of the browser window. The URL path is the same as in the address box, so the hyperlink will request this PHP script again. However, the query string includes two name-value pairs:

- surname=s ensures that the same search criteria are passed to the script second time round
- start=4 tells the script that it should start from row number 4 (the fifth row of the result set).

Figure 7.6 shows the key lines of code from the PHP script that generated the web page in Figure 7.5. Lines 76 to 80 show the actual SQL select statement. The where clause

Figure 7.5 Delivering the results of a database search using multiple web pages.

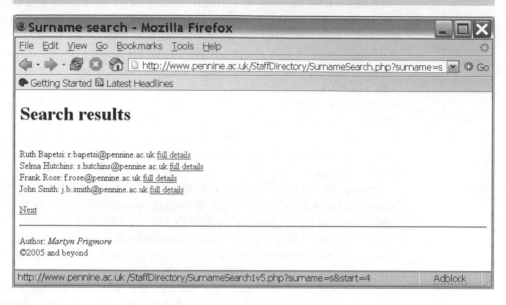

Figure 7.6 Version 1.5 of the SurnameSearch.php script, showing how to deliver a result set over multiple pages.

```
67   //STEP 3 Query the database
68   if (empty($_GET["start"]))
69     //This is the first page of results
70     $start = 0;
71   else
72     //This is not the first page, so get the offset of the first row
73     $start = cleanse_data($_GET["start"]);
74   define('MAX_ROWS', 4);
75   //Use the MySQL specific LIMIT clause to retrieve the specified rows
76   $sqlStatement = "SELECT staffNo, fName, lName, email
77               FROM Staff
78               WHERE lName LIKE '%$surname%'
79               ORDER BY lName, fName, staffNo
80               LIMIT $start, " . MAX_ROWS;
81   $result = mysql_query($sqlStatement, $connection);
82   //Report any errors that occurred when communicating with the MySQL DBMS
83   if ($result == FALSE)
84     exit("SQL statement failed.
85           \n<br />$sqlStatement
86           \n<br />MySQL error " . mysql_errno() . " : " . mysql_error());
87   else
88     echo "\n<!-- Notice: SQL statement \n$sqlStatement \nworked. -->\n";
89   //STEP 4 Fetch the rows
90   $numRows = mysql_num_rows($result);
91   for ($i=1; $i<=$numRows; $i=$i+1)
92   {
93     $row = mysql_fetch_array($result, MYSQL_ASSOC);
94     //STEP 5 Display the data from the row
95     echo "\n<br />", $row["fName"], " ", $row["lName"], ": ", $row["email"];
96     $url="StaffDetail.php?staffNo=" . rawurlencode($row["staffNo"]);
97     echo " <a href=\"$url\">full details</a>";
98   }
99   //Set up page navigation
100  $start=$start+MAX_ROWS;
101  $nextUrl ="SurnameSearch1v5.php?surname=" . rawurlencode($surname) . "&start=" . rawurlencode($start);
102  echo "\n<p> <a href=\"$nextUrl\">Next</a>";
```

has a single like comparison that matches any surname that includes the string entered by the end user. For example, if the end user entered 'Smith', he or she would see everyone whose surname was 'Smith', 'Shoesmith', 'Smithson' and so on.

The order by clause first orders staff by surname, then by first name and finally by staff number. This means that the several members of staff called 'John Smith' will appear in staff number order. It is always sensible to include a candidate key in the order by clause when delivering a result set over multiple web pages. A candidate key is unique to each row, so ensures that the rows of the result set *always* come out in the same order.

The limit clause uses the PHP variable $start and the PHP constant MAX_ROWS to define the offset and the number of rows to deliver. MAX_ROWS is defined in line 74, with the value 4. If, later on, it's decided to deliver six rows on each web page, then it is easy to change the definition of this constant and the script will work with no further changes.

Setting the value of $start is a little trickier. When the script is first called by the SurnameSearch.html form, there is a single name-value pair in the URL (check the address box in Figure 7.5) and so a single GET parameter – surname. When it is called using the 'Next' hyperlink, there are two name-value pairs in the URL – surname and start (check the status bar of Figure 7.5), so two GET parameters. Lines 68–73 use this difference to identify whether the script is being called for the first time or not. If $_GET["start"] is empty, this must be the first time through, so the script sets $start to 0 (line 70). This means that the select statement's limit clause will be LIMIT 0, 4. This is just what is needed, as it will retrieve just the first four rows of the result set. If $_GET["start"] is *not* empty, then this is *not* the first time through, so $_GET["start"] holds the value of the offset for the limit clause. Line 73 uses the cleanse_data() function to circumvent any hacking attempts and stores the offset in the local variable $start. Clicking on the 'Next' hyperlink in Figure 7.5 means $_GET["start"]=4 and so the limit clause will be LIMIT 4, 4. Again, this is just what is needed on the second page – start from the fifth row and deliver four rows in total.

The rest of the script is unchanged until line 100. Line 100 resets $start to the offset required for the *next* page in the sequence by adding the constant MAX_ROWS to the current offset. Remember, $start=$start+MAX_ROWS means 'set the new value of $start to be the old value of $start plus the value of MAX_ROWS'.

Line 101 uses this *new* offset to set up the URL for the 'Next' hyperlink on the page being generated and line 102 actually writes out the hyperlink. Note that the rawurlencode() function is used to ensure that the *values* in the query string do not cause problems (see Chapter 4). It is important to use rawurlencode() only on the *values*. If the whole URL is encoded, then the '?', '=' and '&' characters used to separate the parts of the query string will also be replaced by their hexadecimal character codes, and the URL will be unusable.

Version 1.5 of the SurnameSearch.php script is about as simple as page navigation gets. It only implements a 'next page' mechanism – end users can only navigate forwards through the result set. There is no attempt to stop when all the rows have been displayed – a 'Next' hyperlink is always created, even when the value of the offset is greater than the number of rows in the result set. Finally, a more sophisticated navigation mechanism would include numbered links to pages, as well as the 'previous page' and 'next page' links. Adding these features is left as an exercise.

Figure 7.7 Problems caused by a single quote mark.

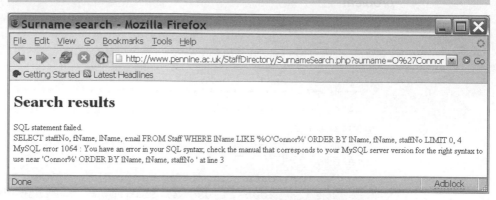

Before leaving Version 1.5 of SurnameSearch.php, it's worth pointing out a bug in the code. When users search for 'O'Connor', they see the web page in Figure 7.7. The text on this web page is generated by the debugging code in lines 84–86 (see Figure 7.6) and it tells us that the syntax of the SQL select statement is incorrect. The debugging code shows the full select statement in the second line (repeated in Code listing 7.2.2) and the MySQL DBMS error message on the next two lines. The problem is in the where clause. There are *three* single quote marks in `'%O'Connor%'` – the two single quote marks that delimit the string literal, plus the apostrophe character that is part of the string literal. The MySQL DBMS interprets the first single quote as the start of a string literal and the second as the end of the string literal, even though the second is actually an apostrophe, not a delimiter. So, the MySQL DBMS thinks that the string literal is `'%O'`. The rest of the string literal – `Connor%'` – is assumed to be a syntax error.

Code listing 7.2.2   The offending SQL select statement

```
SELECT staffNo, fName, lName, email
FROM Staff
WHERE lName LIKE '%O'Connor%'
ORDER BY lName, fName, staffNo
LIMIT 0, 4
```

This problem with single quote marks was mentioned in Chapter 3. To include an apostrophe as part of an SQL string literal, use two single quote marks – `'%O''Connor%'` rather than `'%O'Connor%'`. This suggests another function for the include file DataCleansing.inc, which would replace all single apostrophes in a string literal with two apostrophes, as shown in Code listing 7.2.3.

A similar problem can sometimes arise with double quote marks – often used around the house name in an address, such as 'Mr P. Smith, "Sunnydale Barn", Upper Cumberworth, West Yorkshire'. Whether or not double quote marks also cause a problem depends on the particular DBMS being used. If there is a problem, it can usually be solved in the same way.

Code listing 7.2.3   A user-defined PHP function to solve the SQL apostrophe problem

```
function sqlApostrophe($value)
{
  /*-- Begin function header
  --
  ****************************************************
  -- Comment Replaces a single apostrophe with two
apostrophes.
  --          Needed to avoid problems with SQL string
literals
  -- Version Date       Author         Comment
  -- 0.1     2005-11-05 M. Prigmore    First draft
  --
  ****************************************************
  -- End function header */
  if (empty($value))
    return "";
  else
    return str_replace("'", "''", $value);
}
```

7.3 Single script database modifications and data validation

Database modifications involve gathering data from the end user with an HTML form, then, in a server-side script, using this data to modify the database. Chapter 4 showed how to add a new support session to the database. The solution used two separate web resources – a static HTML form to gather the data and a server-side PHP script to write this data to the database. It is more common for web applications to use a single server-side script to achieve both tasks. When the user first requests the script, it delivers the HTML form to gather the data. The action attribute of the form points to the same server-side script. So, when the user clicks the submit button, the script is called for a second time. This time the script uses the form data to modify the database instance.

Delivering different content depending on whether or not the server-side script has been run before is a common approach. It was used above, with one script delivering several different pages of content, and will be used again. There are two reasons for taking this approach. First, all processing for a particular application behaviour is contained in a single script, so it is easier to maintain. Second, reporting data validation errors can be more user-friendly, with error messages appearing next to the HTML form control with the error. Figure 7.8 (a) shows a portion of Version 0.2 of the SupportSessionInsert.php server-side script.

Figure 7.8 Generating the HTML form in SupportSessionInsert.php Version 0.2.

```
29 <!DOCTYPE html PUBLIC "-//W3C//DTD XHTML 1.1//EN"
30     "http://www.w3.org/TR/xhtml11/DTD/xhtml11.dtd">
31 <html>
32 <head>
33   <meta http-equiv="Content-Type" content="text/html; charset=utf-8" />
34   <title> Pennine University Staff Directory </title>
35 </head>
36 <body>
37 <?php
38   if (empty($_GET["staffNo"]) or empty($_GET["day"]) or empty($_GET["start"]) or empty($_GET["end"]))
39   {
40     //The user has not entered the required data, so display the form.
41 ?>
42 <h1> Add a new support session </h1>
43
44 <form method="GET" action="<?php echo $_SERVER["PHP_SELF"]; ?>">
45 <p> Staff number: <input type="text" name="staffNo" size="5" maxlength="5"  /> </p>
46 <p> Day: <input type="text" name="day" size="10" maxlength="9"  /> </p>
47 <p> Start time: <input type="text" name="start" size="5" maxlength="5"  /> </p>
48 <p> End time: <input type="text" name="end" size="5" maxlength="5"  /> </p>
49 <p> <input type="submit" /> </p>
50 </form>
51
52 <?php
53   }
54   else
55   {
```

(a) The PHP code.

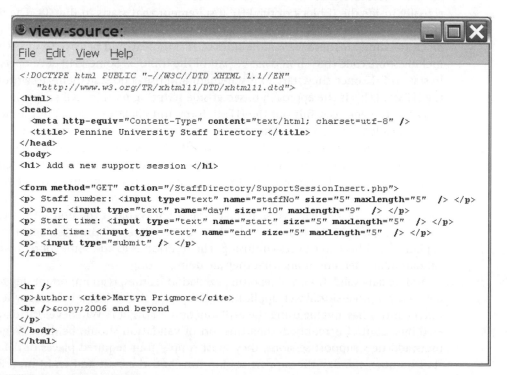

(b) The HTML form it generates.

The server-side script begins with the usual HTML, then slips into PHP in line 37. The if statement in line 38 checks if any data has been entered into the HTML form controls (notice that the script assumes data is passed from the HTML form using the GET method). If any of the expected values are missing, then the end user has not entered the required data, so the script delivers the HTML form. Rather than using an echo statement to write each line of HTML to the HTTP response message, the script drops out of PHP in line 41. The PHP application server writes lines 42 and 43 directly to the HTTP response message. It also writes out the first part of line 44, but part way along the line it encounters the PHP start tag '<?php', so, once again, begins to interpret the PHP statements. There is just one:

```
echo $_SERVER["PHP_SELF"];
```

$_SERVER[] is another of the PHP superglobal arrays. It works just like the $_GET and $_POST superglobal arrays, but holds information passed to PHP from the HTTP server. $_SERVER["PHP_SELF"] holds the (relative) URL of the PHP script itself. This URL is written out as the value of the action attribute of the HTML form, ensuring that the HTML form submits its data back to this same script. This is clearly visible in the HTML source shown in Figure 7.8 (b). The PHP end tag '?>' drops the script back out of PHP. The last two characters of line 44, '">', are written straight to the HTTP response message, as are lines 45–51.

This approach to coding PHP, dropping in and out of PHP as and when it suits, makes it very easy to code server-side scripts and is one reason for the popularity of PHP as a server-side scripting language. Much of the server-side script looks, and behaves, like plain HTML. However, it does look rather odd. The non-PHP code in lines 42–51 is actually inside the if block of the PHP if statement that starts in line 38. The if block only ends in line 53, with the closing curly bracket (notice, too that there is an else block to come). If there were more lines of HTML, it would be easy to miss this and include some code that should *not* be part of the if block. Some PHP developers prefer to stay in PHP once they start an if statement and use echo statements to write out all the HTML. (This is the approach to server-side scripting used in CGI scripts.)

When the end user fills out the HTML form and clicks on the submit button, the script is called for a second time. Assuming all the required data was entered, the if condition in line 38 is false, so PHP skips over the if block to the else block (Figure 7.9). The code here is the same as that in Version 0.1 (except that version 0.1 used POST rather than GET). The script writes the data gathered from end users to the database and delivers a success (or error) message.

The main problem with Version 0.2 of the script is that if the user forgets to enter data for any one of the four controls, then the script shows the form again, with no explanation. This will be very confusing. The solution is to add some more robust data validation and tell end users what they are doing wrong.

Adding data validation, and reporting validation failures, is an important step towards delivering a professional web application. Chapter 4 showed how to check whether or not a control has a value using the PHP function empty(). Whenever the data gathered by a control is required, then this sort of validation should be done. When end users add new support sessions, they must supply four required pieces of data: their staff number, the day the support session runs and the start and end times. Each of these data items is required.

Figure 7.9 Dealing with the form data in SupportSessionInsert.php Version 0.2.

```
54  else
55  {
56    $staffNo = cleanse_data($_GET["staffNo"]);
57    $day = cleanse_data($_GET["day"]);
58    $start = cleanse_data($_GET["start"]);
59    $end = cleanse_data($_GET["end"]);
60    //STEP 1 connect to the DBMS
61    $connection = mysql_connect('localhost', 'martyn', 'martynpassword');
62    //Report any errors that occurred when communicating with the MySQL DBMS
63    if ($connection==FALSE)
64      exit("\nCould not connect to MySQL DBMS. \n<br />MySQL error " . mysql_errno() . " : " . mysql_error());
65    else
66      echo "\n<!-- Notice: Succesfully connected to MySQL DBMS. -->";
67    //STEP 2 specify which database to use
68    $database = mysql_select_db('StaffDirectory', $connection);
69    //Report any errors that occurred when communicating with the MySQL DBMS
70    if ($database == FALSE)
71      exit("Unable to locate the database. \n<br />MySQL error " . mysql_errno() . " : " . mysql_error());
72    else
73      echo "\n<!-- Notice: Using specified database. -->";
74    //STEP 3 Modify the database
75    $sqlStatement = "INSERT INTO SupportSession (staffNo, dayOfWeek, startTime, endTime)
76                VALUES ('$staffNo', '$day', '$start , '$end')";
77    $result = mysql_query($sqlStatement, $connection);
78    //STEP 4 Confirm successful execution or report any errors that occurred when communicating with the MySQL DBMS
79    if ($result == TRUE)
80    {
81      echo "\n<!-- Notice: SQL statement \n$sqlStatement \nworked. -->\n";
82      echo "\n<h1>New support session added</h1>";
83      echo "\n<p>The following support session data has been successfully added to the database:";
84      echo "\n<br />Staff number: $staffNo";
85      echo "\n<br />Day: $day";
86      echo "\n<br />Start time: $start";
87      echo "\n<br />End time: $end</p>";
88    }
89    else
90      exit("\nSQL statement failed.
91           \n<br />$sqlStatement
92           \n<br />MySQL error " . mysql_errno() . " : " . mysql_error());
93    //STEP 5 Close the connection
94    mysql_close($connection);
95  }
96  ?>
```

Leaving a text box empty is not the only way end users could enter invalid data. Each text box requires additional data validation:

- staff numbers must be numeric
- days must be one of Monday, Tuesday, Wednesday, Thursday or Friday
- start times and end times must be in the format hh:mm, such as 12:15, 9:30 and 09:45.
- start times must be 09:00 or later.
- end times must be before 18:00.

In a traditional GUI application, each control's value would be validated as the end user moved the cursor to the next control. For example, as the end user moved from 'Staff number' to 'Day', the application would check that the value entered in 'Staff number' was valid. If not, it would move the cursor back to the 'Staff number' and warn the end user that the data entered was invalid. To use this model of data validation in a server-side script, the HTML form would need to submit its data to the web server every time the user moved off a control. This is not how HTML forms work, so another approach is needed.

For the 'Day' control, there are only five valid values. A very effective way to prevent invalid data is simply to list these values in an HTML select control. The HTML select control shows end users a list of values and allows them to select one. This means that the only way end users can submit invalid data is if they forget to select one of the available values. A similar approach works for the time, provided the hours and minutes are selected separately. Web applications make extensive use of this technique to avoid the problem of data validation. If end users can only select from a list of valid values, then the server-side script only needs to check that they did actually select one.

When it isn't possible to list all the valid data values, as with the staff number, then the actual values entered must be validated. Some developers prefer to check time values themselves anyway. To illustrate data validation, the 'Add new support session' form uses dropdown menus for the day and start time, but text boxes for the staff number and end time.

Figure 7.10 (a) shows the form itself and Figure 7.10 (b) the HTML source. Notice that the dropdown menu for the day shows the text 'Choose a day . . . '. HTML select controls display the *first* of the options by default. If this first option is a valid data value, users may forget to change it, and submit incorrect data. For example, they might have meant to add a support session starting at 10:30 on Tuesday, but accidentally add one starting at 09:00 on Monday. One common solution to this problem is to make the first option something like 'Choose a day . . . '. If end users click on the submit button too soon, the PHP script realizes that there has been some kind of mistake and redisplays the form. A similar approach is taken with the start time, which has dropdown

Figure 7.10 The HTML form used to gather data from end users to add a new support session.

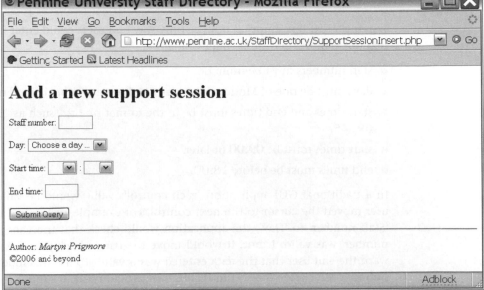

(a) The form as it appears in the Firefox web browser.

Figure 7.10 (*Continued*)

```
view-source:                                              _ □ X

File  Edit  View  Help

<h1> Add a new support session </h1>
<form method="get" action="/StaffDirectory/SupportSessionInsert.php">
<p>
Staff number: <input type="text" name="staffNo" size="5" maxlength="5" />

</p>
<p>
Day: <select name="day" size="1">
        <option>Choose a day ...</option>
        <option>Monday</option>
        <option>Tuesday</option>
        <option>Wednesday</option>
        <option>Thursday</option>
        <option>Friday</option>
     </select>
</p>
<p>
Start time: <select name="startHour" size="1">
               <option></option>
               <option>09</option>
               <option>10</option>
               <option>11</option>
               <option>12</option>
               <option>13</option>
               <option>14</option>
               <option>15</option>
               <option>16</option>
               <option>17</option>
            </select>
          : <select name="startMinute" size="1">
               <option></option>
               <option>00</option>
               <option>15</option>
               <option>30</option>
               <option>15</option>
            </select>
</p>
<p>
End time: <input type="text" name="end" size="5" maxlength="5" />
</p>
<p> <input type="submit" name="Insert"/> </p>
</form>
```

(b) The HTML source code.

select controls for both the hours and minutes. The first option for each select control is empty – <option></option>. Again, if users click on the submit button before choosing a valid start time, the PHP script recognizes this and redisplays the form.

Remember that the HTML source code in Figure 7.10 (b) is generated by the PHP script SupportSessionInsert.php, but does not contain any PHP. It is important to keep this in mind. When SupportSessionInsert.php is requested for the first time, it generates the form in Figure 7.10 (a). This form gathers data from end users and submits the

Figure 7.11 Validating the first three HTML form controls.

```
34  <!DOCTYPE html PUBLIC "-//W3C//DTD XHTML 1.1//EN"
35      "http://www.w3.org/TR/xhtml11/DTD/xhtml11.dtd">
36  <html>
37  <head>
38      <meta http-equiv="Content-Type" content="text/html; charset-utf-8" />
39      <title> Pennine University Staff Directory </title>
40  </head>
41  <body>
42  <?php
43      $validationFail = false;  //Used to indicate that a data value failed validation
44      $validationMessage = array();  //Array to store validation messages for each control
45      if (empty($_GET["staffNo"]))
46      {
47          $validationFail = true;
48          $validationMessage["staffNo"]="Please enter a staff number.";
49      }
50      elseif (!is_numeric(cleanse_data($_GET["staffNo"])))
51      {
52          $validationFail = true;
53          $validationMessage["staffNo"]="Staff number must be numeric.";
54      }
55      if ($_GET["day"]=="Choose a day ...")
56      {
57          $validationFail = true;
58          $validationMessage["day"]="Please choose a day.";
59      }
60      if (empty($_GET["startHour"]))
61      {
62          $validationFail = true;
63          $validationMessage["startHour"]="Please choose the start hour.";
64      }
65      if (empty($_GET["startMinute"]))
66      {
67          $validationFail = true;
68          $validationMessage["startMinute"]="Please choose the start minute.";
69      }
```

data back to SupportSessionInsert.php, which adds it to the database and generates a *different* web page, this time displaying a success message. This is an important point. The URL shown for the form in Figure 7.10 (a) is http://www.pennine.ac.uk/StaffDirectory/ SupportSessionInsert.php, but the source code in Figure 7.10 (b) is *not* the PHP code for SupportSessionInsert.php. Chapter 4 explained how server-side scripts generate HTTP response messages and it is worth rereading this if the distinction between the server-side script and the web pages it generates isn't clear.

Version 0.3 of the SupportSessionInsert.php file implements validation for each of the four HTML form controls shown in Figure 7.10 (a). Validation is the first thing the PHP script does after writing out the start of the HTML document (Figure 7.11). Line 43 declares a Boolean variable $validationFail and sets it to FALSE. If any of the controls fail data validation, then this variable is set to TRUE, indicating that the user entered invalid data.

Line 44 declares an array $validationMessage, which is used to store messages that explain to end users what they have done wrong. Each **validation test** in Figure 7.11 works by using Boolean conditions to ask the question 'Is the data invalid?' So, for example, in line 60, the if statement if (empty($_GET["startHour"])) asks the question 'Is the data invalid because the end user forgot to submit a value for the start hour?' If the answer to this questions is 'Yes' then the data fails validation. This can seem confusing because *satisfying* the condition means *failing* the validation test.

It is also possible to write validation tests that ask 'Is the data valid?' In this case, satisfying the condition means *passing* the validation test. For example, the valid values for day are the string literals 'Monday' to 'Friday'. The if statement:

```
if ($_GET["day"]=="Monday" or
    $_GET["day"]=="Tuesday" or
    $_GET["day"]=="Wednesday" or
    $_GET["day"]=="Thursday" or
    $_GET["day"]=="Friday")
```

asks if the value of $_GET["day"] is one of these valid values. If the value satisfies the condition, then it passes the validation test.

When the data satisfies the condition in line 60 (that is, fails the validation test), PHP executes the code block in lines 61–64. This code sets $validationFail to TRUE (line 62) and adds an element to the $validationMessage array (line 63). The element key is startHour, which indicates that this validation failure relates to the startHour control, and the element value is Please choose the start hour, which explains what users have done wrong. In contrast, when users choose a valid hour from the select control, the data does not satisfy the condition and so passes validation. In this case, because there is no else block, PHP moves on to the next statement in line 65. This is correct – if the data passes validation then there is nothing to do.

The same sort of validation test is applied to startMinute (lines 65–69). In both these cases, it makes sense to check that there is actually some data, because the first option in the HTML select controls is empty – it is <option></option>. Users could easily choose this empty option by mistake. The validation for the day select control is different. None of the options for this select control is empty, so it seems reasonable to assume that there is no need to test for the empty string (it turns out that this is not so reasonable). Instead, the validation test in line 55 is whether or not the value submitted is the default – Choose a day . . . . If it is, then there has been a mistake and a validation message is added to $validationMessage.

One problem with this is that the form uses the HTTP GET method, so the controls' values are passed as name-value pairs in the URL query string. There is nothing to stop end users typing values directly into the address bar. For example, they could type the query string:

```
?staffNo=12345&day=&startHour=09&startMinute=15&end=10:15
```

The web server would happily use these name-value pairs to initialize PHP's $_GET superglobal array and the value of $_GET["day"] will be empty! Similarly, there is nothing to stop end users giving a start hour of 57. In both cases, the data is invalid, but the validation tests in Figure 7.11 do not pick up the mistake. This means that the data validation for the select controls is not sufficiently robust. The Exercises section at the end of this chapter tighten the validation so that even hand-typed data values are validated effectively.

Another option is to use the HTTP POST method as it does not send the data via the URL, so end users can't easily circumvent the PHP script's validation tests.

Lines 45–54 validate the staffNo control using a PHP if . . . elseif statement (Figure 7.12) rather than a plain if statement. The if . . . elseif statement allows for a sequence of tests, rather than just one. When the if condition is not satisfied, PHP

Figure 7.12 The PHP if . . . elseif statement for checking a sequence of separate conditions.

```
if (this Boolean expression is true)
{
  do this statement;
  and do this statement;
}
elseif (this Boolean expression is true)
  do this statement;
elseif (this Boolean expression is true)
{
  do this statement;
  and do this statement;
}
else
  do this statement;
```

skips to the first `elseif` keyword and checks the condition there. If this condition is also not satisfied, it skips to the next `elseif` keyword and so on.

There can also be a final `else` keyword, followed by a block of code telling PHP what to do when none of the conditions has been satisfied. However, once a condition is satisfied, the code block immediately following it is executed and the remainder of the if . . . elseif statement is ignored.

To see how this works in practice, consider what happens when end users do *not* submit a value for the `staffNo` control. The condition in line 45 of Figure 7.11 is satisfied, so PHP executes the code block in lines 46–49. It sets `$validationFail` to `TRUE` (line 47) and adds an element to the `$validationMessage` array (line 48). It then ignores the rest of the if . . . elseif statement, skipping straight to line 55.

A second possibility is that end users submitted a value such as `Peter`. The condition in line 45 would not be satisfied, so PHP would then look for an `elseif` (or, failing that, just an `else`) keyword. It would find one in line 50 and check whether this condition has been satisfied. The value 'Peter' is first passed to the user-defined function `cleanse_data()` to remove any potentially harmful characters. The value returned by `cleanse_data()` is passed straight to the PHP built-in function `is_numeric()`, which will check whether or not a string of characters is a numeric literal (see Chapter 4, Section 4.3). As the string of characters `Peter` is definitely *not* a numeric literal, the `is_numeric()` function returns the value `FALSE`. The Boolean-not operator, '`!`' turns this value to `TRUE` and the condition is satisfied. PHP then executes the block of code on lines 51–54, indicating that the data submitted by an end user failed validation because it is not a numeric literal.

The third possible scenario is that an end user submits a value such as `12345` for the `staffNo`. Again, this value does not satisfy the condition in line 45. Nor does it satisfy the condition in line 50 as `12345` is a numeric literal. As there are no more `elseif` or `else` keywords, PHP skips to line 55 without doing anything.

The `end` control is also a text box, so it is possible that end users could fail to submit data for this control, too. The first validation test in this section, in lines 70–74 in

Figure 7.13 Validating the end time.

```
70   if (empty($_GET["end"]))
71   {
72     $validationFail = true;
73     $validationMessage["end"]="Please enter the time the support session ends.";
74   }
75   else
76   {
77     //Need to check the format of the end time
78     $end = cleanse_data($_GET["end"]);
79     $separator=strpos($end, ":");
80     if ($separator===false or $separator===0 or $separator===strlen($end)-1)
81     {
82       //No colon, or starts with colon, or ends with colon, so not a valid time
83       $validationFail = true;
84       $validationMessage["end"]="Please enter the time in the format hh:mm.";
85     }
86     else
87     {
88       //Correct format, so check hour and minute are valid
89       $hour=substr($end, 0, $separator);
90       if (!is_numeric($hour))
91       {
92         $validationFail = true;
93         $validationMessage["end"]="The hour must be a number.\n<br />";
94       }
95       elseif ($hour>18 or $hour<9)
96       {
97         //Support sessions must end by 18:00
98         $validationFail = true;
99         $validationMessage["end"]="The hour must be between 09 and 18.\n<br />";
100      }
101      $minute=substr($end, $separator+1);
102      //If the hour failed validation, need to keep these messages.
103      //This means lines 109, 114 and 19 may generate a notice "Undefined index: end"
104      if (!is_numeric($minute))
105      {
106        $validationFail = true;
107        $validationMessage["end"]=$validationMessage["end"] . "The minute must be a number.\n<br />";
108      }
109      elseif ($minute>59)
110      {
111        $validationFail = true;
112        $validationMessage["end"]=$validationMessage["end"] . "The minute must be 59 or less.\n<br />";
113      }
114      elseif (strlen($minute)<2)
115      {
116        $validationFail = true;
117        $validationMessage["end"]=$validationMessage["end"] . "The minute must be two digits.\n<br />";
118      }
119    }
120  }
```

Figure 7.13, is very similar to the preceding examples. When end users enter a value into the end control, the else block in lines 75–120 is executed.

Validating the end time is a lot more complex than any of the validation seen so far. When users submit data for the end control, it must go through the following sequence of validation tests:

1 check that the data value is in the format hh:mm, a one- or two-digit hour, followed by the colon character, followed by a two-digit minute.

2 check that the hour is a numeric literal (note that PHP will treat '09' as a numeric literal).

3 check that the numeric hour value lies between 9 and 18.

4 check that the minute is a numeric literal.

5 check that the numeric minute value lies between 0 and 59.

Figure 7.14 Character positions in a string.

Position: 0 1 2 3 4 5 6 7 8 9
Character: a b c d e f g h i j

This is too complex a sequence of tests to do in a single if . . . elseif statement. Instead, the code uses nested if statements, where the code blocks of one if statement include further if or if . . . elseif statements.

The first thing to do with a non-empty value for the end time is remove any potentially harmful characters. Line 78 does this and places the cleansed data into the local variable $end. Once this has been done, the first validation test checks that the value of $end is in the format hh:mm. Line 79 uses the built-in PHP function strpos() to look for the colon character. If there is no colon in $end, then strpos($end, ":") returns the Boolean value FALSE. Otherwise, it returns the position of the colon within the string $end. PHP counts from zero, so the first character is at position 0, the second at position 1 and so on (see Figure 7.14 and the note below).

The value returned from strpos($end, ":") is stored in the variable $separator. There are three values for $separator that indicate an invalid value for $end:

1 $separator is the Boolean value FALSE – in this case $end does not include a colon, so can't possibly be in the format hh:mm

2 $separator is the first character – in this case there is no hour.

3 $separator is the last character – in this case there is no minute.

Any other value of $separator indicates that the end times submitted by end users are in the correct format.

At this point, PHP's relaxed attitude to data types causes a problem. The Boolean value FALSE is equal to the integer 0. This means that the condition $separator==FALSE is true for cases 1 and 2. Similarly, Boolean TRUE is equal to the integer 1, so it is possible that cases 1 and 3 also overlap. To make it absolutely clear what the comparisons are saying, line 80 uses the comparison operator '===', which checks that the value *and* the data type are the same. With this comparison operator, Boolean FALSE and the integer 0 are different as they are different data types. The first condition, $separator===FALSE, is true in case 1. The second, $separator===0, is true in case 2. The third condition, $separator===strlen($end)-1, needs a little explanation.

The built-in PHP function strlen() calculates the number of characters in a string. The position of the *last* character will be one less than the number of characters, so, when this condition is true, $separator is the last character – this is the third invalid case. Any value of $end that is not in the format hh:mm will fail the validation test in line 80.

> Figure 7.14 shows the ten-character string 'abcdefghij', with the positions of each character indicated above them. The last of the ten characters is at position 9. It should be clear from this that, for any string, the position of the last character is one less than the length of the string.

When the value of $end is in the format hh:mm, it does not satisfy the condition in line 80 and so PHP skips to the else block (lines 86–119). The else block must validate the hour and minute parts of $end separately. Line 89 uses the built-in PHP function substr() to pull the hour part from the front of $end. The function description is:

```
string substr(string str, integer start [,integer length])
```

The substr() function extracts a sequence of characters from a string. The first parameter is the string itself, the second gives the position of the character to start from and the (optional) third parameter states how many characters to extract. The function returns the extracted characters as a string. So, for example, substr("adcdefghij", 4, 3) returns the string "efg" – e is the character in position 4 (check this in Figure 7.14) and the extracted string is three characters long. To see how line 89 extracts the hour, suppose that $end has the value "11:35". In this case, the value of $separator, set in line 79, is 2 – the colon is the third character, which is position number 2. Hence, line 89 reads:

```
$hour=substr("11:35", 0, 2);
```

It's clear that $hour is set to the string value "11". When $end has the value "9:35", $separator is 1 and the colon is the second character. The code in line 89 will once again correctly extract the hour portion of $end.

> Manipulating strings in this way is something most web database applications have to do. It's important to remember that PHP numbers the character positions from *zero* and to carefully test which characters a substr() function *actually* extracts as it is easy to be one position out. Tracking down bugs like that can be very tricky.

The remainder of the validation is pretty straightforward. The condition in line 90 asks if the hour is numeric and, in line 95, whether or not it falls in the valid range. Line 101 extracts the minute portion of the end time and subsequent lines validate it.

The condition in line 114 is a bit picky. It means that a time of '12:5' is considered invalid as it should be '12:05'.

One important point about the validation messages for the minutes is that they are stored in the same element of the array $validationMessage as those for the hour. This means that any messages about the minutes must be concatenated on to this element to avoid overwriting messages about the hour.

If the hour passes validation, then, in line 107, the $validationMessage array does not have an element with the key "end". If the minute fails validation, then PHP will generate a notice message for line 107, stating that there is no "end" element in the array $validationMessage (the same is true of lines 112 and 117). To avoid these notices, use separate "endHour" and "endMinute" elements.

Figure 7.15 Delivering validation messages to the end user.

```
122   if ($validationFail)
123   {
124     //The user has not entered the required data, so display the form with validation failure messages.
125     ?>
126 <h1> Add a new support session </h1>
127 <form method="get" action="<?php echo $_SERVER["PHP_SELF"]; ?>">
128 <p>
129 <?php //Report staffNo validation failures
130   if (array_key_exists("staffNo", $validationMessage))
131     echo "<em>", $validationMessage["staffNo"], "</em>\n<br />";
132 ?>
133 Staff number: <input type="text" name="staffNo" size="5" maxlength="5" />
134 </p>
135 <p>
136 <?php //Report day validation failures
137   if (array_key_exists("day", $validationMessage))
138     echo "<em>", $validationMessage["day"], "</em>\n<br />";
139 ?>
140 Day: <select name="day" size="1">
141       <option>Choose a day ...</option>
142       <option>Monday</option>
143       <option>Tuesday</option>
144       <option>Wednesday</option>
145       <option>Thursday</option>
146       <option>Friday</option>
147     </select>
148 </p>
```

Once the data submitted by users has been validated, the script must decide what to do next. If any of the data failed validation, then the script should display the form again, but this time showing the validation messages. Line 122 (Figure 7.15) checks the value of the Boolean variable $validationFail. If any of the data submitted failed validation, this will be TRUE and the PHP script will display the HTML form with appropriate validation messages. Otherwise, it writes the valid support session data to the database (not shown in Figure 7.15).

Consider the staffNo form control, created by the HTML in line 133. If the data submitted for this form control failed validation, there will be an element of the $validationMessage array with key "staffNo". The function call:

```
array_key_exists("staffNo", $validationMessage)
```

in line 130 returns TRUE when the $validationMessage array includes an element with the key "staffNo" and FALSE when it does not. Hence, the validation message in line 131 is only written to the HTTP response when the data submitted for the staffNo form control failed validation. This same approach is used to deliver validation messages for all the form controls. For controls that pass validation, there is no message.

Figure 7.16 shows the Add a new support session HTML form with validation messages. Figure 7.10 (a) shows the original form and it seems clear that this approach to validation is an effective way to improve the usability of the form. However, there are a few problems with the PHP script as it stands.

The first problem is that the validation only checks the values submitted for individual form controls. This is necessary, but often not sufficient as the value of one control may affect the validity of values for another. For example, if the start time is 13:00 it makes no sense to have an end time of 12:45.

Another problem is that the web page shown in Figure 7.16 is actually what is delivered by the *first* call to the script SupportSessionInsert.php. In other words, some

Figure 7.16 Validation messages for each form control.

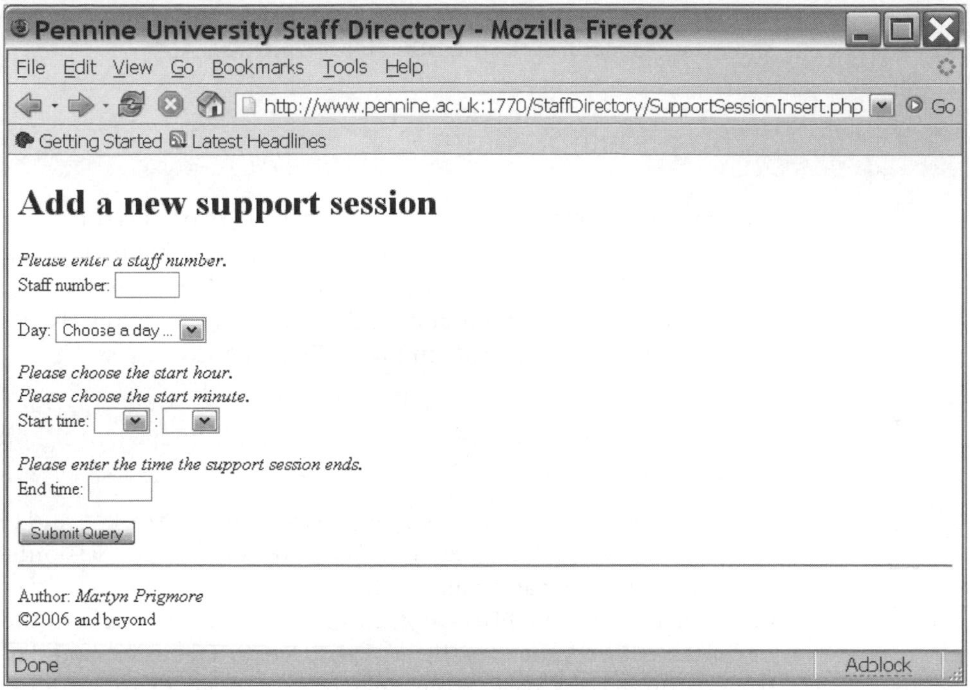

validation messages appear before the user has had a chance to submit any data. This happens because, on the first call of any PHP script, the $_GET (and $_POST) array has no elements. Consequently, any control that is tested to see if a value was submitted will fail this validation. Only the day control is not tested for missing values, so it is the only control in Figure 7.16 with no validation message.

One way around this is to use the fact that the $_GET (and $_POST) array has no elements when the script is first called, but will have elements when the user clicks on the submit button. Even if the controls are all empty when the end user clicks on the submit button, the $_GET (and $_POST) array will have an element with the control's name as the key and the control's value (possibly empty) as the value. Enclosing the validation tests within an if statement with the condition:

```
if (count($_GET)<>0)
```

ensures that the validation *doesn't* happen the first time the script is called.

The third significant problem with the solution as it stands is that, when there are validation failures, the original data submitted by end users is lost (it is not included in the form controls when the form is redelivered). This will annoy end users, who will have to rekey all the data, not just the invalid data. It is easy to solve this problem. For example, to redisplay the data entered in the staffNo control, use PHP to echo back the current value of $_GET["staffNo"]:

```
<input type="text" name="staffNo" size="5" maxlength="5"
value="<?php echo $_GET["staffNo"];?>" />
```

303

As it stands, this line will cause PHP to generate a notice the first time the script runs as there will be no element with the key `staffNo`. To avoid this, use an if statement so that the echo statement is only executed if `$_GET["staffNo"]` has a value. Similar techniques work with other form controls.

7.4 The reload problem

The **reload problem** can affect any web page that processes data gathered from end users, but is a particular problem when the HTTP GET method is used to send the data to the web server. When end user fills out the HTML form in Figure 7.10 (a) with valid data and click on the submit button, the web browser uses the HTML form data to create an HTTP request. The URL in this HTTP request is:

```
http://www.pennine.ac.uk/StaffDirectory/SupportSession
Insert.php?staffNo=31213&day=Wednesday&startHour=09&start
Minute=00&end=10%3A00
```

This URL identifies the web server – www.pennine.ac.uk – and the requested resource – the script file located at StaffDirectory/SupportSessionInsert.php. It also includes four name-value pairs in the query string to pass data from the HTML form to the PHP script. The PHP script uses this data to add a row to the `SupportSession` table, then generates the 'success page' in Figure 7.17 (a). Look at the address bar on this success page, which has been scrolled to show the query string. The address bar contains the URL that the web browser used in the HTTP request and it has all the values entered into the form as name-value pairs in its query string. If end users click on the refresh button, then the web browser uses the success page URL to create another HTTP request. This second HTTP request is exactly the same as the one created when the user clicked on the form's submit button. The

Figure 7.17 The reload problem.

(a) A new support session has been successfully added.

Figure 7.17 *(Continued)*

(b) What users see when they click on the refresh button on the web page in (a).

upshot is that the data is submitted twice and the PHP script tries to add it to the database for a second time.

> In Figure 7.17 (a) the colon character '– : –' in the end time part of the name-value pair in the URL has been replaced by its character reference, '%3A'. The web browser does this to all data submitted from a form, but the HTTP server translates it back before passing the value to the PHP application server.

Because the `SupportSession` table has a primary key, the DBMS reports an error. The PHP code for handling DBMS communication errors comes into play and, this time, SupportSessionInsert.php generates the web page shown in Figure 7.17 (b). Notice that the actual SQL insert statement is perfectly valid – it has only been rejected because there is already a row in the `SupportSession` table with this primary key and duplicate primary key values are not allowed. The same problem can occur if users bookmark the success page. That is because the query string is kept as part of the bookmark and SupportSessionInsert.php tries to add this data to the database every time the bookmark is used.

It is worth reflecting on how the approach to gathering data from end users has evolved. Initially, the HTML form to gather data was part of the static file Support-SessionInsert.html. The form submitted its data to a PHP script, Version 0.1 of SupportSessionInsert.html. This script both validated the data, reporting any validation failures, and generated a success page. Its success page was also vulnerable to the reload problem as the form data was submitted using the HTTP GET method. The combined script developed in the previous section could generate the HTML form to gather the data, report validation failures on the HTML form itself and generate a success page. Again, the success page was vulnerable to the reload problem. In fact, the reload problem arises because the same script that receives the data also generates the success page. This suggests an obvious solution: have one script to receive and validate the data and do the database modification, but use a second script to generate the success page. As this second script does not perform the database modification, users can click on refresh as often as they like and nothing untoward will happen.

Notice that the web page in Figure 7.17 (b), which shows the DBMS error message, will also suffer from the reload problem. Each time the user hits the refresh button, SupportSessionInsert.php tries to add the same new support session to the database and, each time, the DBMS reports the same error. The simplest solution is to have the script that delivers the success page report any DBMS communication errors, too.

> The HTTP POST method is less susceptible to the reload problem as, if users refresh the form, the web browser will warn them that they are about to resend data that has already been sent. Also, a bookmark would not include the data, so only refresh causes the problem. However, using the HTTP POST method is not a complete solution to the reload problem, so it is better to create a separate success page.

In a traditional GUI application, this sort of thing is simple. The code that did the database modification would simply load up the form that delivered the success message (or reported the DBMS communication error). This is not possible on the Web. In a web application, the web browser requests a particular resource from the web server. The web server responds to this request by supplying the requested resource. The web server cannot respond by supplying a *different* resource from the one requested. However, the web server can ask the web browser to request a different resource. It does this by sending a **location header** in the HTTP response. Location headers are used quite a bit when a website is reorganized and important resources (such as a home page) are moved or renamed. Any end user with a bookmark to the resource will be using the old URL to request it. The web server recognizes the old URL and uses a location header in the HTTP response to tell the web browser where the requested resource has moved to. It is up to the web browser to send a second HTTP request, this time requesting the resource from its new location.

The structure of the header section, and, in fact, each HTTP header, is shown in Figure 7.18 (see Chapter 2 for a discussion of the structure of HTTP messages). The header name is followed by a colon and a space, then the header value. A typical location header looks like this:

```
Location: SupportSessionInsertSuccess.html
```

Figure 7.18 The structure of an HTTP message.

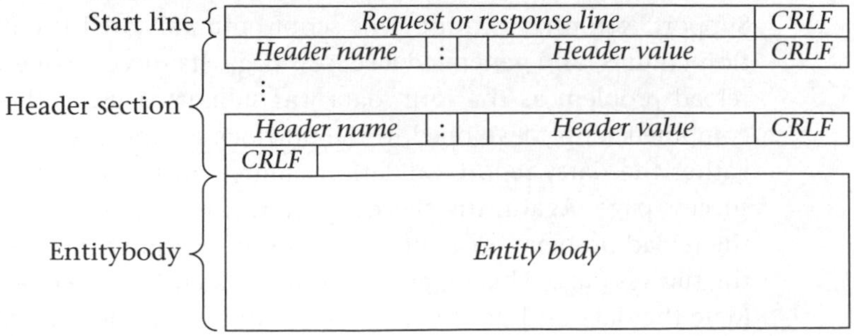

It begins with the header name 'Location', then gives a URL – in this case, a relative URL. Location headers are usually combined with a response line of the form:

```
HTTP/1.1 301 Moved permanently
```

The status of 301 tells the web browser that the requested resource has been permanently moved to a new location. The web browser will expect to find a location header giving the URL for this new location.

As discussed in Chapter 4, PHP writes the output of echo and print statements and any data outside of a <?php ... ?> tag to the entity body. To allow the application developer to write data to the header section, PHP provides the header() function. The description of this functions is:

```
void header ( string header [, bool replace [, int
http_response_code]] )
```

The return type void means that the function does not actually return a value (so, strictly speaking, isn't a function, but we'll let that pass). The only required parameter is *header*, which contains the actual HTTP header text. The parameter *replace* indicates whether or not this header replaces any previously written headers of this type or adds to them. *http_response_code* is the status code to write in the HTTP response line. For location headers, the header() function will automatically write an HTTP response line with status code 302, meaning that the resource has been moved temporarily. This is the best status to use when redirecting the web browser to a success (or DBMS error) page, so it's best to omit *http_response_code* when the header is a location header.

Figure 7.19 shows a first attempt at solving the reload problem using the header() function. Only step 4 of the process is affected (lines 225–237). In earlier versions of the PHP script, step 4 either confirmed that the database modification had succeeded or reported a DBMS communication error. In Version 1.1, step 4 writes location headers to the HTTP response, asking the web browser to request a resource from a different location. If the database modification succeeds, the location header points to a success page, but, if not, it points to a page that reports DBMS communication errors.

The success page is a static HTML page that informs end users that their database modification has succeeded. It is a lot less informative than previous success messages,

Figure 7.19 Using the location header to redirect a web browser to a different PHP script.

```
221  //STEP 3 Modify the database
222  $sqlStatement = "INSERT INTO SupportSession (staffNo, dayOfWeek, startTime, endTime)
223             VALUES ('$staffNo', '$day', '$start', '$end')";
224  $result = mysql_query($sqlStatement, $connection);
225  //STEP 4 Confirm successful execution or report any errors that occurred when communicating with the MySQL DBMS
226  if ($result == TRUE)
227  {
228    //Database modified successfully, so redirect to the success page
229    header("Location: SupportSessionInsertSuccess.html");
230  }
231  else
232  {
233    //Database communication error, so redirect to the DBMS-error page
234    //Note use of URL re-writing to send the error details
235    header("Location: ReportDbmsError.php?errno=\"" . mysql_errno()
236             . "\"&error=\"" . rawurlencode(mysql_error()) . "\"");
237  }
238  //STEP 5 Close the connection
239  mysql_close($connection);
```

which also told them what data had been added. However, line 229 shows how easy it is to use the header () function. Reporting a DBMS communication error is a little more complex. Lines 235–236 use the functions mysql_errno () and mysql_error () to create a URL for the location header that includes a query string. When there is a DBMS communication error, the web browser is sent a location header like:

```
Location: ReportDbmsError.php?errno="1062"&error="Duplicate
entry '1-Monday-17:00:00' for key 1"
```

This location header gives a relative URL, so the web browser assumes that the web resource ReportDbmsError.php is on the same path as the original resource. The web browser uses this to create a URL for a new HTTP request and includes the query string. This ensures that the MySQL error number and error description are passed to ReportDbmsError.php.

Be careful when passing string data to the header () function. If the header string includes new line characters, then PHP will generate a warning as HTTP headers cannot include new line characters.

This technique could also be used to pass data to a more sophisticated success page. However, there is a problem with that. Although the HTTP protocol doesn't set a limit on the length of a URL, many web browsers do, though it isn't easy to find out what that length is. Rather than use the query string to pass all the data entered by users to the success page, it is better to pass just the primary key values. The success page can then query the database to retrieve the record that was just added and display it to the end user.

Manually writing HTTP headers can cause a very annoying problem. When PHP creates the HTTP response message, it needs to write the HTTP headers *before* it writes anything to the entity body, for obvious reasons. So, when a PHP script writes something to the entity body – either because there is HTML code outside the <?php ... ?> tag or because of an echo or print statement – the PHP application server assumes that there are no more headers to come. It writes out a response line and any headers it thinks are required, then starts writing the entity body, line by line. If there is a subsequent call to the header () function, PHP generates a warning message:

```
Warning: Cannot modify header information - headers already
sent by (output started at SupportSessionInsert.php:226) in
SupportSessionInsert.php on line 237
```

The key information in this message is that, because the PHP application server has already written headers to the HTTP response message, it cannot write any more. It also indicates at which line it first wrote the headers – line 226 in this message – and which line there was a subsequent attempt to write headers – here, line 237.

The simplest solution to this problem is to avoid writing anything to the HTTP response before using the header () function. Careful use of if statements can achieve this. However, even a single blank line before the <?php ... ?> tag can lead to headers being sent. PHP provides special output buffering functions to allow greater control over when the PHP application server writes data to the HTTP response message. Output buffering is an advanced feature of PHP programming, so is not covered in this book.

7.5 # Gathering complex data using wizards

Adding data to a single table is a relatively simple process. Some web database applications need to gather quite complex data from end users and use this data to modify a number of different tables. The simplest solution is to use a long web page, with lots of form controls. This is not very user-friendly and may lead to more validation failures and, hence, users becoming frustrated.

The alternative is to have a number of related web pages, each gathering a small portion of the data required. When users have completed one page, they submit the data and move on to the next web page, which gathers the next portion of the data. Once all the data has been submitted, the application can modify the database. Applications that gently guide end users through a complex process in this way are often called **wizards**. Wizards are sometimes used for user registration and often used for opening Internet bank accounts or similar financial transactions.

At the Pennine University, there is a wizard to help students enrol on their chosen course at the start of the year. The first step asks end users to enter their student ID (Figure 7.20 (a)). This is passed to the next web page (Figure 7.20 (b)), which uses it to

Figure 7.20 The self-enrolment wizard.

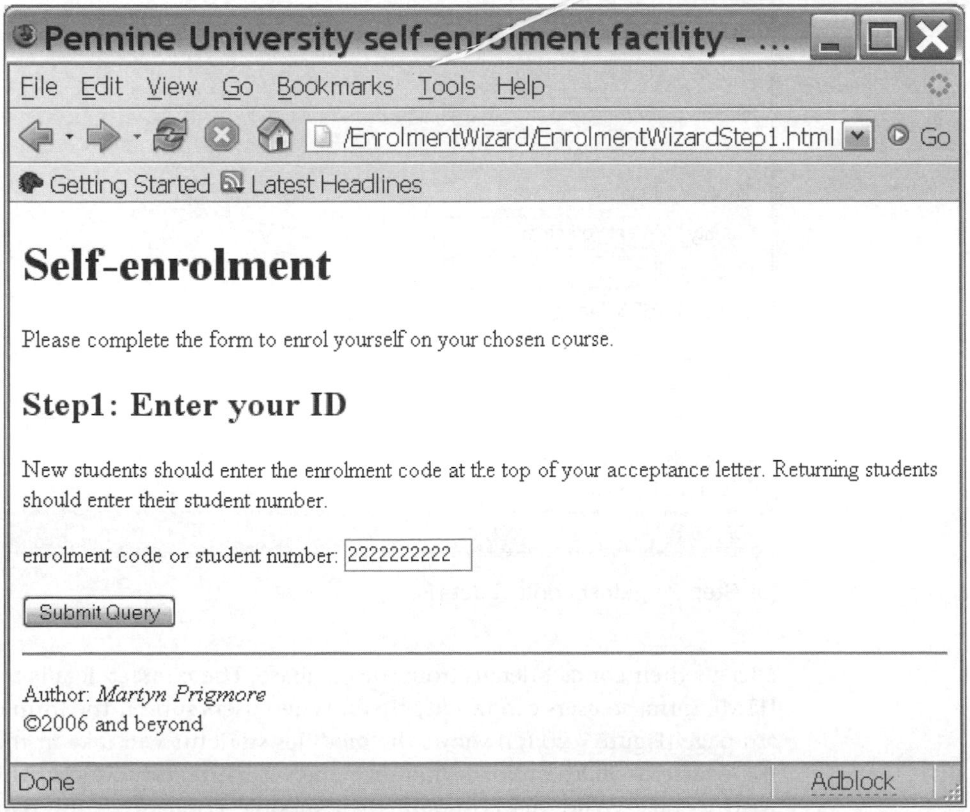

(a) Step 1 : gather the student ID number.

Figure 7.20 (*Continued*)

Pennine University self-enrolment facility - ...

File   Edit   View   Go   Bookmarks   Tools   Help

/EnrolmentWizard/EnrolmentWizardStep2.php   Go

Getting Started   Latest Headlines

Self-enrolment

Step 2: Check your contact details

We currently hold the following contact details. Please check them and click the "Confirm" button to proceed.

Student number: 2222222222

Given name	Shafaq
Family name	Aziz
Phone	09876 987654
email	s.aziz@pennine.ac.uk
House	The Pines
Street	Shaw Street
	Lower Houses
Town	Holmfirth
County	West Yorkshire
Country	UK
Postcode	HD5 7AA

Confirm

Author: *Martyn Prigmore*
©2006 and beyond

Done   Adblock

(b) Step 2 : gather contact details.

retrieve their contact details from the database. The contact details are delivered as an HTML form, so users can modify them. When users submit the form data, a third wizard page (Figure 7.20 (c)) shows the modules students will take in the coming year. If the course includes optional modules, then students can choose which options they wish to take. When users submit their module choices, all the data gathered from these three web pages is used to modify the database instance.

Figure 7.20 (*Continued*)

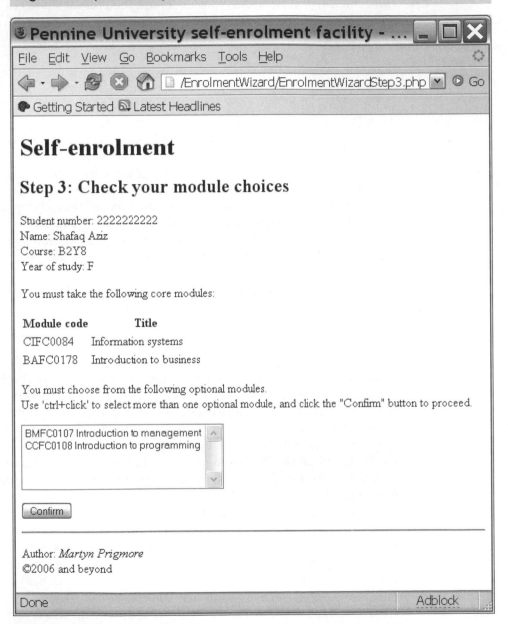

(c) Step 3 : gather module choices.

Strictly speaking, modifying contact details and module choices could be done independently, but the enrolment process provides a good example of a wizard in a web database application.

The main problem with wizards is ensuring that data gathered on one wizard page is available to all subsequent wizard pages. The self-enrolment wizard illustrates why. Changes made to the contact details are submitted to the third wizard page, but this page does not write these changes to the database. Instead, it simply gathers more data from end users – their module choices. It must then pass all the data – module choices *and* contact details – to a final script and it is that which performs all the database modifications.

This is the old problem of maintaining state across multiple stateless HTTP interactions. One solution has already been discussed: URL rewriting. URL rewriting is effective for keeping track of which part of a large result set should be displayed (Section 7.2) or for passing data to an error-reporting web page (Section 7.4). It is less effective for wizards, however, as there is usually far too much data.

Another problem is that data sent via the URL query string is not secure. The best solution is to store the data in the database at each stage and have subsequent wizard pages retrieve it as required. All that needs to be passed from wizard page to wizard page is some form of unique identifier. Sessions provide probably the best way to implement this approach and they are discussed in the next section. One problem with this approach is that repeatedly retrieving the data from the database can degrade performance. If there isn't too much data (just too much for a URL) and security isn't a major problem, then **hidden form controls** offer an alternative mechanism to sessions and URL rewriting for maintaining state.

Hidden form controls are just that – controls on an HTML form that have a value, but are hidden from the end users. They are defined using the HTML input element. For example:

```
<input type="hidden" name="studentNo" value="2222222222" />
```

defines an input control of type hidden (that is, a hidden form control). Its name is `studentNo` and its current value is `2222222222`. When the web browser displays the web page with this input element, there is nothing visible on the form. However, the control is part of the form, so, when end users submit the form data, the web browser also submits the data stored in the hidden form control. A PHP script can rewrite the value of a hidden form control just as easily as it can rewrite the query string of a URL and this is how a wizard can use hidden form controls to pass data from page to page.

The self-enrolment wizard queries four database tables. The `Student` table holds data about each student – their names and contact details, the courses they are studying and their year of study. The `Course` and `Module` tables hold data on courses and modules respectively. Finally, the table `CourseModule` holds data about which module is used on which course and whether it is a core or optional module on that course. The `CourseModule` table is known as a **link table**.

Link tables allow a relational database to deal with situations where many rows of one table are linked to many rows of another. This is the case with the `Course` and `Module` tables as one course will have many modules, but each module may be taken on many courses. (Link tables are discussed in detail in Chapter 9.) The table schema are:

```
Student (studentNo:VARCHAR, fName:VARCHAR, lName:VARCHAR,
         phone:VARCHAR, email:VARCHAR, house:VARCHAR,
         street:VARCHAR, street2:VARCHAR, town:VARCHAR,
         county:VARCHAR, country:VARCHAR, postcode:VARCHAR,
         course:CHAR, stage:CHAR)
```

```
PRIMARY KEY (studentNo)
FOREIGN KEY (course) REFERENCES Course (code)

Course (code:CHAR, title:VARCHAR, leadDepartment:VARCHAR,
        minorDepartment:VARCHAR, level:VARCHAR,
        qualification:VARCHAR, mode:VARCHAR)
PRIMARY KEY (code)

Module (code:CHAR, title:VARCHAR, department:VARCHAR,
        level:CHAR, preReq:VARCHAR)
PRIMARY KEY (code)

CourseModule (module:CHAR, course:CHAR, type:VARCHAR)
PRIMARY KEY: (module, course)
FOREIGN KEY (course) REFERENCES Course (code)
FOREIGN KEY (module) REFERENCES Module (code)
```

The first wizard page is static HTML rather than a PHP script. It simply gathers student ID numbers from end users and submits this data to the second wizard page. Figure 7.21 shows the HTML source code. The form control starts in line 14. Notice that it uses the HTTP POST method to send its data to EnrolmentWizardStep2.php. This particular page could use GET instead as there will only be one data value to submit. The HTML has been validated, so conforms to the the XHTML 1.1 standard.

The second wizard page receives the student ID numbers and uses them to retrieve the contact details and deliver them for modification by end users (Figure 7.20 (b)). The script follows the usual structure for such a script. First, the data validation code checks that a student ID number was entered. If not, a validation failure message is written to the HTTP response, with a link back to the first wizard page. If the student ID number passes validation, then the script connects to the DBMS and chooses the correct database, with appropriate code to handle DBMS communication errors.

Figure 7.21 The HTML code for the first page of the self-enrolment wizard.

```
1  <!DOCTYPE html PUBLIC "-//W3C//DTD XHTML 1.1//EN"
2      "http://www.w3.org/TR/xhtml11/DTD/xhtml11.dtd">
3  <html>
4  <head>
5    <meta http-equiv="Content-Type" content="text/html; charset=utf-8" />
6    <title> Pennine University self-enrolment facility </title>
7  </head>
8  <body>
9  <h1> Self-enrolment </h1>
10 <p>Please complete the form to enrol yourself on your chosen course.</p>
11 <h2>Step1: Enter your Id</h2>
12 <p>New students should enter the enrolment code at the top of your acceptance letter.
13 Returning students should enter their student number.</p>
14 <form method="post" action="EnrolmentWizardStep2.php">
15 <p> enrolment code or student number: <input type="text" name="studentNo" size="10" maxlength="10" /> </p>
16 <p> <input type="submit" /> </p>
17 </form>
18 <hr />
19 <p>Author: <cite>Martyn Prigmore</cite>
20 <br />&copy;2005 and beyond
21 </p>
22 </body>
23 </html>
```

The next task is to retrieve students' contact details, together with which courses they are on and which stage (year of study). All this information is held in the Student table, so the SQL select statement in lines 63–66 in Figure 7.22 does the job.

The studentNo column is the primary key for the Student table. Because the select statement uses an equality match on this primary key, there will only be one row in the result set (this first draft of the script does not attempt to deal with an incorrect student ID number). This simplifies the script as there is no need to loop through the result set.

Line 75 in Figure 7.23 fetches the single row from the result set into the associative array $row. After a couple of lines that write information, line 81 starts the form. Line 82 writes out the student ID number $row["studentNo"] – as plain text (end users cannot change this value on this web page). Line 83 writes the student ID number out again, but this time as the value of a hidden form control:

```
echo "\n<input type=\"hidden\" name=\"studentNo\"
         value=\"".$row["studentNo"]."\" />;
```

Figure 7.22 Retrieving the data for the second wizard page.

```
63  $sqlStatement = "SELECT studentNo, fName, lName, phone, email,
64                      house, street, street2, town, county, country, postcode, course, stage
65              FROM Student
66              WHERE studentNo='$studentNo'";
67  $result = mysql_query($sqlStatement, $connection);
68  //Report any errors that occurred when communicating with the MySQL DBMS
69  if ($result == FALSE)
70    exit("SQL statement failed. \n<br />MySQL error " . mysql_errno() . " : " . mysql_error());
71  else
72      echo "\n<!-- Notice: SQL statement worked. -->\n";
```

Figure 7.23 Writing out the form to allow end users to amend their contact details.

```
73
74  //STEP 4 Fetch the row - there will only be one as studentNo is the primary key
75  $row = mysql_fetch_array($result, MYSQL_ASSOC);
76
77  //STEP 5 Display the data from the row
78  echo "\n<h2>Step 2: Check your contact details</h2>";
79  echo "\n<p>We currently hold the following contact details.
80          Please check them and click the \"Confirm\" button to proceed.</p>";
81  echo "\n<form method=\"post\" action=\"EnrolmentWizardStep3.php\">";
82  echo "\n<p>Student number: ", $row["studentNo"];
83  echo "\n<input type=\"hidden\" name=\"studentNo\" value=\"" . $row["studentNo"] . "\" />";
84  echo "\n<input type=\"hidden\" name=\"course\" value=\"" . $row["course"] . "\" />";
85  echo "\n<input type=\"hidden\" name=\"stage\" value=\"" . $row["stage"] . "\" />";
86  echo "\n</p>";
87  //Show personal details for modification
88  echo "\n<table>";
89  echo "\n<tr><td>Given name</td><td><input type=\"text\" name=\"fName\" value=\"" . $row["fName"] . "\" /></td></tr>";
90  echo "\n<tr><td>Family name</td><td><input type=\"text\" name=\"lName\" value=\"" . $row["lName"] . "\" /></td></tr>";
91  echo "\n<tr><td>Phone</td><td><input type=\"text\" name=\"phone\" value=\"" . $row["phone"] . "\" /></td></tr>";
92  echo "\n<tr><td>email</td><td><input type=\"text\" name=\"email\" value=\"" . $row["email"] . "\" /></td></tr>";
93  echo "\n</table>";
94  //Show address for modification, but in a separate table
95  echo "\n<table>";
96  echo "\n<tr><td>House</td><td><input type=\"text\" name=\"house\" value=\"" . $row["house"] . "\" /></td></tr>";
97  echo "\n<tr><td>Street</td><td><input type=\"text\" name=\"street\" value=\"" . $row["street"] . "\" /></td></tr>";
98  echo "\n<tr><td></td><td><input type=\"text\" name=\"street2\" value=\"" . $row["street2"] . "\" /></td></tr>";
99  echo "\n<tr><td>Town</td><td><input type=\"text\" name=\"town\" value=\"" . $row["town"] . "\" /></td></tr>";
100 echo "\n<tr><td>County</td><td><input type=\"text\" name=\"county\" value=\"" . $row["county"] . "\" /></td></tr>";
101 echo "\n<tr><td>Country</td><td><input type=\"text\" name=\"country\" value=\"" . $row["country"] . "\" /></td></tr>";
102 echo "\n<tr><td>Postcode</td><td><input type=\"text\" name=\"postcode\" value=\"" . $row["postcode"] . "\" /></td></tr>";
103 echo "\n</table>";
104
105 echo "\n<p><input type=\"submit\" value=\"Confirm\" /></p>";
106 echo "\n</form>";
```

When end users click on the submit button, the web browser sends the name and value of this hidden form control to the third wizard page. Without this hidden form control, the third wizard page would not know the value of the student ID number entered on the first wizard page. Lines 84 and 85 also use hidden form controls to pass the course code and year of study to the third wizard page.

It is worth noting that all this data is enclosed in an HTML paragraph element, starting in line 82 and ending in line 86. The form element cannot appear inside a paragraph element, but paragraph elements can appear inside the form element. (This is one of the many nesting rules of the XHTML 1.1 standard.) The elements that define the form controls *must* appear inside a paragraph element (or some similar element). So, the standard approach to creating a form is that the form element contains a paragraph element, which contains form control elements.

Similar nesting rules apply to HTML tables, so are applied in lines 88–93. These write out an HTML table with four row elements – `<tr>` . . . `</tr>` – each of which has two table data elements – `<td>` . . . `</td>`. Table data elements define the columns for each row in an HTML table. (There are also table header elements – `<th>` . . . `</th>` – that define the column headings. These are used on the wizard page.)

The HTML table is used to improve the presentation of the student contact details. The first column contains a label for a data item. The second column contains the current value of that data item in a text box control (note that there is no need for a paragraph element here as an input element can appear inside a table data element as well as inside a paragraph element). For example, in line 89, the label is 'Given name' and the text box contains the value `$row["fName"]`.

Using tables is a standard way to achieve a tidier web page. Note how the first four text boxes in Figure 7.20 (b) line up nicely. A second HTML table makes the seven text boxes used for the address line up nicely, too.

An HTML table is a structure within the HTML document. It is nothing to do with the database.

The address has been split into seven separate data items. There is a reason for this. Many applications now use special software to retrieve the correct address based on the house name, or number, and postcode. It is easier to get end users to split the address up than to try and use the string manipulation functions to extract the house name or number and the postcode from one long address value. It also facilitates data mining to find out, for example, how many students come from EU countries. If the country is buried inside a single string value for the address, such questions cannot easily be answered.

The third wizard page – EnrolmentWizardStep3.php – receives 14 name-values pairs via the HTTP POST method – 3 from hidden form controls and 11 from visible controls. It first validates the data, ensuring that the required data has been submitted. Then the values of `$_POST["course"]` and `$_POST["stage"]` (from hidden form controls) are used to retrieve a list of core and optional modules. Figure 7.20 (c) shows how these are delivered. The core modules are shown as text and the optional modules in an HTML select element.

Figure 7.24 Retrieving details of core and optional modules.

```
81   //STEP 3 Query the database
82   /*Use a join query to retrieve modules at the correct level
83     (i.e. stage) and on the correct course for this student.
84     Use order-by clause to ensure compulsory modules (i.e. type='Core')
85     appear before optional modules in the result set
86   */
87   $sqlStatement    = "SELECT code, title, level, type
88                         FROM Module, CourseModule
89                         WHERE Module.code=CourseModule.module
90                         AND CourseModule.course='$course'
91                         AND Module.level='$stage'
92                         ORDER BY CourseModule.type, Module.title";
93   $result = mysql_query($sqlStatement, $connection);
94   //Report any errors that occurred when communicating with the MySQL DBMS
95   if ($result == FALSE)
96     exit("SQL statement failed. \n<br />MySQL error " . mysql_errno() . " : " . mysql_error());
97   else
98       echo "\n<!-- Notice: SQL statement worked. -->\n";
```

The script structure for this page follows the usual six steps to query a database from a server-side script. Figure 7.24 shows the SQL select statement used in step 3. It is a join query, joining the tables `Module` and `CourseModule`. The first condition in the where clause is the join condition. The second condition uses the value of `$_POST["course"]`, copied to the local variable `$course`. This value identifies the course being taken by the student. So, this condition ensures that only modules taken on that course are retrieved. The third condition uses the same approach to ensure that only modules relevant to the student's current year of study are retrieved. The order by clause gets the DBMS to order the rows so that the core modules (where the value of `type` is `'Core'`) come before the optional modules (`type` is `'Option'`) and that core and optional modules are then ordered alphabetically by title.

In Figure 7.20 (c), the course is identified only by its code, passed from the previous wizard page. It would be better to retrieve the full course details from the database and deliver these as text. The student should not be able to modify course details during enrolment. This means running two separate SQL queries in the one script, which is easy enough – simply repeat steps 3, 4 and 5 for each database query in turn.

Once the SQL statement has been run successfully, the script sets up the HTML form, creating hidden form controls for each of the 14 items of data that were passed to it. This ensures that the data is passed on to the next wizard page. It then writes the core modules to the web page, using an HTML table to line up the data, and sets up the optional modules as items in a list that end users can select from.

Figure 7.25 shows the PHP code to achieve both of these tasks. Lines 125 and 126 set up the table to display the core modules. Notice that the first row in the table, in line 125, has columns defined using the table heading element – `<th> ... </th>` – not the table data element.

Line 129 fetches the first row of the result set and line 130 starts a while loop to loop through the rows one at a time. The condition on this while loop has two Boolean expressions. The first – `$row <> FALSE` – tests that there is a row to process.

Figure 7.25 Delivering the module data (core modules are listed as text, optional modules as choices in a list box).

```
123   //Show core modules
124   echo "\n<p>You must take the following core modules:</p>";
125   echo "\n<table>";
126   echo "\n<tr><th>Module code</th><th>Title</th></tr>";
127   //STEP 4 Loop through the result set
128   //First list core modules as plain page content
129   $row = mysql_fetch_array($result, MYSQL_ASSOC);
130   while ($row <> FALSE and $row['type']=='Core')
131   {
132     //STEP 5a Display core module details
133     echo "\n<tr><td>{$row['code']}</td><td>{$row['title']}</td></tr>";
134     $row = mysql_fetch_array($result, MYSQL_ASSOC);
135   }
136   echo "\n</table>";
137   //Now list optional modules in a select control
138   //NOTE: Listing both code and title will make it harder to use the controls value,
139   //      since will need to extract code and title from the one string value
140   echo "\n<p>You must choose from the following optional modules.
141         \n<br />Use 'ctrl+click' to select more than one optional module,
142         and click the \"Confirm\" button to proceed.</p>";
143   echo "\n<p><select name=\"module[]\" multiple=\"multiple\" size=\"5\">";
144   while ($row <> FALSE)
145   {
146     //STEP 5b Use optional module details to create select list option elements
147     echo "\n<option>{$row['code']} {$row['title']}</option>";
148     $row = mysql_fetch_array($result, MYSQL_ASSOC);
149   }
150   echo "\n</select></p>";
151   echo "\n<p><input type=\"submit\" value=\"Confirm\" /></p>";
152   echo "\n</form>";
153
154   //STEP 6 Close the connection
155   mysql_close($connection);
```

The second – `$row['type']=='Core'` – tests whether the value of the `type` column for this row is `'Core'`. When both Boolean expressions are TRUE, PHP executes the echo statement in line 133. This writes out the HTML to create a new row in the table, with the module's code and title in the table data elements. Line 134 fetches the next row and PHP loops back to line 130. This process continues until the value for the `type` column in the current row is no longer `'Core'` (which means that it will be `'Option'`). When this happens, all the core modules must have been dealt with because the order by clause in line 92 (Figure 7.24) ensures that core modules appear first in the result set.

As all core modules will now have been dealt with, the script writes the end table tag (line 136) and moves on to deal with the optional modules. End users need to be able to choose which options to take, so they are displayed as HTML option elements within an HTML select element. Line 143 writes the select element's start tag. On the web page generated by this script, the start tag will be:

```
<select name="module[]" multiple="multiple" size="5">
```

The `size` attribute tells the web browser how many list items to display at one time. If there are more than five, it will automatically add a scroll bar to the list. The `multiple` attribute allows users to select more than one item from the list. In older versions of HTML, it was sufficient just to give the attribute name, but, in XHTML, *all* attributes must have a *value*, hence the rather clumsy name-value pair `multiple="multiple"`.

The name attribute is the interesting one. Because the select element allows multiple selections, it needs to pass multiple data values to the next PHP script. This PHP script – for the fourth wizard page – expects the form controls to come via the $_POST superglobal array. As superglobals are associative arrays, each element has a key and a value. The key of the $_POST array element is the name of the HTML form control element. The value of the $_POST array element is the value of the HTML form control element and, by default, this is a string. If the name attribute is defined as name="module", then the value of $_POST["module"] is a string that holds information on only *one* of the selected items. Adding the square brackets to the HTML select element's name attribute informs PHP that the value of $_POST["module"] is an array, *not* a string. Because PHP now expects the value of $_POST["module"] to be an array, it correctly adds every item chosen by end users to this array.

This is quite a complex situation – $_POST is an array. Most of its elements are strings, but the element $_POST["module"] is itself an array. The elements of the array $_POST["module"] are strings – the list items chosen by end users. Figure 7.26 presents a picture of the $_POST superglobal array. The key-value pairs are as they would be when end users click on the 'Confirm' button shown in Figure 7.20 (c) and the fourth wizard page is called. The first 14 elements – $_POST["studentNo"], $_POST["course"], ..., $_POST["postcode"], all have character string values. The fifteenth – $_POST["module"] – has an indexed array as its value. In the image shown, the indexed array has two elements and indicates that this end user selected *both* optional modules shown in the list in Figure 7.20 (c).

Returning to the code in Figure 7.25, line 144 starts another while loop. This while loop picks up where the previous one left off. At this point, $row must hold the row of data for the first optional module (the previous while loop dealt with all the core modules). Because of the order by clause (line 92, Figure 7.24), the rest of the rows in the result set will also be optional modules ('Core' and 'Option' are the only possible values

Figure 7.26 A picture of the $_POST **array, showing its key value pairs for the web page in Figure 7.20 (c).**

Key	Value		
studentNo	2222222222		
course	B2Y8		
...			
postcode	HD5 7AA		
module		Index	Value
		0	BMFC0107 Introduction to management
		1	CCFC0108 Introduction to programming

of the column `CourseModule.type`). So, this while loop simply runs through the remaining rows of the result set, writing each out as an HTML option element.

Lines 150–153 (Figure 7.25) close the select element, write out a submit button and close the form element. Line 155 closes the connection to the DBMS.

The final wizard page (not shown) receives all the data gathered from each end user and writes it to the database. This means updating the `Student` table with the new contact details and updating the timetable database with the list of optional modules chosen by the student.

This example has demonstrated how to use hidden form controls to pass data along a chain of PHP scripts, ensuring that data gathered on the web page generated by the first PHP script is available to all subsequent scripts. Without hidden form controls, the data would only be available to the *next* script in the chain.

There are some problems with the self-enrolment wizard as it is currently coded. One significant improvement would be to write the contact details to the database on the third wizard page before retrieving the module details. From a business perspective, changing contact details and choosing optional modules are both part of the same process – enrolment. From the database perspective, they are quite independent actions, so there is no need to insist that both changes are made at the same time. This would mean that only the student ID number, course code and year of study would need to be passed along using a hidden form control, simplifying the code.

It's also possible to generate all the wizard pages from a single PHP script. This would make the validation more user-friendly. At the moment, any validation failures mean going back to the first wizard page and starting the self-enrolment process from scratch.

7.6 Managing application state with sessions

A **session** is a mechanism designed specifically to maintain application state between HTTP requests. Unlike URL rewriting and hidden form fields, which store application state on the web browser, the application state is stored on the web server as **session variables**. The web browser only needs to store the **session ID**. Figure 7.27 uses a UML sequence diagram to illustrate the process. When a web browser first requests a resource from the application, it does not have a session ID. That is how the application server knows this is the first request from this web browser, so initializes a session for it. Initializing a session involves creating a unique session ID and a set of session variables to hold the application state. These session variables can be stored in a file on the web server or in the database. File storage tends to be the default option and the simplest to use. The application server generates the HTTP response message and passes it to the HTTP server, along with the session ID. The HTTP server sends these to the web browser. At this point, the web browser has the requested resource, plus a session ID for this web server. When the web browser requests a second page from this same web server, it sends the session ID as part of the HTTP request message. The HTTP server passes the HTTP request, including the session ID, to the application server. It uses the session ID to retrieve the session variables for this web browser and carry out any necessary processing, returning the processed resource to the HTTP server. The second web page is delivered to the web browser, again with the session ID attached. This

Figure 7.27 Using sessions to maintain application state.

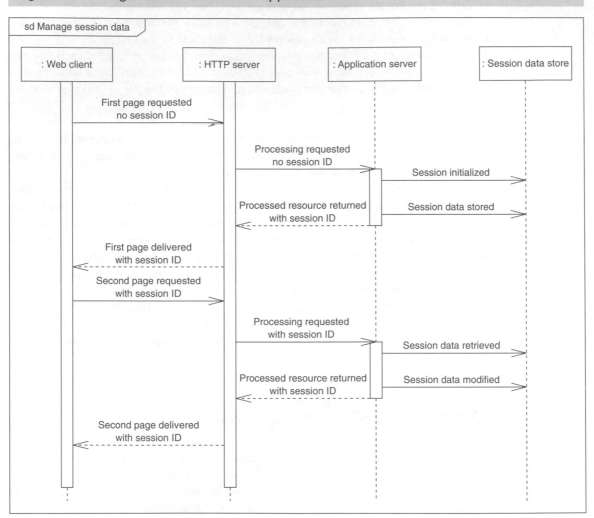

continues until the end user requests that the session ends or until there has been no HTTP request with this session ID for a fixed length of time. Once ended, the application server destroys the session ID and session variables and gets the web browser to destroy its copy of the session ID.

Sessions can be a much simpler mechanism for the application developer to use than URL rewriting and hidden form fields. There is no need for them to write code to embed complex URL query strings or hidden form controls into the web page. The application server itself maintains the application state, and the HTTP server and web browser automatically send the session ID to each other in their HTTP messages. Even if many different end users request the same script at the same time, the web server just creates an instance of the script for each end user and ensures that each instance receives the correct application state for that user. All the application developer need do is create and use session variables, knowing that the right ones will be available each time the script is called by a particular end user.

As a mechanism, sessions is also more secure than URL rewriting and hidden form fields because, as application state data never leaves the application server, they cannot be intercepted. Thus, common uses of sessions include storing shopping basket data, and managing user logins (though HTTP authentication provides an alternative login mechanism).

When sessions are used to personalize websites, the session variables are usually stored in a database, so data values can persist even after a particular session closes. Once a user logs in, he or she can see information about past interactions with the application and perhaps suggestions as to future actions, such as buy certain products or sign up for a newsletter.

PHP makes using sessions very easy. Any script that needs to access session data should begin by calling the built-in PHP function `session_start()`. The function has no parameters and always returns true. When a script calls `session_start()`, the PHP application server checks to see whether or not the HTTP request message came with a session ID. If it did not, then it initializes a new session by creating a unique session ID. This session ID is sent to the web browser in the HTTP response, typically as a **cookie** (see note below), though, as some end users block all cookies, it can also be sent using URL rewriting (see PHP Documentation Group (2005) for details). Once `session_start()` has initialized a session, the script can add session variables. In PHP version 5, the session variables are all elements of the `$_SESSION` superglobal array. To create session variables, simply add an element, key and value, to this array.

When PHP receives an HTTP request that *does* include a session ID, `session_start()` behaves differently. Instead of initializing a new session, it retrieves any existing session variables from the session data store and makes them available via the `$_SESSION` superglobal array. The script can add new session variables, change the value of existing session variables or remove them. The session ends automatically when the user closes the browser. To end a session manually takes some doing, though. First, the `$_SESSION` superglobal array needs to be cleared out, then the web browser needs to be told to remove the cookie from the client computer, then finally the built-in PHP function `session_destroy()` removes all trace of the session from the web server. The PHP user manual (PHP Documentation Group, 2005) has some useful user-contributed comments on how to end sessions.

A **cookie** is a set of data stored by a web browser on its client computer. Each cookie is associated with a particular Internet domain. Cookies set by the Pennine University's website, for example, could be associated with the domain 'www.pennine.ac.uk' domain or with 'pennine.ac.uk'. (The second is broader as it includes the mail server and other Internet-accessible servers.) The web server specifies which domain a cookie is associated with, along with other cookie information, and sends this information to the web browser using special HTTP headers.

When the web browser creates an HTTP request for a resource in a given domain (because the end user clicked on a hyperlink, for example), it automatically includes in the HTTP request any cookie data for cookies associated with that domain. Again, the cookie data is sent using HTTP headers.

Persistent cookies are stored in a file on the computer's hard disk and persist until their expiry date, when the web browser will remove them. Session cookies are removed when the web browser closes.

A nice, simple example of a web database application that can only really be implemented using sessions is the 'My list' feature of the Pennine University's Library Catalogue. The library has a web-based catalogue, allowing people to search for books they want to take out on loan. Figure 7.28 (a) shows the result of searching the catalogue with the title keyword 'database' (generated by the TitleSearch.php script). The search results give the title of the book and the class mark, which is enough to find it on the shelves.

Notice that this search application uses the same multiple page mechanism as the Staff Directory search application discussed above. In fact, the code for the two search applications is almost identical. It is quite common that two applications are similar enough to share a lot of code, but different enough to be separate applications. Good application developers turn the common code into functions, such as the `cleanse_data()` function discussed in Chapter 4, and reuse it whenever they can. This reduces the likelihood of faults as many of the functions used in an application will already have been used, and so tested, in existing systems.

Object-orientated software engineering takes this approach much further and is arguably a more effective approach to application development than procedural programming with functions. Those who are familiar with the object-orientated approach could recast some of the example web database applications into object-orientated ones as an exercise as PHP 5 supports this approach.

Figure 7.28 The Library Catalogue.

(a) The search results page, with URL for 'Details' hyperlink in status bar.

Figure 7.28 (*Continued*)

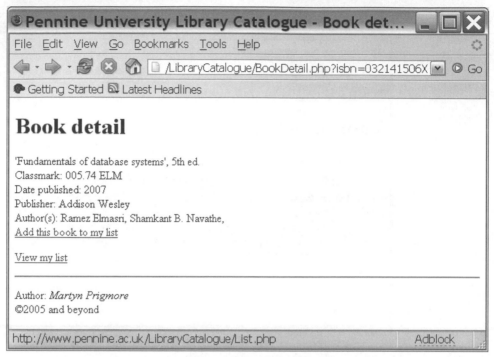

(b) The book detail page, with URL for 'View my list' hyperlink in status bar.

TitleSearch.php uses URL rewriting to maintain application state. It manages pagination by writing the search criteria and offset into the 'Next' hyperlink (Figure 7.28 (a), just as the Staff Directory search script did. The 'Details' hyperlink, after each search result, encodes the book's ISBN (used as the primary key for the Book table). The mouse was hovering over the first of these hyperlinks when the screenshot was taken, so the URL is shown in the status bar. These hyperlinks offer end users choices. They make a choice by clicking on a hyperlink. When they click on the 'Details' hyperlink, they cause the web browser to pass the ISBN to the BookDetail.php script. A web page generated by the BookDetail.php script is shown in Figure 7.28 (b).

This example uses the ISBN as the primary key for the Book table. Obviously this isn't realistic. A library will hold many copies of a book and each copy has the same ISBN. However, for the purposes of this example, ISBN will do as a primary key for the Book table as two different books will have different ISBNs and we can assume that the borrower won't care which copy of any particular book is picked.

Look closely at the list of authors on the Book detail web page in Figure 7.28 (b). There is a superfluous comma after the second author's name. This appears because each author is listed on a separate line in the result set for the database query. The BookDetail.php script writes out the authors one at a time and doesn't know how many there are altogether. Adding a comma after each name sets the line up for the *next* author. However, the last author in the list always has a superfluous comma after their name. The script should really trim this off.

Figure 7.29 Adding a book to the booklist using Version 0.1 of List.php.

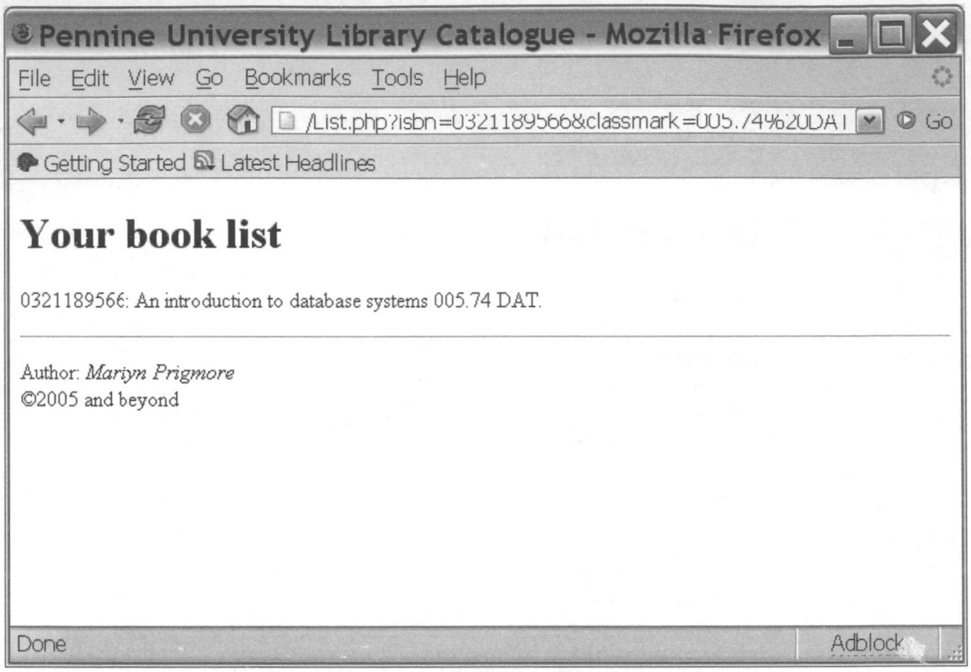

So far, the application has not needed to maintain data about users' choices on the web server. However, the librarians were always being asked for pens and paper, so that people could write down details of books they wanted. This led to lots of lost pens and wasted time. To help out, the 'My list' feature was added to the catalogue. The 'Add this book to my list' hyperlink calls the List.php script, passing it details of the book being displayed. The effect of this is to add the book's ISBN, class mark and title to the session data store and display an end user's current book list (Figure 7.29). End users can do further searches and add other books to their lists. When they have all the books they want on their lists, they can print them out and carry the printout with them as they search the shelves for these books. Because each book list can be as long as end users want, it is impractical to use URL rewriting or hidden form controls to maintain this data. Storing the data in the session data store is clearly the best solution.

Figure 7.30 shows the code for Version 0.1 of List.php. The script calls session_start() in line 22. This establishes, or re-establishes, the session. Any data stored in the session store can be accessed via the $_SESSION superglobal array and new data can be added to this array simply by adding a new element.

From line 25 to line 33 there is the usual start to a web page at the Pennine University. Line 35 tests whether or not any data was passed to the script via the HTPP GET method. (This is rather weak data validation and should be improved before the script is deployed.)

If there is some data, then it will be details of a book to add to the list – specifically, the ISBN, class mark (the library catalogue number) and title. Lines 38–40 add this data to the $_SESSION superglobal array as a new element. First, line 38 cleanses the ISBN and stores it in the variable $key, then, in line 39, the ISBN becomes the key to

Figure 7.30 Version 0.1 of the List.php script.

```
22 session_start();
23 include 'DataCleansingOv2.inc';
24 ?>
25 <!DOCTYPE html PUBLIC "-//W3C//DTD XHTML 1.1//EN"
26     "http://www.w3.org/TR/xhtml11/DTD/xhtml11.dtd">
27 <html>
28 <head>
29   <meta http-equiv="Content-Type" content="text/html; charset=utf-8" />
30   <title> Pennine University Library Catalogue </title>
31 </head>
32 <body>
33 <h1>Your book list</h1>
34 <?php
35 if (!empty($_GET))
36 {
37   //Add new book to the book list, before displaying it
38   $key=cleanse_data($_GET["isbn"]);
39   $_SESSION[$key]= cleanse_data($_GET["title"]) . " "
40              . cleanse_data($_GET["classmark"]) . ".\n";
41 }
42 //Display the book list
43 if (empty($_SESSION))
44   echo "<p>You have no books on your list</p>";
45 else
46 {
47   foreach ($_SESSION as $key => $value)
48   {
49     echo "\n<p>";
50     echo $key . ": " . $value;
51     echo "\n</p>";
52   }
53 }
54 ?>
```

a new element in the $_SESSION array. The value of this new element is formed by concatenating the (cleansed) values of the book's title and class mark. This is all that needs to be done to add the data to the session data store. PHP will ensure that the data is available when this session is re-established. Note that if the same book is added for a second time, then there is already an element of $_SESSION with its ISBN as the element key. In this situation, what happens in line 39 is that the value of the *existing* element is overwritten (with exactly the same information, so nothing actually changes). This means that no book ever appears twice in the book list. This rather elegant feature avoids the script having to check $_SESSION for identical data each time a book is added to the list.

Lines 43–53 display the book list itself, using a standard PHP foreach loop to run through the elements of the $_SESSION superglobal array. Note that both the key (the ISBN) and the value (the title and class mark) of each element are displayed on the web page. This happens each time a book is added to the list and also when the end user clicks on a 'View my list' hyperlink (see, for example, Figure 7.28 (b)). Figure 7.29 shows a web page generated by Version 0.1 of List.php, with just one book on the list.

One interesting point about sessions is that only scripts that need to access the session data store have to start a session. Neither the TitleSearch.php script, which generated the list of books in Figure 7.28 (a), nor the BookDetail.php script, which generated Figure 7.28 (b), uses session data, so neither script calls the session_start() function. Even so, when end users request either of these resources from the Library Catalogue, the web browser will send the session ID in the HTTP request.

Figure 7.31 Clearing the book list by destroying all session data: Version 0.1 of ClearList.php.

```
20  session_start();
21  $_SESSION=array();
22  if (isset($_COOKIE[session_name()]))
23  {
24      setcookie(session_name(), '', time()-42000);
25  }
26  session_destroy();
27  header("Location: TitleSearch.html");
28  ?>
29  <!DOCTYPE html PUBLIC "-//W3C//DTD XHTML 1.1//EN"
30      "http://www.w3.org/TR/xhtml11/DTD/xhtml11.dtd">
31  <html>
32  <head>
33    <meta http-equiv="Content-Type" content="text/html; charset=utf-8" />
34    <title> Pennine University Library Catalogue </title>
35  </head>
36  <body>
37  <h1>Clear book list</h1>
38  <p> Your book list has been cleared. </p>
39  <p> Your browser should automatically re-direct you to the
40      <a href="TitleSearch.html">search page</a>
41  </p>
42  </body>
43  </html>
```

If end users browse off to another website, then the web browser will *not* send the session ID. This is because, by default, PHP sets the domain of the cookie that stores the session ID to the web server's domain – www.pennine.ac.uk. Any resource requested from this domain is sent the Library Catalogue session ID.

If other applications, such as the Web Timetable, also use sessions, then the application developer needs to set different domains – for example, 'www.pennine.ac.uk/LibraryCatalogue' for the Library Catalogue session ID and 'www.pennine.ac.uk/WebTimetable' for the Web Timetable session ID. The PHP user manual (PHP Documentation Group, 2005) describes how to do this.

It is common to allow users to end a session, clearing out any session data on the web server and removing the cookie from the client machine. Version 0.1 of the script ClearList.php (Figure 7.31) does this. Add a 'Clear list' hyperlink to the book list web page to allow users to clear their lists (Figure 7.32). The ClearList.php script includes all its PHP code *before* it outputs any HTML. This is because most of the statements cause PHP to write an HTTP header to the HTTP response message. Remember, all HTTP headers need to be written before any of the HTTP entity body – that is, before any HTML.

At present, the only way to remove data from the list is to clear it out entirely. It would be nice to include a 'Remove this book' feature so that end users could remove individual entries from their lists.

To do this, the script would have to remove an element from the $_SESSION array. PHP provides the built-in function unset(), which achieves this. For example, to remove the first book in the list in Figure 7.32, use the PHP statement:

```
unset($_SESSION["0321189566"]).
```

This works because the book's ISBN – 0321189566 – was used as the key of the element.

Figure 7.32 The booklist web page with a 'Clear list' hyperlink.

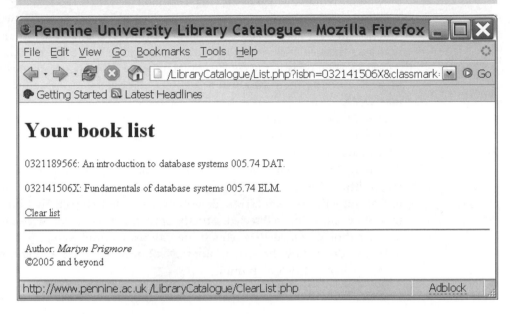

Line 20 (Figure 7.31) starts the session. This is necessary as the script will alter the session data (by removing it all). Line 21 sets the value of the $_SESSION superglobal array to the empty array. This is the line that gets rid of all the session data from the web server.

Lines 22–25 deal with the cookie on the client machine. It is possible that the cookie hasn't yet been set – the end user may have bookmarked the ClearList.php page or a page that contains a hyperlink to it and got to this point before the web server sends the session ID to the client machine. When PHP first sets the cookie that stores the session ID, it gives it a default name. That name is always accessible, using the built-in PHP function session_name(). When a session ID *has* been sent, there will be an element in the $_COOKIE superglobal array and the key for it is the name of the *current* session. The built-in PHP function isset() checks whether or not a variable or array element has been given a value, so isset($_COOKIE[session_name()]) returns true when there is a cookie with the name of the current session. This confirms that a cookie has been set on the client machine. In this case, line 24 uses another built-in PHP function to set an HTTP header that instructs the web browser to destroy this cookie.

It's worth examining this function:

```
setcookie(session_name(), '', time()-42000)
```

The first parameter is the name of the cookie, which is how the web browser knows which of its many cookies to destroy. The second parameter sets the value of the cookie to the empty string, erasing all the cookie's data. The third parameter is the expiry date, in the standard UNIX time format (number of seconds since 1 January 1970). The built-in PHP function time() gets the current date and, subtracting a number of seconds, ensures that the expiry date will be in the past. This will force the browser to

327

destroy the cookie. (There are other parameters to the `setcookie()` function, but they aren't required when destroying a cookie.)

Erasing *and* destroying the cookie may seem like overkill, but remember that this function doesn't actually do either of these things. It merely sends an HTTP header that asks the *web browser* to do them. By asking the web browser to erase the cookie data first, then destroy the cookie completely, there is a better chance that the information stored in the cookie will actually be removed – if one action fails, the other may well succeed.

Line 26 calls the built-in PHP function `session_destroy()` which destroys the remaining session information on the web server (the session variables themselves were unset in line 21).

Finally, line 27 sends an HTTP header redirecting the web browser to the Title-Search.html web page. This is the page that gathers the catalogue search criteria. The rest of the script is plain HTML, describing a simple web page that informs end users that they are being redirected. Strictly speaking this is not necessary as the web browser should immediately request the TitleSearch.html web page. End users see the web page defined by the code in lines 29–43 only if it takes a long time for the web server to deliver TitleSearch.html.

7.7 Identifying and authenticating users

The session created in the 'My list' example allowed anonymous browsing – there was no need for users to identify themselves before adding books to their lists. Many applications, however, require users to identify themselves before they can use the application.

First, each end user must be registered with the application. Registration involves issuing each end user with username and password. Some web database applications allow users to register themselves. They usually provide some basic information, such as their names and e-mail addresses, and choose their own usernames and passwords. These applications are, in effect, open access as anyone can register. However, once registered, end users' behaviour can be monitored.

There are many reasons for an application monitoring the behaviour of end users. For example, an organization might want to identify which parts of a website are most popular, prevent misuse of the application, gather information about users for direct marketing purposes or facilitate personalization of a website. When a web database application is not open access, then the application or database administrator will issue usernames and passwords. These act as a barrier to entry as well as allowing the administrator to monitor end users.

Once registered, end users can login each time they return to the website. To login, they identify themselves with their usernames and authenticate their identity with their passwords. Once logged in, the application must keep track of each end user's identity from one HTTP request to the next. This is where sessions can be useful. When users first come to the website, a simple HTML form allows them to login. For each user, the username is stored in a session variable, so is available to the application for subsequent HTTP requests. Each script in the application must check that the 'username' session variable exists and, if not, display the login page (for example, by using redirection). There should also be a 'logout' button or hyperlink on each web page. This calls a script to destroy the session.

HTTP authentication provides an alternative way to keep track of the identity of end users. HTTP authentication is built in to the HTTP protocol and it is possible to set up the the web server so that it checks that an end user is logged in before dealing with the HTTP request. The HTTP server automatically makes the login details (username and password) available to PHP.

A good example of an open access application that wants to track its end users is the Pennine University's Course Catalogue. Prospective students can browse the online catalogue anonymously, but must register to receive a printed copy. Once registered, they can log in and the application will keep track of those pages they have visited. It can use this information to suggest other courses that they might be interested in. Many web applications currently use similar techniques to personalize web pages for registered users. Logging in also gives the prospective students access to parts of the website that are not open access. For example, they can track the progress of their application and view some of the online learning materials used in the courses that they are interested in.

This section covers gathering registration data and managing HTTP authentication from within PHP scripts. Once these techniques are understood they can be combined with sessions and storing information on the database to develop scripts that implement much more sophisticated functionality than the examples discussed here.

7.7.1 Gathering registration data

Figure 7.33 shows the registration page for the course catalogue. The page uses an HTML table to ensure that the text boxes line up neatly. There are two form controls that haven't been used previously – the textarea control and the password control.

The textarea form control allows end users to type their full address across a number of lines – a simpler approach than that used in the enrolment wizard, which split the address up into its component parts (it is also less effective as it is difficult to validate the address).

The textarea form control is defined as follows:

```
<textarea name="address" cols="37" rows="5"
wrap="virtual"></textarea>
```

Unlike the input form control, there is no short tag for the textarea control – the end tag must always be present. The textarea form control has four important attributes:

- the `name` attribute is required, as usual
- the `cols` and `rows` attributes control how wide and how tall the textarea is on the web page
- the `wrap` attribute determines whether or not text typed into the text area 'wraps' on to a new line at the edges of the control.

Figure 7.33 Course catalogue registration page showing password text boxes.

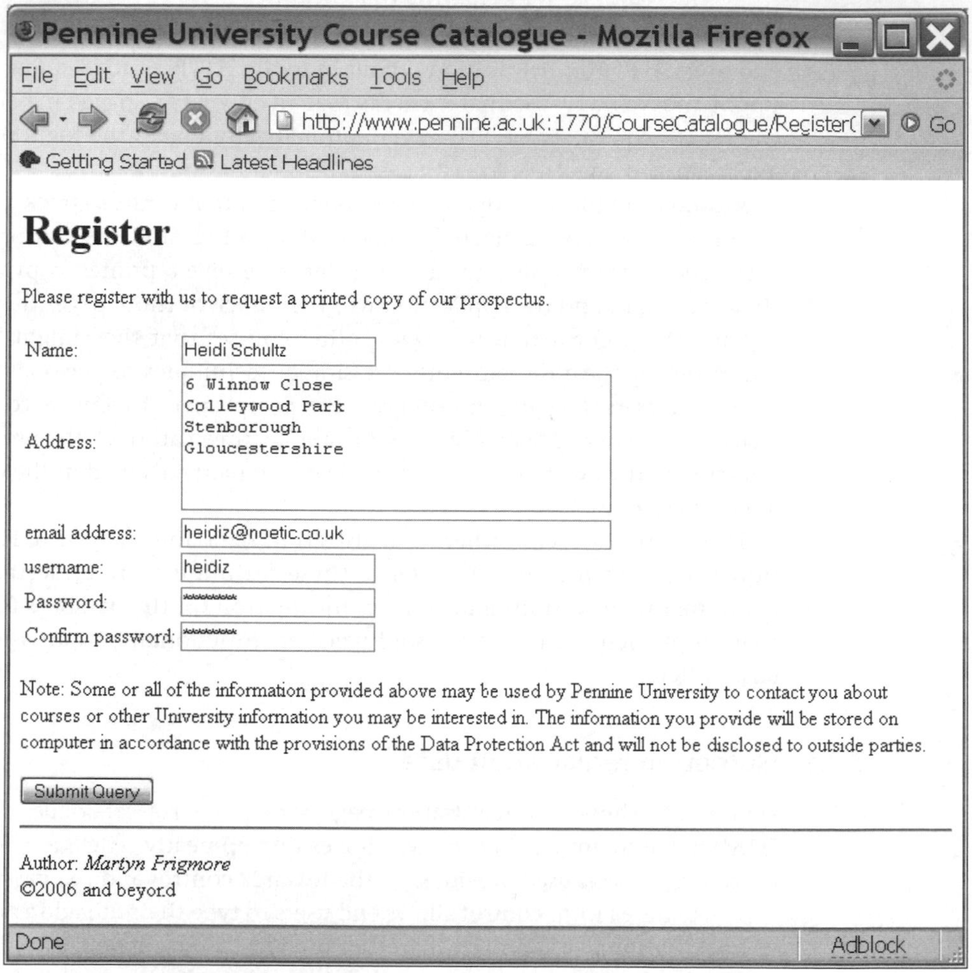

There are three possible values:

- "virtual" means that the text wraps on the web page, but only new line characters actually typed by end users are sent as part of the control's data
- "physical" means that the web browser actually adds new line characters to the data wherever it needs to wrap the text
- "off" means that the text is not wrapped, so end users must type new line characters to start a new line.

Notice that the label 'Address' is not aligned with the top of the address textarea. Web applications now use cascading stylesheets to alter the web browser's default presentation, but, as this technology has not been covered, the examples stick with the default presentation.

> When the web browser submits the data from the textarea form control, it correctly sends the new line character, encoded as %0D%0A (this is actually two characters – 'carriage return' followed by 'linefeed'). When PHP uses this data as part of an insert statement, the new line characters are included as part of the address. When the data is inserted into TEXT or the VARCHAR column of a MyISAM table, the MySQL DBMS is quite happy with this, correctly storing the new line characters in the address. When the data is later retrieved from the table, it will again correctly include the new line characters. This may not be the case with every MySQL storage engine, nor other DBMS.

The other new form control is the password control. The form controls labelled 'Password:' and 'Confirm password:' in Figure 7.33 actually have the word 'password' typed into them, but password form controls never display the actual data they hold, only a sequence of '*' or '•' characters (depending on the web browser). This means that users can enter their passwords without worrying that someone could read over their shoulder what they have typed. The password form control is defined using the HTML input element:

```
<input type="password" name="password1" size="20"
maxlength="20" />
```

Of course, hiding the text from end users also presents a problem. For example, if Heidi had meant to type 'password' but accidentally mistyped it as 'passeord', then she cannot see her mistake. That is why there is a 'Confirm password:' control. It is unlikely that end users will make the same typing error twice, so asking them to type their passwords twice and comparing the two values is a good way of preventing this sort of mistake.

Code listing 7.7.1.1 shows how to cross-validate two password controls. (See Section 7.3 for a fuller discussion of validation.)

Code listing 7.7.1.1 Validating the two password controls on a user registration page

```
if (empty($_POST["password1"])
   or empty($_POST["password2"])
   or $_POST["password1"]<>$_POST["password2"])


{
  $validationFail = true;
  $validationMessage["password"]="There was a problem with
the password. Please try again.";
}
```

Once the user registration data has been gathered, it is usually stored in the database. It is good practice to encrypt password data before storing it. There are a number of encryption algorithms available, but the simplest approach is to use a **hash function**. Hash functions take a string of characters and return another string, usually of hexadecimal digits. Given a particular input string, the hash function always returns the same output string. For example, consider the SHA-1 hash function. Given the **clear text value** password as input, the SHA-1 hash function always returns the **hashed value** 5baa61e4c9b93f3 f0682250b6cf8331b7ee68fd8 as output. Hash functions are designed so that it is not feasible to retrieve the original clear text value from the hashed value. Given the hashed value 5baa61e4c9b93f3f0682250b6cf8331b7ee68fd8, there is no easy way to work out that this represents the clear text value password.

Hash functions provide a useful mechanism for encrypting passwords. When a user chooses a password during registration, it is the hashed value, not the clear text value, that is stored on the database. This means that it is not possible for anyone to discover another user's password simply by looking in the database. When an end user comes to login, he or she types the clear text password into the login form, the application uses this to generate the hashed value and compares this hashed value to the one stored in the database. If they match, then the user has entered the correct password.

The MySQL DBMS implements the SHA-1 hash function as the value function SHA1(). This function expects a single string value as input and outputs another string value:

string **SHA1**(string *str*)

So, for example:

SHA1('password')='5baa61e4c9b93f3f0682250b6cf8331b7ee68fd8'

Note that the single quote marks around a clear text and hashed values are *not* part of the string value but the usual SQL string delimiters.

Adding an encrypted password to a database is relatively straightforward. Figure 7.34 shows the code from Register.php, which deals with valid registration data. First, the

Figure 7.34 Dealing with data from the registration form.

```
122  else
123  {
124    $name = cleanse_data($_POST["name"]);
125    $address = cleanse_data($_POST["address"]);
126    $email = cleanse_data($_POST["email"]);
127    $username = cleanse_data($_POST["username"]) ;
128    $pwd = cleanse_data($_POST["password1"]);
129    //STEP 1 connect to the DBMS
130    $connection = mysql_connect('www.pennine.ac.uk', 'martyn', 'martynpassword');
131    //Report any errors that occurred when communicating with the MySQL DBMS
132    if ($connection==FALSE)
133      exit("\nCould not connect to MySQL DBMS. \n<br />MySQL error " . mysql_errno() . " : " . mysql_error());
134    //STEP 2 specify which database to use
135    $database = mysql_select_db('test', $connection);
136    //Report any errors that occurred when communicating with the MySQL DBMS
137    if ($database == FALSE)
138      exit("Unable to locate the database. \n<br />MySQL error " . mysql_errno() . " : " . mysql_error());
139    //STEP 3 Modify the database
140    $sqlStatement = "INSERT INTO User (name, address, email, username, password)
141               VALUES ('$name', '$address', '$email', '$username', SHA1('$pwd'))";
142    $result = mysql_query($sqlStatement, $connection);
143    //STEP 4 Confirm successful execution or report any errors that occurred when communicating with the MySQL DBMS
144    if ($result == TRUE)
145    {
146      //Database modified successfully, so re-direct to the login page
147      header("Location: Login.php");
148    }
149    else
150    {
151      //Database communication error, so create an error message
152      $status = mysql_errno();
153      $message = mysql_error();
154      header("Location: RegisterMsg.php?status=$status&message=$message");
155    }
156    //Now redirect the web browser to the success/DBMS-error page
157    //STEP 5 Close the connection
158    mysql_close($connection);
```

data is cleansed and stored in local variables, then the script establishes a connection to the DBMS.

Lines 140 and 141 are the interesting ones. These set up an SQL insert statement to add the registration data to a table called `User`. The values added are simply those entered into the registration form by the end user, apart from the value for the `password` column. The value for this column is `SHA1('$pwd')`. This applies the MySQL function to the value of the PHP variable `$pwd`.

It is worth looking a little more closely at these two lines as it is important to understand what the SQL insert statement actually looks like.

Code listing 7.7.1.2 (a) shows the PHP code that builds the SQL insert statement. When the PHP application server processes this statement, it will replace each of the variable names inside the string literal with their values. In particular, it replaces `$pwd` with the value `password`, entered by the end user into the password control on the registration form. The result is the SQL insert statement shown in Code listing 7.7.1.2 (b). Note that this SQL statement includes the MySQL function `SHA1()`. It is the MySQL DBMS that encrypts the password, not PHP.

Code listing 7.7.1.2 Using the MySQL DBMS function SHA1 () to encrypt the password

(a) The PHP code

```
$sqlStatement = "INSERT INTO User (name, address, email,
                        username, password)
                 VALUES ('$name', '$address', '$email',
                        '$username', SHA1('$pwd'))";
```

(b) The SQL insert statement built by the PHP code given the data shown in Figure 7.33

```
INSERT INTO User (name, address, email, username, password)
VALUES ('Heidi Schultz',
        '6 Winnow Close
        Colleywood Park
        Stenborough Gloucestershire',
        'heidiz@noetic.co.uk',
        'heidiz',
        SHA1('password'))
```

PHP also includes a function called `sha1()`. This behaves in exactly the same way as the MySQL function `SHA1()`. Using the PHP `sha1()` function means encrypting the password *before* sending it to the DBMS.

Code listing 7.7.1.3 (a) shows one way to use the PHP `sha1()` function, while (b) shows the SQL insert statement. The difference between Code listings 7.7.1.2 (b) and 7.7.1.3 (b) should be obvious.

Code listing 7.7.1.3 Using the PHP function sha1 () to encrypt the password

(a) The PHP code

```
//First encrypt the password
$pwd=sha1($pwd);
```

```
$sqlStatement = "INSERT INTO User (name, address, email,
                      username, password)
               VALUES ('$name', '$address', '$email',
                      '$username', '$pwd')";
```

(b) The SQL insert statement built by the PHP code given the data shown in Figure 7.33

```
INSERT INTO User (name, address, email, username, password)
VALUES ('Heidi Schultz',
        '6 Winnow Close
         Colleywood Park
         Stenborough Gloucestershire',
        'heidiz@noetic.co.uk',
        'heidiz',
        '5baa61e4c9b93f3f0682250b6cf8331b7ee68fd8')
```

In the examples given of functions implementing the SHA-1 algorithm, the MySQL function is always written in upper case and the PHP function in lower case. In fact, both function names can be written in either case. It does make sense, though, to consider always writing MySQL functions in upper case and PHP functions in lower case. As with everything, this is a matter of personal style.

Lines 144–157 use relocation to avoid the reload problem. In this case, when the data has been successfully added to the database, it makes sense to send the user to the login page. If there is a problem, an error page is displayed instead.

7.7.2 Controlling HTTP authentication with PHP

As mentioned, it is possible to configure the HTTP server to require users to login before they can access certain resources. The details for how to do this depend on which HTTP server is being used. One problem with this approach is that the application developer needs to alter the configuration of the HTTP server. In some cases, this may not be possible. The application may share an HTTP server with others and be limited to the default configuration or may be hosted by a third party, leaving the developer with no way to modify the configuration files.

An alternative is to manage HTTP authentication using PHP. Again, there are limitations as the code required is different for different web servers and, when PHP is installed as a CGI application, it cannot manage HTTP authentication. Even so, it is worth looking at a simple example of HTTP authentication managed within a PHP script as it illustrates most of the issues that any implementation must address.

HTTP authentication uses the term **security realm** to mean a set of related web resources that can only be accessed by authorized users. When the web server receives an HTTP request for a resource in a particular realm, the web server checks whether or not the HTTP request includes the authorization header. When it is present, the authorization HTTP request header holds the username and password supplied by the end

Figure 7.35 An HTTP authentication prompt from the Firefox web browser.

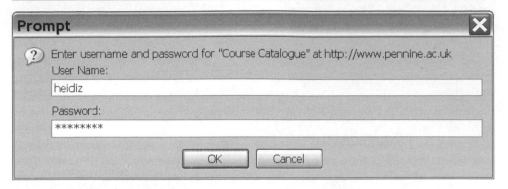

user for this particular security realm. If the HTTP request does not have an authorization header, the web server responds with a **challenge**.

A challenge is simply an HTTP response message with status code 401, meaning 'You need to login to get this resource', and the WWW-Authenticate HTTP response header set appropriately. The WWW-Authenticate HTTP header tells the web browser how to login. This response message also includes an entity body. Typically, the entity body is a simple web page stating that the requested resource can only be accessed by authorized users. When the web browser receives the challenge, it displays a prompt like the one shown in Figure 7.35. The user can either click on the 'Cancel' button or enter his or her login details and then click on 'OK'. When an end user clicks on 'Cancel', the web browser displays the web page that came as the entity body of the challenge (Figure 7.36).

When the end user enters their login details and clicks on 'OK', two things happen (Figure 7.37). First, the login details are stored by the web browser in its authentication cache. Second, they are sent to the web server in the authorization header of a *second* HTTP request for the same resource. This time, the web server should check the details in the authorization header. If the login details are not valid, then the web server sends another challenge. If the login details are valid, however, the web server responds by supplying the requested resource. Note that, in this case, the entity body of the challenge is never displayed to the end user.

Once logged in, the web browser sends the login details, as an authorization header, with all future HTTP requests for web resources from the same domain (just as it does with the session ID). Thus, HTTP authentication uses the same basic mechanism as sessions to overcome the statelessness of the HTTP protocol and track authenticated users from one request to the next. However, HTTP authentication is much more limited in the application state information that it holds. Only the username and password are maintained, nothing else.

> The web browser stores login details for each *domain*, not for each security realm. It will send the login details with every request for a resource from that domain. It will *not* send the login details with requests for resources from a different domain.

Figure 7.36 Cancelling a request for a protected web resource.

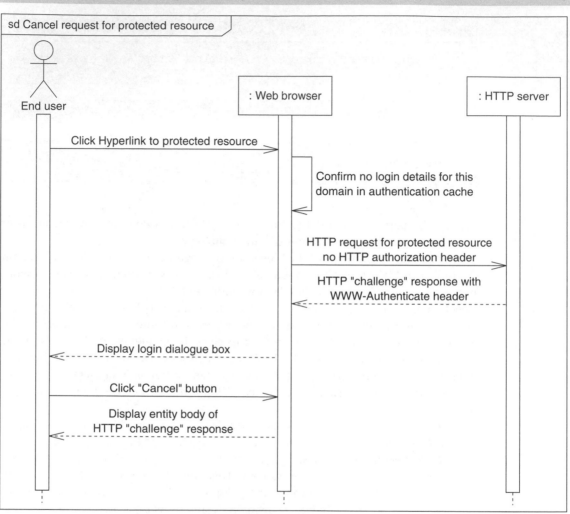

The HTTP authentication process described in Figures 7.36 and 7.37 is relatively straightforward, and so is managing HTTP authentication with PHP. The HTTP authentication process provides the PHP script with a username and password. The PHP script uses the username and password to apply a security policy, asking. 'Is this user authorized to view this web page?'

Figure 7.38 shows Version 0.1 of the PHP script Login.php. In this case, the security policy is very simple: if the end user has provided a username and password, *any* username and password, then he or she is authorized. This is not a realistic security policy, but is a good starting point as it keeps things as simple as possible. The script generates different HTTP responses for authorized and unauthorized users, just as it would with a more realistic security policy.

The username and password typed into the HTTP authentication prompt (Figure 7.35) are sent to the HTTP server, which makes them available to the PHP script in the

Figure 7.37 Retrieving a protected web resource by supplying valid authorization details.

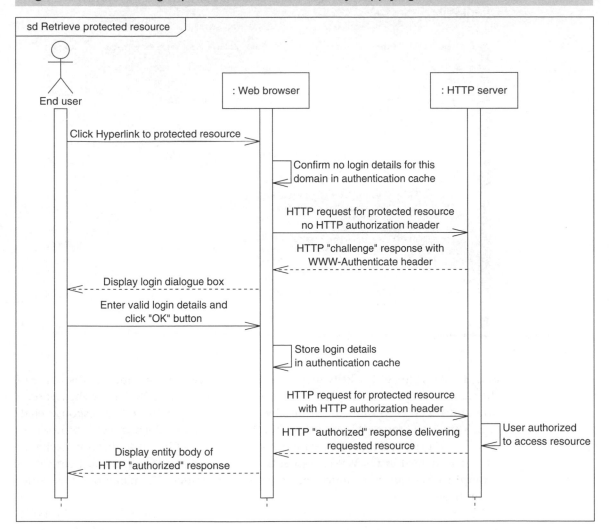

$\_SERVER[\ ]$ superglobal array. The username is held in $\_SERVER[\ "PHP\_AUTH\_\ USER"]$ and the password in $\_SERVER[\ "PHP\_AUTH\_PW"]$. Line 25 tests if either of these is empty – that is, whether or not the user failed to type either a username or password. If so, then, in line 27, the script uses the built-in PHP function header() to set the response line (Figure 7.18), specifying a status of 401, with the reason phrase 'Unauthorized'.

Line 28 uses the header() function a second time. This time it sets the WWW-Authenticate HTTP header. The WWW-Authenticate HTTP header includes two pieces of information. The first is the name of the authentication protocol being used. Line 28 specifies the basic authentication protocol. This is the simplest of the two authentication protocols included in HTTP. It is not secure as the password is sent from the web browser to the HTTP server in clear text, but it is widely implemented by web browsers

337

Figure 7.38 Managing HTTP authentication with PHP: Version 0.1 of Login.php.

```
23  include 'DataCleansingOv2.inc';  //Functions to cleanse user data before processing
24
25    if (empty($_SERVER['PHP_AUTH_USER']) or empty($_SERVER['PHP_AUTH_PW']))
26    {
27      header('HTTP/1.0 401 Unauthorized');
28      header('WWW-Authenticate: Basic realm="Course Catalogue"');
29      include 'DocHeader.inc';
30      echo "<h1>Login required</h1>";
31      echo "<p>The web page you requested is restricted to authorised users only.
32            You can either try again to <a href=\"{$_SERVER['PHP_SELF']}\">login</a>
33            or <a href=\"RegisterOv1.php\">register</a>.";
34    }
35    else
36    {
37      $username = cleanse_data($_SERVER['PHP_AUTH_USER']);
38      $password = cleanse_data($_SERVER['PHP_AUTH_PW']);
39      include 'DocHeader.inc';
40      echo "<h1>Login test</h1>";
41      echo "<p>Hello $username.</p>";
42      echo "<p>You entered '$password' as your password.</p>";
43    }
44  ?>
45  <hr />
46  <p>Author: <cite>Martyn Prigmore</cite>
47  <br />&copy;2006 and beyond
48  </p>
49  </body>
50  </html>
```

and HTTP servers, so is widely used. The second piece of information is the name of the security realm – `realm="Course Catalogue"`, in line 28. Setting the response line and the WWW-Authenticate header will ensure that the HTTP response challenges the web browser to provide authentication details. When the web browser receives an HTTP response with a status of 401, it clears out its authentication cache for the realm named in the WWW-Authenticate header and displays the authentication prompt to the end user. Notice that this prompt includes the name of the security realm (Figure 7.35).

The rest of this code block (lines 29–33) describes the entity body of the HTTP response. This is the web page that will be displayed when end users clicks on 'Cancel' on the authentication prompt.

Line 29 is interesting. It is an include statement, instructing the PHP application server to insert the contents of DocHeader.inc into the script at this point. Figure 7.39 shows the contents of DocHeader.inc. They are the first eight lines written to the entity

Figure 7.39 The DocHeader.inc include file.

```
1  <!DOCTYPE html PUBLIC "-//W3C//DTD XHTML 1.1//EN"
2     "http://www.w3.org/TR/xhtml11/DTD/xhtml11.dtd">
3  <html>
4  <head>
5    <meta http-equiv="Content-Type" content="text/html; charset=utf-8" />
6    <title> Pennine University Course Catalogue </title>
7  </head>
8  <body>
```

Figure 7.40 The web page delivered with the HTTP challenge – it is only seen if end users click on Cancel on the authentication prompt.

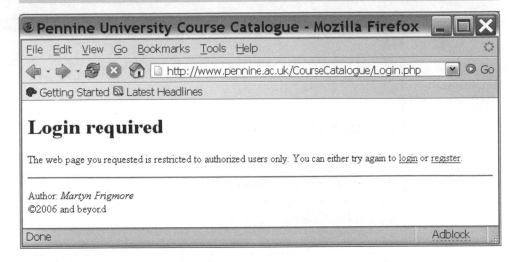

body of the HTTP response by the PHP script. When the PHP application server encounters the include statement, it assumes that the include file will begin with plain HTML rather than PHP. (That is why previous include files, which actually contained PHP, enclosed all their content in the PHP tag – `<?php ... ?>`.) Thus, the PHP application server will write the whole of DocHeader.inc to the entity body of the HTTP response message. When it returns to line 30 of Login.php, it assumes that it is back to processing PHP, so correctly interprets the PHP echo statement.

Lines 30–33 (Figure 7.38) write out a helpful message. The message is delivered as part of the entity body of the HTTP challenge.

Lines 45–50 finish off the entity body. Remember, this web page (Figure 7.40) is only ever seen when end users click on 'Cancel' on the authentication prompt.

If end users enter both a username and a password, then they have met the security policy enforced by this PHP script. In this case, the else block is executed instead (lines 36–43). This cleanses the data entered into the username and password text boxes and stores them in local variables. It then includes the DocHeader.inc file, just as the if block did. This HTML needs to be written to the entity body regardless of whether or not end users meet the security policy. It cannot be written before line 25 as the if block writes HTTP headers, which must be written before anything is written to the entity body. So, it must be written independently in both blocks. Extracting the HTML into an include file is a more elegant solution than copying it out twice.

Lines 40–42 write a message telling end users what username and password they typed. Again, this isn't realistic behaviour, but does demonstrate that the script has successfully gathered the authentication details.

Finally, lines 45–50 again finish off the entity body. A web page generated by the script after one user has successfully entered her username and password is shown in Figure 7.41.

A more realistic security policy would be to compare usernames and passwords to those stored on the database. In the Course Catalogue database, these details are stored

Figure 7.41 The web page delivered when an end user provides valid authentication details.

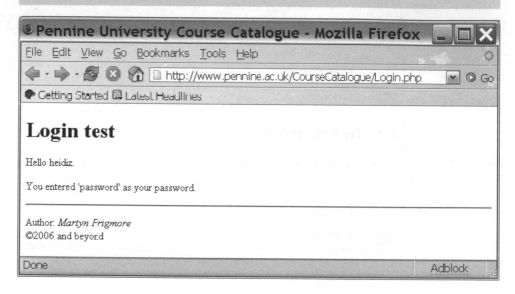

in the `username` and `password` columns of the `User` table. Passwords are encrypted by the DBMS before storing, using the SHA-1 algorithm.

It is reasonably simple to use the techniques developed over the last four chapters to write a PHP script that implements this security policy. The script must check that the username and password text boxes are not empty *and* are present on the database. Figure 7.42 shows the relevant portion of Version 0.2 of the Login.php script.

Lines 26–53 implement the security policy by validating the values of `$_SERVER` `["PHP_AUTH_USER"]` and `$_SERVER["PHP_AUTH_PW"]`.

Line 27 checks whether or not an end user entered a username and password. If not, line 28 sets the variable `$validationFail` to `TRUE`. If the end user did enter a user-name and password, lines 31–50 validate this data against the list of registered users stored on the database.

The SQL statement (lines 40–43) retrieves those rows of the `User` table where the `username` column has the same value as `$_SERVER["PHP_AUTH_USER"]` and the `password` column has the value output by the MySQL function `SHA1()` when the input is the value of `$_SERVER["PHP_AUTH_PW"]`. (The `$_SERVER` ele-ment values are copied to local variables before being used.) Remember, the registra-tion process encrypts the password before storing it on the database, but `$_SERVER` `["PHP_AUTH_PW"]` is the clear text password. If line 43 read:

```
AND password='$password';
```

then no user would be able to login because the encrypted data stored in the `password` column will never match the clear text data stored in the local PHP variable `$password`.

Line 44 retrieves the data from the database, and line 49 validates it. If there are no matching rows, then there is no registered user with the username and password sup-plied, so line 50 sets `$validationFail` to `TRUE`.

Figure 7.42 Validating authentication details against the database: Version 0.2 of Login.php.

```
26  $validationFail = false;  //Used to indicate that a data value failed validation
27  if (empty($_SERVER['PHP_AUTH_USER']) or empty($_SERVER['PHP_AUTH_PW']))
28    $validationFail = true;
29  else
30  {
31    //End user has provided username and password, so check whether they are registered
32    $username = cleanse_data($_SERVER['PHP_AUTH_USER']);
33    $password = cleanse_data($_SERVER['PHP_AUTH_PW']);
34    $connection = mysql_connect('www.pennine.ac.uk', 'martyn', 'martynpassword');
35    if ($connection==FALSE)
36      exit("\nCould not connect to MySQL DBMS.\n<br />MySQL error ".mysql_errno()." : ".mysql_error());
37    $database = mysql_select_db('test', $connection);
38    if ($database == FALSE)
39      exit("Unable to locate the database.\n<br />MySQL error ".mysql_errno()." : ".mysql_error());
40    $sqlStatement = "SELECT username
41                     FROM User
42                     WHERE username='$username'
43                     AND password=SHA1('$password')";
44    $result = mysql_query($sqlStatement, $connection);
45    //Report any errors that occurred when communicating with the MySQL DBMS
46    if ($result == FALSE)
47      exit("SQL statement failed.\n<br />MySQL error ".mysql_errno()." : ".mysql_error());
48    //If no rows were returned, the user is not registered
49    if(mysql_num_rows($result)==0)
50      $validationFail = true;
51    //STEP 6 Close the connection
52    mysql_close($connection);
53  }
54
55  if ($validationFail)
56  {
57    header('HTTP/1.0 401 Unauthorized');
58    header('WWW-Authenticate: Basic realm="Course Catalogue"');
59    include 'DocHeader.inc';
60    echo "<h1>Login required</h1>";
61    echo "<p>The web page you requested is restricted to authorised users only.
62          You can either try again to <a href=\"{$_SERVER['PHP_SELF']}\">login</a>
63          or <a href=\"RegisterOv1.php\">register</a>.";
64  }
65  else
66  {
67    include 'DocHeader.inc';
68    echo "<h1>Login test</h1>";
69    echo "<p>Hello $username.</p>";
70    echo "<p>You entered '$password' as your password.</p>";
71  }
```

Line 55 checks the value of $validationFail. If it is true, then the user is challenged to supply a valid username and password. If it is false, then the username and password supplied have passed validation and the user gets to see the requested resource, which is generated by the else block in lines 65–71.

There are some difficulties with HTTP authentication. One difficulty many developers have had has been with implementing a 'logout' process. As the authentication details are stored on the web browser, not the web server, the only way to log a user out is to force the web browser to clear its authentication cache. As mentioned above, sending an HTTP response with the status code 401 does this. It is relatively easy to create a logout script that sets this in motion. It should simply rechallenge the web browser. Lines 57 and 58 in Figure 7.42 show how to set up the HTTP response message to do that.

A more serious problem is that, with the Basic HTTP authentication scheme, the authentication details are transmitted across the network as clear text (though see the note below). Anyone with suitable software can intercept these HTTP messages and discover the usernames and passwords of registered users. One option is to use the more secure digest authentication scheme, but even this is not considered that secure. Web database applications that need robust security should use a version of secure HTTP, which encrypts the whole HTTP message (see, for example, Gourley and Totty (2002) for an overview).

The basic authentication scheme sends data as clear text, but it is *encoded*, using what is called Base-64 encoding. The goal of Base-64 encoding is to ensure that the data can be transmitted correctly, without any characters being mangled on the way. This is a little like the URL encoding discussed earlier. Base-64-encoded data is very easy to decode and it is *not* an encryption mechanism.

Chapter summary

■ This chapter has examined a number of issues and techniques commonly used in web database applications. The focus has been on how to maintain application state despite the statelessness of the HTTP protocol. Three general techniques have been discussed:

- URL rewriting
- hidden form controls
- sessions.

■ In addition, the special case of authentication details, which can be managed using HTTP authentication, has been discussed.

■ The examples used to illustrate these techniques also demonstrated:

- multiple page result sets
- server-side data validation
- single script solutions to gathering data
- how to solve the reload problem
- wizards
- how to use a DBMS function to encrypt a password.

■ This is quite a lot to cover in one chapter and was only achieved by focusing on the general concepts rather than production-quality solutions. The 'Further reading' section suggests a few places to look for such solutions. Understanding the underlying concepts will help you to understand these.

Further reading

There are several good books on PHP and MySQL, though most of them give pretty sparse coverage of database issues. Bulger et al. (2004) is a good practitioners' book and includes several fully worked case studies. Williams and Lane (2004) is an excellent introduction to web application development. Welling and Thompson (2005) has a gentler pace, but covers very similar ground.

If none of these appeals, then simply browse the shelves at your library or any good bookshop. Online resources are equally plentiful.

Review questions

7.1 What is application state? Summarize the three main approaches to storing application state in a web database application.

7.2 Using suitable examples, explain what will cause each of the following kinds of PHP errors:
(a) parse error
(b) warning
(c) fatal error
(d) notice.

7.3 Explain why setting the default error reporting level so that the PHP application server reports only parse errors on the web page is a sensible approach for a shared PHP application server.

7.4 Explain the purpose of the `LIMIT` clause – a MySQL extension to the select statement.

7.5 Describe the function of the PHP superglobal array `$_SERVER`.

7.6 Explain the purpose of the PHP comparison operator `'==='`.

7.7 Explain the reload problem.

7.8 What is an HTTP location header and how is it used to solve the reload problem?

7.9 Draw a diagram to explain the process of HTTP authentication.

7.10 What is a hash function? Why might you use one?

Exercises

7.11 Using Version 1.5 of SurnameSearch.php as a basis, complete the code to display the result set across multiple pages. In particular, include the following features.
(a) Validate string and numeric data using the functions you wrote in Exercise 4.13 (d). Deal with search criteria that include single apostrophes in the string literal.
(b) Display a count of the number of matching rows at the start of the page. (*Hint*: The PHP built-in function `mysql_num_rows()` counts the number of rows in the *result set*. If there is a limit clause, then this will not be the total number of matching rows. Try using an aggregate query.)

(c) Display the rows in an HTML table element so that, for each row, the forename, surname and e-mail and the 'Full details' hyperlink appear in separate columns. Alternatively, if you are familiar with CSS, use CSS to achieve this layout. (*Hint:* See solution to 4.14 (d)). Consider writing a suitable function to do this for *any* result set.

(d) Add a 'Prev' hyperlink, allowing users to navigate to the previous page of the result set. This link should *not* be enabled on the first page, nor should the 'Next' link be enabled on the last page.

(e) Make the forename column heading a hyperlink. When this hyperlink is clicked on, redisplay the search results ordered by forename. Allow end users to cycle through three states – ascending order, descending order and unordered. Do the same for the surname and e-mail columns.

(f) The web page now includes up to six hyperlinks, each encoding different items of application state. The page navigation and ordering hyperlinks must be properly synchronized. Critically evaluate how effective URL rewriting is as a mechanism for maintaining application state as the number of items increases.

7.12 Suppose Paul and Helene are both using the Staff Directory application. Paul is searching the directory and receives a two-page result set. Helene is modifying the database instance. Describe a scenario in which Helene's modifications mean that Paul does not see all the rows that match his search criteria. How could you guard against such problems?

7.13 Tidy up Version 0.3 of SupportSessionInsert.php, dealing with the following issues:
(a) ensure that the form displays without validation error messages when first requested
(b) tighten the validation to deal with the situation in which the user types name-value pairs directly into the URL query string
(c) when there are validation errors, ensure that any valid data is redisplayed in the relevant form control
(d) when both the start and end time are valid times, check that the duration of the support session is at least one hour
(e) ensure that the script does not suffer from the reload problem.

7.14 Make the following improvements to the self-enrolment wizard.
(a) Validation failures at any stage in the running of the self-enrolment wizard generate a message directing the end user back to the very first wizard page. Address this by rewriting the wizard as a single script solution.
(b) Implement the self-enrolment wizard using sessions rather than hidden form controls to maintain application state. Again, make this a single script solution.

7.15 Make the following improvements to the MyList application discussed in Section 7.6.
(a) Each web page in the Library Catalogue application should include a message telling end users how many books are currently on their lists. Amend the TitleSearch.php, BookDetail.php and List.php scripts to include this information.
(b) Allow users to remove a single item from their lists.

7.16 Secure the MyList application discussed in Section 7.6.
(a) Users should have to log in before they can use the MyList application. If users are not logged in when they try to view their lists or add books to them, use HTTP authentication to gather login information. (*Note:* For a quick solution, apply a

very simple security policy, such as allowing any username and password. For a more realistic security policy, compare each username and password supplied by users to suitable user details stored on the database.)

(b) Allow users to log out. Remember to clear out their session data.

Investigations

7.17 Investigate the more advanced facilities now offered by PHP to handle errors in PHP code. Areas to investigate include the 'try . . . catch' mechanism for handling exceptions and custom-built error-handling functions.

7.18 Investigate output buffering, which allows greater control over when HTTP headers are written.

7.19 In the examples discussed in this chapter, the session data is stored in data files on the PHP server. Investigate approaches to storing session data on the database.

7.20 Write a PHP script that will check the syntax of an SQL statement. Things you could check include (but aren't limited to) that keywords are spelt correctly, required parts of the statement are present, clauses appear in the correct order and parentheses nest properly. Try extending your script to check for basic semantic errors, such as misspelt table or column names, type mismatches between literals and columns and so on. (*Note:* To do this, you will need to query the data dictionary.)

8 Conceptual database design

Chapter objectives

→ To discuss the three stages of database design – conceptual, logical and physical.

→ To introduce the ER diagram as a means of documenting the conceptual database design.

→ To explain some problems with ER diagrams and discuss solutions.

Chapter outline

Web database applications deliver web pages the content of which is generated dynamically by merging data drawn from a database (the dynamic content) with static content. A simple web database application, such as the Pennine University's Staff Directory, would usually be written without any formal designs. The application developer would work out a solution in his or her head and validate it by talking through ideas with the end user. Even in this situation, though, the application developer would still produce a design, it just wouldn't be documented. This approach can be fast, and effective, but does assume that the end user is always available and the application developer is an expert.

When the end user is too busy to be closely involved, or for novice developers and those using unfamiliar technologies, documenting the design is part of the process of developing a solution. Alternative solutions can be worked out without the need to code anything and a decision made about how best to proceed.

For large web database applications with many different developers it is crucial that all the design decisions are documented. If someone leaves the development team and hasn't documented his or her work, then that knowledge leaves the team. A fully documented design is both a record of the decisions taken and a means of evaluating these decisions against users' requirements. This makes a clear understanding of effective design techniques a must for all serious application developers.

Designing a web database application involves two distinct tasks. First, the design must describe a database that meets the information requirements of end users. Second, it must describe a collection of web pages that allow users to access the database. This may be to deliver data from the database instance to end users or allow end users to modify the database instance.

Traditionally, database designers were not involved in such user interface design. Databases often served several different applications, so could not be tailored to any particular one. Similarly, web designers often knew little about database design, focusing on the important issues of website usability and good looks. The distance between what database designers and website designers do is shrinking and both need to understand something of the other's territory. The UML helps by providing a common language for both database and web design.

Database design is split into three distinct phases. **Conceptual database design** produces a model showing the business artefacts and behaviour needed to realize users' requirements. The description of the data requirements is not based on any particular data model but simply documents the different kinds of things that the database will hold data about and the connections between them. This demonstrates that the application will meet the users' requirements without going into the technicalities of how. Because it avoids technical issues, end users can usually easily understand, and comment on, a conceptual database design.

Logical database design begins to deal with how the database will be organized. It takes the data requirements identified in the conceptual design and represents them using the data structures available in a particular data model. Separating conceptual and logical database design means that end users don't need to understand the particular data model used. As even the relational data model can be hard to grasp, this is a good thing.

Physical database design adapts the logical design to use particular technologies – the MySQL DBMS rather than the Oracle database (remember, Oracle calls its DBMS a 'database'), for example. Although each DBMS organizes its data structures according to a particular data model, there are often differences in how they do this.

The process of website design is less mature than that of database design and there is no single approach that commands wide acceptance. Even so, the conceptual–logical–physical split makes sense here, too. Conceptually, there is little difference between a user interface using web technologies and one using a more traditional graphical user interface (such as Microsoft Visual Basic forms or Java Swing classes). Logically, however these two approaches have significant differences – in particular whether the connection between user interface and database is stateful or stateless. The physical design of the website will identify the particular web technologies used. Chapter 11 uses the conceptual–logical–physical split to introduce an approach to website design for web database applications.

- Section 8.1 outlines the database design process and sets it within the context of the software development lifecycle introduced in Chapter 1.

- Section 8.2 uses the Staff Directory to introduce the basic features of an ER diagram and discusses how to use the requirements analysis to identify what data needs to be held on the database.

- Sections 8.3–8.5 elaborate on the material in Section 8.2, discussing more advanced notations for ER diagrams.
- Section 8.6 discusses association multiplicity constraints. It is an important topic that needs to be understood before ER diagrams can be used effectively. The section considers the UML outer multiplicity constraint first, then contrasts it with the inner multiplicity constraint, which is probably more widely used in database design.
- Section 8.7 discusses generalization relationships.
- Section 8.8 concludes the chapter by considering ways to validate an ER diagram.

8.1 The database design process

This chapter, and the following two, focus on database design. There are three stages in database design:

- conceptual
- logical
- physical.

The conceptual database design produces a high-level design for the database that is not tied to any formal data model, yet organizes the data required by the application efficiently and effectively. The fragmentary data requirements documented in the use cases are collected and represented in a single, coherent, high-level overview of requirements.

> **Conceptual database design** Shows the structures required to organize the data mentioned in the users' requirements specification.

The conceptual database design describes what data structures are required, the connections between them and any constraints imposed on the data by business rules. The focus is very much on *what* rather than *how*. It forms the basis of the database designer and end users discussions about the data requirements. To serve this purpose, the conceptual database design must be intelligible to end users.

The **entity-relationship (ER) diagram** is a popular choice for conceptual design. It organizes data into structures called entities. Each **entity** is something that the application must hold data about. The particular data held is represented as **attributes** of an entity. Connections between entities are represented by **relationships** (hence the name 'entity-relationship diagram').

Logical database design begins to deal with how the application will meet the users' requirements. It takes the data requirements identified in the conceptual design and represents them using the data structures available in a particular data model. Settling on a particular data model means reconsidering the way data is organized.

> **Logical database design** Shows how to use a particular data model to meet the end users' data requirements.

Separating conceptual and logical database design means the end users don't need to understand the particular data model used. As even the relational data model can be hard to grasp (foreign keys are a particular sticking point), this is a good thing. Chapter 9 discusses logical database design for the relational data model and Chapter 12 examines logical database design for a database using XML. In both cases the conceptual ER diagram can be adapted to represent only data structures appropriate to the chosen data model. Another design technique, called normalization, helps the database designer to organize the data into structures that minimize redundant data. Problems caused by redundant data are one motivation for using databases in the first place (see Chapter 1), so minimizing redundant data within a database is a good idea.

Physical database design considers how the requirements identified in the logical database design can be met using a particular DBMS. Issues in physical database design include what data types are actually available, how business rules can be implemented and what data storage structures are available. This makes physical database design a much more diverse process than either conceptual or logical database design.

> **Physical database design** Shows how to implement the logical database design using particular software and hardware technologies.

Although each DBMS organizes its data structures according to a particular data model, there are often differences in how they do this. Non-standard extensions to SQL are common and a DBMS usually offers control over the data storage structures or provides other facilities not defined in the data model. For example, the Oracle database allows the DBA to specify which disk a table should be stored on or even to split a single table across more than one disk. The MySQL DBMS offers a choice of different storage structures (called storage engines), each with its own benefits and drawbacks. There are also some general techniques that allow the DBA to optimize the performance of most databases. One is denormalization, which reintroduces redundant data to the database in a controlled way. The idea is that, while redundant data causes problems, it is sometimes better to allow *some* redundancy to improve performance. The trade-off is that the situation must be carefully managed to avoid the problems such redundant data can bring. Chapter 10 discusses physical database design.

All three stages of database design lie within the 'design solution' phase of the information systems lifecycle discussed in Chapter 1. There is no intent at this stage to actually build anything – no code is written, no application software deployed. The tools and techniques discussed in this and the three following chapters can all be applied using pencil and paper, though software is often used to support the designer. This may be a simple drawing package or a fully functional, UML-compliant software engineering tool. However, one of the best approaches for the novice is to take a blank sheet of paper, a pencil and an eraser and sketch out solutions to some sample problems. When the basics of the actual techniques have been grasped, it is easier to tackle the occasionally baroque complexity of the software engineering tools.

8.2 Introduction to entity-relationship (ER) diagrams

In this book, ER diagrams are drawn using the UML notation. This notation was itself influenced by earlier notations for ER diagrams (particularly the IDEF1X notation) and incorporates some of the best features of these earlier notations. This makes it a good choice for anyone learning to use ER diagrams for the first time.

> For those familiar with UML, an ER diagram uses the class diagram notation, but without the strictly object-orientated features such as attribute and operation visibility. It also adds some features, such as candidate keys, which are not always used in object-orientated approaches to database design.

The ER diagram is the main technique used in conceptual database design. The Staff Directory web database application makes a good introductory case study for ER diagrams. Although it does not include all the features that can be represented in an ER diagram, it has the main ones. This version of the Staff Directory database can also support the requirements of the School of Computing's Staff List application, discussed in Chapters 1 and 2.

In an ER diagram, an **entity** represents a set of things of interest in the scenario being modelled. A particular one of these things is called an **occurrence** of the entity. To qualify as an entity, there must be more than one occurrence of it, at least in principle. So, in the Staff Directory, there could be an entity to represent members of staff as there are lots of these, but there will not be an entity to represent the directory itself. There is only *one* staff directory, so it is *not* represented as an entity.

All occurrences of an entity share the same properties. These shared properties are represented as **attributes** of the entity. From the database perspective, an entity represents something that the database holds data about, while the attributes represent the actual data held. A database also holds information about connections between different entities. In an ER diagram, these are represented as a **relationship**. In some cases, a relationship will have attributes of its own.

These three simple abstractions – entity, attribute and relationship – allow the ER diagram to model the data requirements of any web database application.

> **Entity** A set of things about which the information system must hold, or process, data. Each entity has a name that is unique within the ER diagram.
>
> **Entity occurrence** A particular instance of an entity.

In the Staff Directory database, there will be an entity to represent members of staff as the set of members of staff is clearly of interest. The simplest representation of an entity in an ER diagram is as a rectangle enclosing the entity name and the **stereotype**

Figure 8.1 An entity, with name and stereotype indicated.

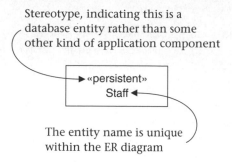

Figure 8.2 An ER diagram with two entities and a relationship.

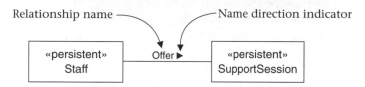

«persistent», as shown in Figure 8.1. Note that the curved arrows are *not* part of the ER diagram – they simply point to the interesting features.

Stereotypes distinguish between the different kinds of application component. The stereotype «persistent» indicates that the entity's data persists in the database even after the computer is switched off. The entity name can be a noun, as in Figure 8.1, or a noun phrase. Staff is a good name for an entity representing members of staff. SupportSession is a suitable name for the entity representing support sessions offered by members of staff. An entity name can include letters, digits and underscores and is written with no spaces and each word capitalized, so we have SupportSession rather than support_session or Support session. It is usually singular, too, so SupportSession rather than SupportSessions.

Each relationship also has a name. It has the same format as an entity name, but is usually a verb or verb phrase. For example, there is a meaningful connection between the entities Staff and SupportSession – each support session is offered by a particular member of staff. This is represented as the relationship Offer, drawn as a straight line between the two entities (Figure 8.2).

The relationship name is written close to the line (above, below or beside the line are all fine) and includes a name direction indicator, which is the arrowhead in Figure 8.2. The name direction only indicates how to read the relationship name. In this case, the relationship name is to be read as 'Staff offer support sessions' rather than 'Support sessions offer staff'. The relationship itself can be traversed in either direction – from a particular occurrence of Staff to an occurrence of SupportSession that he or she will Offer or from a particular occurrence of SupportSession to the occurrence of Staff who will Offer the SupportSession.

Relationship Represents a meaningful connection between entities, which are said to participate in the relationship.

Relationship occurrence A particular instance of a relationship. Links together one occurrence of each entity that participates in the relationship.

Relationships are best drawn as horizontal or vertical lines or else lines that turn 90-degree corners (see examples in the figures later in this chapter). It is a good idea to avoid representing relationships with diagonal lines, reserving these for other uses within the ER diagram.

An entity is something that the database holds data about, and that data is represented as the entity's attributes. This means that an entity has at least one attribute, which can also be included in the ER diagram. The attributes of the Staff entity represent such things as the staff number, parts of each person's name, e-mail address and so on. The SupportSession entity has attributes to represent the day a support session runs and its start and end times. It does not have an attribute to represent which member of staff offers a particular support session – that is, there is no 'foreign key'. This job is done by the Offer relationship. Some database designers do include foreign keys in the conceptual database design, but the information is redundant as the relationships indicate meaningful connections between entities, so foreign keys are not required.

The attribute name is a noun or noun phrase and can include letters, digits and underscores, but not spaces. The first letter is not capitalized, but second and subsequent words are, so we have startTime rather than StartTime or start_time. This helps to distinguish attribute names from entity names.

Attributes of an entity are listed in the **attribute compartment**. This compartment can be left off an ER diagram (as in Figures 8.1 and 8.2), but, when it is included it sits directly below the entity's **name compartment** (which holds the name and the stereotype «persistent»). Both compartments are shown in Figure 8.3, which shows a simple

Figure 8.3 An ER diagram showing two entities with their attributes and a relationship between them.

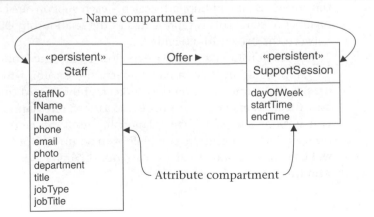

ER diagram with two entities, each having attributes, and a relationship between the entities. Some relationships can have attributes of their own. This is not shown in Figure 8.3, though is discussed below.

Within an entity (or relationship) each attribute must have a unique name. However, two attributes of *different* entities (or relationships) can have the same name.

> **Attribute** A property of an entity or relationship. Each attribute has a name, which must be unique within the entity or relationship.

The database designer must decide whether each thing mentioned in the users' requirements is an entity or an attribute. Consider the e-mail address of a member of staff. Each e-mail address has two parts – the username and mail server address. In the e-mail address 'p.smith@pennine.ac.uk', 'p.smith' is the username and 'pennine.ac.uk' is the mail server address. As it has identifiable properties, the e-mail address could be modelled as an entity. However, an e-mail address has no *interesting* properties (at least, not in the scenario being modelled). End users need both parts of the e-mail address to use it – they have no use for the username or the mail server address alone. This means that the e-mail address is not something the database holds data about. Rather, it is data *about* members of staff, so is modelled as an attribute of the Staff entity.

Using these three simple abstractions – entity, attribute and relationship – it is possible to produce a conceptual database design that organizes the required data effectively and efficiently. The diagrams themselves are simple enough to explain, so can form the basis for discussions between the database designer and end users. This allows end users to verify that their requirements are actually being met by the proposed database design. However, simple ER diagrams such as the one in Figure 8.3 provide only basic information about the database. The notation for ER diagrams is much richer than that. An ER diagram can also include information on an attribute's data type, business rules and database constraints, and different kinds of relationship. This richer notation is explored in the following sections. Table 8.1 summarizes the definitions of the three basic structures and their characteristics.

Table 8.1 The basic data structures used in an ER diagram.

ER diagram data structure	Definition	Characteristics
Entity	A set of things about which the information system must hold, or process, data.	Name is unique within the ER diagram. Must have at least one attribute. The name compartment is always shown, the attribute compartment may be hidden.
Relationship	A meaningful connection between entities.	Name is unique within the ER diagram. May have attributes, but most do not.
Attribute	A property of an entity or relationship.	Name is unique within the entity or relationship.

To create an ER diagram, the database designer needs to identify entities, attributes and relationships. Typically, there will be a users' requirements specification to work from. (If not, then the database designer will need to speak directly with the end users and produce his or her own requirements specification.)

As discussed in Chapter 1, requirements specifications are often documented by means of use cases. Entities represent things of interest in the scenario being modelled, so such things will be mentioned in the use case. As 'things' have names, any nouns or noun phrases in the use case could potentially be used to name an entity – a member of staff, a support session, for example. Alternatively, these could suggest names for some property of one of these things, such as an e-mail address or the day on which a support session runs. This means that nouns and noun phrases in the use case specifications could indicate entities *or* attributes.

Consider the specification for the use case Get support sessions from the Staff Directory application.

Get support sessions

The application provides a list of support sessions offered by an academic member of staff. This is expected to be used mostly by students, but is available to other users.

The user will have accessed the full contact details for an academic member of staff and will request a list of that person's support sessions. The day, start time and end time of all the support sessions are displayed. If there are no support sessions for the chosen academic, a message stating this is displayed.

To identify possible entities and attributes, simply scan through this use case and highlight any nouns or noun phrases. Next, consider whether or not each will be an entity or, if not, an attribute of an entity. If the noun indicates an entity, then check that it is not one covered by an already identified entity – for example, an 'academic' is also a 'member of staff'. Table 8.2 lists every noun and noun phrase in the use case specification, together with a comment on whether it is an entity or an attribute. Where possible, an attribute is assigned to one of the entities. Lists like these aren't usually kept, but can be useful for documenting decisions. Here are some important points to note from Table 8.2.

- The application itself is *not* an entity, nor would 'staff directory', 'database' or other such nouns indicate entities. There will only ever be *one* occurrence of each of these things (within the scenario being modelled) so they cannot be entities.

- 'Academic' is not modelled as a separate entity as an academic is simply a particular kind of member of staff. It is possible to model different kinds of thing, using a generalization relationship. If this approach were taken, then there would be an Academic entity. This is discussed below.

- 'User' is not an entity. In this use case, there is no need to store information about users as the Staff Directory application is open access.

- 'Contact details' is regarded as a synonym for 'member of staff'. These appear to represent different things as a person is not usually equated with his or her phone number and e-mail address. However, in the context of the Staff Directory, a 'member of staff' *is* the same as his or her 'contact details'.

Table 8.2 Nouns from the 'Get support sessions' use case specification.

Noun	Is it an entity or an attribute?
The application	No – the database is part of the application, not the other way round!
list	No – this is an output from the application, not persistent data.
support session	Entity – data about support sessions is held on the database.
academic	No – synonym for member of staff. Could model as a separate entity, but no need in this simple application.
member of staff	Entity – data about members of staff is held on the database.
students	No – students will *use* the application, but the database will not hold data *about* them.
users	No – users are outside the system boundary.
contact details	No – synonym for member of staff.
day	Attribute – this is data held about a support session.
start time	Attribute – this is data held about a support session.
end time	Attribute – this is data held about a support session.
message	No – it may make sense to hold messages on the database, but this is an implementation issue, not part of conceptual database design.

Once the entities and attributes have been listed, suitable names can be chosen. The names should be short and meaningful. They need not be any of the nouns identified from the use case specification. None of the synonyms 'member of staff', 'academic' and 'contact details' is as clear and meaningful as 'staff', so the entity that represents the contact details of members of staff (including academic staff) is called Staff. In contrast, 'support session' is perfectly clear, so the entity that represents support sessions is called SupportSession.

Entity and attribute names are often abbreviated as many application developers prefer short names. Many database designers would abbreviate SupportSession to SupSes. There is no technical reason for doing this as the days when identifiers could be only eight characters long are slowly passing into IT legend. There may also be a good business reason for keeping a long name as the abbreviation could be unclear. For example, does Sup stand for 'support' or 'supplementary' or 'supply'? In contrast, the No of 'staffNo' is a recognized abbreviation for 'number'. The attribute names fName and lName are a bit dubious – why not just use forename and surname? The abbreviations were used in this book for a very pragmatic reason – they kept the width of the table images small enough to fit on to a page. In a real system, the longer names would be preferable. The best guidance is to use abbreviations that improve the clarity of the design and avoid those that don't.

Relationships are identified by a second trawl through the use case specifications. This time, the aim is to identify verb phrases that indicate some meaningful connections between entities. There will often be several such phrases indicating each relationship. Occasionally, there may be two different relationships between the same two entities and these will both need to be identified and included in the ER diagram. Table 8.3 lists the verb phrases found in the Get support session use case specification. Again, the name of each relationship should be short and meaningful. For example,

Table 8.3 Verb phrases from the 'Get support session' use case specification.

Verb phrase	Is it a relationship?
support sessions offered by an academic member of staff	Relationship – indicates that the entity representing 'support session' has a meaningful connection with the entity representing 'academic member of staff'.
The user will have accessed the full contact details	No – 'user' is not an entity.
and [the user] will request . . . that person's support sessions	No – 'user' is not an entity.
support sessions for the chosen academic	No – indicates same relationship as first row.

Offer is shorter than OfferedBy, so the relationship name in Figure 8.3 is read Staff Offer SupportSession rather than SupportSession OfferedBy Staff. Remember that this does not alter the meaning of the ER diagram as, however the name is read, the relationship still works in both directions.

ER diagrams provide a concise overview of the data requirements of a particular application. Entities represent things that the application holds data about, attributes the data held and relationships the connections between entities. This overview can lack detail. For example, the simple ER diagram in Figure 8.3 does not indicate whether support sessions are offered by individual staff or groups of staff.

One way to provide more information about a scenario is to use an **object diagram**. This shows particular occurrences of entities and the relationship occurrences that link them. For an entity occurrence, each attribute has a particular value. Figure 8.4 shows an object diagram for the ER diagram in Figure 8.3. In this example, one occurrence of

Figure 8.4 An object diagram.

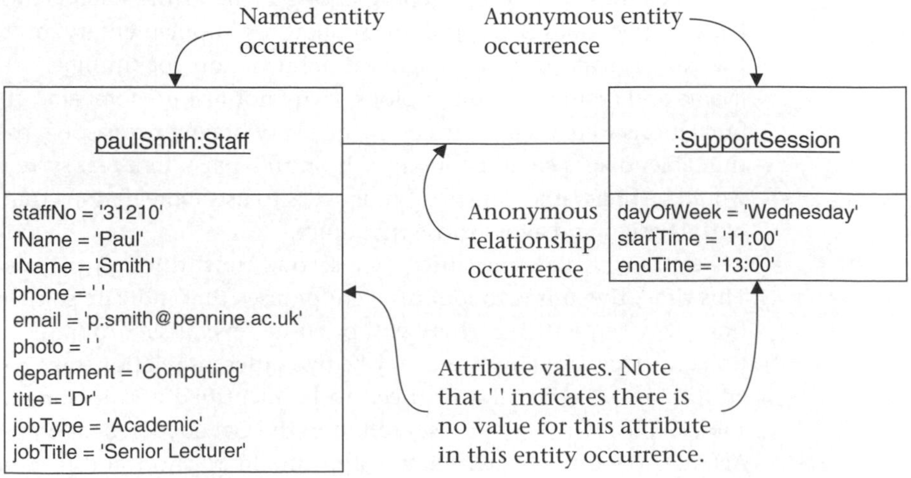

each of the entities and relationships is included in the object diagram. Entity occurrences are distinguished from entities by underlining the entity name and preceding it with a colon. The occurrence of the Staff entity has been given an occurrence name, while the occurrence of the SupportSession entity is anonymous. Naming entity occurrences is not necessary, but may be useful in some situations. Each attribute is shown with a particular value. Where an entity occurrence has no value for an attribute, this is shown as an empty literal – ' '.

Object diagrams are a useful tool for analysing a scenario more closely. By showing sample data, they can illustrate which attributes are required and which are optional. They can also provide examples of how many relationship occurrences a particular entity occurrence participates in. For example, is it possible for a particular member of staff to offer no, one or more than one support session? Once these issues have been investigated, they can be noted on the ER diagram using the more advanced notation discussed in the following sections

8.3 Attributes

An attribute is a property of an entity or relationship. Every attribute has a name. It also has a multiplicity and data type and may have a default value or a property string. This section discusses these additional features of attributes and explains how to represent them on an ER diagram.

On an entity occurrence, each attribute will either have a value or not (be null). Sometimes an attribute may hold more than one value. This is called a **multivalued attribute**. A multivalued attribute is a simple way of modelling data with a non-scalar data type. The notation for a multivalued attribute is similar to that for declaring an array in programming languages such as C++, Java and PHP. Arrays are the obvious way to implement a multivalued attribute, but sets and multisets are also options.

For example, the Web Timetable database holds data about students. Each student has at least one, possibly two or more, forenames. This data is held in the fName attribute. The UML notation for this is fName [1..*]. The notation [n..m] – for integers m and n – shows the lower and upper bounds on the number of attribute values and is called the **attribute multiplicity**. An asterisk – * – indicates an upper bound of 'many'. Another multivalued attribute is email. It holds at least one, and at most two, e-mail addresses for each student, thus email [1..2].

The attribute multiplicity can also indicate when an attribute value is optional (can be null) as in such a case the lower bound will be zero. For example, some students provide the university with a contact telephone number, but some do not. The attribute is written phone [0..1]. If no multiplicity is specified, then the attribute will hold exactly one data value. Students have exactly one surname, held in the lName attribute, which is usually written lName. This is equivalent to writing the attribute lName [1..1]. All these attributes are shown in Figure 8.5, with the left-hand version being the preferred one and the right-hand version showing all the attribute multiplicities.

Data items and, hence, attributes also have a data type. The data type is written after the attribute name and its multiplicity (if this is shown) separated by a colon.

Figure 8.5 Two equivalent versions of the Student **entity showing attribute multiplicity constraints.**

«persistent» Student
studentNo
fName [1..*]
lName
email [1..2]
phone [0..1]

«persistent» Student
studentNo [1..1]
fName [1..*]
lName [1..1]
email [1..2]
phone [0..1]

Figure 8.6 Attribute data types for the Student **entity.**

«persistent» Student
studentNo : Char(10)
fName [1..*] : Varchar
lName : Varchar
email [1..2] : Varchar
phone [0..1] : Varchar

Different information systems will need different data types. For example, a geographical information system will need data types for points, lines, polygons and so on, while an accounting information system probably won't. The data types used should be documented by the database designer, either in a UML package or listed in a table. In this book, the scalar data types discussed in Chapter 3 are the ones used during conceptual database design.

The most common data type is the character string. Character strings can be of a fixed or varying length – abbreviated to Char and Varchar respectively. In database design, it is common to state a maximum length for the data values of character string attributes. For example, on the Student entity, the attribute studentNo is a fixed-length character string, which always has ten characters. This is written studentNo : Char(10). It is not necessary to include a length, so, for example, the lName attribute is a varying length character string with no maximum length, written lName : Varchar. Figure 8.6 shows all the attribute data types for the Student entity. For numeric attributes, the scale and precision can be specified.

Attributes may have a **default value** (sometimes called an initial value). The default value for an attribute is the value used in an entity occurrence when end users don't specify a value for the attribute. The duration attribute of the TeachingSession entity has a data type of interval and a default value of '1h' as, at the Pennine University, most teaching sessions last for one hour. In the ER diagram, the attribute will be written duration : Interval=1h. This default value is only used when end users don't supply a value for a particular occurrence of TeachingSession. So, in an occurrence of TeachingSession that represents a two-hour tutorial, duration will have the *value* 2h, even though the *default* is 1h.

Few DBMS will accept **1h** as a valid interval literal, but it is fine during conceptual design. It is easy to explain to the end users and easy to convert to a valid interval literal during physical design.

It is common to have attributes with fairly small sets of allowed values. The day attribute of the TeachingSession entity has only seven possible values. To model this, include an **attribute constraint**. Adding constraints to an attribute is one use of the **property list**. The property list for an attribute is a list of constraints, tagged values (discussed below) and comments that apply to the attribute. It appears in braces – {...} – after the default value. The attribute constraint can also be written in a note and attached to the attribute by a dashed line. Figure 8.7 shows attributes with default values and attribute constraints. The constraint on the day attribute is documented in a note. The duration attribute has both a default value and a constraint, though in this case the constraint is documented in the attribute's property list. Note that this constraint uses mathematical notation – 1h <= duration <= 3h. This expresses the business rule that every teaching session lasts at least one hour, but may not last more than three hours. The TeachingSession entity is unusual because most of its attributes have constraints. The Student entity in Figure 8.6 is more typical as none of its attributes has a constraint.

The dashed line joining a note to the part of the ER diagram it relates to can be drawn at a diagonal. This helps to distinguish it from the relationships in the diagram, which are not drawn as diagonal lines.

Some entities have **derived attributes**. For each entity occurrence, the value of its derived attributes can be derived (or calculated) from the values of the other attributes. In an ER diagram, a derived attribute has a forward slash – / – before its name.

The TeachingSession entity has two derived attributes – /endTime and /runsFor (Figure 8.7). For an occurrence of TeachingSession, the value of the derived attribute /endTime will be the result of adding the value of duration to the value of startTime. The way to calculate a derived attribute is noted as a comment in the attribute's property list or in a note attached to the attribute.

Figure 8.7 Some complex attribute definitions.

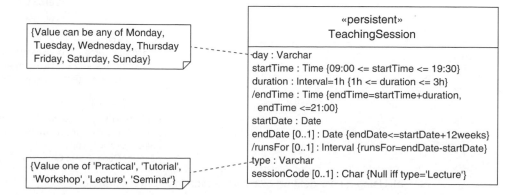

For /endtime, the property list includes two pieces of information. The first – endTime=startTime+duration – indicates how to derive the value of this attribute from other attribute values. The second – endTime<=21:00 – places a constraint on the possible values of the derived attribute. Note that a constraint on a derived attribute is really a constraint on the attributes its value is derived from. In this case, the constraint endTime<=21:00 on /endTime really says the value of startTime+duration must not be greater than 21:00. It is not possible to write separate constraints on the startTime and duration attributes that capture this.

The multiplicity of a derived attribute depends on that of the attributes it is derived from. If all the attributes involved always have a value (that is, they have multiplicity [1..n] for some integer n), then the derived attribute will always have a value, too. The particular derivation will determine the upper bound of the multiplicity. So, for example, endTime has a multiplicity [1..1] as its value can always be derived and a teaching session can have at most one end time. In contrast, the value of runsFor depends on the value of endDate. This has a multiplicity of [0..1], so on some entity occurrences there is no value for endDate. On these entity occurrences there cannot be any value for runsFor either, so its multiplicity is [0..1].

An alternative to using an attribute constraint to restrict what values an attribute can hold is to declare a user-defined type. This is commonly done when many different attributes will share the same constraint. Figure 8.8 (a) uses a UML class diagram to declare the user-defined type SessionType. This user-defined type is the set of all the different kinds of teaching session at the Pennine University.

Figure 8.8 Declaring and using a user-defined type.

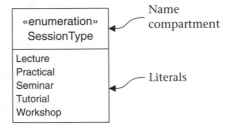

(a) Declaring an enumeration data type in UML.

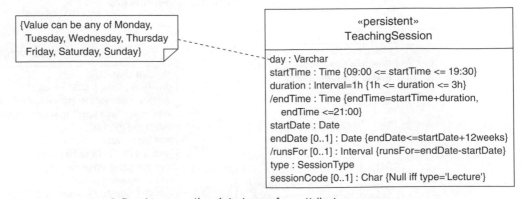

(b) Using a user-defined type as the data type of an attribute.

The stereotype «enumeration» indicates that this UML class diagram models a user-defined type, not a database entity. The name compartment contains the stereotype and the user-defined type's name.

The lower rectangle is *not* a list of attributes. Instead, it lists all of the literals that represent allowed data values for the data type. Figure 8.8 (b) shows how to use this as the data type for the attribute type in the TeachingSession entity.

User-defined types are a more advanced feature of the UML, and are not often used in relational database design. However, when several attributes share a common set of allowed values, and the list is long, then it's worth considering using this feature. Some DBMS already allow the DBA to define enumeration data types of this sort (the MySQL DBMS is one) and ISO SQL:2003 includes support for user-defined types.

Once all the attributes have been identified, it is useful to have a list of them. This forms part of the **application glossary**, which lists all the entities, attributes and relationships.

A key purpose of an application glossary is to provide a central repository of information about the design. It includes a description of each item and any synonyms (different names for the same thing). A good modelling tool will be able to generate an application glossary from the ER diagrams, but, if necessary, a separate document can be maintained. In this case, it is important to be clear whether it is the application glossary that is definitive or the ER diagrams as it is likely that they will get out of step at some point in the development cycle.

It is common to keep an application glossary in table format. Table 8.4 shows *part* of the application glossary for the Web Timetable application. It lists the attributes of the TeachingSession entity and includes all the information about each attribute shown in Figure 8.7.

8.4   Entities

An entity is a set of things of interest to the organization that share the same properties. To the database designer, they are those things the database must hold information about. Each occurrence of an entity is distinct from all other occurrences. Even two entity occurrences with the same attribute values are distinct from one another. When an entity can have two distinct occurrences but the attribute values are the same, it is called a **weak entity**. In contrast, every occurrence of a **strong entity** is distinct from all other occurrences. Figure 8.9 uses an object diagram to show that, in the Staff Directory database, SupportSession is a weak entity. Two different support sessions, offered by different members of staff, occur on the same day and at the same time, so have exactly the same attribute values. The Staff entity, though, is a strong entity – for example, the value of staffNo is different for each entity occurrence (all members of staff have a different staff number). This leads to the following definition of strong and weak entities.

Strong entity An entity that can be uniquely identified by its attribute values.

Weak entity An entity that cannot be uniquely identified by its attribute values.

Table 8.4 Extract from the application glossary showing information on attributes.

Entity	Attribute	Description	Synonym	Multiplicity	Data type	Default value	Constraint	Tagged value	Comment
TeachingSession	day	The day on which the teaching session runs.	day of week	1..1	Varchar		Any day of the week.		
	startTime	The time the teaching session begins.	start	1..1	Time		Between 09.00 and 19.30.		
	duration	The length of the session.	length	1..1	Interval	1 hour	Between 1 and 3 hours.		
	/endTime	The time at which the teaching session ends.	end	1..1	Time		No later than 21.00.		Derived as startTime + duration.
	startDate	First day the session runs.		1..1	Date				
	endDate	Date of final session.		0..1	Date		No more than 12 weeks after startDate.		
	/runsFor	Number of weeks the session runs for.		0..1	Interval				Derived as difference between startDate and endDate.
	type	What type of session this is.		1..1	Varchar		One of practical, tutorial, workshop, lecture or seminar.		
	sessionCode	Used to distinguish between different sessions for the same module.	tutor group	0..1	Char		Null whenever type is lecture, not null for other types.		

Figure 8.9 Strong and weak entities in the Staff Directory database.

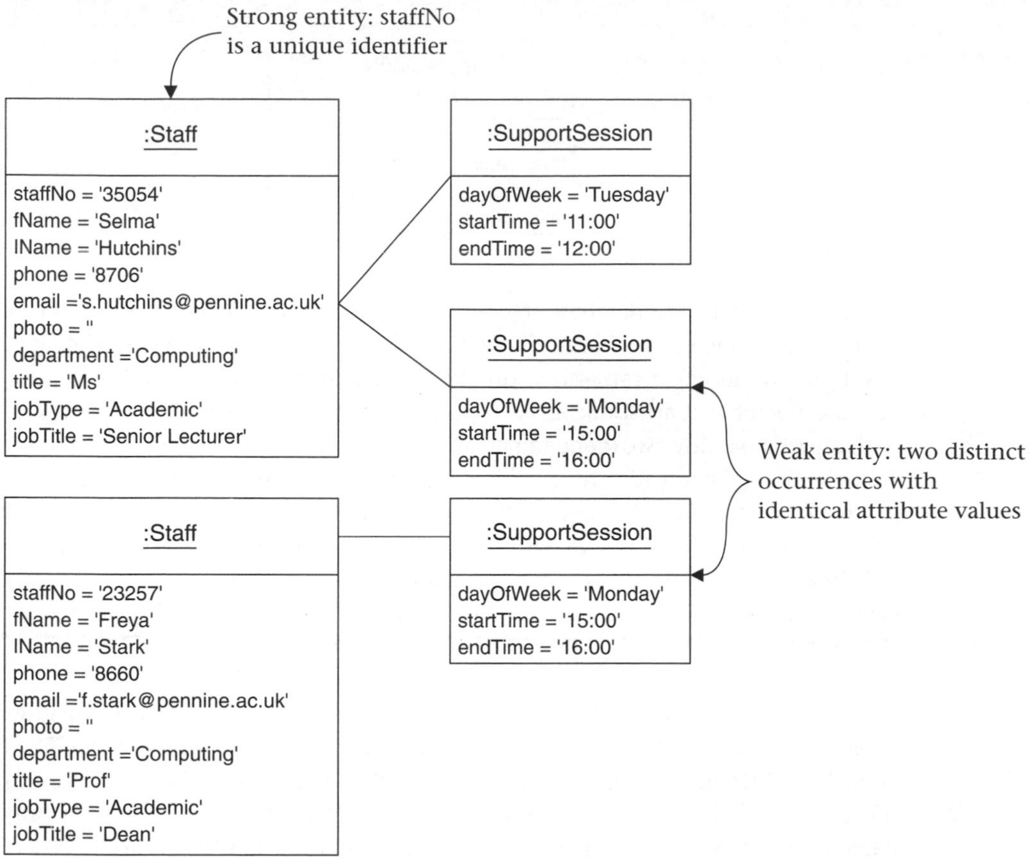

Strong entity: staffNo
is a unique identifier

:Staff

staffNo = '35054'
fName = 'Selma'
lName = 'Hutchins'
phone = '8706'
email ='s.hutchins@pennine.ac.uk'
photo = ''
department ='Computing'
title = 'Ms'
jobType = 'Academic'
jobTitle = 'Senior Lecturer'

:SupportSession

dayOfWeek = 'Tuesday'
startTime = '11:00'
endTime = '12:00'

:SupportSession

dayOfWeek = 'Monday'
startTime = '15:00'
endTime = '16:00'

Weak entity: two distinct
occurrences with
identical attribute values

:Staff

staffNo = '23257'
fName = 'Freya'
lName = 'Stark'
phone = '8660'
email ='f.stark@pennine.ac.uk'
photo = ''
department ='Computing'
title = 'Prof'
jobType = 'Academic'
jobTitle = 'Dean'

:SupportSession

dayOfWeek = 'Monday'
startTime = '15:00'
endTime = '16:00'

Drawing an analogy between the relational data model and ER diagrams, an entity corresponds to a table – both hold data about some 'thing' that the organization is interested in. Attributes correspond to columns and each occurrence of an entity corresponds to a row in the table – both hold the actual data for a particular instance of the 'thing' in question. In the relational data model, a set of columns the values of which are unique to a particular row of the table is called a candidate key. The candidate key acts as a unique identifier for a row. So, a set of attributes that uniquely identifies an entity occurrence can also be thought of as a candidate key. It follows from the definition that every strong entity has at least one candidate key and that a weak entity has no candidate keys.

This illustrates an important difference between the relational data model and ER diagrams. In the relational data model, *every* table has a primary key, as there can be no duplicate rows. In an ER diagram *some* entities may not have a primary key as there can be duplicate entity occurrences.

> This analogy forms the basis for the process of deriving a relational database design from an ER diagram.
>
> A conceptual ER diagram does not include foreign keys because the relationships indicate connections between entities.

Figure 8.10 Using tagged values in the property list to indicate candidate keys.

«persistent» Module
code : Char(7) {PK} title : Varchar {CK=1} department : Varchar {CK=1} level : Varchar

In the Web Timetable database, Module is a strong entity as each occurrence can be uniquely identified by the value of code, so {code} is a candidate key for the Module entity. Entity occurrences can also be uniquely identified by combinations of values of the title and department attributes as, within a department, there will be only one module with a particular title. So, {department, title} is also a candidate key for the Module entity.

It can be useful to indicate candidate keys on the conceptual ER diagram and distinguish the primary key. The way to do this is to include a **tagged value** in the attribute property list. Tagged values are written as a name-value pair – name=value. Each candidate key may have several attributes in it and there may be several candidate keys. For each candidate key, place a tagged value – CK=n – in the property list of each attribute that is part of the candidate key. The value of n indicates which candidate key the attribute is part of.

In Figure 8.10, the candidate key {department, title} is indicated by including the tagged value CK=1 in the property list for the attributes department and title. The tagged value PK is included in the property list of the attribute code to show that this is part of (in fact, the whole of) the primary key. The tagged value for the primary key only has a name – there is only one primary key, so there is no need to use the value. Where a primary key has two or more attributes, each has the tagged value PK in its property list.

> Tagged values are a standard part of the UML but the particular tagged values CK=n and PK are *not* part of the UML standard. They are introduced specifically to use in ER diagrams.

There is an alternative notion of strong and weak entities. This approach defines a weak entity as one the existence of which depends on another entity. For example, in the Staff Directory database, the SupportSession entity depends on the Staff entity – an occurrence of SupportSession cannot exist except when linked to an occurrence of Staff. However, the Staff entity is *not* existence dependent on SupportSession – there may be occurrences of Staff that are not linked to any occurrences of SupportSession. Basing the definition of strong and weak entities on existence dependence is not equivalent to the definition based on primary keys. For example, in the Web Timetable database, every module has a module leader (Figure 8.11). Thus, an occurrence of the Module entity cannot exist unless it is associated with an occurrence of the Staff entity. This suggests that Module is a weak entity, yet both the Module and Staff entities have primary keys. It is possible, on the existence dependence definition, to argue that

Figure 8.11 Every module has a module leader, but is Module existence dependent on Staff?

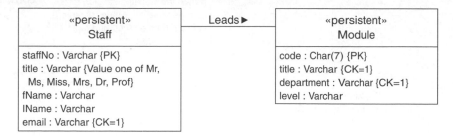

Module *is* a weak entity. The module leader writes the module specification, delivers the lectures and marks the assignments. Without the leader the module cannot run, so Module is existence dependent on Staff. It is also possible to argue that Module *is not* a weak entity. If a module leader resigns unexpectedly, the module does not cease to exist simply because there is no module leader. Whether Module is, or is not, a weak entity seems to depend on the way the Pennine University deals with the unexpected loss of a module leader. If a new module leader is appointed immediately, then it is arguable that Module *is* existence dependent on Staff, but otherwise it is not.

If the distinction between strong and weak entities is to be useful, then it should be clear, so the definition in terms of candidate keys is preferred. This does not mean that existence dependence is not an important concept. The UML has an alternative way of modelling existence dependence, using special kinds of relationship, and these are discussed below.

> The evolution of the concepts 'weak entity' and 'existence dependence' illustrate how the discipline of computing tends to proceed. A concept is articulated in one form, discussed by the community and refined. As it is refined, it may be split into several simpler, though related, concepts. Eventually these may lead to new approaches to doing computing or be entirely superseded by new concepts. Those studying, or working in, the discipline must develop strategies to cope with this process of continual change. One is standardization. The ISO standard for SQL and the OMG standard for the UML, for example, both seek to control the rate of change. The existence of such standards ensures some continuity, so learning them is not a waste of time.

Business rules are important in database design. Many can be modelled using attribute constraints or tagged values. This is the best approach when a business rule constrains the value of one attribute (possibly based on the values of others). The attribute constraints on TeachingSession (Figure 8.7) all implement business rules that constrain the value of one attribute. Some business rules are more complex. Consider the following business rule at the Pennine University:

> When a teaching session runs on a Saturday or Sunday, it must not start before 10:00 and must finish by 16:00, but otherwise, a teaching session must start at 09:00 or later and must finish by 18:00.

Figure 8.12 Constraints attached to attributes and the entity itself.

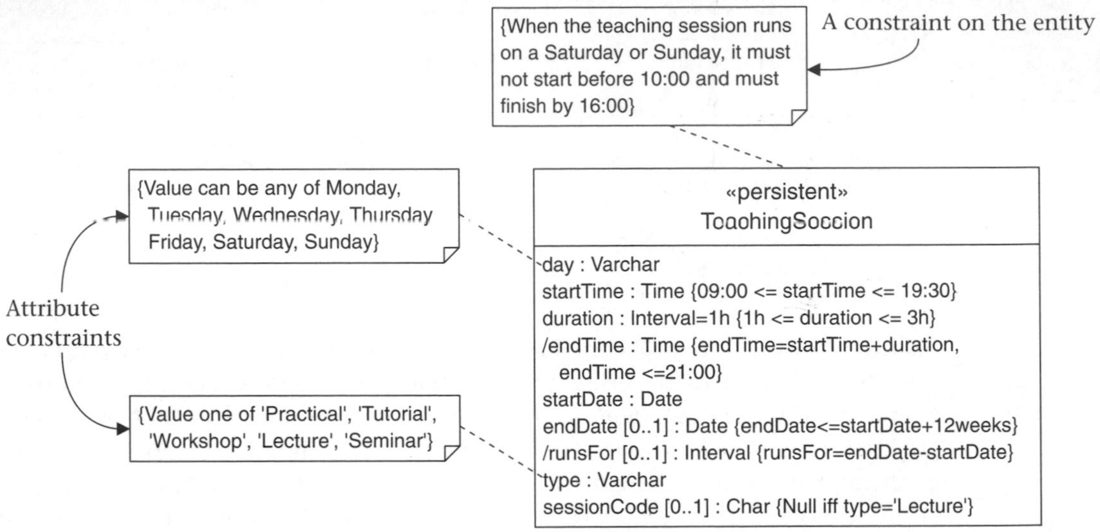

{When the teaching session runs on a Saturday or Sunday, it must not start before 10:00 and must finish by 16:00}

A constraint on the entity

{Value can be any of Monday, Tuesday, Wednesday, Thursday Friday, Saturday, Sunday}

Attribute constraints

{Value one of 'Practical', 'Tutorial', 'Workshop', 'Lecture', 'Seminar'}

«persistent»
TeachingSession

day : Varchar
startTime : Time {09:00 <= startTime <= 19:30}
duration : Interval=1h {1h <= duration <= 3h}
/endTime : Time {endTime=startTime+duration, endTime <=21:00}
startDate : Date
endDate [0..1] : Date {endDate<=startDate+12weeks}
/runsFor [0..1] : Interval {runsFor=endDate-startDate}
type : Varchar
sessionCode [0..1] : Char {Null iff type='Lecture'}

This business rule involves a conditional constraint – that is, if the value of the day attribute is a weekday, then apply one constraint to the value of the startTime and duration attributes, but otherwise apply a different constraint. Conditional statements like this cannot easily be implemented using database integrity constraints, but should be noted in the conceptual ER diagram. A good way to record such complex constraints is in a note attached to the entity, rather than against a particular attribute. Figure 8.12 shows the TeachingSession entity with three constraints written in notes – two attached to attributes (as they were in Figure 8.7) and one to the entity itself.

Other business rules place constraints on what entity occurrences are valid, rather than attribute values. Candidate and primary key constraints (Figure 8.10) are one example of such a business rule as no two occurrences of the entity can have the same attribute values for a candidate key. It would be possible to document candidate keys using notes attached to the entity, but the resulting ER diagram would be rather cluttered, so tagged values are used instead. Another example would be:

every module must have at least two hours of contact time each week.

This constraint involves both the Module and TeachingSession entities as it insists that for any occurrence of the Module entity, there are linked occurrences of TeachingSession, such that the sum of their duration attribute values is at least two hours. (This is a rather naïve constraint – what if there are three practicals, lasting an hour each, but students can only attend one?) To indicate that the constraint involves both entities, simply attach the note to them both. If there are lots of these business rules, then, again, the ER diagram can become cluttered. If this happens, it may be better to draw a separate ER diagram to document such constraints and hide the attribute compartments of the entities, as has been done in Figure 8.13.

The UML was developed to help design object-oriented applications, so includes an ability to record the behaviour associated with an entity. Traditional database design techniques have not considered behaviour – what the application does with the

Figure 8.13 A constraint on two entities.

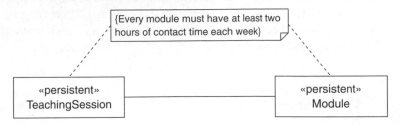

Figure 8.14 An entity with an operation and the operation's method note.

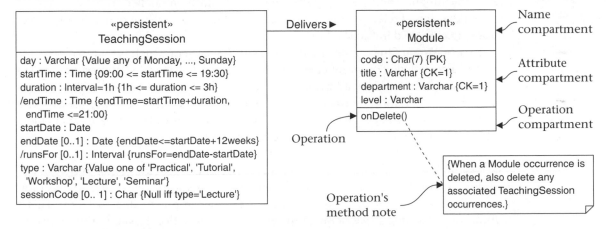

data – only how best to organize the data. With the advent of stored procedures, which allow the DBMS to manage behaviour as well as data organization (see Chapter 11), it can be useful to include some application behaviour in the ER diagram.

Behaviour is modelled using **operations**, with each operation belonging to an entity. Operations are listed in the **operations compartment**, which, if it is shown, comes immediately below the attribute compartment.

Another possible use of operations is to document referential actions. Referential actions were discussed as part of the relational data model and again as part of the SQL DDL create table statement (Chapters 3 and 5 respectively). They can be applied more widely however, as whenever there is a relationship between two data structures it is useful to know what to do when an occurrence of one of them is removed. Figure 8.14 shows the Module entity with an operation onDelete( ). Whenever an occurrence of the Module entity is removed, it seems reasonable to insist that every associated occurrence of TeachingSession is also removed. Otherwise there will be teaching sessions scheduled for a module that isn't running.

In an ER diagram, there is no counterpart of the ON UPDATE referential action. This is concerned with ensuring that when a candidate key column value changes, so does any matching foreign key's column value. ER diagrams do not include foreign keys, so there is no equivalent action.

367

Operation names have the same format as attribute names, but are followed by parentheses – '( )'. The parentheses can include a list of parameters, which are values passed to the operation each time it is executed. There is no need to specify how the operation will actually work, but it is useful to include a **method note** for each operation that explains its purpose.

8.5 Associations

The commonest kind of relationship between entities is the **association** relationship. Any meaningful connection between entities could be modelled as an association. (The other sort of relationship that is used in an ER diagram is the **generalization relationship**, discussed in Section 8.7.)

An association can connect a number of entities, each of which is said to participate in the association. The number of participating entities is called the **degree of the association**. Traditionally an association between two entities is called a **binary association**. An association between three or more entities is called an **n-ary association**. When an association has just one participating entity, it is called a **unary association**. These definitions are not perfect and are refined below.

Associations have no special meaning beyond the simple notion that they represent a meaningful connection between entities. They do have additional properties to those discussed so far. Many of these properties apply to just one end of the association. For example, sometimes an entity plays a particular role in an association. This is indicated by adding a **role name** at the end of the association linked to that entity. In Figure 8.15, the Staff entity plays the role of module leader in the Leads association, so the role name ModuleLeader is added to the Staff end of the Leads association (compare this with Figure 8.11, where there is no role name). It indicates that each occurrence of Leads links a particular occurrence of Module with the occurrence of Staff representing the actual module leader. The association now reads, 'A member of staff, acting in the role of module leader, leads a module'. Role names do not change the meaning of the diagram – the Leads association still represents the same meaningful connection between the Staff and Module entities – but it does provide additional information on how to interpret the meaning. Role names have the same syntax as entity names.

Figure 8.15 A role name on an association.

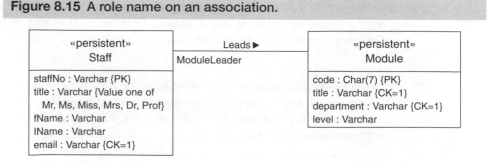

Figure 8.16 Binary and unary associations using the same role name.

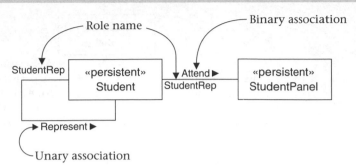

One situation in which role names become useful is when an association connects an entity with itself – a unary association. The association Represent in Figure 8.16 is an example of a unary association – it connects the Student entity with itself.

Note that, like a binary association, a unary association has two ends. Each occurrence of a unary association links two occurrences of the entity (possibly, though not necessarily, the same entity occurrence).

The ER diagram models how students make their views about courses known. Each year, the students on each course elect a student representative. Student representatives are themselves students, but they attend student panels to raise any concerns expressed by the students they represent. The role name StudentRep at one end of the unary association Represent emphasizes that the occurrences of Student at the different ends play different roles – a student, acting in the role of student representative, represents all the students on the course.

Unlike entity names and association names, role names need not be unique. In fact, it makes sense to reuse them as an entity may play the same role in more than one association. Student representatives also attend student panels, so there is a binary association, Attends, connecting Student with StudentPanel. Obviously, an occurrence of Student who participates in this association is also playing the role of StudentRep and this is indicated by including the same role name at the Student end of the Attend association (Figure 8.16). This is read, 'Student, acting in the role StudentRep, Attend StudentPanel'. When two *different* entities play similar roles, though, they should be given different role names to avoid possible confusion.

An association can connect three or more entities – an n-ary association. This situation is less common than a unary association, but most organizations will have examples of associations between three entities.

An n-ary association is shown as a diamond with lines from the diamond to the entities involved. The association name is written inside the diamond. With n-ary associations, there is no name direction indicator. Figure 8.17 shows the BookEquipment association. This association connects the three entities Staff, Equipment and TeachingSession and models the fact that staff may book additional equipment to use in a particular teaching session. Notice that BookEquipment has *three* association ends – one for each entity. Each of these association ends could be given a role name, though, in this example, there is no need.

Figure 8.17 An n-ary association connecting three entities.

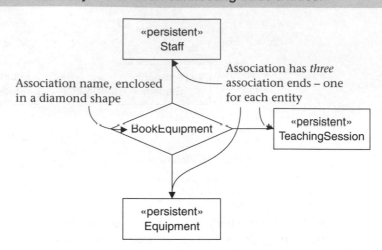

N-ary associations like that shown for BookEquipment model situations that cannot be modelled using binary associations alone. Consider the ER diagram in Figure 8.18 (a). This attempts to use binary associations to capture the same scenario modelled by Figure 8.17. The binary association Book is intended to indicate that a member of staff books additional equipment, but it is not clear which teaching session this equipment is needed for. The binary association For can show that a member of staff wants additional equipment in a particular teaching session, but it cannot show *which* equipment is required. Similarly, UsedIn can show which equipment is required for a teaching session, but not who booked it.

The problem is that there is no way to tie together the information captured by these three separate binary associations. It is possible, for example, that an occurrence of Book exists even though there are no occurrences of the other two associations. These ambiguities cannot be resolved using binary associations alone.

They can be resolved, however, by introducing a new entity, EquipmentBooking, and three binary associations Figure 8.18 (b). The new entity represents a particular equipment booking. In business terms this could be a paper booking form, filled out by staff who want to book additional equipment for their teaching sessions. The idea is that each occurrence of EquipmentBooking is linked to exactly one occurrence of the other three entities – that is, one member of staff books one piece of equipment for one teaching session. This is exactly the same situation as Figure 8.17.

When developing a conceptual ER diagram, the database designer can choose whether or not to use n-ary associations. If they are not used, then there will be entities like EquipmentBooking, the purpose of which is to link together other entities. A special feature of link entities is that they might not have any attributes. This breaks the rules, but is generally tolerated.

The terms unary, binary and n-ary are useful guides to the complexity of the situation modelled by an association, but they are not clear cut. It is possible to conceive of an association in which two entities participate, but is really closer to an n-ary association. For example, at the Pennine University, a member of staff, acting as

Figure 8.18 Representing complex associations with simpler structures.

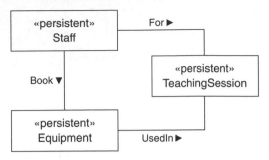

(a) Incorrect use of binary associations to represent a connection between three entities.

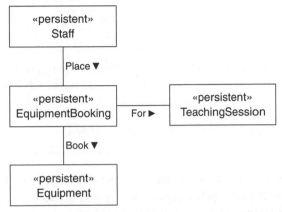

(b) Correct use of link entity and binary association to represent connections between three entities.

module leader, leads a team of module tutors (each of whom is also a member of staff) to deliver a particular module.

The ER diagram representing this situation is shown in Figure 8.19. Only two entities participate in the association, so it conforms to the definition of a binary association. However, it has three association ends, so is much more like an n-ary association. The clinching argument is that, during logical design, this association will have to be treated as an n-ary association. So, it seems that there should be a tighter definition of these terms.

Binary association An association with two ends.

Unary association A special kind a binary association where both association ends are attached to the same entity.

N-ary association An association with three or more ends.

Figure 8.19 Is this a binary or an n-ary association?

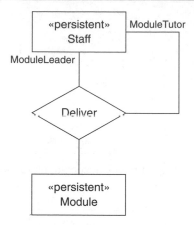

The ER diagram in Figure 8.19 is not the only way to model this situation. A better way might be to have two separate binary associations between the entities **Staff** and **Module** – one called **Leads** and one called **Teaches**. However, the point is that associations like the one shown are possible, but do not fit into the traditional definitions of unary, binary and n-ary associations.

In a conceptual ER diagram, an association can have attributes of its own. In data modelling, such associations are less common than associations without attributes, but common enough that there is a special notation for them. To give you an example, suppose that the Web Timetable application holds data for more than one academic year. Then, it would be possible that the module leader for a module would change from one year to the next. The database would then need to store additional information about module leaders – in which academic year they led a particular module.

This is simple enough to model. Add an academicYear attribute to hold this piece of information. The problem, though, is where to add it. Suppose the academicYear attribute is added to the Staff entity. Some members of staff lead more than one module and in more than one year, so this must be a multivalued attribute with repeated values allowed. Figure 8.20 shows an object diagram with the academicYear attribute added to Staff. Selma Hutchins is a module leader of two modules in the academic year 2004–2005, but of only one in 2005–2006. However, there is no way of deciding which of the two modules she is still leading in 2005–2006. This shows that academicYear cannot be an attribute of Staff. A similar argument shows that academicYear is not an attribute of Module.

The problem occurs because the academicYear attribute provides information about the link between an occurrence of Staff and an occurrence of Module – that this link is valid only for the specified academic years. This means that it is an attribute of the Leads association itself, not of the two entities that participate in the association.

Figure 8.21 shows how to model this on an ER diagram. The association attributes are listed in an entity-like box, drawn near the association. This attribute box is

Figure 8.20 Object diagram illustrating that academicYear cannot be an attribute of Staff.

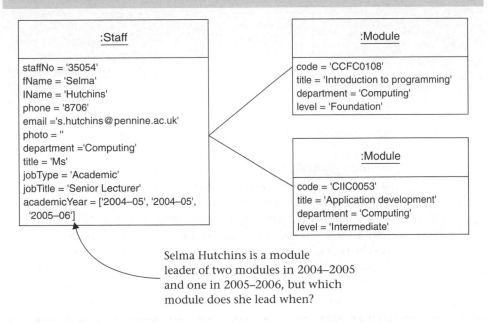

Selma Hutchins is a module
leader of two modules in 2004–2005
and one in 2005–2006, but which
module does she lead when?

Figure 8.21 Binary association with attributes.

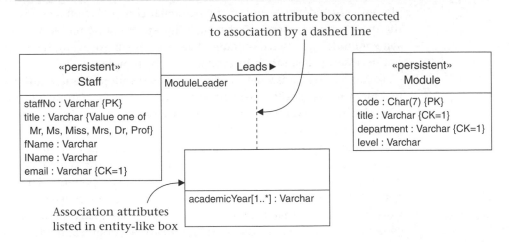

connected to the association by a dashed line. Notice that association attributes can have all the features of entity attributes. In Figure 8.21 academicYear is a multivalued attribute as a particular member of staff may lead a particular module in more than one academic year. For an n-ary association, the attribute box is connected to the diamond, again by a dashed line. There is no rule about where to place the attribute box on the ER diagram – above, below or beside the association are all fine.

Figure 8.22 An aggregation association representing a whole–part relationship between Course and Module.

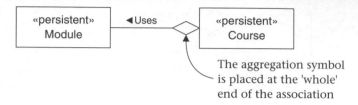

The aggregation symbol is placed at the 'whole' end of the association

An **aggregation association** is a special sort of association relationship indicating that one entity forms a part of another. This whole–part relationship is indicated by adding a diamond to the end of the association attached to the 'whole'. For example, at the Pennine University, a Course is made up of Modules, so the Course is the whole and the Module is the part. This is indicated by placing an open diamond at the Course end of the association between these two entities (Figure 8.22). The aggregation association indicates that, at the Pennine University, there is a stronger association between courses and modules than between courses and students. Although a course won't run if there are no students, it would still be in the university's prospectus. The courses and students therefore exist independently of one another. In contrast, a course is made up of modules, so if there were no modules, there could be no courses. Each course is a collection of modules and the aggregation association captures this fact.

Aggregation represents a loose collection – it is possible for the whole to exists without the parts or for the parts to exist independently of the whole. For example, a module can exist independently of any particular course. When a course is removed from the prospectus, the modules remain valid and may be reused in new courses. Also, some modules are offered on more than one course, so, again, removing a course does not necessarily mean that the modules will be removed.

To model situations where a part *cannot* exist independently of the whole, the UML includes the **composition association**. Composition is a stronger form of aggregation. It models the situation where the existence of one entity depends on the existence of another (discussed in Section 8.4).

Consider the way in which module leaders at the Pennine University develop coursework assignments. Each module can have at most one coursework assignment, but this assignment can have several coursework components. The coursework components cannot exist independently – it simply does not make sense to have a coursework component that isn't part of a coursework assignment. Nor can the same component be reused in a different assignment as modules should test different learning outcomes. To emphasize this stronger form of aggregation, the diamond symbol is filled in, as shown in Figure 8.23.

One way to think of the difference between aggregation and composition is to consider the lifetimes of the entity occurrences within the database. When an occurrence of the Coursework entity is deleted, the occurrences of the Component entities that are a part of it are also deleted. When an occurrence of the Course entity is deleted, the occurrences of the Module entity that were a part of it can stay in the database (they may be used on other courses).

Figure 8.23 A composition association – the part cannot exist independently of the whole.

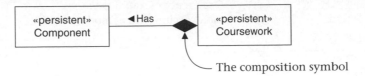

The composition symbol

Aggregation and composition are particularly useful during logical database design when the target data model is XML. Composition indicates that the element representing the part should be included within the element representing the whole. Aggregation indicates that element inclusion is a feasible approach to implementing the association. A plain association could be implemented using keys. Logical database design for XML is discussed in Chapter 12.

8.6 Association multiplicity constraints

Most organizations have business rules of the form 'one occurrence of this entity may be linked to this many occurrences of this other entity'. Examples from the Web Timetable application include:

- one member of staff may lead many modules or none
- one module is led by exactly one member of staff
- one student, acting as student representative, represents many other students
- one student is represented by exactly one student acting as student representative.

Such business rules can be illustrated by object diagrams.

Figure 8.24 shows that one member of staff may lead many modules. Here, Selma Hutchins is module leader for 'Introduction to programming' and 'Application development'. It also shows that one member may not lead any modules. The occurrence of Staff representing Freya Stark is not linked to any occurrences of Module. This is summed up in the first business rule above.

Object diagrams are a useful way to illustrate such rules, but are too cumbersome to document them. For example, Figure 8.24 only shows that one member of staff may lead up to two modules. It does not show that staff may lead three or more modules. To document these business rules, a **multiplicity constraint** is added to an association end.

Multiplicity constraints on an association end are a powerful technique for capturing business rules. Like the notion of strong and weak entities, ideas about association multiplicity constraints have developed over time. This section explains the UML version of association multiplicity constraints first, then explains a popular alternative. In both cases, some shortcomings of the approach are examined. If a database designer chooses to use the UML notation for ER diagrams, but the earlier version of association multiplicity constraints, then this should be clearly indicated. A suggested notation for this is included below.

375

Figure 8.24 Object diagram illustrating the multiplicity constraint for the end of the Leads association attached to the Module entity.

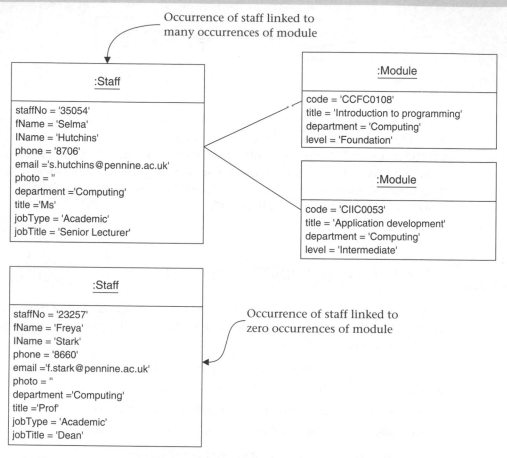

Occurrence of staff linked to many occurrences of module

:Staff

staffNo = '35054'
fName = 'Selma'
lName = 'Hutchins'
phone = '8706'
email ='s.hutchins@pennine.ac.uk'
photo = ''
department ='Computing'
title ='Ms'
jobType = 'Academic'
jobTitle = 'Senior Lecturer'

:Module

code = 'CCFC0108'
title = 'Introduction to programming'
department = 'Computing'
level = 'Foundation'

:Module

code = 'CIIC0053'
title = 'Application development'
department = 'Computing'
level = 'Intermediate'

:Staff

staffNo = '23257'
fName = 'Freya'
lName = 'Stark'
phone = '8660'
email ='f.stark@pennine.ac.uk'
photo = ''
department ='Computing'
title ='Prof'
jobType = 'Academic'
jobTitle = 'Dean'

Occurrence of staff linked to zero occurrences of module

8.6.1 Multiplicity constraints in the UML

The formal definition of an association multiplicity constraint in the UML2.0 specification has changed from earlier versions. In 2003, the then current public draft of the specification read:

For an association with N ends, choose any N-1 ends and associate specific instances with those ends. Then the collection of links of the association that refer to these specific instances will identify a collection of instances at the other end. The multiplicity of the association end constrains the size of this collection. (OMG, 2003, p. 113)

This details an algorithm for identifying the multiplicity constraint. In the final release of the UML2.0 standard, the definition has changed to:

Traversal of an n-ary association towards a navigable end requires that objects first be identified for the remaining n-1 ends. The result of traversal is a collection of objects for the navigable end derived from links in which the other n-1 objects participate. For binary associations, n=2, in which case traversal proceeds from one object at the other end to a collection of objects at the navigable end. The multiplicity of the association end constrains the size of this collection. If the end is marked as ordered, this collection will be ordered. (OMG, 2005 p. 113)

Although it seems more complicated, the final definition describes what is essentially the same process. To calculate the multiplicity constraint for an association end, ask the following two questions.

1 What is the lower bound on the number of occurrences of the entity at the chosen association end that could be linked, by occurrences of the association, to a given set of occurrences of entities from each of the other ends of the association?

2 What is the upper bound on the number of occurrences of the entity at the chosen association end that could be linked, by occurrences of the association, to a given set of occurrences of entities from each of the other ends of the association?

The answers to these questions establish a lower bound and an upper bound for the multiplicity constraint and will depend on the meaning of the association. This form of multiplicity constraint on an association end is sometimes called the **outer multiplicity constraint**, though in UML (and this subsection), it is simply referred to as *the* multiplicity constraint on an association end.

> **Outer multiplicity constraint on an association end** Represents the lower and upper bounds on the number of occurrences of the entity at this association end that may be linked, by occurrences of the association, to a given set of occurrences of entities consisting of one entity occurrence from each of the other ends of the association.

At this point, an example is absolutely essential.

Multiplicity constraints on binary associations are by far the simplest to calculate. Consider the Leads association indicated between the Staff and Module entities (Figure 8.15). To calculate the multiplicity constraint for the Module end of the Leads association, simply ask the above two questions. As there is only one entity at the other end of the association, the first question becomes as follows.

1 What is the lower bound on the number of occurrences of Module that could be linked, by occurrences of the association, to a given occurrence of Staff?

The object diagram in Figure 8.24 can help here. Some staff don't lead modules – Freya Stark, for example. An occurrence of Staff representing someone who is not a module leader will not be linked to any occurrences of Module. This gives a lower bound on the multiplicity constraint of zero.

Now consider the upper bound.

2 What is the upper bound on the number of occurrences of Module that could be linked, by occurrences of the association, to a given occurrence of Staff?

Again, this is easy enough to answer. Some members of staff are module leaders for several modules. An occurrence of Staff representing someone who is a module leader for several modules will be linked to many occurrences of Module. For example, in Figure 8.24 Selma Hutchins leads two modules. Other staff may lead more. This gives an upper bound on the multiplicity constraint of many, written '*'. The complete multiplicity constraint, therefore, is written '0..*' and placed at the Module end of the Leads association, as shown in Figure 8.25. Note that there are no square brackets around the multiplicity constraint on an association end.

The ER diagram in Figure 8.25 is read:

> any particular occurrence of Staff is linked by occurrences of Leads to a lower bound of zero and an upper bound of many occurrences of Module

or, in plain English:

> a particular member of staff may not lead any modules, but they may lead many.

This is, bar minor rewording, the first of the business rules listed at the start of this section.

Calculating the multiplicity constraint at the Staff end of the Leads association involves following the same process. First, consider the lower bound.

1 What is the lower bound on the number of occurrences of Staff that could be linked to a given occurrence of Module?

This is easy. Every module has a module leader and a module leader is a member of staff. Thus, there is always an occurrence of Staff linked to a given occurrence of Module. This gives a lower bound on the multiplicity constraint of one.

Now consider the upper bound.

2 What is the upper bound on the number of occurrences of Staff that could be linked to a given occurrence of Module?

The Leads association models the connection between a module and the member of staff leading that module. There is only one module leader for any one module, so, at most, one member of staff is linked to any given occurrence of Module by occurrences of the Leads association. This is despite the fact that several members of staff might *teach* the module. The Leads association does *not* model this 'staff teaches module' relationship.

The final ER diagram showing both the multiplicity constraints on the Leads association is shown in Figure 8.26.

Figure 8.25 The multiplicity constraint for the end of the Leads association attached to the Module entity.

Figure 8.26 The Leads association with both its multiplicity constraints.

Figure 8.27 The Sits association with its multiplicity constraints.

As a second example, consider the Sits association between Student and Module (Figure 8.27). This association represents students sitting modules in a particular academic year. First, calculate the multiplicity constraint at the Student end of the association.

1 What is the lower bound on the number of occurrences of Student that could be linked to a given occurrence of Module?

Once teaching starts, all modules will have some students taking them or the module will not be on the timetable. However, the timetable is created before the start of the academic year, so only data about students in the second or later years is available. First year modules will not have any students taking them at that point, but must still be timetabled. This means that an occurrence of Module that represents a first year module may not have any occurrences of student linked to it, so the lower bound will be zero.

2 What is the upper bound on the number of occurrences of Student that could be linked to a given occurrence of Module?

A typical module will have many students, so an occurrence of Module may be linked to many occurrences of Student. The upper bound is 'many'.

At the Module end of the Sits association, the lower bound of the multiplicity constraint is calculated by asking this question.

1 What is the lower bound on the number of occurrences of Module that could be linked to a given occurrence of Student?

At the Pennine University, every student must sit one module in each academic year. This means that the lower bound is one.

To calculate the upper bound, ask the following question.

2 What is the upper bound on the number of occurrences of Module that could be linked to a given occurrence of Student?

At the Pennine University no student can sit more than seven modules in any one year. Consequently, the upper bound is seven. Figure 8.27 shows the ER diagram that captures this information.

The multiplicity constraints on a unary association are calculated in the same way, though the fact that there is only one entity involved can make it a little confusing. Consider the Represent association in Figure 8.16 (shown again in Figure 8.28), which associates the Student entity with itself. The role name is useful for distinguishing between the two ends of the association.

To calculate the multiplicity constraint for the StudentRep end of the Represent association, ask the two questions again.

1 What is the lower bound on the number of occurrences of Student at the StudentRep end of the association that could be linked to a given occurrence of Student at the opposite end of the association?

Figure 8.28 Multiplicity constraints on a unary association.

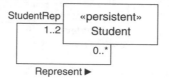

Represent ▶

2 What is the upper bound on the number of occurrences of Student at the Student-Rep end of the association that could be linked to a given occurrence of Student at the opposite end of the association?

As every student has a student representative, any occurrence of Student is linked by an occurrence of Represent to the occurrence of Student who is his or her StudentRep. The lower bound is one. On large courses, the students elect two student representatives, so some occurrences of Student are linked to two distinct occurrences of Student acting as StudentRep. No student has more than two student representatives, though, so the upper bound is two.

The multiplicity constraint at the end of the Sits association that has no role name answers these two questions.

1 What is the lower bound on the number of occurrences of Student that could be linked to a given occurrence of Student at the StudentRep end of the association?

2 What is the upper bound on the number of occurrences of Student that could be linked to a given occurrence of Student at the StudentRep end of the association?

At this point, it is tempting to argue as follows. An occurrence of Student at the Student-Rep end of the association must be a student representative, so he or she will represent at least one student. This is incorrect, however. Just as some staff are not module leaders, some students are not student representatives. A student who is not a student representative will not represent anyone, just as a member of staff who is not a module leader will not lead any modules. Hence, the lower bound on this multiplicity constraint is zero.

The upper bound will be 'many'. An occurrence of Student at the StudentRep end of the association who happens to be a student representative will represent all the students on his or her course. Clearly this can be many students. Figure 8.28 shows the Represent association with its multiplicity constraints.

As another example, consider the classic for a unary association – line management within an organization.

At the Pennine University, each member of staff has exactly one line manager. Even the Vice Chancellor, who is otherwise at the top of management hierarchy, has a designated line manager for performance review purposes. Some members of staff do not manage anyone else, but some manage several other members of staff. Representing this as an ER diagram, there is a single entity, Staff, and a single association, Manages, connecting this entity to itself. The ER diagram is shown in Figure 8.29, and is read 'Staff, acting in the role of LineManager, Manage other Staff'.

Figure 8.29 A unary association modelling line management.

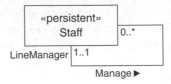

Manage ▶

To calculate the multiplicity constraint at the LineManager end of the association consider these questions.

1   What is the lower bound on the number of occurrences of Staff at the LineManager end of the association that could be linked to a given occurrence of Staff at the opposite end of the association?

2   What is the upper bound on the number of occurrences of Staff at the LineManager end of the association that could be linked to a given occurrence of Staff at the opposite end of the association?

As stated above, every member of staff has a line manager, so the lower bound is one. Any member of staff has at most one line manager, so the upper bound is also one. This gives a multiplicity constraint of 1..1.

For the multiplicity constraint at the other end of the association, ask these questions.

1   What is the lower bound on the number of occurrences of Staff that could be linked to a given occurrence of Staff at the LineManager end of the association?

Don't be misled into considering only occurrences of Staff acting in the role LineManager. As some members of staff are not line managers and so do not manage anyone, the answer to this question is zero.

2   What is the upper bound on the number of occurrences of Staff that could be linked to a given occurrence of Staff at the LineManager end of the association?

This upper bound will be many as those members of staff who *are* line managers may manage several other staff. The multiplicity constraints are shown in Figure 8.29.

Unlike attribute multiplicity, there is no default multiplicity constraint. When there is no multiplicity constraint on an association end, it means that the multiplicity is not known. The commonest multiplicity constraints, and their UML representations, are shown in Table 8.5. Other ranges are possible, though less common. For example,

Table 8.5 Common association multiplicity constraints.

Range	UML notation
Zero or more	0..* (sometimes abbreviated to *)
One or more	1..*
Zero or one	0..1
Exactly one	1..1 (sometimes abbreviated to 1)

'three to seven' is written 3..7 and 'three or five or more than 10' is written 3, 5, 10..*. On the ER diagram itself, the multiplicity constraint should be written close to the appropriate association end. Writing both multiplicity constraints on the same side of the line representing the association and on the opposite side to the association name can improve the clarity of the ER diagram. Although the two commonest multiplicity constraints – 0..* and 1..1 – have abbreviations, it is best not to use these in a conceptual ER diagram. End users are unlikely to be familiar with these abbreviations, so using them could impede a key purpose of the ER diagramming technique – to help end users evaluate the database design.

Multiplicity constraints have been used to characterize unary and binary associations. Associations like Leads (Figure 8.26) are called **one-to-many** associations. A one-to-many association is one where the upper bound on the multiplicity constraint at one association end is 1, while the upper bound at the other end is greater than one (it might be '*' or an integer greater than 1). A typical object diagram has one occurrence of Staff linked with many occurrences of Module, as shown in Figure 8.30 (a).

Figure 8.30 Characterizing associations by their multiplicity.

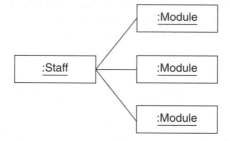

(a) Object diagram for the one-to-many association `Leads`.

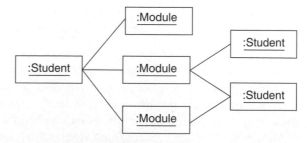

(b) Object diagram for the many-to-many association `Sits`.

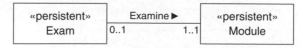

(c) ER diagram for the one-to-one association `Examine`.

(d) Object diagram for the one-to-one association `Examine`.

Not all associations are one-to-many. The Sits association (Figure 8.27) is **many-to-many**. A many-to-many association is one where the upper bound on the multiplicity constraint at both association ends is greater than one. A typical object diagram has many occurrences of Student linked with many occurrences of Module, as shown in Figure 8.30 (b).

The only other possibility is that the upper bound on the multiplicity at *both* association ends is equal to one. Unsurprisingly, these are called **one-to-one** associations. Here is an example.

At the Pennine University, a module may be assessed by an exam. Some modules do not have an exam, but those that do only have one exam. Each exam examines exactly one module. The ER diagram for this one-to-one association is shown in Figure 8.30 (c), with a typical object diagram shown in Figure 8.30 (d).

The multiplicity for each association end of an n-ary association is calculated in the same way as multiplicity for binary and unary associations. The complicating factor is that there are now two (or more) other ends to worry about.

Consider the n-ary association BookEquipment, which has three participating entities (Figure 8.17). At the Equipment end of this association, the lower bound on the multiplicity constraint is obtained by answering this question.

1 What is the lower bound on the number of occurrences of Equipment that could be linked, by occurrences of the association, to a given set of occurrences of Staff and TeachingSession?

To answer it, consider the possible sets of occurrences of Staff and TeachingSession (where it's implied that there is one occurrence of each entity). Any occurrence of Staff could be paired with any occurrence of TeachingSession. When the chosen member of staff does not teach the chosen teaching session, there will be *no* additional equipment booked by that person for the teaching session. This means that the lower bound will be zero.

For the upper bound, consider the following question.

2 What is the upper bound on the number of occurrences of Equipment that could be linked, by occurrences of the association, to the given set of occurrences of Staff and TeachingSession?

Again, consider the possible sets of occurrences of Staff and TeachingSession. When the chosen occurrence of Staff *does* teach the chosen occurrence of TeachingSession, it is possible that he or she will have booked lots of additional equipment for this particular teaching session, so the upper bound is many. Figure 8.31 shows this multiplicity constraint on the ER diagram.

The multiplicity constraint at the TeachingSession end of the BookEquipment association is calculated similarly. This time, consider the possible sets of occurrences of Staff and Equipment. First, ask this question.

1 What is the lower bound on the number of occurrences of TeachingSession that could be linked, by occurrences of the association, to a given set of occurrences of Staff and Equipment?

Any occurrence of Staff could be paired with any occurrence of Equipment. It is possible that the chosen member of staff may never have booked this particular

Figure 8.31 The multiplicity at the Equipment end of the BookEquipment association.

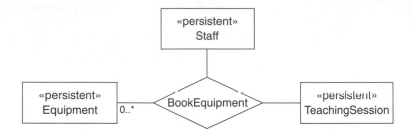

piece of equipment, so the lower bound is zero. For the upper bound, consider this question.

2 What is the upper bound on the number of occurrences of TeachingSession that could be linked, by occurrences of the association, to a given set of occurrences of Staff and Equipment?

It is conceivable that a particular member of staff books the same piece of equipment for every single one of his or her teaching sessions, so the upper bound will be many. The multiplicity constraint 0..* is therefore added to the TeachingSession end of the BookEquipment association.

The third association end is that with the Staff entity attached. To calculate the multiplicity at this association end, consider the possible sets of occurrences of TeachingSession and Equipment. For the lower bound, ask the following question.

1 What is the lower bound on the number of occurrences of Staff that could be linked, by occurrences of the association, to a given set of occurrences of TeachingSession and Equipment?

Any occurrence of TeachingSession could be paired with any occurrence of Equipment. It is possible that the chosen piece of equipment has not been booked for this particular teaching session, so the lower bound is zero.

For the upper bound, ask this question.

2 What is the upper bound on the number of occurrences of Staff that could be linked, by occurrences of the association, to a given set of occurrences of TeachingSession and Equipment?

When a particular piece of equipment *is* booked for a particular teaching session, it can only be booked *once*. The upper bound, therefore, is one and so the multiplicity constraint 0..1 is added to the Staff end of the BookEquipment association. Figure 8.32 shows the association with all three of its multiplicity constraints.

The UML definition of multiplicity is phrased in terms of entity occurrences – given a set consisting of one entity occurrence from each of the other ends, how many entities from the chosen end are linked to these by occurrences of the association? For n-ary associations this means that the lower bound on a multiplicity constraint will almost always be zero. To see why, consider what a multiplicity constraint of 1..* at the

Figure 8.32 UML multiplicity constraints on the BookEquipment n-ary association.

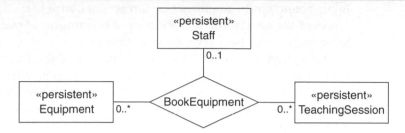

Figure 8.33 The n-ary association for the Ballroom Dancing Society.

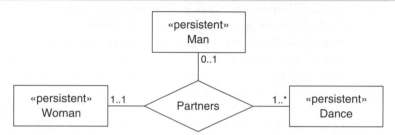

TeachingSession end of the BookEquipment association means. It means that every pair of occurrences of Staff and Equipment is linked to some occurrence of Teaching-Session by an occurrence of the BookEquipment association. In other words, *every* member of staff books *every* piece of equipment for *some* teaching session. Obviously, in the case of equipment bookings, this statement is not true. Some staff never book equipment and those who do are unlikely to have booked every possible piece of equipment at some time, even if they have worked at the Pennine University for 40 years.

There are some n-ary associations for which every pair of occurrences of two entities *will* be associated with at least one occurrence of the third, though they are less common. One example, though, comes from the Ballroom Dancing Society at the Pennine University.

The society is quite small and there are always more women than men at the dances. To ensure that everyone gets to dance with everyone else, there are a few rules:

1 each man dances with each woman at least once during the evening

2 some couples have more than one dance together, but some only one

3 as there are always fewer men than women, men participate in every dance, but some women have to sit some dances out.

The n-ary association Partners (with its multiplicity constraints) is shown in Figure 8.33.

To calculate the multiplicity constraints, ask the questions as before to establish the lower and upper bounds for each one. The multiplicity constraint at the Dance end of the Partners association captures information about how many dances a couple may have together. The lower bound on the number of occurrences of Dance that could be linked, by occurrences of the association, to a given set of occurrences of Man and Woman is one – every possible couple has at least one dance (as per rule 1, above). The upper bound on the number of occurrences of Dance that could be linked, by occurrences of the association, to a given set of occurrences of Man and Woman is many – some couples may have several dances (rule 2).

The multiplicity constraint at the Woman end of the Partners association captures information about how many dance partners a man may have in a particular dance. The lower bound on the number of occurrences of Woman that could be linked, by occurrences of the association, to a given set of occurrences of Man and Dance is one as, given a particular man and a particular dance, there will be a woman partnering that man for the dance (rule 3). The upper bound on the number of occurrences of Woman that could be linked, by occurrences of the association, to a given set of occurrences of Man and Dance is also one – a man can only dance with one woman at a time (this is ballroom dancing, so there is no swapping of partners).

The multiplicity constraint at the Man end of the Partners association captures information about how many dance partners a woman may have in a particular dance. The lower bound on the number of occurrences of Man that could be linked, by occurrences of the association, to a given set of occurrences of Woman and Dance is zero – some women must sit out some dances as they have no partner and so do not dance (rule 3). The upper bound on the number of occurrences of Man that could be linked, by occurrences of the association, to a given set of occurrences of Woman and Dance is one as a woman can only dance with one man at a time (again, no partner swapping).

8.6.2 Other approaches to association multiplicity

The UML approach to association multiplicity constraints is not the only one. Another approach is to express the multiplicity constraints in terms of the chosen entity's participation in an association. This is the approach taken in the Merise method and by many database textbooks.

It is worth examining this approach for two reasons. First, it is widely used in textbook discussions of ER diagrams and by practising database designers. Second, in the case of n-ary associations, it provides quite different information about the association to that provided by UML's outer multiplicity constraint.

To distinguish between the two approaches, this section always refers to the UML multiplicity constraint as the **outer multiplicity constraint** and the Merise multiplicity constraint as the **inner multiplicity constraint**.

To calculate the inner multiplicity constraint for an association end, ask the following two questions.

1 For a given occurrence of the entity at the chosen end of the association, what is the lower bound on the number of occurrences of the association it could participate in?

2 For a given occurrence of the entity at the chosen end of the association, what is the upper bound on the number of occurrences of the association it could participate in?

The answers to these questions establish a lower bound and an upper bound for the inner multiplicity constraint and, just as for the outer multiplicity constraint, will depend on the meaning of the association.

> **Inner multiplicity constraint on an association end** Represents the lower and upper bounds on the number of occurrences of the association that a single occurrence of the entity at this association end may participate in.

This definition is simpler than the definition of the outer multiplicity constraint. Only the entity at the chosen association end, and the association itself, are mentioned. There is no need to worry about the other entities that participate in the association.

Consider again the Leads association between the Staff and Module entities (Figure 8.15). To calculate the inner multiplicity constraint for the Module end of the Leads association, simply ask the two questions.

For the lower bound, ask the following.

1 For a given occurrence of Module, what is the lower bound on the number of occurrences of Leads it could participate in?

Notice that there is no mention of the Staff entity, though obviously any occurrence of Leads will have an occurrence of Staff at one end. To answer the question, note that every module has a module leader, so any given occurrence of Module must participate in at least one occurrence of Leads – the one linking it to the occurrence of Staff representing the module leader. The lower bound in the inner multiplicity constraint, therefore, is one.

For the upper bound, ask the following question.

2 For a given occurrence of Module, what is the upper bound on the number of occurrences of Leads it could participate in?

Again, the meaning of the association provides the answer – there is only one module leader for any module, so the upper bound is also one. Thus, the inner multiplicity constraint for the Module end of the Leads association is 1..1.

To calculate the inner multiplicity constraint at the Staff end of the Leads association, consider a particular occurrence of Staff. It's possible that this particular member of staff does not lead any modules, so the lower bound on the inner multiplicity constraint is zero. It is also possible that this particular member of staff leads several modules, so the upper bound is many. Thus, the inner multiplicity constraint for the Staff end of the Leads association is 0..*.

There is no special notation in the UML to express inner multiplicity constraints. The ER diagram in Figure 8.34 uses the 'constraint in a note' approach to document the inner multiplicity constraints at each end of the Leads association. (This approach was also used with entity and attribute constraints, for example, in Figures 8.12 and 8.13.)

Notice that in Figure 8.34, the inner multiplicity at one end of the binary association is the same as the outer multiplicity at the other end. For binary (and unary) associations, this is always the case. For n-ary associations, inner and outer multiplicity constraints can be quite different, with no simple equivalence between them.

Consider the n-ary association BookEquipment. To calculate the inner multiplicity constraint at the Equipment end of this association, consider a particular occurrence of

Figure 8.34 An ER diagram showing both outer and inner multiplicity constraints on a binary association.

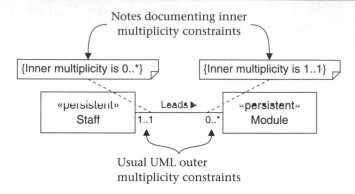

Equipment. It is possible that this particular piece of equipment has never been booked, so the lower bound is zero. Equally, it is possible that it is booked regularly, so the upper bound is many and the inner multiplicity constraint is 0..*. Similarly, a particular occurrence of Staff may not have booked any additional equipment or may have made many bookings, so the inner multiplicity constraint on Staff is also 0..*. Finally, a particular occurrence of TeachingSession may not have any additional equipment booked or may have several such items booked, so, again, the inner multiplicity constraint is 0..*.

The inner multiplicity constraints on BookEquipment are shown, using standard UML notation, in Figure 8.35(a). This standard UML notation is a little cumbersome and leads to cluttered ER diagrams. Génova et al. (2002) suggest changes to the UML notation to allow both inner *and* outer multiplicity constraints to be shown in an ER diagram without using notes. Their proposal is that, for:

1 binary and unary associations, only show the outer multiplicity constraints (as the inner multiplicity constraints add no new information)

2 n-ary associations, show the outer multiplicity constraints in their usual place and locate the inner multiplicity constraints where the association end meets the diamond.

This enhanced notation for n-ary associations is shown in Figure 8.35(b). It seems a reasonable proposal, but, it must be emphasized, this suggestion has *not* been incorporated in the UML standard.

Now consider the inner multiplicity constraints on the Partners association. It is relatively straightforward to calculate these. For the Man entity, every man partners a woman in the first dance of the evening, so the lower bound is one. Every man then partners a woman in every other dance, so the upper bound is many. Similarly, a woman is guaranteed a dance with every man, so will participate in at least one occurrence of the Partners association and may participate in many. Finally, a given dance will involve at least one couple (or it isn't a dance) and possibly many couples. These inner and outer multiplicity constraints are shown in Figure 8.36.

Figure 8.35 An n-ary association with inner and outer multiplicity constraints.

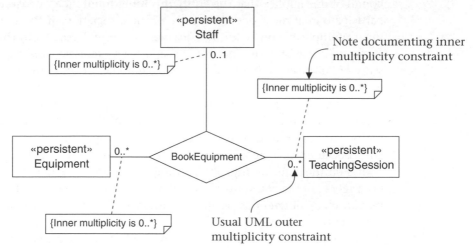

(a) Using standard UML notation.

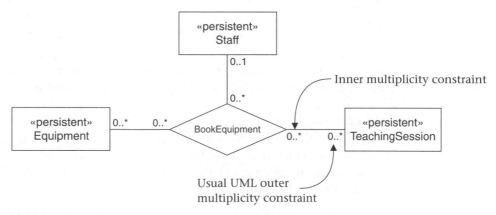

(b) Using the enhanced notation proposed in Génova et al. (2002).

Figure 8.36 ER diagram showing inner and outer multiplicity constraints on Partners.

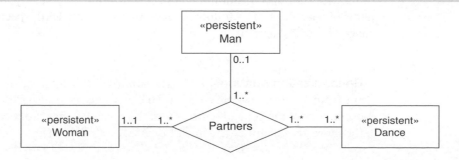

The two examples given above illustrate a problem with inner multiplicity constraints similar to that with outer multiplicity. It is that the upper bound on the inner multiplicity constraints of an n-ary association is almost always many. An upper bound of one implies that the entity this inner multiplicity constraint applies to will participate in at most one occurrence of the association. If the upper bound on the inner multiplicity constraint on Equipment was one (Figure 8.35) then there would be at most one pair of occurrences of Staff and TeachingSession associated with any occurrence of Equipment – that is, any piece of equipment could only be booked once. This is clearly unrealistic.

The situation regarding the two kinds of multiplicity constraint can be summed up as follows. The lower bound on the inner multiplicity indicates whether or not a given entity participates in the association, while the upper bound limits how many different association occurrences a given entity occurrence can participate in. The lower bound on the outer multiplicity constraint indicates whether or not any given set of occurrences of the *other* entities participates in the association. The upper bound limits how many different association occurrences this set of entity occurrences can participate in.

For binary associations, there is an easy equivalence between inner and outer multiplicity – the inner multiplicity constraint at one end of an association equals the outer multiplicity constraint at the other end. For n-ary associations, the inner and outer multiplicity constraints provide different information about the association. Furthermore, for n-ary associations the lower bound on the inner multiplicity constraint usually provides the most interesting information, as the upper bound is often many. In contrast, the upper bound of the outer multiplicity constraint usually provides the more interesting information for this type of association as the lower bound is often zero.

Given the above, it seems sensible to include both inner and outer multiplicity constraints in the ER diagram for n-ary associations, and two viable notations (one standard UML, one extending the UML) have been suggested. The database designer can choose whether to use one, or both, types of multiplicity constraint, but must be very clear about which he or she is using.

8.7 Generalization relationships

After multiplicity constraints, generalization relationships will be a breeze.

Generalization models the situation where one thing is a special kind of some other thing. The UML specification defines generalization very clearly, though it does so in terms of 'classifiers'. The following definition casts the UML specification in the language of the ER diagram.

Generalization relationship A taxonomic relationship between a more general entity and a more specific entity. Each occurrence of the specific entity is also an occurrence of the general entity. Thus, the specific entity indirectly has features of the more general entity (Adapted from OMG, 2005 p. 51).

The idea is that all occurrences of an entity share some common attributes. However, certain occurrences of the entity have some additional attributes, while others do not. Those with the additional attributes are examples of the more specific, or specialized, entity. All are examples of the more general entity.

An association can represent any kind of relationship. A generalization only represents the 'is a kind of' relationship. In this sense, generalization has a more specific meaning than association. Generalization is used a lot in object-orientated design, but can be useful in conceptual database design. Note that a generalization relationship always has two distinct participating entities – the more general and the more specific entity.

Consider the Room entity from the Web Timetable application. All rooms have the same attributes – building, roomNo and capacity. The building and roomNo identify its location, while capacity indicates how many students the room can accommodate. Regardless of whether the room is a general teaching room, suitable for seminars and tutorials, or a lecture theatre, music room or laboratory, it has a location and a capacity. Laboratories also have workstations. Each workstation is a place where one or more students work. It may be a computer workstation, designed for one student to use, or a lab bench in a science or engineering laboratory, some of which are designed for two students to share. Hence, the number of workstations may be lower than the room's capacity. Rather than include a workstations attribute for the Room entity, which is not relevant for most occurrences of Room, it makes sense to create a *new* entity, Laboratory, and indicate that this is a specific *type* of Room, with an additional attribute – workstations.

This situation is shown in the ER diagram in Figure 8.37. The generalization relationship is distinguished from an association by placing a triangle at the more general end of the relationship. The attributes common to all occurrences of Room are included in the more general entity Room. The additional attribute relevant to the more specific entity occurrences is included in the Laboratory entity. It is important to realize that an occurrence of Room *does not* have a workstations attribute. However, an occurrence of Laboratory *does* have a building, roomNo and capacity attribute as well as a workstations attribute. The more specific entity inherits the attributes (and operations) of the more general entity.

In the Web Timetable, the Room entity actually has three more specific entities – Laboratory, LectureTheatre and MusicRoom.

A music room may or may not have a piano, electronic keyboard or organ in it. Staff and students need to known which rooms do and which don't. They also want to know what type of keyboard is in the room. This suggests the more specific entity MusicRoom with two additional attributes – keyboard and description.

Figure 8.37 A generalization relationship.

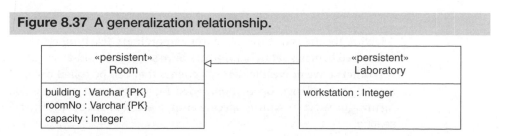

Figure 8.38 Two equivalent representations of a generalization hierarchy with two levels.

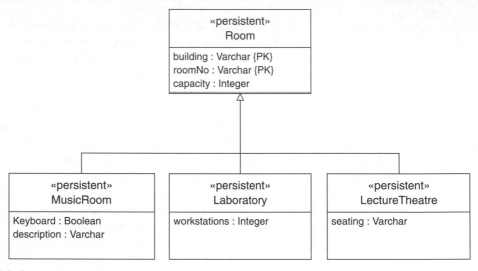

(a) Converging paths.

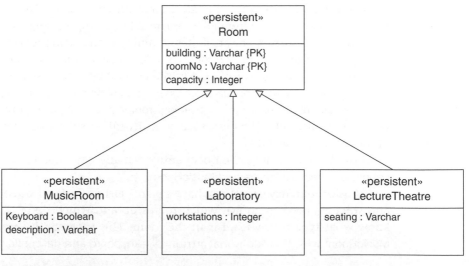

(b) Separate paths.

A lecture theatre is distinguished from an ordinary teaching room by its seating. Some have fixed benches set in tiers, others have seats with fold-away tables on the arms and still others have moveable tiers of benches that can be rolled back, turning the lecture theatre into a large, open room, used for sports such as basketball or badminton. Again, this suggests a more specific entity LectureTheatre with the additional attribute seating.

Two equivalent representations of these generalization relationships are shown in Figures 8.38 (a) and (b). In the first, the paths from the more specific to the more general entity are shown converging on a single triangle. All three are more specific versions of the Room entity. An alternative is to show a separate generalization relationship for each of the more specific entities. In both cases, the diagrams represent *three* generalization relationships – one between MusicRoom and Room, one between Laboratory and Room and one between LectureTheatre and Room.

Generalization relationships can be quite complex. They can form hierarchies of increasingly more specific entities. For example, the Laboratory entity has two more specific entities – ComputingLab and ScienceLab.

A computing lab has a computer at each workstation and specialist software installed on each computer. This may be computing software (such as programming languages), engineering software (such as CAD/CAM applications) or scientific software (such as chemical analysis applications).

A science lab is a room where experiments take place. These experiments may involve hazardous procedures, so must be assessed under health and safety legislation and given a safety rating. They may also need safe usage notes. Ordinary computing labs don't need such an assessment.

The full hierarchy is shown in Figure 8.39. Note that, for example, ComputingLab is a more specific kind of Laboratory, which is itself a more specific kind of Room. So, each occurrence of ComputingLab has the attributes specialistSoftware, workstations, building, roomNo and capacity. It inherits workstations from Laboratory and building, roomNo and capacity from Room. It does not inherit any attributes from MusicRoom or LectureTheatre as neither of these has a generalization relationship with ComputingLab, although they are higher up the hierarchy.

Generalization relationships do not have multiplicity constraints. It would not make sense to ask how many occurrences of Room had a generalization relationship with a particular occurrence of Laboratory. Each occurrence of Laboratory *is* an occurrence of Room. Generalization relationships connect entities, not entity *occurrences*. They capture a relationship at a higher level of abstraction than that captured by an association.

There are two constraints that apply to generalization relationships. In fact, they actually apply to the set of generalization relationships for which an entity is the more general entity. The first is the **disjoint constraint**. This indicates whether or not the occurrence of the more general entity can, at the same time, be an occurrence of more than one of its more specific entities. For example, an occurrence of Room can be an occurrence of MusicRoom or it can be an occurrence of Laboratory, but it cannot be both at the same time. This is indicated by placing the UML keyword 'disjoint' in parentheses at the more general end of the generalization relationships. It is important to emphasize that this constraint relates to the set of three generalization relationships that have Room as their more general entity, not just to one of them.

The other sort of constraint often used in ER diagrams is not part of the UML, but can be included in the list of constraints on a set of generalization relationships. The **participation constraint** indicates whether or not every occurrence of the more general entity is also an occurrence of one of the more specific entities. For example, some occurrences of Room are just teaching rooms, they are not occurrences of MusicRoom, Laboratory or LectureTheatre. The keyword 'optional' is included in the

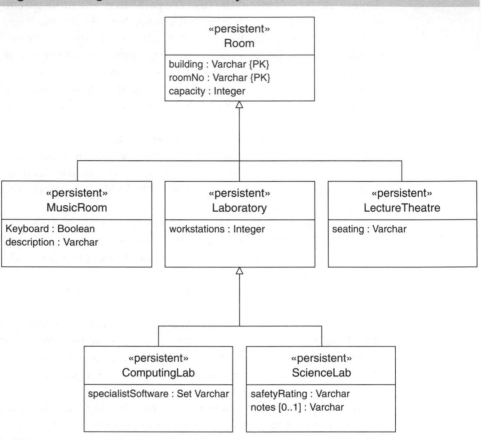

Figure 8.39 A generalization hierarchy.

list of constraints on these generalization relationships. In an ER diagram using converging paths for the generalization relationships, the list of constraints {disjoint, optional} is placed by the single triangle (Figure 8.40 (a)). If separate paths are used for each generalization relationship, then a dotted line is drawn across these relationships and the constraint placed near the dotted line (Figure 8.40 (b)).

The generalization relationships for Room illustrate a {disjoint, optional} constraint. Those for Laboratory illustrate the opposite. An occurrence of Laboratory can be both a ComputingLab and a ScienceLab at the same time. For example, the chemical engineering laboratory is a ScienceLab as students use hazardous chemicals in their experiments. It is also a ComputingLab as each workstation has a computer with specialist chemical analysis software installed on it. The disjoint constraint thus has the value 'overlapping' rather than 'disjoint'.

In terms of participation constraint, every laboratory must be either a ComputingLab or a ScienceLab (or both), so participation is 'mandatory'. The constraint {overlapping, mandatory} on the generalization relationships with Laboratory as the more general entity is shown in Figure 8.40 (a).

Figure 8.40 Constraints on a set of generalization relationships.

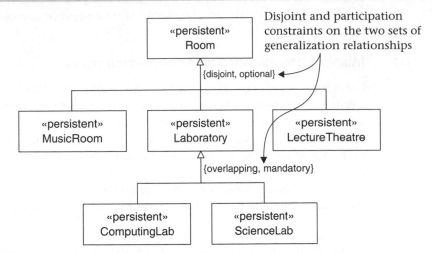

(a) With converging paths.

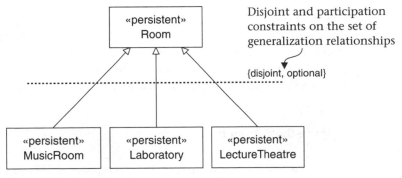

(b) With separate paths.

8.8 Validating an ER diagram

The purpose of an ER digram is to document the business artefacts and behaviour needed to realize the users' requirements. ER diagrams are quite good at this, but it is possible to draw an ER diagram that *looks* convincing but fails to do its job properly. There are three broad areas of concern.

First, there are the **connection traps**. A connection trap is when associations between entities in the ER diagram do not fully capture the different links between occurrences of those entities.

A second problem occurs when an association represents a connection between entities that is already represented by other associations. The ER diagram can be simplified by removing such **redundant associations**.

The third area of concern is that the ER diagram may not allow users to make all the database queries they require. **Access path analysis** can verify that the ER diagram represents a database design that can support all required database queries.

8.8.1 Missing associations and connection traps

Connection traps occur when the database designer has failed to identify that there is a direct connection between two entities that needs to be represented by an association. Sometimes the structure of the ER diagram misleads the database designer into thinking that there is a connection between two entities via a third entity when there isn't. Where such a structure occurs, the database designer should carefully examine the ER diagram to ensure that all the connections between entities are fully captured by the associations. Sometimes there are no clues and only carefully reflecting on the intended meaning of the ER diagram will find a missing association.

> **Connection trap** A structure in an ER diagram where a connection between two entities is not adequately represented by existing associations.

Consider the ER diagram shown in Figure 8.41 (a). The ER diagram does not include an association between Module and TeachingSession. Instead, it implies that the connection can be made indirectly, going via Staff. Given an occurrence of TeachingSession, navigate along the Teaches association to find which member of staff teaches this session, then navigate along the WorksOn association to find which module that person

Figure 8.41 A fan trap.

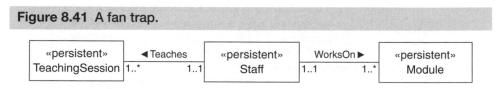

(a) Two one-to-many associations 'fan out' from a single entity.

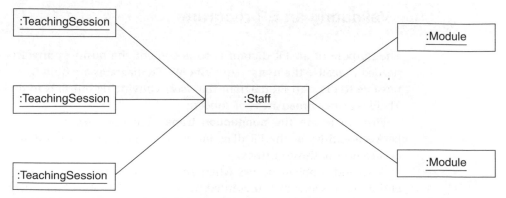

(b) Which teaching session is linked with which module?

Figure 8.42 Resolving a fan trap by adding the missing association.

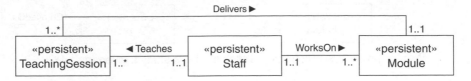

Figure 8.43 Two potential fan traps, which aren't.

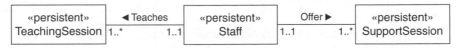

(a) No connection trap – the ER diagram correctly represents the scenario being modelled.

(b) Not a fan trap, but a connection trap nonetheless.

works on. Of course, as the object diagram in Figure 8.41 (b) illustrates, this is not possible. Links from many occurrences of TeachingSession converge on a single occurrence of Staff, from which links to many occurrences of Module emerge. There is no way of deciding which occurrence of TeachingSession is linked with which occurrence of Module. The characteristic fan shape gives this sort of connection trap its name – the **fan trap**.

Fan traps may occur when two one-to-many associations fan out from the same entity. While these two associations accurately reflect the connections between the participating entities, they don't capture the connection between the two outermost entities. In the example, there was a connection between TeachingSession and Module that could not be captured by the associations Teaches and WorksOn. The obvious solution is to add this 'missing' association to the ER diagram, as shown in Figure 8.42. This solution is used to resolve all connection traps, though it often introduces a new problem – one of the three associations in Figure 8.42 is now unnecessary. Redundant associations are dealt with in the next subsection.

The intended meaning of the ER diagram is crucial when deciding whether or not a potential connection trap is a problem. The ER diagrams in Figures 8.43 (a) and (b) involve two one-to-many associations fanning out from a single entity, but neither represents a fan trap.

The ER diagram in Figure 8.43 (a) models the connections between members of staff and their teaching and support sessions. Although the structure of the ER diagram is exactly the same as that in Figure 8.41 (a), the meaning in Figure 8.43 (a) is quite different. There is no implied connection between teaching and support sessions, other

Figure 8.44 A connection trap.

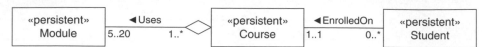

(a) A connection trap – which students study a given module?

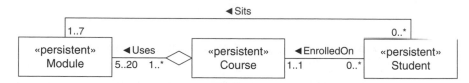

(b) Resolving the connection trap with the `Sits` association.

than that they happen to involve the same member of staff – that is, there is no *missing* association between TeachingSession and SupportSession.

The ER diagram in Figure 8.43 (b) is not a fan trap either. It *would* be a fan trap if it suggested that it was possible to navigate from an occurrence of TeachingSession to the occurrences of Equipment used in that teaching session. The lower bound on the (outer) multiplicity constraint at the Equipment end of KeptIn makes it clear that this is not always possible – some equipment is not kept in any room.

The ER diagram does suffer from a connection trap, though. When an entity participates in two associations and one or more of the multiplicity constraints has a lower bound of zero, then a second sort of connection trap – called a **chasm trap** – can occur. The optional participation of Equipment in KeptIn means that it is not always possible to find what equipment is needed for a teaching session using the two associations shown. If this information is required, then a *new* association should be added between TeachingSession and Equipment.

Another example of a connection trap (which is neither a fan trap nor a chasm trap) is shown in Figure 8.44 (a). Each Student enrols on exactly one Course, which Uses at least five Module. The modules taken on a course will cover all years of the course, so a student will only sit some of these modules in any one year. As the Web Timetable is intended to model a single academic year, the ER diagram has a connection trap – it is not possible to identify which modules any given student is taking this year. Notice that this problem would arise even if the the lower bound on the multiplicity constraint at the Student end of EnrolledOn were one.

The problem is that the database designer has failed to notice that there is a direct connection between Module and Student. The solution is to add the Sits association, as shown in Figure 8.44 (b).

Notice that the existence of a connection trap in Figure 8.44 (a) is due to the intended interpretation of the ER diagram – that it represents modules taken by students in a particular academic year. If the ER diagram was instead intended to represent *all* the modules a student takes during his or her entire course of study, then there would be no connection trap as the link between a particular module and a particular student can be made via the course. That is unless, for example, a course has optional modules.

Then, there would be a connection trap again as it isn't possible to identify which students take a particular optional module. It is worth thinking carefully before declaring a connection trap and adding a new association.

8.8.2 Redundant associations

The opposite problem to connection traps occurs when an association adds no new information to an ER diagram as the connection it represents is already adequately represented by other associations. Such **redundant associations** can be removed from an ER diagram, simplifying the conceptual design.

Resolving a fan trap usually creates a redundant association. Consider the ER diagram in Figure 8.45 (a) (a copy of Figure 8.42). The associations form a closed loop or circuit – staff teach teaching sessions, which deliver modules, which are worked on by staff. Such circuits *may* indicate that one of the associations is redundant, so should be examined carefully. As with connection traps, the intended meaning of the ER diagram will determine whether or not a given association is actually redundant.

Consider the Delivers association. This was introduced to resolve a fan trap, so it is clearly not redundant (removing it would reintroduce the fan trap). The Teaches association is not redundant either. To see this, consider what happens when it is removed, as shown in Figure 8.45 (b). Teaches captured information about which member of staff taught a particular teaching session. A particular occurrence of TeachingSession is now linked by an occurrence of the Delivers association to exactly one occurrence of Module. Unfortunately, this occurrence of Module may be linked to many different occurrences of Staff (by occurrences of WorksOn). This means that it is no longer possible to identify which member of staff teaches a given teaching session. Similarly, given a particular member of staff, it is not possible to identify which teaching sessions he or she teaches.

Figure 8.45 Removing a redundant association.

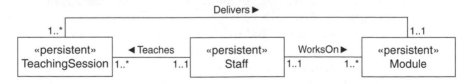

(a) A closed loop of associations indicates a possible redundant association.

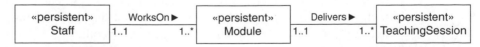

(b) `Teaches` is not redundant.

(c) The ER diagram redrawn with the redundant association `WorksOn` removed.

399

The last association is WorksOn. WorksOn captures information about which members of staff work on which modules. Figure 8.45 (c) shows the ER diagram with this association removed and it turns out that this ER diagram is equivalent to the original. Given a particular occurrence of Module, navigate along the Delivers association to find all the occurrences of TeachingSession that are linked to it. For each occurrence of TeachingSession navigate along Teaches to find which occurrence of Staff is linked to it. This provides a list of *all* staff working on the module as, if they work on the module, they must teach one of the teaching sessions. Similarly, for a given occurrence of staff, it is possible to use Teaches and Delivers to find which modules he or she works on. Hence, the WorksOn association in Figure 8.45 (a) is redundant.

8.8.3 Access path analysis

An ER diagram is intended to document a database design capable of meeting the information requirements of the end users. These requirements imply that certain database queries must be possible. **Access path analysis** (also called **transaction path analysis**) checks whether or not the entities and associations in the ER diagram can support a particular database query. The basic approach is for the database designer to think through the behaviour of the DBMS in response to a query. The designer should identify which entities hold the required data and consider how to navigate from one entity to the other via the associations in the ER diagram. The basic idea is to map out how to access the required information. If there is no way to access the required information, then the ER diagram must be incomplete.

The best approach to documenting that the ER diagram can support a particular database query is to draw the access path itself, showing the entities and associations that the DBMS would need to access to answer the query. For example, in the Web Timetable, it is reasonable to ask which staff teach a particular course. Clearly this data is held in the Course and Staff entities.

Figure 8.46 (a) shows an extract from the Web Timetable ER diagram, which includes all the relevant entities and associations. There is no association between the Course and Staff entities, but it is possible to navigate from Course along the Uses association to Module and then along Leads to Staff – an access path consisting of just two associations.

Unfortunately, this access path does not answer the question asked. Instead, it identifies those staff who *lead* a module of the course, but not those staff who only teach the module.

An alternative is to navigate from Course along the Uses association to Module, but then along Delivers to TeachingSession and finally along Teaches to Staff. This access path *does* answer the question asked, so the ER diagram can support this database query. Figure 8.46 (b) shows this access path drawn out.

As a database application may involve hundreds of different queries it is rarely possible to check them all. Instead, the database designer should identify those queries that are particularly important for the behaviour of the finished application. These may include:

- queries that are important to end users
- queries that will be run frequently
- complex queries.

Figure 8.46 Access path analysis for the query 'List all staff who teach on a particular course'.

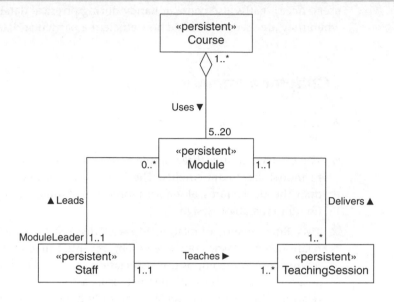

(a) Extract from the Web Timetable ER diagram showing the relevant entities and associations.

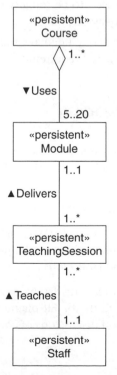

(b) The actual access path for the query.

Identifying such queries can be difficult, but it is worth making the effort. Even if only a few access paths are developed, they provide some reassurance that the ER diagram represents a database design that will meet the core requirements of the end users. Access paths also come in handy during physical database design (Chapter 10), when they are used to estimate how efficient a particular database query will be.

Chapter summary

- The main focus of this chapter has been on conceptual database design using ER diagrams.

- The ER diagram uses three simple abstractions – entity, relationship and attribute – to model data requirements. The UML class diagram notation has been used to draw the ER diagrams, along with some non-standard additions that are particularly useful for database design.

- Two different sorts of relationship were discussed – association and generalization relationships. Associations represent meaningful connections between entities. Aggregation and composition associations are special forms of association. Generalization relationships are distinct from associations, representing 'is a kind of' relationships, which are most commonly met in object-orientated approaches to application development.

- The important topic of association multiplicity constraints has been covered in depth. Two kinds of multiplicity constraints – inner and outer – were identified. These were seen to be roughly equivalent for binary associations, but quite different for n-ary associations.

- The chapter concluded by suggesting approaches to validating an ER diagram against the users' requirements.

Further reading

Muller (1999) covers database design with the UML in depth and includes logical design for data models other than the relational data model (our Chapter 9) and XML (our Chapter 12).

Connolly and Begg (2004) also use the UML notation for ER diagrams.

There are many books on UML itself and all cover class diagrams, which form the basis for the ER diagrams in this chapter. Good introductory UML texts include Bennett et al. (2005) and Holt (2001).

There are many existing database textbooks that cover the database design process, but use other notations for ER diagrams. Kroenke (2006) and Hoffer et al. (2004) have particularly good discussions of conceptual database design.

The research paper by Génova et al. (2002) forms the basis for the comparison of inner and outer multiplicity in Section 8.6. It is a reasonably clear discussion, though, as it is a research paper, may be considered a little heavy going. The distinction between inner and outer multiplicities is not often made in database textbooks, but it is essential to understand it if the UML notation is used.

Review questions

8.1 Describe the three stages of database design.

8.2 Define the following terms used in ER diagramming:
(a) entity
(b) entity occurrence
(c) attribute
(d) relationship
(e) relationship occurrence.

8.3 Describe three of the additional features of attributes and give an example of each.

8.4 Explain the purpose of a derived attribute. How are these indicated in the ER diagram?

8.5 Distinguish between a strong and a weak entity.

8.6 Explain each of the following terms used in ER diagramming:
(a) association relationship (often just called an association)
(b) degree of an association
(c) binary association
(d) unary association
(e) n-ary association.

8.7 Explain the differences between an association, aggregation association and composition association. How are aggregation and composition associations indicated in the ER diagram?

8.8 What is the purpose of a multiplicity constraint?

8.9 Explain the difference between one-to-one, one-to-many and many-to-many associations.

8.10 Explain each of the following terms used in ER diagramming:
(a) generalization relationship
(b) disjoint constraint
(c) participation constraint.

Exercises

8.11 For each of the following descriptions, draw an ER diagram showing an entity and its attributes.

(a) When they enrol at the Pennine University, students are each allocated a ten-character student ID number, which acts as a unique identifier. The first name(s), preferred name and family name are recorded for each student. Each is allocated a university e-mail address, and optionally may provide an additional e-mail address and phone number.

(b) Each course has a unique, four-character course code and a title. The level of the course (access, undergraduate or postgraduate), the exit qualification and the mode of study (full- or part-time) are all recorded. The name of the department(s) delivering the course is also included (there are at most two departments involved). The title and mode uniquely identify a course.

(c) Each teaching session runs on a particular day (Monday to Friday), between two given times. No teaching session starts before 09.00 or after 18.00. Teaching sessions last between one and three hours (the usual length is one hour). Each teaching session is timetabled to run between two fixed dates and runs for between 1 and 12 weeks. The type of the session is lecture, tutorial, practical, workshop or seminar. For sessions that are *not* lectures, there is a session code, to distinguish between classes that run in parallel.

(d) Write at least two similar descriptions of entities based on a business or organization that you are familiar with and draw an appropriate ER diagram.

8.12 For each of the following descriptions, draw an ER diagram showing one or more entities (without their attributes) joined by a single association (possibly with attributes) or a generalization relationship. Include the (outer) multiplicity constraints in your diagram.

(a) A member of staff teaches one or more teaching sessions and each teaching session is taught by exactly one member of staff.

(b) A student may act as student representative for, at most, one course and each course has one or more student representatives. As there is supposed to be one student representative for each year of study on a course, which student represents which year is also recorded.

(c) An exam consists of one or more questions, with each question appearing on zero or more exams. (*Hint:* Use an aggregation association.)

(d) Questions may themselves be composed of many other questions, with each of these subsidiary questions belonging to exactly one main question. (*Hint:* Use a generalization relationship *and* a composition association.)

(e) An online chess tournament has 10 professionals and 100 amateurs taking part. Each game is played between one amateur and one professional. Each professional will play every amateur. If an amateur wins a game, he or she can play a second game against that professional. Any amateur winning two games against a professional is awarded a prize.

(f) Write at least two similar descriptions of associations or generalizations based on a business or organization that you are familiar with and draw an appropriate ER diagram.

8.13 Analyse the 'View timetable' use case for the Web Timetable case study in Appendix B, using the approach outlined in Section 8.2 and Appendix A. Draw up an application glossary using the style of Appendix A. Draw an initial conceptual ER diagram based on your analysis of the 'View timetable' use case.

8.14 Complete the conceptual database design for the Web Timetable case study by analysing the remaining use cases.

8.15 Validate your solution to Exercise 8.14, identifying and removing connection traps and redundant relationships.

8.16 Use transaction path analysis to verify that your conceptual database design for the Web Timetable supports each of the following transactions.
(a) View a timetable for a particular course.
(b) View a timetable for a particular academic, including his or her support sessions.
(c) List all equipment stored in a particular room.
(d) List all portable equipment available for use in a particular teaching session on a particular date.
(e) List all tutorial, practical and seminar group teaching sessions for a particular course. Do not include teaching sessions that have four or fewer places left.

Investigations

8.17 Almost every database textbook includes a discussion of ER diagrams. Investigate the notation used by a range of different database textbooks, comparing the different approaches. Pay particular attention to how they model association multiplicity and whether they use the inner or outer multiplicity constraint.

8.18 Investigate the benefits, and the drawbacks, of including operations in the ER diagram. What sorts of operations can be included? Why do traditional approaches to conceptual database design avoid such behavioural modelling? (Muller (1999) is a good starting point for this.)

8.19 Choose a business or organization that you know well and develop a conceptual database design that meets its information requirements. If the organization is large, focus on one aspect of its activities.

8.20 ER diagrams are one of a number of techniques for conceptual database design. Object Role Modelling (ORM) (Halpin, 2001) is one alternative, the Semantic Object Data Model (Kroenke, 2006) another. Investigate one of these alternative approaches to conceptual database design, contrasting it with the ER diagramming approach.

9 Logical database design

Chapter objectives

→ Discuss how to transform a conceptual ER diagram into a logical ER diagram for the relational data model.

→ Describe how to generate table schema (a relational database design) from a logical ER diagram.

→ Introduce normalization as an alternative database design technique.

Chapter outline

A conceptual database design demonstrates that an application will meet the users' data requirements, without going into the details of how. Logical database design begins to deal with how. It takes the data requirements identified in the conceptual database design and represents them using the data structures available in a particular data model, and this chapter focuses on the relational data model. Separating conceptual and logical database design means that the end users don't need to understand the particular data model used. Instead, the simple, and intuitive, abstractions of an ER diagram form the basis for discussion between designer and users. As formal data models, even the relatively simple relational data model, can be hard to grasp, this can be a successful approach.

The problem is that settling on a particular data model means reconsidering the way data is organized. An ER diagram uses three structures to organize data:

● entity
● attribute
● relationship.

The relational data model has only two:

● table
● column.

It is clear that an entity will become a table and each attribute of the entity will be a column in this table (the rows of the table are the entity occurrences – the actual data). This leaves the associations.

In an ER diagram, an association represents a connection between entities. In the relational data model, a connection between tables is represented by a foreign key column. However, associations can have attributes and foreign key columns cannot. This means that the translation from ER diagram to relational database design is not straightforward. This is the price paid by the database designer for a freer discussion of data requirements during conceptual database design.

- Section 9.1 introduces the standard approach to logical database design, showing how to translate the ER diagram for the Staff Directory into a set of table schema (the relational database design). This section is intended to introduce the key ideas of logical database design before discussing those features of ER diagrams that don't have direct counterparts in the relational model.

- Section 9.2 shows how to remove these features from an ER diagram while maintaining the original intentions of the designer. The result is called a logical ER diagram, targeting the relational data model.

- Section 9.3 introduces some refinements to logical database design. In particular, it discusses how to derive default values and referential actions from the logical ER diagram. It ends with a summary of the logical database design process.

- Section 9.4 discusses an alternative database design technique called normalization. This was developed specifically for the relational data model and is an important tool for validating the relational database design.

9.1 Introducing logical database design

During logical database design, the entities, attributes and relationships of the conceptual database design are translated into the data structures of a particular data model.

> **Logical database design** Shows how to use the organization structures of a particular data model to meet the end users' data requirements.

The simpler structures used in an ER diagram usually have direct counterparts in the chosen data model, so the translation is pretty straightforward. For a relational database, entities become tables, single-valued attributes become columns and one-to-many associations with no attributes are represented by foreign keys. Provided an ER diagram only uses these three simple structures, the database designer can write down a set of table schema that meet the end users' data requirements.

The conceptual design for the Staff Directory database, shown in Figure 9.1, is such an ER diagram. It has two entities, each of which has a number of single-valued attributes. There is a single one-to-many association, which has no attributes of its own.

The earlier chapters on the relational data model and the relational data language SQL suggest that the logical database design should include the characteristics of

Figure 9.1 ER diagram representing the conceptual database design for the Staff Directory database.

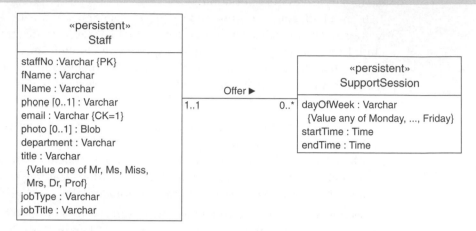

tables and columns listed in Table 9.1. These are all documented in the conceptual database design. The conceptual database design can also include a number of business rules. Whether these business rules can be implemented or not depends on the particular DBMS used, so they are considered during physical database design.

The first thing to do is write down an initial table schema for each entity. This should include the table name and column descriptions that form the table heading. The table name will usually be the same as the entity name. Columns will usually have the same name and data type as the attribute they implement. Any default values can be noted after the data type. An attribute with multiplicity [0..1] may not have a value on some entity occurrences. This means that the column implementing this attribute may be null on some rows of the table. All other columns have multiplicity [1..1] so will be not null. The column description should clearly indicate whether a column can or cannot be null.

Occasionally the database designer will want to choose a different name for the table or column than that used for the corresponding entity or attribute. The main reason for changing a table or column name is that the name used in the ER diagram is not a valid SQL identifier. For example, it might be a reserved word in the dialect of SQL used by the target DBMS. Another potential problem might be that the target DBMS doesn't support a particular data type. These issues are dealt with during physical database design. Another reason for changing a name is if the end users insisted on an unnecessarily long or confusing name during conceptual design. Now they are out of the picture, the database designer could change this to something shorter or more

Table 9.1 Characteristics of tables and columns.

Relational data structure	Characteristics
Table	Name and table constraints, such as primary, candidate and foreign keys.
Column	Name, data type, default value and not-null constraint.

meaningful. Code listing 9.1.1 shows the initial table schema for the `Staff` and `SupportSession` tables.

Code listing 9.1.1   Initial table schema for the `Staff` and `SupportSession` tables

```
Staff (staffNo VARCHAR NOT NULL,
        fName VARCHAR NOT NULL,
        lName VARCHAR NOT NULL,
        phone VARCHAR NULL,
        email VARCHAR NOT NULL,
        photo BLOB NULL,
        department VARCHAR NOT NULL,
        title VARCHAR NOT NULL,
        jobType VARCHAR NOT NULL,
        jobTitle VARCHAR NOT NULL)

SupportSession (dayOfWeek VARCHAR NOT NULL,
                startTime TIME NOT NULL,
                endTime TIME NOT NULL)
```

In the relational data model, each table should have a primary key. The **Staff** entity is a strong entity (Figure 9.1) and its primary key becomes the primary key of the `Staff` table. The **SupportSession** entity is a weak entity so does not have a primary key. The `SupportSession` *table* will have a primary key, but, at the moment, it cannot be identified. Primary keys are noted below the table heading, as shown in Code listing 9.1.2.

Code listing 9.1.2   Initial table schema showing primary keys

```
Staff (staffNo VARCHAR NOT NULL,
        fName VARCHAR NOT NULL,
        lName VARCHAR NOT NULL,
        phone VARCHAR NULL,
        email VARCHAR NOT NULL,
        photo BLOB NULL,
        department VARCHAR NOT NULL,
        title VARCHAR NOT NULL,
        jobType VARCHAR NOT NULL,
        jobTitle VARCHAR NOT NULL)
PRIMARY KEY (staffNo)

SupportSession (dayOfWeek VARCHAR NOT NULL,
                startTime TIME NOT NULL,
                endTime TIME NOT NULL)
PRIMARY KEY NOT YET IDENTIFIED
```

Both table schema look a little like an SQL create table statement. This is intentional. As most relational DBMS use SQL as their data language, it makes sense to write

Figure 9.2 An alternative approach to documenting table schema.

Table name	Staff		
Column name	*Data type*	*Default*	*Null*
staffNo	VARCHAR		No
fName	VARCHAR		No
lName	VARCHAR		No
phone	VARCHAR		Yes
email	VARCHAR		No
photo	BLOB		Yes
department	VARCHAR		No
title	VARCHAR		No
jobType	VARCHAR		No
jobTitle	VARCHAR		No
Constraints			
Primary key	staffNo		

the table schema so that they can be easily turned into SQL create table statements. However, some database designers feel that table schema should have a more polished look to them.

An alternative is to set out the table schema in a way similar to that shown in Figure 9.2. This is another of those times when personal preference (or a manager's preference) will decide which approach to use.

The next step deals with the one-to-many associations. Each one-to-many association generates a foreign key and its associated foreign key constraint. The question is, which of the two tables gets the foreign key?

Consider the Offer association between Staff and SupportSession. This tells us that each occurrence of the SupportSession entity is linked by a single occurrence of the Offer association to a single occurrence of the Staff entity. In contrast, one occurrence of the Staff entity may be linked to many different occurrences of the Offer association to occurrences of the SupportSession entity. Translating this into the relational data model, each row of the SupportSession table should be linked to a single row of the Staff table, while a single row of Staff may be linked to many rows of SupportSession. Clearly the SupportSession table is the one that needs the foreign key – a foreign key always links back to a single row in the referenced table. Figure 9.3 shows the ER diagram and relational database tables side by side and illustrates the process of translating a one-to-many association into a foreign key relationship between two tables.

One-to-many associations are always dealt with in this way – the table that implements the entity at the 'many' end of the one-to-many association gets the foreign key. In the example, the matching candidate key in the Staff table is {staffNo},

Figure 9.3 Translating a one-to-many association into a foreign key relationship.

Staff

staffNo:Varchar	fName:Varchar	lName:Varchar	phone:Varchar	email:Varchar	photo:BLOB	department:Varchar	title:Varchar	jobType:Varchar	jobTitle:Varchar
10780	John	Smith	NULL	j.b.smith@pennine.ac.uk	[BLOB]	Catering	Mr	Support	Cheif
25447	John	Smith	5104	j.smith@pennine.ac.uk	[BLOB]	Music	Mr	Administration	Secretary
25448	Judith Anne	Smith	7709	j.a.smith@pennine.ac.uk	[BLOB]	Estates	Mrs	Support	Estates Manager
31210	Paul	Smith	NULL	p.smith@pennine.ac.uk	[BLOB]	Computing	Dr	Academic	Senior Lecturer
77712	Frank	Rose	8871	f.rose@pennine.ac.uk	[BLOB]	Computing	Mr	Technical	Technician
14443	Helen	Abbot	8032	h.abbot@pennine.ac.uk	[BLOB]	Computing	Mrs	Administration	Secretary
23257	Freya	Stark	8660	f.stark@pennine.ac.uk	[BLOB]	Computing	Prof	Academic	Dean
33935	Padma	Brar	6641	p.brar@pennine.ac.uk	[BLOB]	Health	Ms	Administration	Administrator
35054	Selma	Hutchins	8706	s.hutchins@pennine.ac.uk	[BLOB]	Computing	Ms	Academic	Senior Lecturer
45965	Mikhail	Sudbin	5553	m.sudbin@pennine.ac.uk	[BLOB]	Music	Mr	Academic	Lecturer
35155	Helene	Chirac	NULL	h.chirac@pennine.ac.uk	[BLOB]	Health	Miss	Technical	Technician
55776	Gurpreet	Choudhury	5454	g.choudhury@pennine.ac.uk	[BLOB]	Music	Dr	Academic	Senior Lecturer
56893	Ruth	Bapetsi	8022	r.bapetsi@pennine.ac.uk	[BLOB]	Health	Mrs	Academic	Senior Lecturer
56673	Joshua	Bittaye	7782	j.bittaye@pennine.ac.uk	[BLOB]	Computing	Mr	Academic	Senior Lecturer
89987	Dan	Lin	8514	d.lin@pennine.co.uk	[BLOB]	Computing	Dr	Administration	Senior Administrator
78893	Jo Karen	O'Connor	8871	j.k.oconnor@pennine.ac.uk	[BLOB]	Health	Miss	Administration	Administrator
33509	Helen	Timms	8661	h.timms@pennine.ac.uk	[BLOB]]	Music	Mrs	Technical	Technician

Matching candidate key column already exists in table at the 'one' end of the one-to-many association

Foregin key relationship in relational database design implements the one-to-many Offer association of the conceptual ER diagram

SupportSession

staffNo:Varchar	dayOfWeek:Varchar	startTime:Time	endTime:Time
56673	Friday	15:30:00	16:30:00
56673	Thursday	15:30:00	16:30:00
35054	Monday	09:00:00	10:00:00
45965	Wednesday	11:00:00	12:00:00
31210	Wednesday	11:00:00	13:00:00
35054	Monday	15:00:00	16:00:00
56893	Thursday	09:00:00	10:00:00
45965	Monday	11:00:00	12:00:00
23257	Monday	15:00:00	16:00:00
55776	Monday	14:00:00	16:00:00
56893	Tuesday	14:00:00	15:00:00
56673	Friday	10:00:00	11:00:00
35054	Tuesday	11:00:00	12:00:00

Foregin key column added to table at the 'many' end of the one-to-many association

«persistent» Staff

staffNo :Varchar (PK)
fName : Varchar
lName : Varchar
phone [0..1] : Varchar
email : Varchar (CK=1)
photo [0..1] : Blob
department : Varchar
title : Varchar
{Value one of Mr, Ms, Miss, Mrs, Dr, Prof}
jobType : Varchar
jobTitle : Varchar

1..1

Offer ▶

0..*

«persistent» SupportSession

dayOfWeek : Varchar
{Value any of Monday, ... Friday}
startTime : Time
endTime : Time

so a copy of the `staffNo` column is added to the `SupportSession` table. If the matching candidate key has two or more columns, a copy of each of these columns is added to the other table to form the new foreign key.

The name of the foreign key column does not need to be the same as the matching primary key column. For example, the `staffNo` column in the `SupportSession` table could be called `staff`. In contrast, the data type of the foreign key columns must be *exactly the same* as the data type of the matching candidate key column. This includes them being the same length, although column lengths aren't always included in the logical database design. So, if the `staffNo` column in the `Staff` table was a `Varchar(10)`, the `staffNo` column in the `SupportSession` table would also be `Varchar(10)`.

It's also possible to determine whether or not the foreign key columns should have a not-null constraint. If the one-to-many association has a multiplicity of 0..1 at the 'one' end, then the foreign key columns can be null. If, however, the multiplicity at the 'one' end is 1..1, then the foreign key columns cannot be null. Consider, for example, the Offer association in Figure 9.3. The multiplicity at the 'one' end is 1..1. This means that, for any particular occurrence of the SupportSession entity, there *must* be an occurrence of the Staff entity associated with it via the Offer association. In the language of the relational data model, this says that every row of the `SupportSession` table is associated via its foreign key with a row of the `Staff` table – the foreign key column cannot be null.

The only other part of the column description is the default value. Foreign key columns don't often have a default value. When they do, it indicates that there is some particular row of the referenced table that should be associated with any 'unclaimed' rows of the referencing table. Suppose that a new row is added to the `SupportSession` table by an end user but that user forgets to say which member of staff offers the support session. Is there a particular member of staff who can be associated with this unclaimed support session? Clearly not, so there is no default value for the foreign key column `staffNo` in the `SupportSession` table.

Code listing 9.1.3 shows the amended table schema for the `SupportSession` table, with the full column description for the new foreign key column `staffNo` and the associated foreign key constraint.

Code listing 9.1.3   Including a foreign key constraint in a table schema

```
SupportSession (staffNo VARCHAR NOT NULL,
                dayOfWeek VARCHAR NOT NULL,
                startTime TIME NOT NULL,
                endTime TIME NOT NULL)
PRIMARY KEY NOT YET IDENTIFIED
FOREIGN KEY (staffNo) REFERENCES Staff(staffNo)
```

Adding the `staffNo` column to the `SupportSession` table means that each row of this table is now unique – staff members only offer one support session at any given time. As discussed in Chapter 3, the primary key of the `SupportSession` table is {`staffNo, dayOfWeek, startTime`}. Typically, the primary key of a table that implements a weak entity will include *all* the foreign key columns. The final table schema is shown in Code listing 9.1.4.

Code listing 9.1.4   Table schema for the SupportSession table

```
SupportSession (staffNo VARCHAR NOT NULL,
                dayOfWeek VARCHAR NOT NULL,
                startTime TIME NOT NULL,
                endTime TIME NOT NULL)
PRIMARY KEY (staffNo, dayOfWeek, startTime)
FOREIGN KEY (staffNo) REFERENCES Staff(staffNo)
```

At this point, most of the information about entities, their attributes and the one-to-many associations, has been included in the table schema. What's missing is any mention of the candidate keys and business rules. One option is simply to leave these things out of the logical database design. They are fully documented in the conceptual design and it is possible that they cannot be implemented on the target DBMS, so it would make sense to consider them during physical design. On the other hand, this means that the logical design (the set of table schema) is not a complete specification of the end users' data requirements. It will need to be read in conjunction with the conceptual design. Rather than have the data requirements specified in two different places, it is better to note any outstanding data requirements in the logical design itself. Candidate keys and other constraints can be noted after the foreign key constraints. Code listing 9.1.5 shows the final logical design for the Staff Directory database.

Code listing 9.1.5   Final logical design for the StaffDirectory database

```
Staff (staffNo VARCHAR NOT NULL,
       fName VARCHAR NOT NULL,
       lName VARCHAR NOT NULL,
       phone VARCHAR NULL,
       email VARCHAR NOT NULL,
       photo BLOB NULL,
       department VARCHAR NOT NULL,
       title VARCHAR NOT NULL,
       jobType VARCHAR NOT NULL,
       jobTitle VARCHAR NOT NULL)
PRIMARY KEY (staffNo)
CANDIDATE KEY (email)
BUSINESS RULE title must be one of {'Mr', 'Ms', 'Miss',
        'Mrs', 'Dr', 'Prof'}

SupportSession (dayOfWeek VARCHAR NOT NULL,
                startTime TIME NOT NULL,
                endTime TIME NOT NULL)
PRIMARY KEY (staffNo, dayOfWeek, startTime)
FOREIGN KEY (staffNo) REFERENCES Staff(staffNo)
CANDIDATE KEY (staffNo, dayOfWeek, endTime)
BUSINESS RULE dayOfWeek must be one of {'Monday',
        'Tuesday', 'Wednesday', 'Thursday', 'Friday'}
```

9.2 Logical ER diagrams

As a conceptual ER diagram may include structures that are not compatible with the target data model, a sensible first step is to remove them. They can be replaced with structures that are compatible with the target data model and broadly model the same situation. In most cases, this will mean replacing a structure that has a complex meaning (such as an n-ary association) with some combination of simpler structures (such as entities and binary associations). The goal is to produce an ER diagram that can easily be used to write down a logical database design.

The commonest structure in a conceptual ER diagram that is not compatible with the relational data model is the many-to-many association. Consider the many-to-many association Uses, which relates a course and the modules taught on that course (Figure 9.4). The obvious way to try and implement this as a foreign key in a relational database is to include a foreign key column `course` in the `Module` table (Figure 9.5). The problem is that a column can only hold *one* value, so the foreign key column `course` can only associate a particular module with one course. This isn't good enough as a module may be used by two or more courses. For example, the matching primary and foreign keys in Figure 9.5 associate the module 'Introduction to programming' with the full-time ICT course, but *cannot* show that it is *also* associated with the part-time ICT course (which it is). The same reasoning shows that a foreign key column `module` in the `Course` table could only ever indicate that a particular `Course` used one module. Again, this isn't good enough because a course needs to have at least four modules. A many-to-many association cannot be represented by a foreign key.

There are two other structures that occur in ER diagrams but have no direct equivalent in the relational data model. These are n-ary associations for n ≥ 3 (a foreign key can represent a link between, at most, two tables) and multivalued attributes (a column can hold, at most, one value of the given data type). The following subsections illustrate how these three structures can be replaced in the ER diagram by a combination of 'simpler' structures that *do* have direct equivalents in the relational data model. The resulting ER diagram is called a **logical ER diagram**.

Figure 9.4 A many-to-many association.

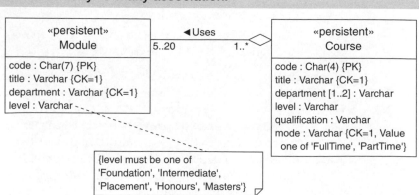

Figure 9.5 A foreign key cannot implement a many-to-many association.

Module					
code:varchar	title:varchar	department:varchar	level:char	preReq:varchar	course:char
CCFC0108	Introduction to programming	Computing	F	NULL	C3F5
CIFC0084	Information systems	Computing	F	NULL	C3F8
BAFC0178	Introduction to business	Business	F	NULL	B4T1
BMFC0107	Introduction to management	Business	F	NULL	B2Y6
CIIC0053	Application development	Computing	I	CCFC0108	C3F5
CCIC7009	Computing mathematics	Computing	I	NULL	C2Z1
CCHO0418	Formal specification	Computing	H	NULL	C2Z1
BAIC3427	Business audit	Business	I	BAFC0178	B4T1
CCH09668	Advanced programming	Computing	H	CCIC7009	C2Z1
CIHO6008	Soft systems	Computing	H	NULL	C3F5

———— Matching primary and foreign keys ————

Course					
code:char	title:varchar	department:varchar	level:varchar	qualification:varchar	mode:varchar
C3F5	ICT	{Computing}	Undergraduate	BSc	Full time
C3F8	ICT	{Computing}	Undergraduate	BSc	Part time
B4T1	Business studies	{Business}	Undergraduate	BA	Full time
B2Y6	Management	{Business}	Undergraduate	BA	Full time
B2Y8	Business computing	{Computing, Business}	Undergraduate	HND	Part time
B2Y9	Business computing	{Computing, Business}	Undergraduate	HND	Full time
C2Z1	Computer science	{Computing}	Undergraduate	BSc	Full time

> Some relational database designers, recognizing that these features will cause them problems later, choose not to use them at all. Others prefer to use them though, as they help to make conceptual design more intuitive and flexible. Which approach to take is, once again, a matter of personal preference.

It is important to realize that a logical ER diagram is simply a first step towards a logical database design. It is a tool used by the database designer and the database designer alone. It isn't seen by the users – they see the conceptual design. It isn't seen by the application developers – they see the final logical database design (which, for a relational database, is a set of table schema). This means that the logical ER diagram is a work-in-progress and, as such, can break a few of the rules that a conceptual ER diagram must obey. In particular, some associations are left without a name and some new entities don't have any attributes.

9.2.1 How to deal with multivalued attributes

In the relational data model, a column has, at most, one value of the specified data type on each row. This means that an attribute with a multiplicity greater than one cannot be implemented directly in a relational database as a column with the same data type as the attribute. There are three approaches to dealing with these multivalued attributes:

- use a non-scalar data type, such as set, multiset or array, the members of which have the same data type as the attribute

- replace the multivalued attribute with two or more single-valued attributes on the same entity

- replace the multivalued attribute with a new entity and a one-to-many association from the original entity.

The simplest approach is to use a non-scalar data type.

Consider the entity Course from the Web Timetable database (Figure 9.6). The attribute department has multiplicity [1..2], so is a multivalued attribute. The attribute multiplicity indicates that at least one and, at most, two departments are involved in running a particular course.

The business rule that motivates this constraint concerns how the Pennine University deals with courses that include a major–minor combination. For example, the course 'Business computing' is offered jointly by the business and computing departments. Two-thirds of the teaching and most of the course administration is done by the business department. The rest is done by the computing department. The business department is therefore said to be the 'lead department' for the course, with the computing department the 'minor department'.

This situation can be modelled using a non-scalar data type, as shown in the logical ER diagram in Figure 9.6. Here, the department attribute has a data type Varchar Array [2], indicating that its value is an array that has, at most, two members (this is an SQL-style

Figure 9.6 Modelling a multivalued attribute using a non-scalar data type.

Multivalued attribute with scalar data type

Single-valued attribute with non-scalar data type

```
            «persistent»                      «persistent»
              Course                            Course

 code : Char(4) {PK}              code : Char(4) {PK}
 title : Varchar {CK=1}           title : Varchar {CK=1}
 department [1..2] : Varchar      department : Varchar Array [2]
 level : Varchar                     {Must have 1 or 2 elements}
 qualification : Varchar          level : Varchar
 mode : Varchar {CK=1, Value one  qualification : Varchar
   of 'FullTime', 'PartTime'}     mode : Varchar {CK=1, Value one
                                    of 'FullTime', 'PartTime'}
```

Conceptual ER diagram   Logical ER diagram

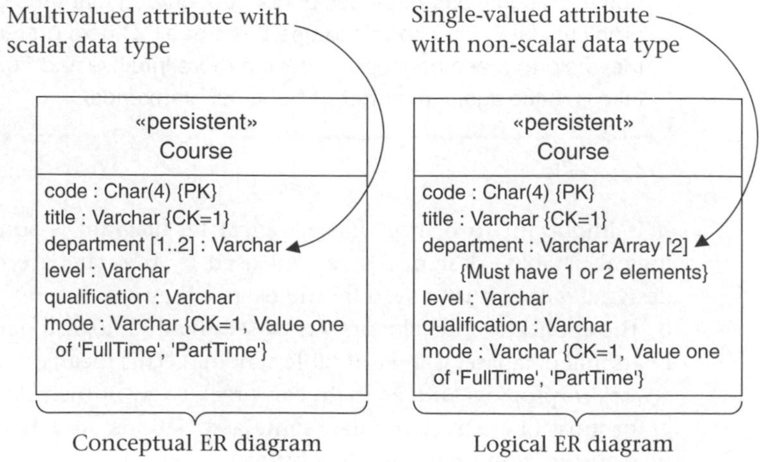

array, rather than a C-style array), each of which is a varying length character string. Note that an array has an upper bound on the number of members – in this case two – but no lower bound. The lower bound of the original multiplicity constraint has to be specified in an attribute constraint. It's clear that the logical ER diagram is equivalent to the conceptual ER diagram in terms of their meaning. The logical ER diagram simply gives more guidance on how to implement the data requirement for a multivalued attribute.

Code listing 9.2.1.1 shows the table schema based on this logical ER diagram. Note that the not-null constraint on the `department` column will not ensure that the array members are not null – `department = [NULL, NULL]` assigns a valid, not-null value for this column. This is why there is a new business rule noted for the `department` column.

Code listing 9.2.1.1   Table schema derived from the logical ER diagram in Figure 9.6

```
Course (code CHAR(4) NOT NULL,
        title VARCHAR NOT NULL,
        department VARCHAR ARRAY [2] NOT NULL,
        level VARCHAR NOT NULL,
        qualification VARCHAR NOT NULL,
        mode VARCHAR NOT NULL
       )
PRIMARY KEY (code)
CANDIDATE KEY (title, mode)
BUSINESS RULE department has at least 1 member
BUSINESS RULE mode must be one of {'Full-time', 'Part-time'}
```

The non-scalar data types are a fairly recent innovation in relational database technology. The SQL standard only includes multiset and array data types and even these are still not widely supported by commercial DBMS. Because of this, it makes sense to avoid using them unless it's known that they will definitely be available on the target DBMS. As there are, at most, two values held by the department attribute, it is possible in this case to replace it with two new single-valued attributes – leadDepartment and minorDepartment. These are shown in Figure 9.7. This approach can provide more information than using a multivalued attribute. In the current example, when the two departments are held in a single multivalued attribute, there is no way to identify which is the lead department and which the minor department. With two separate attributes, doing so is easy.

The multiplicity of the new attributes depends on the specific data requirements of the application being modelled. In the example, where only one department is involved in running a course, there will be no minor department, so the multiplicity of minorDepartment must be [0..1]. Because the department attribute always has at least one value, one of the two new attributes must have multiplicity [1..1] and this must be leadDepartment. Again, this reflects a business rule – that there is always at least one department involved in running a particular course. The table schema is shown in Code listing 9.2.1.2.

Figure 9.7 Replacing a multivalued attribute with two new single-valued attributes.

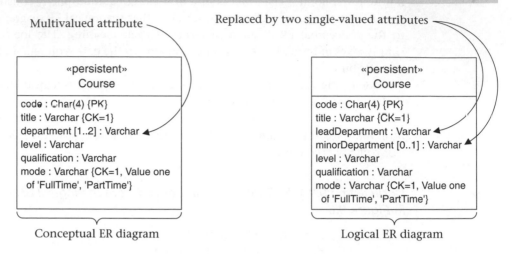

Multivalued attribute

Replaced by two single-valued attributes

Conceptual ER diagram

Logical ER diagram

Code listing 9.2.1.2   Table schema derived from the logical ER diagram in Figure 9.7

```
Course (code CHAR(4) NOT NULL,
        title VARCHAR NOT NULL,
        leadDepartment VARCHAR NOT NULL,
        minorDepartment VARCHAR NULL,
        level VARCHAR NOT NULL,
        qualification VARCHAR NOT NULL,
        mode VARCHAR NOT NULL
       )
PRIMARY KEY (code)
CANDIDATE KEY (title, mode)
BUSINESS RULE mode must be one of {'Full-time', 'Part-time'}
```

Replacing a multivalued attribute with a number of single-valued attributes will only work where the maximum number of values is fixed. If the maximum is many ('*'), then there is no way of knowing how many single-valued attributes are required. It is also only really feasible where the maximum is a small number, so multivalued attributes with a maximum of four values can be dealt with in this way. For example, a person may have up to four phone numbers – home phone, work phone, mobile and fax. It would be acceptable to store each of these in a separate attribute.

In many cases it is more effective to extract the multivalued attribute into a new entity. This approach to multivalued attributes creates a **look-up entity**. The multiple values of the original attribute are held in a separate entity and can be 'looked up' by following an association between the original entity and the look-up entity. Figure 9.8 demonstrates this process, showing the original entity with its multivalued attribute from the conceptual ER diagram and how it is represented in the logical ER diagram. Note that there is no department attribute on the Course entity in the logical ER

Figure 9.8 Replacing a multivalued attribute with a look-up entity and one-to-many association.

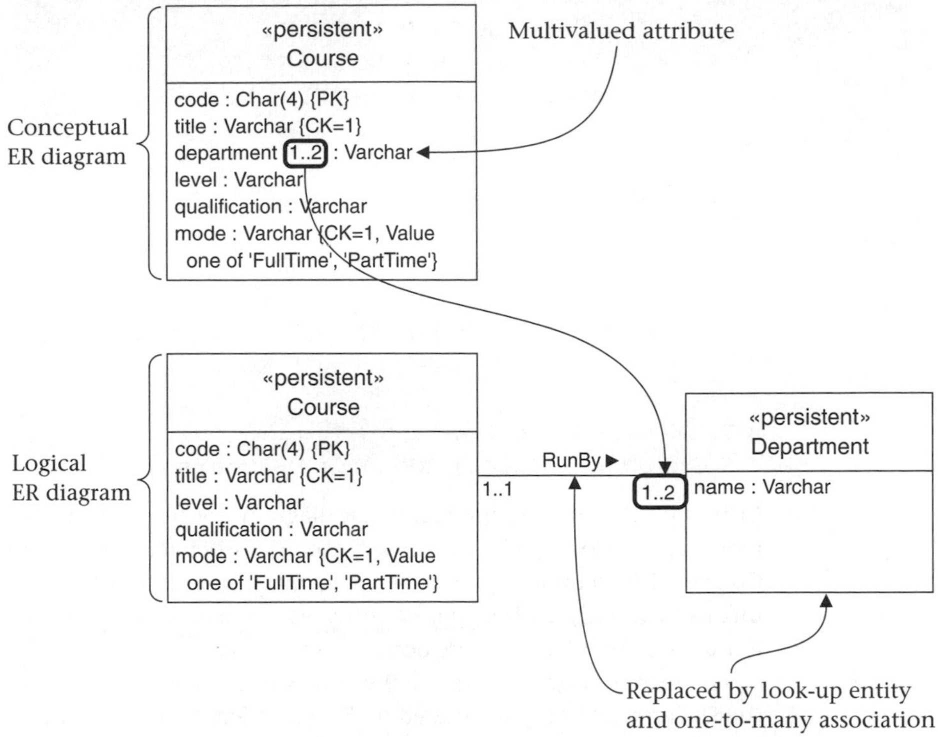

diagram. Instead, each occurrence of Course is associated with at least one, and possibly two, occurrences of the new Department entity. This entity has a single attribute, name, which is just a renamed copy of the department attribute on the Course entity. This is equivalent to the situation in the conceptual ER diagram where each occurrence of Course has at least one, and possibly two, values for the department attribute.

Whenever a multivalued attribute is extracted into a look-up entity, the look-up entity has just the one attribute. The look-up entity will also be a weak entity – in the example, two courses may be run by the same department, so there can be two occurrences of Department that have the same value for the name attribute, but are associated with different occurrences of Course.

The multiplicity constraint at the look-up entity end of the association is the same as the multiplicity constraint on the original multivalued attribute. The multiplicity constraint at the other end of the association is *always* 1..1. A particular occurrence of the look-up entity Department is supposed to hold one value from the department attribute on some particular occurrence of the Course entity. This value was associated with a single occurrence of Course, so an occurrence of the look-up entity must also be associated with a single occurrence of Course.

The table schema for this logical ER diagram are shown in Code listing 9.2.1.3. The one-to-many association RunBy leads to the inclusion of a foreign key column `code` in the `Department` table and, hence, the primary and foreign key constraints.

Code listing 9.2.1.3 Table schema derived from the logical ER diagram in Figure 9.8

```
Course (code CHAR(4) NOT NULL,
        title VARCHAR NOT NULL,
        level VARCHAR NOT NULL,
        qualification VARCHAR NOT NULL,
        mode VARCHAR NOT NULL
      )
PRIMARY KEY (code)
CANDIDATE KEY (title, mode)
BUSINESS RULE mode must be one of {'Full-time', 'Part-time'}

Department (code CHAR(4) NOT NULL,
            name VARCHAR NOT NULL
          )
PRIMARY KEY (code, name)
FOREIGN KEY (code) REFERENCES Course(code)
```

In this particular case, the logical ER diagram doesn't seem to be right. Each occurrence of the look-up entity Department is associated with a single occurrence of Course. This seems to suggest that a department offers only one course, which is clearly incorrect. In fact, the Department entity, as we have seen and like every look-up entity, is a weak entity. Two or more occurrences can have identical attribute values.

The object diagram in Figure 9.9 shows two distinct, but identical, occurrences of the Department entity associated with two different occurrences of the Course entity. This means that, as with the logical ER diagram in Figure 9.8, there will always be

Figure 9.9 Object diagram demonstrating that `Department` is a weak entity.

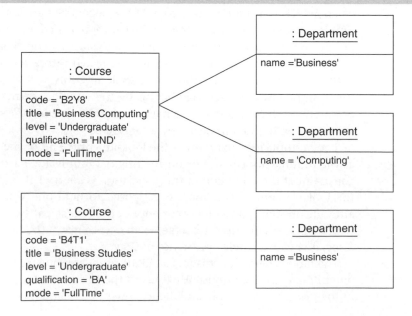

duplicate data about departments held on the database. Note, though, that the only information held about a department is its name.

To avoid even this small amount of duplication, the binary association RunBy could be modelled as a many-to-many association. The next section explains how to transform many-to-many binary associations so that they can be implemented in the relational data model and revisits this example to see what difference modelling the RunBy association as a many-to-many association makes to the logical database design.

9.2.2 Resolving a many-to-many association

Each many-to-many association is replaced by an entity, called a **link entity**. The link entity's name is usually a combination of the names of the two entities it links together.

Figure 9.10 shows how the many-to-many association Uses becomes the link entity CourseModule in the logical ER diagram. (Note that only the primary key attributes of the two entities are shown – Figure 9.4 shows all the attributes).

A new association is created between the link entity and each of the two entities that participated in the old many-to-many association. Each of these new associations is a one-to-many association, so can be implemented in the relational data model as a foreign key. This process is known as **resolving the many-to-many association** as the problem raised by many-to-many associations has been resolved by replacing it with a link entity and two one-to-many associations.

The multiplicity constraints on the two new one-to-many associations are derived from those on the original many-to-many association. In effect, the multiplicity constraints of the many-to-many association 'hop over' the link entity, as shown in Figure 9.10.

To see that the two ER diagrams model the same situation, consider what they actually mean. In the conceptual ER diagram, each occurrence of Course is associated with between 5 and 20 occurrences of Module. This situation is preserved in the logical ER diagram as each occurrence of Course is associated with between 5 and 20 occurrences of the new link entity CourseModule, each of which is associated with exactly one Module. Similarly, in the conceptual ER diagram, a particular occurrence of Module is associated with between 1 and many (*) occurrences of Course. In the logical ER

Figure 9.10 Resolving a many-to-many association.

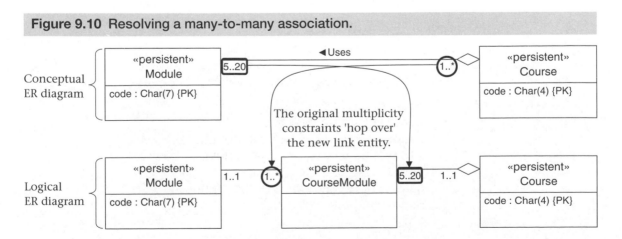

421

diagram, it is associated with between 1 and many (*) occurrences of CourseModule, each of which is associated with exactly one Module. With respect to the relationship between the Course and Module entities, the two ER diagrams are equivalent.

The logical ER diagram in Figure 9.10 breaks two rules. First, neither of the two new one-to-many associations is named. Naming them would be simple enough, but, as they are about to be turned into foreign keys, pretty pointless.

The second rule broken is that the link entity CourseModule has no attributes. This is more serious. An entity is something an information system holds data about. The attributes are the actual data held. If a link entity doesn't have any attributes, then no data needs to be held, so why include the entity at all?

This is the key difference between a logical ER diagram and a conceptual ER diagram. The conceptual ER diagram only models *what* data needs to be held in the database and *what* relationships there are between the data. The logical ER diagram begins to model *how* the data will be held and *how* the relationships will be implemented. A link entity indicates how the many-to-many association between Course and Module can be implemented. Because the link entity CourseModule is concerned with *how* rather than *what*, it is allowed to have no attributes.

Code listing 9.2.2.1 shows the table schema derived from the logical ER diagram in Figure 9.10, implementing the multivalued attribute department as two single-valued attributes (probably the best approach in this particular case). Note that, although the CourseModule link entity has no attributes, the CourseModule table has two columns. These are both foreign key columns, derived from the two one-to-many associations of the logical ER diagram, as discussed in Section 9.1. In this case, as the primary keys of both the Course and Module tables are named code, the new foreign key columns in CourseModule have to be renamed. The foreign key constraint indicates which column is a foreign key to which table.

Code listing 9.2.2.1 *Table schema derived from the logical ER diagram in Figure 9.10*

```
Module (code CHAR NOT NULL,
        title VARCHAR NOT NULL,
        department VARCHAR NOT NULL,
        level VARCHAR NULL
        )
PRIMARY KEY (code)
CANDIDATE KEY (department, title)
BUSINESS RULE level must be one of {'Foundation',
        'Intermediate', 'Placement', 'Honours', 'Masters'}

Course (code CHAR NOT NULL,
        title VARCHAR NOT NULL,
        leadDepartment VARCHAR NOT NULL,
        minorDepartment VARCHAR NULL,
        level VARCHAR NOT NULL,
        qualification VARCHAR NOT NULL,
        mode VARCHAR NOT NULL
        )
```

```
PRIMARY KEY (code)
CANDIDATE KEY (title, mode)
BUSINESS RULE mode must be one of {'Full-time', 'Part-time'}

CourseModule (course CHAR NOT NULL,
              module CHAR NOT NULL
             )
PRIMARY KEY (course, module)
FOREIGN KEY (course) REFERENCES Course(code)
FOREIGN KEY (module) REFERENCES Module(code)
```

Figure 9.11 shows an instance of these three tables and illustrates how the link table `CourseModule` works. Any row in the `Module` table can be associated with several rows in the `CourseModule` table and, through these, to several rows in the `Course` table. The dashed arrows indicate how the module 'Introduction to programming' is associated with both the full- and part-time ICT courses. Similarly, any row in the `Course` table can be associated with several rows in the `CourseModule` table and, through these, to several rows in the `Module` table. The solid arrows indicate how the course 'Business computing, full-time' is associated with three modules – 'Information systems', 'Introduction to business' and 'Application development'.

There are two further points to make about resolving many-to-many associations. Where the many-to-many association involves aggregation or composition, then so does *one* of the new associations. In the conceptual ER diagram in Figure 9.10, the many-to-many association Uses involved aggregation – an occurrence of Course is made up of occurrences of Module. This is carried through into the logical ER

Figure 9.11 The link table `CourseModule` in action.

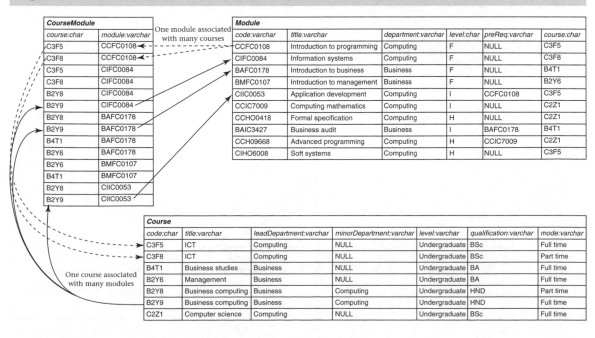

diagram, where the association between the Course entity and the new link entity CourseModule involves aggregation. Note that the aggregation symbol does not move, but remains attached to the same entity, even though it is a new association. Again, the original meaning of the conceptual ER diagram is retained in the logical ER diagram. An occurrence of Course is made up of occurrences of CourseModule, each of which is associated with exactly one occurrence of Module.

Some many-to-many associations have attributes of their own. In this case, the association's attributes become attributes of the link entity in the logical ER diagram. For example, at the Pennine University, each course is reviewed every five years and, at each review, the modules that can be taken for a course may change. This means that the link between an occurrence of Course and an occurrence of Module is time-limited. The dates between which each occurrence of the Uses association is valid are clearly attributes of the association itself.

This situation is shown in Figure 9.12, as is the result of resolving the many-to-many association. Note how the association's attributes become attributes of the link entity. One-to-many binary associations never have attributes of their own as such attributes can always be included on one or other of the two entities involved in the association.

> There is no need to model the dates between which a module for a course can be taken in the conceptual ER diagram for the Web Timetable database application. The Web Timetable database represents which modules are taught for which courses during a particular year. There is no need to indicate future changes to modules as such changes will be incorporated into the database instance before the timetable is published. However, for a database holding more general information about courses and modules, the validation period is an important piece of data and would need to be included in the model.

Figure 9.12 Resolving a many-to-many association that has attributes of its own.

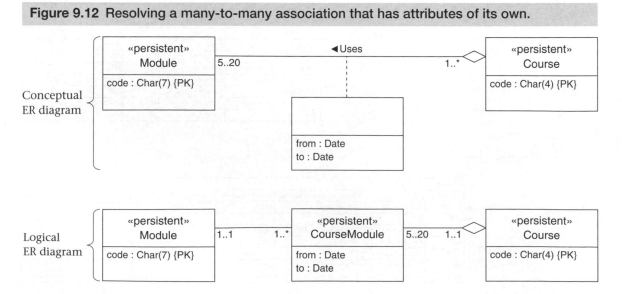

Figure 9.13 Resolving a unary many-to-many association.

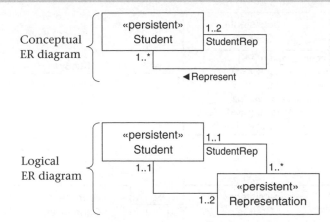

One situation that can puzzle novices is how to deal with a unary many-to-many association. The approach is exactly the same as for a binary many-to-many association.

Consider the unary many-to-many association Represent in Figure 9.13. This models how student representation works at the Pennine University. Each year group elects one or two student representatives, who attend meetings to represent the views of students in their year to the university. The multiplicity constraints capture this situation. Any student acting as a StudentRep will represent one or more students. Each student is represented by at least one, possibly two, students acting as a StudentRep.

In the logical ER diagram, the unary many-to-many association is replaced by the link entity Representation and two one-to-many *binary* associations. Again, note that the original multiplicity constraints 'hop over' the link entity.

At this point, it's worth returning to the problem of how to model the relationship between a course and the department offering that course. The logical ER diagram in Figure 9.8 seemed wrong because the obvious way to model an association between the Course and Department entities is as a many-to-many association. The conceptual ER diagram in Figure 9.14 does this.

Notice that the name is now the primary key as each occurrence of Department will be unique. In the logical ER diagram, the many-to-many association is replaced by a link entity and two new one-to-many associations, which, again, is shown in Figure 9.14.

It's possible to write down the table schema derived from the three entities in this logical ER diagram. They are shown in Code listing 9.2.2.2.

Code listing 9.2.2.2   Table schema derived from the logical ER diagram in Figure 9.14

```
Course (code CHAR(4) NOT NULL,
        title VARCHAR NOT NULL,
        level VARCHAR NOT NULL,
        qualification VARCHAR NOT NULL,
        mode VARCHAR NOT NULL
        )
```

Figure 9.14 A many-to-many association involving an entity with just one attribute.

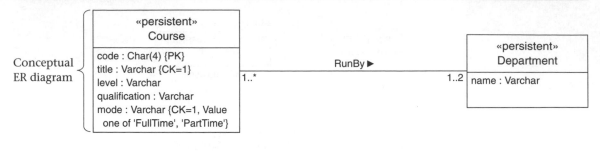

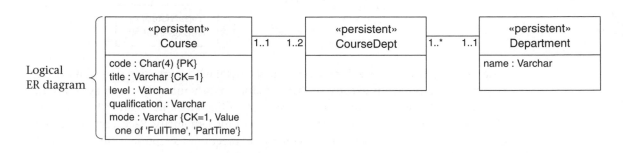

```
PRIMARY KEY (code)
CANDIDATE KEY (title, mode)
BUSINESS RULE level must be one of {'Certificate',
               'Intermediate', 'Honours', 'Masters',
               'Doctoral'}
BUSINESS RULE mode must be one of {'Full-time', 'Part-time'}

CourseDept (code CHAR NOT NULL,
            name VARCHAR NOT NULL
            )
PRIMARY KEY (code, name)
FOREIGN KEY (code) REFERENCES Course(code)
FOREIGN KEY (name) REFERENCES Department(name)

Department (name VARCHAR NOT NULL)
PRIMARY KEY (name)
```

In this logical database design there seems to be no point to the Department table. All it does is duplicate the list of department names, which could easily be found in the table CourseDept by simply creating a view based on the select statement SELECT DISTINCT name FROM CourseDept. As the table provides no new information, it can be omitted from the database.

Code listing 9.2.2.3 shows the modified logical design. There are just the two tables Course and CourseDept, with CourseDept having lost one of its foreign key constraints.

Code listing 9.2.2.3 *Removing the unnecessary table* Department

```
Course (code CHAR(4) NOT NULL,
        title VARCHAR NOT NULL,
        level VARCHAR NOT NULL,
        qualification VARCHAR NOT NULL,
        mode VARCHAR NOT NULL
        )
PRIMARY KEY (code)
CANDIDATE KEY (title)
BUSINESS RULE mode must be one of {'Full-time', 'Part-time'}

CourseDept (code CHAR(4) NOT NULL,
            name VARCHAR NOT NULL
            )
PRIMARY KEY (code, name)
FOREIGN KEY (code) REFERENCES Course(code)
```

Comparing Code listing 9.2.2.3 with Code listing 9.2.1.3, it is clear that the two logical designs are identical, except for the name of the second table. This demonstrates that the original approach to creating a look-up entity to replace a single-valued attribute was correct – create a look-up entity with a single attribute and a one-to-many association from the original entity to the look-up entity. What made this *seem* wrong was the name given to the look-up entity in Figure 9.8. The name Department suggests that the look-up entity holds data about university departments, but it doesn't. Its sole purpose is to act as an 'overflow' container to hold data from the Course entity. The Web Timetable application does not require any data about a *department* other than its name, which is why it was originally modelled as an attribute. It is data held about a *course* that is required.

9.2.3 Replace n-ary associations

The third, and final, structure from a conceptual ER diagram that can't be represented directly in the relational model is the n-ary association, for $n \geq 3$.

The relational data model represents associations between entities with foreign keys. The foreign key columns hold the value of a matching candidate key on some other table. A single foreign key cannot hold values for matching candidate keys on different tables, so cannot directly represent an n-ary association.

The obvious solution is to have separate foreign keys, linking each table to the others. The question is, how exactly to do this.

As discussed in Chapter 8, it is possible to replace an n-ary association with a new link entity and *n* binary associations. This means that the representation of an n-ary association in the logical ER diagram must also involve a new entity. The approach is similar to dealing with the many-to-many association. Each n-ary association is replaced with a link entity and *n* binary associations, one between the link entity and each entity that participates in the original n-ary association. If the n-ary association has attributes of its own, then these become attributes of the link entity. The interesting question is how to derive the multiplicity constraints on the new binary associations.

Figure 9.15 A three-ary association.

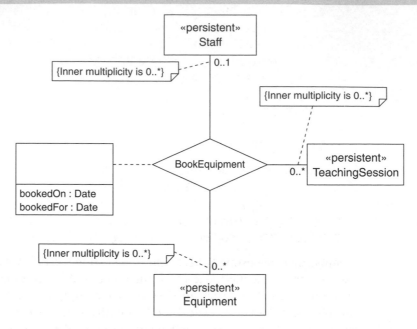

The best way to answer this question is to give an example. The BookEquipment association from the Web Timetable is a three-ary association. It is shown in Figure 9.15 with both the UML outer multiplicity and the inner multiplicity constraints. It also has attributes of its own, so is about as complex as an association gets.

In Figure 9.16, the BookEquipment association of the conceptual ER diagram is replaced by the link entity EquipmentBooking in the logical ER diagram. This link

Figure 9.16 The three-ary association from Figure 9.15 resolved by deriving multiplicity constraints from scratch.

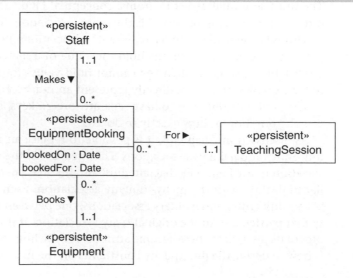

entity inherits the two attributes bookedOn and bookedFor. Three new binary associations are created, associating BookEquipment to each of the three original entities – Staff, TeachingSession and Equipment. The three binary associations are named here to make it easier to discuss them, but this is not necessary.

So far, the transformation has been straightforward. The n-ary association has been replaced by a link entity and three binary associations. The association attributes have been absorbed into the link entity. The final task is to calculate the multiplicity constraints on each of the three binary associations.

An occurrence of the link entity EquipmentBooking should be equivalent to an occurrence of the association BookEquipment. By definition, an occurrence of an association links together exactly *one* occurrence of each of the participating entities. Hence, a single occurrence of BookEquipment must be associated with exactly one occurrence of each of the other three entities. So, a particular occurrence of BookEquipment must be associated with exactly one occurrence of Staff. This means that the multiplicity constraint at the Staff end of the Makes association must be 1..1. Similarly, the multiplicity constraint at the Equipment end of the Books association must be 1..1, as it must also be at the TeachingSession end of the For association. All three 1..1 multiplicity constraints are shown in the logical ER diagram in Figure 9.16.

To calculate the multiplicity constraints at the EquipmentBooking end of the three binary associations, ask the usual questions to establish lower and upper bounds for each one. The lower bound of the multiplicity constraint is calculated by asking this question.

1 What is the lower bound on the number of occurrences of EquipmentBooking that could be linked to a given occurrence of Staff?

As some staff may never book additional equipment for their teaching sessions, the lower bound is zero. To calculate the upper bound ask the next question.

2 What is the upper bound on the number of occurrences of EquipmentBooking that could be linked to a given occurrence of Staff?

Some staff may regularly make such bookings, so the upper bound is many and the multiplicity constraint is 0..*. Note that this multiplicity constraint is the same as the inner multiplicity constraint at the Staff end of the original n-ary association. This will always be the case. For each of the binary associations, the inner multiplicity at the link entity end will be the same as the inner multiplicity at the end of n-ary association attached to the binary association's other participating entity.

Similar reasoning leads to the conclusion that the two remaining multiplicity constraints are also 0..* – a particular teaching session may not require any additional equipment or may require lots and a particular piece of equipment may never be booked or may be booked many times. Figure 9.16 shows these multiplicity constraints.

The transformation from a conceptual to a logical ER diagram loses information on the outer multiplicity constraints on the original n-ary association. Because of this, the logical ER diagram in Figure 9.16 is not equivalent to the conceptual ER diagram in Figure 9.15. It is actually very difficult to show the outer multiplicity constraints of the n-ary association in the logical ER diagram. For example, the outer multiplicity constraint on the Staff end of the BookEquipment association tells us that, for any pair of occurrences of TeachingSession and Equipment, there is at most one occurrence of

BookEquipment linking them to an occurrence of Staff. In the logical ER diagram, this translates into the rule that any pair of occurrences of TeachingSession and Equipment are linked together by at most one occurrence of EquipmentBooking. This constraint involves three entities and two associations and would need to be included using the 'constraint in a note' mechanism of UML. However, there is actually no way to enforce this constraint on most relational DBMS so it is probably not worth including. Bear in mind, though, that in some circumstances the logical ER diagram may not be equivalent to the conceptual ER diagram.

9.3 The process of relational database design

The preceding sections have discussed all the tools required to develop a logical database design targeted at the relational data model. This section outlines a two-stage process for applying these tools, discusses some refinements of the logical design and summarizes what is left to be done during physical database design.

The conceptual ER diagram for the web timetable (Figure 9.17) forms a case study as it illustrates most of the issues that need to be considered. The first stage is to create the logical ER diagram. This removes those features of the conceptual ER diagram that

Figure 9.17 A conceptual ER diagram for the Web Timetable database.

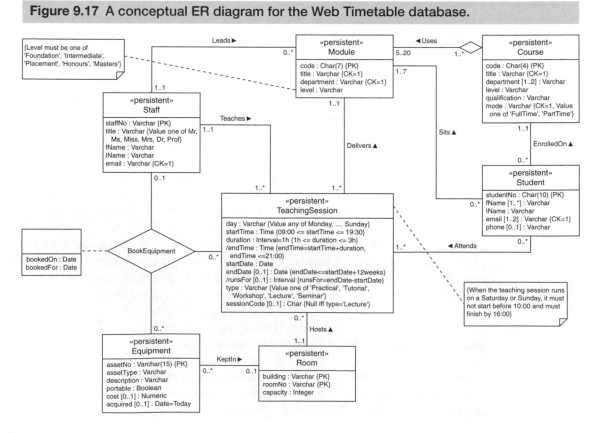

cannot be translated directly into features of the relational data model. The second stage generates the actual table schema.

9.3.1 Create a logical ER diagram

There are three tasks to complete in this stage. In increasing order of difficulty they are:

1 replace multivalued attributes

2 resolve many-to-many unary and binary associations

3 resolve n-ary associations for n ≥ 3.

Table 9.2 summarizes the three possible approaches to replacing multivalued attributes. A non-scalar data type seems the natural solution, but unfortunately is not widely supported. As relational DBMS implement the ISO SQL:2003 array and multiset data types, it may become a more popular option.

The commonest solution is the look-up entity (see Figure 9.8). This replaces the multivalued attribute with a new entity – the look-up entity – and a one-to-many binary association. The look-up entity has exactly one single-valued attribute. A single one-to-many association connects the original entity to the look-up entity. The multiplicity at the look-up entity end of this association is the same as that of the original attribute's multiplicity constraint. At the other end, the multiplicity is always 1..1.

Resolving many-to-many associations is quite straightforward. Resolving n-ary associations may require a little more thought. However, both processes can be done mechanically. Table 9.3 summarizes these processes, although 'writing down' the multiplicity constraints requires care.

To see these rules in action on a reasonably substantial example, consider the Web Timetable conceptual ER diagram (Figure 9.17). Table 9.4 summarizes the changes needed to turn this into a logical ER diagram.

The details of these changes have mostly been discussed above. Resolving the Sits and Attends many-to-many binary associations were not, but both are straightforward.

Figure 9.18 shows the logical ER diagram for the Web Timetable database. Notice that the link entity that resolves the Attends many-to-many association is called Attendance rather than StudentTeachingSession. This name is a little more natural. The link entities that resolve the other two many-to-many associations are named after the two entities they connect.

Table 9.2 Dealing with multivalued attributes.

Option	When to use
Non-scalar data type	Only use if the target DBMS is known to support non-scalar data types.
Multiple attributes	Can be used when the upper bound on the multiplicity is small (four or fewer).
Look-up entity	Use when the upper bound on the multiplicity is large or unlimited.

Table 9.3 Resolving troublesome associations.

Association	How to resolve it
Many-to-many binary association	Replace the many-to-many binary association with a link entity, which includes any attributes of the original association. Create a new one-to-many association between the link entity and each of the entities participating in the original many-to-many association. Write down the multiplicity constraints.
Many-to-many unary association	Replace the many-to-many unary association with a link entity, which includes any attributes of the original association. Create two new one-to-many associations between the link entity and the original entity. Write down the multiplicity constraints.
N-ary association	Replace the n-ary association with a link entity, which includes any attributes of the original association. Create a new one-to-many association between the link entity and each of the entities participating in the original n-ary association. Write down the multiplicity constraints.

9.3.2 Write down table schema

Once a logical ER diagram is available, it is fairly straightforward to write down the table schema. There are four tasks associated with this stage.

1 For each entity, create an initial table schema.
    (a) Write down the table name.
    (b) For each attribute of the entity, add a column description. Include the name, data type, default value and not-null constraint. Include any derived attributes, indicated by the leading '/'.
    (c) If the entity is a strong entity, add a primary key constraint.
    (d) Note any business rules or operations associated with the entity or its attributes.

Table 9.4 Transforming the conceptual ER diagram in Figure 9.17 into a logical ER diagram.

Structure in conceptual ER diagram	Action required
Multivalued attribute Course.department	Replace with two single-valued attributes.
Many-to-many binary association Uses	Resolve by introducing link entity and two one-to-many binary associations.
Many-to-many binary association Sits	Resolve by introducing link entity and two one-to-many binary associations.
Many-to-many binary association Attends	Resolve by introducing link entity and two one-to-many binary associations.
Three-ary association BookEquipment	Resolve by introducing link entity and three one-to-many binary associations.

Figure 9.18 Logical ER diagram derived from the conceptual ER diagram in Figure 9.17.

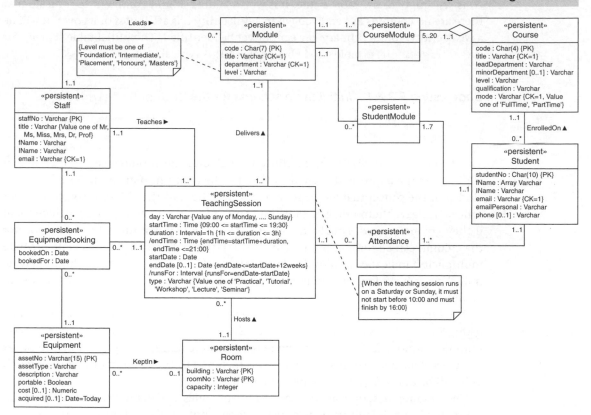

2 For each association in the logical ER diagram:
  (a) decide which entity represents the referenced table and which the referencing table
  (b) add a foreign key to the referencing table by copying the primary key columns from the referenced table
  (c) add a foreign key constraint to the referencing table.

3 For each generalization relationship, determine how to represent this relationship using tables and foreign keys.

4 For each table representing a weak entity, identify an appropriate primary key once all foreign keys have been added.

Consider the first task. In the initial table schema, the table name will usually be the same as the entity it represents. Similarly, attribute names are usually the same. If, for some business reason, an entity or attribute name is a reserved SQL keyword, then change the name at this stage. For example, the SQL keywords 'order', 'time', 'date' and 'group' are all fairly common nouns used by businesses to describe their data requirements so may have been used in the conceptual ER diagram. If there is no obvious synonym, then use a compound noun, such 'PurchaseOrder' or 'CustomerOrder' instead of 'Order'.

Some link entities do not have any attributes. For these, the initial table schema consists simply of the table name. It is worth adding a brief comment to indicate that there are no columns as yet. Even when a link entity has attributes of its own, it will be a weak entity, so the primary key cannot yet be identified. The initial table schema for the `CourseModule` table (Code listing 9.3.2.1) is typical.

Code listing 9.3.2.1   Initial table schema for the `CourseModule` table

```
CourseModule (COLUMNS NOT YET IDENTIFIED FOR THIS LINK TABLE)
PRIMARY KEY NOT YET IDENTIFIED
```

The data types of attributes in the conceptual ER diagram should have counterparts in SQL, so use the appropriate SQL data type for the column. If attribute lengths are included in the conceptual ER diagram, then note them in the column description, but otherwise, leave them out. The same rule holds for default values – only include them if they are mentioned. Finally, the attribute multiplicity will indicate whether or not the column can be null. A multiplicity of [1..1] (remember, this is the default attribute multiplicity) indicates a not-null column and [0..1] indicates that the column may be null. Always include a clear indication of whether the column is, or is not, allowed to be null.

The Equipment entity (Figure 9.17) includes attributes with all these features. Code listing 9.3.2.2 shows an initial table schema for the `Equipment` table. In the first column description, for `assetNo`, the length of the column values is known to be, at most, 15 characters, so this information is included in the column description, much as it will be in the SQL create table statement.

The column description for `acquired` includes a default value. Note that, in Figure 9.17, the default value is noted as Today, but, in the column description, it is `CURRENT_DATE`. This is the name of the appropriate SQL value function. As SQL is the likely implementation language, there is no harm in using the SQL terminology.

The cost and acquired attributes both have multiplicity [0..1], hence the `cost` and `acquired` columns are both allowed to be null. This is noted by including the keyword NULL at the end of the column descriptions. The other attributes have multiplicity [1..1], so the associated column descriptions end with the keywords NOT NULL.

Code listing 9.3.2.2   Initial table schema for the `Equipment` table

```
Equipment (assetNo VARCHAR(15) NOT NULL,
           assetType VARCHAR NOT NULL,
           description VARCHAR NOT NULL,
           portable BOOLEAN NOT NULL,
           cost NUMERIC NULL,
           acquired DATE DEFAULT CURRENT_DATE NULL
           )
PRIMARY KEY (assetNo)
```

The initial table schema in code listing 9.3.2.2 includes the primary key constraint. As any business rules will translate into table constraints, it makes sense to include them in the initial table schema, too. This means that candidate keys and attribute constraints should also be noted down.

Code listing 9.3.2.3 shows the initial table schema for the `Module` table, with its candidate key noted down.

Code listing 9.3.2.3   Initial table schema for the `Module` table

```
Module (code CHAR(7) NOT NULL,
        title VARCHAR NOT NULL,
        department VARCHAR NOT NULL,
        level VARCHAR NOT NULL
        )
PRIMARY KEY (code)
CANDIDATE KEY (department, title)
```

The second task deals with the associations. The logical ER diagram can include only unary or binary associations. Furthermore, the multiplicity can only be one-to-many or one-to-one. This leads to a number of cases. The simplest case is a one-to-one binary association with a lower bound of 1 on both multiplicity constraints, as shown in Figure 9.19. In this case, merge the two entities into a *single* table. Each attribute from both of the entities will have a corresponding column in this single table. This may involve some renaming of columns, but is otherwise straightforward.

All other cases lead to a foreign key and a foreign key constraint. Section 9.1 explained how the entity at the 'many' end of a binary one-to-many association becomes the referencing table, and the entity at the 'one' end becomes the referenced table. A copy of the primary key columns of the referenced table are added to the referencing table. If the referenced table is itself a weak entity, then first deal with the associations of which it is at the 'many' end. This will ensure that its primary key can be identified. For example, in Figure 9.18 TeachingSession is a weak entity, so the Teaches, Delivers and Hosts associations must be dealt with before the associations with the link entities EquipmentBooking and Attendance.

For the association KeptIn, the `Equipment` table is the referencing table, so gets a copy of the primary key columns of the `Room` table.

Code listing 9.3.2.4 shows the table schema for both tables. Notice that, as `Room` has a composite primary key, the foreign key on `Equipment` is also composite. As noted before, the names of the foreign key columns do not need to be the same as the matching primary key column. Here, the `Equipment` table's `room` column matches the `Room` table's `roomNo` column. The data type *must* be the same, though, even down to the length specified for data values. Whether or not the foreign key columns can be null is determined by the multiplicity constraint at the referenced table end of

Figure 9.19 Binary one-to-one association that becomes a single table.

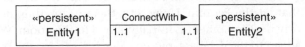

the association. If the lower bound is 0 (i.e. the multiplicity constraint is 0..1), then the foreign key columns may be null. Otherwise, the lower bound is 1 (the multiplicity constraint is 1..1) and the foreign key columns may not be null.

Code listing 9.3.2.4   Table schema for the `Room` *and* `Equipment` *tables showing the foreign key*

```
Room (building VARCHAR NOT NULL,
      roomNo VARCHAR NOT NULL,
      capacity NUMERIC NULL
      )
PRIMARY KEY (building, roomNo)

Equipment (assetNo VARCHAR(15) NOT NULL,
           assetType VARCHAR NOT NULL,
           description VARCHAR NOT NULL,
           portable BOOLEAN NOT NULL,
           cost NUMERIC NULL,
           acquired DATE DEFAULT CURRENT_DATE NULL,
           building VARCHAR NULL,
           room VARCHAR NULL
           )
PRIMARY KEY (assetNo)
FOREIGN KEY (building, room)
    REFERENCES Room(building, roomNo)
```

Each link entity is at the 'many' end of two or more one-to-many associations. Each of these leads to a set of foreign key columns in the corresponding link table. The primary key of the link table is always the set of *all* foreign key columns. For example, the two associations that the CourseModule link entity participates in lead to two sets of foreign key columns – one linking it with the Course table, the other linking it with the Module table.

Code listing 9.3.2.5 shows the final table schema for this link table. The foreign key columns have to be renamed as both the matching primary key columns are called `code`. Neither of the foreign key columns can be null as the multiplicity at the 'one' end of both associations is 1..1.

Code listing 9.3.2.5   Foreign key columns on a link table

```
CourseModule (course CHAR(4) NOT NULL,
              module CHAR(7) NOT NULL)
PRIMARY KEY (course, module)
FOREIGN KEY (course) REFERENCES Course(code)
FOREIGN KEY (module) REFERENCES Module(code)
```

Occasionally there will be a default value for the columns of a foreign key. Suppose that, at the Pennine University, there is an equipment store room, say in Locke 12. Any new equipment is initially stored in this room. When a new piece of equipment is added to the database, but no value is given for the `building` or `room` columns, it is safe to assume that the equipment is stored in Locke 12. This fact would have to be recorded on the ER diagram in a note. In the table schema, it can be recorded as the default value of the foreign key columns, as shown in Code listing 9.3.2.6.

There are two problems to note. First, if users really wanted to add a piece of equipment that was not associated with any room (such as a plasma screen mounted in a foyer), they would need to tell the DBMS to make the building and room columns null.

The second problem is subtler. Suppose a user creates a new row in the Equipment table and gives the DBMS a value for building, Wilson say, but not for room. The DBMS will use the default value for the room in this row and deduce that the equipment is stored in Wilson 12. If there is no such room, the insert statement will fail. If there is, the database will hold incorrect information. It may be better *not* to include the default values in the foreign key after all.

Code listing 9.3.2.6 *A foreign key with a default value*

```
Equipment (assetNo VARCHAR(15) NOT NULL,
           assetType VARCHAR NOT NULL,
           description VARCHAR NOT NULL,
           portable BOOLEAN NOT NULL,
           cost NUMERIC NULL,
           acquired DATE DEFAULT CURRENT_DATE NULL,
           building VARCHAR DEFAULT 'Locke' NULL,
           room VARCHAR DEFAULT '12' NULL
           )
PRIMARY KEY (assetNo)
FOREIGN KEY (building, room)
    REFERENCES Room(building, roomNo)
```

The precise structure of the association will provide guidance on what referential actions are associated with a foreign key constraint. Table 9.5 indicates the most likely referential actions for a foreign key, based on information about the association it represents. Aggregation and composition indicate a whole–part relationship, so, as far

Table 9.5 Most likely referential actions for a foreign key constraint.

Structure in conceptual ER diagram	Referential action
Composition	ON DELETE CASCADE ON UPDATE CASCADE
Aggregation with multiplicity 1..1 at referenced table end	Any ON DELETE referential action *except* SET NULL is possible. ON UPDATE CASCADE
Aggregation with a multiplicity 0..1 at referenced table end	Any ON DELETE referential action is possible. SET NULL is most likely. ON UPDATE CASCADE
Association with multiplicity 1..1 at referenced table end	Any referential action *except* SET NULL is possible.
Association with multiplicity 0..1 at referenced table end	Any referential action is possible.

as possible, the part (the referencing table) should be kept in step with the whole (the referenced table). For composition, which indicates that the part cannot exist independently, the only choice is CASCADE. For plain associations, with no aggregation or composition, consider the multiplicity constraint associated with the referenced table. Where this is 0..1, rows of the referencing table can exist independently, so SET NULL is an option. Otherwise, SET NULL cannot be used.

For the Equipment table, the multiplicity at the 'one' end of the KeptIn association is 0..1, so any referential action is possible. In this situation, consider the meaning of the situation being modelled. If a room number or building name is changed, it doesn't affect the equipment in that room. This suggests ON UPDATE CASCADE is a good choice. By contrast, if a room is removed from the database, it is important to know what has happened to the equipment in that room. Then, ON DELETE NO ACTION prevents a room from being deleted until the user has reallocated all equipment to new rooms. Code listing 9.3.2.7 shows the revised table schema.

Code listing 9.3.2.7   Including referential actions

```
Equipment (assetNo VARCHAR(15) NOT NULL,
            assetType VARCHAR NOT NULL,
            description VARCHAR NOT NULL,
            portable BOOLEAN NOT NULL,
            cost NUMERIC NULL,
            acquired DATE DEFAULT CURRENT_DATE NULL,
            building VARCHAR NULL,
            room VARCHAR NULL
            )
PRIMARY KEY (assetNo)
FOREIGN KEY (building, room)
    REFERENCES Room(building, roomNo)
    ON DELETE NO ACTION
    ON UPDATE CASCADE
```

The discussion so far has focused on binary one-to-many associations. The decisions about whether or not to include not-null constraints or default values, and what referential action to use, can be applied to other types of association in the logical ER diagram. What might change is where to place the foreign key. For a unary one-to-many association, the table representing the entity is both the referenced and the referencing table. This means that it must include a copy of its own primary key.

Consider the association Manages (Figure 9.20), which represents line management at Pennine University. Each member of staff has exactly one line manager (even the Vice Chancellor, who is otherwise at the top of management hierarchy, has a designated line manager for performance review purposes). Some members of staff do not manage anyone else, but some manage several other employees.

The initial table schema is shown in Code listing 9.3.2.8 (a). The final table schema, including the foreign key and associated foreign key constraint, is shown in Code listing 9.3.2.8 (b). The foreign key column lineManager is a copy of the primary key column staffNo. There is no default value, as this would not make business sense. The foreign key column is not null as the multiplicity at the 'one' end of the Manages

Figure 9.20 A unary one-to-many association representing line management at the Pennine University.

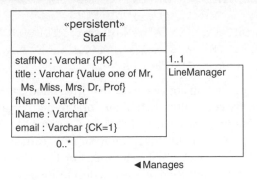

association is 1..1. If the multiplicity were 0..1, then the foreign key columns could be null. The referential actions are chosen to reflect the business situation. Everyone must have a designated line manager, so no member of staff can be removed from the database until all the employees that person manages have been given a new line manager. If, for some reason, the staff number of a member of staff changes, that manager will still be managing the same staff, so this change is cascaded through to the values of the foreign key column.

Code listing 9.3.2.8   Initial, and final, table schema representing the `Staff` *entity in Figure 9.20*

(a) Initial table schema

```
Staff (staffNo VARCHAR NOT NULL,
       title VARCHAR NOT NULL,
       fName VARCHAR NOT NULL,
       lName VARCHAR NOT NULL,
       email VARCHAR NOT NULL
       )
PRIMARY KEY (staffNo)
CANDIDATE KEY (email)
BUSINESS RULE title must be one of {'Mr', 'Ms', 'Miss',
    'Mrs', 'Dr', 'Prof'}
```

(b) Final table schema with self-referencing foreign key

```
Staff (staffNo VARCHAR NOT NULL,
       title VARCHAR NOT NULL,
       fName VARCHAR NOT NULL,
       lName VARCHAR NOT NULL,
       email VARCHAR NOT NULL,
       lineManager VARCHAR NOT NULL
       )
```

439

```
PRIMARY KEY (staffNo)
CANDIDATE KEY (email)
BUSINESS RULE title must be one of {'Mr', 'Ms', 'Miss',
    'Mrs', 'Dr', 'Prof'}
FOREIGN KEY lineManager REFERENCES Staff(staffNo)
    ON DELETE NO ACTION
    ON UPDATE CASCADE
```

The discussion above covers the three main cases – binary one-to-one with both multiplicity constraints 1..1; binary one-to-many; and unary one-to-many.

The first three rows of Table 9.6 summarize this discussion. The different types of association are illustrated by means of abstract logical ER diagrams. In each case, the multiplicity p..1 may be either 0..1 or 1..1. The multiplicity n..m can be any valid multiplicity, unless there is a restriction in the comment.

There are five other kinds of association that could occur in a logical ER diagram. Each involves a one-to-one association. One-to-one associations can easily be represented in the relational data model by using foreign keys. The problem is deciding which is the referencing table. For binary one-to-one associations, the lower bound of the multiplicity constraint can help you decide. A multiplicity of 1..1 indicates that the entity at the *other end* of the association always participates in the association. In this case, it is the best candidate for the referencing table as the foreign key column will never be null. Unary one-to-one associations can be treated exactly the same as unary one-to-many associations.

Table 9.6 Logical design for associations.

Type of association			Referenced table	Referencing table	Comment
«persistent» Entity1 — ConnectWith ▶ p..1 n..m — «persistent» Entity2			Entity1	Entity2	For n ≤ m and m ≥ 2.
«persistent» Entity1 n..m p..1 ConnectWith ▶			Entity1	Entity1	Create a single table with a foreign key that references the same table's primary key.
«persistent» Entity1 — ConnectWith ▶ 1..1 1..1 — «persistent» Entity2			None	None	Create a single table to represent both entities.
«persistent» Entity1 — ConnectWith ▶ 1..1 0..1 — «persistent» Entity2			Entity1	Entity2	Entity1 may exist independently, but Entity2 cannot.
«persistent» Entity1 — ConnectWith ▶ 0..1 0..1 — «persistent» Entity2			Either	Either	Depends on the business scenario being modelled.

Figure 9.21 A unary one-to-one association.

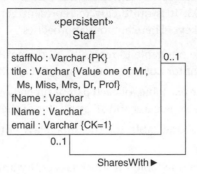

SharesWith ▶

For example, consider the unary one-to-one association SharesWith, which indicates that two *academic* members of staff share an office (Figure 9.21). The association does not model information about non-academic staff. Adding a foreign key to represent this association leads to the table schema shown in Code listing 9.3.2.9. The foreign key consists of the single column {sharer}. The foreign key column can be null as some staff do *not* share an office. The referential actions capture the business scenario outlined above. When a member of staff leaves, whoever they shared the office with will now have an office to themselves, so the foreign key can be set to null. If a staff number changes, the new staff number designates the same person, who shares an office with the same colleague, so the foreign key should be updated to the new staff number.

Code listing 9.3.2.9   Table schema representing the Staff entity in Figure 9.21

```
Staff (staffNo VARCHAR NOT NULL,
       title VARCHAR NOT NULL,
       fName VARCHAR NOT NULL,
       lName VARCHAR NOT NULL,
       email VARCHAR NOT NULL,
       sharer VARCHAR NULL
       )
PRIMARY KEY (staffNo)
CANDIDATE KEY (email)
BUSINESS RULE title must be one of {'Mr', 'Ms', 'Miss',
    'Mrs', 'Dr', 'Prof'}
FOREIGN KEY sharer REFERENCES Staff(staffNo)
    ON DELETE SET NULL
    ON UPDATE CASCADE
```

As the association only applies to *academic* members of staff and many of them do not share an office, the sharer column will be null for *most* rows in the table. This is not a particularly efficient design, but it is logical. Chapter 10 considers ways in which to make the database design more efficient.

A conceptual ER diagram may include generalization relationships as well as association relationships. As ISO SQL:2003 now includes object-orientated features, it is possible to implement generalization relationships directly. This is not the approach taken here as not all relational DBMS incorporate the object-relational features of SQL:2003. It is quite easy to represent generalization relationships using tables and foreign keys. There are four approaches.

- Create one table to represent all the entities. For each subclass entity, include a **discriminator column** to indicate which subclass a particular row represents.

- Create *one* table for each pair of superclass and subclass entities. Include all attributes of the superclass and all attributes of the particular subclass.

- Create one table for the superclass entity and a look-up table for *each* subclass entity.

- Create one table for superclass entity and a *single* look-up table to represent all the subclass entities.

Each of these approaches can be illustrated by the generalization relationships shown in Figure 9.22 between the Room superclass entity and its subclasses MusicRoom, Laboratory and LectureTheatre. Where the generalization relationship forms part of a larger ER diagram, there will be initial table schema for each of these four entities, possibly including foreign keys that implement associations. In this case, the different approaches describe how to merge these table schema or add further foreign keys or both, to model the generalization relationship without breaking any of the existing foreign key relationships. If there are lots of generalization relationships, it may be worth dealing with them before dealing with the associations.

Taking the first approach, there is a single table called Room. The table includes one column for each attribute on each of the four entities. Columns representing attributes from the superclass entity inherit their default value and not-null constraint from the corresponding attribute. Columns representing attributes from the subclass entities *never* have a default value and can *always* be null. This is because one row of the table will represent an occurrence of one of the entities from the hierarchy – only the columns from the main superclass are present on every such occurrence.

Figure 9.22 The Room entity and its subclasses.

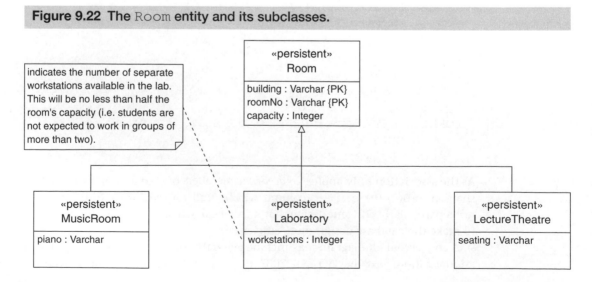

The table also includes three discriminator columns, `musicRoom`, `laboratory` and `lectureTheatre`, which indicate whether or not a particular row of the table represents an occurrence of the MusicRoom, Laboratory or LectureTheatre entities.

Code listing 9.3.2.10 shows an initial table schema. Note that the primary key is the primary key of the main superclass entity.

Code listing 9.3.2.10   Single table representing the entities in Figure 9.22

```
Room (building VARCHAR NOT NULL,
      roomNo VARCHAR NOT NULL,
      capacity VARCHAR NOT NULL,
      piano VARCHAR NULL,
      workstations NUMERIC NULL,
      seating VARCHAR NULL,
      musicRoom BOOLEAN NOT NULL,
      laboratory BOOLEAN NOT NULL,
      lectureTheatre BOOLEAN NOT NULL
      )
PRIMARY KEY (building, roomNo)
```

This version of the `Room` table can obviously represent any occurrence of the Room entity and any occurrence of each of the three subclasses. Even so, the translation is not wholly satisfactory. There is no way of ensuring that rows representing an occurrence of the MusicRoom entity do not have values for the `workstations` or `seating` columns. The business rule that ensures this would be something like:

whenever `musicRoom` is TRUE, then `workstations` and `seating` are null.

To implement this requires an `if ... then` statement, so the business rule could be implemented using procedural code (such as in the PHP script that gathers data on rooms from end users and writes it to the database or in an SQL trigger).

The second approach is really a refinement of the first. Rather than lumping together *all* the subclasses in one table, have a separate table for each of them. There is no need for a discriminator column as each table represents a single subclass.

Code listing 9.3.2.11 shows the table schema. Notice that, in this approach, the default value and not-null constraint for *all* columns, whether representing an attribute of the superclass or subclass entity, is the same as for the corresponding attribute. This is because, for example, a row in the `MusicRoom` table always represents an occurrence of the MusicRoom entity. This approach works well when an occurrence of the superclass *must* be an occurrence of one of the subclasses – that is, when every room is either a music room, a laboratory or a lecture theatre.

Code listing 9.3.2.11   Representing the entities in Figure 9.22 with one table for each superclass–subclass pair

```
MusicRoom (building VARCHAR NOT NULL,
           roomNo VARCHAR NOT NULL,
           capacity VARCHAR NOT NULL,
           piano VARCHAR NOT NULL
           )
```

```
                PRIMARY KEY (building, roomNo)

      Laboratory (building VARCHAR NOT NULL,
                  roomNo VARCHAR NOT NULL,
                  capacity VARCHAR NOT NULL,
                  workstations NUMERIC NOT NULL
                  )
                PRIMARY KEY (building, roomNo)

      LectureTheatre (building VARCHAR NOT NULL,
                      roomNo VARCHAR NOT NULL,
                      capacity VARCHAR NOT NULL,
                      seating VARCHAR NOT NULL
                      )
                PRIMARY KEY (building, roomNo)
```

Sometimes an occurrence of the superclass does not have to be any of the subclasses. In this situation, it is better to create a single, main table to represent the superclass and one or more look-up tables to hold data about the various subclasses. The most comprehensive version of this approach creates one look-up table for each subclass entity. A single entity occurrence, which will include attributes from both the subclass and superclass entities, is represented as two separate tables, with attributes from the superclass being held in the main table and those of the subclass in the look-up table.

Code listing 9.3.2.12 shows the table schema for the main table Room and *three* look-up tables – MusicRoom, Laboratory and LectureTheatre. Each look-up table gets a copy of the primary key of the Room table. Not only is this a foreign key to the Room table, it is also the primary key of the look-up table. This is because each occurrence of a subclass entity is *also* an occurrence of Room, so can be identified by the primary key for Room.

Code listing 9.3.2.12   Representing the entities in Figure 9.22 as one table for the superclass entity and one look-up table for each of the subclass entities

```
      Room (building VARCHAR NOT NULL,
            roomNo VARCHAR NOT NULL,
            capacity VARCHAR NOT NULL
            )
      PRIMARY KEY (building, roomNo)

      MusicRoom (piano VARCHAR NOT NULL,
                 building VARCHAR NOT NULL,
                 roomNo VARCHAR NOT NULL
                 )
      PRIMARY KEY (building, roomNo)
      FOREIGN KEY (building, roomNo)
          REFERENCES Room (building, roomNo)

      Laboratory (workstations NUMERIC NOT NULL,
                  building VARCHAR NOT NULL,
                  roomNo VARCHAR NOT NULL
                  )
```

```
PRIMARY KEY (building, roomNo)
FOREIGN KEY (building, roomNo)
    REFERENCES Room (building, roomNo)

LectureTheatre (seating VARCHAR NOT NULL,
               building VARCHAR NOT NULL,
               roomNo VARCHAR NOT NULL
               )
PRIMARY KEY (building, roomNo)
FOREIGN KEY (building, roomNo)
    REFERENCES Room (building, roomNo)
```

The advantage of this approach is that few, if any, rows have columns that are null. The disadvantage is that there are many more foreign keys, so there will be more duplicated data.

The final approach reduces the number of foreign keys by having a single look-up table. The columns of this look-up table represent the attributes of all the subclass entities, so discriminator columns are required to indicate that a particular row represents a particular subclass entity occurrence.

Code listing 9.3.2.13 shows the table schema. Note that the columns representing attributes from the subclasses have no default values and can always be null.

Code listing 9.3.2.13   Representing the entities in Figure 9.22 as one table for the superclass entity and one look-up table for all the subclass entities

```
Room (building VARCHAR NOT NULL,
      roomNo VARCHAR NOT NULL,
      capacity VARCHAR NOT NULL
      )
PRIMARY KEY (building, roomNo)

RoomType (building VARCHAR NOT NULL,
          roomNo VARCHAR NOT NULL,
          piano VARCHAR NULL,
          workstations NUMERIC NULL,
          seating VARCHAR NULL,
          musicRoom BOOLEAN NOT NULL,
          laboratory BOOLEAN NOT NULL,
          lectureTheatre BOOLEAN NOT NULL
          )
PRIMARY KEY (building, roomNo)
FOREIGN KEY (building, roomNo)
    REFERENCES Room (building, roomNo)
```

As with associations, the constraints on the generalization relationship help decide which approach to take. Generalization relationships do not have multiplicity constraints, but do have disjoint and participation constraints. Table 9.7 indicates how to use these constraints to decide which of the four approaches to take.

The final step in writing down the table schema is to identify the primary keys of any weak entities. Typically, the primary key of a weak entity will include all the

Table 9.7 Deciding how to represent superclass and subclass entities and generalization relationships.

Generalization constraint	Logical design
{overlapping, mandatory}	Single table with one discriminator column for each subclass entity.
{disjoint, mandatory}	Create *one* table for each pair of superclass and subclass entities. Include all attributes of the superclass and all attributes of the particular subclass.
{disjoint, optional}	Create one table for the superclass entity and a look-up table for *each* subclass entity.
{overlapping, optional}	Create one table for the superclass entity and a *single* look-up table to represent all the subclass entities.

foreign key columns. This is because a weak entity is only unique relative to its associated strong entities. For example, the combination of the day and times of the support sessions of each staff member will be unique, though two different staff members may offer support sessions on the same day at the same time. Once this final step has been resolved, the translation of the conceptual ER diagram into an initial logical database design is complete.

This section has explained how to represent most of the features of the conceptual ER diagram in the table schema of the logical database design. There are three features that it has not covered:

1 business rules, expressed as constraints on an attribute or entity

2 derived attributes

3 operations.

Although business rules and derived attributes were noted in the table schema, operations were not discussed. The capabilities of the particular DBMS used to implement the database will determine how these features can be implemented. Accordingly, they are considered during physical database design.

9.4 Normalization

ER diagrams are a top-down design technique. The technique first identifies the entities – the *main* things that the system holds information about – then asks what particular information is held – the attributes and relationships. ER diagrams start from the general and move down towards the particular.

Normalization is a bottom-up technique. It begins with the particular – what specific items of information will be held in the database? Each item of data will be held in a column. Once the list of all columns is available, they can be organized into tables.

Normalization was developed specifically for the relational data model, and is still mostly used to organize relational databases. The goal of normalization is to minimize repeated data and, hence, avoid the potential anomalies that can arise when repeated data is modified in one place, but not another.

As with the relational data model itself, there is a formal mathematical theory underlying the process of normalization. This guarantees that the process will generate an efficient database structure for the given set of columns. The main drawback is that the initial set of columns can be dauntingly large. Another limitation is that normalization works best when there is good sample data. In practice, normalization is often used to validate the table schema generated from a logical ER diagram, rather than to generate the table schema themselves. Another common use is to turn a spreadsheet into a relational database, because spreadsheets tend to have a limited number of columns and ample sample data. The examples in this section are based on spreadsheet data, but the approach can be applied to any set of data items.

Consider the spreadsheet shown in Figure 9.23 (a). There are four problems that can arise when this spreadsheet is modified. First, when a new hall of residence is built, there is no way of including information about it in the spreadsheet until a student actually rents a room there. If the information about halls of residence were kept separately from information about rental agreements, then it would be easy to add information about a new hall. The second problem is the mirror of the first. In the

Figure 9.23 The `StudentRental` spreadsheet.

studentNo	name	accomId	hall	room	rentStart	rentFinish	rent	staffNo	bursar
2005453125	Peter Harris	WM107	William Morris	123	11 Sep 2005	10 Jun 2006	550	56673	Joshua Bittaye
		MC078	Marie Curie	14	10 Sep 2006	9 Jun 2007	500	35054	Selma Hutchins
2004023401	Alice Clough	WM107	William Morris	123	12 Sep 2004	11 Jun 2005	450	56673	Joshua Bittaye
		MW031	Maurice Wilkins	46	11 Sep 2005	10 Jun 2006	550	35054	Selma Hutchins
		MW042	Maurice Wilkins	51	10 Sep 2006	9 Jun 2007	575	35054	Selma Hutchins
2004892857	Jamie Smith	MC078	Marie Curie	14	12 Sep 2004	11 Jun 2005	400	35054	Selma Hutchins
		WM107	William Morris	123	12 Jun 2005	10 Sep 2005	450	56673	Joshua Bittaye

(a) An image of the actual spreadsheet. Blanks indicate implied information.

studentNo	name	accomId	hall	room	rentStart	rentFinish	rent	staffNo	bursar
2005453125	Peter Harris	WM107	William Morris	123	11 Sep 2005	10 Jun 2006	550	56673	Joshua Bittaye
2005453125	Peter Harris	MC078	Marie Curie	14	10 Sep 2006	9 Jun 2007	500	35054	Selma Hutchins
2004023401	Alice Clough	WM107	William Morris	123	12 Sep 2004	11 Jun 2005	450	56673	Joshua Bittaye
2004023401	Alice Clough	MW031	Maurice Wilkins	46	11 Sep 2005	10 Jun 2006	550	35054	Selma Hutchins
2004023401	Alice Clough	MW042	Maurice Wilkins	51	10 Sep 2006	9 Jun 2007	575	35054	Selma Hutchins
2004892857	Jamie Smith	MC078	Marie Curie	14	12 Sep 2004	11 Jun 2005	400	35054	Selma Hutchins
2004892857	Jamie Smith	WM107	William Morris	123	12 Jun 2005	10 Sep 2005	450	56673	Joshua Bittaye

(b) The same spreadsheet with the blanks filled in.

data shown, if all rental agreements with Alice Clough are deleted, then there is no longer any mention of Maurice Wilkins hall.

There can also be problems when existing data is changed. Suppose that Joshua Bittaye retires, and a new Bursar is appointed. There will be many different rows in the spreadsheet that need to be changed. If one is missed, then the data is inconsistent. The spreadsheet data will also be inconsistent if, when a new rental agreement is recorded, the wrong Bursar is named.

All these problems arise because the same data is stored in more than one row of the spreadsheet. Normalization is guaranteed to produce a set of table schema that avoids these problems. It generates separate tables to hold information about each distinct thing, so the first two problems do not arise. More importantly, in a fully normalized database, only the foreign key columns hold duplicate data. The DBMS can automatically monitor this duplicate data and prevent the problems discussed above. In fact, this is one of the main motivations for using databases rather than files to hold an organization's data (see Chapter 1).

Normalization begins with a *single* table of data. This single table has a column for each data item that will be held in the system. Normalization is the process of identifying **repeating groups** of columns and generating a new table for each repeating group. The notion of a repeating group has a formal definition, which is explored later in this section, but, for now, it is defined as follows.

Repeating group A set of two or more columns, such that the data in these columns repeats across two or more rows.

The idea is that a repeating group of columns should actually be a separate table. The repeating group is pulled out into a separate table and a foreign key is left behind on the original table. The foreign key links each row in the original table to the data in the new table that has been pulled out of this row. Of course, any duplicate rows in the new table are eliminated, so data duplication is reduced. Obviously, for this to work, the repeating group should have a candidate key. If there is no candidate key, then it is likely that there are other columns that form part of the repeating group.

This notion of a repeating group of columns is not very precise, but an example should make things clear. The Accommodation Office at the Pennine University keeps data on student rentals in a spreadsheet. Each worksheet within a spreadsheet is just a table of data and can be normalized. A sample of the spreadsheet data in the StudentRentals worksheet is shown in Figure 9.23 (a). On spreadsheets, the empty cells do not necessarily represent missing information (that is, empty cells are not necessarily null). Empty cells can represent *implied information*. For example, in the second row, the studentNo is 2005453125 and the name is Peter Harris. These values aren't shown because it is obvious from the structure of the worksheet that the cell values are the same as those in the row above it. This is a common feature of spreadsheet data. However, it does mean that empty cells in a worksheet can either represent implied information or indicate that the data is not known for this row.

To avoid confusion, it helps to fill in any implied information, leaving only cells with genuinely missing information blank. Thus, Figure 9.23 (b) shows the same spreadsheet data with the implied information filled in.

If this latter spreadsheet data was simply loaded into a database table, the table would have the description shown in Code listing 9.4.1. Looking at the data, `{studentNo, rentStart}` is a candidate key and this will do as the primary key of the table. There are other candidate keys, but they will be easier to spot once the normalization process has been completed.

Code listing 9.4.1   Table schema for the original table, before normalization

```
StudentRental(studentNo, name, accomId, hall, room,
    rentStart, rentFinish, rent, staffNo, bursar)
PRIMARY KEY (studentNo, rentStart)
```

It is clear (in Figure 9.23) that the set of columns `{studentNo, name}` forms a repeating group – that is, two columns, the combined data in which is identical in two or more rows. For example, in the first two rows, these columns have the values `studentNo` = '2005453125' and `name` = 'Peter Harris' and the next three have `studentNo` = '2004023401' and `name` = 'Alice Clough'. Normalization seeks to minimize repeated data by extracting such repeating groups into a new table. There are two actions for each such repeating group:

1 write down a description for a new table, consisting of the columns of the repeating group and identify the primary key of this table

2 write down a description for the original table, but leave out all the non-primary key columns of the repeating group – the primary key columns of the repeating group remain in the original table as a foreign key.

The primary key for the repeating group `{studentNo, name}` is `{studentNo}` as it is possible that two students will have the same name, so `name` cannot be a candidate key. Notice that this argument holds despite the fact that, in Figures 9.23 (a) and (b) all the students have different names. This is because the sample data is just that – a sample. It can only indicate the sort of data likely to be held. A comprehensive set of data would include an example illustrating that two different values of `studentNo` can be associated with the same value of `name`. The table schema is shown in Code listing 9.4.2.

> Implied information in a spreadsheet always indicates a repeating group, but not all repeating groups are indicated by implied information.

Removing the non-primary key columns from the original table simply means removing the `name` column. This leaves `studentNo, accomId, hall, room, rentStart, rentFinish, rent, staffNo` and `bursar`. The `studentNo` column will be a foreign key to the new `Student` table.

The revised table schema is also shown in Code listing 9.4.2. Figure 9.24 shows the sample data after removing this first repeating group. Notice that removing the repeating group means that there is less data repetition as student names are now stored once, and once only, rather than being repeated in several rows.

Figure 9.24 The sample data after removing the first repeating group.

StudentRental

studentNo	accomId	hall	room	rentStart	rentFinish	rent	staffNo	bursar
2005453125	WM107	William Morris	123	11 Sep 2005	10 Jun 2006	550	56673	Joshua Bittaye
2005453125	MC078	Marie Curie	14	10 Sep 2006	9 Jun 2007	500	35054	Selma Hutchins
2004023401	WM107	William Morris	123	12 Sep 2004	11 Jun 2005	450	56673	Joshua Bittaye
2004023401	MW031	Maurice Wilkins	46	11 Sep 2005	10 Jun 2006	550	35054	Selma Hutchins
2004023401	WM042	Maurice Wilkins	51	10 Sep 2006	9 Jun 2007	575	35054	Selma Hutchins
2004892857	MC078	Marie Curie	14	12 Sep 2004	11 Jun 2005	400	35054	Selma Hutchins
2004892857	WM107	William Morris	123	12 Jun 2005	10 Sep 2005	450	56673	Joshua Bittaye

Student

studentNo	name
2005453125	Peter Harris
2004023401	Alice Clough
2004892857	Jamie Smith

Code listing 9.4.2   Table schema after removing the repeating group, name

```
Student(studentNo, name)
PRIMARY KEY (studentNo)
StudentRental(studentNo, accomId, hall, room, rentStart,
    rentFinish, rent, staffNo, bursar)
PRIMARY KEY (studentNo, rentStart)
FOREIGN KEY (studentNo) REFERENCES Student (studentNo)
```

There are clearly no more repeating groups in the Student table, but there is another obvious one in StudentRental. The values for the columns accomId, hall and room repeat across rows. For example, in the first, third and seventh rows, these three columns have the same values – accomId = 'WM107', hall = William Morris and room = '123'. As these three columns are listed next to each other in the sample data, this is easy to spot. What is less obvious is that the staffNo and bursar columns are part of this repeating group. On the first, third and seventh rows, staffNo = '56673' and bursar = 'Joshua Bittaye'. The second and sixth rows also have identical values in these five columns, as do the fourth and fifth. This means that the repeating group includes the columns {accomId, hall, room, staffNo, bursar}. Figure 9.25 shows the StudentRental table with its columns reordered so that the repeating group {accomId, hall, room, staffNo, bursar} is obvious.

This repeating group is dealt with in the same way as the first. A new table, named Accommodation, is defined as shown in Code listing 9.4.3 with the primary key accomId. This makes business sense as accomId uniquely identifies a particular room for rent. More importantly, the value of accomId determines the values of the other columns in the repeating group, so is a candidate key. The StudentRental

Figure 9.25 A repeating group.

StudentRental								
studentNo	accomId	hall	room	staffNo	bursar	rentStart	rentFinish	rent
2004892857	**MC078**	**Marie Curie**	14	35054	**Selma Hutchins**	12 Sep 2004	11 Jun 2005	400
2005453125	**MC078**	**Marie Curie**	14	35054	**Selma Hutchins**	10 Sep 2006	9 Jun 2007	500
2004023401	MW031	Maurice Wilkins	46	35054	Selma Hutchins	11 Sep 2005	10 Jun 2006	550
2004023401	MW042	Maurice Wilkins	51	35054	Selma Hutchins	10 Sep 2006	9 Jun 2007	575
2004023401	**WM107**	**William Morris**	123	56673	**Joshua Bittaye**	12 Sep 2004	11 Jun 2005	450
2004892857	**WM107**	**William Morris**	123	56673	**Joshua Bittaye**	12 Jun 2005	10 Sep 2005	450
2005453125	**WM107**	**William Morris**	123	56673	**Joshua Bittaye**	11 Sep 2005	10 Jun 2006	550

table loses the four columns `hall`, `room`, `staffNo` and `bursar` and gains a foreign key constraint to the `Accommodation` table.

Code listing 9.4.3   Table schema after removing the repeating group
```
{accomId, hall, room, staffNo, bursar}

    Student(studentNo, name)
    PRIMARY KEY (studentNo)

    StudentRental(studentNo, accomId, rentStart, rentFinish,
        rent)
    PRIMARY KEY (studentNo, rentStart)
    FOREIGN KEY (studentNo) REFERENCES Student(studentNo)
    FOREIGN KEY (accomId) REFERENCES Accommodation(accomId)

    Accommodation(accomId, hall, room, staffNo, bursar)
    PRIMARY KEY (accomId)
```

The data in these three tables is shown in Figure 9.26. There are no more repeating groups of columns in the `StudentRental` table, but there is one in `Accommodation`. The data in the last two rows shows that the group of columns {`hall`, `staffNo`, `bursar`} forms a repeating group (highlighted in Figure 9.26).

Code listing 9.4.4 shows the table schema, and Figure 9.27 the sample data, after removing this repeating group. In this case, the new table is called `Hall` and, to avoid confusion, the column `hall` from the original table is renamed `name`. The `Accommodation` table gets a foreign key.

Code listing 9.4.4   Table schema after removing the repeating group
```
{hall, StaffNo, bursar}

    Student(studentNo, name)
    PRIMARY KEY (studentNo)

    StudentRental(studentNo, accomId, rentStart, rentFinish,
        rent)
    PRIMARY KEY (studentNo, rentStart)
```

Figure 9.26 The sample data after removing the second repeating group.

StudentRental

studentNo	accomId	rentStart	rentFinish	rent
2005453125	WM107	11 Sep 2005	10 Jun 2006	550
2005453125	MC078	10 Sep 2006	9 Jun 2007	500
2004023401	WM107	12 Sep 2004	11 Jun 2005	450
2004023401	MW031	11 Sep 2005	10 Jun 2006	550
2004023401	MW042	10 Sep 2006	9 Jun 2007	575
2004892857	MC078	12 Sep 2004	11 Jun 2005	400
2004892857	WM107	12 Jun 2005	10 Sep 2005	450

Student

studentNo	name
2005453125	Peter Harris
2004023401	Alice Clough
2004892857	Jamie Smith

Accommodation

accomId	hall	room	staffNo	bursar
WM107	William Morris	123	56673	Joshua Bittaye
MC078	Marie Curie	14	35054	Selma Hutchins
MW031	**Maurice Wilkins**	46	**35054**	**Selma Hutchins**
MW042	**Maurice Wilkins**	51	**35054**	**Selma Hutchins**

Figure 9.27 The sample data after removing the third repeating group.

StudentRental

studentNo	accomId	rentStart	rentFinish	rent
2005453125	WM107	11 Sep 2005	10 Jun 2006	550
2005453125	MC078	10 Sep 2006	9 Jun 2007	500
2004023401	WM107	12 Sep 2004	11 Jun 2005	450
2004023401	MW031	11 Sep 2005	10 Jun 2006	550
2004023401	MW042	10 Sep 2006	9 Jun 2007	575
2004892857	MC078	12 Sep 2004	11 Jun 2005	400
2004892857	WM107	12 Jun 2005	10 Sep 2005	450

Student

studentNo	name
2005453125	Peter Harris
2004023401	Alice Clough
2004892857	Jamie Smith

Accommodation

accomId	hall	room
WM107	William Morris	123
MC078	Marie Curie	14
MW031	Maurice Wilkins	46
MW042	Maurice Wilkins	51

Hall

name	staffNo	bursar
William Morris	56673	Joshua Bittaye
Marie Curie	35054	Selma Hutchins
Maurice Wilkins	35054	Selma Hutchins

```
FOREIGN KEY (studentNo) REFERENCES Student(studentNo)
FOREIGN KEY (accomId) REFERENCES Accommodation(accomId)

Accommodation(accomId, hall, room)
PRIMARY KEY (accomId)
FOREIGN KEY (hall) REFERENCES Hall(name)

Hall(name, staffNo, bursar)
PRIMARY KEY (hall)
```

The new table, Hall, also has a repeating group of columns – {staffNo, bursar}.

Removing this fourth repeating group leads to the table schema in Code listing 9.4.5. Note that the new table is called Bursar, so the bursar column in the original table is renamed name. The sample data is shown in Figure 9.28. At this point, all the repeating groups have been dealt with, so the normalization process is now complete. The set of table schema in Code listing 9.4.5 is said to have been **normalized**.

Code listing 9.4.5 Table schema after removing the repeating group {staffNo, bursar}

```
Student(studentNo, name)
PRIMARY KEY (studentNo)

StudentRental(studentNo, accomId, rentStart, rentFinish,
    rent)
```

Figure 9.28 The sample data after removing the fourth repeating group.

StudentRental

studentNo	accomId	rentStart	rentFinish	rent
2005453125	WM107	11 Sep 2005	10 Jun 2006	550
2005453125	MC078	10 Sep 2006	9 Jun 2007	500
2004023401	WM107	12 Sep 2004	11 Jun 2005	450
2004023401	MW031	11 Sep 2005	10 Jun 2006	550
2004023401	MW042	10 Sep 2006	9 Jun 2007	575
2004892857	MC078	12 Sep 2004	11 Jun 2005	400
2004892857	WM107	12 Jun 2005	10 Sep 2005	450

Student

studentNo	name
2005453125	Peter Harris
2004023401	Alice Clough
2004892857	Jamie Smith

Accommodation

accomId	hall	room
WM107	William Morris	123
MC078	Marie Curie	14
MW031	Maurice Wilkins	46
MW042	Maurice Wilkins	51

Hall

name	staffNo
William Morris	56673
Marie Curie	35054
Maurice Wilkins	35054

Bursar

staffNo	name
56673	Joshua Bittaye
35054	Selma Hutchins

```
PRIMARY KEY (studentNo, rentStart)
FOREIGN KEY (studentNo) REFERENCES Student(studentNo)
FOREIGN KEY (accomId) REFERENCES Accommodation(accomId)

Accommodation(accomId, hall, room)
PRIMARY KEY (accomId)
FOREIGN KEY (hall) REFERENCES Hall(name)

Hall(name, staffNo)
PRIMARY KEY (hall)
FOREIGN KEY (staffNo) REFERENCES Bursar(staffNo)

Bursar(staffNo, name)
PRIMARY KEY (staffNo)
```

It is important to realize that there may be more than one way to normalize data. When a repeating group is pulled out into a new table, there may be more than one candidate key. In this situation, the choice of primary key will affect which columns are left behind in the original table. For example, the second repeating group – {accomId, hall, room, staffNo, bursar} – has two candidate keys – {accomId} and {hall, room}. If {hall, room} had been chosen as the primary key, then the process of normalization would have led to a different normalized set of table schema.

To use normalization effectively, there needs to be some way to identify repeating groups of columns. Given the table of data in Figure 9.23 (b), some of the repeating groups seemed obvious, others less so. The insight that makes it a little easier to identify repeating groups is that each group becomes a table and that table has a primary key. This means that, even in the original table, the data in the repeating group is determined by the data in those primary key columns.

For example, in any row of the table in Figure 9.23 (b), the value of the accomId column determines the values of hall, room, staffNo and bursar. Whenever accomId is 'WM107' then, in that row, the value for hall is 'William Morris', room is '123', staffNo is '56673' and bursar is 'Joshua Bittaye'.

However, the value of accomId does not determine the value of *every* column for a row. For example, in the first and third rows of the table in Figure 9.23 (b), accomId is 'WM107', but the value of the columns studentNo, name, rentStart, rentFinish and rent are not the same.

The column accomId is called a **functional determinant**. Functional determinants are candidate keys in waiting – they determine the values of a *subset* of columns in the table called the **dependent columns**. The repeating group consists of the dependent columns *and* the columns of the functional determinant.

> **Functional determinant** A set of columns that forms a 'candidate key' for a subset of the columns in the table. The columns which have their value determined are called the *dependent* columns.

This definition means that every candidate key is a functional determinant as a candidate key determines the values of *all* the other columns and, in maths, the whole set is also considered a subset of itself. This leads to a clear definition of when to stop the normalization process – when every functional determinant is a candidate key, there are no more repeating groups.

> **Normalized** A table is said to be normalized when every functional determinant is a candidate key. This is also called *Boyce-Codd normal form.*

> Many textbooks teach a stepped approach to normalization. In this stepped approach, Boyce-Codd normal form lies between what are called third and fourth normal form. There is also a fifth normal form and something called domain key normal form. For most practical purposes, Boyce-Codd normal form is sufficient.

The relationship between a functional determinant and the columns it determines the values of is written using mathematical notation. For example, the relationship between the functional determinant `accomId` and its dependent columns `hall`, `room`, `staffNo` and `bursar` is written:

`{accomId}` → `{hall, room, staffNo, bursar}`

This is read 'The value of `accomId` determines the values of `hall`, `room`, `staffNo` and `bursar`'. The set of columns `{accomId}` is the functional determinant. The set of columns `{hall, room, staffNo, bursar}` is the set of dependent columns. The union of these two sets, `{accomId, hall, room, staffNo, bursar}`, is the repeating group identified in the informal approach to normalization above. The set of dependent columns *must* include every column in the table that holds values determined by the functional determinant.

With the notion of functional determinants as candidate keys in waiting, it's possible to set about systematically identifying repeating groups. Begin with individual columns. For each individual column, examine the data in the table to see whether or not its values determine the values of any other columns. If it does, then the chosen column is a functional determinant.

For example, the first column in the `StudentRental` table is `studentNo`. It is clear from the sample data (Figure 9.29) that the value of `studentNo` in any given row determines the value in the `name` column for that row. There is no counterexample to this claim – that is, there are no two rows of the table that have the same value in `studentNo` but *different* values in `name`. This fact means that `{studentNo}` is a functional determinant, with `name` a dependent column.

In contrast, there are two rows of the table that have the same value in `studentNo` but *different* values in `accomId` (as shown in Figure 9.29), so `accomId` is *not* determined by `studentNo` and, therefore, is not one of the dependent columns. Nor

Figure 9.29 Checking whether or not the value in one column determines the values of other columns.

Same `studentNo` but
different `accomId`

StudentRental										
studentNo	name	accomId	hall	room	rentStart	rentFinish	rent	staffNo	bursar
2005453125	Peter Harris	WM107	William Morris	123	11 Sep 2005	10 Jun 2006	550	56673	Joshua Bittaye
2005453125	Peter Harris	MC078	Marie Curie	14	10 Sep 2006	9 Jun 2007	500	35054	Selma Hutchins
2004023401	Alice Clough	WM107	William Morris	123	12 Sep 2004	11 Jun 2005	450	56673	Joshua Bittaye
2004023401	Alice Clough	MW031	Maurice Wilkins	46	11 Sep 2005	10 Jun 2006	550	35054	Selma Hutchins
2004023401	Alice Clough	MW042	Maurice Wilkins	51	10 Sep 2006	9 Jun 2007	575	35054	Selma Hutchins
2004892857	Jamie Smith	MC078	Marie Curie	14	12 Sep 2004	11 Jun 2005	400	35054	Selma Hutchins
2004892857	Jamie Smith	WM107	William Morris	123	12 Jun 2005	10 Sep 2005	450	56673	Joshua Bittaye

Same `studentNo` but
different `rentStart`

are any of the other columns. Choose any other column and there are two rows that have the same value in `studentNo` but *different* values in the chosen column. This means that `name` is the *only* dependent column. This is written:

{studentNo} → {name}

Whenever a functional determinant is written down, it must show *all* the dependent columns.

A similar argument shows that, based on the data in Figure 9.29:

{room} → {staffNo, bursar}

This illustrates the main problem with using sample data to identify functional determinants – it is often incomplete, so leads to incorrect conclusions. Clearly, the room number alone should not determine who the bursar is. In the scenario being modelled, bursars are in charge of halls of residence. They are responsible for running a particular hall and so are responsible for all the rooms in that hall. This means that Joshua Bittaye is responsible for room 14 in William Morris hall, but this room is not included in the sample data in Figure 9.29. In contrast, Selma Hutchins is responsible for room 14 in Marie Curie hall. This means that there is no way the room number alone can tell us which bursar is responsible for that room. Whenever sample data suggests a particular functional determinant, question whether this makes sense in terms of the scenario being modelled.

Just as candidate keys can have more than one column, so can functional determinants. The set of columns {hall, room} is a functional determinant. Examine the data in Figure 9.23 (b) and it is clear that:

{hall, room} → {accomId, staffNo, bursar}

This also makes sense in the context of the Accommodation Office's spreadsheet. Within any particular hall, there will only be one room with a particular room number, so {hall, room} must determine the value of accomId, which uniquely identifies a room. Similarly, each hall is managed by a particular bursar, so {hall, room} also determines the values of staffNo and bursar. As {accomId} $\rightarrow$ {hall, room, staffNo, bursar}, we've shown that the functional determinants {accomId} and {hall, room} are two different 'candidate keys' for the same repeating group. Each repeating group will be dealt with once, so the database designer must decide which of these two functional determinants is the main one for the repeating group. This is just like deciding which of a table's candidate keys becomes the primary key.

In theory, each set of columns should be examined to see whether or not it forms a functional determinant. For a table with 10 columns there are $2^{10} - 2 = 1022$ sets of columns that are potentially a functional determinant. For a table with n columns, there are $2^n - 2$. This means that the size of the task increases exponentially with the size of the table. Clearly, it is just not practical to check all the possible functional determinants by hand, even if the sample data could be guaranteed to be complete and comprehensive.

There are computer programs that will do this job, but their accuracy is limited by the quality of the sample data, and their speed by the size of the original table.

A better approach is for the database designer to use his or her understanding of the scenario being modelled to identify likely functional determinants and use the sample data to check these. For example, any column the name of which indicates that it is an identifier of some sort is likely to be a functional determinant. For example, accomId is an identifier for a particular room in a particular hall of residence, studentNo identifies a student and staffNo identifies a bursar.

It is worth running through the normalization of the StudentRental data again, using the notion of a functional determinant to help identify repeating groups. This will show that the order in which the repeating groups are removed does not change the final result (though the choice of the main functional determinant for a repeating group does). Nor should the order of the rows and columns in the spreadsheet change which repeating groups are identified, though it may make some repeating groups easier to spot.

The Accommodation Office at the Pennine University actually has two versions of the data in the StudentRental spreadsheet. The version shown in Figure 9.23 (a) is sorted by student and allows Accommodation Office staff to quickly see the rental history of a particular student. The other, RoomRental, sorts the data by room (Figure 9.30). This allows staff to check on room usage over a number of years.

The table schema is shown in Code listing 9.4.6. Note that the primary key is {accomId, rentStart} and {studentNo, rentStart} is still a candidate key for the data, but, simply because of the structure of the spreadsheet, {accomId, rentStart} is easier to spot.

Code listing 9.4.6   The RoomRental table

```
RoomRental(accomId, room, hall, bursar, staffNo,
    rentStart, rentFinish, rent, studentNo, name)
PRIMARY KEY (accomId, rentStart)
```

Begin with the column staffNo. It seems clear that this is intended to identify a particular member of staff and the data supports the assertion that the value of staffNo

Figure 9.30 The RoomRental **spreadsheet – a reordered version of the** StudentRental **spreadsheet data.**

accomId	room	hall	bursar	staffNo	rentStart	rentFinish	rent	studentNo	name
MC078	14	Marie Curie	Selma Hutchins	35054	12 Sep 2004	11 Jun 2005	400	2004892857	Jamie Smith
					10 Sep 2006	9 Jun 2007	500	2005453125	Peter Harris
MW031	46	Maurice Wilkins	Selma Hutchins	35054	11 Sep 2005	10 Jun 2006	550	2004023401	Alice Clough
MW042	51	Maurice Wilkins	Selma Hutchins	35054	10 Sep 2006	9 Jun 2007	575	2004023401	Alice Clough
WM107	123	William Morris	Joshua Bittaye	56673	12 Jun 2005	10 Sep 2005	450	2004892857	Jamie Smith
					12 Sep 2004	11 Jun 2005	450	2004023401	Alice Clough
					11 Sep 2005	10 Jun 2006	550	2005453125	Peter Harris

Figure 9.31 Dealing with the first functional determinant.

RoomRental

accomId	room	hall	bursar	staffNo	rentStart	rentFinish	rent	studentNo	name
MC078	14	Marie Curie	Selma Hutchins	35054	12 Sep 2004	11 Jun 2005	400	2004892857	Jamie Smith
MC078	14	Marie Curie	Selma Hutchins	35054	10 Sep 2006	9 Jun 2007	500	2005453125	Peter Harris
MW031	46	Maurice Wilkins	Selma Hutchins	35054	11 Sep 2005	10 Jun 2006	550	2004023401	Alice Clough
MW042	51	Maurice Wilkins	Selma Hutchins	35054	10 Sep 2006	9 Jun 2007	575	2004023401	Alice Clough
WM107	123	William Morris	Joshua Bittaye	56673	12 Jun 2005	10 Sep 2005	450	2004892857	Jamie Smith
WM107	123	William Morris	Joshua Bittaye	56673	12 Sep 2004	11 Jun 2005	450	2004023401	Alice Clough
WM107	123	William Morris	Joshua Bittaye	56673	11 Sep 2005	10 Jun 2006	550	2005453125	Peter Harris

Repeating group (functional determinant plus dependent columns) becomes a new table

Functional determinant remains on RoomRental as a foreign key

Bursar

staffNo	name
35054	Selma Hutchins
56673	Joshua Bittaye

RoomRental

accomId	room	hall	staffNo	rentStart	rentFinish	rent	studentNo	name
MC078	14	Marie Curie	35054	12 Sep 2004	11 Jun 2005	400	2004892857	Jamie Smith
MC078	14	Marie Curie	35054	10 Sep 2006	9 Jun 2007	500	2005453125	Peter Harris
MW031	46	Maurice Wilkins	35054	11 Sep 2005	10 Jun 2006	550	2004023401	Alice Clough
MW042	51	Maurice Wilkins	35054	10 Sep 2006	9 Jun 2007	575	2004023401	Alice Clough
WM107	123	William Morris	56673	12 Jun 2005	10 Sep 2005	450	2004892857	Jamie Smith
WM107	123	William Morris	56673	12 Sep 2004	11 Jun 2005	450	2004023401	Alice Clough
WM107	123	William Morris	56673	11 Sep 2005	10 Jun 2006	550	2005453125	Peter Harris

determines the value of `bursar`. The data in the first and third rows shows that this is the only dependent column, so:

```
{staffNo} → {bursar}
```

Now create a new table consisting of all the columns in the functional determinant and all its dependent columns. Finally, remove the dependent columns from the `RoomRental` table. Figure 9.31 shows the transformation from a single `RoomRental` table to a `RoomRental` table *plus* a `Bursar` table. Code listing 9.4.7 shows the table schema.

Code listing 9.4.7 Table schema after dealing with the functional determinant `{staffNo} → {bursar}`

```
RoomRental(accomId, room, hall, staffNo, rentStart,
      rentFinish, rent, studentNo, name)
PRIMARY KEY (accomId, rentStart)
FOREIGN KEY (staffNo) REFERENCES Bursar(staffNo)

Bursar(staffNo, name)
PRIMARY KEY (staffNo)
```

Next, consider the column `studentNo`. Both the data and the scenario suggest a functional determinant `{studentNo} → {name}` and the data in the third and fourth rows indicates that `name` is the only dependent attribute.

Code listing 9.4.8 and Figure 9.32 show the tables at this stage of the normalization process.

Figure 9.32 The `RoomRental` data after two functional determinants have been dealt with.

RoomRental

accomId	room	hall	staffNo	rentStart	rentFinish	rent	studentNo
MC078	14	Marie Curie	35054	12 Sep 2004	11 Jun 2005	400	2004892857
MC078	14	Marie Curie	35054	10 Sep 2006	9 Jun 2007	500	2005453125
MW031	40	Maurice Wilkino	35054	11 Sep 2005	10 Jun 2006	550	2004023401
MW042	51	Maurice Wilkins	35054	10 Sep 2006	9 Jun 2007	575	2004023401
WM107	123	William Morris	56673	12 Jun 2005	10 Sep 2005	450	2004892857
WM107	123	William Morris	56673	12 Sep 2004	11 Jun 2005	450	2004023401
WM107	123	William Morris	56673	11 Sep 2005	10 Jun 2006	550	2005453125

Bursar

staffNo	name
35054	Selma Hutchins
56673	Joshua Bittaye

Student

studentNo	name
2004892857	Jamie Smith
2005453125	Peter Harris
2004023401	Alice Clough

Code listing 9.4.8   Table schema after dealing with the functional determinant {studentNo} → {name}

```
RoomRental(accomId, room, hall, staffNo, rentStart,
     rentFinish, rent, studentNo)
PRIMARY KEY (accomId, rentStart)
FOREIGN KEY (staffNo) REFERENCES Bursar(staffNo)
FOREIGN KEY (studentNo) REFERENCES Student(studentNo)

Bursar(staffNo, name)
PRIMARY KEY (staffNo)

Student(studentNo, name)
PRIMARY KEY (studentNo)
```

The next obvious candidate for a functional determinant is {accomId} as, like staffNo and studentNo, it is clearly some form of unique identifier. Figure 9.32 indicates that {accomId} → {room, hall, staffNo}. This is not quite the same repeating group as that identified when normalizing the StudentRental version of this data. There, the repeating group also included the column bursar (see Figure 9.25 and Code listing 9.4.3). This time, the bursar column has already been extracted into a separate table, becoming the Bursar table's name column.

Dealing with the functional determinant {accomId} leads to a new table, Accommodation. The process is a little trickier than previously because the dependent column staffNo is a foreign key (see Code listing 9.4.8). When the staffNo

Figure 9.33 Sample data after dealing with the functional determinant
`{accomId}` → `{room, hall, staffNo}`.

RoomRental

accomId	rentStart	rentFinish	rent	studentNo
MC078	12 Sep 2004	11 Jun 2005	400	2004892857
MC078	10 Sep 2006	9 Jun 2007	500	2005453125
MW031	11 Sep 2005	10 Jun 2006	550	2004023401
MW042	10 Sep 2006	9 Jun 2007	575	2004023401
WM107	12 Jun 2005	10 Sep 2005	450	2004892857
WM107	12 Sep 2004	11 Jun 2005	450	2004023401
WM107	11 Sep 2005	10 Jun 2006	550	2005453125

Student

studentNo	name
2004892857	Jamie Smith
2005453125	Peter Harris
2004023401	Alice Clough

Accommodation

accomId	room	hall	staffNo
MC078	14	Marie Curie	35054
MW031	46	Maurice Wilkins	35054
MW042	51	Maurice Wilkins	35054
WM107	123	William Morris	56673

Bursar

staffNo	name
35054	Selma Hutchins
56673	Joshua Bittaye

column is copied to the new table `Accommodation`, so is the associated foreign key constraint. Then, as `staffNo` is a dependent attribute, the column *and its associated foreign key constraint* are removed from `RoomRental`. This leads to the table schema in Code listing 9.4.9 and the sample data in Figure 9.33.

Code listing 9.4.9 Table schema after dealing with the functional determinant `{accomId}` → `{room, hall, staffNo}`

```
RoomRental(accomId, rentStart, rentFinish, rent,
    studentNo)
PRIMARY KEY (accomId, rentStart)
FOREIGN KEY (studentNo) REFERENCES Student(studentNo)
FOREIGN KEY (accomId) REFERENCES Accommodation(accomId)

Accommodation(accomId, room, hall, staffNo)
PRIMARY KEY (accomId)
FOREIGN KEY (staffNo) REFERENCES Bursar(staffNo)

Bursar(staffNo, name)
PRIMARY KEY (staffNo)

Student(studentNo, name)
PRIMARY KEY (studentNo)
```

There is one last functional determinant to deal with, which is on the `Accommodation` table – that of {hall} → {staffNo}.

Unlike the other functional determinants, which clearly made sense, this one needs to be questioned. It's clear that, over time, the same hall will have more than one bursar. Consequently, although the same member of staff has been the bursar in each hall throughout the period covered by the sample data, this won't always be true. Eventually, for example, Selma Hutchins will retire and so there will have to be a new bursar for the Marie Curie and Maurice Wilkins halls. When this point was put to members of staff in the Pennine University's Accommodation Office, they pointed out that it doesn't matter to them who was bursar at the time a rental was agreed. What matters is who is bursar *now* as that is the person who will deal with any queries. This means that, in the scenario being modelled, there really is only ever one bursar for each hall. The functional determinant is correct after all.

This leads to the final set of table schema, in Code listing 9.4.10. Again, the foreign key associated with the dependent column `staffNo` moves from the original table `Accommodation` to the new table `Hall`, along with the dependent column itself. The name of the `hall` column is changed to `name` in the `Hall` table, though it is unchanged in the `Accommodation` table.

The sample data is shown in Figure 9.34. Comparing this to the sample data in Figure 9.28, there are some superficial differences – the name of the table is `RoomRental` table instead of `StudentRental` and the order of the rows and columns are different.

Figure 9.34 The fully normalized `RoomRental` data.

RoomRental

accomId	rentStart	rentFinish	rent	studentNo
MC078	12 Sep 2004	11 Jun 2005	400	2004892857
MC078	10 Sep 2006	9 Jun 2007	500	2005453125
MW031	11 Sep 2005	10 Jun 2006	550	2004023401
MW042	10 Sep 2006	9 Jun 2007	575	2004023401
WM107	12 Jun 2005	10 Sep 2005	450	2004892857
WM107	12 Sep 2004	11 Jun 2005	450	2004023401
WM107	11 Sep 2005	10 Jun 2006	550	2005453125

Student

studentNo	name
2004892857	Jamie Smith
2005453125	Peter Harris
2004023401	Alice Clough

Accommodation

accomId	room	hall
MC078	14	Marie Curie
MW031	46	Maurice Wilkins
MW042	51	Maurice Wilkins
WM107	123	William Morris

Hall

name	staffNo
Marie Curie	35054
Maurice Wilkins	35054
William Morris	56673

Bursar

staffNo	name
35054	Selma Hutchins
56673	Joshua Bittaye

Comparing the table schema in Code listings 9.4.5 and 9.4.10, there is one significant difference. In Code listing 9.4.10, the `RoomRental` table has a primary key `{accomId, rentStart}`, while the equivalent `StudentRental` table in Code listing 9.4.5 has a primary key `{studentNo, rentStart}`. Whenever there is a choice of candidate keys, there will be different normalized sets of table schema.

Code listing 9.4.10   Fully normalized table schema

```
RoomRental(accomId, rentStart, rentFinish, rent,
    studentNo)
PRIMARY KEY (accomId, rentStart)
FOREIGN KEY (studentNo) REFERENCES Student(studentNo)
FOREIGN KEY (accomId) REFERENCES Accommodation(accomId)

Accommodation(accomId, room, hall)
PRIMARY KEY (accomId)
FOREIGN KEY (hall) REFERENCES Hall(name)

Bursar(staffNo, name)
PRIMARY KEY (staffNo)

Student(studentNo, name)
PRIMARY KEY (studentNo)

Hall(name, staffNo)
PRIMARY KEY (name)
FOREIGN KEY (staffNo) REFERENCES Bursar(staffNo)
```

A table is fully normalized when all functional determinants are candidate keys. The final step in the normalization process is to check that each table is fully normalized. In the `Student` table, only the primary key `{studentNo}` is a functional determinant. Hence, in `Student`, every functional determinant is a candidate key, so the table is fully normalized. The same is true for `Hall` and `Bursar`. The only functional determinant is the primary key, so both tables are fully normalized. `Accommodation` has two functional determinants – `{accomId}` and `{hall, room}`, with `{accomId}` the primary key and `{hall, room}` a candidate key (this was discussed above). This means that `Accommodation` is also fully normalized.

The `RoomRental` table is what is left of the original data. Now that a lot of the columns have gone, it is easier to spot the functional determinants in this table. Clearly `{accomId, rentStart}` is a functional determinant and is the primary key. Equally `{studentNo, rentStart}` is a functional determinant and a candidate key – it was used as the primary key when normalizing the `Student-Rental` version of the spreadsheet data. Finally `{accomId, rentFinish}` and `{studentNo, rentFinish}` are also functional determinants, the values of which determine all the other column values and so both are candidate keys. The data suggests that `{accomId, studentNo}` is also a functional determinant. However, this is simply due to the sample data being incomplete. If a particular student rented the same room in two different years, there would be two different rows in the spreadsheet with different start and finish dates and possibly different rents (inflation means rents may go up, while competition between landlords means that they may come down). Thus {accomId, studentNo} is *not* a functional determinant. In fact, there are no other functional determinants and so the RoomRental table is also fully normalized.

As has been demonstrated, provided *all* the dependent columns are identified for each functional determinant, then it does not matter in which order the repeating groups are dealt with. Where there are two or more functional determinants for a single repeating group, the choice of primary key for the new table will affect the final table schema. However, the difference is not significant for the logical design as any candidate key *could* be used as the primary key. Thus, normalization can proceed according to the following steps.

1 Identify a functional determinant and *all* its dependent columns. Always ensure that for each dependent column columnName the claim 'the functional determinant determines the value of columnName' makes sense within the scenario being modelled.

2 Create a new table consisting of the columns in the functional determinant and all its dependent columns.
   (a) Make the functional determinant the primary key of this table.
   (b) If the dependent columns include the columns of a pre-existing foreign key, then include the foreign key constraint on the new table.

3 Remove the *dependent columns* from the original table, but leave the columns of the functional determinant behind.
   (a) If the dependent columns include the columns of a foreign key, then remove the foreign key constraint on the original table.
   (b) Add a new foreign key constraint on the original table to indicate that the functional determinant references the primary key of the new table.

Chapter summary

- This chapter has discussed logical database design for the relational data model, demonstrating how to develop a relational database schema from a conceptual ER diagram. The task was broken down into two basic steps. First, create a logical ER diagram by eliminating those features that could not be expressed directly using the organization structures of the relational data model. Next, write down a set of table schema. The process is a little involved, but largely mechanical.

- The chapter has concluded with a discussion of normalization. This is an alternative approach to relational database design that is particularly useful in situations when an existing data set (such as a spreadsheet) needs to be stored in a new database. Both an informal, and formal, approach to normalization have been described. The approach to normalization allowed for the repeating groups to be dealt with in any order. There is an alternative approach, which distinguishes different kinds of repeating group and deals with them in a strict order. See the Further reading section, next, for sources on this stepped approach to normalization.

Further reading

Logical database design for the relational data model is a well-established process. The steps described in this chapter are also covered by most database textbooks. The approach to normalization taken here is based on that described in Howe (2001). Other books – Date (2004), Connolly and Begg (2004), Elmasri and Navathe (2007) – use the stepped approach to normalization.

Review questions

9.1 Explain how logical database design differs from conceptual database design. Why are they kept separate?

9.2 Explain the purpose of the logical ER diagram. How does it differ from the ER diagram for the conceptual database design?

9.3 In logical database design for a relational database, how can the designer deal with multivalued attributes?

9.4 Explain the use of the following in a logical ER diagram:
(a) look-up entity
(b) link entity.

9.5 Explain why including default values in foreign key columns can lead to the database holding incorrect data. Under what circumstances would it be safe to include default values?

9.6 Explain how to derive the referential action for a foreign key from the structure of the logical ER diagram.

9.7 What is a discriminator column and when would you use one?

9.8 In the context of normalization, what is a repeating group and how is it dealt with?

9.9 Explain the following terms:
(a) functional determinant
(b) dependent column
(c) Boyce-Codd normal form.

9.10 Explain how the ER diagram can help to determine whether or not a foreign key column may be null.

Exercises

9.11 Many-to-many associations can't be implemented by adding a foreign key column to either one of the tables concerned. Using a diagram, show why adding a foreign key column to *both* tables won't work either.

9.12 Write down logical designs for all the entities in Figure 12.4, the logical ER diagram for the Web Timetable application.

9.13 Figure E.1 is a conceptual ER diagram for the Pennine University's Accommodation Office.
(a) Draw the corresponding logical ER diagram.
(b) Write down the table schema.

Figure E.1 A conceptual ER diagram for the Pennine University's Accommodation Office.

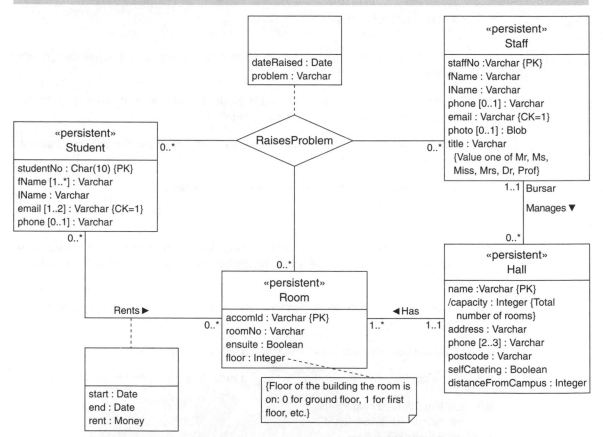

9.14 An analysis of the different sorts of students who attend the Pennine University led to the generalization hierarchy shown in Figure E.2. This exercise examines portions of the generalization hierarchy before attempting to write down a complete set of table schema.
(a) An Undergraduate must be either a Foundation student (studying a Foundation degree) or a Bachelors student (studying a Bachelors degree). Foundation students will have a workplace and a workplace mentor while Bachelors students may be studying on a sandwich course. Write down the table schema for these three entities (ignore the other entities for now). Ensure that you take account of the constraint on the generalization relationships.

Figure E.2 Generalization hierarchy for students at the Pennine University.

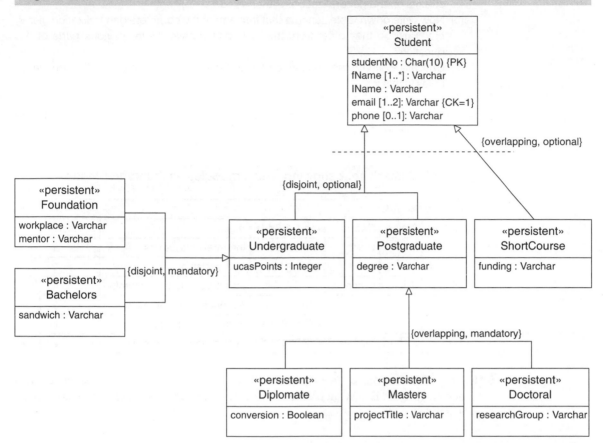

(b) A `Postgraduate` must be either a `Diplomate` student (studying a postgraduate Diploma), a `Masters` student (studying for a Masters degree) or a `Doctoral` student (doing research for a doctorate). `Diplomate` students may be conversion students, studying a different area from that of their first degree, `Masters` students must do a project and `Doctoral` students will be attached to a research group. Some `Doctoral` students also take a Masters degree in their first year and some `Masters` students may also be registered for a Diploma (in case they decide not to complete the project). Write down table schema for these four entities (ignore the other entities for now). Ensure that you take account of the constraint on the generalization relationships.

(c) Consider the generalization relationships between `Student`, `Undergraduate` and `Postgraduate`. Write down table schema for these three entities (ignore the other entities for now). Ensure that you take account of the constraint on the generalization relationships.

(d) Consider the generalization relationships between `Student`, `Undergraduate`, `Postgraduate` and `ShortCourse`. Note that some students are none of these (such as students taking an access course). Also, a student cannot be an undergraduate *and* postgraduate at the same time, but undergraduates and postgraduates can take short courses. Write down table schema for these four entities (ignore the other entities for now). Ensure that you take account of both the constraints on the generalization relationships.

(e) Now write down table schema that implement the complete generalization hierarchy. How do they differ from the table schema written in previous parts of this question?

(f) Critically evaluate the benefits and drawbacks of modelling generalization hierarchies in this way.

9.15 Use normalization to develop a set of table schema from the spreadsheet data shown in Figure E.3.

Figure E.3 Spreadsheet showing which modules each lecturer leads.

LecturerModule

staffNo	fName	lName	moduleCode	module	semester
31210	Paul	Smith	CIFC0084	Information systems	1
			CIHO6008	Soft systems	2
35054	Selma	Hutchins	CCFC0108	Introduction to programming	1
			CCH09668	Advanced programming	2
			CCHO0418	Formal specification	2
56673	Joshua	Bittaye	CIFC0084	Information systems	2

9.16 Use normalization to develop a set of table schema from the spreadsheet data shown in Figure E.4. What problem with the normalization process does this example illustrate?

Figure E.4 Spreadsheet showing programmes of study by department.

ProgrammeOfStudy

department	head	name	programme	pManager	pManagerName	course	courseTitle	cDirector	cDirectorName
Business	12231	John Smith	Foundation	81134	Emmy Noether	B2Y6	Management	76674	Paul Dirac
						B4T1	Business studies	81134	Emmy Noether
			Bachelors	43188	Jeff Smith	B5Y7	Management	43188	Jeff Smith
						B4R1	Business studies (top-up)	81134	Emmy Noether
Computing	23257	Freya Stark	Foundation	31210	Paul Smith	C1F8	Software engineering	67884	David Davies
			Bachelors	31210	Paul Smith	C5T1	Software engineering	56673	Joshua Bittaye
						C2Z1	Computer science	31210	Paul Smith
			Postgraduate	35054	Selma Hutchins	C3M5	Information systems	35054	Selma Hutchins
						C2M3	Computer science	31210	Paul Smith

Investigations

9.17 Investigate the stepped approach to normalization (first, second and third normal forms), summarizing the process and explaining the similarities and differences to the approach used in this chapter.

9.18 Although spreadsheets are a good starting point for normalization, the process can be used with other initial sources of data. All that is needed is a list of data items (the columns). Investigate how to use normalization when the initial source of data is a set of entities and their attributes, a form (such as university application form) and items on the form, and a web page for an e-commerce retailer.

9.19 In Investigation 8.19, you developed a conceptual database design for an organization you know. Use the ER diagram to create a logical database design, including a logical ER diagram and a set of table schema.

9.20 In Investigation 8.20, you investigated an alternative approach to conceptual database design. How is logical database design dealt with in this alternative approach?

10 Physical database design

Chapter objectives

→ To reconsider the organization structures of the logical database design in the light of:

- DBMS-specific design choices
- general physical design issues.

→ To document the physical database design.

→ To assess the likely performance of a database design.

→ To understand the data storage structures available to the DBMS.

Chapter outline

Physical database design takes the logical database design and investigates how the facilities provided by a particular DBMS can best be used to implement it. It is a much more diverse process than either conceptual or logical database design. Some decisions are relatively straightforward, such as which data types provided by the DBMS best match the data types of the logical design. Others could have been made during the logical design process, but were postponed because different DBMS offer different solutions – how to implement derived attributes and business rules, for example. There are also more general physical design decisions, such as whether or not to reintroduce redundant data to help improve performance. The common thread linking these decisions is that they are reliant on the facilities provided by the chosen DBMS and improved performance is an important goal.

A crucial step is that of understanding the design's non-functional requirements, such as the volume of data to be stored, response times and the processing power needed to run database transactions. Analysing storage requirements and transactions can offer some useful guidance for database designers and developers, but the conclusions are indicative, rather than prescriptive. Most commercial DBMS have powerful, built-in optimization strategies and additional features designed to improve perfor-mance. To create a genuinely efficient physical database design, the database designer needs a thorough working knowledge of the DBMS being used, not just a theoretical understanding of physical database design issues.

The websites of most DBMS vendors offer white papers and training materials on how to get the best from their technology. There are also specialist training courses and most serious database designers and administrators will have sat the certification exams for their particular DBMS.

This chapter discusses some common issues in physical database design rather than seeking to replicate vendor-specific design guidance. It introduces the issues and high-lights common solutions, but is not a tutorial on how to implement a particular data-base using a particular DBMS. That said, some of the issues discussed in this chapter will need to be addressed in most database applications, and most database designers will address most of these issues at some point in their careers. Understanding the basic issues should make it easier to make use of the more powerful solutions offered by commercial DBMS.

One issue that must be considered during physical database design is application partitioning (see Chapter 2). The logical database design may include requirements such as derived attributes and business rules that cannot be implemented in the cho-sen DBMS. The difficulty may be that the DBMS doesn't support the appropriate func-tionality or does but only at the cost of degraded performance. As these requirements are part of the database design, they are closely concerned with managing the data on the database instance. If it is possible to implement them efficiently using the facilities provided by the DBMS, then that is the best option. If not, then they should be imple-mented using application code on the web server, such as server-side scripting with PHP. If this is not an option, then, as a last resort, the functionality could be imple-mented on the web client using browser-side scripting. This really *is* a last resort for a web database application as there is no guarantee that an end user's web browser will support browser-side scripting. This chapter explores solutions available in the data-base tier of the application.

■ Section 10.1 completes the translation of the conceptual design into a design that can be implemented on a relational DBMS. It discusses how to map the data types used in the conceptual and logical designs to those supported by a particular DBMS. It also discusses how to implement derived attributes and business rules. These issues were not considered during logical database design as the choice of DBMS affects which options are available. The section concludes by suggesting one way to document the physical database design using SQL DDL statements. The ap-proach in this section leads to a *first draft* of the physical database design. As with the chapters on conceptual and logical design, this first section provides an overview of the basic tasks, rather than a comprehensive description of physical database design.

■ Section 10.2 considers how to assess the likely performance of the database design. It introduces techniques for assessing the likely data storage capacity required by individual tables and, hence, the database as a whole, and for assessing the perfor-mance of individual database transactions (SQL DML statements). The techniques can be applied to *either* the logical database design *or* the first draft of the physical database design. The conclusions may lead the database designer to reassess the first draft of the physical database design or even change the target DBMS.

■ Section 10.3 considers some general issues that the database designer should consider during physical database design. These include whether or not to introduce surrogate keys, how to deal with binary data and whether or not to introduce controlled redundancy.

■ The first three sections described above are all focused on how best to design tables and manage the data they hold using features defined in the ISO SQL standard. Section 10.4 considers the data storage structures and underlying data files used by the DBMS to hold the database instance. It outlines the three basic ways in which to organize records within data files – heap, ordered and hash files. It then discusses the role of indexes in managing data.

■ Section 10.5 concludes the chapter with a discussion of database security issues, based on the security model of the ISO SQL:2003 standard.

10.1 Physical table designs

This section deals with those pieces of information from the conceptual database design that were set aside during logical database design. It uses features of the ISO SQL:2003 standard that are available on most DBMS, though the particulars of implementation may vary.

10.1.1 Data types

The data types used in the chapters on conceptual and logical database design were the most common business data types – character strings, numeric data, dates, times and intervals. Most DBMS include the ISO SQL data types and further data types for specific purposes. Obviously, which particular data type is used will depend on what the target DBMS provides. This section seeks to highlight the typical design decisions a database designer faces at this point in physical database design. A summary of data type choices available in the MySQL DBMS, Oracle database and ISO SQL:2003 standard is included in Table 10.1.

For character string data, the CHAR and VARCHAR data types seem to be ubiquitous (though the Oracle database uses the keyword VARCHAR2 instead of VARCHAR). Many DBMS also include a special data type for columns that hold a lot of character string data. What counts as 'a lot' varies as it is any character string with more characters than can be held in a VARCHAR column.

There is a little more variety in **numeric** data types. Numeric data types can be **exact numeric**, meaning that the value stored will always be exactly the same as the literal or expression representing it, or **approximate numeric**, where there may be rounding errors. For example, the number ½ can be represented exactly as the decimal literal 0.5, but ⅓ cannot be represented exactly as a decimal literal, so must be stored as an

Table 10.1 Differences in data types between ISO standard and two commercial DBMS.

General data type	ISO SQL:2003	MySQL DBMS	Oracle database
Character string	CHAR VARCHAR CLOB	CHAR VARCHAR TEXT (four sizes)	CHAR VARCHAR2 CLOB
Exact numeric	INTEGER (three sizes) NUMERIC DECIMAL	INTEGER (five sizes) NUMERIC DECIMAL	NUMBER
Approximate numeric	REAL DOUBLE PRECISION FLOAT	REAL DOUBLE PRECISION FLOAT	BINARY_DOUBLE BINARY_FLOAT
Date and time	DATE TIME TIMESTAMP	DATETIME DATE TIME TIMESTAMP YEAR	DATE TIMESTAMP

Interval – year, month	INTERVAL YEAR
	INTERVAL MONTH
	INTERVAL YEAR
	  TO MONTH
			INTERVAL YEAR
			  TO MONTH

Interval – day, time	INTERVAL DAY
	INTERVAL HOUR
	INTERVAL MINUTE
	INTERVAL SECOND
	INTERVAL *MAJOR*
	  TO *MINOR*
		TIME	INTERVAL DAY
			  TO SECOND

Boolean	BOOLEAN	BOOL, BOOLEAN	
Binary	BLOB	BLOB (four sizes)	BLOB
Non-scalar	ARRAY MULTISET	SET	VARRAY

approximate numeric value. Most business applications only need exact numeric data, but scientific applications will need to use approximate numerics.

The variations on date and time data types are greater than for the other data types. The ISO SQL and MySQL DBMS DATE and TIME hold a date and a time respectively. The Oracle database's DATE data type and the MySQL DBMS DATETIME data type both hold a date *and* time, such as '21 January 2006 18:36:00'. The idea of the TIMESTAMP data types is that the values provide precision down to fractions of a second (not provided by the Oracle DATE or MySQL DATETIME data types). Support for time zones and automatic time stamping varies for the data types on different DBMS.

The INTERVAL data types of the ISO SQL standard offer a comprehensive and flexible approach to dealing with intervals of time. Year and month intervals can be expressed as a number of years, months or both. Day and time intervals can deal with days, hours, minutes, seconds or some subsequence of these, such as days, hours and hours, minutes, seconds (this is expressed in Table 10.1 as INTERVAL *MAJOR TO MINOR*).

The Oracle database offers the same coverage with a more compact syntax, so INTERVAL YEAR TO MONTH holds intervals such as '3 years and 7 months', '2 years' and '5 months'. INTERVAL DAY TO SECOND can hold intervals such as '2 days, 4 hours, 17 minutes and 27.35 seconds', '12 seconds', '1 hour, 7 minutes' and so on.

The MySQL DBMS allows limited support for hour, minute and second intervals with its TIME data type and greater for support for intervals in the functions used to manipulate dates and times.

Support for the Boolean data type is patchy, which is odd as it is the only type of data that is actually required by the relational data model. It was included in ISO SQL:1999 and is implemented in the MySQL 5.1 DBMS as a synonym for TINYINT(1) – that is, a single-digit integer. This is a common approach when the Boolean data type is not available – simply designate a single digit (or character) to represent 'True' and all others to represent 'False'.

Non-scalar data types also have patchy support. The ISO SQL standard defines ARRAY and MULTISET. The Oracle database implements the VARRAY data type. The MySQL DBMS implements the SET data type, though the possible elements of the set must be defined when the table is created, so this is closer to an enumeration than a true set data type.

The ISO SQL:2003 standard includes the ability for users to define their own data types. User-defined types are supported by the Oracle 10g database (through its object type), though they are not supported in the MySQL 5.1 DBMS. In many relational databases, the system-defined data types are all that are needed.

One common use for user-defined data types is ensuring that foreign key columns have exactly the same data type as their matching primary key column. The ISO SQL:2003 **distinct types** can be used for this. A distinct type is created as a restriction of an existing system-defined type. Code listing 10.1.1.1 shows how to do this for the Staff Directory database tables. A new distinct type, called StaffNo, is defined using the CREATE TYPE statement and used as the data type for the staffNo columns in the Staff and SuportSession tables.

As SQL enforces strong typing on user-defined types, it is not possible to compare, for example, a StaffNo value to a CHAR(5) value, even though these two data types have the same set of possible values. There are facilities to cast a user-defined type back to its underlying system-defined type. Check the manual for the target DBMS before using this facility, though.

Code listing 10.1.1.1 Using user-defined data types for primary and foreign key columns

```
CREATE TYPE StaffNo AS CHAR(5) FINAL;

CREATE TABLE Staff(
staffNo StaffNo NOT NULL ,
```

```
fName VARCHAR(20) NOT NULL ,
lName VARCHAR(20) NOT NULL ,
phone VARCHAR(20) ,
email VARCHAR(30) NOT NULL ,
photo BLOB ,
department VARCHAR(30) NOT NULL ,
title VARCHAR(4) ,
jobType VARCHAR(15) ,
jobTitle VARCHAR(30) ,
CONSTRAINT pkStaff PRIMARY KEY (staffNo)
);

CREATE TABLE SupportSession(
staffNo StaffNo NOT NULL ,
dayOfWeek VARCHAR (9) NOT NULL ,
startTime TIME NOT NULL ,
endTime TIME NOT NULL ,
CONSTRAINT pkSupportSession
    PRIMARY KEY (staffNo, dayOfWeek, startTime)
);
```

> The same advice applies for those thinking of using ISO SQL:2003 **structured types**. These provide many of the features of classes from object-orientated programming languages, but there is one important difference. To SQL, every instance of a user-defined type is a *value* and it isn't possible to distinguish between two different instances that have the same value. In a fully object-orientated language, every instance of a class has a unique identifier, so two instances with the same value can still be distinguished. Structured types are beyond the scope of an introductory database textbook.

10.1.2 Derived attributes

The logical ER diagram may include derived attributes for some entities. The value of a derived attribute is calculated from the values of other attributes (usually, though not always, other attributes of the same entity).

There are two basic approaches to dealing with derived attributes. The first is to store a value for the derived attribute on the database instance. The second is to recalculate a value for the derived attribute each time end users ask for it.

If the value is stored on the database, then it is quick and easy to retrieve it. On the other hand, a derived attribute is redundant data, so is subject to the usual problem – the value for the derived attribute must be recalculated whenever the values of the other attributes change.

In contrast, if the value of the derived attribute is recalculated each time it is *requested,* there is no redundant data stored on the database, but then if the calculation is lengthy users will experience a slower response from the application.

When the value of a derived attribute is stored in a column, the database application needs to maintain the redundant data. When a row is added to the database, or modified, no value is supplied for the derived attribute. Instead, the application calculates the correct value based on the other values. If necessary, this calculation can be done by the database client (such as the web server) before submitting the database transaction to the DBMS. A better way is by using a database **trigger**.

Each SQL DML data modification statement causes a **database event** to occur. A trigger is a piece of application code that is executed when some *specified* database event occurs on a named table.

There are three database events that can cause a trigger to execute. An **insert event** occurs when data is added to a table (typically using an insert statement, but a database import may also cause an insert event). An **update event** occurs when data on a table is modified and a **delete event** when data is removed.

A trigger that executes just once in response to a database event is called a **statement-level trigger**. A **row-level trigger** executes once for each affected row. For example, suppose an update statement affects three rows. A statement-level update trigger would execute once, whereas a row-level update trigger would execute three times. (If the affected table did not have an update trigger, then nothing would happen.)

One additional piece of flexibility offered by triggers is that they can be timed to execute either before or after the database event. This is where their usefulness for dealing with derived data comes in. Before a new row is added to a table, a row-level before insert trigger can calculate the value of any derived data from the values supplied for the other columns. Similarly, the trigger can ensure that derived data is correctly modified when the other column values on a row change.

Figure 10.1 shows the general form of the ISO SQL create trigger statement. It begins with the keywords `CREATE TRIGGER` followed by the name of the trigger. The `triggerEvent` indicates what actions by users cause the trigger to execute (`INSERT`, `UPDATE` or `DELETE`). The `triggerTime` is either `BEFORE` or `AFTER`.

Each trigger is associated with changes to a *single* table and this is specified in the on clause. The referencing clause allows the database developer to define correlation names for the columns being changed and access both the old and new values of the

Figure 10.1 The ISO SQL:2003 syntax for creating a trigger.

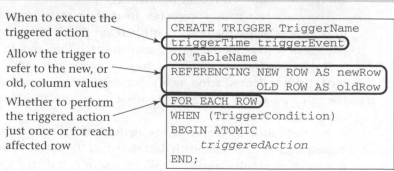

columns. Thus, in the *triggeredAction*, the identifier `newRow.column1` would refer to the value the SQL statement had supplied for `column1` (the new value). Similarly, `oldRow.column1` would refer to the value for `column1` *currently* stored in the database table (the old value). Obviously there are no old values for an insert event and no new values for a delete event.

Neither the MySQL DBMS nor the Oracle database support the referencing clause. Instead, both include standard correlation names `NEW` and `OLD`.

The statement in Figure 10.1 creates a row-level trigger, using the keywords `FOR EACH ROW`. To create a statement-level trigger, use `FOR EACH STATEMENT` instead. It also includes a **trigger condition**.

Trigger conditions allow finer control over when a trigger is executed. The `TriggerCondition` is a Boolean expression. When the triggering event occurs, the DBMS checks the trigger condition. If it is true, then the triggered action is carried out, but otherwise no further action is taken.

As an example of using triggers to maintain duplicate data, the logical design for the TeachingSession entity on the Web Timetable database includes two derived attributes. The value of endTime is calculated by adding duration to startTime. The value of `runsFor` is calculated by subtracting `startDate` from `endDate`. Code listing 10.1.2.1 shows the create table statement for the `TeachingSession` table with both these derived attributes implemented as columns. It also shows the before insert and before update triggers that maintain the redundant data. Although insert and delete events always affect whole rows, update events may affect only a single column. It would be pointless recalculating the value of `endTime` unless one of duration or startTime had changed. The trigger event for an update trigger can include a list of column names and, then, only if one of these is affected is the trigger executed.

Notice that each trigger is triggered by a separate database event. The MySQL DBMS also insists on this, but the Oracle database allows multiple database events to cause one trigger to execute. The before insert trigger `tbiTeachingSession` (`tbi` stands for 'trigger, before insert') has two statements in its triggered action that calculate the two redundant data values. The before update triggers `tbuTeachingSessionEndTime` and `tbuTeachingSessionRunsFor` calculate the redundant data value for one column each and are only triggered by changes to the values of the relevant columns.

Code listing 10.1.2.1 Including a derived attribute as a column in the base table

```
CREATE TABLE TeachingSession(
moduleCode CHAR(7) NOT NULL,
staffNo VARCHAR(5) NOT NULL,
building VARCHAR(10) NOT NULL,
roomNo VARCHAR(4) NOT NULL,
day VARCHAR(9) NOT NULL,
startTime TIME NOT NULL,
```

```
          duration INTERVAL MINUTE NOT NULL,
          endTime TIME NOT NULL,
          startDate DATE NOT NULL,
          endDate DATE NULL,
          runsFor INTERVAL DAY NULL,
          type VARCHAR(9) NOT NULL,
          sessionCode CHAR(1) NULL,
          CONSTRAINT priModule PRIMARY KEY
              (moduleCode, building, roomNo, day, startTime)
          );

          CREATE TRIGGER tbiTeachingSession
          BEFORE INSERT ON TeachingSession
          REFERENCING NEW ROW AS newRow
          FOR EACH ROW
          BEGIN ATOMIC
           newRow.endTime=newRow.startTime+newRow.duration;
           newRow.runsFor=newRow.endDate-newRow.startDate;
          END;

          CREATE TRIGGER tbuTeachingSessionEndTime
          BEFORE UPDATE OF startTime, duration ON TeachingSession
          REFERENCING NEW ROW AS newRow
          FOR EACH ROW
          BEGIN ATOMIC
           newRow.endTime=newRow.startTime+newRow.duration;
          END;

          CREATE TRIGGER tbuTeachingSessionRunsFor
          BEFORE UPDATE OF startDate, endDate ON TeachingSession
          REFERENCING NEW ROW AS newRow
          FOR EACH ROW
          BEGIN ATOMIC
           newRow.runsFor=newRow.endDate-newRow.startDate;
          END;
```

In general, triggered actions can involve multiple statements and use the full SQL procedural language (if statements, loops and so on.).

In Code listing 10.1.2.1, there are a lot of semicolons. Each statement in the triggered action must end with a semicolon. This is called a delimiter as it delimits the statement (it shows where one statement ends and the next begins). The semicolon is also the delimiter for SQL DDL statements. Although the DBMS should be able to sort out what each semicolon means, be aware that it may be necessary to use a different statement delimiter for the SQL DDL to avoid confusion. This is the case with the MySQL DBMS.

Implementing a derived attribute as a column, the value of which is maintained by application code, is not always the best route. In the case of the TeachingSession table, the calculations required to derive the data are very simple. In such cases, it may be more efficient to have the DBMS recalculate the values each time they are requested (this will depend on how often the data is likely to be requested). Relational views are the best way to implement this approach.

Code listing 10.1.2.2 shows the create table statement to create the TeachingSession base table with columns only for the non-derived attributes – the endTime and runsFor columns are omitted. Once this base table has been created, the view vwTeachingSession is created, which includes all the columns in the base table TeachingSession, plus the two derived columns endTime and runsFor. The values of these columns are calculated by expressions in the select statement that define the view. The end users will always query the view vwTeachingSession rather than the base table TeachingSession. It is even possible to modify the base table instance through this view, provided the insert or update statement does not supply values for endTime or runsFor.

Code listing 10.1.2.2   Implementing derived attributes using a view

```
CREATE TABLE TeachingSession(
moduleCode CHAR(7) NOT NULL,
staffNo VARCHAR NOT NULL,
building VARCHAR NOT NULL,
roomNo VARCHAR NOT NULL,
day VARCHAR NOT NULL,
startTime TIME NOT NULL,
duration INTERVAL NOT NULL,
startDate DATE NOT NULL,
endDate DATE NULL,
type VARCHAR NOT NULL,
sessionCode CHAR(1) NULL,
CONSTRAINT priModule PRIMARY KEY (moduleCode, building,
roomNo, day, startTime)
);

CREATE VIEW vwTeachingSession (moduleCode, staffNo,
    building, roomNo, day, startTime, endTime, duration,
    startDate, endDate, runsFor, type, sessionCode)
AS SELECT moduleCode, staffNo, building, roomNo, day,
    startTime, startTime+duration, duration,
    startDate, endDate, endDate-startDate,
    type, sessionCode
    FROM TeachingSession;
```

If, for whatever reason, it isn't possible to use views to calculate the redundant data values on demand, then they must be calculated in the application code. Most DBMS now implement **stored routines** that, like triggers, include procedural code in the database. If these are not available, then implement the application code on the web server by, for example using server-side scripting in PHP. As a last resort, implement the calculation using browser scripting on the web browser.

10.1.3 Business rules

The table schema of the logical design document the primary and foreign key constraints, candidate keys and other business rules. All relational DBMS support primary key constraints. Foreign key constraints are usually supported, too. The purpose of the foreign key constraint is to ensure that the value of a foreign key on the referencing table also occurs in the matching candidate key of the referenced table. If the table instances never (or very rarely) change, then there is no real need to check this constraint.

The MySQL DBMS uses this fact to offer a choice of data storage structures (called storage engines), some of which support foreign key constraints and some of which don't. Those that don't, provide much faster access to the table instance. These different storage engines are discussed later in this chapter.

Candidate key constraints can usually be enforced by means of a combination of the SQL unique and not-null constraints. The unique constraint ensures that each row has a unique candidate key, while the not-null constraints ensure that none of the candidate key columns is ever null.

Other business rules include both state and transition constraints. Many state constraints can be implemented using the ISO SQL check constraint, though this is not supported by the MySQL DBMS. Its ENUM data type offers some support for state constraints that limit the valid values to a specified set (a simpler version of ISO SQL distinct types). For example, the day column in the TeachingSession table must be one of the days of the week. This business rule can be enforced by either using the MySQL DBMS ENUM data type or an ISO SQL check constraint. Code listing 10.1.3.1 shows both approaches. Examples of more complex ISO SQL check constraints were given in Chapters 5 and 6.

Code listing 10.1.3.1 *A simple state constraint limiting column values to a specified set*

(a) Using the ISO SQL check constraint

```
ALTER TABLE TeachingSession
 ADD CONSTRAINT chkDay
 CHECK (day IN ('Monday', 'Tuesday', 'Wednesday',
        'Thursday', 'Friday', 'Saturday', 'Sunday'));
```

(b) Using the MySQL ENUM data type

```
CREATE TABLE TeachingSessionBase(
moduleCode CHAR(7) NOT NULL,
staffNo VARCHAR NOT NULL,
building VARCHAR NOT NULL,
roomNo VARCHAR NOT NULL,
```

```
day ENUM ('Monday', 'Tuesday', 'Wednesday', 'Thursday',
          'Friday', 'Saturday', 'Sunday') NOT NULL,
startTime TIME NOT NULL,
duration INTERVAL NOT NULL,
startDate DATE NOT NULL,
endDate DATE NULL,
type VARCHAR NOT NULL,
sessionCode CHAR(1) NULL,
CONSTRAINT priModule PRIMARY KEY
    (moduleCode, building, roomNo, day, startTime)
);
```

Some business rules cannot be implemented using the ISO SQL check constraint. State constraints that involve choices and transition constraints are the main examples. They are usually enforced using application code. Then, triggers or stored routines on the database server and server-side scripting on the web server are all valid approaches. Which approach will be best in any one situation will depend on the facilities available on the web and database servers. Where possible, it makes sense to keep data-centric application code on the database server. This might not be possible, though, or it might be decided that the database server already has enough to do, in which case the application code should be implemented on the web server.

10.1.4 SQL statements as physical table designs

Decisions about data types, derived attributes and business rules can be documented by rewriting the logical table schema. However, this would require written descriptions of the triggers or views used to implement a derived attribute and the application code used to implement the business rules.

A better approach is simply to write the SQL DDL statements that implement the design (as has been done above) and include comments explaining their purpose.

Code listing 10.1.4.1 shows logical table schema for the Room and Equipment tables. The logical table schema for the Room table includes an additional, derived attribute – /equipmentValue – which holds the total value of all equipment in the room. It also has an extra business rule – that all rooms on the Web Timetable database are teaching rooms and can accommodate at least 20 people. The Equipment table has also acquired a derived attribute – /age – which is calculated as the number of days since purchase. The rule for calculating the derived attributes is noted using the SQL comment style.

Code listing 10.1.4.1   Two logical table schema

```
Room (building VARCHAR NOT NULL,
      roomNo VARCHAR NOT NULL,
      capacity NUMERIC NULL,
      /equipmentValue NUMERIC NULL -- total value of
       equipment in this room
      )
PRIMARY KEY (building, roomNo)
BUSINESS RULE capacity is at least 20, or null
```

```
Equipment (assetNo VARCHAR(15) NOT NULL,
           assetType VARCHAR NOT NULL,
           description VARCHAR NOT NULL,
           portable BOOLEAN NOT NULL,
           cost NUMERIC NULL,
           acquired DATE DEFAULT CURRENT_DATE NULL,
           /age INTERVAL NULL, -- number of days since
               purchase date
           building VARCHAR NULL,
           room VARCHAR NULL
           )
PRIMARY KEY (assetNo)
FOREIGN KEY (building, room)
    REFERENCES Room(building, roomNo)
```

The physical design for these two tables takes the form of a commented SQL script that creates the base tables, views and triggers required to implement the logical design.

One important change is that column lengths missing from the logical table schema must be decided at this stage. Any that were specified in the logical database design are honoured and others are added, based on the database designer's understanding of the data.

The create table statements implement the column descriptions and the primary key constraints. The candidate and foreign key constraints, as well as the constraints implementing business rules, are implemented separately using alter table statements. This avoids the problem of having to create any referenced tables before the associated referencing tables (remember, both foreign key constraints and check constraints can reference other tables).

The base table Equipment has an associated view – vwEquipment – used by all database queries. This view implements the derived attribute /age.

The trigger taiEquipment maintains the value of the derived column Room.equipmentValue when new rows are added to the Room table. It uses an update statement with a correlated subquery, which recalculates the value of Room.equipmentValue for each row of the Room table. This is a little heavy handed as, typically, a single row will be added to Equipment, meaning that the value of equipmentValue would change in, at most, one row of Room. Furthermore, a trigger to deal with the situation when a row is updated is missing from Code listing 10.1.4.2. These deficiencies are addressed in the exercises.

Code listing 10.1.4.2   Physical table design for the logical table schema in Code listing 10.1.4.1 as an SQL script

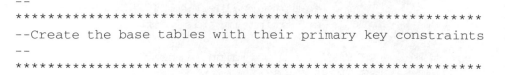

```
--
****************************************************************
--Create the base tables with their primary key constraints
--
****************************************************************
```

```
CREATE TABLE Room (
  building VARCHAR(15) NOT NULL,
  roomNo VARCHAR(4) NOT NULL,
  capacity INTEGER NULL,
  equipmentValue DECIMAL(9,2) NULL, -- DERIVED: total value
       of equipment in this room
  CONSTRAINT priRoom PRIMARY KEY (building, roomNo)
);

CREATE TABLE Equipment (
  assetNo(15) VARCHAR(15) NOT NULL,
  assetType(15) VARCHAR NOT NULL,
  description(50) VARCHAR NOT NULL,
  portable BOOLEAN NOT NULL,
  cost DECIMAL(7,2) NULL,
  acquired DATE DEFAULT (CURRENT_DATE) NULL,
  building(15) VARCHAR NULL,
  room(4) VARCHAR NULL,
  CONSTRAINT priEquip PRIMARY KEY (assetNo)
);


--
**********************************************************
-- Add foreign keys
--
**********************************************************
ALTER TABLE Equipment
  ADD CONSTRAINT frnEquipRoom
  FOREIGN KEY (building, room) REFERENCES Room(building,
roomNo);


--
**********************************************************
-- Implement candidate keys and business rules
--
**********************************************************
ALTER TABLE Room
  ADD CONSTRAINT chkRoomCapacity CHECK (capacity >= 20);


--
**********************************************************
-- Create views
--
**********************************************************
```

```
-- vwEquipment implements the derived attribute /age
CREATE VIEW vwEquipment AS
  SELECT assetNo, assetType, description, portable, cost,
    acquired, CURRENT_DATE-acquired AS age, building, room
  FROM Equip;


--
*************************************************************
-- Create triggers
--
*************************************************************
-- taiEquipment maintains the derived column
Room.equipmentValue
CREATE TRIGGER taiEquipment
AFTER INSERT ON Equipment
FOR EACH STATEMENT
BEGIN ATOMIC
  UPDATE Room
  SET equipmentValue =
        (SELECT SUM(cost)
         FROM Equipment
         WHERE
         Equipment.building=Room.building
         AND Equipment.room=Room.roomNo);
END;
```

The structure outlined in Code listing 10.1.4.2 provides a reasonable approach to documenting the physical database design. It also provides a first draft of the actual database implementation script. An alternative approach is to have a more detailed written description of the physical table designs. This can include information on data volumes and performance. The following section discusses how to assess the performance of a physical database design.

10.2 Analysing database usage and performance

Before deciding on a particular DBMS, it is useful to know whether it will be able to cope with the demands of the application. Can it store the volume of data required? Can it service the number of database transactions that are expected? Understanding the effects of these non-functional requirements on the performance of the database application will influence the choice of the DBMS and the hardware it runs on. A small database with a light load will need less powerful technology than a large database with a heavy load – an obvious comment, but it is surprising how often organizations overlook it. When the database application is replacing an existing application, the database designer may have access to good statistics on how heavily the current system is used. If these statistics are not available, then the database designer must make some reasonable assumptions about database usage.

10.2.1 Analysing data storage requirements

One simple and effective approach to understanding the data storage requirements is to estimate the size of each table. The total size of the database, calculated by summing all the tables, will indicate the disk space requirements of the database server. Similarly, a decision to store image files outside the database might mean that more disk space is needed on the web server. Estimating the size of database is a simple but effective way to ensure that the right decisions are made.

Consider the Staff Directory application. The column definitions for the Staff table are shown in Code listing 10.2.1.1. (Note that these include the length of the column's data value. If lengths were not specified during logical database design, then they should be specified before beginning this calculation.) The idea is quite simple – calculate the maximum length of a single row, then multiply this by an estimate of the number of rows in the Staff table. As a single character is generally stored as a single byte, this gives a good estimate of the size of the table in bytes.

Code listing 10.2.1.1   Physical table design for the Staff *table*

```
CREATE TABLE Staff(
  staffNo CHAR(5) NOT NULL ,
  fName VARCHAR(50) NOT NULL ,
  lName VARCHAR(20) NOT NULL ,
  phone VARCHAR(20) ,
  email VARCHAR(50) NOT NULL ,
  photo BLOB ,
  department VARCHAR(20) NOT NULL ,
  title VARCHAR(5) ,
  jobType VARCHAR(20) ,
  jobTitle VARCHAR(30) ,
  CONSTRAINT pkStaff PRIMARY KEY (staffNo)
);
```

For example, the CHAR and VARCHAR columns in the Staff table have a total, maximum length of 220 characters, giving a maximum of 220 bytes of character data in each row. The photo column has data type BLOB and stores a JPEG with maximum size of 100 kB. This gives an estimated total size for each row of 102,620 bytes (remember, 1kB = 1024 bytes, and 1MB = 1,048,576 bytes). There are, at most, 1200 staff working at the university, so a maximum of 1200 rows in the Staff table. Thus, the Staff table has a maximum size of 123,144,000 bytes, which is roughly 117 Mb.

It is also useful to do the calculation without any binary columns as one common design decision in web database applications is to store image files (and other binary data) on the web server, rather than the database server. In this situation, the photo column would store a URL to the appropriate image file (see below). Assuming that the photo column has data type VARCHAR(30), a row of the Staff table has a maximum size of 250 bytes and the table itself a maximum size of 300,000 bytes, or roughly 293kB. Clearly, removing the binary data from the database dramatically reduces the size of the Staff table.

This calculation takes no account of the fact that some columns may be null or that the length of the VARCHAR columns is a *maximum*. A more sophisticated approach would also consider the *average* length of data values in each column, with null having a length of zero. These give the average row size. With an estimate of the average number of rows in the table instance at any time, it is possible to calculate the average size of the table. Good sample data is essential, but otherwise the calculation remains pretty simple. Figure 10.2 shows a spreadsheet for calculating this data. Note that the photo column is included twice – once as a BLOB and once as a VARCHAR. The calculations only use *one* of these different versions.

There are two more technical problems to face when calculating data volumes. First, modern character sets may use more than one byte for some, or all, character encodings. A two-byte character encoding doubles the amount of storage needed for a character column. It is worth checking which character set is used to store data and

Figure 10.2 Spreadsheet calculating maximum and average data volumes for a table in bytes.

Row size

Column name	Data type	Maximum length	Average length
staffNo	CHAR	5	5
fName	VARCHAR	50	15
lName	VARCHAR	20	8
phone	VARCHAR	20	4
email	VARCHAR	50	24
photo	BLOB	100000	90000
photo	VARCHAR	30	14
department	VARCHAR	20	12
title	VARCHAR	5	3
jobType	VARCHAR	20	15
jobTitle	VARCHAR	30	20
	Excl. binary	*250*	*120*
	With binary	*100220*	*90106*

Table size

Maximum rows 1200

Average rows 1100

	Excl. binary	With binary
Maximum size	300000	120264000
Average size	132000	99116600

considering whether or not this affects the assumption that one character equates to one byte. Second, numeric data can be stored in a range of formats – integer, floating point, decimal – and these use different numbers of bytes, as do dates and times. The technical documentation for the DBMS should provide information on this, though often an estimate based on the size of literals will suffice (as literals usually take up more space than the actual data values, this gives a generous estimate of disk space requirements).

10.2.2 Entity transaction matrices

Another important analysis tool identifies which database transactions (queries and data modifications) use which tables. Database transactions can be identified from the use cases of the requirements specification. They form part of the design of the behaviour of the application, which is done in parallel with the design of the database. They are not often included in the database design itself, but should be available in documentation from other parts of the development team. Occasionally database transactions are included as operations on an entity (see Chapter 8). One problem with analysing database transactions, which was noted in Chapter 8, is that there are often too many of them. In such cases, it's sensible to consider those database transactions that are particularly important. Important database transactions include those used regularly by end users and that perform crucial data management operations (such as extracting statistical data, creating reports and so on).

> Database transactions were considered briefly in the section on access path analysis in Chapter 8.

The way a table is used can affect choices about its data storage structures (the internal level of the ANSI/SPARC architecture). A table that is only ever queried or populated by a database import is effectively read-only. Some DBMS offer very fast data storage structures for read-only tables.

Tables containing data that is modified regularly may need careful design to ensure efficient performance. The careful choice of indexes is particularly important as they speed up some database transactions but slow down others. A **QUID matrix** (QUID stands for query, update, insert, delete) records whether a database transaction queries a table, inserts a new row, updates an existing row or deletes a row. It is reasonable to expect every table to have database transactions that insert a row, query the table and delete a row.

Occasionally a table will be created as a data export from another database, in which case the database transaction inserting the rows would be part of another application.

Occasionally a table will never have data deleted, such as an archive table. Otherwise, a table that is never queried or that is not used by any database transaction, suggests that either a database transaction has been missed or the table is unnecessary.

Figure 10.3 shows an extract from the QUID matrix for the Web Timetable database. The tables (including link tables) are shown down the left-hand side and four database

Figure 10.3 An extract from the QUID matrix for the Web Timetable database application.

		Transaction			
		Import timetable data	Book equipment	View staff timetable	Choose teaching session
Entity	Attendance				I
	Course	UID			
	CourseModule	UID			
	Equipment		Q		
	EquipmentBooking		QUID		
	Module	UID		Q	Q
	Room				
	Staff	UID	Q	Q	
	Student				Q
	StudentModule				Q
	TeachingSession	UID		Q	Q

transactions are shown across the top. So, for example, the 'Book equipment' transaction queries the `Equipment`, `EquipmentBooking` and `Staff` tables and may insert, update or delete from the `EquipmentBooking` table. The idea is that this transaction represents one behaviour captured by the use cases. It is a relatively coarse-grained transaction as the insert, update and delete behaviour are rolled into one.

The database transaction 'Choose teaching session' is more fine-grained as it only represents a student choosing which teaching sessions to attend; separate database transactions (not shown) would allow them to change their minds.

> Its important to realize that a transaction to insert rows into a table may use an SQL `INSERT` statement or an import facility of the DBMS. It is the behaviour of the *transaction* that is important, not the actual SQL statement used to carry it out.
>
> Other names for the QUID matrix include CRUD (create, read, update, delete) and IRUD (insert, read, update, delete).

10.2.3 Transaction path analysis and transaction workloads

Just as it was important to estimate how large the database tables could be, it is important to understand how many DBMS resources a database transaction will require. Access path analysis is sometimes used to analyse a database transaction. It was introduced in Chapter 8 as a means of validating the conceptual database design.

During physical database design, the access paths are revisited and used to estimate the performance overheads of particular transactions. Information on how often the transaction runs and how many rows are accessed is added to the access path. The idea is that the more rows a transaction reads, the more work the DBMS must do and the longer the transaction will take to execute. A transaction that reads many rows and runs frequently is a good candidate for careful performance tuning.

Access paths are based on the logical ER diagram rather than the table schema. (Remember, there is a one-to-one correspondence between entities in the logical ER diagram and table schema.) Consider the database query 'List all staff who teach on courses in the computing department' (a variant of the query considered in Chapter 8; see, for example, Figure 8.46 (b)).

An access path based on the conceptual database design will not include any link or look-up entities created during logical database design, so the access path should be redrawn as shown in Figure 10.4. As before, the access path indicates which tables must be accessed by the DBMS to respond to the query. Given a particular course in the computing department, all modules that could be taken on that course are identified via the `CourseModule` and `Module` tables. For each module, a list of teaching sessions for that module is compiled from the `TeachingSession` table. Finally, for

Figure 10.4 An access path.

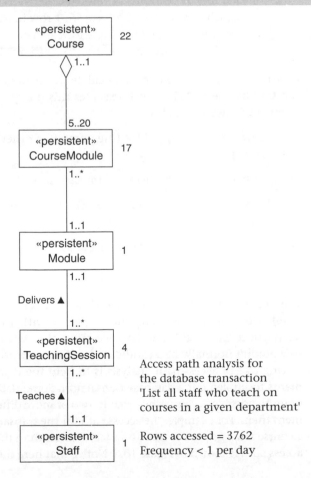

Access path analysis for the database transaction 'List all staff who teach on courses in a given department'

Rows accessed = 3762
Frequency < 1 per day

each teaching session, the single member of staff who teaches that session is identified from the `Staff` table.

For each table, the number on the right-hand side is an estimate of the average number of rows accessed by the DBMS for each row of the table above it in the access path. The first table is a special case – the number beside it estimates the average number of rows initially accessed by the DBMS. The query requires a list of all courses run in the computing department and the staff teaching them. The department offers 22 different courses, so the number 22 is written beside the `Course` entity on the access path.

Moving down the access path, for *each* course at the Pennine University, there are typically 17 modules (6 each in years 1 and 2, 5 in the final year). This means that, for one row of **Course**, the DBMS will need to access 17 rows of **CourseModule**. (For some courses the number will be higher, for others lower, but 17 is the typical number.) In turn, each row of **CourseModule** is linked to exactly one row of `Module`, hence the 1 beside that entity. A typical module has four teaching sessions – one lecture and two tutorials. Again, this will vary, but four is a reasonable estimate to place beside `TeachingSession`. Finally, each teaching session is taught by a single member of staff. This can be summarized by noting that the DBMS must access:

- 22 rows from `Course`
  - for each row in `Course`, 17 rows in `CourseModule`
    - for each row in `CourseModule`, 1 row in `Module`
      - for each row in `Module`, 4 rows in `TeachingSession`
        - for each row in `TeachingSession`, 1 row in `Staff`.

It is now a simple exercise to calculate an estimate for the total number of rows accessed by the DBMS when it executes this query. The calculation is recursive. The number of rows accessed is:

(22 rows in `Course`) + 22 × (the number of other rows accessed for *each* row in `Course`)

The number of other rows accessed for each row of `Course` is:

(17 rows in `CourseModule`) + 17 × (the number of other rows accessed for *each* row in `CourseModule`)

and so on. This leads to the final calculation:

$$22 + 22 \times (17 + 17 \times (1 + 1 \times (4 + 4 \times 1))) = 3762$$

The access path diagram should include a description of the transaction, the total number of rows accessed and the frequency with which the transaction is run. The transaction shown in Figure 10.4 accesses only a few rows and runs very infrequently, so wouldn't normally be a candidate for close scrutiny.

One role of access path analysis is to help the database developer write SQL statements to implement a database transaction. Some database transactions will have two or more possible access paths – that is, two or more different SQL statements that implement them. For example, the access path for the transaction to list all staff who teach on a course *could* go via the `Student` table rather than the `Module` table. This alternative access path is shown in Figure 10.5. Notice that here the number of rows accessed is four

Figure 10.5 An alternative access path to that shown in Figure 10.4.

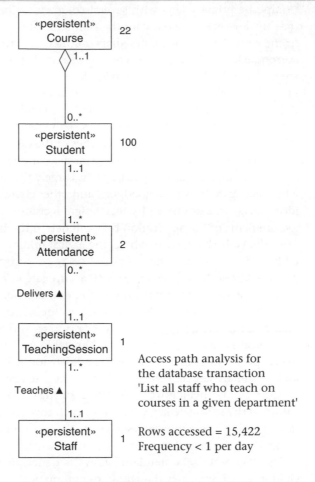

times greater than the access path in Figure 10.4. As both these access paths translate into different SQL SELECT statements, it makes sense to use the one that implements the most efficient access path.

10.3 General issues in physical database design

Some physical database design decisions need to be made regardless of the chosen DBMS. These decisions usually involve trading off improved performance of database queries against poorer performance of database modifications. It is crucial that the database designer properly assesses the implications of any change, to ensure that it does not worsen the situation. The analysis techniques discussed above can help to assess the strengths and weaknesses of the alternative designs, but differences between DBMS mean that decisions can only really be made by someone who understands the technical capabilities of the target DBMS in detail. It is worth emphasizing this as a general textbook cannot substitute for a DBMS manual or training course. That said, the *issues* are the same, it's just the solutions that might be different.

10.3.1 Surrogate keys

Composite primary keys with several columns, or primary keys with the data values that are large are not as easy for the DBMS to handle as primary keys that are numeric. In the early days, database designers routinely replaced the logical primary key with a **surrogate key**. A surrogate key consists of a single numeric column, the values of which are set by the DBMS itself. All foreign keys referencing a table would use the surrogate key as the matching candidate key. The logical primary key (the primary key identified during logical database design) is treated as a candidate key – unique and not null, but not usually referred to by foreign keys. This speeds up table joins by simplifying the join condition and can speed up searches of the table using the surrogate key.

Surrogate keys have provoked a great deal of debate among database professionals and the arguments continue to this day. Largely this is because there are circumstances when surrogate keys are a good idea and other circumstances in which they are a bad idea. This is true of many physical design decisions, so, in the end, it is the particular requirements of the application that will determine the best physical database design.

In the Web Timetable database, the logical primary key of the `TeachingSession` table is {`moduleCode`, `day`, `startTime`, `sessionCode`}. Replacing the composite primary key of the logical design with a surrogate key would improve the performance of the database by simplifying the join conditions needed to join `TeachingSession` with the `Attendance` and `EquipmentBooking` tables. Of course, it also means replacing the foreign keys on the `Attendance` and `EquipmentBooking` tables (see the logical ER diagram for the Web Timetable in Figure 9.18). The complexity of the logical primary key makes it a good candidate for being replaced by a surrogate key. The logical primary key remains one of the candidate keys.

Most DBMS include ways to define surrogate keys that mean the DBMS assigns values to the surrogate key column for each row. As an example, Code listing 10.3.1.1 (a), (b) and (c) show three ways to create the `Room` table using a surrogate key `roomId` rather than the logical primary key {`building`, `roomNo`}.

The ISO SQL:2003 standard allows a **generation clause** (replacing the default clause), which instructs the DBMS to automatically generate a unique value for new rows (Code listing 10.3.1.1 (a)). The MySQL DBMS uses the **auto increment** property of a column to achieve the same effect (Code listing 10.3.1.1 (b)).

The Oracle database takes a different approach, using a **sequence** to generate values. A sequence is a separate database object, so one sequence can generate values for different columns in different tables. The value is guaranteed to be unique *within the database*. Because the sequence is a different database object, the database application must first get the next value from the sequence, then insert that value into the surrogate key column. One way to do this is with a database trigger (Code listing 10.3.1.1 (c)).

Code listing 10.3.1.1 Defining surrogate keys on the Room *table*

(a) ISO SQL:2003, IBM DB2 DBMS

```
CREATE TABLE Room (
roomId      INTEGER GENERATED ALWAYS AS IDENTITY NOT NULL,
building    VARCHAR(10) NOT NULL,
roomNo      VARCHAR(4) NOT NULL,
```

```
capacity    INTEGER,
CONSTRAINT priRoom PRIMARY KEY (roomId)
);
```

(b) MySQL DBMS

```
CREATE TABLE Room (
roomId     INTEGER NOT NULL AUTO_INCREMENT,
building   VARCHAR(10) NOT NULL,
roomNo     VARCHAR(4) NOT NULL,
capacity   INTEGER,
CONSTRAINT priRoom PRIMARY KEY (roomId)
);
```

(c) Oracle database uses sequences

```
CREATE TABLE Room (
roomId     INTEGER NOT NULL,
building   VARCHAR(10) NOT NULL,
roomNo     VARCHAR(4) NOT NULL,
capacity   INTEGER,
CONSTRAINT priRoom PRIMARY KEY (roomId)
);

CREATE SEQUENCE roomIdSeq;

CREATE TRIGGER triRoomPk
BEFORE INSERT ON Room FOR EACH ROW
BEGIN
 SELECT roomIdSeq.nextval
 INTO :new.roomId
 FROM DUAL;
END;
```

There are problems with using surrogate keys. First, the DBMS assigns the value of the surrogate key so it rarely has any meaning for end users (note that staff numbers, module codes and so on are *not* surrogate keys as such values are dictated by the users, not the DBMS). This can actually *increase* the complexity of some database transactions. The database transaction 'List all equipment and the rooms they are located in' could be answered by querying a single table in the logical design – all the required data is in the `Equipment` table as the `building` and `roomNo` columns are included in this table as a foreign key. With a surrogate key on the `Room` table, the `building` and `roomNo` columns no longer appear in the `Equipment` table as foreign key columns. The surrogate key appears instead. In this design, to find which room equipment is stored in requires a table join.

The situation is even more complicated when the foreign key is a part of the referencing table's primary key. Replacing the referenced table's primary key with a surrogate key will alter the structure of the referencing table's primary key. One solution is to give the referenced table a surrogate key as well. Another is to use the referenced table's logical primary key, which is still a candidate key, as the foreign key on the referencing table. This has the benefit of a surrogate key on the referenced table and a meaningful foreign key on the referencing table.

One final problem arises when data is copied, or imported, into a table with a surrogate key. If this data already has values for the surrogate key column, then the DBMS may struggle to cope. The ISO standard allows GENERATED ALWAYS to be replaced by GENERATED BY DEFAULT. In this latter case, the DBMS will only generate a value for the surrogate key if none is supplied. However, there is no guarantee that the supplied values comply with the primary key constraint. If they do not, then the inserts will be rejected.

10.3.2 Binary data

Modern DBMS are quite capable of storing binary data, whether it is an image, sound, video or anything else. However, it is not always a good idea. It is clear from the data storage analysis above (see Figure 10.2), that binary data can significantly increase the database's storage requirements. This is not balanced out by any particular benefits, other than the tidiness of keeping all an application's data in one place. For web database applications, storing binary data on the database can actually cause problems. Web pages include images and other binary data by including a URL for the file that contains the data. If the data is inside a DBMS, this becomes tricky. A URL must actually point to a server-side script that retrieves the binary data from the database and uses it to assemble a suitable HTTP response.

A better solution stores images and other binary data on the web server rather than on the database, as web servers are designed to handle such things.

This raises the problem of how to connect an image (or other binary data) with the row of the database from which it has been removed.

Consider the Staff table. Code listing 10.2.1.1 showed the physical table schema earlier in this chapter. The photo column is a BLOB. In any row of the Staff table, this column's value will be an image of the member of staff concerned, so, if no image is available, the column is null for this row.

Code listing 10.3.2.1, below, shows a revised physical table schema. Here, the photo column is a VARCHAR(100). In any row of the Staff table, this column's value will be a URL that points to an image file of the member of staff concerned. When a web page is generated from data in this table, the value of the photo column can be used directly to generate an HTML img element with the correct URL. The web server does the rest.

A further advantage of this approach is that the photo column has a default value – a standard image to display when there is no photograph of the member of staff available (a BLOB column cannot have a default value).

Code listing 10.3.2.1   Revised column definitions for the Staff *table*

```
CREATE TYPE StaffNo AS CHAR(5) FINAL;

CREATE TABLE Staff(
staffNo StaffNo NOT NULL ,
fName VARCHAR(20) NOT NULL ,
lName VARCHAR(20) NOT NULL ,
```

```
phone VARCHAR(20) ,
email VARCHAR(30) NOT NULL ,
photo VARCHAR(100)
 DEFAULT
 'http://www.pennine.ac.uk/StaffDirectory/NoPhoto.jpg'
 NOT NULL ,
department VARCHAR(30) NOT NULL ,
title VARCHAR(4) ,
jobType VARCHAR(15) ,
jobTitle VARCHAR(30) ,
CONSTRAINT pkStaff PRIMARY KEY (staffNo)
);
```

10.3.3 Controlled redundancy

In the logical design for a relational database, every table will be normalized (as described in Chapter 9). The aim is to reduce repeated data to a minimum as, in a normalized relational database, only data in foreign key columns is repeated. This avoids the problems that data duplication brings, but creates problems of its own. In particular, it means that there are many more join queries than would otherwise be the case.

Another issue is what to do about aggregate queries. These present statistical information, such as how many students attend a teaching session, how much time staff devote to support sessions and so on. Under some circumstances it may make sense to introduce repeated data to reduce joins, or derived data to avoid recalculating statistical information. The careful reintroduction of controlled redundancy can significantly improve performance, just as uncontrolled redundancy can significantly degrade performance. The key is to control the process by normalizing first, *then* assessing the impact of reintroducing specific redundant data. If the benefits outweigh the problems, then introducing redundant data to the physical database design is justified.

The simplest case to consider is a two-table join. Typically, data in the referencing table is subsidiary to that in the referenced table. The Staff and SupportSession tables in the Staff Directory database are good examples of this. The referencing table SupportSession holds data that is additional to that held in the referenced table Staff. One common database query from the Staff Directory application is:

provide an alphabetical listing of staff support sessions.

No information about contact details is needed, just the staff member's name and the days and times of their support sessions. However, details of the staff member's name are held in the Staff table, so this query must be answered using the join statement given in Code listing 10.3.3.1.

Code listing 10.3.3.1   A join query showing details of staff support sessions

```
SELECT fName || ' ' || lName AS name, dayOfWeek, startTime,
  endTime
FROM Staff, SupportSession
WHERE Staff.staffNo = SupportSession.staffNo
ORDER BY lName, fName;
```

An alternative is to repeat the staff member's name in the SupportSession table and Code listing 10.3.3.2 (a) shows the revised physical table schema for this. Note that both the fName and lName columns are repeated, rather than a single name column. This is to preserve the order by clause. Code listing 10.3.3.2 (b) shows the revised SQL statement. This time there is no need to perform a join, meaning this query will place less of a burden on the DBMS.

Code listing 10.3.3.2   A join query showing details of staff support sessions

(a) Physical table schema for SupportSession *with the* fName *and* lName *columns of* Staff *duplicated*

```
CREATE TABLE SupportSession(
staffNo StaffNo NOT NULL ,
dayOfWeek VARCHAR (9) NOT NULL ,
startTime TIME NOT NULL ,
endTime TIME NOT NULL ,
fName VARCHAR(20) NOT NULL ,
lName VARCHAR(20) NOT NULL ,
CONSTRAINT pkSupportSession
  PRIMARY KEY (staffNo, dayOfWeek, startTime)
);
```

(b) The revised SQL statement to list details of staff support sessions

```
SELECT fName || ' ' || lName AS name, dayOfWeek, startTime,
  endTime
FROM SupportSession
ORDER BY lName, fName;
```

Another occasion when controlled redundancy may improve performance is when statistical information is required. For example, consider the database query:

provide a list of all teaching sessions showing the room, the room's capacity and the number of students attending that teaching session.

This query requires data from the TeachingSession and Room tables even before starting to calculate the number of students attending a teaching session. It would make sense to add a noOfStudents column to the TeachingSession table to store the number of students attending each teaching session as this value is unlikely to change after the start of term. This last is an important point – if statistical data is likely to change frequently, then it is better to recalculate it on demand rather than attempt to store the derived data.

One important point about repeated and derived data is that it must be maintained. If a member of staff gets married and changes her name, then her data in both the Staff and SupportSession tables must be modified. Similarly, if a student changes tutorial group, then the value of the derived data in the noOfStudents column in the TeachingSessions table would need to be recalculated. There is a trade-off between better performance of database queries and more work involved during data modification.

The impact of maintaining repeated and derived data must be considered carefully. It can actually be costlier to maintain the redundant data than it is to run the original join and aggregate queries. If this is the case, then don't introduce redundant data. The section on derived attributes examined how to present such data using views and this is a good alternative approach when data is likely to change regularly.

Creating duplicate data by copying information between tables linked by a foreign key is sometimes called denormalization. Strictly speaking, it isn't. Denormalization occurs when a table created as part of the normalization process is reabsorbed into the table it came from. During normalization, each repeating group is extracted into a new table, with a foreign key referencing the original table. Denormalization reverses this – two tables linked by a foreign key are joined back together into a single table.

Consider the Student Rental database, designed by normalization in Chapter 9. The normalized table schema is shown in Code listing 10.3.3.3. There are three very small tables – Student, Hall and Bursar – and all have just two columns. It's worth asking if it makes sense to have separate tables to hold this data.

Code listing 10.3.3.3   The logical table schema for the fully normalized Student Rental database

```
Student(studentNo, name)
PRIMARY KEY (studentNo)

StudentRental(studentNo, accomId, rentStart, rentFinish,
rent)
PRIMARY KEY (studentNo, rentStart)
FOREIGN KEY (studentNo) REFERENCES Student(studentNo)
FOREIGN KEY (accomId) REFERENCES Accommodation(accomId)

Accommodation(accomId, hall, room)
PRIMARY KEY (accomId)
FOREIGN KEY (hall) REFERENCES Hall(name)

Hall(name, staffNo)
PRIMARY KEY (hall)
FOREIGN KEY (staffNo) REFERENCES Bursar(staffNo)

Bursar(staffNo, name)
PRIMARY KEY (staffNo)
```

Consider the Bursar table. This holds information about the *current* bursar for each hall of residence. Figures 10.6 (a) and (b) show table instances for the normalized and denormalized versions of this data. The advantages of the normalized version are that, if the name of a bursar changes, just *one* row of the Bursar table needs to be updated and the name of each bursar is stored only once.

In this particular case, neither of these advantages is significant. There are only a small number of halls of residence, so storing the bursars' names more than once is not a big issue. Also, the names of bursars don't change that often.

Figure 10.6 Data on halls of residence and their bursars.

Hall	
name	staffNo
William Morris	56673
Marie Curie	35054
Maurice Wilkins	35054

Bursar	
staffNo	name
56673	Joshua Bittaye
35054	Selma Hutchins

(a) The normalized data.

Hall		
name	staffNo	bursar
William Morris	56673	Joshua Bittaye
Marie Curie	35054	Selma Hutchins
Maurice Wilkins	35054	Selma Hutchins

(b) The denormalized data.

The disadvantages come from having to perform table joins to find the name of each hall's bursar. In fact, the `Bursar` table is only ever queried as part of a table join with the `Hall` table. Under these circumstances the normalized logical database design is unnecessarily complex. Denormalizing the database, by merging the two tables back into one, is a sensible decision. Figure 10.6 (b) shows the denormalized table.

In contrast, it does not make sense to denormalize the database by merging the `Hall` and `Accommodation` tables. Some halls have over 200 rooms, so there would be a lot of redundant data (bursars' details repeated over and over again). Also, the hall name is a foreign key on the `Accommodation` table, so queries about accommodation that only need the hall name can be made without actually using the `Hall` table.

With the table designs shown in Code listing 10.3.3.3, it would probably also make sense to merge the `Student` table back into `StudentRental`. However, it seems unlikely that the *only* data held about a student is his or her name. It is much more likely that the student's home address, contact phone numbers and so on are also held in the database. If this is true, then it would not be a good idea to merge these tables. The lack of this data is a point that should be raised with the end users during conceptual database design. (It was left out of the example purely for practical reasons – it makes the data set too large to fit on a page!)

The situation discussed here is analogous to that when surrogate keys are used. Surrogate keys and the controlled reintroduction of redundant data are useful techniques, but both can lead to more join queries. These are harder work for the DBMS than single table queries. In many cases, the DBMS will easily cope with the extra work, but, when a particular join query will take up a lot of a DBMS resources, there is a case for reconsidering the design.

Access path analysis can highlight join queries that are likely to cause problems. Whenever redundant data is introduced into the physical database design, the complexity of data modification operations will increase. Some form of application code must be written to ensure that all copies of the redundant data are modified at the same time. This could be DBMS triggers or code on the application server. The added costs of this code should be balanced against the reduced query complexity that results from introducing redundant data.

10.3.4 Structured codes and missing attributes

Structured codes are character strings that contain embedded information. A familiar structured code is the e-mail address. Each e-mail address is a character string consisting of a user's name, the '@' character and a mail server address. National phone numbers begin with an area code, then the actual telephone number. British postcodes have even more structure. Each postcode has two parts – the in code and the out code. When a letter is collected from a post box, the in code identifies which sorting office it should be sent to. Once at the sorting office, the out code identifies the delivery round. So, the postcode 'HD1 1AA' has an in code of 'HD1', identifying the Huddersfield sorting office, and '1AA' is the out code, identifying a particular delivery round.

> Both e-mail addresses and British postcodes actually have more structure than described here, but these details aren't important unless an application actually has to decode them.

Both the telephone number and British postcode predate computer technology and were developed as structured codes that people could easily use. However the idea of structured codes was enthusiastically adopted by early application developers and they are widely used in computerized information systems.

The module and course codes at the Pennine University are structured codes. Module codes begin with two letters indicating the department and subject area that delivers the module, followed by a third letter indicating the level, then a letter and four digits. The first letter of a course code indicates the department offering the course.

In applications that use flat files to store data, structured codes have a number of benefits. They have a regular structure that can simplify data processing, they store complex information compactly, reducing disk space requirements, and are often easy for experienced staff to use.

These benefits do not apply in contemporary database applications. The reduced data storage is insignificant in most cases – disk space is cheap and plentiful. A commercial DBMS can process separate data items efficiently enough that structured codes become an impediment. For example, if the computing department were to change its name to the informatics department, it would be easy to make this change on the database. It would be much harder to change the first character of all the module codes from 'C' to 'I'. Another problem arises when users wish to see a list of all modules offered by the information systems subject area. The DBMS needs to find all those modules that have the module code 'I' as their second character. In both these situations, the string manipulation functions discussed in Chapters 5 and 6 allow the DBMS to parse the string (pull it apart and reassemble it), but there are significant performance problems associated with doing so.

Despite the difficulties with structured codes and the fact that they are not really necessary in contemporary information systems, end users can be very attached to them. Changing the codes means changing working practices and that is rarely something people welcome. So, during the conceptual and logical database design processes, many systems will include structured codes. A good physical design will seek to minimize the need for the DBMS to parse strings, so should try to avoid structured codes.

The simplest approach is to split the structured code into separate attributes and manage each part of the code separately. In this approach, the `Module` table would lose its `code` column and acquire four new columns – `deptCode`, `subjectCode`, `levelCode` and `sequenceId`. This also means that there is now no need for a separate column called `level` as it simply duplicates information included in the module code. The logical and physical table schema are shown in Code listing 10.3.4.1. The end users can be shown the original structured code easily – just create a suitable SQL view to merge the four columns back into one. However, this won't help when data is inserted into the database. End users will expect to type in a single string for the module code, so the application program will need to parse this string before passing the four parts to the DBMS.

Code listing 10.3.4.1   Splitting up a structured code

(a) The original logical table schema – the column `code` is a structured code

```
Module (code CHAR(8) NOT NULL,
        title VARCHAR NOT NULL,
        department VARCHAR NOT NULL,
        level VARCHAR,
        leader CHAR NOT NULL
        )
PRIMARY KEY (code)
CANDIDATE KEY (department, title)
FOREIGN KEY leader REFERENCES Staff(staffNo)
BUSINESS RULE level must be one of {'Foundation',
'Intermediate', 'Placement', 'Honours', 'Masters'}
```

(b) The physical table schema – the column `code` has been replaced by its constituent parts and `level` removed

```
CREATE TABLE Module (
deptCode CHAR(1) NOT NULL,
subjectCode CHAR(1) NOT NULL,
levelCode CHAR(1) NOT NULL,
sequenceId CHAR(5) NOT NULL,
title VARCHAR(100) NOT NULL,
department VARCHAR(20) NOT NULL,
leader CHAR(5) NOT NULL,
CONSTRAINT priModule PRIMARY KEY
  (deptCode, subjectCode, levelCode, sequenceId)
);
```

```
ALTER TABLE Module
ADD CONSTRAINT unqDepartmentTitle
UNIQUE (department, title);

ALTER TABLE Module
ADD CONSTRAINT frnModuleStaff
FOREIGN KEY (leader) REFERENCES Staff(staffNo)
ON UPDATE CASCADE
ON DELETE NO ACTION;
```

Splitting the module code into four parts creates a very complex primary key (code listing 10.3.4.1 (b)). As the module code is used as a foreign key on three other tables, this is not a sensible approach to dealing with this particular structured code.

An alternative is to define a new, structured data type that holds a *single* value for the structured code, but allows users access to the subparts. The ability to define structured data types is one of the advanced features of the ISO SQL:2003 standard.

Code listing 10.3.4.2 shows how to define the user-defined type `moduleCode` and the revised physical table schema for the `Module` table. Any foreign key columns referencing the `Module` table's `code` column must also have data type `moduleCode`. With structured data types, the application developer has access to the subparts of the structured code, but the DBMS and end users see it as a single value for database queries and foreign key constraints. Data modifications, however, present the same problem as do separate columns.

Code listing 10.3.4.2   A user-defined type used to define a structured code

(a) The user-defined type

```
CREATE TYPE moduleCode AS (
deptCode CHAR(1),
subjectCode CHAR(1),
levelCode CHAR(1),
sequenceId CHAR(5)
);
```

(b) The revised physical table schema (without the business rules)

```
CREATE TABLE Module (
code moduleCode NOT NULL,
title VARCHAR(100) NOT NULL,
department VARCHAR(20) NOT NULL,
leader CHAR(5) NOT NULL,
CONSTRAINT priModule PRIMARY KEY (code)
);
```

If structured types are not supported by the target DBMS, then it makes more sense to stick with the original definition of the `Module` table. In this case, the application program will need to deal with the structured code.

Usually, the application developer will create one function that can parse a structured code into its component parts and a second to reassemble the parts into a single string.

These functions could be implemented using stored routines on the database server or server-side scripting on the application server. They could even be implemented on the client, though, in a web database application it would not be a sensible approach.

Yet another possibility is to introduce a surrogate key as the primary key of the module table and include the component parts of the actual module code as separate columns (see Code listing 10.3.4.3). In this case, a unique constraint should be placed on the candidate key {deptCode, subjectCode, levelCode, sequenceId}.

Code listing 10.3.4.3   Using a surrogate key on the module table

```
CREATE TABLE Module (
moduleId INTEGER GENERATED ALWAYS AS IDENTITY NOT NULL,
deptCode CHAR(1) NOT NULL,
subjectCode CHAR(1) NOT NULL,
levelCode CHAR(1) NOT NULL,
sequenceId CHAR(5) NOT NULL,
title VARCHAR(100) NOT NULL,
department VARCHAR(20) NOT NULL,
leader CHAR(5) NOT NULL,
CONSTRAINT priModule PRIMARY KEY (moduleId)
);
```

Structured codes are closely related to another problem – missing attributes. For example, the structure of the module code suggests that there is an attribute missing from the Module table – the subject area. If subject areas were important enough to be included in the structured code, why aren't they an attribute of the Module table?

It may be that, in the Web Timetable application, there is no need to include information on subject areas. However, if the Web Timetable application needs to list modules by subject area, it should be added as an attribute to the Module table. The alternative is to parse the value of Module.code, but it will be much less efficient than simply storing the subject area in the table.

10.3.5   Dealing with a surfeit of nulls

Another issue that needs to be addressed during physical database design is the problem of **sparse tables**. A sparse table is one where the table instance includes a lot of nulls.

In early DBMS, sparse tables took up as much space as if the table had no nulls at all. Contemporary DBMS are much more efficient at optimizing data storage, and sparse tables are not such a problem. Because of this, some database designers are quite happy to have sparse tables in their database, but others still prefer to avoid them. With a contemporary DBMS, the choice is very much down to personal preference.

Consider the situation with the Room and Equipment tables (first discussed in Chapter 3). The Equipment table includes a foreign key to the Room table. This shows where a particular piece of equipment is located. For portable equipment, the foreign key columns are null. If there is a lot of portable equipment, this means lots of nulls in the Equipment table. In this case, it makes sense to split the Equipment table into two tables – FixedEquipment for equipment located in a particular room and `PortableEquipment` for the rest. With this design, the foreign key columns in `FixedEquipment` are never null and there is no foreign key on `PortableEquipment`.

A similar situation occurs in the `Staff` table. In the logical ER diagram, the unary one-to-one association **SharesWith** indicates that two *academic* members of staff share an office. The association does not model information about non-academic staff. Adding a foreign key to represent this association leads to the physical table schema shown in Code listing 10.3.5.1.

The foreign key consists of the single column {`sharer`}. The foreign key column can be null as some staff do not share an office. The referential actions capture the business scenario that when a member of staff leaves, whoever they shared the office with will now have an office to themselves, so the foreign key can be set to null. If a staff number changes, the new staff number designates the same person, who shares the office with the same colleague, so the foreign key should be updated to the new staff number.

Code listing 10.3.5.1   A table with a self-referencing foreign key

```
CREATE TABLE Staff(
   staffNo CHAR(5) NOT NULL ,
   title   VARCHAR NOT NULL,
   fName   VARCHAR(50) NOT NULL ,
   lName   VARCHAR(20) NOT NULL ,
   email   VARCHAR(50) NOT NULL ,
   sharer  CHAR(5) ,
   CONSTRAINT pkStaff PRIMARY KEY (staffNo)
);

ALTER TABLE Staff
ADD CONSTRAINT frnStaffStaff
FOREIGN KEY (sharer) REFERENCES Staff(staffNo)
ON DELETE SET NULL
ON UPDATE CASCADE;
```

As only office shares by *academic* staff are included and many academics do not share an office, the `sharer` column will be null in *most* rows of the table. This is not an efficient design.

A better solution in this situation is to create a look-up table to capture information on who shares with whom. This `StaffShare` table has two columns – `staff1` and `staff2`. Both hold the staff number of a member of staff. The table has one row for each pair of academics who share an office, so each column is a candidate key (each academic has at most one office, so at most one sharer). Both columns are foreign keys to the `Staff` table. If either member of staff leaves, then the other is left with an office to themselves, so the `StaffShare` row should be deleted when either member of staff has his or her data deleted form the `Staff` table.

This leads to the physical table schema shown in Code listing 10.3.5.2. This is a less elegant design than the self-referencing foreign key, but provides an effective way to cut down nulls.

Code listing 10.3.5.2 Removing a self-referencing foreign key by creating a look-up table

```
CREATE TABLE Staff(
   staffNo CHAR(5) NOT NULL ,
   title   VARCHAR NOT NULL,
   fName   VARCHAR(50) NOT NULL ,
   lName   VARCHAR(20) NOT NULL ,
   email   VARCHAR(50) NOT NULL ,
   CONSTRAINT pkStaff PRIMARY KEY (staffNo)
);

CREATE TABLE StaffShare (
   staff1 VARCHAR NOT NULL,
   staff2 VARCHAR NOT NULL )
   CONSTRAINT pkStaff PRIMARY KEY (staff1)
   CONSTRAINT unqStaff UNIQUE (staff2)
);

ALTER TABLE StaffShare
ADD CONSTRAINT frnStaffStaff
FOREIGN KEY (staff1) REFERENCES Staff(staffNo)
ON DELETE CASCADE
ON UPDATE CASCADE;

ALTER TABLE StaffShare
ADD CONSTRAINT frnStaffStaff
FOREIGN KEY (staff2) REFERENCES Staff(staffNo)
ON DELETE CASCADE
ON UPDATE CASCADE;
```

10.3.6 Writing efficient SQL queries

Many database practitioners believe that the most effective approach to physical database design is not to redesign the table schema, but redesign the database queries. To write the most efficient SQL DML, the application programmer needs a knowledge of how the target DBMS actually processes, and optimizes, SQL DML statements.

However, even without such knowledge it is possible to improve the performance of database queries by following some simple guidelines. For example, where a query can be fulfilled by more than one access path, choose the access path that hits the fewest rows. End users don't care how the data is retrieved, so the application developer is free to choose a select statement that uses the most efficient access path. There will be several different select statements for each access path. Which to choose depends largely on the target DBMS. Follow any guidance given in the manual on optimizing SQL and always test the different queries using a test database with a reasonable sample of data.

Although it isn't possible to give general advice on optimizing SQL statements here, there are general guidelines on what to avoid. First, only include conditions in the where clause that are actually needed. This can be a particular problem where a select statement includes an SQL view in the from clause.

Consider the SQL view `ComputingCourse` that only includes courses involving the computing department as the lead department (Code listing 10.3.6.1 (a)). The select statement in Code listing 10.3.6.1 (b) queries this view, but its where clause is unnecessary as it simply repeats the where clause in the select statement that creates the view.

Code listing 10.3.6.1   A redundant where condition arising from the meaning of an SQL view

(a) The SQL view

```
CREATE VIEW ComputingCourse AS
   SELECT code, title, leadDepartment, minorDepartment,
          level, qualification, mode
   FROM Course
   WHERE leadDepartment = 'Computing';
```

(b) This query returns all rows from the view

```
SELECT code, title, qualification, mode
FROM ComputingCourse
WHERE leadDepartment='Computing';
```

It is not always so clear that a where condition is unnecessary. In particular, it will often depend on the particular business rules that apply. For example, at the Pennine University, the e-mail address of a member of staff always includes his or her last name. This means that the second condition in the where clause in Code listing 10.3.6.2 (a) is unnecessary. Less obviously, the where clause in Code listing 10.3.6.2 (b) is also unnecessary. Only rooms with a capacity of 25 or greater appear in the `Room` table, so *every* row satisfies the condition in the where clause.

It is important to use business knowledge carefully, though. What happens when a member of staff gets married? Does her e-mail address change to reflect her new surname? If not, then the select statement in Code listing 10.3.6.2 (a) is actually the *correct* version – removing the condition on the e-mail address may bring back different rows.

Beware writing database transactions that rely on assumptions about how end users interpret their data. If in doubt, check with them and be aware that they may well change their minds.

Code listing 10.3.6.2   Two SQL statements with possibly unnecessary conditions in the where clause

(a) The two conditions will always return the same rows

```
SELECT staffNo, fName, lName, email
FROM Staff
WHERE lName = 'Smith'
OR email LIKE '%smith%';
```

(b) Only rooms with a capacity of 25 or greater appear on the Room table

```
SELECT building, roomNo, capacity
FROM Room
WHERE capacity>=25;
```

The application developer is on surer ground with the next guideline – only include tables in the from clause that are actually needed. Which columns appear in which table is entirely within the control of the database designer.

Consider the query in Code listing 10.3.6.3. There is actually no need to include the Room table here as the only columns required exist as foreign key columns on the Equipment table. Rewriting this query so that it retrieves all columns from the Equipment table will improve performance on *any* DBMS.

Code listing 10.3.6.3   An unnecessary join

```
SELECT e.assetNo, e.assetType, r.building, r.roomNo
FROM Equipment e, Room r
WHERE e.building=r.building
AND e.room=r.roomNo;
```

The third general guideline for writing efficient SQL statements is to use equality conditions wherever possible. For example, Code listing 10.3.6.4 (a) lists all equipment bookings between two dates. It is the sort of select statement that might lie behind a web form. The actual date literals in the where clause are gathered from an end user and the select statement built using PHP. When those two dates are the same, it is worth writing the application code in such a way that it actually builds the select statement in Code listing 10.3.6.4 (b). There is a trade-off here, between more complex application code and a more efficient SQL statement, but it is usually worth the effort. Testing whether or not two date literals are equal in PHP will take a lot less time than testing whether the value of the bookedFor column is both greater than or equal to *and* less than or equal to the same date literal.

Code listing 10.3.6.4   Use equality conditions whenever possible

(a) A select statement implementing a date range query where the range is a single day

```
SELECT staffNo, assetNo, bookedFor
FROM EquipmentBooking
WHERE bookedFor >= '2006-10-12'
AND bookedFor <= '2006-10-12';
```

(b) A better approach

```
SELECT staffNo, assetNo, bookedFor
FROM EquipmentBooking
WHERE bookedFor = '2006-10-12';
```

The fourth guideline is to use the group by and having clauses with care. Always be sure that the query *really* needs to group data, rather than simply list it in some particular order. If the group by clause involves a primary key, then each group will consist of a single row. In this case, the correct approach is to use an order by clause instead. These general guidelines will not ensure that the *most* efficient SQL statement is used, but will avoid the most obvious flaws.

Even when SQL statements have been optimized for a particular DBMS, it is worth listening to users' feedback on the performance of the database application and continuing to tune the database transactions to ensure peak performance. This is particularly true of applications that begin with an empty database instance – as the data is added by end users, the performance is likely to degrade. Any serious problems should be addressed as soon as they are reported.

10.4	Designing data storage

So far, the physical design decisions have affected the organization structures of the logical and external views of the ANSI/SPARC architecture. In this section, the focus is on the data storage structures of the internal view and the data files of the underlying physical level. It covers features that are generally implemented in DBMS-specific ways as it is in the internal view that DBMS vendors can compete most effectively. This may be via data storage structures that offer high performance or special features for a niche market. The ISO SQL:2003 standard mentions some of these features, but leaves a lot of leeway in how DBMS vendors implement them.

Before examining the data storage structures of the internal view, it is useful to delve a little deeper and consider how data is actually stored at the physical level.

10.4.1 Data files

Most databases store the data they hold as **data files** on hard disk drives. There may be one data file for each database table or some more complex data storage structure. For simplicity, this section assumes that each table is stored in a single data file. A row of the table is stored in the data file as a **record**, with each column a **field** within the record. Typically, the DBMS uses the underlying operating system to read data from, and write data to, the data files on disk. The operating system stores each data file in one or more equal-sized chunks called **blocks**. A block is simply a contiguous strip of the hard disk that can be read in a single action. It's a bit like a single web page that can be read by scrolling down, with no need to navigate to other pages for extra information, so there are no delays in getting the information. One data file may consist of many different blocks and these blocks may be in different physical locations on the hard disk. A data file that has blocks scattered across the hard disk like this is said to be fragmented. The operating system can overcome this by defragmenting data files – that is reorganize the hard disk so that each data file takes up a contiguous series of blocks. As rows can vary in length, so can records, meaning that some blocks may hold more records than others. It is also possible to split records across more than one block. To keep the discussion simple, though, assume that this does *not* happen.

When the DBMS needs to search a table, one block at a time is copied from the relevant data file into memory. The DBMS turns the block into a table, with each record becoming a row. If the required row is not present, then the next block is read, then the next until the required row is found. When the table instance is modified, the DBMS uses the same process to read the relevant data block into memory. It makes the required changes to the data in memory, then gets the operating system to rewrite the *entire* block back to the same place on the hard disk, overwriting the original block. At the physical level, it is blocks, not records, that are manipulated.

There are three basic kinds of data file. The simplest is called a **heap file**. Heap files are exactly what they sound like – an unordered heap of records. When a new row is added to a table, the new record is appended to the last block in the table's data file. If this block is full, then the operating system allocates the data file a new block and the record is added to that block. This makes inserting a new row into a table stored as a heap file very fast indeed. The downside is that it is very time-consuming to find, update or delete a row as the data file must be searched one block at a time for the relevant record.

In an **ordered file** (also called a sequential file, though, confusingly, this term is sometimes used for heap files) the records are ordered according to the value of some designated field – the **ordering field**. Figure 10.7 shows the Staff table and the ordered file that actually stores the data on disk. The file (and, hence, the table instance) is ordered by lName. The data file starts with a file header, which holds information such as the number of blocks used for the file, plus the location of each block on the hard disk (as a pointer to the start of a block). In the example shown, each block holds up to four records, and the first four blocks are full. The records are shown as comma-separated values for convenience (the three dots – '. . .' – indicate that not all the record's fields are shown in the illustration), though, in reality, a more sophisticated record structure is likely.

Tables stored as ordered files can quickly be searched using the column that corresponds to the ordering field, because the DBMS can hop around rather than searching each block in order. For instance, in this example, to find the first record with the value 'Stark' in the ordering field, the DBMS actually starts at the middle block, Block 3. It checks the ordering field of the *first* record, which is 'O'Connor', and finds that the required record must come *after* this record. It now checks the last record of Block 3 and finds that the required record must be in a later block. The DBMS has now eliminated the entire first half of the data file, simply by checking one block. In an actual example with hundreds of blocks, this is a major saving in time. The DBMS continues by reading the *middle* block of the last half of the data file – Block 4 in the example. Again, it compares the required value to the ordering field of the *first* record in this block, which is 'Smith', and finds that the required record must come after this record. It now checks the last record of Block 4, and finds that the required record must be in the block. It can now scan the block for the required record.

Mathematicians reading this will recognize that this search mechanism is based on the bisection method for finding the root of an equation.

In contrast, searching in other columns is as slow as searching a heap file. Inserting a row is tricky, too. First, the correct position within the data file is found. Then this

Figure 10.7 The `Staff` table mapped to an ordered file.

Data file header	
No of blocks: 5	
Block 1: <pointer to block 1>	
Block 2: <pointer to block 2>	
Block 3: <pointer to block 3>	
Block 4: <pointer to block 4>	
Block 5: <pointer to block 5>	

Data file

Database table

Block 1

14443, Helen, Abbot, …
56893, Ruth, Bapetsi, …
56673, Joshua, Bittaye, …
33935, Padma, Brar, …

Block 2

35155, Helene, Chirac, …
55776, Gurpreet, Choudhury, …
35054, Selma, Hutchins, …
89987, Dan, Lin, …

Block 3

78893, Jo Karen, O'Connor, …
77712, Frank, Rose, …
31210, Paul, Smith, …
25448, Judith Anne, Smith, …

Block 4

25447, John, Smith, …
10780, John, Smith, …
23257, Freya, Stark, …
45965, Mikhail, Sudbin, …

Block 5

33509, Helen, Timms, …

Staff

staffNo:Varchar	fName:Varchar	lName:Varchar	…
14443	Helen	Abbot	…
56893	Ruth	Bapetsi	…
56673	Joshua	Bittaye	…
33935	Padma	Brar	…
35155	Helene	Chirac	…
55776	Gurpreet	Choudhury	…
35054	Selma	Hutchins	…
89987	Dan	Lin	…
78893	Jo Karen	O'Connor	…
77712	Frank	Rose	…
31210	Paul	Smith	…
25448	Judith Anne	Smith	…
25447	John	Smith	…
10780	John	Smith	…
23257	Freya	Stark	…
45965	Mikhail	Sudbin	…
33509	Helen	Timms	…

block, and all subsequent blocks, need to be rewritten as the new record pushes all subsequent records 'down' the data file. Clever ordered file structures leave some additional space in each block to allow for new records. However, this only postpones the reorganization. Eventually the block fills up and, when a new record needs to be added, the data file must be reorganized just as before. Deleting a row from the table also causes problems. The relevant record is removed, leaving a gap in the block. Again, the data file will need to be reorganized, though this can be postponed until a later date (for example, the 'compact and repair' facility in Microsoft Access reorganizes the underlying data files to remove such gaps only when the user requests it). Updating the value of the column that corresponds to the ordering field causes *both* problems as the original record must be deleted and a new record inserted at the appropriate point in the data file.

Even faster access to records can be achieved using a **hash file**. This places each record in a particular block based on the value of one of the fields. A **hash function** takes the field value as input and outputs the address of one of the blocks in the data file. The same field value *always* gets the same block address. Thus, to read a particular record, the DBMS simply uses the hash function to find the correct block. It copies this block into memory and scans it for the required data. This avoids the need to read all the preceding blocks, which happens with a heap file, or to hop around in search of the right block, as with an ordered file.

10.4.2 Indexes

An **index** provides a way to locate required information quickly. This book has an index. To find a particular topic, use the index. The index entry will indicate on which page(s) of the book the topic is discussed. In a similar way, a database column can have an index. To find a particular column value, use the index. The index entries indicate on which row(s) of the table the required column value occurs. In a relational database, an index is stored in a table, but one that the DBMS recognizes as an index table rather than a data table. The index table is itself stored on disk as an ordered file, with each index entry a record in this file. This means that searching the index is very quick (see the discussion above). Thus, when an index is defined on a database table, the DBMS can copy the index file into memory and search it, rather than copy the table's data file. As the index will be smaller than the data file, this provides a significant performance improvement for database searches, but only when the search criteria uses the indexed column. An index can be defined on almost any combination of columns, but the concept is most easily explained by considering indexes on a single column. Indexes can be used whether the table is stored as an ordered file or a heap file. For an ordered file, there is a difference between the way indexes work when the indexed column is the ordering field of the file and when it is not. This situation is discussed first.

When a database uses an ordered file as the data storage structure for a particular table, it almost always includes an index on the ordering field of the data file. When the ordering field is a candidate key on the table, the index is called the **primary index** of the ordered file. (Only ordered files can have a primary index.) Rather than keep an index record for each data file record, it makes more sense to keep an index record for each *block* of the data file.

This situation is shown in Figure 10.8, where the ordering field is staffNo (the primary key of the Staff table). Each record in the index file consists of two fields. One field holds a pointer to a block in the data file. The other field holds a copy of the value of the ordering field in the *first* record of that block. So, in Figure 10.8, the first index record holds a pointer to the first block of the data file and the value 10780, which is the value of the ordering field in the first record of the first block of the data file. The second index record points to the second block of the data file and holds the value 25448, the value of the first record of the second block, and so on. Note that only *some* values of the indexed column are present in the index itself.

Searching for a particular row in the table using the value of staffNo is easy. For example, suppose the DBMS wishes to retrieve the row of the table where the staffNo value is 33935. Rather than searching the data file itself, the DBMS searches the index file for an index record with this value. It doesn't find one, but it does find

Figure 10.8 The primary index on an ordered data file.

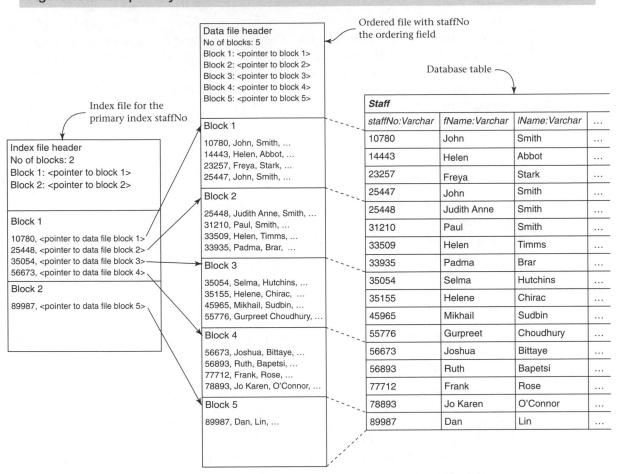

index records with `staffNo` values 25448 and 35054. As the data file is ordered by `staffNo`, the data file record with `staffNo` value 33935 must lie between the data file records with values 25448 and 35054. As both these data file records appear at the start of a block (that is why they are in the index), the required data file record must be in the block that starts with the data file record with `staffNo` 25448.

Searching using the primary index will generally be much faster than searching the ordered file itself. The index file *always* has fewer blocks than the data file, so the standard search procedure for ordered files will be faster on the index file. There are fewer blocks for two reasons. First, the index file has fewer records – only one index record for each data file block – and, second, each index record is smaller than the data file record, so there are more index records per block (this is not shown in Figure 10.8). However inserting or deleting rows and updating the value of the column that corresponds to the ordering field are all slower as both the data file *and* the index file must be modified in each case.

The ordering field of an ordered file does not have to be a candidate key on the table. In this situation, several rows of the data file will have the same value in the ordering field. Figure 10.9 shows the data for the Staff table stored in an ordered file, but this time the ordering field is the department. There can be many rows with the same value in this ordering field – there are six rows with the value 'Computing', for example. Rows with the same value in the ordering field appear in a contiguous cluster of records within the data file. There are five such clusters in Figure 10.9, one for each distinct value of department. Note that some clusters start in one block, but stretch into another. In practice, one cluster could span several blocks in the data file. This data storage structure makes it very easy to find a particular cluster of records – find the *first* record with the required value in the ordering field, then simply read through the file until a record with a different value is encountered. Storing the Staff table as an ordered file with the department as the ordering field makes it very easy to find all staff in a particular department. If this query is run frequently, then this data storage structure makes sense.

When many rows can have the same value in the ordering field, a different approach to creating an index is needed. Rather than have the index records point to the start of a block in the data file, it makes more sense to have the index records point to the start of a cluster. Such an index is called a **clustering index**.

In practice, the index records of a clustering index point to the data file block where the *first* record of the cluster occurs. This means that two index records may point to the same block in the data file. For example, the first and second index records in Figure 10.9 point to block 1. Also, some blocks will not have an index record pointing to them – block 5 does not have any clusters *starting* in it.

In a clustering index, there is one index record for each cluster. This means that there is exactly one index record for each distinct value of the data file's ordering field. This is not true of a primary index, where some values of the data file's ordering field do not appear in the index.

A clustering index provides similar advantages to those of a primary index and suffers from similar problems when rows are inserted, deleted or have the data in the ordering field changed. In the example given in Figure 10.9, some blocks of the data file include records from two different clusters. A refinement of this data storage structure only allows records from the same cluster in any one block. This means that there is usually space available to add a new record to a cluster, but does mean that the data file is larger than necessary.

> The terms 'cluster' and 'clustering' are also used to mean a cluster of *databases* rather than a cluster of *records*. This is an advanced database technology offered by some DBMS manufacturers, but is beyond the scope of an introductory textbook.

A table stored in an ordered file can have *either* a primary index or a clustering index, but not both. Which of these two it has depends on the ordering field chosen. If the ordering field is a candidate key, then the table will have a primary index, but, if the ordering field is *not* a candidate key, then the table will have a clustering index.

There is another kind of index called a **secondary index** that can be defined on any column *except* a column used as an ordering field. Apart from this restriction, the table's

Figure 10.9 The clustering index on an ordered data file.

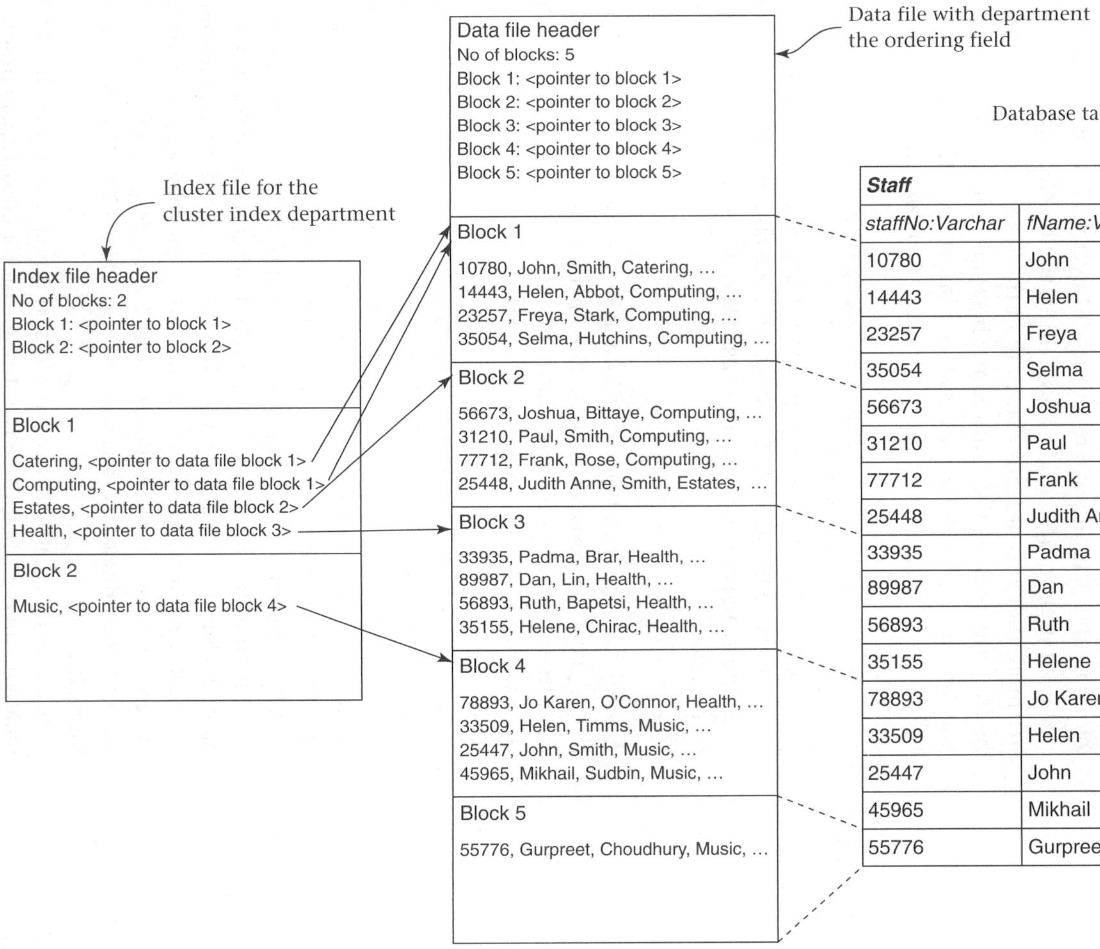

Database table

Staff

staffNo:Varchar	*fName:Varchar*	*lName:Varchar*	*department:Varchar*	…
10780	John	Smith	Catering	…
14443	Helen	Abbot	Computing	…
23257	Freya	Stark	Computing	…
35054	Selma	Hutchins	Computing	…
56673	Joshua	Bittaye	Computing	…
31210	Paul	Smith	Computing	…
77712	Frank	Rose	Computing	…
25448	Judith Anne	Smith	Estates	…
33935	Padma	Brar	Health	…
89987	Dan	Lin	Health	…
56893	Ruth	Bapetsi	Health	…
35155	Helene	Chirac	Health	…
78893	Jo Karen	O'Connor	Health	…
33509	Helen	Timms	Music	…
25447	John	Smith	Music	…
45965	Mikhail	Sudbin	Music	…
55776	Gurpreet	Choudhury	Music	…

data storage structure doesn't limit the choice of secondary indexes – tables stored as heap, ordered and hashed files can all have secondary indexes. The index file is itself an ordered file, so the fast search process for ordered files can be used to quickly search the index file.

Figure 10.10 shows a secondary index defined on the email column of the Staff table (the pointers are shown as arrows, but only for block 1 of the index file as including arrows for *all* the pointers makes the diagram difficult to read). The table's data storage structure is a heap file (unordered), so the email column is definitely *not* used as an ordering field for the data file. Inspection of Figure 10.10 should show that the value of the email field does not affect the position of a record within the data file. There is one index record for each data file record (each row of the table).

As usual, the index record has two fields. One field holds a copy of the value of the data file record's index field (in Figure 10.10, this is the e-mail address). The other field holds a pointer to the data file. In Figure 10.10, the index pointer points to the block in the data file where the record occurs. It's also possible to have the index pointer point at the actual record within the block. Notice that in Figure 10.10 there are more index records in a block than there are data file records. This will typically be the case, making the index a much smaller file and so quicker to search. Even so, the file for a secondary index is always larger than that for a primary index, because there is one index record for every data file *record* rather than one index record for each data file *block*.

> In Figure 10.10, the underlying data storage structure is a heap file. The secondary index would be basically the same if it were an ordered file with some other column acting as the ordering field, or a hash file with some other column providing the hashing value.

A secondary index can be created for as many columns (or combinations of columns) as the database designer desires. This includes a non-candidate key column. In this case, there are different ways to structure the index file to deal with repeated values in the indexed field. The simplest is to stick with one index record for each data file record, which means that some index records have the same value but a different pointer. Secondary indexes speed up data retrieval, but, like all indexes, they must be maintained, so have the effect of slowing down insert, delete and update operations.

The main reason for defining any sort of index is to improve the performance of database queries. The index can do this in two ways. First, it speeds up select statements that use the indexed column in the where clause. For example, searching the Staff table for the member of staff with a particular e-mail address will be quicker if there is an index on the email column than if the DBMS must search the underlying data file. Similarly, indexing a foreign key will speed up a table join.

Second, some queries can be evaluated simply be looking at the index, with no need to read any records from the data file. For example, to find out if the e-mail address 'j.smith@pennine.ac.uk' has already been taken, the DBMS only needs to search the index file.

If indexing a particular column (or combination of columns) will speed up several database queries, then there is a strong case for creating the index.

Figure 10.10 A secondary index for a column in a table that has a heap file as its underlying data storage structure.

Pointers shown only for index records in block 1 (or the diagram gets too cluttered)

Data file with *no* ordering (a heap file)

Database table

Staff

staffNo:Varchar	email:Varchar	...
10780	j.b.smith@pennine.ac.uk	...
25447	j.smith@pennine.ac.uk	...
33935	p.brar@pennine.ac.uk	...
89987	d.lin@pennine.co.uk	...
77712	f.rose@pennine.ac.uk	...
14443	h.abbot@pennine.ac.uk	...
23257	f.stark@pennine.ac.uk	...
25448	j.a.smith@pennine.ac.uk	...
35054	s.hutchins@pennine.ac.uk	...
45965	m.sudbin@pennine.ac.uk	...
35155	h.chirac@pennine.ac.uk	...
55776	g.choudhury@pennine.ac.uk	...
56893	r.bapetsi@pennine.ac.uk	...
56673	j.bittaye@pennine.ac.uk	...
31210	p.smith@pennine.ac.uk	...
78893	j.k.oconnor@pennine.ac.uk	...
33509	h.timms@pennine.ac.uk	...

Data file header
No of blocks: 5
Block 1: <pointer to block 1>
Block 2: <pointer to block 2>
Block 3: <pointer to block 3>
Block 4: <pointer to block 4>
Block 5: <pointer to block 5>

Block 1
10780, j.b.smith@pennine.ac.uk, ...
25447, j.smith@pennine.ac.uk, ...
33935, p.brar@pennine.ac.uk, ...
89987, d.lin@pennine.co.uk, ...

Block 2
77712, f.rose@pennine.ac.uk, ...
14443, h.abbot@pennine.ac.uk, ...
23257, f.stark@pennine.ac.uk, ...
25448, j.a.smith@pennine.ac.uk, ...

Block 3
35054, s.hutchins@pennine.ac.uk, ...
45965, m.sudbin@pennine.ac.uk, ...
35155, h.chirac@pennine.ac.uk, ...
55776, g.choudhury@pennine.ac.uk, ...

Block 4
56893, r.bapetsi@pennine.ac.uk, ...
56673, j.bittaye@pennine.ac.uk, ...
31210, p.smith@pennine.ac.uk, ...
78893, j.k.oconnor@pennine.ac.uk, ...

Block 5
33509, h.timms@pennine.ac.uk, ...

Data file header
No of blocks: 5
Block 1: <pointer to block 1>
Block 2: <pointer to block 2>
Block 3: <pointer to block 3>

Block 1
d.lin@pennine.co.uk, <pointer to data file block 1>
f.rose@pennine.ac.uk, <pointer to data file block 2>
f.stark@pennine.ac.uk, <pointer to data file block 2>
g.choudhury@pennine.ac.uk, <pointer to data file block 3>
h.abbot@pennine.ac.uk, <pointer to data file block 2>
h.chirac@pennine.ac.uk, <pointer to data file block 3>
h.timms@pennine.ac.uk, <pointer to data file block 5>

Block 2
j.a.smith@pennine.ac.uk, <pointer to data file block 2>
j.b.smith@pennine.ac.uk, <pointer to data file2 block 1>
j.bittaye@pennine.ac.uk, <pointer to data file block 4>
j.k.oconnor@pennine.ac.uk, <pointer to data file block 4>
j.smith@pennine.ac.uk, <pointer to data file block 1>
m.sudbin@pennine.ac.uk, <pointer to data file block 3>
p.brar@pennine.ac.uk, <pointer to data file block 1>

Block 3
p.smith@pennine.ac.uk, < pointer to data file block 4>
r.bapetsi@pennine.ac.uk, < pointer to data file block 4>
s.hutchins@pennine.ac.uk, < pointer to data file block 3>

The main reason for not creating an index is that it will usually slow down data modifications as changes to the table's underlying data file usually entail changes to the index file as well. Insert statements will normally be slower.

The effect of an index on update and delete statements is more complex. The increased search speed will mean that the affected records are found faster than they would be otherwise, but the need to maintain the index can mean that the actual data modification is slower.

It is important to consider the cost of maintaining the index, too, and weigh this against the advantages of faster database searches. Sometimes the most effective way to do this is to create the table with and without indexes, add a good helping of sample data and try the queries out.

Most DBMS will automatically define an index on the primary key of a table. There are two reasons for this. First, the primary key is chosen as the main way to uniquely identify a row. This suggests that most select statements using the table will use the primary key in their where clause, so it makes sense to index it. Second, the DBMS must enforce the primary key constraint. This means checking that the primary key value on a new row is distinct from the primary key value on all existing rows. It's clearly going to be easier to do this if there is an index. In fact, this is one circumstance where an index can actually speed up insert statements, too. For a DBMS using SQL as its data language, columns defined as UNIQUE would also benefit from being indexed, for the same reason.

The unique constraint is used to define candidate keys (see above). If the table's underlying data storage structure is an ordered file and the primary key columns (or UNIQUE columns) correspond to the ordering fields, then the DBMS could define a primary index for the column. Otherwise, it must use a secondary index.

In most other circumstances, the database designer or DBA will instruct the DBMS when to create an index. Although not part of the ISO SQL standard, most DBMS implement the SQL DDL create index statement. The SQL DDL create index statement will create a secondary index on the specified columns. It cannot normally be used to define primary or clustering indexes, though, as they are tied to the structure of the underlying data file (but check the documentation of your DBMS).

Code listing 10.4.2.1 shows the typical format of this statement. Code listing 10.4.2.1 (a) shows how to create a secondary index on the Staff table's email column. Code listing 10.4.2.1 (b) creates a secondary index on the combination of columns lName and fName. Within the index file, index records will include a value for *both* columns and a pointer to the appropriate block (or record) in the data file. The index records will be ordered first by the value of lName and then by the value of fName, which is how names are sorted in most telephone directories.

Code listing 10.4.2.1   The SQL DDL create index statement

(a) Creating an index on the Staff **table's** email **column**

```
CREATE INDEX idxStaffEmail ON Staff(email);
```

(b) Creating an index on the Staff **table's** Name, fName **columns**

```
CREATE INDEX idxStaffName ON Staff(lName, fName);
```

> The create index statement can include the keyword UNIQUE, as in CREATE UNIQUE INDEX, and this has the same effect as adding a unique constraint and indexing the column all in one go. For preference, use the unique constraint rather than the unique index as most developers would look in the data dictionary for the constraint rather than the index. Also, the DBMS may be able to use a primary index on the columns with the unique constraint – the CREATE UNIQUE INDEX statement will create a secondary index.

As mentioned above, the create index statement is not normally used to create clustering indexes as not all DBMS support clustering indexes. One that does is the Oracle database. Creating a clustering index for a table in Oracle involves three steps. First, use the Oracle-specific create cluster statement to inform the Oracle database that a clustering index is about to be used. This reserves space for the ordered file on disk. Next, use the SQL DDL create table statement to create the table, but include a cluster clause to indicate how to cluster data in the ordered file just created. Finally, create an index on the *cluster*.

Code listing 10.4.2.2 shows how to implement the clustering index shown in Figure 10.9. The create cluster statement must indicate the data type of the column with the clustering index and this must match the data type of the associated column in the create table statement (the name of the column in the create cluster statement is not significant). In the create table statement, the cluster clause comes *after* the list of columns and constraints. It names the cluster being used and indicates which column in the table is used for the clustering index. Finally, the clustering index itself is created.

Code listing 10.4.2.2   *Creating a clustering index in the Oracle database*

```
CREATE CLUSTER cluStaffDepartment (department VARCHAR(20));

CREATE TABLE Staff(
  staffNo CHAR(5) NOT NULL ,
  fName VARCHAR(50) NOT NULL ,
  lName VARCHAR(20) NOT NULL ,
  phone VARCHAR(20) ,
  email VARCHAR(50) NOT NULL ,
  department VARCHAR(20) ,
  CONSTRAINT pkStaff PRIMARY KEY (staffNo)
)
CLUSTER cluStaffDepartment (department);

CREATE INDEX idxcluStaffDepartment ON CLUSTER
cluStaffDepartment;
```

The Oracle database allows a further refinement to the structure of a data file with a clustering index. It allows data from *two or more tables* to be clustered in the *same* data file.

This is particularly useful where there is a foreign key linking the tables and one of the tables is derived from a weak entity. For example, the `Staff` and `SupportSession` tables fall into this category. Data from `SupportSession` is not much use without data from `Staff`. As `SupportSession` data will usually be retrieved at the same time as the associated `Staff` data, it might make sense to store the data in the same file.

Figure 10.11 shows a sample data file. Notice how it includes records for both `Staff` and `SupportSession` data. The clever bit is that support sessions offered by

Figure 10.11 A two-table ordered data file with a clustering index.

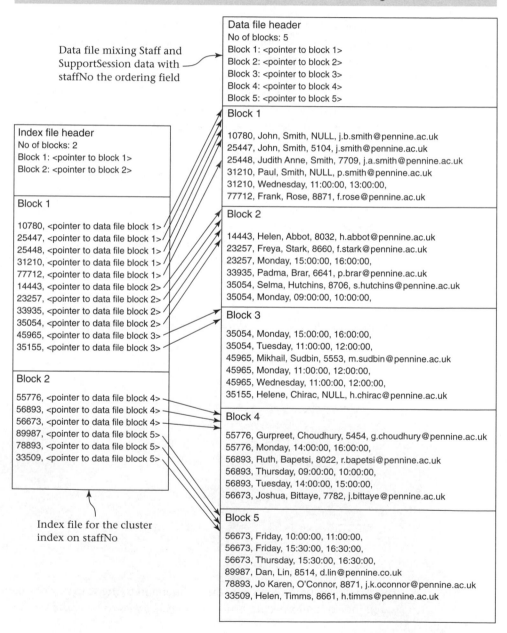

a particular member of staff are stored *immediately after* their `Staff` record. For example, in Block 2 of the data file, the `Staff` record for Freya Stark is followed by her single `SupportSession` record. Selma Hutchins' `Staff` record is followed by her three `SupportSession` records, with one in Block 2 and two more in Block 3. The associated clustering index is also shown, with a single index record for each distinct value of `staffNo` and a block pointer pointing to the block each cluster starts in.

Code listing 10.4.2.3 shows the SQL DDL to instruct the Oracle database to create this data storage structure.

Code listing 10.4.2.3   Creating a clustering index for a two-table cluster in the Oracle database

```
CREATE CLUSTER cluStaffSuppSess (staffNo CHAR(5));

CREATE TABLE Staff(
 staffNo CHAR(5) NOT NULL ,
 fName VARCHAR(50) NOT NULL ,
 lName VARCHAR(20) NOT NULL ,
 phone VARCHAR(20) ,
 email VARCHAR(50) NOT NULL ,
 CONSTRAINT pkStaff PRIMARY KEY (staffNo)
 )
CLUSTER cluStaffSuppSess (staffNo);

CREATE TABLE SupportSession(
staffNo CHAR(5) NOT NULL ,
dayOfWeek VARCHAR (9) NOT NULL ,
startTime TIME NOT NULL ,
endTime TIME NOT NULL ,
CONSTRAINT pkSupportSession
   PRIMARY KEY (staffNo, dayOfWeek, startTime)
)
CLUSTER cluStaffSuppSess (staffNo);

CREATE INDEX idxcluStaffSuppSess ON CLUSTER
cluStaffSuppSess;
```

10.4.3 Storage engines

Most DBMS allow the DBA and database designer some different storage structures to choose from for tables. Each storage structure is a combination of a particular kind of data file (heap, ordered, hashed) and additional structures, such as index files, that allow the DBMS fast access to the data held in the data file. These storage structures are part of the internal level of the ANSI/SPARC architecture.

In the past, such storage structures were called table types. When structured data types were added to SQL, the term 'table type' came to mean the data type a table was based on.

The MySQL DBMS documentation calls data storage structures **storage engines**, emphasizing that they are about data storage (internal view) rather than data organization (logical and external views), so this is the term adopted here. Understanding the basics of data files and indexes is a pre-requisite for understanding storage engines, but the discussion above is only an introduction to this topic.

Choosing the correct storage engine for a table can significantly improve performance as each storage engine is optimized for a particular role. For example, the MyISAM storage engine of the MySQL DBMS is optimized for data retrieval. It uses ordered data files and indexes to achieve this. The MyISAM storage engine does not support commit and rollback functionality – there is no 'undo' facility for modifications to the table instance. Nor does the MySQL DBMS remember, or enforce, foreign key constraints on a MyISAM table (though it will happily check the SQL DDL statements that define them and point out your syntax errors). If foreign keys or commit and rollback support are required, one of the other storage engines should be used, such as the InnoDB storage engine.

When deciding on which storage engine to use, the DBA and database designer should work together to match the storage engine features to the requirements of the application.

All DBMS have a default storage engine, though this can usually be changed by the DBA. A standard ISO SQL create table statement will use the default storage engine as the underlying data storage structure for a table. The default storage engine of the MySQL DBMS is the MyISAM storage engine. Each DBMS will provide its own way of specifying which storage engine to use.

Code listing 10.4.3.1 shows how to create the `Room` table using the InnoDB storage engine on the MySQL DBMS.

Code listing 10.4.3.1   Specifying storage engines in a create table statement for the MySQL DBMS

```
CREATE TABLE Room (
  building VARCHAR(15) NOT NULL,
  roomNo VARCHAR(4) NOT NULL,
  capacity INTEGER NULL,
  equipmentValue DECIMAL(9,2) NULL, -- total value of
    equipment in this room
  CONSTRAINT priRoom PRIMARY KEY (building, roomNo)
)
ENGINE = InnoDB;
```

10.5   Security

It is usually important to keep an application's data secure. Often, applications create their own security procedures to control access to the application itself. Users who don't provide a valid username and password cannot access the application. In a web database application, this usually means including a login web page and not letting users see any other web pages until they have successfully logged in.

The DBMS has its own security procedures and these are usually a lot more sophisticated than a simple login screen. From the database perspective, there are two main security issues. These are deciding who is allowed to connect to the DBMS and what they are allowed to do once they have connected.

Deciding who is allowed to connect to the database is done by means of the processes of **identification** and **authentication**. Identification states who you are and authentication proves it. Typically, users identify themselves by their usernames and authenticate their usernames with passwords.

The process of deciding what users are allowed to do once connected is called **authorization**. Each time users request a particular action, such as query a table or create an index, the DBMS checks whether or not they are authorized to make the request. If they are, it complies, but, if not, it rejects the request with a suitable error message.

The ISO SQL standard does not specify how a DBMS should identify and authenticate its users. It simply assumes that this is done. Once users have successfully identified themselves and connected to the DBMS, unique authorization identifiers are associated with their connections. In ISO SQL, the CURRENT_USER value function returns authorization identifiers for users on their current connection. Many DBMS include the SQL DDL create user statement to allow the DBA to assign authorization identifiers, in the form of usernames, to end users.

Code listing 10.5.1 (a) shows the basic create user statement. It begins with the keywords CREATE USER, followed by a string literal representing the authorization identifier (username) for a new user – in this case, the authorization identifier is 'angela'. The keywords IDENTIFIED BY are optional and used to define the initial password for this user, the string literal '89gleo06'. Some DBMS provide extensions on this basic scheme, such as a password expiry date, while others eschew the create user statement and use a graphical user interface to manage user accounts. A variation on the ubiquitous DROP statement removes a user (Code listing 10.5.1 (b)).

Code listing 10.5.1   User management statements

(a) Creating a user with the SQL DDL create user statement

```
CREATE USER 'angela' IDENTIFIED BY '89gleo06';
```

(b) Removing a user

```
DROP USER 'angela';
```

> The ISO SQL standard uses the term 'authorization identifier' instead of 'username' to allow for more sophisticated identification and authentication schemes than the traditional username and password. For example, users might identify themselves to the system by means of a biometric smart card and authenticate the smart card information with an iris scan or thumb print.

The process of identification and authentication provides a first line of defence for the database by controlling who can connect to the DBMS. A DBMS can manage many databases, each of which can have many tables. Most users only need access to a portion of this data, hence the need for the authorization process.

The ISO SQL **privilege system** offers a relatively straightforward way for the DBA to limit what users can do once they've connected to the DBMS. First, users have full control of any databases (SQL schema) or database objects (tables, views and so on) that they have created. Each is called the **owner** of the database or database object. Once a database has been created the owner is the *only* user who may create tables, views and so on within the database. The ISO SQL standard is quite clear about this – only the database owner can use SQL DDL statements to create or alter objects within the database.

This restriction radically simplifies the problem of defining who can do what. Authorization of (almost) all data definition actions are now dealt with. However, it is a little too radical a simplification for most DBMS, which, instead, extend the privilege system to allow many users to create objects within the same database.

Authorizing other actions on the database – in particular, data manipulation actions – is done via the privilege system. Users who don't own a particular database object can't do anything with it until the object's owner grants them suitable privileges. So, for example, no user can query the Staff table in the Staff Directory database until the owner grants them the privilege to run a select statement on this table. A user who does not have this privilege but tries to run a select statement with the Staff table in the from clause will be told that there is no such table – users who don't have the privilege to access a table cannot even know that it exists.

The ISO SQL standard specifies four data manipulation privileges:

- select privilege
- insert privilege
- update privilege
- delete privilege.

These allow users to use the obvious SQL DDL statement. There are two privileges related to data definition that need to be mentioned. The trigger privilege allows users to create a trigger on a specified table. The references privilege allows users to add a foreign key or check constraint to a table they own that references a table they don't own. An example of this situation was included in Chapter 6 in the section discussing subqueries and the alter table statement is repeated in Code listing 10.5.2. The statement adds a check constraint to the Web Timetable database's Equipment table. The check condition refers to the Asset Tracking database's AssetType table. The owner of the Asset Tracking database must grant the references privilege on the AssetType table to the owner of the Web Timetable database or the alter table statement will not work.

Code listing 10.5.2   An alter table statement that requires the references privilege

```
ALTER TABLE Equipment
ADD CONSTRAINT chkEquipmentAssetType
  CHECK (assetType IN (SELECT type
                        FROM AssetTracking.AssetType));
```

Table 10.2 Six ISO SQL privileges.		
Privilege	*SQL keyword*	*Applies to following database objects*
Select privilege	SELECT	Tables, columns
Insert privilege	INSERT	Tables, columns
Update privilege	UPDATE	Tables, columns
Delete privilege	DELETE	Tables
Trigger privilege	TRIGGER	Tables
References privilege	REFERENCES	Tables, columns

Table 10.2 lists these six privileges, the associated SQL keyword and states whether the privilege can apply to tables and columns or just tables. For example, it is possible to give a user the select privilege on only *some* columns in a table. This provides an alternative to the view mechanism for hiding information from users.

The owner of a database object grants other users privileges to use that object with the SQL **grant statement**. Code listing 10.5.3 shows a typical grant statement, giving two users – 'angela' and 'peter' – select and update privileges on the two tables of the Staff Directory database. It begins with the keyword GRANT, followed by a comma-separated list of the privileges being granted. The keyword ON is followed by a comma-separated list of the database objects affected. Then, the keyword TO is followed by a comma-separated list of the users being granted these privileges. The list of users can be replaced by the keyword PUBLIC to grant the listed privileges on the listed database objects to all DBMS users. The select, update, insert and references privileges can be restricted to individual columns (see Code listing 10.5.6, below, for an example).

Code listing 10.5.3 *A typical grant statement*

```
GRANT SELECT, UPDATE
ON Staff, SupportSession
TO angela, peter;
```

Code listing 10.5.4 illustrates one additional feature of the grant statement. The keywords WITH GRANT OPTION allow the listed users to pass on to others the privileges that they are being granted. So, the user Angela can grant other users the select privilege on the Staff table. The user Angela cannot grant the select privilege on the *SupportSession table* to other users, even though she has this privilege herself (from the grant statement in Code listing 10.5.3).

Code listing 10.5.4 *Granting a user the right to pass on her privileges*

```
GRANT SELECT
ON Staff
TO angela
WITH GRANT OPTION;
```

To remove privileges from a user, use the revoke statement. Code listing 10.5.5 (a) shows how to remove the update privilege on the Staff table from user Peter.

Code listing 10.5.5 (b) shows how to remove the right of user Angela to pass on her select privilege on the Staff table. Angela still has the select privilege on Staff herself, but can no longer pass it on to others.

Code listing 10.5.5   The revoke statement

(a) Revoking a privilege

```
REVOKE UPDATE
ON Staff
FROM peter;
```

(b) Removing the right to pass on privileges

```
REVOKE GRANT OPTION FOR SELECT
ON Staff
FROM angela;
```

> A problem arises concerning what to do about users who were previously granted their privileges by Angela. Do they retain them or should their privileges also be revoked?
>
> The ISO SQL standard does define this behaviour, but it is complicated and not all DBMS follow the standard. Read the manual for the particular DBMS you are using carefully before setting out to revoke privileges and always think very carefully before allowing anyone other than the DBA to grant privileges to others.

Two significant problems with granting privileges to individual users are that it can be time-consuming and difficult to manage. The situation illustrated in Code listings 10.5.3 and 10.5.4 is fairly common – a standard set of privileges for all users and additional privileges for some of them. Managing this situation is helped by introducing the notion of a **role**.

A role is a similar to a UML actor – it represents a particular way of using the system, rather than a particular user. Some users will play several different roles and one role can be played by many users. Adding roles to the security model adds complexity, but does make it easier to manage users and privileges. The DBA creates roles to represent different kinds of users and grants privileges to the role rather than one or more individuals. Then, the DBA tells the DBMS which users play which roles and they get all the privileges of the roles they play.

Code listing 10.5.6 illustrates the steps involved. First, it creates two roles – UnivMember and Academic. Then, it grants the select privilege to the tables of the Staff Directory database to both roles. The second grant statement allows academics to modify data on SupportSession. The third, to change the data in the fName, lName and phone columns of the Staff table. The final grant statement grants the *roles* UnivMember and Academic to two users. These users then have *all* the privileges associated with those roles.

Code listing 10.5.6   Managing privileges using roles

```
CREATE ROLE UnivMember;

CREATE ROLE Academic;

GRANT SELECT
ON Staff, SupportSession
TO UnivMember, Academic;

GRANT INSERT, UPDATE, DELETE
ON SupportSession
TO Academic;

GRANT UPDATE (fName, lName, phone)
ON Staff
TO Academic;

GRANT UnivMember, Academic
TO angela, peter;
```

Roles can be removed from a particular user using the revoke statement, just as individual privileges can. The role itself remains as an object in the database, even if no users currently have that role.

Roles can be permanently removed from the database with a drop role statement, which automatically revokes the role from all users. This is different from the usual behaviour of the drop statement as, in general, a drop statement on a database object fails if there are other database objects that refer to it. For roles, the drop statement has an automatic cascade option that cannot be circumvented. Use with care.

Most DBMS implement a privilege system that follows the general intent of the ISO SQL standard. Many, including the MySQL DBMS, include privileges that relate to data definition actions, such as a create table privilege to allow users to create tables in a database that they do not own. Not all DBMS implement roles, and the details of how privileges and roles interact, especially with respect to the revoke statement, will vary.

Chapter summary

- This chapter has discussed a wide range of issues related to the physical design of a database. The issues either must or should be considered before beginning to implement a database application.

- Much of the chapter has focused on changes to the logical and external views of the ANSI/SPARC architecture – that is, to tweaking the logical design to fit a particular DBMS. The section on data files, indexes and storage engines delved a little deeper into the internal view of the ANSI/SPARC architecture and the underlying data files. The chapter concluded by discussing the ISO SQL standard's security model.

Further reading

Most database textbooks cover physical database design. Kroenke (2006) has a couple of good chapters and Connolly and Begg (2004) provide a nice summary of the process.

The websites of DBMS suppliers provide useful material on physical design for their particular products. It is only possible to give a brief introduction to data files and indexing in an introductory textbook, so take a look at these websites. In particular, there's been no discussion of how best to implement the index file itself. Needless to say, a simple ordered file is *not* the best way to store an index file.

Elmasri and Navathe (2007) and Silberschatz et al. (2002) provide a more technical discussion of these issues. Silberschatz et al. (2002) also have interesting case studies of three of the major commercial DBMS – the Oracle database, IBM DB2 Universal Database and Microsoft SQL Server. Troels Arvin (2006) is developing a comparison of the facilities provided by the ISO SQL:2003 standard and various commercial DBMS and publishing it as a web page.

Review questions

10.1 List the data types of the ISO SQL:2003 standard, including its distinct types, together with a brief summary of how they should be used.

10.2 Outline the two main approaches to implementing columns that hold derived data.

10.3 Explain the purpose of a QUID (IRUD, CRUD) matrix.

10.4 What is a surrogate key and how does it differ from a logical primary key? When would you use one?

10.5 Outline the usual approach to storing binary data in a web database application.

10.6 Explain the following terms, carefully distinguishing between them:
   (a) derived data
   (b) repeated data
   (c) controlled redundancy
   (d) denormalization.

10.7 What is a structured code? Why is it best avoided?

10.8 Describe the record structure of each of the following types of data file:
   (a) heap
   (b) ordered
   (c) hash.

10.9 Explain the following terms:
   (a) index
   (b) primary index
   (c) clustering index
   (d) secondary index.

10.10 Explain the following terms used in SQL database security:
   (a) identification
   (b) authentication
   (c) authorization
   (d) privilege
   (e) role
   (f) authorization identifier.

Exercises

10.11 Code listing 10.1.4.2 documents the physical design for the `Room` and `Equipment` tables. Correct the following weaknesses in this design.
   (a) When a new row is added to the `Equipment` table, the equipment is stored in, at most, one room. This means that the value of the column `Room.equipmentValue` will change in, at most, one row. Replace the statement-level after insert trigger `taiEquipment` with a row-level after insert trigger, so that, when new rows are added to the `Equipment` table, only the corresponding row in the `Room` table has the value of the column `equipmentValue` recalculated.
   (b) Write a new trigger to maintain the value of the column `Room.equipmentValue` when the `cost` column in a row of the `Equipment` table is updated.
   (c) Write a new trigger to maintain the value of the column `Room.equipmentValue` when a row of the `Equipment` table is deleted.

10.12 Estimate the storage requirements for the `Room` and `Equipment` tables in Code listing 10.1.4.2. You will need to make estimates of the maximum and average number of rows for each table. Note that all teaching rooms have an OHP, a PC and a digital projector.

10.13 Consider the transaction:

> provide a list of all teaching sessions showing the room, the room's capacity and the number of students attending that teaching session.

The idea is to check that each room has sufficient capacity for each teaching session timetabled to take place in it.
   (a) Draw an access path and calculate the transaction workload based on the physical table schema below and the following assumptions:
   • there are 4000 teaching sessions
   • there are, on average, 25 students per teaching session.

```
--*************************************************************
-- Create the base tables with their primary key constraints
--*************************************************************
CREATE TABLE TeachingSession(
moduleCode CHAR(7) NOT NULL,
staffNo VARCHAR(5) NOT NULL,
building VARCHAR(10) NOT NULL,
roomNo VARCHAR(4) NOT NULL,
day VARCHAR(9) NOT NULL,
startTime TIME NOT NULL,
duration INTERVAL MINUTE NOT NULL,
endTime TIME NOT NULL,
startDate DATE NOT NULL,
endDate DATE NULL,
runsFor INTERVAL DAY NULL,
type VARCHAR(9) NOT NULL,
sessionCode CHAR(1) NULL,
CONSTRAINT priModule PRIMARY KEY
   (moduleCode, building, roomNo, day, startTime)
);

CREATE TABLE Room (
building VARCHAR(10) NOT NULL,
roomNo   VARCHAR(4)  NOT NULL,
capacity INTEGER,
CONSTRAINT priRoom PRIMARY KEY (building, roomNo)
);

CREATE TABLE Student(
studentNo CHAR(10) NOT NULL,
fName VARCHAR(30) NOT NULL,
lName VARCHAR(30) NOT NULL,
email1 VARCHAR(50) NOT NULL,
email2 VARCHAR(50) NOT NULL,
phone VARCHAR(15),
CONSTRAINT priStudent PRIMARY KEY (studentNo)
);

CREATE TABLE Attendance(
studentNo CHAR(10) NOT NULL,
moduleCode CHAR(7) NOT NULL,
building VARCHAR(10) NOT NULL,
roomNo VARCHAR(4) NOT NULL,
day VARCHAR(9) NOT NULL,
startTime TIME NOT NULL,
CONSTRAINT priAttendance PRIMARY KEY
   (studentNo, moduleCode, building, roomNo, day, startTime)
);
```

```
--   *********************************************************
-- Add foreign keys
--   *********************************************************
ALTER TABLE TeachingSession
  ADD CONSTRAINT frnTeachingSessionRoom
  FOREIGN KEY (building, roomNo)
  REFERENCES Room (building, room)

ALTER TABLE Attendance
  ADD CONSTRAINT frnAttendanceStudent
  FOREICN KEY (studentNo) REFERENCES Student (studentNo)

ALTER TABLE Attendance
  ADD CONSTRAINT frnAttendanceTeachingSession
  FOREIGN KEY
    (moduleCode, building, roomNo, day, startTime)
  REFERENCES TeachingSession
    (moduleCode, building, roomNo, day, startTime)
```

(b) Amend the physical table schema for the `TeachingSession` table to include a `noOfStudents` column, holding derived data. Repeat the transaction path analysis for the database query.

(c) Amend the physical table schema for the `TeachingSession` table, replacing the composite primary keys with surrogate keys. What effect does this have on your transaction path analysis?

10.14 The table instances in Exercise 10.13 rarely change after the start of the academic year. Given this fact, answer the following questions.

(a) Outline the benefits and drawbacks of using surrogate keys and derived data on the `TeachingSession` table.

(b) Explain which kind of data file (heap, ordered or hashed) you would recommend for the four tables. If an ordered file, what would you choose as the ordering fields?

(c) What secondary indexes would you recommend to improve the performance of the query examined in Exercise 10.13? Why?

(d) What other factors need to be considered before deciding between the different physical table schema for the `TeachingSession` table? Which design would you recommend, and why?

10.15 Using Code listing 10.3.4.1 as a guide, implement *two* versions of the `Module` table – one with the single `code` column to hold a structured code and one with structured code implemented as four separate columns (its constituent parts).

(a) Write SQL select statements for *both* tables that list all 'F' (Foundation) level modules, all modules offered by the computing department (code is 'C') and all modules offered by the information systems subject area (subject area code 'I').

(b) For each table, write a PHP script that allows end users to search for modules by department, subject area and level.

(c) For each table, write a PHP script that allows end users to add a new module or modify an existing one, including modifying the module code.

(d) Which table is easiest to use? Why?

10.16 Examine your solutions to Exercises 9.15 and 9.16. Would it be appropriate to denormalize the database schema? Explain your reasoning.

Investigations

10.17 Choose one or more of the physical database design issues discussed in this chapter and investigate the advice given in the manuals or technical support documentation for two commercial DBMS. What facilities does each DBMS provide to deal with the issue? Write a short, technical report explaining your findings and evaluating the facilities provided by the two DBMS to deal with your chosen design issues.

10.18 The discussion of indexes in this chapter has focused on the underlying concepts rather than the technicalities of implementation. One popular approach to implementing indexes is the B-tree index. Using the resources suggested in the Further reading section, investigate this approach. Write a short report explaining B-tree indexes and discussing their strengths and weaknesses.

10.19 In Investigation 9.19, you developed a logical database design for an organization you know. Develop a physical database design for your DBMS. Write a report documenting your design decisions and the evidence that informed them.

10.20 Choose a particular DBMS and investigate its security mechanisms. What security threats do these mechanisms guard against? What security threats are not dealt with? How does the approach compare to that of the ISO SQL:2003 standard?

Web data design

Chapter objectives

→ To discuss the purpose of web data design.

→ To extend the conceptual ER diagram to model how data is delivered to end users via a web page.

→ To extend the logical ER diagram to model the split between client and server pages.

→ To introduce wrapper functions and persistent connections.

Chapter outline

Database design is only one part of the design for a web database application. In particular, it only considers those aspects of the application's behaviour that directly affect the structure of the database, such as referential actions and triggers that maintain redundant data. It does not address the application's behaviour in general, nor does it replicate the user experience design.

There are good reasons for this 'divide and conquer' approach to application design. The different aspects require different skills, so different members of the design team can work in parallel on these different aspects. This speeds up the development process and can lead to all the designs being completed at around the same time. The drawback is that, once all the designs have been completed, it's necessary to check that they all fit together.

On a well-managed project, the different design teams will seek to ensure that their designs are compatible as they go along. Even so, it is always worth checking things through before beginning to implement the design. Mapping the other designs on to the final database design provides an effective means of comparing them. Mismatches could indicate that one or other of the designs has missed or misinterpreted a requirement or that the users were not clear about them in the first place. If this is spotted, then the design can be corrected before implementation.

In this book the process of reconciling the different design is called **web data design** as it shows how the database design supports the web application's data requirements. As yet, there is no standard name for this process.

Web data design works best when there is a design for both the database and the application's behaviour. Sometimes, though, the database design is completed before any of the other design tasks have started. This is always true when a web database application uses an existing database. In such a case, the web data design can be based on the use cases. The designer scans the use cases to identify an initial set of **data-centric** web pages – web pages that draw their content from, or allow users to modify, the database instance. (This technique is also used to identify entities, attributes and relationships, as we saw in Chapter 8). Consider the Get staff contact details use case, part of the users' requirements for the Staff Directory (see Figure A.5, Appendix A). It includes the sentences, 'This allows any user to get the contact details (name, phone and e-mail) for a named member of staff at the university' and 'The user can see the full contact details for any entry in the list, along with a photo of the member of staff if one is available, by selecting that entry.' Together, these two sentences clearly suggest that data about an *individual* member of staff is delivered to users. The second sentence also suggests that the user interface includes a way to list members of staff. Producing a model showing both the database and user interface structures provides additional reassurance that the database design can support the users' requirements.

Web data design can be split into conceptual, logical and physical stages, just like database design. The **conceptual web data design** models what data is delivered to, or gathered from, end users and where in the database it comes from or goes to. It shows the links between the database entities and those parts of the user interface that interact directly with them. The design is documented as a UML class diagram (in effect, an enhanced ER diagram), but should also be included in the application glossary (see Chapter 7). At this stage, there is no Web-specific terminology and so the resulting model *could* be used as a basis for developing a traditional GUI application. It's this independence from the specific approach to developing a user interface that suggests the name *conceptual* web data design.

The **logical web data design** focuses on the particular approach to implementing a user interface taken by web technology and also on the chosen application architecture. It's logical by analogy with the logical database design, which focuses on a particular approach to data organization. In both cases, it is the approach, rather than particular technologies, that are important. So, for example, decisions about which browser technologies to support or which server-side scripting language to use are not relevant at this stage.

As most web database applications follow a three-tier architecture, the logical web data design needs to recognize the split between browser-side and server-side processing. The browser side deals with the presentation of data-centric content to users. This may be delivering data drawn from the database or gathering it from users to store in the database. The server side deals with the actual communication with the DBMS.

Physical web data design recognizes that each screen will be implemented using web pages and these will use certain web technologies. Several screens may be used to build a single web page. For example, the login screen *may* appear as part of every web page on a website. Thus, physical web data design tries to ensure that the communication between the web pages and the database is as efficient as possible. It is focused closely on data-centric issues and does not attempt to provide a full physical design for the website.

An important issue in physical web data design is whether or not to define database views, and stored functions, so that each web page queries a single database object. This simplifies the implementation of the server-side processing on the web server by shifting data-centric tasks firmly on to the database server. The performance implications of the alternative approaches should be assessed before a decision is made.

Another issue for physical web data design is whether or not to implement paging for database queries that will return many rows. Delivering thousands of results in a single web page will not endear the application to users.

There is no single, widely use approach to designing web database applications, so no single diagramming technique for web data design. Atzeni et al. (1999) suggest an approach that adds symbols for web pages to the traditional ER diagram (the same approach is used in Eaglestone and Ridley, 2001). The WebML initiative (www.webml.org) is a similar attempt to extend ER diagramming. It uses its own specialized diagramming notation to allow conceptual design for both the database and the website to be carried out in parallel (see Ceri et al., 2003). Conallen (2003) suggests extensions to the UML designed to facilitate web application design in its entirety. All three approaches recognize the need to model:

- what data is delivered by a web page
- which part of the database this data comes from
- navigation between data-centric web pages
- how the data is transported from the database to the web page.

The first three requirements are appropriate to the conceptual or logical stages of design. The fourth is closely related to the chosen implementation technologies, so is more of a physical design issue. It's important to model navigation because data-centric behaviour may involve more than one web page. For example, in the Staff Directory application, members of staff can update their support sessions. This entails first listing the support sessions for a member of staff. After they have chosen one, its details are displayed ready to be updated. This can involve two separate web pages. Notice that there is no consideration of the actual presentation of the web pages – only their data-centric content is considered during web data design. Conallen's work provides the basis for the approach discussed in this chapter as UML is the modelling language used in the rest of the book.

- Section 11.1 introduces the notion of a **screen** and explains its use in conceptual web data design. It discusses examples of screens to model web search pages, result pages and data entry forms.
- Section 11.2 examines the split between client-side and server-side behaviour.
- Section 11.3 considers some issues that arise during physical design. In particular, it introduces the notion of wrapper functions for database updates.

11.1 Conceptual web data design

Conceptual web data design expands the traditional ER diagram to include screens to represent those parts of the user interface that deliver data to end users. A screen may represent only a portion of a web page (or other GUI) that gathers data from, or delivers data to, end users. In both cases, the screen may manipulate the data in some way. It is important to emphasize that, in web data design, screens model data-centric behaviour only.

Consider the Get staff contact details use case (see Figure A.5, Appendix A). As mentioned above, the sentence 'This allows any user to get the contact details (name, phone and e-mail) for a named member of staff at the university.' and 'The user can see the full contact details . . . along with a photo of the member of staff if one is available . . .' suggest the need for a screen to deliver the contact details for a *single* member of staff. This screen is represented in the diagram as a class with the stereotype «screen». Each screen has a set of attributes that represent its dynamic content – that is, the data it gathers from or delivers to users. In Figure 11.1 (a), the conceptual design for the StaffDetail screen has four attributes. Note that the data types of the screen's attributes are different from those used for an entity's attributes. Rather than the data types typically available in a DBMS, they are the data types available on web pages. PCData is parsed character data – the data type of plain text content in an HTML document. The photograph of a member of staff has data type image as HTML documents treat images separately from character data. Other kinds of content, such as audio, video and so on, could be given the catch-all HTML data type Object or a more explicit data type, such as Video. The multiplicity constraint on the photo attribute indicates that a photograph of the member of staff is optional. Static content is *not* taken from the database, so is omitted from the screens of the conceptual web data design.

Using UML class diagrams is not the only possible approach to web data design. Another is to use HTML prototypes. These are better for modelling the static rather than the dynamic content, but can be used to model both. Figure 11.1 (b) shows the StaffDetails web page modelled using an HTML prototype. The image placeholder and hyperlink in Figure 11.1 (b) are dynamic content, but also indicate positioning on the final web page (not an issue covered by web data design). The labels 'Name', 'Phone' and 'Email' indicate positioning for the other dynamic content. If more information about the dynamic data is needed, then the image is annotated, typically by hand.

Figure 11.1 Designs for dynamic and static aspects of the Staff Details web page.

```
        «screen»
        StaffDetails
    ─────────────────
    name: PCData
    phone: PCData
    email: PCData
    photo: [0..1]: Image
```

(a) The conceptual web data design for the StaffDetails screen, showing dynamic content.

Figure 11.1 (*Continued*)

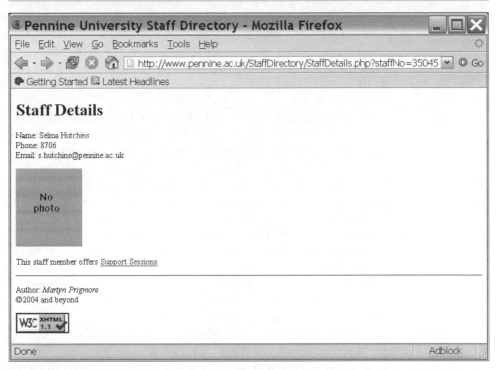

(b) An HTML prototype design for the `StaffDetails` web page, showing static and dynamic content.

Figure 11.2 A directed association between a screen and a database entity.

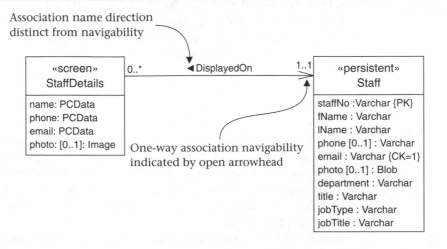

Each screen either delivers data drawn from the database to end users or gathers data from them to query or modify the database instance. This means that a screen is always associated with one or more database tables. Figure 11.2 shows the DisplayedOn association between the StaffDetails screen and the Staff entity. Unlike associations between two entities, this association can be navigated in one direction only – from screen to entity. Clearly an occurrence of the screen needs access to data held by an occurrence of the entity as it is the entity occurrence that holds the official version of these details. The screen merely delivers the data, it does not store it – screen data is transient, not persistent. That is why an occurrence of the entity does not need access to data delivered to end users by the screen. To indicate that the association is navigable in one direction only, an arrowhead is added to the association end by the Staff entity.

Don't mix up association navigability and the association name direction. In Figure 11.2, the association is navigable from screen to entity, but the association name is read in the other direction. Association navigability changes the meaning of the diagram. Making the DisplayedOn association navigable in one direction only means that the Staff entity cannot access the attributes or operations of the StaffDetails screen. The association name direction does not alter the meaning, so, renaming the association Displays, say, would change the name direction but not the meaning.

Another common mistake is to assume that the arrow notation indicates the direction that data flows between the two classes. In fact, the actual data flow in Figure 11.2 is in the *opposite* direction to the association navigation. The StaffDetails screen can access the attributes of the Staff entity to display data about a member of staff. Thus, the data must flow from the Staff entity to the StaffDetails screen – the opposite direction to the association navigability. In fact, in general, data can flow in either direction even if the association is navigable in one direction only. Suppose the StaffDetails screen was supposed to add details for a new member of staff to the database. It would still need to access the Staff entity, so the association would be navigable in the same direction. However, data now flows from the StaffDetails screen to the Staff entity! UML class diagrams are static models – the system is at rest, with no data flowing and no messages being passed. A one-way navigable association indicates that one class has *access to* the attributes and operations of the other class, but there is no such accessibility in the other direction. It says nothing about data flow.

Association navigability is important when it comes to implementing the design. The DisplayedOn association is navigable in one direction only, so there is no need to implement a mechanism to give the Staff entity access to the StaffDetails screen. On the other hand, the application developer must implement some mechanism to give the StaffDetails screen access to the Staff entity. As the StaffDetails screen displays a single member of staff, it must query the database using a candidate key.

A simple mechanism to implement the association is to ensure that the web page implementing the StaffDetails screen has, in addition to the listed attributes, a copy of the appropriate staffNo (or other candidate key for the Staff entity). This is not explicit in the use case description of the behaviour, but is a reasonably obvious solution. Just as foreign keys aren't included in ER diagrams, the staff number is not included as an attribute of the StaffDetails screen as it is an implementation mechanism, not a part of the conceptual design.

The multiplicity constraints on the DisplayedOn association provide additional information. Each occurrence of the StaffDetails screen displays a *single* occurrence of the Staff entity. A particular occurrence of the Staff entity may be displayed on zero or many occurrences of the StaffDetails screen – if no one asks the application for a person's details, then they will never be displayed, but if many users ask for those details, they will be displayed on many different occurrences of the screen.

Information about screens can be described using text rather than UML diagrams. Simply adapt the application glossary to hold information on screens and associations between screens and entities. Text-based approaches to web data design work well with prototyping, as it is awkward to add this information to a prototype web page. HTML comments could be used, but it is difficult to gather the information together.

The conceptual web data design will include a screen for each data-centric behaviour, just as the ER diagram includes an entity for each data organization structure. Typically, a use case mentions several related pieces of data-centric behaviour. For example, the Get staff contact details use case includes the following information:

- 'The user provides the staff member's surname and first initial and requests his or her contact details' – implying a screen that gathers data from users
- 'A list showing the name and phone number of each member of staff matching the search criteria is delivered, together with a count of the number of matches from the Staff Directory' – implying a screen that lists several members of staff.

In fact, these two pieces of behaviour are closely related. The first – gathering data from users – provides the search criteria for the second – listing staff who match these criteria. Thus, although this situation could be modelled as two separate screens, it makes sense to recognize that this is a single piece of data-centric behaviour consisting of two related actions. Modelling these as a single screen leaves open the option of splitting them at a later stage.

It is also possible to implement all the screens from the Get staff contact details use case as a single web page. The web page would consist of an HTML form to gather the search criteria, a section to list matches and a section to display details for a chosen match. The conceptual web data design does not limit the implementation options.

The Get staff contact details use case states that 'A list showing the name and phone number of each member of staff matching the search criteria is delivered, together with a count of the number of matches from the Staff Directory.' The screen for this behaviour clearly lists data from several occurrences of the Staff entity – a group of repeated data.

One simple approach to modelling a group of repeated data is to use attribute multiplicity. Figure 11.3 shows the StaffList screen modelled using this approach. The

Figure 11.3 Modelling repeating groups with attribute multiplicity.

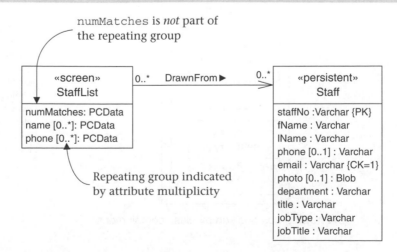

attributes name and phone both have a multiplicity of [0..*], indicating that they are part of the repeating group of data. The single-valued attribute numMatches tells users how many members of staff match their search criteria. Notice that its data type is PC-Data, rather than Numeric as there is no way to distinguish between character and numeric data on a web page.

This approach is simple to use, but has its drawbacks. There is no easy way to insist that each attribute repeats the same number of times, for example. An entity constraint attached as a note would do this, but seems a little inelegant. Also, if there were two or more different repeating groups on the same screen, more notes would be required.

The alternative, more sophisticated, approach to repeating groups is to include two screens. Figure 11.4 (a) shows how this is done. The original StaffList screen retains

Figure 11.4 Modelling repeating groups with composition.

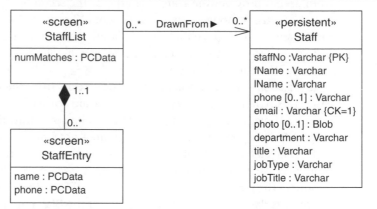

(a) A standard composition association.

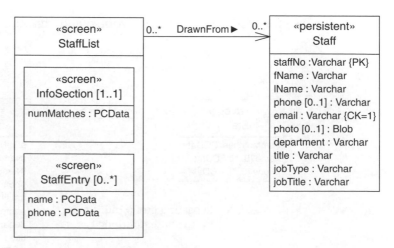

(b) Showing composition by class containment.

the single-valued attributes, while the attributes of the repeating group are extracted into a subscreen, StaffEntry. The attributes of StaffEntry are single-valued because each occurrence of StaffEntry represents a *single entry* on the list of staff members matching the search criteria. The composition association joining StaffList with StaffEntry indicates that the StaffEntry screen is really a part of the StaffList screen and does not have an independent existence. The multiplicity on this composition association says that the StaffList screen may contain zero or more StaffEntry on its list of staff members. This is what makes it a repeating group. The DrawnFrom association is still between the StaffList screen and the Staff entity. Because StaffEntry is a part of StaffList, it has access to the Staff entity via StaffList.

Figure 11.4 (b) shows an alternative way to model composition, which is by drawing the subscreens inside the main screen. In this case, an additional subscreen, InfoSection, is used to hold the non-repeating attributes. Also, each subscreen is given a multiplicity constraint in the name compartment. Thus, for each occurrence of StaffList, there is exactly one occurrence of InfoSection and zero or many occurrences of StaffEntry. This alternative to modelling composition is a little closer to the prototyping approach to web data design.

Screens such as StaffDetails and StaffList deliver data drawn from the database to end users. Clearly this involves a database query. The association identifies the target entity, but there is no explicit indication of the search criteria. When the multiplicity at the entity end of the association is 0..1 or 1..1, it's clear that the screen must identify which data it wants using the entity's candidate key (as discussed above). When the upper bound on the multiplicity is greater than one, it clearly does not use a candidate key. In this case, it is useful to indicate what the search criteria are. The mechanism for this is the **association qualifier**. Figure 11.5 shows an association qualifier at the StaffList end of the DrawnFrom association. The association qualifier has two attributes – lName and initial. They represent the search criteria specified in the use case 'The user provides the staff member's surname and first initial and requests his or her contact details.' The attributes of an association qualifier could be given a data type, though this is not done in Figure 11.5.

Figure 11.5 Using association qualifiers to model search criteria.

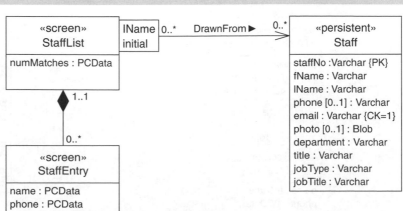

When an association end has a qualifier, the meaning of the multiplicity constraint at the other end alters. It now represents the number of occurrences of the Staff entity linked with the StaffList screen for particular values of the qualifier attributes. In this case, adding the association qualifier hasn't changed this multiplicity constraint as the search criteria will match zero or more occurrences of Staff. Multiplicity at the end of the association with the qualifier is not affected.

The attributes of the association qualifier are part of the association itself, and provide additional information on the data requirements of the application. Notice that the attributes of the association qualifier need not be attributes of either of the classes that participate in the association. Neither the StaffList screen nor the Staff entity has an attribute called initial. This allows for the situation where the final web page does not display the search criteria to end users. In other situations, the search criteria will be displayed on the final web page.

Suppose that the Staff Directory application includes a screen SuppSessSearch that allows users to enter a day and time and lists all staff who offer support sessions at that time. It makes sense to echo back the search criteria in this situation, so the screen SuppSessSearch includes searchDay and searchTime attributes (Figure 11.6). Notice that these screen attributes have the data type PCData, while the association qualifier attributes have data types appropriate to data drawn from the database.

The screens named **StaffEntry** in Figures 11.5 and 11.6 are identical. It would be feasible, in a combined diagram, to use a single **StaffEntry** screen and give it composition associations with both **StaffList** and **SuppSessSearch**. The alternative is to rename one of the screens.

The SuppSessSearch screen draws its data from the Staff entity, but searches the entity based on attributes of the SupportSession entity. Code listing 11.1.1 shows an

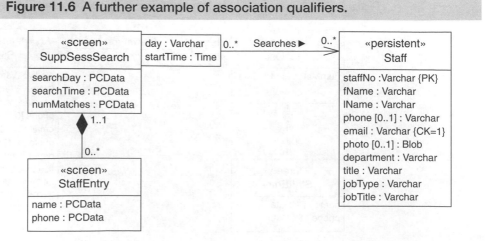

Figure 11.6 A further example of association qualifiers.

SQL select statement that will achieve this for particular values of the day and start time. Hence, this is a viable application behaviour.

Code listing 11.1.1 Querying `Staff` based on data about `SupportSession`

```
SELECT * FROM Staff
WHERE staffNo IN (SELECT staffNo FROM SupportSession
                  WHERE day='Tuesday'
                  AND startTime BETWEEN '11:30' AND '13:30')
```

The data requirements of the search are easily modelled using the association qualifier in Figure 11.6. However, it isn't clear from this diagram that the search criteria of the association qualifier are data drawn from the SupportSession entity – in fact, the SupportSession entity isn't present in the diagram.

One way to model this is to add operations to represent database searches. The operation should be part of the class that actually performs the search, so, in this case, the operation is added to the Staff entity. Figure 11.7 shows the revised class diagram. The Staff entity has a new operation – searchBySupport() – that expects the two parameters day and start.

Figure 11.7 Modelling database searches as operations on the entity being searched.

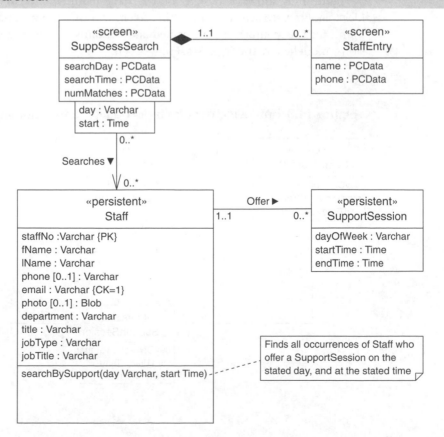

The names of these parameters match the two attributes of the association qualifier. This is the simplest way to indicate that the attributes of the association qualifier are inputs to the searchBySupport( ) operation.

The operation has, as usual, a method note attached to it to document what the operation does. Figure 11.7 also shows that the association qualifier can be attached to any side of the relevant class, as long as its box is drawn a little shorter or narrower than the class itself.

Only data-centric behaviour, such as database searches, should be included in the conceptual web data design. Figure 11.7 could include an operation on StaffEntry to model the merging of the Staff.fName and Staff.lName attributes into the StaffEntry screen's name attribute. An alternative would be to model this as a derived attribute on Staff, possibly with an operation to maintain its value. The SuppSessSearch could also have an operation to calculate its numMatches attribute, although the attribute name alone makes it fairly clear how to calculate this particular value. It is a matter of personal style how far to take this. If the behaviour is already fully worked out in a separate part of the application design, then there is little benefit to be gained from redoing that work during web data design. However, it *is* worth checking that the database design meets the data requirements of any operations already defined.

The examples so far have only involved a screen retrieving data from the database. Some screens will modify the database. For example, members of staff can maintain their support session details.

Figure 11.8 shows a design for the data requirements of this behaviour. The MaintainSuppSess screen is the main screen. It shows the number of support sessions found for the member of staff named and contains a repeating group of support sessions, modelled by the SuppSessEntry screen.

Figure 11.8 Retrieving data from the database for updating.

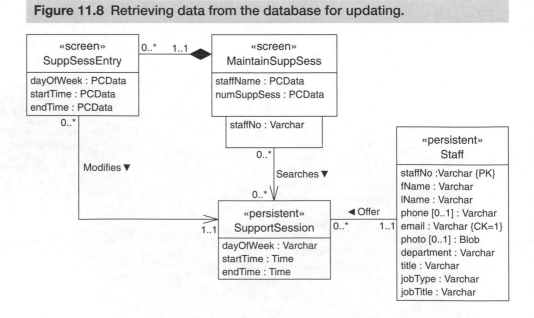

The Searches association indicates that the support session data for MaintainSuppSess and, by composition, for SuppSessEntry too, is retrieved from the SupportSession entity. The association qualifier has an attribute staffNo, so support sessions are retrieved based on their association with a particular occurrence of Staff, via the Offer association.

A separate association, Modifies, models the actual data modification (either adding a new support session or modifying an existing one). As it is the individual support session entries that are modified, this association links SuppSessEntry with SupportSession. Notice that the multiplicity constraint on Searches means that a search may not retrieve any support sessions, while that on Modifies means that each data modification affects exactly one support session.

One last point worth noting. The *conceptual* web data design can actually be based on the *logical* database design. This is because it is concerned with developing a conceptual understanding of the way that the user interface interacts with the database. The logical database design is a better representation of the actual database, so should be used in preference to the conceptual database design. In particular, in a conceptual database design it is possible for associations to have attributes of their own. If a web page needs to deliver these attributes to end users, then there will be an association between the screen and the *association* that has these attributes rather than between the screen and some persistent entity. This is allowed in UML, but looks very odd. In a logical database design, all attributes belong to entities, so the oddity of an association between a screen and another association will not arise.

11.2 Logical web data design

Conceptual web data design identifies what data is required by the user interface. Data delivered to users from the database or gathered from them to update the database is represented as attributes of a screen. Data gathered from users as search criteria are represented as attributes of an association qualifier.

Logical web data design takes these requirements and begins to describe how they will be met. The main focus is on adapting the design to the technology used to deliver a typical three-tier web database application. The logical web data design models the split between the web client and web server. Database communication is carried out by server-side scripts, while the client side deals with user interaction. If the conceptual web data design was based on the conceptual database design, then the first task of logical web data design is to revise the UML class diagram to take account of any changes made in moving from the conceptual to the logical ER diagram. This is mostly concerned with adding new link and look-up entities and considering how they affect associations between the screens and database entities. Once this has been done, the main task of logical web data design begins.

Each screen in the conceptual web data design communicates with the database, so there will be a **server page** in the logical web data design. The server page is represented

Figure 11.9 The client page and server page generated from the StaffDetails screen.

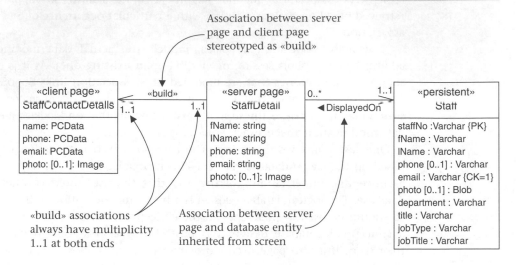

Association between server page and client page stereotyped as «build»

«build» associations always have multiplicity 1..1 at both ends

Association between server page and database entity inherited from screen

as a class with the stereotype «server page», as shown in Figure 11.9. The server page inherits the original screen's association with the database entity. As before, this association is navigable in one direction only – from the server page to the database entity.

The attributes of the StaffDetail server page in Figure 11.9 are slightly different from those of the StaffDetail screen in Figure 11.2. The staff member's name is modelled as fName and lName rather than the single attribute name. This is a minor change and simply emphasizes that the server page will need to combine the fName and lName values drawn from the Staff entity to deliver the required data to end users. The data types of these attributes are different from those of the screen and entity and are the ones likely to be supported by a server-side scripting language (string, float, int and so on).

> There is no restriction on which technology implements the server page. It might be a PHP script, CGI program, ColdFusion script or any other server-side processing technology capable of communicating with the database.

Each screen also communicates with end users. This aspect of the screen's behaviour is modelled as a **client page** – a class with the stereotype «client page» (Figure 11.9).

In the logical web data design, a client page will always be built by some server page. This reflects how server-side scripting works. An end user actually requests the server page and this builds an HTTP response, which the web server sends to the end user as a client page (see Chapter 4). To indicate this, an association stereotyped «build» is drawn between the client page and the server page that builds it.

The **build association** is navigable from the server page to the client page. An occurrence of the server page builds the associated occurrence of the client page, line by line. Clearly, the server page needs access to the client page, but the client page does not even need to know which server page built it. The multiplicity constraints on a build association are always 1..1 at both ends. Each occurrence of the server page is executed by the web server in response to a single HTTP request and builds a single occurrence of the client page as the HTTP response. Similarly, each occurrence of the client page is an HTTP response to a single HTTP request, so was itself built by a single server page.

In fact, Figure 11.9 represents the simplest possible situation – one screen from the conceptual web data design has been replaced by a server page and a client page with a build association between them. This is typical of how the screens in the conceptual web data design transform into client pages and server pages in the logical web data design. For each association between a screen and an entity, create a server page associated with that entity. Turn the original screen into a client page and introduce a build association between the server page and the client page.

The conceptual web data design for the StaffList screen (Figure 11.5) provides a more complex example. Here, the screen is split into two parts – StaffList and StaffEntry, joined by a composition association. This division reflects the need to deliver a repeating group of attributes to end users, along with a single-valued attribute numMatches.

Clearly, this is a client-side issue, which is reflected in the design of the client pages in the logical web data design (Figure 11.10). A build association links the main client page, StaffList, to the server page StaffSearch. There is no need to include a build association between the server page StaffSearch and the StaffEntry client page as the composition association indicates that StaffEntry is really just a part of StaffList, so will be built by the same server page.

Figure 11.10 introduces two additional features of the logical web data design:

- a **form** to gather data from users
- a **submit association** showing which server page processes the form data.

Figure 11.10 Logical web data design for searching for staff by surname and initial.

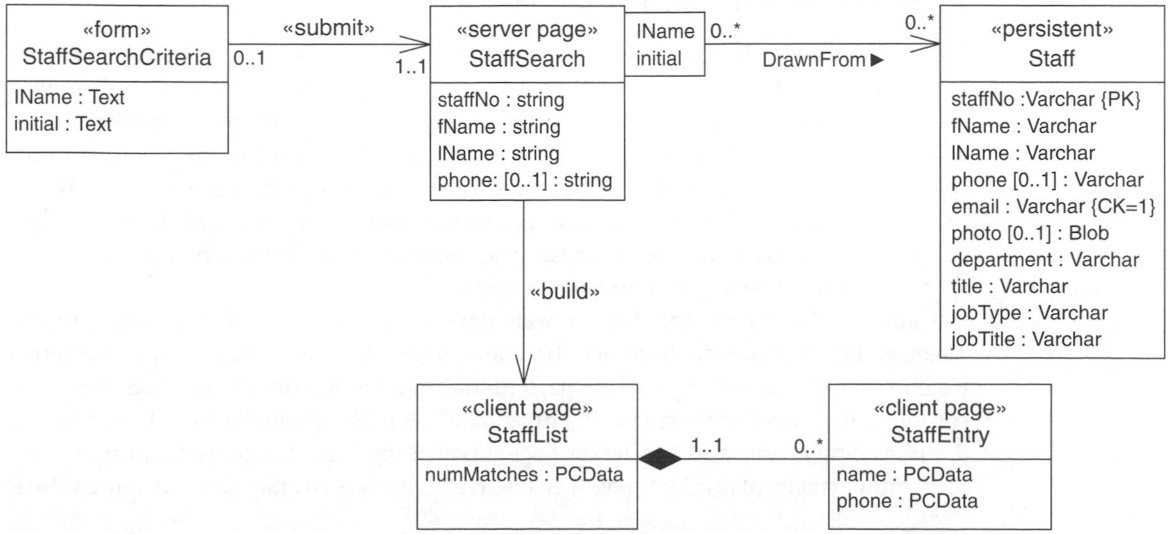

The StaffSearchCriteria class is the form, indicated by the stereotype «form». Notice that the data types of form attributes are different again as they represent the different types of control on an HTML form – text, password, tick box and so on.

Each form gathers data from end users and submits the data to a server page for processing, indicated by a submit association between the form and server page. A submit association is only navigable from the form to the server page. It is the form that calls an occurrence of the server page into existence, so clearly the form needs to access the server page. In contrast, once the server page is up and running, it does not care where its search criteria came from, so does not need access to the form. The multiplicity at the server page end of a submit association is always 1..1. The multiplicity at the form end could be 1..1 or 0..1. The multiplicity 1..1 indicates that the form is the only way to request the server page and 0..1 that there are other ways to request the server page.

It is useful to include forms such as StaffSearch in the logical web data design as they complete the specification of the search behaviour – they gather search criteria from users, use these to search the database and deliver search results back to users. The alternative is to rely on the association qualifier to indicate what search criteria are used by a server page.

Conallen states that a form must be part of a client page as, on a valid web page, an HTML form element is always contained in an HTML element. This is true, but it seems simpler to regard the «form» stereotype as a special kind of «client page» – one that gathers data from end users. As one client page can include other client pages (such as repeating groups), there is no problem with a client page containing a form.

Screens that modify the database instance are more complex again. There are, typically, two pieces of server-side behaviour:

- retrieving data from the database for modification by end users
- writing these modifications back to the database.

Figure 11.8 shows the conceptual web data design for the screen that allows users to maintain support session data. In this case, users are presented with a list of support sessions and can modify any one of them. The main screen, MaintainSuppSess, is involved in retrieving data from the database (the Searches association). Clearly it must split into a client page and a server page. The subscreen SuppSessEntry displays an existing support session, gathers changes to this from users and writes the changed support session back to the database (the Modifies association). It, too, must also split – this time into a form and a server page.

Figure 11.11 shows the logical web data design for the above. The original MaintainSuppSess screen becomes the client page MaintainSuppSess and the server page RetrieveSuppSess. The server page RetrieveSuppSess inherits the Searches association with the SupportSession entity. The SuppSessEntry screen becomes the SuppSessEntry form and the server page ModifySuppSess. SuppSessEntry must be a form rather than a plain client page because it allows users to change its attribute values.

Figure 11.11 Logical web data design for database retrieval and update behaviour.

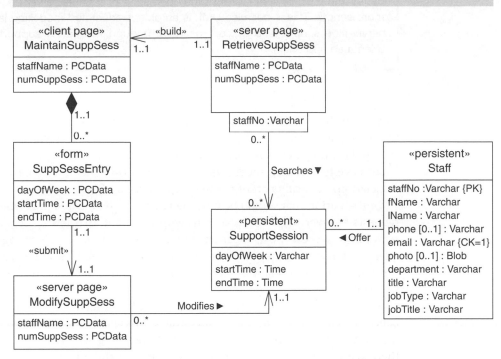

The original SuppSessEntry screen was associated with a database entity via Modifies and, here, the server page ModifySuppSess inherits this association. ModifySuppSess is also associated with the SuppSessEntry form, but it is *not* a build association. The purpose of the server page is to accept data from the form and write it to the database. Hence, the two are connected by a submit association. The composition association between MaintainSuppSess and SuppSessEntry is inherited directly from the conceptual web data design. It implies that SuppSessEntry is part of the MaintainSuppSess client page, so RetrieveSuppSess must build *both* the client page *and* the form it contains.

This example is more complex than that of the search behaviour, but the same general rules clearly apply. Screens associated with a database entity split into a server page, which handles communication with the database, and a client page or form, which handles communication with end users. If the original screen only delivered data to users, then it would become a client page and have a build association with the server page. If the original screen only gathered data from users, then it would become a form and have a submit association with its server page. When, however, a single screen both retrieves data from the database *and* gathers data from end users, it will have two separate associations with the database – one to represent data retrieval and one to represent data modification. The screen itself therefore becomes a form as it must both deliver data to and gather data from end users. Each of the associations generates a server page – one to build the form and one for the form to submit its data to. An alternative approach is to have a single server page and model the different parts of the behaviour as different operations of that page.

> The actual implementation as, for example, PHP scripts may bundle two server pages into a single script, or split the operations of a single server page into two or more scripts. This is because UML is an object-orientated modelling language, but server-side scripts tend to be procedural (though PHP does support the object-orientated approach).

Sometimes it is useful to model associations between client pages. Strictly speaking, these are part of the user experience design as they model navigation paths through the application. Such links are never data-centric. Although data may pass from one client page to the next, there is no communication with the database server, so these associations are really part of the user experience design.

One situation that should be modelled in the web data design is when a client page requests a server page. Forms do this with a submit association, requesting that the server page process the data gathered by the form. Ordinary client pages may also request that a server page carry out some processing. The HTML mechanism for this is the hyperlink, so a **link association** is added to the web data design to model this situation.

Figures 11.9 and 11.10 provide good examples of a client page linking to a server page. In Figure 11.10, end users search the database for staff with a given surname and first initial. The server page builds a list of matching staff entries in response. Users then select one staff entry from the list to request the full contact details for a single member of staff. This is a clear example of a client page linking to a server page using a hyperlink rather than an HTML form. Figure 11.9 shows how these full contact details are retrieved from the database.

Figure 11.12 combines both diagrams to represent the full data requirements of the staff search behaviour. The only *new* information in this diagram is the link association, stereotyped as «link», between the StaffEntry client page and the StaffDetails server page. This link association indicates that the StaffEntry client page can request the StaffDetails server page from the web server. In the final application, such a request results in the web server running the PHP script that implements the StaffDetails server page. Like build associations, the multiplicity at both ends of a link association is always 1..1, so can be omitted from the diagram. Notice that there is no association qualifier on the link association. Association qualifiers indicate that the class at the qualified end of the association searches for particular instances of the class at the other end. In a link association, this is not the case. The client page *does not* search for particular instances of the server page – it requests that the server page search the database.

The logical web data design in Figure 11.12 includes all the features needed to model the way in which the user interface of a web database application communicates with the application's database. It includes a form to gather data from end users, server pages to process this data and client pages to deliver data retrieved from the database. A submit association models the fact that a form must request that a server page process its data, while build associations model the fact that a server page builds a client page as its response to such a request. A link association models the fact that a client page may also request a server page to carry out its processing.

Figure 11.12 Logical web data design for the complete staff search behaviour.

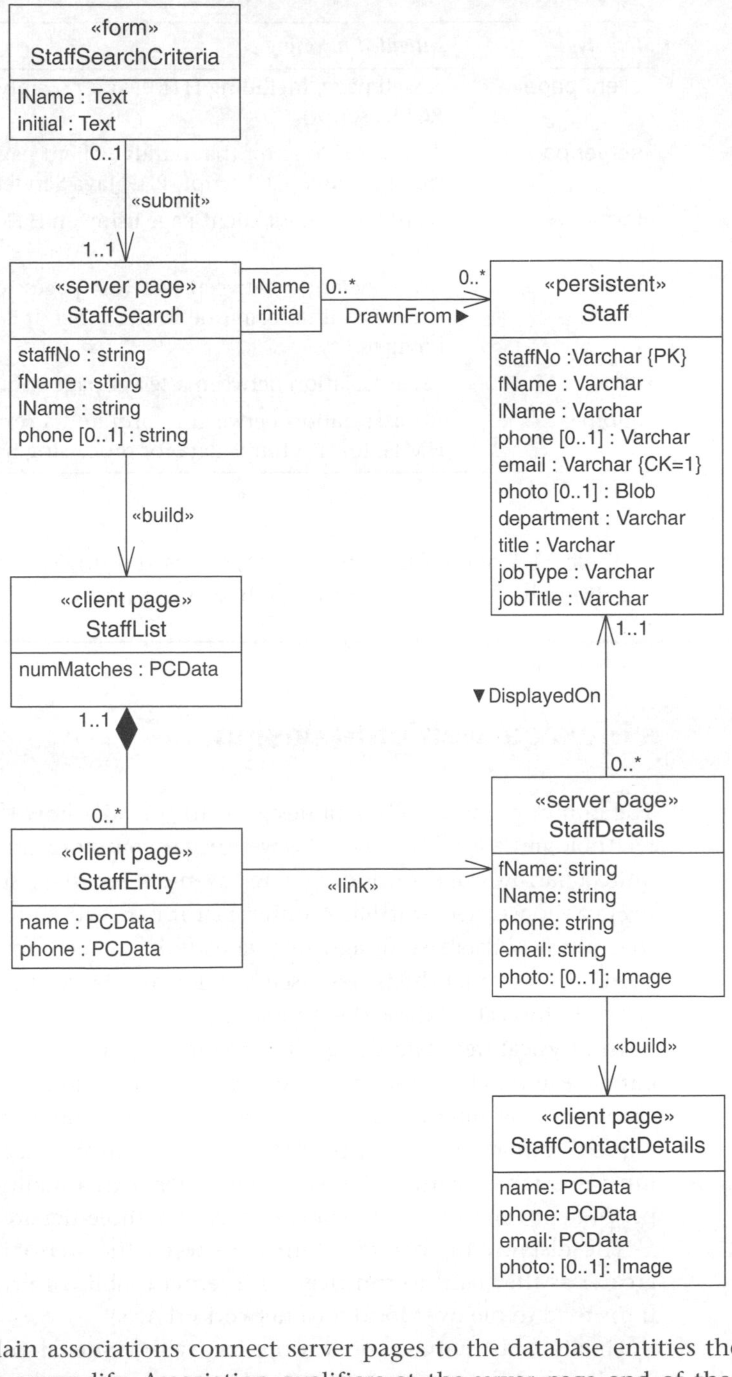

Finally, plain associations connect server pages to the database entities they retrieve data from or modify. Association qualifiers at the server page end of these associations indicate the search criteria (the DrawnFrom association) and where the search is by candidate key the association qualifier is usually omitted (the DisplayedOn association).

Table 11.1 Summary of Conallen's web application extensions to UML used in logical web data design.

Stereotype	Intended meaning
«client page»	A web page, including HTML and possibly browser script logic (such as ECMA script).
«server page»	A server-side script that builds a client page using server-side programming (such as CGI script, PHP, Java Servlet).
«form»	A special kind of client page using an HTML form to gather input from users.
«link»	An association between two web pages (of any kind), indicating that there is a link from one to the other. It can have one-way or two-way navigability.
«build»	An association between a server page and the client page it builds.
«submit»	An association between a form and a server page, indicating that the HMTL form submits data for processing by the server page.

Table 11.1 summarizes the stereotypes used in logical web data design to represent the different elements of a web database application.

11.3 Physical web data design

The aim of physical web data design is to consider how the particular choice of web technologies affects the way the web pages communicate with the database. This is quite a narrow scope, excluding many Web-only matters, such as optimizing the workings of the web server itself. Another factor narrowing the scope of this design task is that physical database design may already have been done (see Chapter 10). If not, then it is likely that the issues discussed here will be considered at the same time as the general physical database design issues.

In physical web data design, improving response times is an important task. Web database applications tend to have slower response times than those using a traditional graphical user interface (GUI). There are three good reasons for this. The stateless request–response model of the HTTP protocol means that web client and web server must re-establish contact for each request whereas a traditional GUI client will have a permanent connection to its server, even in a three-tier architecture.

The distance (in network terms) between the web client and the web server is greater as they tend to run over an internet (public or private) whereas GUI applications tend to run over local area networks (LANs).

Finally, web database applications have a three-tier architecture. The web server will usually need to communicate with the database server before responding to an HTTP request and may need to re-establish a connection first. In a traditional database application, however, the connection is persistent.

One approach to improving the response times for a web page is to ensure that it queries a single database table. Single-table selects tend to be quicker than table joins and are certainly quicker than executing two select statements and trying to combine their data in the PHP (or other server-side) code. This is the approach taken in the Staff Directory – one web page delivers staff contact details and a second delivers details of his or her support sessions (Figures 11.13 (a) and (b)).

However, each separate web page entails an additional HTTP request. If the additional information is viewed infrequently, then the performance cost of the occasional additional HTTP request is probably acceptable. If, instead, it is almost always viewed by end users, then both the performance cost of the additional HTTP request and the plain inconvenience of having to click on that hyperlink will outweigh the cost of implementing a table join. In this latter case, the design should combine staff contact details and support sessions on a single web page.

Once the decision to deliver data from two tables on a single web page has been taken, the design should ensure that the database query is quick and easy. The database designer should certainly consider adding an index on the foreign key columns – the `SupportSession.staffNo` column in this case. Another refinement is to create a view. As mentioned in Chapter 6, the view definition – a join query in this case – is stored in the data dictionary so the DBMS can optimize how the query is

Figure 11.13 Using separate pages for staff details and their support sessions.

(a) The `Staff Details` web page for Selma Hutchins.

Figure 11.13 (*Continued*)

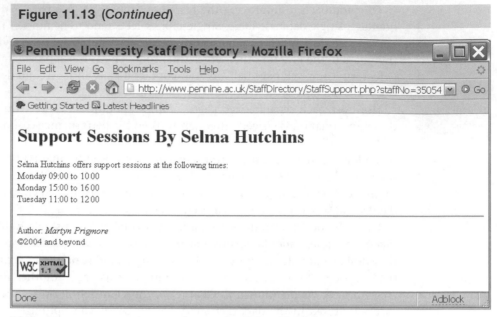

(b) The `Support Sessions` web page for Selma Hutchins.

executed. This means that querying the view will generally be quicker than querying the underlying base tables with a join query. Another benefit of views is that they simplify the server page. The application developer must still write an SQL select statement, but it involves only a single table (remember, a view is a derived table).

Database modification statements can be shifted entirely to the database server by using a **stored function**. A stored function is a piece of application code stored in the database, like a trigger. The main difference is that triggers execute in response to database events, whereas stored functions are executed on the instructions of the database client. SQL stored functions have the same role as PHP functions and are defined in a similar way. The SQL **create function statement** instructs the DBMS to create a stored function on the database. Figure 11.14 shows the structure of the SQL create function statement. It begins with the keywords CREATE FUNCTION, followed by an SQL identifier – the name of the stored function. There is an optional list of parameters, consisting of a parameter name (an SQL identifier as usual) and data type. The parameter list is followed by the keyword RETURNS and the data type of the value returned by the function.

SQL also allows you to create **stored procedures**. These do *not* include a return value. Instead, each parameter declaration begins with one of the three keywords IN, OUT and INOUT. These indicate whether the parameter passes data into the procedure from the calling program or back to the calling program or both. There is no return value from a stored procedure – data can only be passed back to the calling program via OUT and INOUT parameters. Using this mechanism, stored procedures can pass more data back to the calling program.

Figure 11.14 The ISO SQL:2003 syntax for creating a stored function.

A list of parameters
to the function

The code to execute;
may include SQL
procedural and data
manipulation statements

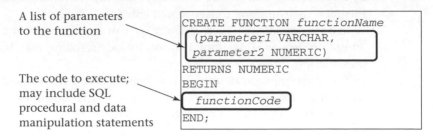

```
CREATE FUNCTION functionName
  (parameter1 VARCHAR,
   parameter2 NUMERIC)
RETURNS NUMERIC
BEGIN
   functionCode
END;
```

Stored functions are often used as **wrapper functions** for SQL insert, update and delete statements. They are particularly useful when data must be validated before an insert or update statement or when a delete statement needs to remove rows from two tables linked by a foreign key. Their main advantage is that they can simplify the coding of server pages. A server page does not need to include the data manipulation statements – it simply passes data to the stored function. Code listing 11.3.1 shows how to create a wrapper function for deleting staff and their support sessions.

Within the function code, each statement is terminated by a semicolon. This causes problems as the first semicolon would usually terminate the create function statement itself! The MySQL DBMS gets round this by allowing the application developer to set a different SQL statement delimiter. The first line in Code listing 11.3.1 shows how to set the SQL statement delimiter to '//' and set it back to the usual ';' at the end. The MySQL DBMS regards the first three semicolons as part of the stored function definition and the '//' on the eleventh line as the create function statement delimiter.

Notice that the parameter names begins with the prefix prm. This is a coding convention to ensure that parameter names and column names don't clash.

Code listing 11.3.1   A stored function to remove a member of staff and all his or her support sessions using the MySQL DBMS

```
DELIMITER //
CREATE FUNCTION DeleteStaff (prmStaffNo VARCHAR)
RETURNS BOOLEAN
BEGIN
  DELETE FROM SupportSession
  WHERE staffNo=prmStaffNo;

  DELETE FROM Staff
  WHERE staffNo=prmStaffNo;
END;
//
DELIMITER ;
```

Some forms and client pages include repeating groups of data. If the maximum number of entries in the repeating group will always be small, then they can easily be delivered on a single web page. This is the case with the list of support sessions offered by a member of staff (Figure 11.13 (b)), but may not be the case with the list of staff members matching some given search criteria.

In a traditional GUI, such repeating groups are displayed in a scrolling list. This is an option here as HTML form controls include scrolling lists, but such lists limit the presentation options.

The most common alternative is to present a long list as a *series* of web pages, each delivering a fixed, maximum number of rows. This complicates the task of the server page, though. First, it will be called repeatedly as the user navigates through the list. Each time, it must retrieve from the database the next set of matches to the original database query and provide a navigation mechanism so that users can move forwards or backwards through the list.

Some DBMS have extended the syntax of the select statement to allow users to specify which rows of the result set to return (see Chapter 7). Code listing 11.3.2 shows the MySQL DBMS limit clause. The select statement will return the sixth to tenth rows of the result set (the first row is row 0, the second row is row 1 and so on). This provides the application developer with a way to control which chunks of the result set the server page displays. On the first page, it will display the first chunk of records, say five, and a link to the 'next' page. This link simply calls the same server page, but instructs it to change the limit clause on the select statement so it shows the next chunk of records.

Code listing 11.3.2   *Specifying which rows of the result set to return using the limit clause of the MySQL DBMS*

```
SELECT staffNo, fName||' '||lName, phone
FROM Staff
WHERE lName='Smith'
AND fName LIKE 'a%'
LIMIT 5,9
```

Deciding whether to present lists as single or multiple web pages involves assessing the performance of the two approaches. Where the results are presented in a single web page, there is a single database query and a single HTTP request. Where results are presented across multiple web pages, there are multiple database queries, which increase the workload of the database server, and multiple HTTP requests, which increase the workload of the web server. For medium-sized result sets, of a few tens of records, the single-page option is clearly more efficient. Even so, the user experience design may include a non-functional requirement banning 'long' web pages. In this case, the elegance of the presentation may outweigh the efficiency gains.

For very large result sets, a single web page may actually be less efficient than multiple web pages. There are two reasons for this. First, an HTTP response is sent across the network as a series of IP packets (see Chapter 2). These must be reassembled at the client into the original HTTP response message. The larger the HTTP response, the more packets there are and the longer it can take to do this and actually display the web page. Sending just the first few rows of the result set will mean that they are displayed quickly and, with luck, users will find what they are looking for on this first page. This is the approach most search engines take – send the top ten results first and you may never have to send the rest. The second reason for multiple pages perhaps being more efficient is that the DBMS will remember the execution plan for the select statement, so, when the second chunk of data is requested, the select statement will execute faster – the additional burden on the database server is therefore not as great as might be expected.

The physical web data design issues discussed above focus on how to improve performance by changing the server-side script's code. However, there is one technical issue that should be considered as part of physical web data design – how to manage connections to the DBMS.

Chapter 4 explained that it is good practice to close a DBMS connection at the end of each PHP script using the `mysql_close()` function. If the application developer does not close the connection, then, usually, the application server will. This is because the DBMS must devote some of its resources to checking all open connections for activity. If there are a lot of open, but unused, connections, then the DBMS is wasting its resources. Thus, it makes sense to close the DBMS connection when a server-side script finishes.

The problem with this is that opening a new DBMS connection also takes up resources, as discussed in Chapter 2. One option is to try and reuse the DBMS connection by having a server-side script open a **persistent connection**. Persistent connections are simply DBMS connections that do *not* close when the server-side script finishes. Instead, the application server keeps the connection open. The next time a server-side script tries to open a connection to the same DBMS using the same authorization identifier, the application server simply reuses the one it currently has open. Persistent connections make sense when a web database application gets a lot of use. In such cases, there is always likely to be a server-side script that can reuse the persistent connection. As the persistent connection is then rarely idle, the DBMS is not wasting resources by checking it for activity. PHP includes the function `mysql_pconnect()` to establish a persistent connection, as shown in the PHP fragment in Code listing 11.3.3.

Code listing 11.3.3 Creating a persistent connection to the MySQL DBMS in PHP

```
$connection = mysql_pconnect('localhost', 'martyn',
'martynpassword');
```

Persistent connections don't provide a stateful link between end users and the database server. Most web database applications don't give end users a DBMS authorization identifier. Instead, the application itself is given a DBMS authorization identifier. All the server-side scripts connect to the DBMS using this authorization identifier, even if they are doing so on behalf of different end users. Thus, the persistent connection could be used by many different end users. Persistent connections can also overload the DBMS. Many web servers are capable of dealing with multiple HTTP requests. They do this by creating multiple 'HTTP subservers', each of which can have a connection to the DBMS. These 'HTTP subservers' tend to hang around even when they have nothing to do. Some DBMS can only support a small number of connections, however, so if there are too many HTTP subservers, then they will use up all the available connections.

> 'HTTP subservers' is not a widely used term, though it captures the general idea. Only multiprocess (such as Apache) or multithreaded (such as Microsoft Internet Information Server) HTTP servers create them.
>
> The specific techniques for managing the HTTP subservers in multiprocess and multithreaded environments isn't important here. What is is the fact that such HTTP servers will hang on to any persistent connections for quite a while. PHP persistent connections cannot be closed by the `mysql_close()` function, either. They really do persist, so use with care.

Chapter summary

- This chapter has discussed web data design, which acts as an additional check that the database design can meet all the requirements of the web database application. It extends the ER diagram, which only includes database objects, to model objects from the user interface using the same UML notation.

- Conceptual web data design gives a good overview of what data is used by which pieces of user behaviour. Logical web data design provides a way to map these data requirements on to the client and server pages of a web database application. Physical web data design considers performance issues. The names for the three stages are not standard, but are used by analogy with the well-established names for the three stages of database design.

Further reading

The stereotypes used in web data design represent only a portion of Conallen's web application extensions for UML. A fuller discussion of his approach is presented in his book on the topic (Conallen, 2003). Ceri et al. (2003) provides the official WebML reference.

Review questions

11.1 Explain what is done during the process of web data design. Distinguish between the conceptual, logical and physical stages of web data design.

11.2 Explain the following concepts used during conceptual web data design:
- (a) screen
- (b) association navigability
- (c) association qualifier.

11.3 Explain the two approaches to representing repeating groups during conceptual web data design.

11.4 Explain the following concepts used during logical web data design:
(a) server page
(b) client page
(c) build association
(d) form
(e) submit association
(f) link association.

11.5 Explain how a screen from the conceptual web data design is represented in the logical web data design.

11.6 Explain the following concepts used during physical web data design:
(a) stored function
(b) wrapper function.

11.7 Explain why it is better to design web pages that query a single table. When might this approach be inappropriate?

11.8 Why would you use a wrapper function?

11.9 Explain the benefits and drawbacks of presenting a result set across multiple web pages.

11.10 What is a persistent connection? Why would you use one?

Exercises

11.11 The Web Timetable case study is documented in Appendix B. Figure 9.18 is a logical ER diagram for this case study. Using this *logical* ER diagram as a basis, do the following.
(a) Develop a *conceptual* web data design for the 'View room facilities' use case in Appendix B.
(b) Develop a conceptual web data design for the 'Book additional facilities' use case in Appendix B. Explain why it is better to use the logical ER diagram in Figure 9.18 as the basis for this conceptual web data design than the conceptual ER diagram in Figure 9.17.
(c) Complete the conceptual web data design for the Web Timetable case study in Appendix B by drawing one or more diagrams for each of the remaining use cases.

11.12 Using your solutions to Exercise 11.11 above as a starting point:
(a) develop a logical web data design for the 'View room facilities' use case
(b) develop a logical web data design for the 'Book additional facilities' use case
(c) complete the logical web data design for this case study.

11.13 In Exercise 9.13 you developed a logical ER diagram for the Pennine University's Accommodation Office. Using that ER diagram as a basis, develop *conceptual* web data designs for the following web pages:
(a) a web page to allow staff to list all rental agreements for a particular student
(b) a web page to allow staff to amend the details of a hall of residence
(c) a web page to allow staff to add a new rental agreement for an existing student to rent an existing room.

11.14 Using your solutions to Exercise 11.13 above as a starting point, develop logical web data designs for each of those web pages.

11.15 What physical design issues should be addressed regarding the web data designs for Exercise 11.14 above?

11.16 Write two sets of server-side scripts to allow users to add, modify and remove support sessions. One set of scripts should code the SQL data modification statements themselves, while the second should use wrapper functions, calling these from the server-side script. Critically evaluate the two approaches. Which is easier to write? Which will be easier to maintain?

Investigations

11.17 Investigate alternative approaches to web data design. Possible sources include Ceri et al. (2003) for WebML, Atzeni et al. (1999) and Eaglestone and Ridley (2001). How do they compare to the approach described in this chapter?

11.18 It should be clear from the exercises that a lot of web data designs follow a similar pattern. The study of such design patterns is a well-established area of research. Investigate the use of design patterns in the context of web database applications.

11.19 In Investigation 9.19 you developed a logical database design for an organization that you know. Use this as the basis for developing a set of conceptual and logical web data designs for a representative range of web application functions (such as search, item details, data modification). What physical web data design decisions would you make for your application?

11.20 Most books on web design pay little attention to the sort of functional design discussed in this chapter. Conversely, this chapter has not covered the user experience design issues that are more familiar to web designers. Investigate the sorts of web design issues more commonly discussed in web design textbooks.

12 XML

Chapter outline

There is a lot of activity around XML at the moment, and a lot of interest in using it as an alternative to relational databases. The pros and cons of XML as a data model were discussed in Chapter 3. This chapter focuses on XML technologies and approaches to database design for XML.

As XML technologies emerged more recently than relational DBMS, there is no stable list of widely used XML technologies. This chapter focuses on two technologies to support the database approach that are now fairly stable.

The RELAX NG schema language for XML allows the XML database developer to specify the general structure of documents for an XML application. Together with a validating parser, it plays a role analogous to the SQL data definition language's create table statement. RELAX NG forms part of a suite of proposed ISO international standards for document schema definition languages, so is likely to be in use for some time.

The XPath language provides a way to locate and, to some extent, extract data from an XML instance document. The analogy with the SQL data manipulation language's select statement is a little more tenuous, though XPath could be regarded as a more powerful version of the where clause. There are more powerful XML query languages, but as yet they are neither widely implemented nor widely used.

Approaches to logical design for XML are more stable. The availability of relational style keys in XML means that many of the techniques used in logical design for the relational data model can be applied, with some tweaks, to logical design for XML. The added complexity of the XDM organization structures allows greater flexibility when translating from the organization structures of the conceptual design to those of the XDM. However, the general approach should be familiar.

Before delving into XML technologies, one omission from the discussion in Chapter 3 needs to be remedied: XML namespaces. They were omitted before as the XDM is complicated enough in itself. Namespaces allow two or more XML languages to be used simultaneously in the same XML document without the parsers getting confused. They are discussed first.

- Section 12.1 discusses XML namespaces.

- Section 12.2 introduces the XML schema language RELAX NG and discusses how to use it to define the structure of an XML document model. It also discusses support for relational style keys by means of the RELAX NG DTD compatibility data type library.

- Section 12.3 introduces the XPath language, as an example of a simple query language for XML. XPath is used in more powerful query languages, such as XQuery and SQL/XML, so makes a good first XML query language.

- Section 12.4 discusses logical design for XML.

12.1 XML Namespaces

A common problem in computing is how to deal with the situation when two different things share the same name. This problem arises in XML because an XML instance document can use mark-up from two or more different document models.

Code listing 12.1.1 shows a fragment of an XML instance document from the Web Timetable database (the line numbers are *not* part of the XML document). This example shows a `module` element from the Web Timetable XML document model. Each `module` element has `code`, `title`, `department` and `level` child elements. The `title` element (lines 4–7) has two child elements, which are a mandatory `mainTitle` element and an optional `subTitle` element.

The `module` element also includes a `leader` child element, which captures information on the module leader. As module leaders are members of staff, the child elements of the `leader` element are drawn from the Staff Directory document model.

Unfortunately, this document model also includes a `title` element. This `title` element contains only text. It is clear to human eyes that the two title elements – in lines 4 and 12 – are different kinds of element that just happen to share a name, but an XML parser expects *all* `title` elements to have the *same* content model.

Code listing 12.1.1   A fragment of an XML instance document with mark-up from two document models

```
1. <!-- No namespace prefixes but two different elements
       with the same name -->
```

```
2.  <module validated="2004-04-21">
3.     <code>CCFC0108</code>
4.     <title>
5.        <mainTitle>Introduction to programming</mainTitle>
6.        <subTitle>C# for beginners</subTitle>
7.     </title>
8.     <department>Computing</department>
9.     <level>F</level>
10.    <leader>
11.       <staffNo>31210</staffNo>
12.       <title>Dr</title>
13.       <name>Paul Smith</name>
14.       <email>p.smith@pennine.ac.uk</email>
15.    </leader>
16. </module>
```

If both `title` elements had the same content model (if both contained only text, for example), then it would be acceptable, from an XML perspective, to reuse the `title` element in these two different contexts. Even so, from the database perspective, the situation could prove confusing as they represent different kinds of title – the title of a module and the title, or honorific, appropriate to a person. When, as in Code listing 12.1.1, two elements with *different* content models have the same *name,* the XML parser needs to know which document model each element belongs to, so that it can check each element's structure against the right document model. If the XML parser checked the `title` element in line 12 against the Web Timetable document model, it would report an error – there is no `mainTitle` child element, and this `title` element cannot itself contain text.

A similar problem occurs with attributes. An XML document model can define attributes independently of elements. This provides a way to reuse attribute declarations. Standard sets of attributes are declared once and used in many different elements. XHTML provides a good example of this. Most of the XHTML elements include the attributes `class`, `id`, `lang`, `style` and `title` and they always have the same meaning. It makes sense to define this list of attributes once and include the whole list in every element that needs it. As one document model can use attribute lists declared in another, there is the potential for two different attributes to share the same name. For XML to work, there must be a mechanism for resolving ambiguous element and attribute names.

The problem of ambiguous names also cropped up in the relational data language SQL. In the `WebTimetable` database, the `Module` and `Course` tables both include a column called `code`. An SQL join query using these two tables must distinguish between these two different `code` columns. The approach taken is to prefix the column name with the name of the table it belongs to – `Course.code` and `Module.code` remove the ambiguity. This solution works because, within a table, all column names must be unique. In an XML document model, all element names must be unique. By analogy, any ambiguity over which document model an element belongs to can be resolved by prefixing the element name with the document model name.

The approach taken with attributes is slightly different. Within an element, attribute names must be unique. This might suggest that, to disambiguate attribute names, they should be prefixed with the element *and* document model names. However, attributes may be declared in a different document model from their parent element. This means that only the document model name is used to disambiguate attribute names.

The XML namespaces specification (W3C, 2004b) implements this general approach to dealing with ambiguous names in mark-up. The name of any element or attribute used in a particular document model is called its **local name**. The document model itself is given a **namespace name**. The namespace name is a globally unique identifier – no two document models will ever share a namespace name. The **expanded name** of any element or attribute consists of its namespace name and its local name. This expanded name uniquely identifies a particular kind of element or attribute. It also tells the XML parser which document model to use to check the element's structure or the attribute's data type.

As namespace names are supposed to be globally unique identifiers, there needs to be a mechanism for ensuring that two document model authors choose different namespace names for their document models. Rather than invent a new set of standards, the W3C decided to use URIs as namespace names. A URI is guaranteed to be globally unique as only the owner of a web domain can use it. There is no intention for the document model to actually exist at the URI used as its namespace name. In fact, there may be nothing at the URI. The URI is simply a convenient, widely used mechanism for defining unique names.

In fact, each namespace name is an internationalized resource identifier (IRI). A URI can only include certain ASCII characters, whereas an IRI can include any Unicode characters. See Duerst and Suignard (2005) for details.

Using URIs as namespace names solves the uniqueness problem, but introduces another. URIs can include characters such as '/', '~' and '%', which cannot be used in XML element and attribute names. For example, the namespace name for the Web Timetable document model is `http://www.pennine.ac.uk/WebTimetable`, but this cannot be used in an XML instance document as part of an element or attribute name.

The solution to this problem is to use a local alias for the namespace name, called the **namespace prefix**. Each XML instance document defines its own namespace prefix for a document model, though each namespace prefix is bound to the same namespace name. So, for example, the namespace name `http://www.pennine.ac.uk/WebTimetable` could sensibly be bound to the namespace prefix `wtt`. Less sensibly it could be bound to the namespace prefix `onlyFoolsUseMeaninglessPrefixes`. The choice is down to the author of the particular XML instance document. The only restriction is that the namespace prefix must be a valid XML name token and cannot include the colon – ':'. Together, the namespace prefix and the local name form the **qualified name**. Within an XML instance document, the format for a qualified name is:

`namespacePrefix:localName`

This is very similar to the SQL qualified identifier, which takes the form *tableName.columnName*. The main difference is that the separator for an XML-qualified name is the colon, not a full stop. (That is why colons are not permitted in the namespace prefix.) Code listing 12.1.2 adds namespace prefixes to the code from Code listing 12.1.1 – wtt for the Web Timetable document model and sdir for the Staff Directory document model. Every element and attribute name in this example is a qualified name.

Code listing 12.1.2   Using the namespace prefix to distinguish between elements and attributes from different document models

```
1.  <!-- With namespace prefixes, but no namespace
        declarations -->
2.  <wtt:module wtt:validated="2004-04-21">
3.    <wtt:code>CCFC0108</wtt:code>
4.    <wtt:title>
5.       <wtt:mainTitle>Introduction to
               programming</wtt:mainTitle>
6.       <wtt:subTitle>C# for beginners</wtt:subTitle>
7.    </wtt:title>
8.    <wtt:department>Computing</wtt:department>
9.    <wtt:level>F</wtt:level>
10.   <wtt:leader>
11.      <sdir:staffNo>31210</sdir:staffNo>
12.      <sdir:title>Dr</sdir:title>
13.      <sdir:name>Paul Smith</sdir:name>
14.      <sdir:email>p.smith@pennine.ac.uk</sdir:email>
15.   </wtt:leader>
16. </wtt:module>
```

Because the namespace name has to be replaced by a namespace prefix, there must be a mechanism for binding namespace prefixes to namespace names. In this way, for example, the author of a particular XML instance document can indicate that the namespace prefix wtt is bound to the namespace name http://www.pennine. ac.uk/WebTimetable. Keep a clear distinction between the mechanism for choosing the namespace name and that for choosing the namespace prefix. The author of the *document model* chooses the namespace name. Anyone using his or her document model must use this namespace name. The author of the *instance document* chooses the namespace prefix to bind to a particular namespace name. Authors of different instance documents can bind different namespace prefixes to the same namespace name.

> In fact, it's possible to bind different namespace prefixes to the same namespace name at different points in an XML instance document. This may be necessary when combining XML mark-up from multiple sources, but remember that unnecessary complexity should be avoided.

The mechanism for binding a namespace prefix to a namespace name is the **namespace declaration**. Namespace declarations appear inside element start tags, along with the element's attributes. Each namespace declaration has the format:

```
xmlns:namespacePrefix="namespaceName"
```

First comes the reserved string of characters 'xmlns:'. Following this comes the namespace prefix, an equals sign, and finally the actual namespace name, enclosed in quotation marks. The XML specification actually describes namespace declarations as 'a family of reserved attributes' (W3C, 2004b). What this means is that, within the mark-up of an XML instance document, namespace declarations are treated just like attributes of the element they appear in. However, a validating XML parser treats namespace declarations quite differently from attributes.

First, a namespace declaration becomes a **namespace node** in the tree representation of the XML document, not an attribute node. Second, an element's descendants inherit its namespace declarations. This means that the namespace prefix declared in a namespace declaration can be used in any child element of the current element and in their child elements and so on. Attributes are definitely *not* inherited by an element's descendants.

> The treatment of namespace declarations is another point at which the designers of XML have chosen a confusing approach. Although you *can* regard namespace declarations as attributes of the element (they are certainly meta-data), they are treated quite differently by XML parsers.

Code listing 12.1.3 includes two namespace declarations in the start tag of the mod-ule element. The first, in line 2, binds the namespace prefix wtt to the namespace name http://www.pennine.ac.uk/WebTimetable. This namespace prefix is used in the qualified name of the module element itself, which comes *before* the namespace declaration. The scope of a namespace declaration is the whole of the element it appears in, including the start tag itself, so this is allowed. Once declared, the wtt namespace prefix can be used to create a qualified name for any descendants and their attributes. Indeed, the scope of the namespace *declaration* includes the module element's descendants and their attributes.

There is another namespace declaration in the module element's start tag. Line 3 binds the prefix sdir to the namespace name http://www.pennine.ac.uk/StaffDirectory. This namespace prefix isn't used until line 13, where it is used in the qualified name sdir:staffNo for the staffNo element. This element is a child of a child of the module element, so is within the scope of the namespace declaration. If the sdir namespace prefix is only ever used in descendants of the leader element, then it might make more sense to declare this namespace in the start tag of the leader element. Whether to declare all the namespaces early in the document tree or only when they are required is a matter of personal style. However, if namespaces are declared further down the document tree, they may need to be declared more than once.

Code listing 12.1.3 *The scope of the namespace declaration and namespace prefix*

```
 1.  <!-- With namespace declarations -->
 2.  <wtt:module xmlns:wtt=
                 "http://www.pennine.ac.uk/WebTimetable"
 3.  xmlns:sdir=
                 "http://www.pennine.ac.uk/StaffDirectory"
 4.              wtt:validated="2004-04-21">
 5.  <wtt:code>CCFC0108</wtt:code>
 6.  <wtt:title>
 7.     <wtt:mainTitle>Introduction to
            programming</wtt:mainTitle>
 8.     <wtt:subTitle>C# for beginners</wtt:subTitle>
 9.  </wtt:title>
10.  <department>Computing</department>
11.  <wtt:level>F</wtt:level>
12.  <wtt:leader>
13.     <sdir:staffNo>31210</sdir:staffNo>
14.     <sdir:title>Dr</sdir:title>
15.     <sdir:name>Paul Smith</sdir:name>
16.     <sdir:email>p.smith@pennine.ac.uk</sdir:email>
17.  </wtt:leader>
18.  </wtt:module>
```

The namespace prefix clearly indicates which namespace an element or attribute belongs to. However, the fact that an element belongs to a particular namespace does *not* mean that its descendants do, too. In line 10, the `department` element's name does not have a namespace prefix. Even though its parent, the `module` element, is in the `http://www.pennine.ac.uk/WebTimetable` namespace, the `department` element is not. In fact, it is not in any namespace. This is a general rule: element and attribute names that do not have a namespace prefix are not in any namespace. Another important point is that if the start tag uses a qualified name, then so must the end tag and if the start tag uses the local name only, so must the end tag.

One problem with the namespace mechanism is that it makes XML documents much harder to read – all those namespace prefixes clutter up the syntax. However, most XML documents have a main document model and use mark-up from other document models only occasionally, so the clutter could be tidied away if there was a way to ensure that local names were correctly bound to the namespace of the main document model. This is not the case in Code listing 12.1.3 where the local name for the `department` element is not bound to any namespace.

The XML namespaces recommendation allows the author of the instance document to declare a **default namespace**. In Code listing 12.1.4, line 2 declares the default namespace to be `http://www.pennine.ac.uk/WebTimetable`. Notice that both the namespace prefix *and* the colon are omitted from the namespace declaration. The effect of this is that every unprefixed *element* name belongs to the `http://www.pennine.ac.uk/WebTimetable` namespace. One way to think of this is that the default namespace declaration binds the empty prefix to the default namespace. Every element name that doesn't have a prefix has an empty prefix, so is bound to the default namespace.

Code listing 12.1.4   The scope of the default namespace declaration (attributes are not included)

```
 1.  <!-- With namespace declarations -->
 2.  <module xmlns="http://www.pennine.ac.uk/WebTimetable"
 3.  xmlns:sdir=
         "http://www.pennine.ac.uk/StaffDirectory"
 4.         validated="2004-04-21">
 5.    <code>CCFC0108</code>
 6.    <title>
 7.      <mainTitle>Introduction to programming</mainTitle>
 8.      <subTitle>C# for beginners</subTitle>
 9.    </title>
10.    <department>Computing</department>
11.    <level>F</level>
12.    <leader>
13.      <sdir:staffNo>31210</sdir:staffNo>
14.      <sdir:title>Dr</sdir:title>
15.      <sdir:name>Paul Smith</sdir:name>
16.      <sdir:email>p.smith@pennine.ac.uk</sdir:email>
17.    </leader>
18.  </module>
```

Unprefixed attribute names are treated differently to unprefixed element names. The attribute `validated` in line 4 does not have a namespace prefix, but it does not belong to the default namespace, `http://www.pennine.ac.uk/WebTimetable`. In fact, it doesn't belong to any namespace. The XML namespaces recommendation states that 'the interpretation of unprefixed attributes is determined by the element on which they appear' (W3C, 2004b). It isn't clear what this means as the recommendation is also quite explicit in stating that 'the namespace name for an unprefixed attribute name always has no value' (W3C, 2004b). The recommendation also includes an example that clearly demonstrates that the namespace for an unprefixed attribute is *not* the namespace of its containing element.

Consider Code listing 12.1.5. There are two namespace declarations in the x element's start tag in lines 2 and 3. The first binds the namespace prefix n1 to the namespace name `http://www.w3.org`. The second makes this same namespace name the default namespace. In line 5, the `good` element's name is unprefixed, so its namespace name must be that of the default namespace, `http://www.w3.org`. The second attribute's name is `n1:a`. The local name is `a` and the namespace prefix is `n1`, so this attribute's namespace name is `http://www.w3.org`. The local name of the first attribute is also `a`. If this attribute belongs to the default namespace, then its namespace name is also `http://www.w3.org`, giving two different attributes with identical expanded names. This is not allowed, so the only possible interpretation is that the first attribute in line 5 does not belong to the same namespace as its parent element. This makes it important to understand how a particular XML processor treats unprefixed attribute names, particularly XML parsers. The documentation for the XML processor you are using should provide guidance on this.

Code listing 12.1.5 Unprefixed attributes are not in the same namespace as their parent element (W3C, 2004b)

```
1. <!-- http://www.w3.org is bound to n1 and is the default
      -->
2. <x xmlns:n1="http://www.w3.org"
3.    xmlns="http://www.w3.org" >
4.    <good a="1" b="2" />
5.    <good a="1" n1:a="2" />
6. </x>
```

12.2 RELAX NG: a schema language for XML

A schema language for XML provides a language for specifying XML document models. Each **schema document** describes the document model for a particular XML application. The structure of an **instance document** of a particular XML document model must match the description in the relevant schema document. A validating XML parser checks the instance document against the schema document. The validating XML parser needs to check that the instance document only contains elements specified in the schema document and the content of these elements is correct. It also needs to check that each element in the instance document has the right attributes. This is the very minimum that a validating XML parser should do, so any schema language for XML must be able to describe elements, their attributes and content models. Most validating XML parsers will ensure that each attribute value has the correct data type and many will do this for text nodes, too, adding another requirement for XML schema languages.

Beyond this basic structural validation, an XML parser may also want to check a range of integrity constraints. The XML analogues of relational candidate and foreign key constraints are a good example. Business rules need to be enforced, too, and it might even be necessary to check that the data in attribute values and text nodes matches a particular pattern (such as a regular expression). Finally, some XML parsers might want to add information to the tree representation of a document as they parse the textual representation. Parsers for the two W3C XML schema languages, DTD and W3C XML Schema, both add default values for attributes, if the attributes were omitted from the textual representation. Parsers for W3C XML Schema also add annotations to attribute and text nodes detailing the data types of these nodes. Parsers for RELAX NG *check* that the data type is correct, but don't add data type information to the tree representation. This only makes a difference if the tree representation is passed to another XML processor that needs detailed data type information, not just an assurance that the data type is correct.

This section focuses on basic structural validation, data types and standard integrity constraints. Basic structural validation is essential since the core purpose of any XML schema language is to support the specification of element content models. Data types are important for database applications, so also need to be covered. The standard integrity constraints, not null, candidate and foreign keys, are all as important in XML databases as they were in relational databases.

The XML schema language used in this section is RELAX NG. As part of an ISO standard, RELAX NG is certainly here to stay, although currently the most widely used XML schema language is W3C XML Schema. RELAX NG has a firm basis in mathematics and is a clean and easy to understand language. There are few ad hoc restrictions and, once the basic ideas have been learnt, applying them is as much a matter of common sense as it is technical facility.

RELAX NG is based on the notion of a **pattern**. In the tree representation of a valid instance document, every node will match a pattern defined in the schema document. 'Matching a pattern' means that the tree structure below the node (the node and all its descendants, plus their attributes) is the same as the structure described by the pattern. A pattern can be written out in English, as in the following example.

This is the pattern for an element node with node name 'session'. This element node contains:

- exactly one element node with node name 'dayOfWeek'
- exactly one element node with node name 'startTime'
- exactly one element node with node name 'endTime'

These three element nodes must occur in the specified order.

Whenever the RELAX NG parser meets a `session` element in the instance document, it checks its content against this pattern. If the content matches the pattern, it is valid. If not, it is not valid. Notice that this pattern doesn't say what the `dayOfWeek`, `startTime` and `endTime` elements look like. There will be separate patterns for these.

One nice feature of patterns is that they can contain other patterns. Here, the pattern specifying the `session` element contains the patterns specifying the `dayOfWeek`, `startTime` and `endTime` elements. Combining patterns in this way makes models with complex content easy to describe. First, the child elements are listed, then patterns for each of them written out. When the content models of two elements share some common structure – for example, a common set of attributes or child elements – a pattern for this common structure can also be defined, given a name and used as part of the content model for both elements. Such common patterns can even be imported from other schema documents. This is the same idea as using functions and include files to share code between two different PHP scripts.

RELAX NG supports two different, but equivalent, syntaxes. The first uses XML, so RELAX NG schema documents written with this syntax are themselves XML documents. This XML syntax is used here. The alternative is the compact syntax, which uses ideas from programming languages and regular expressions. The compact syntax is similar to that of the DTD XML schema language.

Code listing 12.2.1 shows a short snippet of both syntaxes. These two syntaxes are completely equivalent to one another and a schema document written using one can automatically be translated into a schema document written using the other. Choosing between them is a matter of personal preference. Both syntax styles are fairly easy for beginners to interpret. Code listing 12.2.1 reads as follows.

There is an element called 'session'. It contains: an element called 'dayOfWeek' that contains text; an element called 'startTime' that contains text; and an element called 'endTime' that contains text.

This section uses the XML syntax because it is the syntax style of other XML schema languages, so learning to work with this style of syntax is important.

Code listing 12.2.1   The two syntaxes of the XML schema language RELAX NG

(a) The XML syntax, used in the rest of the section

```
<element name="session">
  <element name="dayOfWeek">
    <text />
  </element>
  <element name="startTime">
    <text />
  </element>
  <element name="endTime">
    <text />
  </element>
</element>
```

(b) The compact syntax – a marriage of DTD and Java syntax

```
element session
{
  element dayOfWeek { text },
  element startTime { text },
  element endTime { text }
}
```

Using an XML syntax to specify XML document models could get a little confusing. For example, the first line in Code listing 12.2.1 (a) is an XML element called 'element'. So, in the RELAX NG document model there is an element called 'element', which has an attribute called 'name'. This XML element has an intended interpretation: it specifies an element pattern that is matched by elements in the target document model. For example, this XML element element:

```
<element name="dayOfWeek"> <text /> </element>
```

is intended to be interpreted as follows.

At this point in the instance document, there is an XML element called 'dayOfWeek'. This 'dayOfWeek' element has no attributes and contains ordinary text.

Just keep in mind that, in a RELAX NG schema document, the element element represents a RELAX NG element pattern. The phrase 'element pattern' is used instead of the potentially confusing 'element element'. The document model for the RELAX NG XML syntax has other elements representing other patterns. For consistency, these will always be called 'patterns' rather than 'elements'.

RELAX NG focuses exclusively on specifying the basic structure of XML document models. It supports data type validation by means of datatype libraries. These are external resources used by a RELAX NG validating XML parser to check data types for it. Because RELAX NG uses datatype libraries rather than imposing its own type system on XML documents, application developers are free to choose whichever datatype library best suits their needs. They could even write their own, though this is seldom necessary. RELAX NG schema documents can also be automatically converted to W3C XML Schema schema documents, which is rather handy as RELAX NG is much easier to learn and use than W3C XML Schema, but W3C XML Schema is more widely used. The only problem is that RELAX NG can describe *more* XML document models than W3C XML Schema, so some RELAX NG schema documents can't be translated directly into W3C XML Schema schema documents. (Neither language can describe every possible XML document model.)

12.2.1 Basic patterns

There are four basic patterns in RELAX NG:

- text
- data
- attribute
- element.

A schema document combines these four basic patterns to produce a complete description of an XML document model. It does this by specifying a pattern for the attributes and content model of every element in the document model. The XML parser compares each element in an instance document to the appropriate element pattern in the schema document. If they all match their patterns, then the document is valid. Otherwise, it is invalid. This subsection explains the basic patterns and the next explains how to combine them to create more complex patterns.

A text node, or attribute value, in the instance document *must* match a text pattern or a data pattern in the schema document. Whenever the XML parser encounters a text node, or attribute value, in the instance document, it checks that the pattern of the parent element contains a matching text or data pattern. As text nodes don't have attributes or further content, the text pattern is written as an empty element:

```
<text />
```

Whenever the text pattern appears in a schema document, it means:

at this point in the instance document there is some text.

As a simple example, this fragment of a Staff Directory instance document:

```
<dayOfWeek>Monday</dayOfWeek>
```

matches the pattern for the `dayOfWeek` element:

```
<element name="dayOfWeek"> <text /> </element>
```

as it is an element called 'dayOfWeek', which contains a text value.

As RELAX NG treats the attribute and attribute value as separate nodes, attribute values can also match the text pattern. Although this is a divergence from the XDM (where an attribute value is represented by the value attribute of the corresponding attribute node), it is easy to convert a RELAX NG tree representation of an instance document into an XDM one – simply absorb every attribute value node into its parent attribute node. The RELAX NG approach means that elements and attributes are treated consistently, making the language simpler and easier to use than XDM.

In mixed content models, there may be more than one text node in the content of an element, separated by other element nodes. For example, the content model for the XHTML paragraph element allows the following paragraph elements in an instance document:

```
<p><strong>This paragraph element has no child text
nodes!</strong></p>
```

```
<p>The preceding paragraph element had no child text nodes,
but one child element node: the "strong" element.</p>
```

```
<p>The preceding paragraph element had <strong>one</strong>
child text node and no child element nodes. This paragraph
element has two child text nodes separated by a child
element node.</p>
```

The first paragraph has zero text nodes, the second has one text node and the third has two. To make it easier to define mixed content models, a text pattern in the schema document is matched by zero or more text nodes in the instance document. This situation is discussed in more detail below, when the interleave pattern is explained.

In an XML document, every text node is stored as a string of Unicode characters. Database applications usually want to restrict text values to a specific data type. The data pattern does this by insisting that the value of a text node should be a valid literal for the specified data type. Because mixed content models are considered poor practice in database applications, the data pattern cannot be used in mixed content models.

The data pattern is matched by attribute values and text nodes from the instance document that have the specified data type. The schema document must make clear which data type matching nodes are supposed to have. To achieve this, the data pattern uses two attributes. The value of the type attribute names a particular data type. The value of the datatypeLibrary attribute is a URI that uniquely identifies the datatype library where this data type is defined. The datatypeLibrary attribute is necessary because two different datatype libraries might define different data types with the same name (this is the namespace problem in another guise).

The general format for the data pattern is:

```
<data datatypeLibrary="libraryURI" type="dataTypeName">
</data>
```

Remember, the content of a matching node will be a literal for the specified data type, not an actual data value (check the discussion of this distinction in Chapter 3). Whenever the data pattern appears in a schema document, it means:

at this point in the instance document, there is some data with this data type, which is defined in this datatype library.

As an example, the following data pattern is matched by text nodes and attribute values that contain a date literal, in the format yyyy-mm-dd.

```
<data datatypeLibrary="http://www.w3/org/2001/XMLSchema-
datatypes" type="date" > </data>
```

If the `datatypeLibrary` attribute is omitted, then the built-in RELAX NG data types are used. There are two built-in data types, both of which represent character string data. The `token` data type is the default data type of XML documents. A `token` data value is a character string in which every sequence of white space characters (spaces, tabs, carriage returns and linefeeds) has been replaced by a *single* space character and any leading or trailing spaces have been trimmed. The other data type is `string`. The data values of the `string` data type are character strings in which white space is preserved.

The data pattern can contain other patterns. These further restrict the data values allowed to occur in matching nodes from the instance document. This lets the schema author implement simple user-defined types. However, if there are no restrictions, the data pattern will be empty. As usual, this empty XML element can be abbreviated to:

```
<data datatypeLibrary="libraryURI" type="dataTypeName" />
```

The data type of text nodes matching the text pattern is assumed to be `token`. However, unlike a text pattern, the data pattern is matched by exactly one node. This means that, in general, the data pattern `<data type="token" />` is *not* equivalent to the text pattern `<text />`. The first is matched by exactly one node, the second by zero, one or many nodes. Datatype libraries, data types and the RELAX NG data pattern are discussed in more detail below.

Each attribute in the instance document must match an attribute pattern in the schema document. An attribute in the instance document matches a particular attribute pattern, provided:

1 its name matches the 'name' attribute of the attribute pattern
2 its value matches the text or data pattern contained in the attribute pattern.

For example the attribute pattern:

```
<attribute name="myAttribute"> <text /> </attribute>
```

is matched by any attribute in the instance document that has the name 'myAttribute' and a value that matches the text pattern (that is, the attribute value is plain old text). The attribute pattern can be read as saying:

> At this point in the instance document there is an attribute with the specified name and its value matches this pattern.

RELAX NG recognizes that *most* attribute values will match the text pattern, so the pattern above is equivalent to:

```
<attribute name="myAttribute" />
```

This isn't quite in the spirit of XML, as the 'empty' attribute pattern actually contains a text pattern. Contrast this with the empty text pattern, `<text />`, which is a genuinely empty XML element.

Text, data and attribute patterns are all fairly simple. So is the element pattern. Every element in the instance document must match an element pattern in the schema document. Each element has a name, set of attributes and some content, so an element in the instance document matches a particular element pattern, provided:

1 its name matches the 'name' attribute of the element pattern

2 each of its attributes matches an attribute pattern contained by the element pattern

3 each of its child elements matches a text, data or element pattern contained by the element pattern.

For example, the element pattern:

```
<element name="myElement"> <text /> </element>
```

is matched by any element in the instance document called 'myElement' that has no attributes and contains only text. Whenever the element pattern appears in a schema document, it means:

> at this point in the instance document, there is exactly one element called by this name, with these attributes and its content matches this pattern.

An element's attributes are specified by including attribute patterns as part of the content of the element pattern. For example, the pattern:

```
<element name="myElement">
  <attribute name="myAttribute"> <text /> </attribute>
  <text />
</element>
```

specifies an element called 'myElement'. This element has a single attribute called 'myAttribute' and its value is plain text. The element's content is a single, child text element. A typical instance would be:

```
<myElement myAttribute="SomeValue"> Some text content
</myElement>
```

Elements can contain data patterns. The idea is that the content of the element is a literal for some particular data type, specified by the data pattern. If an element contains a data pattern, then it can only contain the *one* data pattern and cannot contain any text or element patterns (attribute patterns are allowed). There is a good reason for this. If the element is supposed to contain a data literal, then let it do just that – the data, all the data and nothing but the data. If an element needs to contain some text *and* a data literal, then simply wrap the data literal up in a child element. For example the pattern:

```
<element name="startTime">
  <element name="time">
   <data
      datatypeLibrary="http://www.w3/org/2001/
      XMLSchema-datatypes" type="time" />
  </element>
  <text />
</element>
```

is matched by the instance:

```
<startTime> <time> 12:00 </time> (though I might be a bit
late) </startTime>
```

Here, the content model's time element is a single data pattern. It is the startTime element that has a mixed content model.

In an instance document, the content of an element, its child nodes, is ordered in document order (see Chapter 3). RELAX NG assumes that the order of the patterns contained within an element pattern defines the document order for child nodes in the instance document.

Consider the session element defined by the element pattern shown in Code listing 12.2.1.1 (a). An instance of the session element matches this pattern provided that it contain instances of the dayOfWeek, startTime and endTime elements *in that order*. This is also an example of how the basic patterns can be combined to describe complex content models. A single element pattern contains three further element patterns, each of which contains a text pattern. Together, they completely specify the session element and its content model. Code listing 12.2.1.1 (b) shows a valid instance of the session element; all the child elements are present, in the correct number (one of each) and the correct order. Code listing 12.2.1.1 (c) is not valid. Although all the child elements are present in the correct number they are in the wrong order. Code listing 12.2.1.1 (d) is also invalid; the order is correct but there are too many dayOfWeek elements. Similarly, code listing 12.2.1.1 (e) is invalid because the startTime element is missing.

Code listing 12.2.1.1   Element patterns and document order

(a) The element pattern for the session *element*

```
<element name="session">
  <element name="dayOfWeek"> <text /> </element>
  <element name="startTime"> <text /> </element>
  <element name="endTime"> <text /> </element>
</element>
```

(b) A valid instance of the session *element, matching the element pattern in (a)*

```
<session>
  <dayOfWeek>Monday</dayOfWeek>
  <startTime>09:00</startTime>
  <endTime>10:00</endTime>
</session>
```

(c) An invalid instance of the session *element – child elements occur in the wrong order*

```
<session>
  <endTime>10:00</endTime>
  <startTime>09:00</startTime>
  <dayOfWeek>Monday</dayOfWeek>
</session>
```

(d) An invalid instance of the `session` *element – too many* `dayOfWeek` *elements*

```
<session>
  <dayOfWeek>Monday</dayOfWeek>
  <dayOfWeek>Wednesday</dayOfWeek>
  <startTime>09:00</startTime>
  <endTime>10:00</endTime>
</session>
```

(e) An invalid instance of the `session` *element – no* `startTime` *element*

```
<session>
  <dayOfWeek>Monday</dayOfWeek>
  <endTime>10:00</endTime>
</session>
```

Although the order of the text and element patterns for an element's child nodes is significant, the order of attribute patterns is not. This is because XML specifically states that the order of attributes is not significant. Attribute patterns can appear anywhere in the content of an element pattern and will be matched by any instance of the specified element that contains the right attributes, regardless of their order within the start tag.

The next section discusses more complex ways to combine patterns than simple containment. It introduces mechanisms for specifying optional content and allowing more than one instance of a child node to occur in an element's content. It also explains how a RELAX NG schema can allow the content of an element to appear in a random order. Unordered content models are useful for database applications where the order of an element's content is often irrelevant. (Remember, the relational data model makes this explicit – the rows of a table can appear in any order and, in any particular row, the columns can appear in any order).

12.2.2 Complex patterns

Document models often allow elements to appear many times in a particular content model. In the Staff Directory document model, an instance of the `staff` element can have zero or more instances of the `phone` element among its child nodes. A schema language needs to check such multiplicity constraints. The four commonest multiplicity constraints for an XML element are exactly one, zero or one, zero or more and one or more. (These correspond to the UML multiplicities 1..1, 0..1, 0..* and 1..* respectively.)

In RELAX NG the default multiplicity for element patterns is 'exactly one' – that is, an element pattern is matched by exactly one instance of the named element. To match 'exactly two' occurrences, simply include the pattern twice. For example, the instance of the `session` element in Code listing 2.2.1.1 (d) matches the pattern:

```
<element name="session">
  <element name="dayOfWeek"> <text /> </element>
  <element name="dayOfWeek"> <text /> </element>
  <element name="startTime"> <text /> </element>
  <element name="endTime"> <text /> </element>
</element>
```

This pattern insists that there must be *two* dayOfWeek elements at the start of every session element.

Including patterns multiple times is not very efficient. RELAX NG includes the concept of a named pattern, which is simply a pattern that has been named. The name of the pattern is used in content models instead of the pattern itself, ensuring that, if the pattern changes, it only needs to be changed once (just like a PHP function). In this brief introduction to XML schema languages there isn't time to cover named patterns in detail. See the Further reading section at the end of this chapter for books that do.

RELAX NG includes three different patterns to match the other common multiplicities. The optional pattern matches zero or one occurrence of the pattern it contains. Whenever the optional pattern appears in a schema document it means.

> at this point in the instance document, the following pattern may appear at most once, but may not appear at all.

A good example comes from the contacts database used by the Pennine University to track telephone enquiries from potential students. The potential applicant provides a name and phone number and may optionally give an e-mail and home address.

Code listing 12.2.2.1 shows a RELAX NG pattern for this situation. The first optional pattern contains a single element pattern, specifying the email element. An instance of the contact element may contain an email element or it may not.

The second optional pattern contains four element patterns. These four elements are optional *as a group*. To be valid, an instance of the contact element either contains all four child elements, in the specified order, or it contains none of them.

Code listing 12.2.2.1 (c) shows an invalid instance of the contact element. It is invalid because it contains a houseNumber element, so should also contain street, town and postcode elements. This is an important point, so is worth reiterating – part of an instance document matches an optional pattern when it matches the *whole* of the content of that pattern or when the *whole* of the content of the optional pattern is missing.

Code listing 12.2.2.1 *Using the optional pattern for groups of elements that may occur zero or one time in an element instance*

(a) The pattern

```
<element name="contact">
  <element name="name"> <text /> </element>
  <element name="phone"> <text /> </element>
  <optional>
    <element name="email"> <text /> </element>
  </optional>
  <optional>
    <element name="houseNumber"> <text /> </element>
    <element name="street"> <text /> </element>
    <element name="town"> <text /> </element>
    <element name="postcode"> <text /> </element>
  </optional>
</element>
```

(b) A valid instance – optional elements omitted

```
<contact>
  <name> Jeff Bridges </name>
  <phone> 01234 567 890 </phone>
</contact>
```

(c) An invalid instance – if the houseNumber element exists, so must street, town and postcode

```
<contact>
  <name> Jeff Bridges </name>
  <phone> 01234 567 890 </phone>
  <houseNumber> 5 </houseNumber>
</contact>
```

The zeroOrMore pattern works in a similar way, matching zero or more occurrences of the pattern it contains. Whenever the zeroOrMore pattern appears in a schema document it means:

> at this point in the instance document, the following pattern may appear many times or may not appear at all.

Code listing 12.2.2.2 (a) modifies the pattern in Code listing 12.2.2.1 (a) to allow zero or many phone numbers. An instance of the contact element matching this pattern does not *have* to contain a phone element, so the only compulsory element is the name element. This seems a little pointless, so a third pattern, Code listing 12.2.2.2 (b), encloses the element pattern for the phone element in a oneOrMore pattern. Whenever the oneOrMore pattern appears in a schema document it means:

> at this point in the instance document, the following pattern must appear at least once and may appear many times.

This seems to be a more sensible multiplicity constraint for the phone element.

Code listing 12.2.2.2   Allowing many phone elements

(a) Using the zeroOrMore pattern

```
<element name="contact">
  <element name="name"> <text /> </element>
  <zeroOrMore>
    <element name="phone"> <text /> </element>
  </zeroOrMore>
  <optional>
    <element name="email"> <text /> </element>
  </optional>
  <optional>
    <element name="houseNumber"> <text /> </element>
    <element name="street"> <text /> </element>
    <element name="town"> <text /> </element>
    <element name="postcode"> <text /> </element>
  </optional>
</element>
```

(b) Using the oneOrMore pattern

```
<element name="contact">
  <element name="name"> <text /> </element>
  <oneOrMore>
    <element name="phone"> <text /> </element>
  </oneOrMore>
  <optional>
    <element name="email"> <text /> </element>
  </optional>
  <optional>
    <element name="houseNumber"> <text /> </element>
    <element name="street"> <text /> </element>
    <element name="town"> <text /> </element>
    <element name="postcode"> <text /> </element>
  </optional>
</element>
```

Used together, these patterns can produce any multiplicity constraint that can be expressed in UML. For example, to require at least two phone elements, use the pattern:

```
<element name="phone"> <text /> </element>
<oneOrMore>
  <element name="phone"> <text /> </element>
</oneOrMore>
```

To match this pattern, there must be one phone element, to match the first element pattern, and at least one more phone element, to match the oneOrMore pattern. This gives the required minimum of two phone elements.

Sometimes there is a choice between two or more different content models for an element or two different kinds of value for an attribute. The choice pattern represents a choice between different patterns, which are listed as the pattern's content. Part of an instance document matches a choice pattern provided that it matches *one* of the patterns it contains. Whenever the choice pattern appears in a schema document it means:

> at this point in the instance document, there is a choice between the following patterns and the content of the current node *must* match one of these patterns.

There is a problem with choice patterns, nicely illustrated by people's names. Sometimes names are stored as a single character string, with no distinction between first and last names. At other times, the first and last names are stored separately.

Code listing 12.2.2.3 shows two instances of the name element from the Staff Directory database that illustrate the two possibilities. Clearly these are two *different* content models for the *same* element. The content model for the element in Code listing 12.2.2.3 (a) contains a text node, while the content model for the element in Code listing 12.2.2.3 (b) contains two child element node and no text nodes (it is the *child* elements – fName and lName – that contain text nodes).

Code listing 12.2.2.3   Two valid instances of the name *element*

(a) A name *element with text content*

```
<name>Paul Smith</name>
```

(b) A name element with child elements for first and last names

```
<name>
  <fName>Paul</fName>
  <lName>Smith</lName>
</name>
```

The problem arises when trying to write this choice pattern. It must allow the XML parser to choose between two different content models. The first content model is a single text node, so is represented by a text pattern:

```
<text />
```

The second content model consists of one fName element followed by one lName element, both of which contain text, so is the pattern:

```
<element name="fName"> <text /> </element>
<element name="lName"> <text /> </element>
```

A first attempt at writing the complete pattern simply encloses these two inside a choice pattern, thus:

```
<element name="name">
  <choice>
    <text />
    <element name="fName"><text /></element>
    <element name="lName"><text /></element>
  </choice>
</element>
```

However, this isn't correct. A name element matches this pattern if it matches any one of the three patterns contained in the choice pattern – a text node, a single fName element or a single lName element. In fact, the instance in Code listing 12.2.2.3 (b) does *not* match this pattern as matching name elements can only have *either* an fName element *or* an lName element, not both.

The solution is to introduce the group pattern. The group pattern acts like parentheses. Everything inside the group pattern is treated as a single pattern by the enclosing choice pattern. The correct pattern for the name element therefore is:

```
<element name="name">
  <choice>
    <text />
    <group>
      <element name="fName"><text /></element>
      <element name="lName"><text /></element>
    </group>
  </choice>
</element>
```

Now, the choice pattern allows a choice between *two* child patterns. Either the contents of the name element match the text pattern or they match the pattern contained in the group pattern.

Another use for the choice pattern is to define enumerations. Remember, an enumeration is a very simple kind of user-defined data type – the user specifies a list of valid values. To do this, the schema document needs to allow the XML parser to choose between literals for the allowed data values.

The obvious solution is to enclose the list of valid literals in a choice pattern. Each literal is enclosed in a value pattern. The value pattern has a type attribute to indicate the intended data type of the matching literal and a datatypeLibrary attribute (see the description of the data pattern). Its content is a single literal defining the data value. The value pattern is matched by *any* literal representing the same value as the one it contains. So, for example, the string literals '   This string has white space   ' and 'This string has   white space' both match the value pattern:

```
<value type="token"> This string has white space </value>
```

As the data type of the value is token, the XML parser strips out any additional white space characters *before* it compares the text in the instance document to the literal contained by the value pattern. Whenever the value pattern appears in a schema document it means:

at this point in the instance document, this particular data value appears.

In contrast, the data pattern indicates that *some* data value appears at this point in the instance document, without stating which.

The dayOfWeek element is a good example of an element that can be specified by an enumeration as it should only contain text that represents a day of the week. The content of the dayOfWeek element is valid if it matches *one* of the allowed literals. Combining the value and choice patterns gives an enumeration of its allowed content. Code listing 12.2.2.4 shows a pattern for the dayOfWeek element that ensures only dayOfWeek elements containing the name of a day of the week will be accepted by the XML parser. Values are case-sensitive, so a dayOfWeek element with content 'Monday' will match the pattern, whereas one that has 'monday' will not.

Code listing 12.2.2.4   An enumeration

```
<element name="dayOfWeek">
  <choice>
    <value type="token"> Monday </value>
    <value type="token"> Tuesday </value>
    <value type="token"> Wednesday </value>
    <value type="token"> Thursday </value>
    <value type="token"> Friday </value>
  </choice>
</element>
```

Unordered content models are specified with the interleave pattern. The most common unordered content model is one in which two or more elements can appear in any order. This is the usual situation with database applications. For example, to indicate that the contents of the `session` element can appear in any order, enclose them all in an interleave pattern:

```
<element name="session">
  <interleave>
    <element name="dayOfWeek"> <text /> </element>
    <element name="startTime"> <text /> </element>
    <element name="endTime"> <text /> </element>
  </interleave>
</element>
```

Any instance of the `session` element that contains exactly one of each of the `dayOfWeek`, `startTime` and `endTime` elements, in any order, matches this pattern.

The full effect of interleave is rather subtle. To understand how it works, consider the more complex pattern shown in Code listing 12.2.2.5 (a). The idea is that the child elements of the `contact` element ought to be allowed to appear in any order, except for those that are part of the address. These elements must appear in the order `houseNumber`, `street`, `town` and `postcode`. The group pattern ensures that this happens.

The contents of a group pattern within an interleave pattern *must* appear in the specified order. However, the other child patterns of the interleave pattern may be interleaved in between the patterns from the group. This is what has happened in the instance of the `contact` element shown in Code listing 12.2.2.5 (b). The four elements `houseNumber`, `street`, `town` and `postcode` appear in this order, but the other elements are interleaved between them. Notice that these other elements are *not* in the same order as they appear in the pattern.

Code listing 12.2.2.5 *Using the interleave pattern to allow contact details to appear in any order*

(a) The pattern

```
<element name="contact">
  <interleave>
    <element name="name"> <text /> </element>
    <oneOrMore>
      <element name="phone"> <text /> </element>
    </oneOrMore>
    <optional>
      <element name="email"> <text /> </element>
    </optional>
    <optional>
      <group>
        <element name="houseNumber"> <text /> </element>
```

```
        <element name="street"> <text /> </element>
        <element name="town"> <text /> </element>
        <element name="postcode"> <text /> </element>
      </group>
    </optional>
  </interleave>
</element>
```

(b) An instance of the `contact` *element matching the pattern in (a)*

```
<contact>
  <email> jo.carter@emailprovider.com </email>
  <houseNumber> 12 </houseNumber>
  <phone> 079991 998877 </phone>
  <street> High Street </street>
  <town> Otherworth </town>
  <name> Jo Carter </name>
  <phone> 04321 987654 </phone>
  <postcode> HX67 7TH </postcode>
</contact>
```

The interleave pattern allows sequences of nodes matching its child patterns to be interleaved. If the child pattern allows the nodes to be unordered, then any sequence of these nodes that matches this pattern can be interleaved with the other sequences. If the child pattern requires the nodes to be ordered, then only a sequence of nodes in the correct order can be interleaved with the other sequences.

In Code listing 12.2.2.5, the first three child patterns are unordered (there is no group pattern to say that they must appear in a particular order). The fourth child pattern contains a group pattern, so only sequences of nodes in the correct order match this pattern.

Using the full power of interleave makes more sense in mixed content models. Code listing 12.2.2.6 (a) uses an interleave pattern to define a mixed content model (the line numbers are not part of the pattern – they are included to make it easier to discuss this pattern). The aim is to allow the three elements dayOfWeek, startTime and endTime to be interleaved with text, with the proviso that startTime and endTime must appear in this order. As the text pattern matches a sequence of zero or more text nodes, only a single text pattern is needed in the content of the interleave pattern. Code listing 12.2.2.6 (b) shows three instances of the session element that match this pattern.

Consider the first of these. It contains four text nodes and this sequence of text nodes matches the pattern in line 4 of Code listing 12.2.2.6 (a). It also contains a single element called dayOfWeek. The sequence consisting of this single element node matches the pattern in line 3 of Code listing 12.2.2.6 (a). Finally, it also contains one of each of the elements startTime and endTime, in this order – this sequence of two element nodes matches the pattern in lines 5–8. Thus, this particular instance of the session element contains sequences of nodes matching each of the patterns contained in the interleave pattern. This means that it also matches the interleave pattern itself.

Code listing 12.2.2.6   Using the interleave pattern in mixed content models

(a) The pattern

```
1.  <element name="session">
2.   <interleave>
3.    <element name="dayOfWeek"> <text /> </element>
4.    <text />
5.    <group>
6.     <element name="startTime"> <text /> </element>
7.     <element name="endTime"> <text /> </element>
8.    </group>
9.   </interleave>
10. </element>
```

(b) Three instances of the `session` *element matching the pattern in (a)*

```
<session>
I offer support sessions on a
<dayOfWeek>Monday</dayOfWeek>.
They start at <startTime>09:00</startTime> and end at
<endTime>10:00</endTime>. Feel free to drop in.
</session>

<session>
I offer support sessions running from
<startTime>09:00</startTime> to <endTime>10:00</endTime>
on a
<dayOfWeek>Monday</dayOfWeek>. Feel free to drop in.
</session>

<session>
The support session starts at <startTime>09:00</startTime> on
a <dayOfWeek>Monday</dayOfWeek>, and ends at
<endTime>10:00</endTime>. Feel free to drop in.
</session>
```

(c) An instance of the `session` *element that does not match the pattern in (a)*

```
<session>
The support session ends at <endTime>10:00</endTime> on a
<dayOfWeek>Monday</dayOfWeek>. Feel free to drop in. I'll be
there from <startTime>09:00</startTime>.
</session>
```

Each of the instances of `session` shown in Code listing 12.2.2.6 (b) makes perfect sense and there is no good reason to stop end users from using any of these variants. The instance of the `session` element in Code listing 12.2.2.6 (c) does not match the pattern as the `endTime` element appears before the `startTime` element, which is not allowed. It seems reasonable to disallow this example as stating the time that a support session ends *before* saying when it starts could easily confuse people. There are likely to be students turning up at 10:00 to find that their tutor is no longer available.

The patterns optional, oneOrMore, zeroOrMore, interleave and group can be thought of as operators on patterns as they take one or more patterns and operate on them to make a new pattern. The choice pattern allows choices between different patterns. Starting with the simple patterns – text, element, attribute, data and value – it is possible to use the operator patterns and the choice pattern to develop RELAX NG schema to describe almost every possible XML document model. That almost sounds slightly disappointing, but isn't really. It's possible to determine how expressive an XML schema language is. RELAX NG is more expressive than W3C XML Schema, which, in turn, is more expressive than DTD. All these languages describe classes of trees and there are an awful lot of tree structures that no one would ever want to use as document models.

12.2.3 Datatype libraries

Datatype libraries were mentioned briefly above, but they are worth a closer look. Datatype libraries are external resources that the RELAX NG parser draws on to check the data type of text nodes and attribute values. In effect, they allow a RELAX NG schema author to use whichever system of data types is best for the job. Web database developers can even develop their own datatype libraries, though this is rarely necessary. By keeping data type checking out of the core language, RELAX NG can deal with data types from a wider range of situations than some other schema languages, which are tied to their own system of data types.

There are currently two widely used data type libraries. The DTD compatibility library includes the data types defined by the DTD schema language (W3C, 2004f). There are eight of these, including the ID, IDREF and IDREFS data types used to implement relational-style candidate and foreign keys. There is also the facility for the user to define enumeration data types, though this should not be used as RELAX NG has its own version of enumerations. The DTD compatibility library will also check the relational-style primary and foreign key constraints. This topic is covered below.

The W3C XML Schema datatype library includes all the primitive data types defined by the W3C XML Schema recommendation. In all, there are 49 primitive data types (at least, there are in the document XML Schema Part 2: Datatypes – Working draft, 17 February 2006 (W3C, 2006c)). The string and token data types are equivalent to the RELAX NG string and token data types, with the usual string literals. There are equivalents of the DTD data types ID, IDREF and IDREFS, although the W3C XML Schema datatype library does *not* check the associated candidate and foreign key constraints. There are numeric data types, including decimal, integer and double, again with the usual string literals. Boolean is also considered a numeric data type, with two values. The Boolean value 'true' is represented by either of the literals true and 1. The Boolean value 'false' is represented by either of the literals false and 0.

There are a number of date and time data types in the W3C XML Schema datatype library, but the definitions are complex because they ensure the correct handling of time zones. That said, the `date` and `time` data types are broadly similar to the SQL `DATE` and `TIME` data types. The `duration` data type represents a length of time, but is quite different from the SQL `INTERVAL` data type. A `duration` includes year, month, day, hour, minute and second parts in a single value, so mixes the two incompatible time intervals of year and month and of day, hour and minute. The consequence is that, in some cases, two `duration` values are neither longer nor shorter than each other. Handle with care.

The `dataTypeLibrary` attribute specifies the datatype library being used. It's value is a URI, though, like the namespace name, this URI need not actually point to anything. It is simply a globally unique identifier for the datatype library. Most of the patterns in RELAX NG can have a `dataTypeLibrary` attribute in their start tag, not just the data pattern. The `dataTypeLibrary` attribute acts rather like a default namespace declaration – all descendants of the pattern can use the data types from this datatype library, even if they haven't got their own `dataTypeLibrary` attribute. As a simple example, the following attribute pattern is perfectly acceptable:

```
<attribute
  datatypeLibrary="http://www.w3/org/2001/XMLSchema-
  datatypes" name="lastUpdate">
  <data type="date" />
</attribute>
```

The attribute pattern declares that it, and its descendants, will use the W3C XML Schema datatype library. Its child data pattern does so, without restating this fact.

Datatype library declarations in an ancestor of a pattern can easily be overridden. Consider the definition of the `staffMember` element in Code listing 12.2.3.1. The element pattern declares that it and its descendants will use the W3C XML Schema datatype library. The element pattern contains two attribute patterns, each of which contains a data pattern.

The first data pattern *does* use the W3C XML Schema datatype library, although there is no mention of this datatype library in the data pattern itself, just the data type name. The second attribute pattern does *not* use W3C XML Schema datatype library. Instead, it uses its own `datatypeLibrary` attribute to indicate that it is using the DTD Compatibility datatype library.

Code listing 12.2.3.1 *Using two different datatype libraries*

```
<element name="staffMember"
datatypeLibrary="http://www.w3/org/2001/XMLSchema-datatypes"
>
  <attribute name="lastUpdate"> <data type="date" />
  </attribute>
  <attribute name="surrogateKey">
    <data datatypeLibrary=
    "http://relaxng.org/ns/compatibility/datatypes/1.0"
    type="ID" />
  </attribute>
</element>
```

One reason for allowing different datatype libraries is that they offer different features. The DTD compatibility datatype library will check the relational-style candidate and foreign key constraints. The W3C XML Schema datatype library allows the data values for a data type to be further restricted using facets. A facet is simply a Boolean expression that restricts the allowed values for a data type. RELAX NG uses the param pattern to specify a facet. This pattern can only appear in the content of a data pattern.

For example the `minInclusive` facet applies to numeric and date data types and indicates that only values greater than or equal to the given value are permitted. The `maxInclusive` facet is its twin, placing an upper bound on the allowed data values. To restrict an integer to a value between 10,000 and 99,999 inclusive, use the following pattern:

```
<data datatypeLibrary=
    "http://www.w3.org/2001/XMLSchema-datatypes"
    type="integer">
  <param name="minInclusive">10000</param>
  <param name="maxInclusive">99999</param>
</data>
```

There are a lot of facets defined by the W3C XML Schema specification (W3C, 2004e) but they all work the same way. Use them if required, but, if not, leave them be.

12.2.4 A schema for the Staff Directory document model

All the patterns discussed so far are used in the RELAX NG schema describing the document model of the Staff Directory XML database. The process of writing this schema document illustrates how to derive a schema document by critically examining a typical instance document. The basic idea is to start with a sample instance document and follow a process of top-down refinement.

At each node, identify element, attribute and text nodes with the current node as their parent. For element nodes, write down an element pattern, but leave the content of this pattern empty for now. Do a similar thing for attribute nodes – simply write down an empty attribute pattern. Text nodes can be described by a text pattern, a data pattern or a value pattern. Text and value patterns can't contain other patterns, so simply write them down as the pattern for the text node. Data patterns may include param patterns. Even so it is best to write out the full data pattern when it is identified, rather than leave its content for the next stage in the process.

Now consider the attribute and element nodes just listed, in document order. Each attribute has a single child text node – its value. Write down the pattern for that text node. Each element node may have multiple attribute nodes, child element nodes and child text nodes. Write down a pattern for each of the nodes *inside* the pattern of the parent node. Leave the attribute and element nodes empty, just as before. Now repeat the process all over again.

This process does a breadth first traversal of the tree representation, so will eventually define a pattern for every node in the document. To see the process in action, consider Code listing 12.2.4.1. It shows a typical instance document for the Staff Directory XML database. It begins with an XML declaration, but this is not part of the tree representation of the document so does not appear as part of the schema document. There are no comments or processing instructions, but, even if there were, they would be ignored. Otherwise, this is a fairly typical XML document for holding data, though perhaps with fewer attributes than usual.

Code listing 12.2.4.1   A typical instance document for the Staff Directory XML database

```xml
<?xml version="1.0" encoding="utf-8"?>
<staff>
  <staffMember lastUpdate="2006-01-12">
    <staffNo>31210</staffNo>
    <name>Paul Smith</name>
    <email>p.smith@pennine.ac.uk</email>
    <supportSessions>
      <session>
        <dayOfWeek>Wednesday</dayOfWeek>
        <startTime>11:00</startTime>
        <endTime>13:00</endTime>
      </session>
    </supportSessions>
  </staffMember>
  <staffMember lastUpdate="2005-03-07">
    <staffNo>35054</staffNo>
    <name>Selma Hutchins</name>
    <phone>8706</phone>
    <email>s.hutchins@pennine.ac.uk</email>
    <supportSessions>
      <session>
        <dayOfWeek>Monday</dayOfWeek>
        <startTime>09:00</startTime>
        <endTime>10:00</endTime>
      </session>
      <session>
        <dayOfWeek>Monday</dayOfWeek>
        <startTime>15:00</startTime>
        <endTime>16:00</endTime>
      </session>
      <session>
        <dayOfWeek>Tuesday</dayOfWeek>
        <startTime>11:00</startTime>
        <endTime>12:00</endTime>
      </session>
    </supportSessions>
  </staffMember>
  <staffMember lastUpdate="2005-03-07">
    <staffNo>23257</staffNo>
    <name>Freya Stark</name>
```

```
        <phone>8660</phone>
        <phone>8661</phone>
        <email>f.stark@pennine.ac.uk</email>
        <supportSessions>
          <session>
            <dayOfWeek>Monday</dayOfWeek>
            <startTime>15:00</startTime>
            <endTime>16:00</endTime>
          </session>
        </supportSessions>
      </staffMember>
  </staff>
```

In terms of the tree representation, the root node is the document itself and its only child is the staff element.

Code listing 12.2.4.2 uses this simple observation to start off the schema document. Line 1 is an XML declaration as the schema document is itself an XML document. Note that the encoding for this schema document is ISO-8859-1, which is not the same encoding as the instance document. This is perfectly acceptable.

Line 2 is the start tag for an element pattern. The name attribute identifies this as the pattern for the staff element. Thus, the staff element of any instance document *must* match this pattern. The namespace declaration sets the default namespace for the entire XML document to http://relaxng.org/ns/structure/1.0. This is the namespace name for the RELAX NG document model, so an XML parser knows that the mark-up in this document is specified in the RELAX NG document model.

Line 3 is blank, indicating that the pattern for the staff element is missing its content model.

Line 4 is the closing tag </element>, indicating the end of this element pattern.

The RELAX NG document model has its own schema document so that validating XML parsers can check the structure of RELAX NG schemas and ensure that, for example, every choice element in the schema document has at least one child element and every element element in the schema document has a name attribute. The schema document is written using the RELAX NG XML schema language.

Code listing 12.2.4.2   The root element is the staff *element*

```
1. <?xml version="1.0" encoding="ISO-8859-1"?>
2. <element xmlns="http://relaxng.org/ns/structure/1.0"
       name="staff">
3.
4. </element>
```

All the content of the instance document appears inside the staff element, so every pattern in the schema document will be a descendant of the pattern for the staff element. This means that the schema document in Code listing 12.2.4.2 forms a skeleton for the final schema document. All the remaining patterns will appear between the start and end tags of this RELAX NG element pattern.

Having identified that the root node has the `staff` element as its single child node and written down an element pattern for this child node, it is time to move down one level of the tree and consider the content model for the `staff` element. To do this, first identify the child nodes of the `staff` element, but, at this stage, don't bother about *their* content models.

Looking at the instance document in Code listing 12.2.4.1, it is clear that there is only one kind of child node – the `staffMember` element. However, there are several of them. The business rule is that the `staff` element must contain one or more `staffMember` elements and Code listing 12.2.4.3 shows the pattern for that content model. Line 3 now begins the RELAX NG oneOrMore pattern. This pattern contains a single element pattern, for the `staffMember` element. The blank line, line 5, indicates that the content model for the `staffMember` element has yet to be defined.

Code listing 12.2.4.3 *The* `staff` *element contains one or more elements called* `staffMember` *and that's all*

```
1.  <?xml version="1.0" encoding="ISO-8859-1"?>
2.  <element xmlns="http://relaxng.org/ns/structure/1.0"
        name="staff">
3.      <oneOrMore>
4.          <element name="staffMember">
5.
6.          </element>
7.      </oneOrMore>
8.  </element>
```

Once again, there is a single kind of child element, though it could occur many times in the instance document, so the content model for the `staff` element is fully specified by the pattern in code listing 12.2.4.3.

Time to move down a level and consider the content model for the `staffMember` element. Again, the instance document in Code listing 12.2.4.1 provides clues. Every `staffMember` element has an attribute called `lastUpdate`.

Code listing 12.2.4.4 builds on Code listing 12.2.4.3. In RELAX NG, attributes are indicated by an attribute pattern. Line 5 has the start tag for this attribute pattern, with the `name` attribute in this start tag indicating that the attribute pattern is matched by an attribute called `lastUpdate`. Line 6 is left blank to indicate that the pattern for the value of the `lastUpdate` attribute hasn't been specified yet and line 7 is the closing tag for the attribute pattern.

Every `staffMember` element also contains a `staffNo` element. Clearly, there will only ever be one `staffNo` element for each member of staff, so a single element pattern is needed in the content model for `staffMember`, as shown in lines 8–10. The same is true of the `name` and `email` elements and, again, these also have a single element pattern in the content model for `staffMember`.

The `phone element` is trickier. In the instance document shown in Code listing 12.2.4.1 the first `staffMember` element doesn't contain a `phone` element, but the third has two. This suggests a multiplicity of 'zero or more'. Lines 14–18 in Code listing 12.2.4.4 place the zeroOrMore pattern around a single element pattern to capture this part of the content model for staffMember.

The only other child of the staffMember element is the supportSessions element. Every staffMember element in Code listing 12.2.4.1 has a supportSessions element. However, the Staff Directory also includes contact details for non-academic staff. Such staff never offer support sessions, so their staffMember elements won't contain a supportSessions element. This means that the supportSessions element is optional. The pattern in lines 22–26 in Code listing 12.2.4.4 indicates this.

Code listing 12.2.4.4 *The* staffMember *element has a more complex content model*

```
1. <?xml version="1.0" encoding="ISO-8859-1"?>
2. <element xmlns="http://relaxng.org/ns/structure/1.0"
name="staff">
3.    <oneOrMore>
4.      <element name="staffMember">
5.        <attribute name="lastUpdate">
6.
7.        </attribute>
8.        <element name="staffNo">
9.
10.       </element>
11.       <element name="name">
12.
13.       </element>
14.       <zeroOrMore>
15.         <element name="phone">
16.
17.         </element>
18.       </zeroOrMore>
19.       <element name="email">
20.
21.       </element>
22.       <optional>
23.         <element name="supportSessions">
24.
25.         </element>
26.       </optional>
27.     </element>
28.   </oneOrMore>
28. </element>
```

The schema document in Code listing 12.2.4.4 fully describes the content model for both the staff and staffMember elements. The blank lines indicate missing content models, but all these are one level below the staffMember element in the tree representation of the document.

The simplest way to deal with these missing content models is to start at the top of Code listing 12.2.4.4 and work downwards. The first blank line, line 6, indicates that the content model for the `lastUpdate` attribute is missing. The value of the `lastUpdate` attribute is always a date, so use a data pattern with the W3C XML Schema datatype library to define the attribute's value (Code listing 12.2.4.5).

Code listing 12.2.4.5 The content model for the `lastUpdate` attribute

```
5. <attribute name="lastUpdate">
6. <data datatypeLibrary=
       "http://www.w3.org/2001/XMLSchema-datatypes"
       type="date" />
7. </attribute>
```

Line 9 in code listing 12.2.4.4 is also blank, indicating that the content model for the `staffNo` element needs to be defined. At the Pennine University, the staff number is always a five-digit number and there is often a need to list members of staff in staff number order. For this reason, its value should be numeric.

One way to define a five-digit numeric value is to say that it is an integer between 10,000 and 99,999. Code listing 12.2.4.6 shows the relevant data pattern, with its param children already written out. It is always best to deal with data patterns in one go – identify that a data pattern is required and define its content. This is because its child elements are always leaf nodes, so things don't get too complicated. (The line numbers have been adjusted to allow for the extra lines.)

Code listing 12.2.4.6 Restricting data values using the param pattern

```
8. <element name="staffNo">
9.  <data datatypeLibrary=
        "http://www.w3.org/2001/XMLSchema-datatypes"
        type="integer">
10.    <param name="minInclusive">10000</param>
11.    <param name="maxInclusive">99999</param>
12.  </data>
13. </element>
```

The next blank line occurs in line 12 in Code listing 12.2.4.4, indicating that the content model for the `name` element needs to be defined.

The simplest approach is to use the text pattern as it matches all the sample data in the instance document in Code listing 12.2.4.1. However, as discussed above, the `name` element might be split into `fName` and `lName` elements.

Code listing 12.2.4.7 uses the choice pattern to allow either of these two content models in lines 15–25. Note that, the content models for the child elements `fName` and `lName` have been left blank (lines 19 and 22).

The content models for the phone and e-mail elements in lines 16 and 20 in Code listing 12.2.4.4 are simply the text pattern. Both could be specified in more detail as RELAX NG allows a data pattern to be restricted using regular expressions. However, plain old text will do fine for this example. Code listing 12.2.4.7 shows the complete content models for the `phone` and `email` elements.

**Code listing 12.2.4.7   Using the choice pattern to allow different content
models for the** name **element**

```
14.    <element name="name">
15.      <choice>
16.        <text />
17.        <group>
18.          <element name="fName">
19.
20.          </element>
21.          <element name="lName">
22.
23.          </element>
24.        </group>
25.      </choice>
26.    </element>
27.    <zeroOrMore>
28.      <element name="phone">
29.        <text />
30.      </element>
31.    </zeroOrMore>
32.    <element name="email">
33.      <text />
34.    </element>
```

Returning to Code listing 12.2.4.4, the next, and final, blank line occurs in line 24.
This is the content model for the supportSessions element. This element must
always contain at least one session element and may contain several. The session
elements hold details of individual support sessions. Although some staff members do
not offer support sessions, this is captured by making the supportSessions
element optional. When the supportSessions element exists, however, it *must*
contain at least one session element.

Code listing 12.2.4.8 shows how to use the oneOrMore pattern to achieve this.

Code listing 12.2.4.8   Using the oneOrMore pattern

```
35.    <optional>
36.      <element name="supportSessions">
37.        <oneOrMore>
38.          <element name="session">
39.
40.          </element>
41.        </oneOrMore>
42.      </element>
43.    </optional>
```

The content model for the supportSessions element completes the specification
of the content models for attributes and elements at the third level of the tree representation. Now, it's time to go back to line 1 and search for missing content models at

the next level down (the blank lines). Code listings 12.2.4.7 and 12.2.4.8 include all the missing content models.

The first is the content model for the fName element (line 19 in Code listing 12.2.4.7). This element will only ever contain text, as will the lName element (line 22).

This just leaves the content model for the session element (line 39 in Code listing 12.2.4.8). The session element contains exactly one of each of the dayOfWeek, startTime and endTime elements. The startTime and endTime elements must appear in this order, but that is the only restriction on the content model. Code listing 12.2.4.9 shows the RELAX NG pattern for this content model.

Code listing 12.2.4.9   Using the interleave pattern

```
38. <element name="session">
39.   <interleave>
40.     <element name="dayOfWeek">
41.
42.     </element>
43.     <group>
44.       <element name="startTime">
45.
46.       </element>
47.       <element name="endTime">
48.
49.       </element>
50.     </group>
51.   </interleave>
52. </element>
```

At this point, only the content models for the dayOfWeek, startTime and endTime elements are left still to do.

Code listing 12.2.4.10 shows the complete RELAX NG schema document, including these last three content models in lines 32–37. Schema documents like this one are called **Russian doll schema** as the content model of each element appears inside the content model of its parent, just as each Russian doll is contained inside a larger one.

Russian doll schema are not the only approach to writing schema documents and have some problems. In particular, if an element or attribute is used in the content models of two different elements, then it must be defined twice – once for each of its two parent elements. RELAX NG provides facilities to allow pattern reuse. See the Further reading section at the end of this chapter for details of resources that cover these more advanced features.

Code listing 12.2.4.10   The final schema document for the Staff Directory

```
1. <?xml version="1.0" encoding="ISO-8859-1"?>
2. <element xmlns="http://relaxng.org/ns/structure/1.0"
       name="staff">
3.     <oneOrMore>
```

```
4.        <element name="staffMember">
5.          <attribute name="lastUpdate">
6.            <data datatypeLibrary=
             "http://www.w3.org/2001/XMLSchema-datatypes"
             type="date" />
7.          </attribute>
8.          <element name="staffNo">
9.            <data datatypeLibrary=
             "http://www.w3.org/2001/XMLSchema-datatypes"
             type="integer">
10.             <param name="minInclusive">10000</param>
11.             <param name="maxInclusive">99999</param>
12.           </data>
13.         </element>
14.         <element name="name">
15.           <choice>
16.             <text />
17.             <group>
18.               <element name="fName"><text /></element>
19.               <element name="lName"><text /></element>
20.             </group>
21.           </choice>
22.         </element>
23.         <zeroOrMore>
24.           <element name="phone"><text /></element>
25.         </zeroOrMore>
26.         <element name="email"><text /></element>
27.         <optional>
28.           <element name="supportSessions">
29.             <oneOrMore>
30.               <element name="session">
31.                 <interleave>
32.                 <element name="dayOfWeek">
33.                   <choice>
34.                     <value type="token">Monday</value>
35.                     <value type="token">
                     Tuesday</value>
36.                     <value type="token">
                     Wednesday</value>
37.                     <value type="token">
                     Thursday</value>
38.                     <value type="token">Friday</value>
39.                   </choice>
40.                 </element>
41.                 <group>
42.                   <element name="startTime">
```

```
43.    <data datatypeLibrary=
       "http://www.w3/org/2001/XMLSchema-datatypes"
       type="time" />
44.              </element>
45.              <element name="endTime">
46.    <data datatypeLibrary=
       "http://www.w3/org/2001/XMLSchema-datatypes"
       type="time" />
47.                    </element>
48.                  </group>
49.                </interleave>
50.              </element>
51.            </oneOrMore>
52.          </element>
53.        </optional>
54.      </element>
55.    </oneOrMore>
56. </element>
```

12.2.5. Checking relational-style candidate and foreign key constraints

XML has two approaches to modelling relationships between things. The first uses containment – the element representing a support session is physically contained within the element representing the staff member offering that support session.

Physical containment of one element within another creates a tree-structured hierarchy of parent–child relationships. This approach cannot model all possible relationships as some relationships are not inherently hierarchical.

Suppose support sessions in the School of Computing are organized jointly by all staff teaching a module. At a particular time, all these staff turn up to a computer lab and offer one-to-one support to any students who need it. There is no easy way to model this scenario using the hierarchical approach. The simplest is to put a copy of a particular supportSession element into the staff element of every member of staff who will be there. However, this leads to the usual problems with duplicate data. For example, if the day or time of the support session changes, it must be changed in lots of different supportSession elements.

To deal with this, XML includes relational-style primary and foreign keys. These provide a more flexible and powerful mechanism for modelling relationships. It is important to realize that the RELAX NG does not itself support relational-style keys, nor does it enforce candidate and foreign key constraints. RELAX NG focuses solely on checking that the tree structure of XML instance documents matches the patterns in the schema document. The complexity of the XML data model makes this a big enough task in itself. For comparison, the equivalent task in the relational data language SQL is achieved by using the create table and alter table statements and these two simple statements also define the integrity constraints!

Candidate and foreign keys are dealt with by the DTD compatibility datatype library. This is because relational-style candidate and foreign keys were first introduced as part of the DTD schema language. The approach to defining candidate and foreign keys is quite different from the approach taken in the relational data model. First, only *attributes* can be defined as candidate or foreign keys. Second, this is done by assigning the attribute a special data type, rather than by declaring an integrity constraint.

Any attribute with the data type ID from the DTD compatibility datatype library is recognized as representing a candidate key. The value of such an ID attribute must be a character string that meets the definition for an XML name token, with the added restriction that it cannot contain the colon character.

Be careful, here. The value of an ID attribute is not actually a name, it is a value. This value is a character string that just happens to be restricted to the same set of characters as that used for XML element and attribute names (among other things). The XML specifications use the same description of this set of allowed characters for both name tokens *and* values. When a document instance is validated, the DTD compatibility library checks that the data type of the value of any ID attribute is correct. It also checks that the value of each occurrence of an ID attribute is unique within the instance document. This includes ID attributes in *different* elements. Every attribute node in the instance document that has a data type of ID *must* have a value that is unique within the instance document. This makes the ID attribute a kind of global surrogate key. A good analogy for the ID attribute is the sequence object used by the Oracle DBMS to generate values that are unique within a database. Of course, the DTD compatibility data type library does not actually *generate* the values for an ID attribute, but it does check that they are unique.

As usual, there is an example in the Staff Directory as the staff number must be unique. So far, the staff number has been modelled as a staffNo element, a child element of the staffMember element. In RELAX NG there is currently no way to check that the *value* of an *element* is unique within the instance document (the W3C XML Schema language does now support this feature). So, although the content of the staffNo element is a candidate key, there is no way to enforce the candidate key constraint.

To enforce a candidate key constraint on staff numbers, then, they must be modelled as an attribute with the data type ID. Code listing 12.2.5.1 shows how to do this.

Code listing 12.2.5.1 (a) shows the first few lines of the schema document and (b) shows a typical instance document. Note that three changes have been made to the schema document since Code listing 12.2.4.10, lines 4–13. First the staffNo is now defined by an attribute pattern, not an element pattern. Second, its data type has changed from the W3C XML Schema data type integer to the DTD compatibility data type ID (obviously). Third, the data values are no longer constrained by param patterns. This is because the DTD compatibility datatype library does not support facets. With this new schema document, the XML parser will check the value of all the staffNo attributes in an instance document and report an error if there are two the same.

There is also a subtle change to the instance document. Now that staffNo is an attribute with the ID data type, its value must be a valid XML name token. Name tokens cannot start with a digit, so the actual staff number values can't be used. Instead, the staff number needs to be prefixed with a letter or underscore. Code listing 12.2.5.1 (b) therefore prefixes the actual staff number with the letter 's'. This is one of the main problems with using attributes to hold candidate key values.

Code listing 12.2.5.1   Candidate keys in XML

(a) The first ten lines of the schema document

```
<?xml version="1.0" encoding="utf-8"?>
<element xmlns="http://relaxng.org/ns/structure/1.0"
  name="staff">
 <oneOrMore>
   <element name="staffMember">
     <attribute name="lastUpdate">
      <data datatypeLibrary=
      "http://www.w3/org/ 2001/XMLSchema-datatypes"
      type="date" />
     </attribute>
     <attribute name="staffNo">
      <data datatypeLibrary=
      "http://relaxng.org/ns/compatibility/datatypes/1.0"
      type="ID" />
     </attribute>
```

(b) A typical instance document

```
<?xml version="1.0" encoding="utf-8"?>
<staff>
  <staffMember lastUpdate="2006-01-12" staffNo="s31210">
    <name>Paul Smith</name>
    <email>p.smith@pennine.ac.uk</email>
    <supportSessions>
      <session>
        <dayOfWeek>Wednesday</dayOfWeek>
        <startTime>11:00</startTime>
        <endTime>13:00</endTime>
      </session>
    </supportSessions>
  </staffMember>
  <staffMember lastUpdate="2005-03-07" staffNo="s23257">
    <name>Freya Stark</name>
    <phone>8660</phone>
    <phone>8661</phone>
    <email>f.stark@pennine.ac.uk</email>
    <supportSessions>
      <session>
        <dayOfWeek>Monday</dayOfWeek>
        <startTime>15:00</startTime>
        <endTime>16:00</endTime>
      </session>
    </supportSessions>
  </staffMember>
</staff>
```

There are two further problems with the schema in Code listing 12.2.5.1 (a). The first is a conceptual problem. XML attributes are intended to model meta-data, which is data *about* the *element* rather than actual data about the thing the element holds data about. The staff number is clearly *not* meta-data – it is data about a member of staff, so should be part of the content of the staffMember element, not part of its meta-data.

The second problem is a practical one. A staff number should be a five-digit number. The only way to enforce this constraint is to use the W3C XML Schema datatype library. Unfortunately, it is also a candidate key and the only way to enforce this constraint is to use the DTD compatibility datatype library. As each attribute value or text node can only have one data type and that data type can come from only one datatype library, the schema author must choose either to enforce the candidate key constraint or the constraint that data values are five-digit integers.

This second problem can be partially solved by using a surrogate key (see Chapter 10). Code listing 12.2.5.2 shows the first few lines of an amended schema document. The staffMember element has an attribute called surrogateKey with the data type ID. The values of this attribute are guaranteed to be unique, but might not be five-digit integers.

It also has a child element called staffNo. This element contains a five-digit integer, but the values might not be unique. The final twist is to insist that the value of the surrogateKey attribute (minus its leading 's') must be the same as the content of the staffNo element. This will ensure that *both* constraints apply to the attribute's value and the element's content.

Of course, the XML parser won't do this. An additional XML processor needs to be written to do this final check. However, this additional XML processor will be quite simple. All it needs to do is check that, in each staffMember element, the value of the surrogateKey attribute is the same as the content of the staffNo element. It does not need to check that the surrogateKey attribute value is unique within the document, nor that the content of the staffNo element is a five-digit integer as the XML parser (actually, the datatype library) has already done both these checks.

Code listing 12.2.5.2 *Using a surrogate key for the* staff *element*

```
<?xml version="1.0" encoding="utf-8"?>
<element xmlns="http://relaxng.org/ns/structure/1.0"
    name="staff">
  <oneOrMore>
    <element name="staffMember">
      <attribute name="lastUpdate">
        <data datatypeLibrary=
        "http://www.w3/org/2001/XMLSchema-datatypes"
        type="date" />
      </attribute>
      <attribute name="surrogateKey">
        <data datatypeLibrary=
        "http://relaxng.org/ns/compatibility/
        datatypes/1.0"
        type="ID" />
      </attribute>
```

```
<element name="staffNo">
  <data
datatypeLibrary="http://www.w3/org/2001/ XMLSchema-
datatypes" type="integer">
      <param name="minInclusive">10000</param>
      <param name="maxInclusive">99999</param>
  </data>
</element>
```

Attributes with the data type ID play the role of candidate keys. Attributes with the data type IDREF play the role of foreign keys. The value of an IDREF attribute must be an XML name token and must also match the value of some ID attribute in the same instance document.

Code listing 12.2.5.3 shows a typical example of this mechanism in action. Code listing 12.2.5.3 (a) is a RELAX NG schema document for the Staff Directory application. The schema has been simplified to make it easier to see the foreign key mechanism in action. As before, the root element is called staff and this will contain one or more staffMember elements. Each staffMember element has a lastUpdate and a staffNo attribute with the data type ID, so is a candidate key. It contains name, phone and email elements, as before. However, the staffMember element does not contain a supportSessions element. Instead, the staff element may also contain zero or more session elements. The session element has a staffNo attribute with the data type IDREF, so is a foreign key. It contains dayOfWeek, startTime and endTime elements, as before.

This schema models the relationship between members of staff and the support sessions they offer in quite a different way from the earlier ones. Here, elements representing staff and support sessions appear as child elements of the root element. In an instance document, all the staffMember elements come first, followed by all the session elements. The value of the staffNo attribute of each session element will match the value of exactly one staffNo attribute of some staffMember element. Code listing 12.2.5.3 (b) shows a simple document instance, with two members of staff, each offering one support session.

Code listing 12.2.5.3   Foreign keys in XML

(a) The schema document with simplified patterns for staffMember **and** supportSession **elements**

```
<?xml version="1.0" encoding="utf-8"?>
<element xmlns="http://relaxng.org/ns/structure/1.0"
name="staff">
  <oneOrMore>
    <element name="staffMember">
      <attribute name="lastUpdate">
        <data datatypeLibrary=
        "http://www.w3.org/2001/XMLSchema-datatypes"
        type="date" />
      </attribute>
```

```
            <attribute name="staffNo">
              <data datatypeLibrary=
              "http://relaxng.org/ns/compatibility/data
              types/1.0" type="ID" />
            </attribute>
            <element name="name"> <text /> </element>
            <zeroOrMore>
              <element name="phone"> <text /> </element>
            </zeroOrMore>
            <element name="email"> <text /> </element>
              </element>
            </oneOrMore>
            <zeroOrMore>
              <element name="session">
                <attribute name="staffNo">
                  <data datatypeLibrary=
                  "http://relaxng.org/ns/compatibility/data
                  types/1.0" type="IDREF" />
                </attribute>
                <element name="dayOfWeek"> <text /> </element>
                <element name="startTime"> <text /> </element>
                <element name="endTime"> <text /> </element>
              </element>
            </zeroOrMore>
          </element>
```

(b) A typical instance document

```
<?xml version="1.0" encoding="utf-8"?>
<staff>
  <staffMember lastUpdate="2006-01-12" staffNo="s31210">
    <name>Paul Smith</name>
    <email>p.smith@pennine.ac.uk</email>
  </staffMember>
  <staffMember lastUpdate="2005-03-07" staffNo="s23257">
    <name>Freya Stark</name>
    <phone>8660</phone>
    <phone>8661</phone>
    <email>f.stark@pennine.ac.uk</email>
  </staffMember>
  <session staffNo="s31210">
    <dayOfWeek>Wednesday</dayOfWeek>
    <startTime>11:00</startTime>
    <endTime>13:00</endTime>
  </session>
  <session staffNo="s23257">
    <dayOfWeek>Monday</dayOfWeek>
    <startTime>15:00</startTime>
```

```
      <endTime>16:00</endTime>
    </session>
  </staff>
```

There is no need for the element with the ID attribute and that with the IDREF attribute to appear at the same level in the document hierarchy. In fact, ID and IDREF attributes can be used to link an element with one of its descendants.

There is a further twist to the ID and IDREF mechanism for implementing foreign key constraints. There is also an IDREFS data type. An attribute that has the data type IDREFS holds a *list* of space-separated XML name tokens, each of which matches the value of some ID attribute in the same instance document. The IDREFS data type offers a way to solve the problem raised at the start of this subsection. Making the staffNo attribute of the session element an IDREFS means that it can list *all* members of staff who attend this support session. The IDREFS data type provides a mechanism for implementing a foreign key that references multiple candidate keys, directly implementing a many-to-many relationship. This goes beyond the capability of foreign keys in the relational data model. Link tables achieve a similar effect in a relational database, but require two foreign keys, not one.

12.3 An introduction to XPath

The tree representation of an XML document consists of nodes connected by edges. Each **edge** represents the relationship between a node and its parent. Moving through the tree from a parent node to a child or attribute node, or from any node to its parent, traces out a **path** through the tree. Notice that paths can move down the tree or up it or meander up *and* down it in more complex ways.

> The 'or attribute' in the above description is necessary because, in XML, an attribute isn't a child of its parent. Apologies if this is getting tedious, but the distinction is important.

Figure 12.1 shows the tree representation of an instance document for the Staff Directory XML database. The number labelling each node indicates its position in the document order. The instance document holds contact details for two members of staff – Paul Smith and Freya Stark. The dashed lines indicate four different paths through this tree. All four paths start at the root node, though, in general, paths can start from any node in the instance document. All four paths always move down the tree structure, though, again, in general, paths can move back up the tree, too.

The leftmost path in Figure 12.1 passes through the nodes 1, 2, 3 and 5, *in that order*. This means that the path can be described by a sequence of nodes, written (1, 2, 3, 5). The other paths can also be described by the sequences of nodes (1, 2, 3, 7), (1, 2, 11, 13) and (1, 2, 11, 15).

601

Figure 12.1 The tree representation of an instance document for the Staff Directory XML database with four paths indicated.

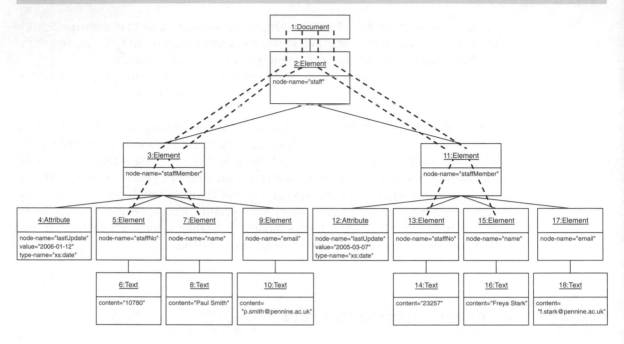

All four paths can be described by the *same* set of instructions, shown in Code listing 12.3.1. These instructions do not define a unique path because, for example, following the instruction in Step 3 leads to two nodes – the two `staffMember` element nodes numbered 3 and 11. The nodes each step leads to form the starting points for the next step. As Step 3 leads to nodes 3 and 11, nodes 3 and 11 form the starting points for step 4. As each step may have a number of starting points, it makes sense to consider them in document order. So, in step 4, first follow the instructions with node 3 as the starting point. This leads to the two nodes 5 and 7. Next, follow the instructions again with node 11 as the starting point. This leads to the two nodes 13 and 15. This means that Step 4 leads to four nodes – the `staffNo` and `name` child elements of node 3, and the `staffNo` and `name` child elements of node 11.

Code listing 12.3.1   Some plain English instructions for navigating a document tree

Step 1: Move to the root node.

Step 2: Move to the child element nodes.

Step 3: Move to the child element nodes.

Step 4: Move to the child element nodes that are called either `staffNo` or `name`.

As sequences of nodes describe both the starting point for a step and where it leads to, they provide a concise description of what happens when the instructions in Code listing 12.3.1 are followed, thus.

Step 1: Starts with the whole document and leads to the sequence of nodes (1).

Step 2: Starts from the sequence of nodes (1) and leads to the sequence of nodes (2).

Step 3: Starts from the sequence of nodes (2) and leads to the sequence of nodes (3, 11).

Step 4: Starts from the sequence of nodes (3, 11) and leads to the sequence of nodes (5, 7, 13, 15).

Clearly, sequences of nodes are a good way to describe both individual paths through a tree and the result of following the instructions that describe a set of similar paths. That is why the formal description of the XPath 2.0 and XQuery 1.0 data model (XDM) uses sequences of nodes as its basic organization structure.

The XPath language is basically a computer language for describing instructions like the ones above. In XPath terminology, each step is called a **location step** and a set of location steps is called the **location path**. The sequence of nodes forming the starting point for a particular location step is the context for that step. The context size is the number of nodes in the context. Each node in the context is considered in turn. At any stage in the evaluation of a location step, the node being considered is called the context node, and the context position is its position in the current context. Each location step equates to a sequence of nodes. The location path also equates to a sequence of nodes – that produced by following each of the location steps in turn.

This means that a location path does not actually equate to a path through the tree. Instead, it describes a *set* of paths through the tree (just as the instructions above do). The sequence of nodes a location path equates to is the sequence of nodes at the end of all the paths it describes.

Before introducing the syntax for XPath, it is worth looking in a little more detail at the concept of a location step. Location steps can be broken up into three distinct parts. Some more examples based on the instance document shown in Figure 12.1 will help illustrate these three parts.

First, consider the location path described by the instructions in Code listing 12.3.2.

Code listing 12.3.2 *A second list of plain English instructions for navigating a document tree*

Step 1: Move to the root node.

Step 2: From the current context, move to the descendant element nodes called staffMember.

Step 3: From the current context, move to the child element nodes that are called either staffNo or name.

These instructions result in the following node sequence.

Step 1: Starts with the whole document and sets the context to the sequence of nodes (1).

Step 2: Starts from the context (1) and sets the context to the sequence of nodes (3, 11).

Step 3: Starts from the context (3, 11) and sets the context to the sequence of nodes (5, 7, 13, 15).

This means that the location path in Code listing 12.3.2 leads to the same sequence of nodes as that in code listing 12.3.1, but with fewer location steps.

The first difference between the two is that in Step 2 in Code listing 12.3.2, the instruction says 'move to the *descendent*', whereas, in Code listing 12.3.1, it says 'move to the *child*'. This illustrates the first way to refine the notion of a location step. Each location step begins at a given context and moves to a new context. The initial move could be from the context nodes to all their child nodes or to all their descendant nodes or some other sequence of nodes defined relative to the context.

In XPath, this initial sequence of nodes for a location step is called the **axis**. The axis is always defined relative to the context. XPath defines 12 different axes.

- The child axis consists of all child nodes of the context node.
- The parent axis consists of the parent node of the context node.
- The self axis consists of the context node.
- The descendant axis consists of all descendant nodes of the context node.
- The ancestor axis consists of all ancestor nodes of the context node.
- The descendant or self axis consists of the context node plus all descendant nodes of the context node.
- The ancestor or self axis consists of the context node plus all ancestor nodes of the context node.
- The attribute axis consists of the attribute nodes of the context node.
- The following sibling axis consists of all sibling nodes of the context node that occur after it in document order. An attribute node has no siblings.
- The preceding sibling axis consists of all sibling nodes of the context node that occur before it in document order. An attribute node has no siblings.
- The following axis consists of all nodes that occur after the context node in document order, other than its descendants.
- The preceding axis consists of all nodes that occur before the context node in document order, other than its ancestors.

Attribute nodes only ever appear in the attribute axis or in the self axis when the context node is an attribute node. The two sibling axes are always empty when the context node is an attribute. The parent, ancestor and ancestor or self axes only ever contain element nodes – only elements can contain other nodes so only elements can be parents. The other axes can contain element nodes, text nodes, namespace nodes, comment nodes and processing instruction nodes.

An XPath axis is either a **forward axis** or a **reverse axis**. The difference between them is that, for a forward axis, the nodes appear in document order, while for a reverse axis they appear in reverse document order. This is important as it determines the order of nodes in the node sequence for this step. The reverse axes are parent, ancestor, ancestor or self, preceding and preceding sibling. The others are all forward axes. Note that the order of attribute nodes in the attribute axis is implementation-defined, but will always be the same.

Returning to the two examples, Step 2 in Code listing 12.3.1 works as follows.

1 Start with the context (1).

2 Use the child axis, so the initial sequence of nodes is (2).

3 Select all the element nodes, so the node sequence is (2).

4 Set the context to the node sequence (2).

In contrast, Step 2 in Code listing 12.3.2 works as follows.

1 Start with the context (1).

2 Use the descendant axis. This means the initial sequence of nodes is (2, 3, 5, 6, 7, 8, 9, 10, 11, 13, 14, 15, 16, 17, 18) – only the two attribute nodes 4 and 12 are not present.

3 Select only the nodes called 'staffMember', so the node sequence is (3, 11).

4 Set the context to the node sequence (3, 11).

This also shows the second way to refine a location step – specify which nodes on the chosen axis should be selected from the initial sequence of nodes identified by the axis. In XPath, this is called a **node test**.

XPath includes two sorts of node test. The first, called a name test, selects nodes by name. Code listing 12.3.2 uses a name test. Name tests only work for element and attribute nodes as they are the only nodes that have names.

The second, called a kind test, selects a particular kind of node. The simplest kind test selects nodes based on the different kinds of nodes allowed in the XDM – text nodes, element nodes or attribute nodes (or comment, processing instruction or namespace nodes). Code listing 12.3.1 uses a simple kind test to select just the element nodes. A more complex sort of kind test selects nodes based on which kind of XDM node they are and what their data type is.

Step 3 in Code listing 12.3.2 (and Step 4 in Code listing 12.3.1) starts with the context (3, 11) and uses the child axis. The children of node 3 are nodes 5, 7 and 9. The children of node 11 are nodes 13, 15 and 17. This gives an initial sequence of nodes (5, 7, 9, 13, 15, 17). Step 3 then has the further information that only element nodes called 'staffNo' or 'name' should be included. This looks like it should be a name test. Unfortunately, a name test can only include *one* name. In fact, it is a general rule that a location step can only have one node test. Using and and or to produce Boolean combinations of node tests simply isn't allowed. That is why a location step can have a **predicate**. A predicate is a Boolean combination of XPath expressions (of location paths or location steps). This is a little odd, because XPath expressions are node sequences, not Boolean values. It is possible because XPath coerces each node sequence into a Boolean value as follows:

- the empty sequence is coerced into being the Boolean value false

- a sequence consisting of a single text node or attribute with Boolean data type is coerced into being the Boolean value the node represents

- a sequence consisting of a single text node or attribute with a string data type is coerced into being the Boolean value true for non-empty strings and false for empty strings

- a sequence consisting of a single text node or attribute with a numeric data type is coerced into being the boolean value `true` for non-zero numbers and `false` for zero or the special value `NAN` (which stands for 'not a number').

- any other non-empty sequence is coerced into being the Boolean value `true`.

This coercion applies to both the results of XPath expressions making up the predicate *and* the result of the predicate itself, if this is a node sequence.

Returning to Step 3 in Code listing 12.3.2, the only way to capture the final requirement – that only element nodes called `staffNo` or `name` should be included in the node set for this step – is to use a predicate. Consider the location path 'From the current context, use the self axis and move to the node called `staffNo`'.

This location path has a single location step, so can be written using just an axis and a node test. For a particular context node, the location path works as follows.

1 Start from the context node.

2 Use the self axis, giving an initial node sequence consisting of just the context node itself.

3 Select only the nodes called `staffNo`. If the context node is called `staffNo`, this leads to the node sequence consisting of just the context node itself; otherwise it leads to the empty sequence.

4 Finally, set the context to this node sequence.

Similarly, the location path 'From the current context, use the self axis and move to the node called `name`' evaluates to a sequence consisting of the context node if the context node is called `name`, but to the empty sequence in all other circumstances. The predicate for Step 3 in Code listing 12.3.2 combines these two location paths with a Boolean `or` operator:

(From the current context, use the self axis and move to the element node called `staffNo`) `or` (From the current context, use the self axis and move to the element node called `name`)

Step 3 in Code listing 12.3.2 works as follows.

1 Start from the sequence of nodes (3, 11).

2 Use the child axis, giving an initial node sequence (5, 7, 9, 13, 15, 17).

3 Apply the node test to select all the element nodes from the node sequence (5, 7, 9, 13, 15, 17). This gives the node sequence (5, 7, 9, 13, 15, 17).

4 For each node in the sequence (5, 7, 9, 13, 15, 17) apply the predicate described above. For nodes 5, 7, 13 and 15, the predicate evaluates to `true`. For nodes 9 and 17, both called `email`, the predicate evaluates to `false`. This gives the node sequence (5, 7, 13, 15).

Using a combination of axis, node test and predicate, a location path can point to *any* node in the XML document. This makes XPath one of the core XML technologies. XPath expressions form the basis for XQuery, are used extensively in XSLT to identify portions of a document for transformation and are used in some XML schema languages to apply constraints to the document structure (W3C XML Schema and Schematron both use XPath expressions).

So far, the discussion of XPath has been at a conceptual level. The syntax for XPath expressions is based on the syntax for the UNIX file system's pathnames. This makes sense, because the UNIX file system is a hierarchical structure and most computing professionals are familiar with the pathname syntax. In UNIX, a pathname is a sequence of directory names, separated by a forward slash, and a final filename. For example, the pathname `/usr/local/httpd/files/index.html` starts at the root directory (the initial forward slash), moves to the directory called `usr`, then the directory called `local`, then the directory called `httpd`, then the directory called `files` and, in that directory, points to the file called `index.html`.

Similarly, an XPath location path is written as a sequence of location steps separated by a forward slash. If there is only one location step in the location path, then there is no need for a trailing forward slash. Each location step has three parts. First comes the axis, represented by its name followed by a double colon – `::`. So, in an XPath location step, the child axis is written `child::` and the follow sibling axis is written `follow-sibling::`. The other axes all follow this pattern.

After the axis comes the node test. Node tests are either name tests or kind tests. The XPath syntax for a name test is simply the name of the node required. If this is a local name, then XPath will determine the namespace from the context. A node satisfies the name test provided its expanded name matches the expanded version of the name given in the name test. There is no need to specify whether the node is an element or an attribute as XPath works this out from the axis. An axis includes attribute nodes if, and only if, it is either the attribute axis or it is the self axis in the context of an attribute node. In these situations, XPath assumes that the name test selects attributes with the given name. In all other situations, it assumes that it selects elements with the given name. This default kind of node for an axis, in a given context, is called the **principal node kind** for that axis in that context.

Name tests can include wildcards. The wildcard symbol is '*' and it selects all nodes of the principal node kind. As node names can be qualified by a namespace prefix, it is possible to use name tests of the form `*:myName`, which selects nodes of the principal node kind called `myName` regardless of their namespace. Similarly, `myPrefix:*` selects nodes of the principal node kind in the namespace with prefix `myPrefix` regardless of their local name.

The XPath syntax for a simple kind test is the kind of the node followed by parentheses. So, the kind test for element nodes is written `element()`. This syntax generalizes to allow more complex kind tests by including further information between the parentheses, but these more complex kind tests are not covered in this book. The `text()` and `attribute()` kind tests are matched by text nodes and attribute nodes respectively. The special kind test `node()` selects any kind of node at all from the nodes matching the axis. The `node()` kind test is useful for emphasizing that *all* nodes from the axis are required, not just the principal node kind.

Putting the syntax together, the XPath syntax for Step 2 in Code listing 12.3.1 – 'Move to the child element nodes' – is:

```
child::element()
```

Note that the XPath expression `child::element()` is equivalent to `child::*`. This is because the principal node kind of the child axis is the element node, so `child::*` says 'select all child element nodes, regardless of their name'. Most XPath developers seem to use `child::*`, presumably because it is easier to type.

For Step 2 in Code listing 12.3.2 – 'From the current context, move to the descendant element nodes called `staffMember`' – the XPath syntax is:

```
descendant::staffMember
```

The final part of a location step is the predicate. The predicate is simply a Boolean combination of location paths, enclosed in square brackets. The final location step in Code listing 12.3.2 – 'From the current context, move to the child element nodes that are called either `staffNo` or `name`' – is written:

```
child::*[self::staffNo or self::name]
```

This location step can be read as follows.

> Select all child nodes of nodes in the current context. From these, select all element nodes (the principal node kind), regardless of their node name (the wildcard '*'). Finally, for each node selected so far, test whether or not it satisfies the predicate 'This node is called either `staffNo` or `name`'.

A single forward slash at the start of a location path selects the root node of the document. This is the first step in our two examples, so completes the syntax required to write XPath expressions for them. The location path described by Code listing 12.3.1 can be written:

```
/child::element()/child::element()
    /child::element()[self::staffNo or self::name]
```

or, using wildcards:

```
/child::*/child::*/child::*[self::staffNo or self::name]
```

Code listing 12.3.2 can be written:

```
/descendant::staffMember
    /child::*[self::staffNo or self::name]
```

XPath can be used as a simple query language for XML documents. Using the instance document in Figure 12.1 as the database instance, the business query 'What is the name of the member of staff with `staffNo` "10780"' gives the answer 'Paul Smith'. The XPath expression that retrieves this data from the instance document is shown in Code listing 12.3.3.

Code listing 12.3.3   Using XPath as a simple query language

```
/child::staff/child::staffMember[child::staffNo
    eq '10780']/child::name/child::text()
```

There is some new syntax here, in the predicate in Step 3 (Step 1 is the initial forward slash, which says, 'Start at the root node'). The predicate is:

```
[child::staffNo eq '10780']
```

This predicate uses the XPath comparison operator eq, which makes equality comparisons between two sequences of values. XPath comparison operators compare XPath expressions, which are always sequences. As XPath doesn't deal with 'raw' values, the literal '10780' actually represents the sequence ('10780'), which is a sequence consisting of a single value. This is a standard feature of XPath syntax – a literal for a 'raw' value is interpreted as the sequence with that single value as its only member.

There is also a problem with the other part of this predicate. The XPath expression child::staffNo doesn't represent a sequence of *values* but a sequence of *element nodes*. XPath automatically converts this into a new sequence before making the equality comparison required by the eq operator. Each element node is replaced by its string value. The string value of an element node (or the root node) is the concatenation of the content of its descendant text nodes into a single string, taking the text nodes in document order. Thus, a sequence of two element nodes is converted into a sequence of two string values before the comparison is made. XPath also converts text nodes and attribute nodes into a single string value – for text nodes this is their content, while for attribute nodes it is their value. In this way every sequence of nodes is replaced by a sequence of string values. This process is known as **atomization**.

> There are two further atomizations, for comment nodes and processing instruction nodes. Each becomes the string representing its text.

Now that both sides of the eq operator have been turned into sequences of string values, XPath compares them according to the following rules:

- if either sequence is empty, the result is the empty sequence, ().
- if either sequence has more than one value, the result is false.
- otherwise, the two values are compared.

There are five other value comparison operators covering the obvious comparisons:

- ne is 'not equal to'
- lt is 'less than'
- le is 'less than or equal to'
- gt is 'greater than'
- ge is 'greater than or equal to'.

For text and attribute nodes that have a data type (those described by a data pattern in the document schema) XPath treats the atomized string values as literals for the appropriate data type. If the string value is not a valid literal, XPath reports a runtime error.

Returning to Code listing 12.3.3, the location path instructs the XPath processor to carry out the following five steps.

Step 1: Start from the document and return the context consisting of the root node (1).

Step 2: From the context (1) select all child element nodes called staff. This leads to the context (2).

609

Step 3a: From the context (2) select all child element nodes called `staffMember`. This leads to the sequence of nodes (3, 11). Now, apply the predicate `child::staffNo eq '10780'` to each node in this sequence.

Step 3b: With node 3 as the context node, evaluate the location path `child::staffNo`. This leads to the sequence of nodes (5) (there is only one child node called `staffNo`). Atomize this sequence. This leads to the sequence of string values ('10780'). Now consider the right-hand side of the `eq` operator. This is the string value '10780', which is converted to the sequence ('10780'). As both sides of the `eq` operator evaluate to the sequence ('10780'), return the value `true`. Node 3 is added to the final context.

Step 3c: With node 11 as the context node, evaluate the location path `child::staffNo`. This leads to the sequence of nodes (13) (there is only one child node called `staffNo`). Atomize this sequence. This leads to the sequence of string values ('23257'). Now consider the right-hand side of the `eq` operator. This is the string value '10780', which is converted to the sequence ('10780'). As the two sides evaluate to single-member sequences with different string values, return the value `false`. Node 11 is not added to the final context.

Step 3d: Finally, pass the context (3) to the next step.

Step 4: From the context (3) select all child element nodes called `name`. This leads to the context (7).

Step 5: From the context (7) select all child text nodes. This leads to the context (8).

As node 8 is the text node with value 'Paul Smith', the XPath expression *does* answer the query.

This example demonstrates the power of predicates. For each node that satisfies the axis and node test of the third location step, the predicate burrows deeper into the tree to test a Boolean condition. Only if this test is satisfied is the node included in the context for the next location step. This is a little like a tourist using a street map to navigate to a hotel in Venice (where there are no cars, only pedestrians and boats). The alleys are the edges and the junctions are the nodes. At each junction, the tourist checks whether or not this alleyway leads to the hotel. If it does, the person turns down the alleyway. If not, the alleyway is ignored.

This introduction to XPath covers the key concepts in the language and introduces the concepts at the heart of XML query languages. Beyond the basic features discussed, XPath provides other comparison operators and a large collection of functions. The Further reading section at the end of this chapter points to resources that can help in exploring the XPath language, along with the more powerful XML query languages XQuery and SQL/XML. XQuery builds on the ability of XPath to locate specific portions of an XML document to deliver an XML query language along the lines of the relational query language SQL. The W3C adopted XQuery as an official recommendation in January 2007. In cases where XML documents or document fragments are stored in relational databases, the SQL/XML query language will also be important. This extends the traditional SQL query language to deal with column values that are one of the XDM data types. SQL/XML has already been at least partially implemented by several commercial RDBMS.

12.4 Designing XML databases

The differences between the relational data model and the XDM do not affect conceptual database design as it doesn't target any particular data model. Even so, if a project is known to be using an XML rather than a relational database, then it would make sense to use data types from the XDM rather than relational model. Other than that, conceptual database design is the same for XML as it is for relational databases.

Logical database design follows a similar process to that for logical design for the relational data model, but targets the XDM. First, any structures in the conceptual ER diagram that cannot be implemented directly using structures from the XDM are removed. This give a logical ER diagram for the XDM. The structures in this logical ER diagram are then implemented using elements and attributes – the core organization structures of the XDM. It's important to note that the UML attributes of the ER diagram do not necessarily become XML attributes – many become XML elements.

Logical database design for the XDM does not aim to produce a complete schema document, like that in Code listing 12.2.4.10. Instead, it produces descriptions for each of the main elements – their names, attributes and content models. This raises the problem of how best to write down these descriptions.

In logical database design for the relation data model, the table schema are written in such a way that they are almost, but not quite, SQL create table statements. The main reason for not going directly to SQL is that table schema are a little simpler than create table statements. XML, and the XDM, are not as simple as the relational data model. In fact, the RELAX NG compact syntax probably provides the simplest language for describing the content models of XML elements. This makes it a strong candidate for the logical design language for XML databases. However, that means learning yet another syntax (the seventh in this book, which has used UML, PHP, SQL, XML, RELAX NG XML syntax and XPath). As the aim here is to understand the *process* of logical database design for the XDM it makes sense to use the RELAX NG XML syntax instead. This leads to slightly longer descriptions for the content models, but avoids cluttering up the discussion with explanations of yet another syntax.

Physical database design for XML turns the element content models produced during logical design into a complete schema document for the database. It also addresses the general physical database design issues discussed in Chapter 10. Physical database design for XML databases is even more closely tied to the choice of DBMS than it is for relational databases. The best general advice is to bear in mind the issues discussed in Chapter 10 and read the documentation for the chosen XML DBMS very carefully. The remainder of this section focuses on logical database design for XML.

Logical database design for the XDM has two main goals. First, it must produce a set of content models for XML elements that implement the requirements documented by the conceptual database design. Second, it should minimize data duplication. This requires a different style of content model from more traditional, document-centric XML applications, with a lot more use of relational style keys. If relational style keys aren't used, then there will be lots of data duplication.

It is important to realize that there is more than one mechanism for implementing relational style keys. Only one mechanism has been discussed in this chapter – that of using attributes with the special data types ID, IDREF and IDREFS. This mechanism matches surrogate keys with single- or multiple-valued foreign keys to manage referential integrity. The surrogate key is a single attribute and its value is unique within the document rather than within the containing element.

The W3C XML Schema language includes this mechanism, but also includes a more flexible mechanism for implementing referential integrity. A schema document written using W3C XML Schema can define a collection of attributes, or child elements with only text or data content, as a key. In effect, each key definition in an element's content model is a candidate key constraint as the combination of data values must be unique within each instance of the containing element. Defining a set of attributes or elements in an element's content model as a keyref is equivalent to defining a foreign key. The keyref definition must explicitly reference a named key and the combination of values in an instance of the keyref must be the same as that in an instance of the matching key.

To complete the set of relational style keys, W3C XML Schema includes a unique constraint – the counterpart of the SQL UNIQUE constraint – that enforces uniqueness but allows the attributes or elements to be optional (the XML equivalent of NULL). All three of these constraints use XPath expressions to identify the set of attributes or elements that comprise the relational style key.

Both these mechanisms for implementing relational style keys in XML (ID/IDREF/IDREFS and unique/key/keyref) only work within a single XML instance document (although the instance document may be stored in more than one physical file).

There is a third mechanism, using the W3C's XLink recommendation, that allows foreign key constraints that apply to elements (and attributes) from two document instances with different document models. Particular XML-based DBMS may provide other mechanisms to implement relational style keys. This means that, during logical design, there is a choice of two general mechanisms for implementing the associations of the conceptual ER diagram – element containment and relational style keys.

The multiple mechanisms for implementing relational style keys mean only a general indication that relational style keys are being used is made during logical database design. The particular implementation mechanism is described during physical database design. Deciding to use an XML schema language or some dedicated hyperlink mechanism, such as XLink, is a task left to the physical design stage.

The organization structures of the XDM are documents, elements and attributes and relational style keys. An XDM relational-style foreign key can reference *multiple* matching candidate keys – something that the relational data model does not allow. This means that the XDM can directly support the many-to-many associations of the conceptual ER diagram. It also directly supports multivalued UML attributes as child elements that may occur more than once. Even so, there are some ER diagram organization structures that are best replaced by simpler structures at the start of the logical design process. These are:

- binary and unary associations that have attributes of their own
- n-ary associations, for n ≥ 3.

As with logical design for relational databases, the first task is to create a logical ER diagram from which these two features have been removed.

Binary and unary associations that have attributes of their own will be many-to-many associations. They are resolved in exactly the same way as they were for the relational data model. The many-to-many association is replaced by a link entity and its attributes are those of the original many-to-many association.

The link entity participates in a one-to-many association with each of the two original entities. Figure 12.2 repeats an example of a binary association seen in Chapter 9 (Figure 9.12). It's important to emphasize that only associations with attributes need to be replaced by a link entity. Many-to-many associations that don't have attributes can be left as they are.

Each n-ary association is also resolved in exactly the same way that it was for the relational data model. The n-ary association is replaced by a link entity and *n* binary associations connecting the link entity to each of the *n* entities that participated in the original n-ary association. Figures 12.3 (a) and (b) repeat an example of how to resolve a three-ary association discussed in Chapter 9 (Figures 9.15 and 9.16).

Figure 12.4 shows the logical ER diagram for the Web Timetable database using the XDM rather than the relational data model. There are far fewer changes here than there were for the logical ER diagram produced in Chapter 9 (Figure 9.17). Only the three-ary association has been replaced as the Uses association in the conceptual ER diagram did not have any attributes of its own. One problem with this logical ER diagram is that the conceptual ER diagram was written using data types appropriate to the

Figure 12.2 Replacing a binary association that has attributes with a link entity.

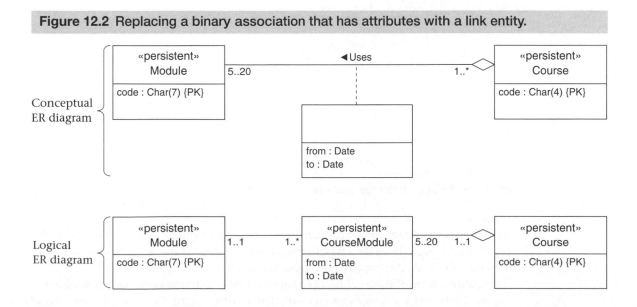

Figure 12.3 Replacing a three-ary association with a link entity and three binary associations.

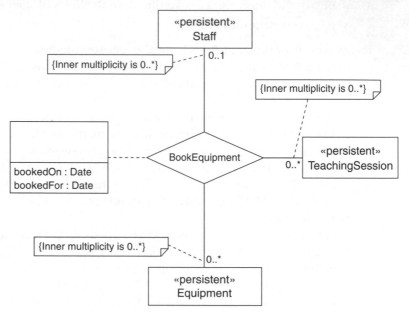

(a) Three-ary association.

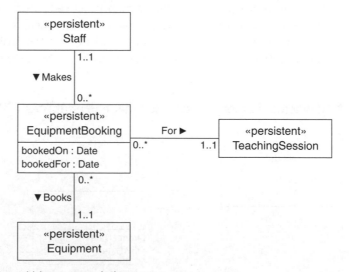

(b) Link entity and binary associations.

relational data model (specifically, to the SQL data language). Rather than redo the conceptual design using data types appropriate to XML, examples of how to translate between SQL and XML data types are discussed.

The move from the logical ER diagram to an XML schema document is reasonably simple. Each entity becomes an element. The entities' attributes either become child

Figure 12.4 The logical ER diagram for the Web Timetable database, targeting the XML data model XDM.

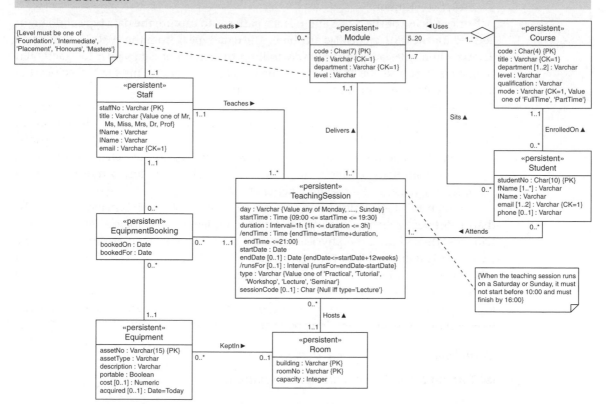

elements or attributes of the element implementing the entity. Deciding which depends on the intended interpretation of the UML attribute. In XML, attributes represent meta-data, and element content represents data. In UML, most attributes represent data, but they can also represent meta-data. UML attributes that represent meta-data should be implemented as XML attributes. Those that represent data should be implemented as XML child elements. Note that, as XML attributes can only have multiplicity 0..1 or 1..1, a UML attribute with any other multiplicity must therefore be implemented as an XML element. UML attribute multiplicity is dealt with using XML element or attribute multiplicity (including optionality). Primary and candidate keys, along with any business rules, are initially recorded as comments. The implementation of these constraints depends on the choice of mechanism for implementing relational style keys, which is a physical design issue.

This first step leads to an initial element pattern for each entity in the logical ER diagram, but doesn't deal with relationships. Consider the Student entity in Figure 12.4. An initial RELAX NG pattern looks like that in Code listing 12.4.1 (a). The entity becomes an XML element, with the same name, apart from the initial lower-case 's'. Both UML and XML are case-sensitive, but have different conventions. UML entity names always begin with an upper-case letter, whereas XML element names tend to begin with a lower-case letter.

The Student entity has six attributes, all of which represent data so all become child elements of the `student` element. Code listing 12.4.1 (b) shows the definition of the `studentNo` element.

Notice the use of the `data` and `param` patterns to capture the data type and length defined for the UML studentNo attribute. The data type is from the W3C XML Schema datatype library because the only way to limit the length of data values to exactly ten characters is to use the W3C XML Schema `length` facet. This facet specifies the length of data values for character string data types.

The data type chosen is `token` rather than `string`. The `string` data type pre serves all white space, including leading and trailing spaces, new lines, tabs and so on. This seems close to the SQL `CHAR` data type, which will pad short values with spaces. However, the value for `studentNo` will *always* have exactly ten characters – this is a Pennine University business rule. As there shouldn't be any white space in a `studentNo` value, `token` seems a better choice.

Although this logical design uses data types from W3C XML Schema, it might be that a different schema language is used to implement the logical design. If that happens, then, during the physical database design, the data pattern in Code listing 12.4.1 (b) is translated into the nearest equivalent data type provided by the chosen schema language. Even if it is known in advance that the available data types will be more restricted than those from W3C XML Schema, it makes sense to document in the logical database design any stronger requirements identified during conceptual database design. The data pattern is a good way to do this.

Code listing 12.4.1   Logical design for the `Student` *entity*

(a) Turning the entity into an element pattern

```
<element name="student"> </element>
```

(b) The UML attribute studentNo *becomes a child element*

```
<element name="student">
  <element name="studentNo">
    <data datatypeLibrary=
      "http://www.w3/org/2001/
      XMLSchema-datatypes"
      type="token">
      <param name="length">10</param>
    </data>
  </element>

</element>
```

The fName, lName, email and phone UML attributes illustrate a range of attribute multiplicities. All can be captured using a combination of the RELAX NG patterns `optional`, `oneOrMore` and `zeroOrMore`, as shown in Code listing 12.4.2. Notice that the complete pattern for the email element is repeated twice – first as a required element and again as an optional element. This achieves the required [1..2] UML multiplicity constraint, but raises a problem. If the element pattern is changed, perhaps adding child elements to reflect the physical structure of an e-mail address, then it must be changed in two different places. Use a RELAX NG named pattern (see below) to overcome this problem.

The content of these elements will be plain text as there is no length specified in the ER diagram. Note that this is subtly different from the SQL VARCHAR, which does not perform white space normalization. If white spaces must be preserved in data values, use the string data type instead.

Another point worth noting is that the RELAX NG pattern for the student element doesn't use the interleave pattern, so the child elements must appear in the order they are defined. Although this isn't required by the UML of the logical ER diagram, it seems a reasonable design decision for an XML database.

Code listing 12.4.2 *Dealing with UML attribute multiplicity*

```
<element name="student">
  <element name="studentNo">
    <data datatypeLibrary=
      "http://www.w3/org/2001/XMLSchema-datatypes"
      type="token">
      <param name="length">10</param>
    </data>
  </element>
  <oneOrMore>
    <element name="fName"> <text /> </element>
  </oneOrMore>
  <element name="lName"> <text /> </element>
  <element name="email"> <text /> </element>
  <optional>
    <element name="email"> <text /> </element>
  </optional>
  <optional>
    <element name="phone"> <text /> </element>
  </optional>
</element>
```

This leaves only the primary and candidate key constraints. As there is a choice of mechanisms for implementing relational-style candidate key constraints in an XML schema document, these can't be specified during logical design. Instead, they are noted, using standard XML comments that are added at the end of the pattern (just as they were added at the end of the table schema).

Code listing 12.4.3 shows the complete initial element pattern for the UML Student entity. Where a UML entity does not have any candidate keys, then its XML element simply doesn't have a primary key constraint. Unlike the relational data model, the XDM does not require every element to have a primary key.

Code listing 12.4.3 *The complete initial element pattern for the UML Student entity*

```
<element name="student">
  <element name="studentNo">
    <data datatypeLibrary=
```

```
            "http://www.w3/org/2001/XMLSchema-datatypes"
            type="token">
            <param name="length">10</param>
        </data>
    </element>
    <oneOrMore>
        <element name="fName"> <text /> </element>
    </oneOrMore>
    <element name="lName"> <text /> </element>
    <element name="email"> <text /> </element>
    <optional>
        <element name="email"> <text /> </element>
    </optional>
    <optional>
        <element name="phone"> <text /> </element>
    </optional>
    <!-- PRIMARY KEY CONSTRAINT: (studentNo) -->
    <!-- CANDIDATE KEY CONSTRAINT: (email) -->
</element>
```

The initial element patterns capture information from the logical ER diagram about entities and attributes. The next step is to capture information about relationships. This is more complex because there is a choice of mechanisms for implementing relationships and it is where XML document models designed to hold data differ most from those designed to hold documents. Data-centric documents make much more use of relational-style keys than document-centric ones. This is because using element containment to implement a relationship may lead to data duplication. For example, in Figure 12.4, there is an aggregation association between the Course and Module entities. This indicates that a Module is part of a Course. It might seem natural to make the corresponding `module` element a child of the `course` element, using containment to implement the association. Unfortunately, at the Pennine University, some modules are used by many courses (indicated by the multiplicity constraints on Uses). To reflect this, a copy of the `module` element must appear in each of the `course` elements using the module, leading to unnecessary data duplication. A key goal of the database approach is to avoid unnecessary data duplication, so, under these circumstance, relational-style keys should be used to implement the association.

Another problem with using containment to represent associations is that sometimes it simply doesn't work. Consider the association KeptIn between the Equipment and Room entities (Figure 12.4). It might seem reasonable to use containment to implement the association and make the `equipment` element a child of the `room` element. Again, this doesn't work – this time because some occurrences of Equipment are not linked to any occurrence of Room (check the lower bound on the multiplicity constraint). This leads to two general rules for guiding us as to whether to use containment or relational-style keys.

1 Where both entities may occur independently of one another, the association *must* be implemented using relational-style keys.

2 Where using containment to implement an association could lead to duplicate occurrences of the child element, use relational-style keys instead.

These rules help to ensure that each of the many different sorts of association can be implemented effectively.

One sort of association that is *always* implemented using element containment is a composition association. This is because composition associations model a whole–part relationship between entities, the part not being able to exist independently of the whole. This is exactly what containment does – the child element is a part of the parent and cannot exist independently. The entity representing the whole is designated the parent element and the entity representing the part is the child element.

There is one unusual circumstance that leads to a problem here. Consider the unary composition association on the Component entity in Figure 12.5. This ER diagram models the scenario of a piece of coursework being made up of components and each component itself being made up of other components. It isn't possible to define recursive content models such as this using the Russian doll style of schema document.

Code listing 12.4.4 shows the RELAX NG syntax for defining a named pattern. Once defined, using the RELAX NG define pattern, it can be referred to anywhere else in the schema document using the RELAX NG ref pattern. Named patterns allow the schema's author to define recursive content models. Code listing 12.4.4 (a) can be read as follows.

There is an element named `coursework`. It includes a `title` element, a `rubric` element and one or more occurrences of the named pattern called `elmComponent`.

There is a definition of a named pattern called `elmComponent`. This is a pattern for an element named `component`. The element includes a `sequenceNo` element, a `title` element and an `instructions` element. It also includes zero or more of the named pattern called `elmComponent`.

Code listing 12.4.4 (b) shows a slightly different version of the define pattern. The idea of this version is that a coursework component can only have *one* component of its own. The problem is that the element pattern actually insists that every component contains a component. This leads to an infinite descent – a component must have a child component, which must itself have a child component, which must itself have a child component, ad infinitum. To avoid this, always enclose a recursive ref pattern in an optional pattern or a zeroOrMore pattern.

Figure 12.5 A unary composition association – each component is made up of other components.

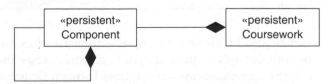

Code listing 12.4.4   Using named patterns to define recursive content models

(a) A recursive content model

```
<element name="coursework">
  <element name="title"> <text /> </element>
  <element name="rubric"> <text /> </element>
  <oneOrMore>
    <ref name="elmComponent" />
  </oneOrMore>
</element>

<define name="elmComponent">
  <element name="component">
    <element name="sequenceNo"> <text /> </element>
    <element name="title"> <text /> </element>
    <element name="instructions"> <text /> </element>
    <zeroOrMore>
      <ref name="elmComponent" />
    </zeroOrMore>
  </element>
</define>
```

(b) An invalid content model for the component ***element that leads to an infinite descent***

```
<define name="elmComponent">
  <element name="component">
    <element name="sequenceNo"> <text /> </element>
    <element name="title"> <text /> </element>
    <element name="instructions"> <text /> </element>
    <ref name="elmComponent" />
  </element>
</define>
```

There are other situations in which using containment in a recursive content model can lead to infinite descents or to infinite loops, where one element contains a second, which contains the first, which contains the second, ad infinitum. When an element must have a recursive content model, it is worth writing out a few element instances, just to check that there are no hidden infinities lurking in the content model.

It may also be possible to implement aggregation associations using containment, but this depends on the multiplicity constraints (see the discussion below). For example, the aggregation association Uses between Course and Module in Figure 12.4 is a many-to-many association, so should be implemented using relational-style keys.

However, when an aggregation association is implemented using containment, the entity representing the whole should again be designated the parent, regardless of the multiplicity constraints.

Most binary one-to-one associations can be implemented using containment. This is because there is never any possibility of data duplication as each occurrence of one entity is linked to, at most, one occurrence of the other. Only use relational-style keys when *both* multiplicity constraints are 0..1 – that is, when both entities may occur independently of one another (again, see the discussion below).

Some one-to-many associations can be implemented using containment. The multiplicity at the 'one' end of the association must be 1..1. This means that the entity at the 'many' end cannot occur independently of the entity at the 'one' end. The entity at the 'one' end is therefore designated the parent and the entity at the 'many' end the child.

A problem arises when an entity participates in more than one association. Consider the EquipmentBooking entity in Figure 12.4. This participates in three one-to-many associations with three distinct entities. Each of these associations has the multiplicity 1..1 at the 'one' end, so each of the entities Staff, Equipment and TeachingSession could potentially be its parent element. Clearly it cannot be a child element of all three possible parents without duplicating the data for each equipment booking three times, which is not a good idea.

One solution is to choose one of the three possible parents to be the actual parent and use relational-style keys to implement the other two associations. Alternatively, use relational-style keys to implement all the associations. One argument in favour of the second approach is that an entity which participates in many different associations really ought to have an independent existence. This suggests the following guideline:

> one-to-many associations should only be implemented using containment when the potential child element is associated with just one potential parent and cannot have an independent existence.

A good example of this situation is the association between the Staff and SupportSession entities in the Staff Directory database. These are the only two entities in the database. Moreover, the SupportSession entity cannot exist independently of the Staff entity The one-to-many association between them is implemented by designating the Staff entity the parent and the SupportSession entity the child. The multiplicity constraint at the "many" end of the association determines the multiplicity of the child element. The child element is optional if the lower bound on the multiplicity constraint is zero. Otherwise it is required.

Code listing 12.4.5 shows three (incomplete) schema demonstrating alternative ways to implement this association using parent–child element containment. Code listing 12.4.5 (a) uses the approach taken in Section 12.2. The whole Staff Directory database is represented by the `staff` element. The Staff entity is implemented as the `staffMember` element. This element contains an optional `supportSessions` element, representing the collection of all support sessions offered by a particular member of staff. The `supportSessions` element itself contains one or more `session` element and it is the `session` element that implements the SupportSession entity.

The `supportSessions` element isn't really necessary. Code listing 12.4.5 (b) makes the `session` elements direct children of the `staffMember` element. This is both simpler and closer to the meaning of the ER diagram.

Code listing 12.4.5 (c) takes this one stage further, dispensing with the `session` element as well and simply including the support session data items as a repeating group of child elements – `dayOfWeek`, `startTime` and `endTime`. This will only work because the content model fixes the *order* of these elements. Any application reading the instance document will see that each `dayOfWeek` element is followed immediately by a `startTime` and `endTime` element and so can treat them as a group. Relying on the order of elements to convey meaning is not a good idea in a database application, so, of the three approaches, the second is probably the best.

Code listing 12.4.5 *Two approaches to implementing an association using containment*

(a) An incomplete pattern for the `staffMember` *element containing an optional* `supportSession` *child element*

```
<element name="staff">
  <oneOrMore>
    <element name="staffMember">

      <optional>
        <element name="supportSessions">
          <oneOrMore>
            <element name="session">
             <element name="dayOfWeek"> </element>
             <element name="startTime"> </element>
             <element name="endTime"> </element>
            </element>
          </oneOrMore>
        </element>
      </optional>
    </element>
  </oneOrMore>
</element>
```

(b) An incomplete pattern for the `staffMember` *element containing zero or more child* `supportSession` *elements*

```
<element name="staff">
  <oneOrMore>
    <element name="staffMember">

      <zeroOrMore>
        <element name="session">
          <element name="dayOfWeek"> </element>
          <element name="startTime"> </element>
          <element name="endTime"> </element>
```

```
        </element>
      </zeroOrMore>
    </element>
  </oneOrMore>
</element>
```

(c) An incomplete pattern for the `staffMember` *element containing optional child elements that capture support session data*

```
<element name="staff">
  <oneOrMore>
    <element name="staffMember">

      <zeroOrMore>
        <element name="dayOfWeek"> </element>
        <element name="startTime"> </element>
        <element name="endTime"> </element>
      </zeroOrMore>
    </element>
  </oneOrMore>
</element>
```

When the lower bound on both multiplicity constraints is zero, the association cannot be implemented using containment. This is because a lower bound of zero on a multiplicity constraint means that the entity at the opposite end may occur independently. The association KeptIn between the Equipment and Room entities (Figure 12.4) is a good example. The lower bound on both multiplicity constraints is zero, which means that both entities can occur independently of each other – some equipment is not kept in any room and some rooms have no equipment kept in them, for example. Clearly, neither entity can be implemented as a child element of the other, so the association must be implemented by relational-style keys. The question is, which element is the referenced element (so gets the 'primary key') and which is the referencing element (getting the 'foreign key')?

The multiplicity constraints provide the answer, just as they did during logical design for the relational model. Consider the KeptIn association between the Equipment and Room entities. The two entities are implemented as separate XML elements – `equipment` and `room`. XML foreign keys can refer to multiple matching candidate key values, so it is *possible* to place a foreign key in the `room` element that references the primary key in the `equipment` element. Each foreign key would include multiple values, matching the primary key value of multiple occurrences of the `equipment` element.

The alternative is to place the foreign key in the `equipment` element. Each foreign key would include a single value, matching the primary key values of a single occurrence of the `room` element.

This second approach is a lot simpler, so is the best one to take. The general rule is as follows.

When the lower bound on both multiplicity constraints is zero, use relational-style keys to implement the association. The entity at the association end with the larger upper bound on its multiplicity constraint is designated the referencing entity. The other is the referenced entity. If the upper bounds are equal, then choose as the referenced entity the one that is more significant in terms of the scenario being modelled (the most important to the business).

A foreign key is added to the element representing the referencing entity. A primary key is added to the element representing the referenced entity (unless it already has one).

Code listing 12.4.6 shows the element schema for the Equipment and Room entities, with comments indicating their primary and foreign keys and describing a default value. Notice that the comment describing the foreign key is limited to mentioning the referenced element. This is because there are at least three possible mechanisms for implementing foreign keys. If the final schema document is written in RELAX NG, then the foreign key will be implemented using the ID/IDREF/IDREFS mechanism. If it is written in W3C XML Schema, then the foreign keys may use its key/keyref mechanism. Some native XML DBMS may use XLink or a proprietary mechanism. Giving a natural language description is the best that can be done during the logical design process.

Code listing 12.4.6 Noting a foreign key

```
<element name="room">
  <element name="building"> <text /> </element>
  <element name="roomNo"> <text /> </element>
  <element name="capacity">
    <data datatypeLibrary=
        "http://www.w3.org/2001/XMLSchema-datatypes"
        type="integer" />
  </element>
  <!-- PRIMARY KEY CONSTRAINT: (building, roomNo) -->
</element>

<element name="equipment">
  <element name="assetNo">
    <data datatypeLibrary=
        "http://www.w3.org/2001/XMLSchema-datatypes"
        type="token">
      <param name="length">15</param>
    </data>
  </element>
  <element name="assetType"> <text /> </element>
  <element name="description"> <text /> </element>
  <element name="portable">
    <data datatypeLibrary=
        "http://www.w3.org/2001/XMLSchema-datatypes"
        type="boolean" />
  </element>
```

```
<optional>
  <element name="cost">
    <data datatypeLibrary=
    "http://www.w3.org/2001/XMLSchema-datatypes"
    type="decimal" />
  </element>
</optional>
<optional>
  <element name="capacity">
    <data datatypeLibrary=
      "http://www.w3.org/2001/XMLSchema-datatypes"
      type="date" />
    <!-- DEFAULT VALUE = Today -->
  </element>
</optional>
<!-- PRIMARY KEY CONSTRAINT: (assetNo) -->
<!-- FOREIGN KEY CONSTRAINT: Single value, references the
     room element -->
</element>
```

Another relationship best implemented using relational-style keys is the unary association. Using relational-style keys avoids defining a recursive content model for the element. Even the unary composition association, discussed above, would probably be better implemented by means of relational-style keys.

Finally, many-to-many associations should *always* be implemented using relational-style keys. Many-to-many associations rely on the ability of XDM foreign keys to refer to multiple matching candidate keys. There are no strict rules on designating the referencing and referenced entities. The entity at the association end with the smallest upper bound on its multiplicity constraint is a good candidate for the referenced entity as this keeps the list of foreign key values on the referencing entity to a minimum. Tables 12.1 and 12.2 summarize the guidance given on when to use containment and when to use relational-style keys.

Generalization relationships are much easier to deal with than associations. One very simple approach is to create an element pattern for the more general entity and include in its content model element patterns for each of its more specialized entities. Disjoint constraints are implemented using the choice pattern, while participation constraints are implemented using the optional pattern. To see this approach on a reasonably complex example, consider the five generalization relationships in Figure 12.6.

Code listing 12.4.7 presents the element schema for the Room entity, although it doesn't include the specializations for the Laboratory entity. The constraints on this first set of three generalization relationships are disjoint and optional. The optional constraint means that an occurrence of the Room entity need not be an occurrence of any of its more specialized versions. This is implemented by the optional pattern, which means that an occurrence of the room element may not contain any of the data for its more specialized versions. The disjoint constraint means that an occurrence of the Room entity can be an occurrence of, *at most, one* of the more specialized versions. The choice pattern achieves this, by insisting that only one of the three child

Table 12.1 Relationships that can be implemented using containment.

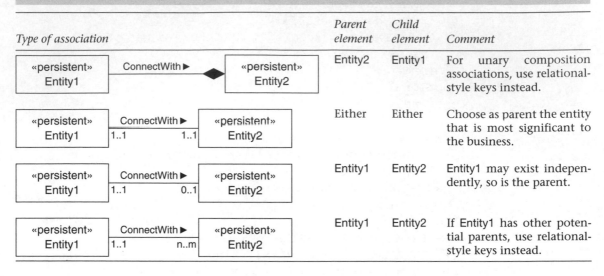

Type of association	Parent element	Child element	Comment
«persistent» Entity1 — ConnectWith ▶ — «persistent» Entity2 (composition)	Entity2	Entity1	For unary composition associations, use relational-style keys instead.
«persistent» Entity1 [1..1] — ConnectWith ▶ — [1..1] «persistent» Entity2	Either	Either	Choose as parent the entity that is most significant to the business.
«persistent» Entity1 [1..1] — ConnectWith ▶ — [0..1] «persistent» Entity2	Entity1	Entity2	Entity1 may exist independently, so is the parent.
«persistent» Entity1 [1..1] — ConnectWith ▶ — [n..m] «persistent» Entity2	Entity1	Entity2	If Entity1 has other potential parents, use relational-style keys instead.

Table 12.2 Relationships that must be implemented using relational-style keys.

Type of association	Referenced element	Referencing element	Comment
«persistent» Entity1 [0..m] — ConnectWith ▶ — [0..n] «persistent» Entity2	Entity1	Entity2	Assuming m<n. If m = n, choose the entity that is most significant to the business as referenced entity.
«persistent» Entity1 [n..m] [p..q] ConnectWith ▶ (unary)	Entity1	Entity1	
«persistent» Entity1 [p..q] — ConnectWith ▶ — [n..m] «persistent» Entity2	Entity1	Entity2	Assuming 1<q<m, so this is a many-to-many association. If q = m, choose the entity that is most significant to the business as referenced entity.

Figure 12.6 Five generalization relationships.

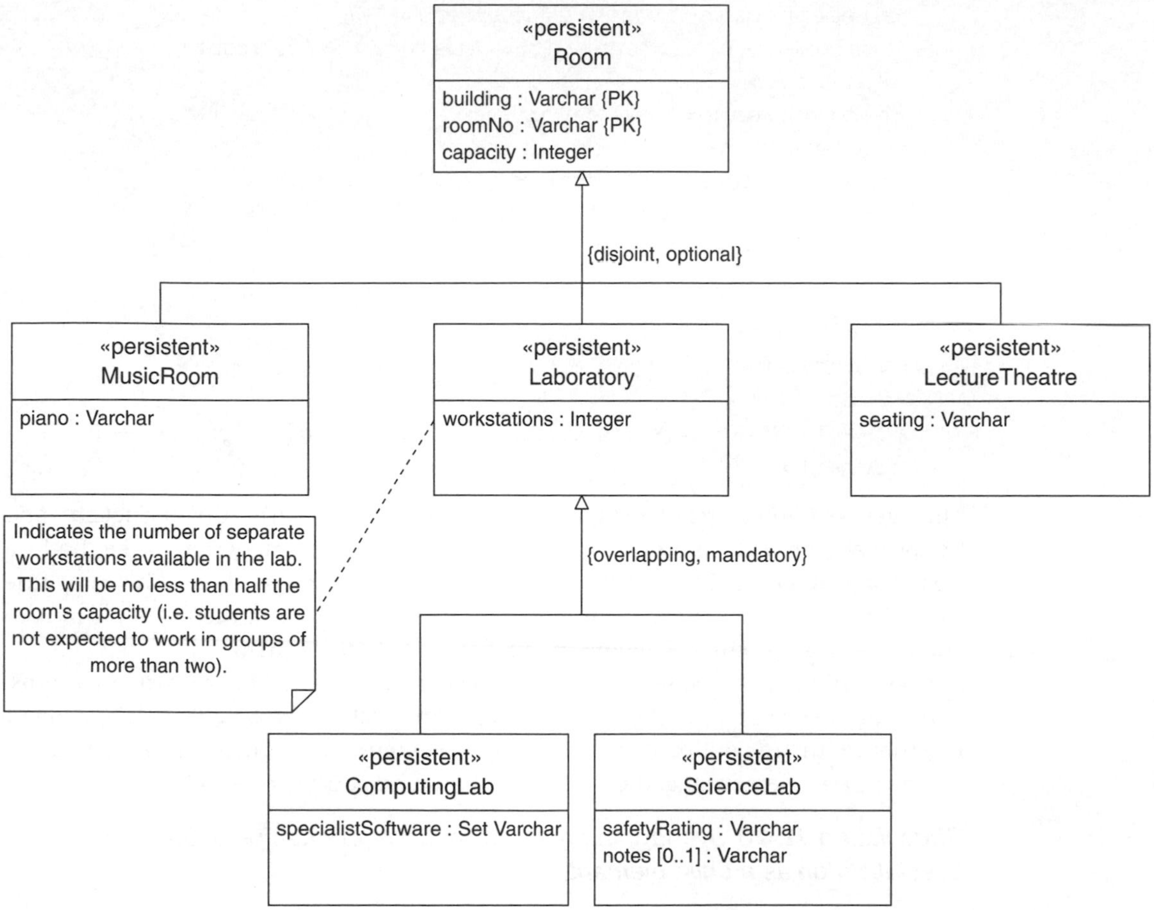

elements – musicRoom, lectureTheatre and laboratory – can occur in any instance of the room element.

Code listing 12.4.7 Implementing the first three generalization relationships using containment with choice and optional patterns

```
<element name="room">
  <element name="building"> <text /> </element>
  <element name="roomNo"> <text /> </element>
  <element name="capacity">
    <data datatypeLibrary=
      "http://www.w3.org/2001/XMLSchema-datatypes"
      type="integer" />
  </element>
      <!-- Specializations -->
      <optional>
        <choice>
          <element name="musicRoom">
```

```
            <element name="piano"> <text /> </element>
          </element>
      <element name="lectureTheatre">
        <element name="seating"> <text /> </element>
      </element>
      <element name="laboratory">
        <element name="workstations">
          <data datatypeLibrary=
             "http://www.w3/org/2001/XMLSchema-datatypes"
             type="integer" />
         </element>

        </element>
       </choice>
      </optional>
      <!-- PRIMARY KEY CONSTRAINT: (building, roomNo) -->
    </element>
```

The generalization relationships linking Laboratory with ComputingLab and ScienceLab are overlapping, so an occurrence of Laboratory might be both a ComputingLab *and* a ScienceLab. Moreover it *must* be one of them. This is a little tricky. The `laboratory` element must include one or other of the `computingLab` and `scienceLab` child elements and may include both of them.

Code listing 12.4.8 achieves this by allowing for a choice between two patterns. *Either* the `laboratory` element includes a mandatory `computingLab` element together with an optional `scienceLab` element *or* it includes a mandatory `scienceLab` element together with an optional `computingLab` element.

Code listing 12.4.8 Overlapping generalization relationships allow either specialization as a child element

```
<element name="laboratory">
  <element name="workstations">
    <data datatypeLibrary=
       "http://www.w3/org/2001/XMLSchema-datatypes"
       type="integer" />
  </element>
  <!-- Specializations -->
  <choice>
   <group>
     <element name="computingLab">
       <element name="specialistSoftware"> <text />
       </element>
     </element>
     <optional>
       <element name="scienceLab">
         <element name="safetyRating"> <text /> </element>
         <optional>
           <element name="notes"> <text /> </element>
```

```
          </optional>
        </element>
      </optional>
    </group>
    <group>
      <optional>
        <element name="computingLab">
        <element name="specialistSoftware"> <text />
        </element>
       </element>
      </optional>
      <element name="scienceLab">
        <element name="safetyRating"> <text /> </element>
            <optional>
                <element name="notes"> <text /> </element>
            </optional>
        </element>
      </group>
    </choice>
  </element>
```

To round off this subsection, here is a summary of the process of logical database design for XML.

1 For each entity in the logical ER diagram, write down an initial element schema.
   (a) Write down the element name.
   (b) Write down an initial content model for the element. For each attribute of the entity, include a child element (or attribute) pattern in the content model. Give this child element the same name as the attribute and indicate its multiplicity. Include a comment about any default value.
   (c) If the entity is a strong entity, add a comment recording primary and candidate keys.
   (d) Add comments to record any business rules associated with the entity.

2 For each binary association in the logical ER diagram, do the following.
   (a) Decide whether the binary association should be represented by containment or by relational-style keys.
   (b) Where the association is best represented by containment, designate one entity to be a child entity. Move the element schema for the child entity into the content model of the element schema for the parent entity. Use the multiplicity constraint at the child end of the original association to determine which multiplicity pattern to enclose the child in.
   (c) Where the binary association is best represented by relational-style keys, designate one element as the referenced element and the other as the referencing element. Add a comment describing the foreign key to the element schema for the referencing element.

3 For each generalization relationship, write down an element schema for the more general entity, which includes the more specialized entities in its content. Use choice and options to implement the disjoint and participation constraints.

One interesting consequence of introducing relational-style foreign keys is that normalization then becomes a useful tool for checking the effectiveness of the logical design. Normalization was invented to ensure that there was no unnecessary data duplication in a logical design for a relational database. It plays the same role in logical design for an XML database. The notion of a functional determinant extends naturally to collections of XML elements as, in XML, a functional determinant is simply a set of elements that forms a 'candidate key in waiting' for some subset of the child elements of a given element. All that needs to be done is to extract the relevant child elements into a new child element of the *root element* and add a foreign key to the original parent element. This approach was illustrated in Code listing 12.2.5.3 for the `session` and `staffMember` elements.

The key difference in XML is that some repeating groups are allowed. Where a relationship can be implemented using containment *without* introducing any repeated data, then the parent element can contain a repeating group of child elements. This is true of the repeating group of `session` elements within a `staffMember` element. The description of the normalization process given in Chapter 9 can be adapted to give a description of normalization for XML.

1 Identify a functional determinant and *all* its dependent elements. Always ensure that, for each dependent element `elementName`, the claim 'the functional determinant determines the value of `elementName`' makes sense within the scenario being modelled.

2 Consider whether or not this repeating group of child elements may lead to unnecessary data duplication. If so, create a new child element of the root element consisting of the elements in the functional determinant and all its dependent elements.
   (a) Note that the functional determinant is a candidate key for this element.
   (b) If the dependent columns include the columns of a pre-existing foreign key, then include the comment documenting the foreign key constraint on the new element.

3 Remove the *dependent elements* from the original element, but leave the elements of the functional determinant behind.
   (a) If the dependent elements include the columns of a foreign key, then remove the comment documenting the foreign key constraint from the original element.
   (b) Add a new foreign key constraint on the original element to indicate that the functional determinant references the candidate key of the new element.

If the foreign key is eventually implemented using the `ID/IDREF/IDREFS` mechanism, then any foreign key elements are *replaced* by an `IDREF/IDREFS` attribute. The candidate key elements are not replaced, but their parent element acquires an additional surrogate key `ID` attribute.

Chapter summary

- This chapter has completed the discussion of the core XML features by discussing XML namespaces. Namespaces are widely used in XML documents, including both schema and instance documents.

- The chapter has introduced RELAX NG as a schema language for XML and XPath as a simple XML query language. Both languages are largely stable and widely implemented. XPath is also used in more sophisticated XML query languages.

- The chapter has concluded with a discussion of XML database design. Conceptual design is unchanged and logical design is very similar to logical design for the relational data model. Because of the lack of standard XML database technologies, physical design is tied closely to the particular XML DBMS being used. Even so, the guidance given in Chapter 10 should prove useful, provided the documentation for the XML DBMS is read carefully first.

Further reading

Bourret (2003) provides a good general introduction to XML databases, though is getting a little out of date.

The early part of Steegmans et al. (2004) provides a more recent version of this material.

Møller and Schwartzbach (2006) is probably the best general introduction to XML and its related technologies. They cover XML for both document and database applications.

Harold and Means (2004) give an overview of the various XML technologies, with emphasis on those developed by the W3C. The W3C website (www.w3.org) is the official source for XML and those related technologies developed by the W3C.

Van der Vlist (2003) covers RELAX NG.

Eisenberg and Melton (2002b, 2005) provide an introduction to XQuery, while some of their other papers (2001, 2002a, 2004) cover SQL/XML.

The approach to logical design for XML is adapted directly from the traditional approach to relational database design. Provost (2002) gives a more detailed account of the value of normalization for designing XML schema documents.

Review questions

12.1 In the context of XML namespaces, explain the following terms:
   (a) local name
   (b) namespace name
   (c) expanded name
   (d) namespace prefix
   (e) qualified name.

12.2 What is the purpose of a namespace declaration? How do you declare a default namespace?

12.3 Explain the difference between an instance document and a schema document. When is an XML document both a schema document and an instance document?

12.4 What are the four basic patterns of RELAX NG? Explain the purpose of each of them.

12.5 Explain the purpose of the following RELAX NG patterns:
(a) optional
(b) zeroOrMore
(c) oneOrMore
(d) group
(e) interleave.

12.6 Which two RELAX NG patterns are used to define an enumeration?

12.7 What is the purpose of the RELAX NG param pattern? When and where can it be used?

12.8 Briefly describe how to implement relational-style foreign keys and foreign key constraints using the RELAX NG DTD compatibility data type library.

12.9 Explain the following terms from the XPath language:
(a) location step
(b) location path
(c) context
(d) axis
(e) node test

12.10 Which structures from a conceptual ER diagram should not be included in the logical ER diagram for the XDM?

Exercises

12.11 Critically evaluate the XML namespaces mechanism.

12.12 For each of the following descriptions, write down a RELAX NG pattern. If no content is specified for an element, assume that it contains text. Assume that elements appear in the order stated unless an unordered content model is specified.
(a) The `book` element has a `contents` element, optional `foreword`, `preface` and `acknowledgements` elements, plus one or more `chapter` elements.
(b) A `chapter` element has an `objectives` element, `introduction` element, `outline` element, one or more `section` elements, `summary` element and `furtherReading` element. The `objectives` element, `outline` element, `summary` element and `furtherReading` element all have a `heading` element and text content.
(c) The `section` element may consist solely of text content, have some text followed by one or more `subsection` elements or consist entirely of

subsection elements. The subsection element has a heading element and text content.

(d) An acknowledgements element contains a mix of text and trademarks elements. Each trademarks element contains one or more trademark elements, one or more company elements (the company/companies holding the trademark) and text. All the trademark elements must come before all the company elements. There may be text between any two child elements of the trademarks element.

12.13 Write down instances of the elements defined by the following RELAX NG patterns, showing the different ways the content can interleave.

(a)
```
<element name="session">
  <interleave>
    <group>
      <element name="term"> <text /> </element>
      <element name="dayOfWeek"> <text /> </element>
    </group>
    <group>
      <element name="startTime"> <text /> </element>
      <element name="endTime"> <text /> </element>
    </group>
  </interleave>
</element>
```

(b)
```
<element name="session">
  <interleave>
    <group>
      <element name="term"> <text /> </element>
      <element name="dayOfWeek"> <text /> </element>
    </group>
    <group>
      <element name="startTime"> <text /> </element>
      <element name="endTime"> <text /> </element>
    </group>
    <text />
  </interleave>
</element>
```

(c)
```
<element name="session">
  <interleave>
    <group>
      <element name="term"> <text /> </element>
      <element name="dayOfWeek"> <text /> </element>
    </group>
    <element name="time">
      <element name="startTime"> <text /> </element>
      <element name="endTime"> <text /> </element>
    </element>
    <text />
  </interleave>
</element>
```

(d)
```
<element name="session">
  <interleave>
    <group>
      <element name="term"> <text /> </element>
      <element name="dayOfWeek"> <text /> </element>
    </group>
    <interleave>
      <element name="time">
        <element name="startTime"> <text /> </element>
        <element name="endTime"> <text /> </element>
      </element>
      <text />
    </interleave>
    <text />
  </interleave>
</element>
```

12.14 The `student` element contains each student's ID number, first and last names, e-mail address and may also contain a phone number. For each of the following additional restrictions, write down a RELAX NG pattern for the `student` element.
(a) The content appears in the order specified.
(b) A student may have several first names and the content appears in the order specified.
(c) A student may have up to two e-mail addresses (one personal, one university) and the content appears in the order specified. (*Hint*: You'll need to define a `type` attribute for the `email` element, the content of which is an enumeration).
(d) The first name must come before the last name, but otherwise no specific ordering is required.
(e) The first and last names must appear in this order with no intervening content, but, otherwise no specific ordering is required.

12.15 Figure 12.4 shows the logical ER diagram for the Web Timetable application, targeting the XDM.
(a) Using RELAX NG, complete the logical design for the Web Timetable application.
(b) Assuming that all the various elements are enclosed in a single `webTimetable` element, write three or more XPath expressions to locate data in your XML database.

12.16 Figure E.1 is a conceptual ER diagram for the Pennine University's Accommodation Office.
(a) Draw the corresponding logical ER diagram for the XDM.
(b) Using RELAX NG, write down a logical design for this database.
(c) What are the significant differences between this logical database design and the logical database design for the relational data model developed in Exercise 9.13?

Investigations

12.17 Evaluate RELAX NG (OASIS, 2001) against one of the other XML schema languages. Possible choices include the W3C XML Schema language (W3C, 2004d, 2004e), DSD2 (Møller, 2002) or Schematron (ISO/IEC JTC 1, 2004).

Figure E.1 A conceptual ER diagram for the Pennine University's Accommodation Office.

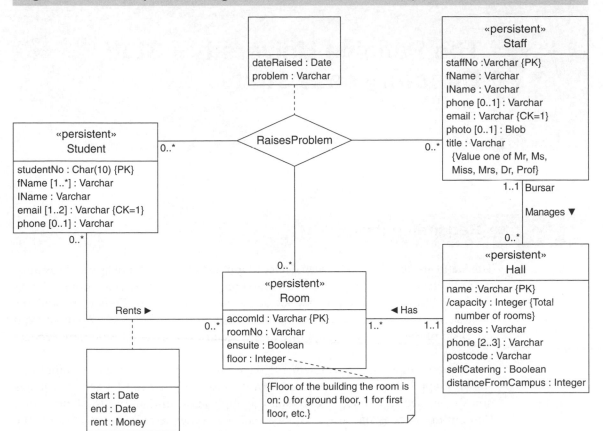

12.18 Investigate one of the more powerful query languages for XML. Choices include XQuery (Eisenberg and Melton, 2002b, 2005), W3C (2005c, 2005e) or SQL/XML (Eisenberg and Melton, 2001, 2002a, 2004).

12.19 In Investigation 8.19, you developed a conceptual database design for an organization you know. Use the ER diagram to create a logical database design targeting the XDM, including a logical ER diagram and a RELAX NG schema document. How does it differ from the logical design targeting the relational data model you developed in Investigation 9.19?

12.20 Investigate the support for XML and its associated technologies offered by commercial DBMS. You should consider both native XML DBMS (DBMS that have as their underlying data model an XML data model such as the XDM) and the relational DBMS, many of which include support for storing XML documents.

The Pennine University's Staff Directory case study

A.1　Requirements

The Staff Directory is a simple web database application, though not as simple as most staff directories. In addition to the usual requirements to deliver staff contact details via a web browser, it must also provide details of support sessions offered to students by academics. The idea for the application was first documented in an e-mail from the Dean of the School of Computing to the head of Library and Computing Services (Figure A.1).

Additional input at the requirements stage came from the School of Computing's Staff List application and the printed staff directory (Figures A.2 (a) and (b)). It was quickly decided to develop a web database application in-house as the Library and Computing Services had the necessary staff and other resources available. All the Schools and Services staff agreed that the Staff Directory would use a database and it would be the definitive source for staff contact details. Accuracy was considered crucial, so a separate administrator's interface would be developed to allow administrative staff to add, modify and remove staff details from the database. An option in this administrator's interface would allow users to generate the printed directory.

Both these requirements were put outside the scope of the first phase of the project, which focused on retrieving staff contact details from a database and delivering them to end users via a web browser. Consequently, in the first phase of the project, there is no requirement to include room numbers on the Staff Directory database.

The requirement to include details of academics' support sessions caused some difficulties. As the times of support sessions might change each term to fit into the academics' new timetables, it was felt that academics themselves should maintain this data. However, doing so raised a security problem – how to ensure that academics' support sessions were not changed by anyone but them. The solution adopted was documented in an e-mail from the head of Library and Computing Services (Figure A.3).

The requirements were documented as use cases. The use case diagram (Figure A.4) provides an overview of who uses the system and how they expect to use it. The use case specifications (Figure A.5) give further details of the expected behaviour. Together, they form the formal definition of users requirements for the Staff Directory web database application.

Figure A.1 Text of an e-mail discussing a new Staff Directory application.

Dilip

It was interesting to chat after yesterday's meeting. You are right that we need a university-wide, searchable staff directory on the intranet. I promised to recount our recent experience of developing a similar web application, so here are the salient details.

Two years ago, our web administrator (Frank Rose) wrote an application to generate a series of web pages listing contact details for staff, filtered by job role – admin, academic, technical and research. All the data were kept in a single text file, accessed using a PHP script (ask Frank!) This is proving difficult to manage. Originally, Frank made the data file accessible to all members of staff, so they could amend their own details. This caused problems, with several instances of data loss or corruption. On one memorable occasion, Frank had just saved the details of seven new researchers, only to lose them all when I overwrote the Staff List data file with the copy I'd been editing in Notepad! Only Frank can access the data file now, but he can't always make immediate changes when staff move offices or new staff arrive.

The application is also a little inflexible – in particular, new staff usually want to search by name, not role. Finally, the academics want it to show the details of their support sessions. These are unbooked 'drop-in' sessions, open to any student (all schools run these, not just computing). As all academics spend at least two hours each week sitting in their offices waiting for students to drop in, they want the times widely publicised. A staff directory seems the sensible place for this.

I hope you find these brief notes useful. If you do decide to sponsor a Staff Directory, I'm sure Frank will be happy to share his experiences with your development team.

Regards
Freya

Figure A.2 Examples of existing staff directory formats at the Pennine University.

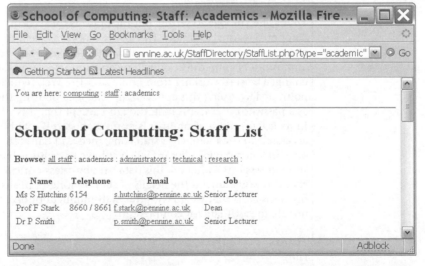

(a) The School of Computing's staff list.

Figure A.2 (*Continued*)

SCHOOL OF COMPUTING					
Wilson 117	**8660**	**Stark**	**F**	**Prof**	**Dean**
Administrative Support					
Wilson 117a	8661	Timms	H	Mrs	PA to Dean
Wilson 100	8010	School Office			
Wilson 100	8011	School Office fax			
Wilson 100	8032	Abbot	H	Mrs	Secretary
Wilson 100	8022	Bapetsi	R	Ms	Administrative Assistant
Technical Support					
Wilson 200	8871	O'Connor	JK	Ms	Technician
Wilson 200	8871	Rose	F	Mr	Technician
Academic					
Wilson 124	7782	Bittaye	J	Dr	Senior Lecturer
Wilson 123	8706	Hutchins	S	Ms	Senior Lecturer
Research					
Wilson 227	8514	Lin	D	Mr	Research Assistant

(b) Extract from the printed staff directory.

Figure A.3 Extract from e-mail confirming how to secure modification of Support Session data.

> Thanks for the memo setting out the options for securing access to the 'Support Sessions' function. The first two options seem to be too complex – asking them to remember another password won't be popular and using OS authentication will mean Support Session data can't be changed by staff working from home over the Web (which was the point of developing this application). The idea of using the staff number as a password/PIN seems best, though I accept that it is a bit of a kludge. In its favour, the staff number is printed on staff ID cards, so is easily accessible to the member of staff concerned and hard for others to find out. Anyone who loses a card will just have to wait to change the support sessions – after all, this data isn't business-critical. Also, support staff can easily amend the details of staff on long-term sick leave. So, my decision is that we go with the 'staff number option'. Can you update the estimate for completion?
>
> Thanks
> Dilip

Figure A.4 Use case diagram for the Staff Directory.

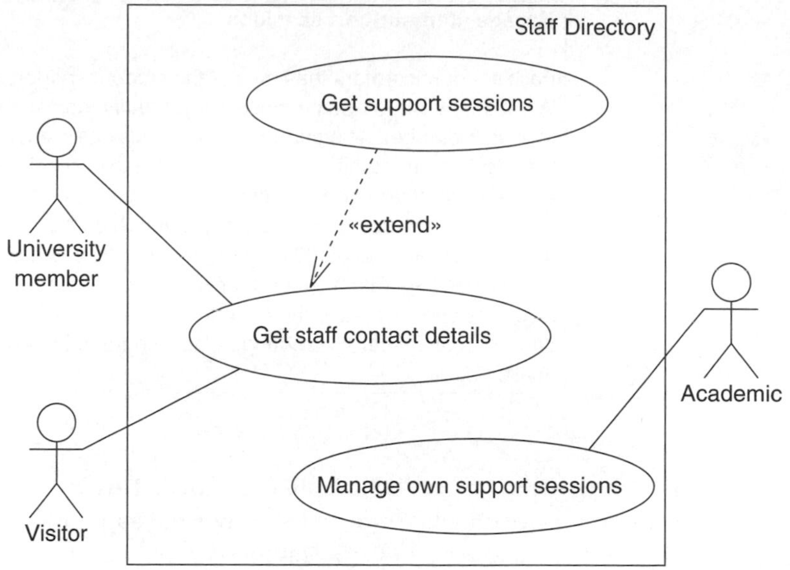

Figure A.5 Staff Directory use case specifications.

Get staff contact details

This allows any user to get the contact details (name, phone and e-mail) for a named member of staff at the university. The user provides the staff member's surname and first initial and requests his or her contact details. A list showing the name and phone number of each member of staff matching the search criteria is delivered, together with a count of the number of matches from the Staff Directory. The user can see the full contact details for any entry in the list, along with a photo of the member of staff if one is available, by selecting that entry. If there are no matches, a message stating this is displayed.

The full contact details for an academic provide access to a list of support sessions offered by him or her.

There is also an option to view a 'help' page, giving instructions on how to use the search facility.

Get support sessions

The application provides a list of support sessions offered by an academic member of staff. This is expected to be used mostly by students, but is available to other users.

The user will have accessed the full contact details for an academic member of staff and will request a list of that person's support sessions. The day, start time and end time of all the support sessions are displayed. If there are no support sessions for the chosen academic, a message stating this is displayed.

(Continued)

Figure A.5 *(Continued)*

Manage staff support sessions

Each academic enters the times of the student support sessions.
When they wish to amend these, they identify themselves using
their staff number. The current support sessions are displayed and
the user allowed to alter them. Existing support sessions may be
altered or removed and new support sessions added. For each support
session, the academic must specify a day (Monday to Friday), start
time (which must be 09.00 or later) and end time (which must be
18.00 or earlier). Each support session should be at least 30 minutes
long. The user can save the changed details, replacing the original
ones, or may discard the changes, leaving the original contact details
unaltered.

Notice that the browse behaviour is omitted. This is because the different schools
could not agree on what browse behaviour the application should support. Computing wanted to browse by job role (as for its current 'staff list'), health alphabetically by
surname and music by instrument. It was agreed that each school would develop its
own browse pages, hosted on its local web server but drawing its data from the central
Staff Directory database. This page would interface with the Staff Directory web database application to deliver full contact details for listed staff.

A.2 Deriving the ER diagram from the use case specifications

The use cases will include descriptions of the data requirements for the application, so
are the *main* source for the conceptual database design. This section suggests a way to
extract information on the entities, attributes and relationships by scanning the use
case specifications. It also suggests how to document these requirements in an application glossary – an alternative to using a UML modelling tool. Note that, during conceptual design, new requirements may be identified. If so, the use cases should be revised.
This is one consequence of recognizing that design is an iterative and incremental
process – earlier stages may need revisiting and their documentation updating in the
light of discoveries later on in the development lifecycle.

A.2.1 Identify and document entities and attributes

Each entity represents a class of things that the database must hold data about. The
particular data held for an entity are its attributes. To identify database entities and attributes, scan the use cases for nouns (and noun phrases). Each noun names a thing. If

it is a thing that the database needs to store data about, then it is an entity. If it is data about a thing, then it is an attribute. Note that most things named in the use case specifications will not be entities or attributes. They might, for example, be users of the application or outputs of it.

The nouns 'name', 'surname' and 'initial' are all identified as attributes and there is clearly some overlap in meaning. For any given member of staff, 'name' refers to his or her full name, so includes the surname, whereas 'initial' is the first letter of their first forename.

Rather than have three separate attributes, it makes sense to store just enough data to allow the application to derive the full name, surname and first initial. The simplest approach is to have surname and forename attributes as the full name and first initial can be derived from these. Derived attributes can be included in the model.

The full name is retrieved from the database in Get staff contact details, so it makes sense to include the derived attribute\fullName in the model. The first initial is gathered from users as part of the search criteria, but not stored in the database, so there is no need to indicate this as an attribute.

There are two ways to document the process of identifying data entities. Figure A.6 shows one of the original use case specifications with comments for each noun and noun phrase. Table A.1 shows the result of a similar analysis of all three use cases, documented in a table. Note that only the *first* occurrence of the noun or noun phrase is commented on. This means that more potential entities are identified in the first use case than in later ones.

Once it's decided which things mentioned in the use cases are entities and which attributes, they are recorded in the **application glossary**. This may be managed within a modelling tool or as a separate document, when a format like that in Tables A.2 and A.3 can be used.

A.2.2 Identify and document relationships between entities

Just as noun phrases may indicate entities or attributes, a verb phrase may indicate an association between entities. Again, scan the use cases to find possible associations and document them by either using a commenting tool (Figure A.7) or entering them in a separate table (Table A.4).

Once the relationships between entities have been identified, they are recorded in the application glossary. Again, this may be managed within a modelling tool or as a separate document, when a format like that in Table A.5 can be used.

For each association and each entity participating in that association, calculate the multiplicity constraint. For generalization relationships, write down the disjoint and participation constraints. Table A.6 presents one approach to recording information on association multiplicity.

Figure A.6 Documenting possible entities using comments within a word-processed document.

Get staff contact details

This allows any [user] to get the [contact details]([name, phone and email]) for a named [member of staff] at the [University]. The user provides the [staff member]'s [surname and first initial] and requests their contact details. A [list] showing the name and phone number of each member of staff matching the [search criteria] is delivered, together with a [count of the number of matches] from the [Staff Directory]. The user can see the full contact details for any [entry] on the list], along with a [photo] of the member of staff if one is available, by selecting that entry. If there are no matches, a [message] stating this is displayed.

The full contact details for an [academic] provide access to a list of [support sessions] offered by them.

There is also an option to view a ["help" page], giving instructions on how to use the [search facility].

Comment: Not an entity - users are outside the system boundary.

Comment: Entity - synonym for "staff member"

Comment: Not entities - this is data held about members of staff: i.e. attributes

Comment: Entity - synonym for "staff member"

Comment: Not an entity - there is only one university, so it cannot be an entity.

Comment: Entity - the application holds contact details, photo and staff number.

Comment: Not entities - this is data held about members of staff: i.e. attributes

Comment: Not an entity - this is an output from the application, not persistent data.

Comment: Not an entity - synonym for "surname and first initial"

Comment: Not an entity - this data will be calculated for each search, so cannot be stored in the database.

Comment: Not an entity - the staff directory is the application, not something the application holds data about.

Comment: Not an entity - this is an output from the application, not persistent data.

Comment: Not an entity - this is data held about members of staff: i.e. an attribute

Comment: Not an entity - it may make sense to hold messages in the database, but this is an implementation issue, not part of conceptual design.

Comment: Not an entity - an academic is a member of staff. Could model them as a separate entity, but no need in this simple application.

Comment: Entity - data about support sessions is held in the database.

Comment: Not an entity - it may make sense to hold help information in the database, but this is an implementation issue, not part of conceptual design.

Comment: Not an entity - the search facility is part of the applications functionality.

Table A.1 Possible entities or attributes mentioned in the Staff Directory use cases.

Noun	Is it an entity or attribute?
User	No – users are outside the system boundary.
contact details	Entity – synonym for 'staff member'.
name	Attribute – this is data *about* a member of staff.
phone	Attribute – this is data *about* a member of staff.
e-mail	Attribute – this is data *about* a member of staff.
member of staff	Entity – synonym for 'staff member'.
university	No – there is only one university, so it cannot be an entity.
staff member	Entity – the database must hold contact details, photo and staff number for each staff member.
surname	Attribute – this is data *about* a member of staff.
initial	Attribute – this is data *about* a member of staff.
list	No – this is an output from the application, not persistent data.
search criteria	No – synonym for 'surname and first initial'.
count of number of matches	No – this data will be calculated for each search, so cannot be stored in the database.
Staff Directory	No – the Staff Directory *is* the application, not something the application holds data about.
entry on the list	No – this is an output from the application, not persistent data.
photo	Attribute – this is data held about members of staff.
message	No – it may make sense to hold messages in the database, but this is an implementation issue, not part of conceptual database design.
academic	No – an academic is a member of staff. Could model them as a separate entity, but no need in this simple application.
support session	Entity – data about support sessions is held on the database.
'help' page	No – it may make sense to hold help information on the database, but this is an implementation issue, not part of conceptual design.
search facility	No – the search facility is part of the applications functionality.
The application	No – the database is part of the application, not the other way round!
students	No – students will use the application, but the database will not hold data about them.
day	Attribute – this is data held about a support session.
start time	Attribute – this is data held about a support session.
end time	Attribute – this is data held about a support session.
student support session	Entity – a synonym for 'support session'.

Table A.2 Extract from Staff Directory application glossary: entities.

Entity	Synonyms	Description
Staff	staff member member of staff academic contact details	Each occurrence of the Staff entity holds identification and contact details for a member of staff.
SupportSession	drop-in session student support session	Each occurrence of the SupportSession entity holds information on when the support session runs.

Table A.3 Extract from Staff Directory application glossary: attributes.

Entity	Attribute	Description	Synonym	Multiplicity	Data type	Default value	Constraint	Tagged value	Comment
SupportSession	day	The day on which the teaching session runs.	day of week	1..1	Varchar		Any day of the week.		
	startTime	The time at which the teaching session begins.	start	1..1	Time		Between 09.00 and 18.00.		
	endTime	The time at which the teaching session ends.	end	1..1	Time		No later than 18.00.		
	/duration	The length of the session.	length	1..1	Interval		Between 1 and 3 hours.		Derived as endTime minus startTime.

Figure A.7 Documenting possible associations using comments within a word-processed document.

Get staff contact details

This allows any [user to get the contact details](name, phone and email) for a named member of staff at the University. The user provides the staff member's surname and first initial and requests their contact details. A list showing the name and phone number of each member of staff matching the search criteria is delivered, together with a count of the number of matches from the Staff Directory. The user can see the full contact details for any entry on the list, along with a photo of the member of staff if one is available, by selecting that entry. If there are no matches, a message stating this is displayed.

The full contact details for an academic provide access to a list of [support sessions offered by them].

There is also an option to view a "help" page, giving instructions on how to use the search facility.

Comment: Not an association between entities. Although "contact details" is a synonym for the Staff entity, "user" is not an entity.

Comment: An association - indicates that academics (who are all members of staff) offer support sessions. Both Staff and SupportSession are entities.

Table A.4 Documenting possible associations using tables.

Verb phrase	Is it an association or generalization relationship?
allows any user to get the contact details	Not a relationship between entities. 'Contact details' is a synonym for the Staff entity, but 'user' is not an entity.
support sessions offered by [an academic]	An association – indicates that academics (who are all members of staff) offer support sessions. Both Staff and SupportSession are entities.

Table A.5 Extract from Staff Directory application glossary: associations between entities.

Relationship	Synonyms	Participating entities	Description
Offer	OfferedBy	Staff, SupportSession	An association. Each occurrence of Offer indicates that a particular support session is offered by a particular academic.

Table A.6 Extract from Staff Directory application glossary: association multiplicity constraints.

Association	Participating entity	Minimum occurrences	Maximum occurrences
Offer	Staff	0	* (many)
		E.g. Padma Brar is a secretary, so does not offer support sessions. For the occurrence of Staff representing Padma's contact details, there is no occurrence of the Offer association.	E.g. Paul Smith offers two support sessions and Mikhail Sudbin offers three. There is no set limit to how many support sessions an academic can offer.
	SupportSession	1	1
		Each support session must be offered by someone, so, for each occurrence of SupportSession, there will always be an occurrence of Offer linking it to an occurrence of Staff.	Each support session is offered by a single academic. Academics may run joint support sessions *in addition to* their individual support sessions. Only individual support sessions are recorded on the database.

A.3   Database creation script

The following code allows you to create a sample Staff Directory database for use with the exercises.

```
-- ************************************************************
-- Create the tables using MySQL Syntax.
-- Use the DROP TABLE statement first, to ensure no name
-- conflicts arise.  Useful if the first version fails
-- half-way through and the script must be run again.
```

```
--
-- NOTES
-- 1) The "IF EXISTS" syntax is MySQL specific.
-- *********************************************************
DROP TABLE IF EXISTS Staff;

CREATE TABLE Staff(
staffNo CHAR(5) NOT NULL ,
fName VARCHAR(50) NOT NULL ,
lName VARCHAR(20) NOT NULL ,
phone VARCHAR(20) ,
email VARCHAR(50) NOT NULL ,
photo BLOB ,
department VARCHAR(20) NOT NULL ,
title VARCHAR(4) ,
jobType VARCHAR(20) ,
jobTitle VARCHAR(30) ,
CONSTRAINT pkStaff PRIMARY KEY (staffNo)
);

DROP TABLE IF EXISTS SupportSession;

CREATE TABLE SupportSession(
staffNo CHAR(5) NOT NULL ,
dayOfWeek VARCHAR (9) NOT NULL ,
startTime TIME NOT NULL ,
endTime TIME NOT NULL ,
CONSTRAINT pkSupportSession PRIMARY KEY (staffNo,
dayOfWeek, startTime)
);

--***************************************************************
-- Add the other constraints.
-- Adding foreign keys after creating all the tables means
-- we can create the tables in any order.
--
-- NOTE The default MySQL table type is MyISAM, which does
--      not enforce the foreign key constraint!
-- *********************************************************
ALTER TABLE SupportSession
ADD CONSTRAINT frnSupportSessionStaff
FOREIGN KEY (staffNo)
REFERENCES Staff (staffNo)
ON UPDATE CASCADE
ON DELETE CASCADE;

--***************************************************************
-- Insert sample data.
--***************************************************************
-- Staff data
--***************************************************************
```

```
INSERT INTO Staff
(staffNo, fName, lName, phone, email, department, title,
jobType, jobTitle)
VALUES
('10780', 'John', 'Smith', NULL,
'j.b.smith@pennine.ac.uk', 'Catering', 'Mr', 'Support',
'Chef');
INSERT INTO Staff
(staffNo, fName, lName, phone, email, department, title,
jobType, jobTitle)
VALUES
('25447', 'John', 'Smith', '5104', 'j.smith@pennine.ac.uk',
'Music', 'Mr', 'Administration', 'Secretary');
INSERT INTO Staff
(staffNo, fName, lName, phone, email, department, title,
jobType, jobTitle)
VALUES
('25448', 'Judith Anne', 'Smith', '7709',
'j.a.smith@pennine.ac.uk', 'Estates', 'Mrs', 'Support',
'Estates Manager');
INSERT INTO Staff
(staffNo, fName, lName, phone, email, department, title,
jobType, jobTitle)
VALUES
('31210', 'Paul', 'Smith',  NULL, 'p.smith@pennine.ac.uk',
'Computing', 'Dr', 'Academic', 'Senior Lecturer');
INSERT INTO Staff
(staffNo, fName, lName, phone, email, department, title,
jobType, jobTitle)
VALUES
('77712', 'Frank', 'Rose', '8871', 'f.rose@pennine.ac.uk',
'Computing', 'Mr', 'Technical', 'Technician');
INSERT INTO Staff
(staffNo, fName, lName, phone, email, department, title,
jobType, jobTitle)
VALUES
('14443', 'Helen', 'Abbot', '8032', 'h.abbot@pennine.ac.
uk', 'Computing', 'Mrs', 'Administration', 'Secretary');
INSERT INTO Staff
(staffNo, fName, lName, phone, email, department, title,
jobType, jobTitle)
VALUES
('23257', 'Freya', 'Stark', '8660', 'f.stark@pennine.
ac.uk', 'Computing', 'Prof', 'Academic', 'Dean');
```

```
INSERT INTO Staff
(staffNo, fName, lName, phone, email, department, title,
jobType, jobTitle)
VALUES
('33935', 'Padma', 'Brar', '6641', 'p.brar@pennine.ac.uk',
'Health', 'Ms', 'Administration', 'Administrator');

INSERT INTO Staff
(staffNo, fName, lName, phone, email, department, title,
jobType, jobTitle)
VALUES
('35054', 'Selma', 'Hutchins', '8706',
's.hutchins@pennine.ac.uk', 'Computing', 'Ms', 'Academic',
'Senior Lecturer');

INSERT INTO Staff
(staffNo, fName, lName, phone, email, department, title,
jobType, jobTitle)
VALUES
('45965', 'Mikhail', 'Sudbin', '5553', 'm.sudbin@pennine.
ac.uk', 'Music', 'Mr', 'Academic', 'Lecturer');

INSERT INTO Staff
(staffNo, fName, lName, phone, email, department, title,
jobType, jobTitle)
VALUES
('35155', 'Helene', 'Chirac', NULL, 'h.chirac@pennine.ac.uk',
'Health', 'Miss', 'Technical', 'Technician');

INSERT INTO Staff
(staffNo, fName, lName, phone, email, department, title,
jobType, jobTitle)
VALUES
('55776', 'Gurpreet', 'Choudhury', '5454',
'g.choudhury@pennine.ac.uk', 'Music', 'Dr', 'Academic',
'Senior Lecturer');

INSERT INTO Staff
(staffNo, fName, lName, phone, email, department, title,
jobType, jobTitle)
VALUES
('56893', 'Ruth', 'Bapetsi', '8022',
'r.bapetsi@pennine.ac.uk', 'Health', 'Mrs', 'Academic',
'Senior Lecturer');

INSERT INTO Staff
(staffNo, fName, lName, phone, email, department, title,
jobType, jobTitle)
VALUES
```

```
('56673', 'Joshua', 'Bittaye', '7782',
'j.bittaye@pennine.ac.uk', 'Computing', 'Mr', 'Academic',
'Lecturer');

INSERT INTO Staff
(staffNo, fName, lName, phone, email, department, title,
jobType, jobTitle)
VALUES
('89987', 'Dan', 'Lin', '8514', 'd.lin@pennine.co.uk',
'Health', 'Dr', 'Administration', 'Senior Administrator');

INSERT INTO Staff
(staffNo, fName, lName, phone, email, department, title,
jobType, jobTitle)
VALUES
('78893', 'Jo Karen', 'O''Connor' , '8871'
,'j.k.oconnor@pennine.ac.uk', 'Health', 'Miss',
'Administration', 'Administrator');

INSERT INTO Staff
(staffNo, fName, lName, phone, email, department, title,
jobType, jobTitle)
VALUES
('33509', 'Helen', 'Timms', '8661',
'h.timms@pennine.ac.uk', 'Music', 'Mrs', 'Technical',
'Technician');


- - *****************************************************
- - SupportSession data
- -*****************************************************

INSERT INTO SupportSession
(staffNo, dayOfWeek, startTime, endTime)
VALUES
('56673', 'Friday', '15:30', '16:30');

INSERT INTO SupportSession
(staffNo, dayOfWeek, startTime, endTime)
VALUES
('56673', 'Thursday', '15:30', '16:30');

INSERT INTO SupportSession
(staffNo, dayOfWeek, startTime, endTime)
VALUES
('35054', 'Monday', '09:00', '10:00');

INSERT INTO SupportSession
(staffNo, dayOfWeek, startTime, endTime)
VALUES
('45965', 'Wednesday', '11:00', '12:00');
```

```
INSERT INTO SupportSession
(staffNo, dayOfWeek, startTime, endTime)
VALUES
('31210', 'Wednesday', '11:00', '13:00');

INSERT INTO SupportSession
(staffNo, dayOfWeek, startTime, endTime)
VALUES
('35054', 'Monday', '15:00', '16:00');

INSERT INTO SupportSession
(staffNo, dayOfWeek, startTime, endTime)
VALUES
('56893', 'Thursday', '09:00', '10:00');

INSERT INTO SupportSession
(staffNo, dayOfWeek, startTime, endTime)
VALUES
('45965', 'Monday', '11:00', '12:00');

INSERT INTO SupportSession
(staffNo, dayOfWeek, startTime, endTime)
VALUES
('23257', 'Monday', '15:00', '16:00');

INSERT INTO SupportSession
(staffNo, dayOfWeek, startTime, endTime)
VALUES
('55776', 'Monday', '14:00', '16:00');

INSERT INTO SupportSession
(staffNo, dayOfWeek, startTime, endTime)
VALUES
('56893', 'Tuesday', '14:00', '15:00');

INSERT INTO SupportSession
(staffNo, dayOfWeek, startTime, endTime)
VALUES
('56673', 'Friday', '10:00', '11:00');

INSERT INTO SupportSession
(staffNo, dayOfWeek, startTime, endTime)
VALUES
('35054', 'Tuesday', '11:00', '12:00');
```

Appendix

B

The Pennine University's Web Timetable case study

B.1 Requirements

The Pennine University teaches a variety of courses at both undergraduate and postgraduate levels. Students study several modules each term. Each week, a module will have a lecture, tutorial, practical or seminar session. Typical arts and humanities modules have one lecture and one tutorial each week, while typical science and engineering modules have a lecture, tutorial and practical. Some modules have two lectures each week – one for day students and one for evening students. Others have no lectures, simply a long seminar session. This makes timetabling very tricky, especially as more students than before are taking combined degrees, so are taking modules with more than one school.

Although the existing timetabling application will continue to be used by the timetable administrators, it has been decided to develop a new approach to allocating students to tutorial groups and so on. Timetables for courses, modules and academic staff will be created with the existing timetabling application, but students will not be allocated to particular tutorial, practical or seminar groups. Instead, a new application will allow students to choose these themselves. For example, where a student takes a module with only one lecture, but a choice of four tutorial slots, he or she *must* attend the lecture but may choose which of the four tutorial slots to go to.

The application must be Web based and accessible to students over the Internet, allowing them to easily sort out their timetable before the start of term. The application must also allow academic staff to book any additional equipment that they may need for specific teaching sessions. The requirements were documented as use cases. The use case diagram (Figure B.1) provides an overview of who uses the system and how they expect to use it. The use case specifications below give further details of the expected behaviour. Together, they form the formal definition of the users' requirements for the Staff Directory web database application.

> These requirements are simplified versions for use with the exercises in Chapter 8. The ER diagrams in Chapters 8 and 9 include many details not mentioned in these use cases, such as attribute and entity constraints.

Figure B.1 The Web Timetable use case diagram.

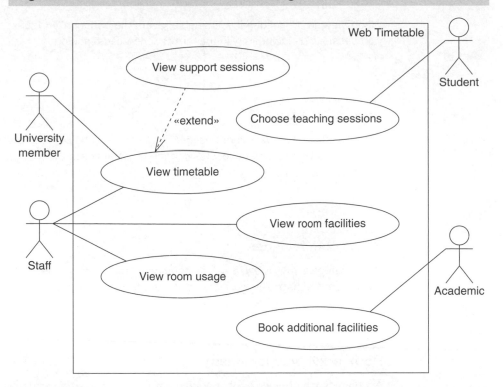

View timetable

A member of the University may ask to view a timetable. Timetables are available for courses, modules, rooms, academics and students. Valid identifiers for particular timetables are, respectively, course code, module code, building and room number, staff number and student ID number. Timetables should include the following information under each heading.

Course timetable: Course code and title, name of school delivering the course.
Module timetable: module code and title, name of module leader.
Room timetable: building and room number.
Academic timetable: staff member's title and name.
Student timetable: Student's name and number and the course he or she is enrolled on.

Provided a valid identifier for the requested timetable is provided by the user, the teaching sessions for that timetable are delivered. For each teaching session, the module code, module title, type of class, building, room and tutor are shown, as well as the start and end time of the session and the teaching weeks for which it runs.

For practical, tutorial, seminar and lab sessions, the group ID is also included to distinguish between teaching sessions that deliver the same lesson, but to different groups of students.

For an academic timetable, users may optionally include details of that staff member's support sessions (see View support sessions).

View support sessions

When viewing an academic's timetable, users may optionally request that their support sessions be included with the formal scheduled teaching.

View room usage

Staff members may view room usage. They enter a valid building and room number and see a cut-down timetable, showing the times at which the room is in use and for which weeks.

View room facilities

Staff members may view a list of equipment that is available in a room. Portable equipment that happens to be stored in that room is not shown, only fixed equipment.

Book additional facilities

Academics may book portable equipment for use on particular dates in a particular teaching session that they deliver. They specify the teaching session and the type of equipment required. They then choose the specific dates on which they wish to book this equipment for the stated teaching session. Only dates on which the teaching session actually runs are allowed (only dates that fall during term time).

For each of the requested dates, the application allocates a suitable item of equipment and records both the date the booking was made and the date on which the equipment is required. If no suitable item is available, then a message stating this is displayed.

Choose teaching sessions

Students may choose which tutorial, practical or seminar groups they attend. They specify which course they are studying and see a timetable for that course. The timetable includes *all* teaching sessions for every module used by the specified course.

For each module, students choose which of the available teaching sessions they wish to attend. Once a teaching session has only four places left, it is considered unavailable. These last four places are allocated by the course leader and allow, for example, students with special needs to be accommodated.

Glossary

absolute URL A *URL* that includes the full address of the *resource*. See *relative URL* and *URL*.

access path analysis See *transaction path analysis*.

actor A role that a user, human or otherwise, of the information system might take.

aggregate function Used in an SQL *select statement* to summarize information for a group of rows.

aggregate query A *select statement* that uses an *aggregate function*.

aggregation association In UML, an *association* indicating that one *entity* forms part of another.

alias In SQL, an alternative name for an *expression* in the *select list*.

alter table statement Alters the structure of a *table*.

alternate key A *candidate key* of a *table* other than the *primary key*.

ancestor In a *tree*, the *parent*, parent of a parent and so on of a particular *node*.

application See *application software* and *information system*.

application glossary A central repository of information about the design of the *application*.

application partitioning The division of responsibilities between the different tiers of a client-server *application*.

application programming interface (API) A set of functions that allows programmers to access the functionality of a piece of software, such as a *DBMS*.

application software Computer software that people interact with, usually via a graphical user interface (GUI), using windows, buttons, menus and so on.

application state Information about the current and previous state of an *application*.

assertion In SQL, an *integrity constraint* that applies to the *database instance* rather than a *table instance*.

association A meaningful connection between, for example, an *actor* and a *use case* in a use case diagram or between *entities* in an *ER diagram*.

association, binary An *association* with two ends.

association, degree of In an *ER diagram*, the number of *entities* that participate in an *association*.

association, n-ary An *association* with three or more ends.

association, unary A *binary association* with one participating *entity*.

association qualifier Attaches *attributes* to an *association* end. It indicates that association occurrences exist only for particular *values* of these attributes, changing the meaning of the *multiplicity constraint* at the other end of the association.

atomization In XPath, the process that converts a sequence of *nodes* to a value.

attribute, in UML A property of an *entity* or *relationship*.

attribute, in HTML or XML A property of an *element*. A *name-value pair* that provides additional information about an *element*. Similar to a *UML tagged value*.

attribute, derived In *UML*, an *attribute* the value of which can be derived (or calculated) from the *values* of the other attributes.

attribute, multivalued In *UML*, an *attribute* that can hold more than one *value*. Similar to a *non-scalar data type*. See *attribute multiplicity*.

attribute compartment In *UML*, that part of the representation of an *entity* where the *attribute* definitions are written.

attribute constraint In *UML*, a limit placed on the *values* taken by an *attribute*.

attribute multiplicity In *UML*, indicates how many *values* an *attribute* may hold. See *attribute, multivalued*.

attribute property list In *UML*, a list of constraints, *tagged values* and comments that apply to the *attribute*.

authentication In *database* security, the way in which users prove their identity to the *DBMS*. See *identification* and *authorization*.

authorization In *database* security, the process by which a *DBMS* determines whether or not a user is allowed to request a particular action.

authorization identifier Unique identifier for a user of an *application*.

auto increment Optional property of a column in the MySQL DBMS used to instruct the *DBMS* to automatically generate a unique *value* for this column in new rows. See *surrogate key*.

axis In XPath, the first sequence of *nodes* reached in a *location step*. See also *node test* and *predicate*.

base table A *table instance* stored on disk. See also *table* and *derived table*. A base table may be a persistent base table or a temporary base table.

binary operator An operator that takes two input *values*. See *operator* and *unary operator*.

block A contiguous strip of the hard disk (or other persistent storage medium) that can be read in a single action.

boiler-plate text The *static content* of a *web page*.

bridge A device that connects two subnetworks, allowing devices in one subnetwork to broadcast messages to the other subnetwork.

build association In *logical web data design*, a *UML stereotyped association* between a *client page* and a *server page* indicating that an occurrence of the *server page* builds the associated occurrence of the *client page*.

business rule A *statement* that describes the information used by an organization or restrictions on how that information is used.

candidate key A set of columns from a *table*, the combination of the *values* of which is unique and irreducible, meaning no subset of those column values is unique.

candidate key constraint An *integrity constraint* that enforces uniqueness and irreducibility for a set of columns.

cardinality of a table The number of rows in the *table instance*.

cascading stylesheet (CSS) A language for controlling the presentation of *HTML elements*.

challenge In *HTTP authentication*, the HTTP response to an unauthorized request for a web *resource*.

char SQL *data type* for a fixed-length character string.

character data The actual content of an *XML* or *HTML document*.

check condition A Boolean expression used to define a *check constraint*.

check constraint In SQL, a constraint used to enforce general *business rules*.

child In a *tree*, a *node* immediately below some other node, called its *parent*.

clear text value The *value before* applying a *hash function*.

client page In *logical web data design*, a *UML stereotyped* class representing a client-side *web page*.

column description The name and *data type* of a column in a *table*.

commit An instruction to the *DBMS* to 'save' all changes made to the *database instance*. After a commit, the changes are made permanent. See also *rollback*.

common gateway interface (CGI) An *application programming interface (API)* supported by most *HTTP* servers.

comparison operators An *operator* that compares two *values* of a given *data type* and returns a Boolean value. See *operator*.

composite candidate key A *candidate key* with two or more columns.

composition association A stronger form of *aggregation association* in which the part cannot exist independently of the containing *entity*.

computer network A group of computing devices connected together to allow sharing of resources.

conceptual database design A model showing the structures required to organize the *data* mentioned in the user requirements specification.

conceptual web data design Shows the links between the *database entities* and those parts of the user interface that interact directly with them.

connection In SQL, a user's link with the *DBMS*. See *session*.

connection trap A structure in an *ER diagram* such that a connection between two *entities* is not adequately represented by existing *associations*.

cookie A set of *data* stored by the *web browser* at the request of the *web server*.

correlation name In an *SQL statement*, an *alias* for a *table*.

correlated subquery A *subquery* that refers to a column of the outer *SQL statement*.

create function statement In SQL, creates an SQL *stored function*.

create schema statement In SQL, creates an *SQL schema*.

create table statement In SQL, creates a *table*.

cross join The simplest, and least useful, sort of *join* in SQL. Joins each row in one *table* to every row in the other.

data The basic facts; something known about a situation.

data-centric A part of the user interface that draws (part of) its content from, or allows the user to modify, the *database instance*.

data cleansing Removing potentially malicious *data* before it is processed by the script.

data communications manager (DCM) Software that works alongside the *DBMS* to allow it to use network system software.

data definition language (DDL) The set of statements for creating and modifying the *database schema*.

data dictionary Maintained by the *DBMS*, the data dictionary holds the description of a *database's* data structures and constraints. Also called the system catalogue.

data file A file on a hard disk or other persistent data storage medium, used to store *data*.

data item A particular fact about a thing.

data language A computer language designed to allow the manipulation of *data* and data structures on a *database*.

data manipulation language (DML) The statements used to manipulate the *database instance*.

data model A general approach to organizing the *data* on a *database*.

data type A named set of *data values*, typically sharing common characteristics and operations. See *user-defined data type* and *system-defined data type*.

data validation The process of correctly interpreting the *data* entered by the user and generating an appropriate response.

database A persistent, self-describing, structured collection of related items of *data*.

database client *Application software* designed to allow end users to interact with the *DBMS*.

database design A description or model of the *data* requirements of a particular organization.

database event An SQL *DML statement* causes a database event to occur. The database events are insert, update and delete.

database instance The actual data held on a *database*.

database management system (DBMS) The software that manages all interaction with the *database*.

database query A request to view selected *data* held on a *database*.

database schema The description of a *database* structure consisting of all the *table schema*.

datagram A chunk of a message being sent using the *IP* internetworking *protocol*.

DBMS See *database management system*.

DCM See *data communications manager*.

DDL See *data definition language*.

degree of a table The number of columns in the *table*.

default namespace In *XML*, if a default namespace is declared, then every unprefixed *element name* belongs to that default namespace.

default value The *value* used (for an *attribute*, column, parameter and so on) when end users do not specify a value.

delete statement An *SQL statement* that allows users to remove rows from a *table instance*.

delete event Occurs when a row is removed from a *table*.

dependent column One for which the *value* is determined by the value *functional determinant*.

derived table A *table instance* that is only ever stored in memory. See *base table, table, view*.

descendant In a *tree*, a *child*, child of a child and so on of a particular *node*.

disjoint constraint On a *generalization relationship*, indicates whether or not the occurrence of the more general *entity* can, at the same time, be an occurrence of more than one of its more specific entities.

distinct type In SQL, a *user-defined data type* created as a restriction of an existing *system-defined data type*.

DML See *data manipulation language*.

DNS See *domain name system*.

docroot see *document root*.

document In *XML*, one of the three structures used to organize data. See also *element* and *attribute*.

document body, in HMTL Contains the *document* content.

document head, in HMTL Contains information about the *document*.

document element In *XML* and *HTML*, the top-level *element* that encloses all the elements and *character data* held in the *document*.

document model Defines the general structure of a *document*'s content.

document order The ordering of *nodes* within an *XML document*.

document root Top-level folder where a *website*'s *resources* are stored.

document type declaration, in HMTL Indicates which version of *HTML* is being used.

domain name An easily remembered alternative to an *IP address*.

domain name system (DNS) Allows an *Internet application* to translate a *domain name* into the corresponding *IP address*.

dynamic content The content of a dynamic *web page* that can change between different instances of that *document*.

edge In a *tree*, an *edge* connects two *nodes*.

element, in HTML Elements define the structure of an *HTML document*. They may contain content such as text or define other structures, such as *form* controls and line breaks.

element In *XML*, elements define the structure of an *XML document*. They may contain other elements, *character data* or a mixture of these.

element, complex An *element* that contains other elements.

element content The actual *data* contained in an *element*.

element name In *XML*, the *node name* of a particular kind of *element*.

element, simple An *element* that contains only *character data*.

empty element An *HTML* or *XML element* that has no content.

enterprise constraint A mechanism for enforcing a more general *business rule*.

entity A set of things about which the information system must hold, or process, *data*.

entity, strong Its occurrences can be uniquely identified by its *attribute values*.

entity, weak Its occurrences cannot be uniquely identified by its *attribute values*.

entity-relationship (ER) diagram One approach to representing a *database design*.

ephemeral port number Any *port number* that is not a *well-known port number*. Value is 1024 or larger.

equi-join A *join* in which the *join condition* is based on an equality match, usually between the columns of a *foreign key* and its matching *primary key*.

ER diagram See entity-relationship (ER) diagram.

escape sequence A sequence of characters used to represent a special character, such as a new line, or 'escape' the special meaning of a character, such as the single quote or dollar sign, in PHP or some other computer language.

expanded name In *XML*, the full name of an *element* or *attribute* consisting of its *namespace name* and its *local name*.

expression A valid combination of *literals*, *operators* and *variables*.

extend relationship Indicates that the behaviour of one *use case* (the extending use case) may be added on to the behaviour of another (the extended use case).

Extensible Mark-up Language (XML) A language for defining the *document model* of other *mark-up* languages.

external view Part of the ANSI/SPARC database systems architecture. Provides a tailored view of a *database* for a group of end users with similar information needs.

extranet A private *internet* used by an organization and its partners.

fantrap A particular kind of *connection trap*.

field Within a *record*, a single item of *data*; the equivalent of a column or *attribute value*.

file transfer protocol An *Internet* application that allows files to be transferred from one computer to another across *the Internet*.

foreign key A column (or set of columns) in one *table*, the *values* of which match those of the *primary key* on some other table. It acts as a link between the two tables.

foreign key constraint An *integrity constraint* that states, for every row of the *referencing table*, the *value* of the *foreign key* column(s) must match those in the *primary key* column(s) in some row of the *referenced table*. Also called a *referential integrity constraint*.

form In *logical web data design*, a *UML stereotyped* class representing an *HTML form*; a special kind of *client page*.

forward axis In XPath, an *axis* in which the nodes appear in *document order*. See also *reverse axis*.

from clause In an SQL *select statement*, indicates which table(s) the columns named in the *select list* come from.

functional determinant A set of columns that forms a *candidate key* for a *subset* of the columns in the *table*. See *dependent column, normalized table, repeating group*.

functional requirement A requirement to hold particular information or support particular behaviour.

generalization relationship A taxonomic relationship between a more general *entity* and a more specific entity.

generation clause Used with a *surrogate key* to instruct the *DBMS* to automatically generate a unique *value* for this column in new rows.

grant statement Allows the owner of a *database* or database object to grant privileges to use that object to other *DBMS* users.

group by clause Allows rows to be grouped by the *value* of one or more columns and summary information calculated for each group. Rows with the same values in the grouping columns are placed in the same group.

hash file File organization that places each *record* in a particular *block* on the hard disk (or other persistent storage medium).

hash function A function that takes a character string and returns a (much longer) unique string of characters. In security, often used to encrypt passwords. In a *hash file*, a hash function determines which *block* a *record* is placed in.

hashed value The *value* returned by a *hash function*.

having clause In an *SQL select statement* indicates which groups have their summary information shown. Only ever used in conjunction with a *group by clause*.

heap file A *data* file in which *records* are stored in no particular order; an unordered heap of records.

hidden form control An *HTML form* control, specifies setting the input *element's* type *attribute* to 'hidden', which is not displayed in the web *browser*, but can be viewed in the HTML source of the *web page*. Used as one technique for maintaining *application state* in a web application by writing hidden form controls at runtime.

host number The part of the *IP address* identifying the particular network device.

HTML See *Hypertext Mark-up Language*.

HTML character entity A special sequence of characters used to represent a character that is hard to type or has a special meaning in *HTML*.

HTTP See *hypertext transfer protocol*.

HTTP authentication A method for *authenticating* users built into the *HTTP* protocol.

HTTP method Allows a *web client* to request specific services of a *web server*.

HTTP request message *HTTP* message sent from the *web client* to the *web server*.

HTTP response message *HTTP* message sent from the *web server* to the *web client*.

HTTP server *Application software* used to manage access to a *website*. Often referred to as the *web server*.

hyperlink A link from one part of a *document* to another or between two documents.

Hypertext Mark-up Language (HTML) The specification of the *document model* for *web pages* and the language used to write them.

hypertext transfer protocol (HTTP) The *application protocol* used by *web clients* and *web servers* to communicate. Aims to facilitate the transfer of web *resources*.

identification In *database* security, the way in which users identify themselves to the *DBMS*. See *authentication* and *authorization*.

identifier In SQL, a valid name for a database object.

identifier, regular In SQL, a valid name for a *database* object that is not case-sensitive.

identifier, delimited In SQL, a valid name for a *database* object that is case-sensitive.

include file A PHP script suitable for inclusion in other PHP scripts.

index Provides a way to quickly locate a *record* within a *data* file based on the *value* of a *field* within that record.

index, clustering An *index* on the *ordering field* of an *ordered file* when that field *does not* correspond to a *candidate key* of the *table* being stored.

index, primary An *index* on the *ordering field* of an *ordered file* when that field corresponds to a *candidate key* of the *table* being stored.

index, secondary An *index* on any field of an *ordered file*, apart from the *ordering field*.

information Some useful combination of facts.

information system '. . . The means by which people and organizations, utilizing technologies, gather, process, store, use and disseminate information' (UKAIS, 1999).

information system's lifecycle The time during which an information system is being planned, developed and used.

inner join A *join* in which *data* for unmatched rows is excluded from the *result set*. See also *equi-join, join, outer join*.

insert statement An *SQL statement* that allows users to add a row of data to a *table instance*.

insert event Occurs when a row is added to a *database table*.

instance document In *XML*, a *document* that conforms to a particular *document model* (possibly held as two or more physical *XML documents*). See also *schema document*.

integrity constraint A statement about the *database instance* that must always be true.

internal view Part of the ANSI/SPARC database systems architecture. Describes what space is available for *data* storage, how the data is stored and what techniques are used to ensure that data are accessed efficiently.

internet An interconnected network; two or more networks, possibly with different physical network infrastructure, that have been connected together.

Internet, The A global network of publicly accessible interconnected networks.

Internet application A client-server *application* that uses *Internet* technologies to connect clients with the server. *The Web* and e-mail are the most familiar Internet applications.

Internet protocol (IP) *Protocol* that interconnects the networks on *the Internet* by providing a common addressing scheme and mechanisms to identify a route from the source to the destination address.

intranet A private *internet* – typically one using the *TCP/IP* suite of internetworking *protocols*.

IP See *Internet protocol*.

IP address A logical network address conforming to the definition in the *IP protocol*.

join A *select statement* that retrieves *data* from two (or more) *tables* or from two (or more) copies of the same table. (See also *inner join, join condition, outer join*.)

join condition A Boolean expression in the *where clause* of a *join* that tells the *DBMS* which rows of the *cross join* should appear in the *result set*.

leaf In a *tree*, a leaf is a *node* with no *child* nodes.

link association In *logical web data design*, a *UML stereotyped association* between a *client page* and a *server page* indicating that an occurrence of the *client page* requests the associated occurrence of the *server page*.

link entity An *entity* in a *logical ER diagram* that replaces a many-to-many *association*. See *link table*.

link table A *table* in a relational *database* that implements a many-to-many *association*. See *link entity*.

literal A human-readable representation of a *data value*.

local area network (LAN) A computer network, usually run by a single organization, in which the networked computers are all located within about 1 kilometre of one another.

local name In *XML*, the name of an *element* or *attribute* used in the *document model* defining that element or attribute.

location header An *HTTP* response message header that instructs the *web browser* to request the *resource* from a different location.

location path In XPath, a sequence of *location steps*.

location step In XPath, a location step is an instruction to move from one sequence of *nodes* to another, within an XML document.

logical data independence The property of the ANSI/SPARC database systems architecture that means changes to the *logical view* need not affect the *external view*.

logical database design Shows how to use a particular *data model* to meet end users' data requirements.

logical ER diagram An *ER diagram* that only uses structures that have direct equivalents in the target *data model*.

logical view Part of the ANSI/SPARC database systems architecture. Provides a complete description of the data structures and *data* on the *database*.

logical web data design Adapts the *conceptual web data design* to reflect the particular approach to implementing a user interface taken by web technology and the chosen *application* architecture.

look-up entity An *entity* (usually in a *logical ER diagram*) that plays a role similar to that of a *multivalued attribute*. Each occurrence of a look-up entity holds a list of *values* associated with a single occurrence of some other *entity*.

mark-up Special text within a *document* that describes its content, especially the structure of document content. Used in *HTML* and *XML*.

many-to-many In an *ER diagram* a *binary association* with an upper bound of *(many) on both *multiplicity constraints*.

matching candidate key In the description of a *foreign key constraint*, this is the *candidate key* of the *referenced table*, the *value* of which matches the foreign key of the *referencing table*.

meta-data *Data* that describes the structure of a *database*.

method note In *UML*, the way to document the specific behaviour represented by an *operation*.

mixed content Refers to an *XML element*, the content of which is a mixture of other elements and text.

multimedia document A *document* combining different media types, such as text, images, sound and video.

multiplicity constraint A *constraint* on an *association* end that restricts the number of occurrences of the *entity* at the chosen end in some way. See *multiplicity constraint, outer* and *multiplicity constraint, inner*.

multiplicity constraint, inner A constraint on an *association* end that limits the number of occurrences of the association that a single occurrence of the *entity* at this association end may participate in.

multiplicity constraint, outer A *constraint* on an *association* end that limits the number of occurrences of the *entity* at this association end that may be linked, by occurrences of the association, to a given set of occurrences of entities from each of the other ends of the association.

name compartment In *UML*, that part of the representation of an *entity* where the entity name and *stereotype* are written.

name server Part of the *domain name system (DNS)*, it maintains a database linking *domain names* to *IP addresses*.

namespace declaration In *XML*, the mechanism for binding a *namespace prefix* to a *namespace name*.

namespace name In *XML*, the globally unique identifier for a *document model*.

namespace node Represents a *namespace declaration* in the *tree* representation of an *XML document*.

namespace prefix In *XML*, a local *alias* for the *namespace name*.

name-value pair A pair consisting of a name for an *attribute*, *variable* or parameter, together with a *literal* giving its *value*.

network address A way to locate a particular computing device attached to a network.

network number The part of the *IP address* that identifies the network the device is connected to.

no value In *XML,* indicates that no *value* has been supplied for a particular property of a *node*.

node A position in a *tree*.

node-name The name of a *node* (such as *element* or *attribute*) in an *XML document*. See also *type name*.

node test In XPath, the second sequence of *nodes* needed in a *location step,* after using the *axis*. See also *predicate*.

non-functional requirement Any requirement not directly tied to what *data* or behaviour an information system should support.

non-scalar data type A *data type* that has *values* with user-accessible subparts.

normalized table A *table* description is said to be normalized if all *repeating groups* have been removed into separate tables. More formally, a table is normalized if every *functional determinant* is a *candidate key*.

not-null constraint States that a particular column cannot be *null*.

null In the relational data model, null is used to indicate that there is no *data* to hold in a column for a particular row.

numeric Numeric *data* is that used in arithmetic or which needs to be sorted into numerical order.

numeric, exact A *numeric data value* that can be represented exactly as a standard decimal literal – 0.2, 1756, 6.5 and so on.

numeric, approximate A *numeric data value* that cannot be represented approximately, such as $\frac{1}{3}$ as 0.333, $\sqrt{2}$ as 1.414, π as 3.141.

object diagram Shows particular occurrences of *entities* and the relationship occurrences that link them. An instance of an *ER diagram*.

occurrence A specific instance of an entity or association.

one-to-many In an *ER diagram* a *binary association* with the upper bound of the *multiplicity constraint* at one association end being 1, and at the other *(many).

one-to-one In an *ER diagram* a *binary association* with an upper bound of 1 on both *multiplicity constraints*.

operator Language construct that takes one or more *values*, manipulates them in some way and outputs a single value.

operation In *UML*, operations document the behaviour of an *entity*. The specific behaviour is documented in a *method note*.

operations compartment In *UML*, that part of the representation of an *entity* where the *operations* are written.

ordered file A *data* file in which *records* are stored in a particular order determined by the *ordering field*.

ordering field The *field* used to order *records* within an *ordered file*.

outer join A *join* in which *data* for unmatched rows from one, or all, *tables* is included in the *result set*. For such rows, the column *values* from the other table are set to *null* in the result set. See also *equi-join, inner join, join*.

owner In *database* terms, the user who created a particular database or database object.

parent In a *tree*, a *node* immediately above some other node, called its *child*.

participation constraint Indicates whether or not every occurrence of the more general *entity* is also an occurrence of one of the more specific entities.

path In a *tree*, a path is a sequence of *nodes* where each node is a *child* of the preceding node.

pattern The basic building block of a RELAX NG *schema*.

physical web data design Adapts the *logical web data design* to use particular web technologies.

persistent connection A *DBMS connection* that does *not* close when the server-side script finishes.

PHP resource A reference to some external *resource*, that is used within a PHP script.

physical data independence The property of the ANSI/SPARC database systems architecture that means changes to the *internal view* need not affect the *logical view*.

physical database design Shows how to implement the *logical database design* using particular software and hardware technologies.

port number A unique identifier for a program using *TCP* to send messages across an *internet*.

precision For *numeric data*, the total number of digits that can be stored, including those after the decimal point.

predicate In XPath, the third way to refine the sequence of *nodes* reached by a *location step*. See also *axis* and *node test*.

primary key The *candidate key* chosen as the main identifier for a *table*.

privilege In SQL, the ability to instruct the *DBMS* to carry out some particular action.

privilege system In SQL, the system of *privileges* that can be assigned to a user.

property list In UML, a list of additional properties for an attribute.

protocol The rules governing communication between members of a group, such as for networked computing devices.

qualified identifier In SQL, a column name prefixed with the name of the *table* and, optionally, the *database* it belongs to, such as `tableName.columnName` or `databaseName.tableName.columnName`. Used to distinguish between two columns, in different tables that have the same name.

qualified name In *XML*, the *namespace prefix* and the *local name* form the qualified name.

QUID matrix Records whether a *database* transaction queries a *table*, inserts a new row, updates an existing row or deletes a row.

RDBMS A *DBMS* that is based on the relational data model.

realm See *security realm*.

record Within a *data file*, holds information on one thing. The equivalent of a row in a *table* or an occurrence of an *entity*.

redundant association One where the connection it represents is adequately represented by other *associations*.

referenced table In the description of a *foreign key constraint*, this is the *table* with the matching *candidate key*.

referential action Tells the *RDBMS* how to maintain *referential integrity* when a user requests changes to *candidate key values* that would violate a *foreign key constraint*.

referential integrity constraint See *foreign key constraint*.

referencing table In the description of a *foreign key constraint*, this is the *table* with the *foreign key*.

relation See *table*.

relationship A meaningful connection between *entities* that are said to participate in the relationship.

relationship occurrence A particular instance of a *relationship*. It links together one occurrence of each *entity* that participates in the relationship.

relative URL A *URL* defined relative to some base URL. See *absolute URL* and *URL*.

reload problem When reloading a *web page* causes a previous action to be repeated – a particular problem for web database *applications* that allow data modification.

repeating group A set of two or more columns such that the *data* in these columns repeats across two or more rows. See *functional determinant*.

requirement Statement of what an information system must do. See also *functional requirement* and *non-functional requirement*.

resolving the many-to-many association A process carried out during *logical database design* that replaces a single many-to-many *association* with a new *entity* (called a *link entity*) and two new one-to-many associations.

resource In PHP, a *data type* for variables used to hold a reference to an external resource being used by a script, such as a *DBMS connection*.

result set The set (or multiset) of rows returned by a *DBMS* in response to a *database query*.

reverse axis In XPath, an *axis* in which the *nodes* appear in reverse *document order*. See also *forward axis*.

role In SQL, this represents a group of users who share the same *privileges*.

role name Indicates that an *entity* plays a particular *role* in an *association*.

rollback An instruction to the *DBMS* to 'undo' all changes made to the *database instance* as the last point at which the instance was made permanent. See also *commit*.

root In a *tree*, the top-level *node*. Every tree has a single root node. Sometimes called the *root node*.

root element See *document element*.

root node See *root*.

router A device that interconnects two or more networks and forwards messages from one network to another.

Russian doll schema An XML *schema document* in which the content model for each *element* appears inside its *parent*.

safe method An *HTTP* method that will not result in any changes on the *web server* other than the *HTTP server* logging the request.

scalar data type A *data type* that has complete *values* – they have no subparts that are directly accessible to end users.

scale For *numeric data*, the number of digits after the decimal point.

schema valid In *XML*, indicates that a particular *XML document* instance meets all the structural requirements set out in the *document model*'s XML schema.

schema document In *XML*, a *document* that holds the description of the document structures allowed by a particular *document model*. Used by a *validating XML parser* to check that a particular *instance document* conforms to the document model.

scheme In a *URL*, the scheme identifies which *Internet* application the URL relates to.

scope The scope of a *variable* is that portion of a program within which the variable can be used.

screen Represents a *data-centric* part of the user interface.

security realm In *HTTP authentication,* a set of web *resources* that can only be accessed by *authorized* users.

select list In an SQL *select statement*, the list of columns the *values* of which should be retrieved for a *database query*.

select statement The *SQL statement* that allows users to query a *database*.

self join A *select statement* that joins two copies of the same *table*.

sequence A database object that generates *numeric values* guaranteed to be unique within the *database*.

server page In *web data design*, a *UML stereotyped* class representing a server-side script.

session (SQL) In SQL, each user's *connection* to the *DBMS* has an associated *session*. Users can set certain default properties for their sessions, such as language, character set, date format and so on.

session In web applications, a technique for maintaining *application state* by storing it on the *web server*.

session ID In web applications, a unique identifier used by the *web browser* and *web server* to determine which *session* a user is associated with.

session variable Variables storing the *application state*.

set function See *aggregate function*.

SGML See *Standard Generalized Mark-up Language*.

SGML application Another name for an *SGML document model*.

SGML document model A *document model* defined using *SGML*.

sibling In a *tree*, a *node's* siblings are the other *child* nodes of its *parent*.

simple candidate key A *candidate key* with a single column.

socket For *TCP*, the combination of *IP address* and *port number* that uniquely identifies the program using TCP to send messages.

sparse table A *table instance* that includes a lot of *nulls*.

SQL catalog A container for *SQL schema*.

SQL schema Term used in the SQL standard to refer to a collection of *tables* of related *data* – that is, an SQL schema is simply a *database*.

SQL statement A statement written in the SQL language, used to instruct a *DBMS*.

Standard Generalized Mark-up Language (SGML) A language for defining the *document model* of other *mark-up* languages.

state constraint A statement about the information held by the information system that must always be true.

stateful application An *application* that maintains a *record* of the current and past state of communications between client and server.

stateless application An *application* that does not maintain a *record* of communications between client and server. Each interaction begins as if the client and server had not previously communicated.

static content The content of a dynamic *web page* that is the same for all instances of that *document*.

stereotype In *UML,* a way to distinguish between the different kinds of *application* components.

storage engine A combination of a particular kind of *data file* (*hash, heap, ordered*) and additional structures such as *index* files.

stored function A piece of application code stored on the *database* and executed as part of an SQL *expression*. Stored functions return a *value* to the calling program. See also *stored procedure* and *trigger*.

stored procedure A piece of application code stored on the database and executed on the instructions of the *database client*. Stored procedures do not return a *value* to the calling program – instead, they use parameters to pass values between the stored procedure and the calling program. See also *stored function* and *trigger*.

stored routine A *stored function* or *stored procedure*.

strongly typed A computer language that has *operators* that will only work for *values* of the correct *data type*.

structured codes Character strings that contain embedded information.

structured type In SQL, a *user-defined data type* with a complex internal structure.

stylesheet A set of formatting instructions for a *document*.

submit association In *logical web data design*, a *UML stereotyped association* between a *form* and a *server page* indicating that an occurrence of the form submits *data* it gathers to the associated occurrence of the *server page* for processing.

subquery A *select statement* that appears as part of another *SQL statement*.

superglobal variable In PHP, a system-defined variable that automatically has global *scope* within a PHP script.

surrogate key A single *numeric* column that has *values* set by the *DBMS* itself, which act as the *primary key* of a *table*. The values of a *surrogate key* have no business significance.

system boundary Separates what is part of the information system from what is not.

system catalogue See *data dictionary*.

system-defined data type A *data type* defined by the *data model*, or database software, usually as part of the *data language*.

system software Computer software that runs the computer hardware and forms the infrastructure for developing *application software*.

table A structure for organizing data into rows and columns.

table heading The set of all *column descriptions* for a *table*. Sometimes called a *table schema*.

table instance The set of all rows in a *table*.

table schema The description of a *table*, its columns and constraints.

tag In a *mark-up* language, tags delimit (mark the start and end of) *elements*. A start tag may contain *attributes*.

tagged value In *UML*, a *name-value pair*.

TCP See *Transmission Control Protocol*.

TCP connection Combination of the source and destination sockets.

transaction A series of modifications to a *database* that must all succeed. If any one fails, then all must be rolled back (see *rollback*).

transaction path analysis A technique for checking if the *entities* and *associations* in the *ER diagram* can support a particular *database query*.

transition constraint A statement restricting the ways in which information can be changed.

Transmission Control Protocol (TCP) A transport *protocol* ensuring that there is a reliable *connection* between networked devices.

tree A mathematical structure consisting of an ordered set of *nodes* connected by *edges*. Each edge connects two nodes called the *parent* and *child*.

trigger A piece of *application* code stored on the *database* and executed when some specified *database event* occurs in a named *table*. See also *stored function* and *stored routine*.

trigger, row-level Fires once for each row affected by the *database event*, either before or after the row is modified.

trigger, statement-level Fires once, either before or after, the *database event* occurs.

trigger condition A Boolean expression that controls whether or not the *trigger* is executed.

type casting Changing the *data type* of a *value*, for example from a *numeric data type* to a character string.

type-name In *XML*, the name of a *data type*.

unary operator An operator that takes one input *value*. See *binary operator* and *operator*.

Unified Modeling Language (UML) 'A visual language for specifying, constructing and documenting the artefacts of systems.' (OMG, 2003, p. 20).

uniform resource locator (URL) Identifies an application server and allows a client to specify exactly which *resource* it wants from that server.

unique constraint Ensures that, in every row of the *table*, the combination of column values is unique or that one of the columns is null.

unknown In *XML*, indicates that it is possible a *value* has been specified for a property of an information item, but is currently inaccessible.

update statement An *SQL statement* that allows users to modify the column *values* in specified rows of a *table instance*.

update event Occurs when *data* in a row in a *database table* is modified.

URL See *uniform resource locator*.

URL rewriting A technique for maintaining *application state* in a web application by appending *name-value pairs* to the URL query string at runtime.

use case A description of one way in which the *information system* is used.

use case diagram *UML* diagram showing the various *use cases*, how they are connected and which *actors* use them.

use case specification A written description of a single *use case*.

user-defined data type A *data type* defined for using as part of a particular *database design*.

user-defined function In PHP, a function written by the programmer for a specific purpose.

user experience design The design of the look and feel of a *website* and the navigation paths through it.

validation test The process of checking that *data* submitted by end users is valid.

validating XML parser An *XML parser* that also checks whether or not an *XML document* satisfies the constraints specified in the appropriate *schema document*.

value The binary number stored on the *database* to represent a particular *data* item.

value function In SQL, a pre-defined function acting on values.

variable A named container for *data values*.

varchar SQL *data type* for a character string of varying length.

view In SQL, a view is a *derived table* and its definition is stored in the *data dictionary*. See also *external view, internal view* and *logical view*.

view definition An SQL *select statement* defining a *view*.

Web, the A distributed collection of *hyperlinked multimedia documents*, accessed using *Internet* technology.

web browser General-purpose *application software* able to display a range of *Internet* content, though primarily *web pages*.

web data design The process of reconciling the *database design* with the design of the rest of the *web database application*. Split into conceptual, logical and physical stages, as with the established approach to database design.

web database applications *Application software* that utilizes web and database technologies.

web page A *multimedia document*, usually containing *hyperlinks*, that is available via *the Internet*.

web server Collection of hardware and software used to manage a *website*. See *HTTP server*.

website A structured collection of *web pages* and other web *resources*.

well-formed XML A *document* that conforms to the well-formedness constraints of the *XML* recommendation.

well-known port number A standard *port number* used by specific programs, such as *web servers*, e-mail servers and so on. Lies in the range 1 to 1023.

where clause Used in several *SQL statements* to indicate which rows of a *table* should be affected by the statement.

wrapper function A programming approach that 'wraps up' SQL data modification statements in a *stored function*.

XML See *Extensible Mark-up Language*.

XML application A particular *XML document model*. A description of the structure of a class of *XML documents*, developed for some specific purpose.

XML declaration A statement at the start of a physical *XML document* indicating that the *document* is XML. States the XML version and character set used and indicates whether or not *data* held in other physical files is required to fully understand the XML document.

XML document A physical, plain text file consisting of Unicode characters that represents *well-formed XML*. Also called an *instance document*.

XML document fragment A portion of a *well-formed XML document*.

XML name A valid name for an *XML element* or *attribute*.

XML parser An *XML processor* that checks whether or not a particular *document* satisfies the well-formedness constraints in the XML specification.

XML processor *Application software* that can read, and correctly interpret, an *XML document*.

XML schema See *schema document*.

References and bibliography

The Harvard style of referencing is used, except in two respects: where the full forename of an author is known, it is included, rather than just their initials; and where there are three or more authors, all are listed. A separate list of websites is also included.

ABRSM (no date) *Guide to Music Medals: Entry and administration*. Available at: <www.musicmedals.org/?page=introduction/entryAdmin.html> [accessed 16 June 2007].

Atzeni, Paolo, Ceri, Stefano, Parabosci, Stefano and Torlone, Riccardo (1999) *Database Systems: Concepts, languages, architectures*. Maidenhead, UK: McGraw-Hill.

Arvin, Troels (2006) *Comparison of Different SQL Implementations*. Available at: http://troels.arvin.dk/db/rdbms [accessed 16 June 2007].

Avison, David, and Fitzgerald, Guy (2003) *Information Systems Development: Methodologies, techniques and tools,* 3rd edn. Maidenhead, UK: McGraw-Hill.

Bennett, Simon, Skelton, John, and Lunn, Ken (2005) *UML*, Schaum's Outlines, 2nd edn. Maidenhead, UK: McGraw-Hill.

Berners-Lee, T. (1994) *RFC1738 – Uniform Resource Locators*. Available at: www.ietf.org/rfc/rfc1738.txt [accessed 16 June 2007].

Bourret, Ron (2003) *XML and Databases*. Available at: www.rpbourret.com/xml/XMLAndDatabases.htm [accessed 16 June 2007].

Bulger, Brad, Greenspan, Jay, and Wall, David (2004) *MySQL/PHP Database Applications,* 2nd edn. Indianapolis, Indiana: Wiley.

Castro, Elizabeth (2007) *HTML, XHTML and CSS Visual Quickstart Guide,* 6th edn. Berkeley, California: Peachpit Press.

Ceri, Stefano, Fraternali, Piero, Bongio, Aldo, Brambilla, Marco, Comai, Sara, and Matera, Maristella (2003) *Designing Data-intensive Web Applications*. San Francisco, California: Morgan Kaufmann.

Conallen, Jim (2003) *Building Web Applications with UML*, 2nd edn. Harlow, UK: Addison-Wesley.

Connolly, Thomas, and Begg, Carolyn (2004) *Database Systems: A practical approach to design, implementation and management*, 4th edn. Harlow, UK: Addison-Wesley.

Date, C. J. (2004) *An Introduction to Database Systems*, 8th edn. Harlow, UK: Addison-Wesley.

Duerst, M., and Suignard, M. (2005) *Request for Comments: 3987 – Internationalized Resource Identifiers (IRIs)*. Available at: www.ietf.org/rfc/rfc3987.txt [accessed 16 June 2007].

Eaglestone, Barry, and Ridley, Mick (2001) *Web Database Systems*. Maidenhead, UK: McGraw-Hill.

Eisenberg, Andrew, and Melton, Jim (2001) 'SQL/XML and the SQLX informal group of companies', *Sigmod Record*, 30(3). Available at: www.sigmod.org/sigmod/record/issues/0109/standards.pdf [accessed 12 April 2006].

Eisenberg, Andrew, and Melton, Jim (2002a) 'SQL/XML is making good progress', *Sigmod Record*, 31(2) pp. 101–8. Available at: www.sigmod.org/sigmod/record/issues/ 0206/standard.pdf [accessed 12 April 2006].

Eisenberg, Andrew, and Melton, Jim (2002b) 'An early look at XQuery', *Sigmod Record*, 31(4). Available at: www.sigmod.org/sigmod/record/issues/0212/AndrewEJimM.pdf [accessed 12 April 2006].

Eisenberg, Andrew, and Melton, Jim (2004) 'Advancements in SQL/XML', *Sigmod Record*, 33(3). Available at: www.sigmod.org/sigmod/record/issues/0409/11.JimMelton.pdf [accessed 12 April 2006].

Eisenberg, Andrew, and Melton, Jim (2005) 'XQuery 1.0 is nearing completion', *Sigmod Record*, 34(4), pp. 78–84. Available at: www.sigmod.org/sigmod/record/issues/0512/ p78-column-eisenberg-melton.pdf [accessed 12 April 2006].

Elmasri, Ramez, and Navathe, Shamkant B. (2000a) *Chapter 10: The network data model and the IDMS system*. Available at: ftp://ftp.aw.com/cseng/authors/elmasri/Dbase3e [accessed 6 June 2007].

Elmasri, Ramez, and Navathe, Shamkant B. (2000b) *Chapter 11: The hierarchical data model and the IMS system*. Available at: ftp://ftp.aw.com/cseng/authors/elmasri/ Dbase3e [accessed 6 June 2007].

Elmasri, Ramez, and Navathe, Shamkant B. (2007) *Fundamentals of Database Systems*, 5th edn. Harlow, UK: Addison-Wesley.

Fielding, R. (1995) *RFC1808 – Relative Uniform Resource Locators*. Available at: www.w3.org/Addressing/rfc1808.txt [accessed 27 September 2005].

Génova, Gonzalo, Llorens, Juan, and Martínez, Paloma (2002) 'The meaning of multiplicity of n-ary associations in UML', *Software and Systems Modeling*, 1(2), pp. 86–97.

Gourley, David, and Totty, Brian (2002) *HTTP: The definitive guide*. Farnham, UK: O'Reilly.

Graves, Mark (2002) *Designing XML Databases*. Upper Saddle River, New Jersey: Prentice Hall.

Halpin, Terry A. (2001) *Information Modeling and Relational Databases: From conceptual analysis to logical design*. San Francisco, California: Morgan Kauffmann.

Harold, Elliotte Rusty and Means, W. Scott (2004) *XML in a Nutshell: A desktop quick reference*, 3rd edn. Farnham, UK: O'Reilly.

Hoffer, J. A, Prescott, M. B. and McFadden, F. R. (2004) *Modern Database Management*, 6th edn. Harlow, UK: Prentice Hall.

Holt, Jon (2001) *UML for Systems Engineering: Watching the wheels*. London: The Institution of Electrical Engineers.

Howe, David (2001) *Data Analysis for Database Design*, 3rd edn. Oxford: Butterworth-Heinemann.

ICANN (2004) *FAQs*. Available at: www.icann.org/faq [accessed 16 June 2007].

IANA (2005) *Port Numbers*. Available at: www.iana.org/assignments/port-numbers [accessed 16 June 2007].

Ince, Darrel (2002) *Developing Distributed and E-commerce Applications*. Harlow, UK: Addison-Wesley.

ISO/IEC JTC 1 (2004) *Document Schema Definition Languages (DSDL) – Part 3: Rule-based validation – Schematron*. Available at: www.schematron.com/iso/dsdl-3-fdis.pdf [accessed 16 June 2007].

Korpela, Jukka (2001) *A Tutorial on Character Code Issues*. Available at: www.cs.tut.fi/~jkorpela/chars.html [accessed 16 June 2007].

Kroenke, David M. (2006) *Database Processing: Fundamentals, design and implementation* (international edn). Harlow, UK: Prentice Hall.

Melton, Jim, and Simon, Alan R. (2002) *SQL:1999 – understanding relational language components*. San Francisco, California: Morgan Kaufmann.

Møller, Anders (2002) *Document Structure Description 2.0*. Available at: www.brics.dk/DSD/dsd2.html [accessed 16 June 2007].

Møller, Anders, and Schwartzbach, Michael (2006) *An Introduction to XML and Web Technologies*. Harlow, UK: Addison-Wesley.

Moore, Adrian (2005) *Multimedia Web Programming*. Houndsmill, Basingstoke, UK: Palgrave Macmillan.

Muller, Robert J. (1999) *Database Design for Smarties: Using UML for data modeling*. San Francisco, California: Morgan Kaufmann.

Musciano, Chuck, and Kennedy, Bill (2002) *HTML & XHTML: The definitive guide*, 5th edn. Farnham, UK: O'Reilly.

MySQLAB (2007) *MySQL 5.1 Reference Manual*. Available at: http://dev.mysql.com/doc/refman/5.1/en/index.html [accessed 16 June 2007].

National Statistics (2004) *More Businesses are Buying over the Internet*. Available at: www.statistics.gov.uk/pdfdir/e-com1104.pdf [accessed 16 June 2007].

NISCC (2006) *Secure Web Applications: Development, installation and security testing*, NISCC Briefing 10/2006, issued 27 April 2006. Available at: www.cpni.gov.uk/docs/secureWebApps.pdf [accessed 16 June 2007].

OASIS (2001) *RELAX NG Specification – Committee Specification 3 December 2001*. Available at www.oasis-open.org/committees/relax-ng/spec-20011203.html [accessed 16 June 2007].

OMG (2003) *UML 2.0 Infrastructure Specification – ptc/2003-09-15*. Available at: www.omg.org [accessed 16 June 2007].

OMG (2005) *UML 2.0 Infrastructure Specification – formal/05-07-05*. Available at: www.omg.org [accessed 16 June 2007].

PHP Documentation Group (2005) *PHP Manual*. Available at: http://uk.php.net/manual/en [accessed 16 June 2007].

Provost, Will (2002) *Normalizing XML*. Available at: www.xml.com/pub/a/2002/11/13/normalizing.html [accessed 16 June 2007].

Ray, Erik T. (2003) *Learning XML*, 2nd edn. Farnham, UK: O'Reilly.

Rodriguez, Adolfo, Gatrell, John, Karas, John, and Peschke, Roland (2001) *TCP/IP Tutorial and Technical Overview*, IBM Redbooks, 6th edn. New York: IBM.

Savage, Ron (2005) *BNF Grammar for ISO/IEC 9075-2:2003 – Database Language SQL (SQL-2003) SQL/Foundation*. Available at: http://savage.net.au/SQL/sql-2003-2.bnf.html [accessed 16 June 2007].

Silberschatz, Abraham, Korth, Henry F., and Sudarshan, S. (2002) *Database System Concepts*, 4th edn. Maidenhead, UK: McGraw-Hill.

Skidmore, Steve, and Eva, Malcolm (2004) *Introducing Systems Development*. Houndsmill, Basingstoke, UK: Palgrave Macmillan.

Steegmans, Bart, Bourret, Ronald, Cline, Owen, Guyennet, Olivier, Kulkarni, Shrinivas, Priestley, Stephen, Sylenko, Valeriy, and Wahli, Ueli (2004) *XML for DB2 Information Integration*, IBM Redbooks. New York: IBM.

UKAIS (1999) *The Definition of Information Systems*. Available at: www.cs.york.ac.uk/ukais/isdefn.pdf [accessed 16 June 2007].

Unicode Consortium (2005) *Unicode-enabled Products*. Available at: www.unicode.org/onlinedat/products.html [accessed 16 June 2007].

van der Vlist, Eric (2003) *RELAX NG*. Available at: http://books.xmlschemata.org/relaxng [accessed 16 June 2007].

Vaswani, Vikram (2004) *PHP101: PHP for the absolute beginner* [on line]. Available at: http://devzone.zend.com/article627-PHP-101-PHP-for-the-Absolute-Beginner [accessed 2 August 2007].

W3C (2001) *XHTML™ 1.1 – Module-based XHTML Second Edition – W36 Working Draft, 16 February 2007*. Available at: www.w3.org/TR/xhtml11 [accessed 16 June 2007].

W3C (2004a) *Why Validate?*. Available at: http://validator.w3.org/docs/why.html [accessed 16 June 2007].

W3C (2004b) *Namespaces in XML 1.1 Second Edition – W3C Recommendation, 16 August 2006*. Available at: www.w3.org/TR/xml-names11 [accessed 16 June 2007].

W3C (2004c) *XML Information Set Second Edition – W3C Recommendation 4 February 2004*. Available at: www.w3.org/TR/2004/REC-xml-infoset-20040204 [accessed 16 June 2007].

W3C (2004d) *XML Schema Part 1: Structures Second Edition – W3C Recommendation, 28 October 2004*. Available at: www.w3.org/TR/xmlschema-1 [accessed 16 June 2007].

W3C (2004e) *XML Schema Part 2: Datatypes Second Edition – W3C Recommendation, 28 October 2004*. Available at: www.w3.org/TR/xmlschema-2 [accessed 16 April 2007].

W3C (2004f) *Extensible Markup Language (XML) 1.0 Third Edition – W3C Recommendation, 4 February 2004*. Available at: www.w3.org/TR/2004/REC-xml-20040204 [accessed 16 April 2007].

W3C (2005a) Markup validation service. Available at: http://validator.w3.org [accessed 16 June 2007].

W3C (2005b) *Tutorial: Character sets & encodings in XHTML, HTML and CSS*. Available at: www.w3.org/International/tutorials/tutorial-char-enc [accessed 16 June 2007].

W3C (2005c) *XQuery 1.0: An XML Query Language – W3C Recommendation, 23 January 2007*. Available at: www.w3.org/TR/xquery [accessed 16 June 2007].

W3C (2005d) *XML Path Language (XPath) 2.0 – W3C Recommendation, 23 January 2007*. Available at: www.w3.org/TR/xpath20 [accessed 16 April 2007].

W3C (2005e) *XQuery 1.0: An XML Query Language – W3C Candidate Recommendation, 3 November 2005*. Available at: www.w3.org/TR/2005/CR-xquery-20051103 [accessed 16 June 2007].

W3C (2005f) *XQuery 1.0 and XPath 2.0 Functions and Operators – W3C Recommendation, 23 January 2007*. Available at: www.w3.org/TR/xpath-functions [accessed 16 June 2007].

W3C (2005g) *XQuery 1.0 and XPath 2.0 Data Model (XDM) – W3C Recommendation, 23 January 2007*. Available at: www.w3.org/TR/xpath-datamodel [accessed 16 June 2007].

W3C (2005h) *XQuery 1.0 and XPath 2.0 Formal Semantics – W3C Recommendation 23 January 2007*. Available at: www.w3.org/TR/xquery-semantics [accessed 16 June 2007].

W3C (2005i) *XSL Transformations (XSLT) Version 2.0 – W3C Recommendation, 23 January 2007*. Available at: www.w3.org/TR/xslt20 [accessed 16 June 2007].

W3C (2006a) *Extensible Stylesheet Language (XSL) Version 1.1 – W3C Candidate Recommendation, 20 February 2006*. Available at: www.w3.org/TR/2006/CR-xsl11-20060220/#d0e155 [accessed 16 June 2007].

W3C (2006b) *XQuery Update Facility – W3C Working Draft, 11 July 2006*. Available at: www.w3.org/TR/xqupdate [accessed 16 June 2007].

W3C (2006c) *XML Schema Part 2: Datatypes Second Edition – W3C Recommendation, 28 October 2004*. Available at www.w3.org/TR/xmlschema-2 [accessed 16 June 2007].

Welling, Luke, and Thompson, Laura (2005) *PHP and MySQL Web Development*, 3rd edn. Indianapolis, Indiana: Sams.

Wikipedia (2005) *Wikipedia*. Available at: http://en.wikipedia.org/wiki/Wikipedia [accessed 16 June 2007].

Wilde, Erik (1999) *Wilde's WWW: Technical foundations of the World Wide Web*. Berlin: Springer.

Williams, Hugh E., and Lane, David (2004) *Web Database Applications with PHP and MySQL*, 2nd edn. Farnham, UK: O'Reilly.

Williams, Rob (2001) *Computer Systems Architecture: A networking approach*. Harlow, UK: Addison-Wesley.

Websites

Apache Software Foundation: www.apache.org

Boxes and Arrows: www.boxesandarrows.com

Document Schema Definition Languages: http://dsdl.org

Free On-line Dictionary of Computing (FOLDOC): http://foldoc.doc.ic.ac.uk/foldoc

Internet Assigned Numbers Authority: www.iana.org

Internet Corporation for Assigned Names and Numbers: www.icann.org

Macromedia: www.adobe.com

UK Academy for Information Systems (UKAIS): www.ukais.org

Unicode consortium: www.unicode.org

W3Schools: www.w3schools.com

Webopedia: www.webopedia.com

Wikipedia, the free encyclopaedia: http://en.wikipedia.org

Index